A Local Assessment Toolkit to Promote Deeper Learning

Transforming Research Into Practice

Karin Hess

Foreword by Jay McTighe

FOR INFORMATION:

Corwin
A SAGE Company
2455 Teller Road
Thousand Oaks, California 91320
(800) 233-9936
www.corwin.com

SAGE Publications Ltd.
1 Oliver's Yard
55 City Road
London EC1Y 1SP
United Kingdom

SAGE Publications India Pvt. Ltd.
B 1/I 1 Mohan Cooperative Industrial Area
Mathura Road, New Delhi 110 044
India

SAGE Publications Asia-Pacific Pte. Ltd.
3 Church Street
#10-04 Samsung Hub
Singapore 049483

Program Director: Jessica Allan
Associate Editor: Lucas Schleicher
Editorial Assistant: Mia Rodriguez
Production Editor: Tori Mirsadjadi
Copy Editor: Diane DiMura
Typesetter: C&M Digitals (P) Ltd.
Proofreader: Scott Oney
Indexer: Maria Sosnowski
Cover Designer: Scott Van Atta
Marketing Manager: Nicole Franks

Copyright © 2018 by Corwin

All rights reserved. When forms and sample documents are included, their use is authorized only by educators, local school sites, and/or noncommercial or nonprofit entities that have purchased the book. Except for that usage, no part of this book may be reproduced or utilized in any form or by any means, electronic or mechanical, including photocopying, recording, or by any information storage and retrieval system, without permission in writing from the publisher.

All trademarks depicted within this book, including trademarks appearing as part of a screenshot, figure, or other image, are included solely for the purpose of illustration and are the property of their respective holders. The use of the trademarks in no way indicates any relationship with, or endorsement by, the holders of said trademarks.

Printed in the United States of America

Library of Congress Cataloging-in-Publication Data

Names: Hess, Karin (Karin K.), author.

Title: A local assessment toolkit to promote deeper learning : transforming research into practice / Karin Hess ; foreword by Jay McTighe.

Description: Thousand Oaks, California : Corwin, 2018. | Includes bibliographical references and index.

Identifiers: LCCN 2017048978 | ISBN 9781506393759 (pbk. : alk. paper)

Subjects: LCSH: Educational tests and measurements—Methodology. | Cognitive learning. | Effective teaching.

Classification: LCC LB3051 .H46 2018 | DDC 371.26—dc23
LC record available at https://lccn.loc.gov/2017048978

This book is printed on acid-free paper.

18 19 20 21 22 10 9 8 7 6 5 4 3 2 1

DISCLAIMER: This book may direct you to access third-party content via Web links, QR codes, or other scannable technologies, which are provided for your reference by the author(s). Corwin makes no guarantee that such third-party content will be available for your use and encourages you to review the terms and conditions of such third-party content. Corwin takes no responsibility and assumes no liability for your use of any third-party content, nor does Corwin approve, sponsor, endorse, verify, or certify such third-party content.

Contents

Foreword from Jay McTighe	xi
Acknowledgments	xiii
About the Author	xv
Introduction	**1**
Module 1: Are My Students Thinking Deeply or Just Working Harder? Infusing Rigor Into Instruction and Assessment: Laying the Groundwork for Deeper Learning for *All* Students	**15**
1.1 What Is Cognitive Rigor?	15
1.2 Developing a Common Understanding of What Cognitive Rigor Is and What It Is Not	16
1.2a Cognitive Rigor Is Making Connections to Consolidate the Learning	17
1.2b Cognitive Rigor Is Applying What You've Learned, Also Known as Transfer	19
1.2c Cognitive Rigor Is Challenge With Support	21
1.2d Cognitive Rigor Is Higher-Order Thinking, Which Usually Means Analyzing, Evaluating, and Creating	23
1.2e Cognitive Rigor Is Engagement, Collaboration, and Discourse That Makes Thinking Visible	25
1.2f Cognitive Rigor Is Triggered by Asking a Different Kind of Question That Shifts Teacher–Student Roles	29
1.3 Seven Common Misconceptions About Rigor	35
1.4 Bloom Meets Webb: Origins of the Hess Cognitive Rigor Matrix	43
Creating the Matrix	43
Proof of Concept and Final Steps in the Development of the Cognitive Rigor Matrix	46
The Thinking Behind the Tools in Module 1	46
Summarizing Key Ideas: Bloom's Taxonomy and Depth of Knowledge	46
Reflections	48
1.5 Getting Started Applying Your Understanding of Rigor and Deeper Learning	48
Part 2: Support Materials for Module 1	**50**
I. A Workshop Plan for Module 1	50
II. The Hess Cognitive Rigor Tools: About the Tools in This Module	51
TOOLS #1–#4 Core Subject CRMs	51
TOOLS #5A–#5D Special Subject CRMs	51
III. Strategies and Tools for Professional Developers and Teacher Planning	61
What's TV Got to Do With DOK?	63
Test Your DOK "IQ" (IQ=I May Still Have Some Questions)	64

Test Your DOK "IQ" Test "Cheat Sheet"	67
Hess Cognitive Rigor Matrix Question-Planning Worksheets	71
IV. Kid Tools: Resources for Use With Students to Support Deeper Thinking	**77**
STRATEGY 1: "I Can Rock the Rigor" Kid Tool	77
STRATEGY 2: Collaborative Inquiry Plan	77
STRATEGY 3: The One-Pager	77
STRATEGY 4: TBEAR and Kid TBEAR	77
STRATEGY 5: Multi-sensory Clustering	78
STRATEGY 6: Sample Turn and Talk Frames	79
STRATEGY 7: Jigsaw to Develop Schemas	79
STRATEGY 8: Text Decks: A Close Reading Strategy	79

Module 2: Is the Task Appropriate to the Text?
Examining and Using Increasingly Complex Texts — 89

2.1 What Makes Texts Complex, and Why Should *Every* Teacher Care?	**89**
2.2 The Thinking Behind the Tools in Module 2	**90**
2.3 Five Key Learnings From a Text Complexity Analysis Process	**92**
2.4 Understanding Quantitative and Qualitative Complexity Measures	**92**
2.5 Unpacking Overall Text Complexity Using a Qualitative Analysis Approach	**94**
STEP 1: Use the Instructional and Assessment Planning Worksheet	94
STEP 2: Determine Rubric Ratings	95
STEP 3: Brainstorm Instructional Strategies and Scaffolding	95
STEP 4: Develop a Local Bibliography of Benchmark Texts	96
2.6 A Detailed Discussion of What to Look for—Eight Qualitative Complexity Factors	**97**
Reflections	**102**

Part 2: Support Materials for Module 2 — 103

I. A Workshop Plan for Module 2	**103**
II. The Hess Text Complexity Tools: About the Tools in This Module	**104**
TOOL #6 Analyzing Qualitative Features Worksheet	104
TOOL #7 Analytic Rubric for Informational Texts	105
TOOL #8 Analytic Rubric for Literary Texts	105
III. The Importance of Teaching About Text Structures	**110**
IV. Sample Instructional Strategies for Teaching About Text Structures	**112**
STRATEGY 1: Providing Frames to Build a Schema for Each Text Structure	112
STRATEGY 2: Using Graphic Organizers to Analyze or Compose Texts	113
STRATEGY 3: Using Text Signals to Analyze and Interpret Intended Meanings	113
STRATEGY 4: Examining How Text Features and Text Structures Support Meaning	113
STRATEGY 5: Building Anchor Charts With Students for Each Structure Studied	113
V. Sample Text-Based Assessment Strategies	**116**
STRATEGY 6: Word Splash (pre-, post-, self-assessment)	116
STRATEGY 7: What Do I Know About These Words? (pre-, post-, self-assessment)	117
STRATEGY 8: Bookmark—As-You-Read (formative assessment)	117
STRATEGY 9: Card Pyramid (orally summarizing before writing)	118
STRATEGY 10: Pattern Folders—Emerging Themes (organizing text evidence)	119
STRATEGY 11: Reading Strategy Use (self-monitoring while reading)	119

STRATEGY 12: Sample Frames for Text-Based Questions
(discussion and writing prompts) — 119
STRATEGY 13: Using Predetermined Assessment Targets to
Develop Comparable Text-Based Questions — 120

Module 3: What Does This Test *Really* Measure? Designing and Refining High-Quality Assessments for Deeper Learning — 131

3.1 What Is a High-Quality Assessment? — 131
3.2 Assessment Purposes and Use: Formative, Interim, and Summative — 135
3.3 Developing and Refining Rubrics and Scoring Guides — 138
Examining Rubric Quality — 141
A Quick Guide to Rubric Development — 146
3.4 What Can You Learn From Analyzing Student Work Products? — 147
What Are Strategically Designed Performance Tasks? — 148
Six Purposes and Uses of Student Work Analysis — 151
3.5 Developing Anchor Papers for Performance Tasks and Anchor Sets for Calibration — 158
Benchmarking: The Big Picture — 158
Selecting Anchor Papers: PLC Tools #13, #14, and #15 — 162
3.6 Cognitive Labs: An Effective and Efficient Alternative to Piloting New Assessments — 165
Why Might Educators Use Cognitive Labs? — 166
What Does a Cognitive Lab Look Like? — 166
General Cognitive Lab Protocols — 167

Cognitive Lab Part 1: Observe and Document—Done While Students Are Working — 169
Cognitive Lab Part 2: Small Group Interview — 170
Cognitive Lab Part 3A: Interpret Student Work Samples and Make Decisions — 171
Cognitive Lab Part 3B: Collaboratively Interpreting Evidence in Student Work — 171

3.7 Guidelines for Creating Task Validation Teams: Analyzing Technical Quality of Assessments — 172
Preparing to Have an Assessment Formally Reviewed — 173
Determining the Makeup of Validation Teams — 173

Local Assessment Cover Page for Task Validation — 177
Analyzing Assessments for Technical Quality: Conducting a Task Validation — 180
Materials for the Validation Panel — 180
Validation Protocols — 180

Reflections — 184

Part 2: Support Materials for Module 3 — 185

I. A Workshop Plan for Module 3 — 185
II. The Hess PLC Tools: About the Tools in This Module — 187
TOOL #9 Task Quality Validation Protocol — 189
TOOL #10 Analyzing Formative Assessments — 192
TOOL #11 Rubric Quality Review Worksheet — 193
TOOL #12 Student Work Analysis — 194
TOOL #13 What Is the Evidence? — 196
TOOL #14 Individual Reviewer Rubric Score Sheet — 197
TOOL #15 Team Rubric Score Sheet — 198
TOOL #16A Task Validation Summary—Short Version — 199
TOOL #16B Task Validation Summary—In-Depth Version — 200

TOOL #17 Cognitive Labs Part 2	203
TOOL #18 Cognitive Labs Part 3A	204
TOOL #19 Cognitive Labs Part 3B	205
TOOL #20 A Guide to Performance Assessment Development	206
TOOL #21 Performance Assessment Overview: Purpose and Use	210

III. Strategies and Tools for Professional Developers and Teacher Planning — 212

The Great American Chocolate Chip Cookie Taste Test	213
Anatomy of an Opinion, Argument, or Critique: Planning Tools for Teachers and Students	216
General Guidelines for the Administration of Progress-Monitoring Performance Assessments in Writing	224
General Guidelines for the Administration of Progress-Monitoring Performance Assessments in Mathematics	228

IV. Sample Formative Assessment Strategies — 235

5 Key Ideas Underlying Effective Formative Assessment	235
Sample Formative Assessment Strategies	237

V. Sample Performance Assessment Design Strategies — 248

PERFORMANCE ASSESSMENT STRATEGY 1: Case Studies and Student-Designed Expeditionary Learning	252
PERFORMANCE ASSESSMENT STRATEGY 2: Task Shells	252

Module 4: Where Do I Start, What Do I Teach Next, Which Supports Work Best? Using Learning Progressions as a Schema for Planning Instruction and Measuring Progress — 281

4.1 What Are Learning Progressions (or Learning Trajectories), and How Can They Be Used to Scaffold Instruction and Guide the Design and Use of Assessments of Deeper Learning? — 281

What a Learning Progression Is and What It Is Not—Building a Working Definition	282
What Exactly Are Learning Progressions?	282

4.2 Four Interrelated Guiding Principles of Learning Progressions — 286

Guiding Principle I—Validated by Research	288
Guiding Principle II—Organized Around "Big Ideas"	289
Guiding Principle III—Describe Increasing Understanding	289
Guiding Principle IV—Align With Formative Assessment	290
Linking Learning Progressions to Assessment Purposes and Formative, Interim, and Summative Uses	297

4.3 Standards, Learning Progressions, and Curriculum: How Are They Related? — 298

How Are Learning Progressions Different From Standards?	299
Potential Benefits of Using a Learning Progressions Schema for Designing Instruction and Assessment	300

4.4 Zooming "In" and Zooming "Out" of Learning Progressions: Two Sides to the Same Coin — 302

4.5 Applying the Four Interrelated Guiding Principles to Better Understand a Learning Progression — 307

Guiding Questions for Developing, Refining, or Validating Learning Progressions	307

4.6 Providing System Coherence: Using Learning Progressions for Instructional and Assessment Planning — 309

First a Little Background About the Learning Progressions Frameworks (LPFs)	309
Three Case Studies Applying Learning Progressions	310

4.7 Lessons Learned—Using Learning Progressions to Guide Instruction and Change Assessment Practices	**317**
4.8 Looking for Increasing Rigor—by Observing Shifts in Teacher and Student Roles	**320**
4.9 Suggested Ways to Get Started Using the "Looking for Rigor" Walk-Through Tool #26	**324**
Reflections	**326**

Part 2: Support Materials for Module 4 — **327**

I. A Workshop Plan for Module 4	**327**
II. The Hess LP Tools: About the Tools in This Module	**329**
TOOL #22 Analyzing Learner Characteristics/Student Work Along a Progression	330
TOOL #23 Guiding Questions for Developing, Refining, or Validating Learning Progressions	332
TOOL #24 Planning Instruction Using a Learning Progressions Mindset	335
TOOL #25 Unit Planning Template: Using Learning Progressions to Guide Formative, Interim, or Summative Assessment	336
TOOL #26 Looking for Rigor Walk-Through Tool: Teacher-Student Roles	338
III. Strategies and Tools for Professional Developers and Teacher Planning	**339**
Checking Understandings—Possible Responses: Learning Progressions Anticipation Guide	340
Two Sample Tasks Illustrating Pre- and Mid-assessments	341
IV. Strategies and Resources for Use With Students	**348**
STRATEGY 1: My Favorite No	348
STRATEGY 2: Flipped Classrooms	348
STRATEGY 3: Infographics	348
STRATEGY 4: Assignment Menus—Quick Tips for Differentiation	349
STRATEGY 5: Note Facts	351

Module 5: Is This a Collection of Tests or an Assessment System? Building and Sustaining a Local Comprehensive Assessment System for Deeper Learning — **359**

5.1 Rethinking What It Means to Have a Comprehensive Local Assessment System	**360**
General Guiding Questions for Review of Individual Assessments	361
5.2 Five Indicators of a Comprehensive Local Assessment System	**364**
5.3 Multiple Measures and Common Assessments	**367**
The Use of Multiple Measures in Local Assessment Systems	367
Teacher Understanding of Purposes and Use of Multiple Assessment Measures	367
5.4 What Exactly Are "Common" Assessments and Where Do They Fit in the Local Assessment System?	**368**
Common Assessments, Common Scoring Criteria	369
Why Should Districts Develop Local Common Assessments?	369
Factors to Consider During the Development of Common Assessments	370
5.5 Revisiting Alignment From a Systems Perspective	**372**
What Makes Assessments Valid or Reliable?	372
Aligned Assessments, Aligned Systems	373
Six Questions Alignment Studies Can Answer	374
Applying Alignment Criteria	376
5.6 Interpreting Results From Local Assessment Analyses	**377**
Reflections	**379**

Part 2: Support Materials for Module 5	380
I. A Workshop Plan for Module 5	380
II. The Hess Alignment Tools: About the Tools in This Module	381
TOOL #27 Year-at-a-Glance: Planning Classroom-Based Assessments Over the School Year	384
TOOL #28 Discussion Questions: Examining Our Local Assessment System	386
TOOL #29 Basic Individual Test Blueprint Analysis Worksheet: One-Way Alignment, Mapping One Assessment Test or Performance Task to Standards and Intended DOK	388
TOOL #30 Assessment System Blueprint—Mapping Content Standards or Proficiencies to Assessments	391
TOOL #31 Advanced Individual Test Blueprint Analysis Worksheets: One-Way Alignment, With Additional Factors to Consider	394
TOOL #32 Text Complexity Analyses Summary	396
TOOL #33 Item or Task Bank Review	398

Appendices

Appendix A: Summary of Hess Tools to Guide Local Assessment Development, Instructional Planning, and PLC Activities	**401**
Appendix B: Instructional and Formative Assessment Strategies to Uncover Thinking	**407**
Appendix C: Troubleshooting Tips When Designing Assessment Items and Tasks	**413**
Appendix D: Sample "What I Need to Do" Rubrics—Science, ELA, Mathematics, Blank Template	**423**
Appendix E: Student Profile: Science Inquiry Learning Progression	**429**
Appendix F: Student Learning Progression Literacy Profile—Grades 7–8	**439**
Appendix G: Writing Persuasively Learning Progression (Strand 7, LPF)	**449**
Appendix H: LPF STRAND 7 (Grades K–2) Sample Lesson Planning Steps Using Learning Progressions	**453**
Appendix I: An Expanded Glossary for Understanding and Designing Comprehensive Local Assessment Systems	**457**
References	**477**
Index	**483**

Visit the companion website at
resources.corwin.com/HessToolkit for downloadable resources.
Additional resources available at **www.karin-hess.com/free-resources.**

Foreword

by Jay McTighe,
Co-author of *Understanding by Design*

The title of this book is revealing. While its pages offer a rich collection of tools and strategies for effective classroom assessment, its reference to deeper learning reminds us that our assessments should serve a larger purpose than simply measurement.

The book would be worthwhile if it simply focused on summative assessments for evaluation and grading. Dr. Hess articulates the principles and technical requirements of sound assessment with the authority and assurance of a scholar to ensure that evaluative assessments and concomitant grades provide fair and valid measures of targeted goals. But the book goes much further in examining the benefits of assessment (and related instructional) practices that promote deeper learning.

To underscore the primacy of learning-focused assessment, the book begins with an exploration of models of learning by Kolb and McCarthy. Hess then "walks her talk" by employing these models overtly thoughout the book. The book is structured to support both individual readers and group reading (e.g., via professional learning communities or study groups). Additionally, she offers suggestions for using the book as a guide in workshops, and the modular structure offers flexibility to readers and leaders alike.

Before launching into assessment-specific tools and strategies, Hess describes her conception of intellectual rigor and introduces the Cognitive Rigor Matrix (CRM), an innovative framework for determining the level of complexity of assessment items and tasks. The Matrix can be used to analyze current assessments, serve as a design tool for constructing more rigorous performance tasks, and guide differentiated instruction. For leaders, the CRM can also be used as a framework for classroom observations and "walk-throughs."

The subsequent section on text complexity is particularly rich, offering a unique window into large-scale assessment design. Hess then translates these technical processes into state-of-the-art tools and protocols that classroom teachers can apply to determine the text complexity of their assignments and assessments.

The heart of the book centers on the design of high-quality performance assessment tasks and associated rubrics. Authentic tasks engage students in applying their knowledge and skills to a realistic issue or challenge, providing evidence of their understanding. Like the game in athletics or the play in theater, quality performance tasks provide clear and relevant targets for learning that can engage and motivate learning, as well as measure it. Hess's many years of experience are on full display as she offers an array of tools and suggested practices for the design and use of rigorous performance assessments.

Another unique contribution of the book reflects Dr. Hess's groundbreaking work of identifying Learning Progressions (LPs) in various disciplines. LPs provide descriptive continuums that chart the learning pathways from novice to expert performance. She illustrates the value of their use as informative guides to planning instruction and assessment based on a logical progression of how learners migrate from basic skills and concepts toward deeper understanding and transfer abilities.

Moving beyond the qualities of individual assessments, Hess makes a strong case for the importance of developing a comprehensive and balanced assessment *system*. As in a patchwork quilt, the whole is greater than the sum of the parts. An assessment system is needed to assess all the outcomes that matter and provide the feedback necessary for systemic, continuous improvement.

The book concludes with an Appendix containing a comprehensive list of all the tools referenced throughout the book. As with a large collection of mechanic's tools, you are not likely to use all of the assets contained in this full-featured toolkit. Throughout each module are tools for teachers and students. Additionally, the appendices contain numerous models and tips to support development of assessments and rubrics. Over time, as your assessment practices expand, you will find a treasure trove of practical resources to promote aligned assessment, deep learning, and continuous improvement. Be prepared to have your own learning deepened as you devour this impressive volume. Most certainly your students will be the beneficiaries.

Acknowledgments

They say it takes a village to raise a child. I think sometimes that can also be true for when writing a book. Throughout my career, I've benefited tremendously from the insights and good will of many people in "my village"—picking up gems of wisdom along the way from my own children and grandchildren, from students in my classroom, from many incredible educational gurus, and from my work with colleagues and school leaders who trusted me to lead longer-term efforts in their states or schools. This book represents more than my vision alone. It attempts to provide some collective thinking about how learning occurs and the many ways that local assessment practices can be implemented across districts, so that in every classroom, assessment is employed to enhance student learning, confidence, and independence.

I've always believed that learning directly from the best thinkers in education would make my ability to translate their ideas into practice much stronger. While too numerous to mention all of them (trust me, it's a long list), there are several who strongly influenced and advanced my thinking to the "next level" when attending their workshops, reading their books and articles, and having thought-provoking conversations with them. I hope I have remained true to their original thinking while striving to integrate and advance their ideas into my work.

Two thought leaders helped me refocus my thinking about best practices in teaching when I was a middle school teacher. After reading Nancy Atwell's classic book, *In the Middle*, and taking a course with Sandra Kaplan, "Differentiating Curriculum for Gifted Learners," I was convinced that differentiation, student-centered learning, and targeted small group instruction could be much more effective in reaching *all learners*, not just the gifted students. That first course with Sandra Kaplan eventually led me to complete my master of science degree in the education of the gifted.

Later, while working at the New Jersey Department of Education, several more national experts rocked my world—among the best were Grant Wiggins, Jay McTighe, and Heidi Hayes-Jacobs.

Before there was the dynamic duo of Wiggins and McTighe, there was Wiggins and there was McTighe. Grant was talking about this wacky idea he called *authentic assessment*. At one of his institutes, he asked us, "What if during the last two weeks of school, you let students identify something they wanted to learn and gave them access to the whole school building and all of the teachers as resources to complete their independent studies?" I raised my hand and volunteered to be an observer at one of those elementary schools to see it firsthand. Grant always helped me to see the bigger picture—a vision of where assessment could take you and your students.

What I learned from Jay was how to design teacher-friendly tools to actually do this work. Call me a pack rat, but I still have that folder he mailed to me years ago with several practical planning templates for developing performance tasks. In large part, I envisioned my book being modeled after the *Understanding by Design Professional Development Workbook*—clear, practical, and revolutionary in its potential impact on teaching, learning, and assessment.

Most people think of curriculum mapping or 21st century skills when they think of Heidi Hayes Jacobs; but that was not what first moved the needle for me. Long before those books, Heidi stood in a school auditorium in Newark, New Jersey, providing a visual metaphor for typical classroom discourse. She tossed a volley ball into the audience to simulate a teacher posing a question. The ball came back to her, simulating a response. After several of these exchanges, she asked, "Who touched the ball the most?" The answer was obvious—the teacher was the most engaged person in that classroom!

From that day forward, I began to attend more to how to structure classroom discourse for deeper thinking and greater student engagement. It should be no surprise then that many years later, when I read Norman Webb's reports and papers about test alignment studies and discovered his thinking about four depth-of-knowledge levels (DOK) when students engage with content, that I made one more important leap forward. It began with designing tools for teacher committees to use when conducting alignment studies of state assessments and led to thinking more about tests designed for deeper thinking and engagement. I further refined my work when integrating the concepts of depth of knowledge with formative uses of assessment. Let me just say that I've learned much from Dylan Wiliam's research in the area of formative assessment.

Collaborations on long-term curriculum and assessment projects while working with colleagues at the Center for Assessment (Dover, NH), the New Hampshire Department of Education, the New York City Department of Education, and the Center for Collaborative Education (Boston) provided me with the "big picture" in finding ways to bridge local assessment with large-scale assessment practices.

Multiyear projects with school leaders and school districts challenged me to develop, rethink, and refine the ideas and materials included in this toolkit. These critical friends always help me to "keep it real" for teachers and kids.

- In Vermont—working with Sue Biggam (Vermont Reads Institute), Bob Stanton (Lamoille Area Professional Development Academy/LAPDA), Jen Miller-Arsenault (Washington Central Supervisory Union), and Michaela Martin (Orleans North Supervisory Union)
- In Connecticut—working with literacy consultants at EASTCONN, Donna Drasch and Helen Weingart
- In Wyoming—working with R. J. Kost (Park County School District #1) and Kelly Hornsby (Campbell County School District #1)
- In Arkansas—working with Megan Slocum and Marcia Smith (Springdale School District)
- In Oregon—having a unique multiyear email relationship with Susan Richmond (Hillsboro School District) as she worked to bring these ideas to teachers in her district and in the process, pushed a lot of my thinking about implementation challenges.

Finally, a special note of thanks for the people at Corwin who always provided helpful direction, insightful comments, and unlimited patience, making me feel as though this book must be the only book being worked on! I'm especially grateful for the support and responsiveness of Jessica Allan, Diane DiMura, Lucas Schleicher, Mia Rodriguez, and Tori Mirsadjadi, who knew exactly how to take my ideas and fashion them into the final "package."

About the Author

Karin Hess has more than 40 years of deep experience in curriculum, instruction, and assessment. She is a recognized international leader in developing practical approaches for using cognitive rigor and learning progressions as the foundation for formative, interim, and performance assessments at all levels of assessment systems.

For almost 15 years at the Center for Assessment, Dr. Hess distinguished herself as a content, assessment, and alignment expert in multiple content areas, K–12. She has effectively guided many states and U.S. territories in the development of grade-level standards and test specifications for general education (e.g., New England Common Assessment Program/NECAP; Smarter Balanced Assessment Consortium/SBAC) and alternate assessments for students with significant cognitive disabilities (e.g., National Center and State Collaborative/NCSC). During this time, she also contributed to Maine's early thinking about how to structure requirements for graduation exhibitions and provided in-depth guidance for local development and use of performance assessments for proficiency-based graduation systems in Rhode Island, Wyoming, and New Hampshire.

Dr. Hess's experiences as a state director of gifted education for New Jersey and as a district curriculum director, building principal, and classroom teacher (15 years) enable her to understand the practical implications of her work while maintaining fidelity to research, technical quality, and established best practices. Dr. Hess has also worked as a program evaluator for the Vermont Mathematics Project and as the developer and editor of Science Exemplars (www.exemplars.com), creating, piloting, and annotating student work samples in science.

Karin has authored and co-authored numerous books, book chapters, articles, and white papers related to cognitive rigor, text complexity, assessment, and student-centered learning. Her ongoing work has included guiding the development and implementation of New Hampshire's K–12 Model Competencies for ELA, Mathematics, and Science and supporting school districts in many states in creating and analyzing use of high-quality performance assessments and performance scales for competency-based learning systems.

Introduction

College- and career-readiness (CCR) standards set expectations for all students to demonstrate deep conceptual understanding through the application of content knowledge and skills in new situations. Unfortunately, content standards provide limited or no guidance as to how, when, or to what degree specific skills and concepts should be emphasized by educators in the classroom. Without a clear direction and use of rich, engaging learning tasks, important CCR skills and dispositions will be, at best, inconsistently or randomly addressed by teachers or forgotten in the design of systemwide programs, curriculum, and instruction. We know that what gets tested is what gets the greatest instructional attention. If assessments of CCR standards only test acquisition and basic application of academic skills and concepts, there will be little incentive for schools to focus instruction and local assessment on deeper understanding and transfer of learning to real-world contexts (Hess & Gong, 2014). And, if deeper understanding and transfer of learning is only an expectation for some students, then we have not done our job in preparing all students for life after high school. Knowing how to think deeply about content and about themselves as learners should be a CCR goal for every student.

From my work with teachers, school districts, and states across the country, I've come to understand that effective local assessment systems are built upon several critical components:

- Ensuring there is a range of assessments (formative, interim, summative) of high technical quality at every grade level
- Providing robust, embedded professional development and leadership to support the use of assessment data that informs instruction and advances learning for each student
- Promoting a belief system that at the center of assessment is helping each student reach full potential

The tools, protocols, and examples presented in the *Local Assessment Toolkit* follow three guiding principles with the overarching goal of deeper learning for all students.

Guiding Principle #1: Assessment Quality Matters

Every day in every classroom, we set expectations for learning and in some way attempt to assess that learning. We buy tests; we buy curricular materials with tests; we develop tests; we spend class time on "test prep" prior to administering large-scale tests; and we worry a lot about test results. Sometimes, we design performance tasks and extended projects to elicit learning at a deeper level than most commercially available assessments can tap. We probably believe that most assessments we use have a higher level of precision and technical quality than they actually do. (I know that I did when I was in the classroom.) In other words, we put a lot of faith in the quality of the assessments we're using, even when we're not sure what they specifically assess; whether they do it sufficiently, effectively, *and fairly*; or how best to use the results to truly advance and deepen learning.

Individual educators and sometimes groups of educators use data from assessments to assign grades, identify and address learning gaps, or to plan next steps for instruction. But when do we actually examine the technical quality of our local assessments? And when does a "collection of tests" across teachers, grade levels, and content areas evolve to become a high-quality, cohesive assessment system? Knowing *why* an assessment is or is not a high-quality assessment is the first step in knowing how to interpret and use the results—even if this means replacing some of your current assessments with more effective ones. Often when I begin working with assessment teams in a school district, giving them honest feedback on their current use of assessments, it's not unusual for me to hear these comments: "I wish you were here 3 years ago when we began this work!" or "You're making us crazy . . . but in a good way."

Why do they say these things? Because assessment quality really does matter.

Guiding Principle #2: Learning Is at the Center of Assessment Design and System Coherence

I spent more than 25 years working *in* schools before I began working full time *with* schools. Schools are busy places. I get it. There is little time to stop and evaluate the quality of each assessment or to examine how well the overall assessment system supports our collective beliefs about student learning or promotes a vision for how students might engage more deeply while they are learning. It's not enough to buy or be handed "good assessments" without understanding what makes them high-quality assessments. And it's not enough to simply assess the skills and concepts that are most easily assessed, while ignoring the importance of deeper understanding.

An assessment system and the assessments in it should align with the philosophy underlying the Assessment Triangle, first presented in *Knowing What Students Know* (National Research Council [NRC], 2001). The assessment triangle focuses on the triad of cognition, observation, and interpretation, as the precursors to the design and use of assessments. In other words, how students typically learn and develop expertise in a content domain should guide assessment design and use of assessment data. Based on my understanding and interpretation of the Assessment Triangle, this is how cognition, observation, and interpretation interact to drive assessment design:

- **COGNITION:** Presents a (cognitive) model of knowing how students learn and develop competence in a subject domain over time
- **OBSERVATION:** Guides development of the kind of tasks or situations that allow one to observe student learning and performance along a learning continuum
- **INTERPRETATION:** Offers a method of knowing how to draw inferences about learning from the performance evidence

Guiding Principle #3: Deep Learning Is an Essential Goal for Every Student

Most students have become accustomed to "learning" as listening to the teacher, reading texts, and practicing what the teacher showed them how to do. Maybe we haven't systemically changed how we teach and assess because teaching for deeper understanding and assessing it is really, really complicated. Deeper learning to develop expertise in a domain of knowledge and performance requires months, or even years, of sustained, deliberate practice. Development of expertise also requires feedback to guide and optimize practice activities. A student with strong interpersonal skills will best understand and apply such feedback to academic learning.

Design Questions Related to the Elements of the Assessment Triangle

Observation-Related Questions:
What will the student do, say, or produce? What strategies are expected to be employed? Is the assessment task designed to measure the most important competencies? Is the task designed to elicit evidence of reasoning or extended thinking?

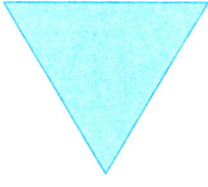

Interpretation-Related Questions:
What do you know for certain, given the evidence in the student's work/response? Does assessment evidence show that the student is moving from Novice performance to Expert performance (over time)? Where/how will you need to probe further for more or different evidence?

Cognition-Related Questions:
How do students acquire, build upon, and represent competence in this content domain? What are the "typical pathways" for developing expertise in the subject area over time? Is the assessment design consistent with a broader theory of learning that allows for diagnosis of learning needs, providing support, and moving students beyond basic understanding?

Source: National Research Council (2001).

Education for Life and Work (NRC, 2012) provides a cognitive science perspective of deeper learning showing how different it is from a more traditional approach.

> We define "deeper learning" as the process through which an individual becomes capable of taking what was learned in one situation and applying it to new situations (also called transfer). Through deeper learning (which often involves shared learning and interactions with others in a community), the individual develops expertise in a particular domain of knowledge and/or performance. . . . While other types of learning may allow an individual to recall facts, concepts, or procedures, deeper learning allows the individual to transfer what was learned to solve new problems. (pp. 5–6)

Deeper learning is supported through rich instructional and assessment practices that create a positive, collaborative learning environment in which students gain content knowledge while developing their intrapersonal and interpersonal skills. For example, developing metacognitive skills—the ability to reflect on one's own learning and make strategic adjustments accordingly—deepens academic content learning as well.

Summary of Recommended Research-Based Teaching Methods in Support of Deeper Learning

Use multiple and varied representations of concepts and tasks, such as diagrams, numerical and mathematical representations, and simulations, along with support to help students interpret them.

Encourage elaboration, questioning, and explanation, for example, by prompting students who are reading a history text to explain the material aloud to themselves or others as they read.

Engage learners in challenging tasks while also supporting them with guidance, feedback, and encouragement to reflect on their own learning processes.

(Continued)

> (Continued)
>
> **Teach with examples and cases,** such as modeling step by step how students can carry out a procedure to solve a problem while explaining the reason for each step.
>
> **Prime student motivation** by connecting topics to students' personal lives and interests, engaging students in problem solving, and drawing attention to the knowledge and skills students are developing and their relevance, rather than grades or scores.
>
> **Use formative assessments,** which continuously monitor students' progress and provide feedback to teachers and students for use in adjusting their teaching and learning strategies.
>
> *Source:* Education for Life and Work: Developing Transferable Knowledge and Skills in the 21st Century (NRC, 2012, pp. 9–10).

When we value deeper learning, we provide the time and strategic supports necessary for all students to be successful. This shift requires that we change how we view the learner, the curriculum, and the learning environment. When we value deeper learning across our school systems, we provide all teachers with the time and tools to collaborate and to deepen their understanding of quality assessment and how assessment results can help us to meet the needs of diverse learners. The *Local Assessment Toolkit* has taken the NRC research and recommendations to heart and put them into user-friendly practice. Using many of these tools and protocols, I've seen teams of teachers dramatically shift perspectives about learning and daily practices in instruction and assessment that can eventually shift the schoolwide norms.

Do you believe that deeper learning is an essential goal for all students *and* that all students can learn to think deeply? If you do, then the strategies and tools in this book should greatly enhance your work and move it forward. If you don't believe it's possible for all students to understand in more meaningful ways, then you can either give the book to a colleague (just kidding) or try one strategy to see if the results change your mind, even if only a little bit at first. This is usually the way change in daily practice begins—one strategy at a time. Once you and your students see that they can produce high-quality work, learning in your classrooms will never be the same. Students will come to know they are capable of that kind of work all the time. They will not be afraid to take on more challenging and complex assignments because they know they will be supported in the struggle. Deeper learning—not grades—becomes the motivation to do better, do more, and go farther.

This last idea was confirmed for me many years ago, both in a workshop with Rick Stiggins when he was discussing research about what motivates learners to want to improve their performance and in his 1997 book, where he states, "If students are to come to believe in themselves, then they must first experience some believable (credible) form of academic success as reflected in a real and rigorous assessment. A small success can rekindle a small spark of confidence, which in turn encourages more trying. . . . Our goal, then is to perpetuate this cycle" (p. 45). During the workshop I attended, he identified the top three motivators for students improving their performance. Here they are, in reverse order:

- **Number 3 Motivator—**When a supportive adult who knows the student well provides appropriate scaffolding, challenge, and encouragement, students come to understand that learning is about being confused and then figuring it out. (Readers of this book fall into this category. Congratulations! You are the third most effective motivator for your students.)

- **Number 2 Motivator**—When a student identifies with another student who is successful at a similar task, he believes that he can also be successful. ("Hey, I'm as smart as she is. I can do that, too!") This will only happen when students play on the same team, when they work and struggle together, and when they know that success is the result of everyone contributing to produce high-quality work and deeper understanding. This is the power of collaboration and is true for both students and teachers.

- **Number 1 Motivator**—When a student can see her own progress over time, it validates that she can learn deeply. This means that the evidence of learning needs to be specific and concrete. A student needs to understand the success criteria for the learning target, match it to her performance to meet the target, and be able to identify what went well and where more work is needed. This is about students having some control of their learning pathway and knowing what and how to learn. This is the power of self-assessment, and it holds true for both students and teachers.

Clint Mathews, secondary English teacher and district ELA curriculum facilitator in Gillette, Wyoming, shared this reflection with me on how a shift in teaching for deeper understanding affected his students' control over their own learning:

One of the biggest changes that has occurred in my classes is the relevance of DOK in day-to-day activities, as well as in formal assessment. As we work through every task, I have a greater self-awareness of who is really doing the work and for what reason. Too often teachers, including myself, often step in and take over much of the work, thinking that we are helping students. I tend to now look at each lesson through a DOK lens and I am much more purposeful in what I have students do and how I help them while still having students shoulder much of the load. I have also found it easier to differentiate some tasks as we move through the lesson in order to push more students toward a DOK 4 from a DOK 3. For example, in a senior British literature class, my students were analyzing several poems by a chosen poet from the Romantic period. In addition, they were tasked with explaining how the author truly represented the literary period. They drew from interpretations of the poems but also incorporated outside sources such as relevant biographical, historical, and critical texts. Several students quickly moved through the readings and even through the preliminary draft. It became obvious that they were on track toward proficiency.

Two of my students excelled throughout the course, but in different ways. Student A worked through each task meticulously and purposefully. He welcomed challenges and willingly worked toward a DOK 4 (synthesizing multiple sources) with minimal prompting. Student B worked methodically through each task and once she demonstrated proficiency, found little reason to go above and beyond; instead, she would rather draw and work on her art—her true passion.

Rather than adding another task to their plates, I used formative assessment to monitor these students and then worked with them independently in order to guide them toward level 4 work. Student A was very devoted to music. His writing addressed all of the requirements for the DOK 3 task, but he went further with the writing and added a comparison component wherein he compared a notable composer to the poet, explicated significant works of each, and explained how while the poet represented the age, the composer actually rebelled against the period and served as an inspiration for the following period. Student B followed a similar path, but with an artist. They each discovered new information by integrating something they were personally passionate about, made original claims, and defended those claims with textual evidence from multiple works—all above and beyond the original assigned task.

The Design, Purpose, and Suggested Uses of the *Local Assessment Toolkit*

The *Local Assessment Toolkit* represents many years working with educators to develop and refine practical tools and protocols that build local capacity by establishing a common language and deeper knowledge of assessment system components and how the system as a whole can become greater than its parts. Because assessment systems include formative uses of assessment, I see the "system" as including instruction and the many related instructional supports. For example, I cannot talk about increasing rigor without suggesting ways to support (scaffold) all students in getting there (e.g., providing strategies for classroom discourse that uncovers thinking or graphic organizers that help students to organize ideas). I cannot talk about designing assessments for and of deeper thinking without providing strategies for interpreting and acting on evidence seen in student work. You cannot do one well without the other.

As the title suggests, the design of assessments and the assessment system should always be based on linking research with day-to-day practices that promote authentic learning and deeper understanding. While these tools can be employed to support any high-quality assessment work, my focus is on knowing how the brain processes information so that thinking can be revealed and understanding deepened. I've linked the tools, protocols, and strategies throughout the toolkit with several areas of research: cognitive science, psychometrics and assessment design, research related to building expertise in the academic disciplines, and interpersonal and intrapersonal skill development.

These tools have had many users—from undergraduate- and graduate-level classes, to in-service professional development activities, to guidance for test item writers and designers of research studies. However, the *Local Assessment Toolkit* was primarily designed as a professional development guide for long-term use by school leaders. The most effective leadership cadre is composed of committed administrators, district curriculum and assessment facilitators, instructional coaches, and teacher leaders. At the end of the day, the outside consultant gets on a plane and goes home. Sometimes the consultant comes back several times or acts as a long-distance mentor to the school leaders; but the people who carry the vision forward and ensure fidelity of the day-to-day implementation are the school leaders. They are the "front runners" who will try things out first in their classrooms and inspire their colleagues by sharing and reflecting on their results. They are the coaches and supervisors who will visit classrooms, looking for and supporting deeper-learning teaching and assessment practices. They are the administrators who can structure time and focus, making collaboration possible for designing and using high-quality assessments. Long-term implementation is about cultivating leadership density—recognizing the potential for leadership within your staff, and weaving connections among teams within the system, so that teachers can acknowledge their own leadership in shaping the vision for the direction in which the school or district is heading. Building leadership density and providing structures for meaningful collaboration are two critical components needed for implementing systemic change (Hess, 2000). Based on my research, a third component necessary for ensuring systemic change is involving every educator and every student in the work.

About the Modules

The five topic-based modules guide assessment teams and professional developers in the use of field-tested, teacher-friendly tools, strategies, and protocols similar to what testing contractors might use in test development, but modified for a local school setting. Each module applies best practices in assessment design and use to what we know about student thinking and understanding. Above all, this assessment toolkit is about learning.

The modules do not have to be used sequentially; however, earlier modules focus on components essential to instruction and assessment design (rigor, alignment, student engagement)—a good starting point. The later modules focus on assessment system development and supporting district or schoolwide use. Most assessment teams that I have worked with find that as they work collaboratively, taking the time to process and test the ideas and examples across classrooms (such as collecting and collaboratively analyzing student work samples), their assessment literacy deepens. Modules are often revisited from time to time to gain new insights about student learning or used for professional learning when new staff are brought on board. Never forget that this work is ongoing and always cyclical and iterative in nature. Here are a few key points about the organization of the *Local Assessment Toolkit*:

- Modules have been organized in what I hope is a thoughtful approach to helping school and district leadership teams analyze and perhaps redesign local assessment systems for greater effectiveness and deeper learning.

- Modules are designed to be used both for individual learning and to frame a series of professional development opportunities, such as local PLC activities. Collaborative learning and implementation will be the most effective way to change the system.

- I always begin with Module 1 (cognitive rigor) and then decide where to focus next. As you unpack the complexities of each module, you'll realize that slowing down implementation allows time for the system to catch up. While some schools may begin with a focus on questioning and classroom discourse, others might focus on developing and using performance assessments. I always recommend setting two goals: a short-term goal that will yield immediate results (e.g., every teacher tries one new strategy in Module 1 to reflect on and share with peers) and a longer-term goal for the school (e.g., school-based validation teams begin to codevelop assessments using Module 3 tools).

- Each module is framed by an essential question and divided into two parts. Part 1 provides a discussion and examples of the "what" (defining key learning and assessment ideas) and the "why" (a research-based rationale for implementation). Part 2 can be thought of as the "how" (how to practice the ideas) and the "what if" (suggesting ways to apply and adapt the ideas to improve your local system).

- Part 2 of each module also includes a suggested workshop plan using the support materials and resources in the module. The 4-stage structure of the suggested professional learning plan synthesizes Kolb's Experiential Learning Cycle with McCarthy's 4MAT learning style system to address the why, the what, the how, and the what if of implementation. A brief description of Kolb and McCarthy's models and my rationale for using them to plan professional development sessions are provided at the end of this section.

- Throughout each module, there are a variety of support materials. Icons are used to indicate specific uses of the information and protocols, and to differentiate teacher versus student tools.

ICON	SUPPORT MATERIALS IN EACH MODULE
	When you see the clipboard, it indicates a potential workshop activity or time for readers to stop and reflect.
	Teacher tools are indicated by a compass icon with a number. Teacher tools include a variety of instructional and assessment planning worksheets and protocols. Tools in each module correspond to a different focus (e.g., Module 1—Cognitive Rigor; Module 2—Text Complexity; Module 3—PLC Tools).

(Continued)

(Continued)

ICON	SUPPORT MATERIALS IN EACH MODULE
	Kid tools are classroom examples to be used by students to uncover thinking and reasoning. They include everything from graphic organizers to student peer- and self-assessment tools.
	Throughout the toolkit, video clips and other professional resources are suggested to further illustrate a concept or demonstrate a protocol. These are resources that school leaders might want to include in locally designed professional learning or PLC activities.

Overview of Module Content

Module 1: (Cognitive Rigor) Are My Students Thinking Deeply or Just Working Harder?

Infusing rigor into instruction and assessment:
Laying the groundwork for deeper learning for all *students*

Module 1 lays the groundwork for developing a common understanding of cognitive rigor and dispels seven common misconceptions about DOK/rigor. Activities, examples, and tools illustrate how to use the Hess Cognitive Rigor Matrices when planning and supporting or coaching instructional and assessment activities.

Module 2: (Text Complexity) Is the Task Appropriate to the Text?

Examining and using increasingly complex texts

Module 2 provides tools for understanding and qualitatively analyzing literary and informational texts before deciding how to best use them. Instructional planning tools and frames for text-based questions are used to explore ways to probe for deeper understanding of print and nonprint texts.

Module 3: (Assessment Design and Use) What Does This Test Really Measure?

Designing and refining high-quality assessments for deeper learning

Module 3 includes numerous tools, protocols, and content-specific examples for designing assessments for formative, interim, or summative use. PLC tools apply research-based technical indicators for rubric design, task validation, and development of common performance assessments. Processes for analyzing student work and selecting and annotating anchor papers are used to build understandings about student learning.

Module 4: (Learning Progressions) Where Do I Start, What Do I Teach Next, Which Supports Work Best?

Using learning progressions as a schema for planning
instruction and measuring progress

Module 4 can be thought of as a course called *learning progressions 101*. Information in this module is designed to help educators clarify what a learning progression is and what it is not. For example, your best guess about how learning might develop is not a *learning* progression; arranging standards across grade levels is not a *learning* progression. True learning progressions are supported by targeted instruction and validated with empirical research and student work analysis. The step-by-step strategies and school-based examples in this module provide guidance in using learning progressions to plan and target instruction, creating pre-, mid-, and postassessments, and measuring progress along a learning continuum.

Module 5: (Building a Comprehensive Assessment System) Is This a Collection of Tests or an Assessment System?

Building and sustaining a comprehensive local assessment system for deeper learning

Modules 1 through 4 have focused mostly on individual assessment design and use, not on building a coherent assessment system. The tools in Module 5 are useful in identifying system strengths and gaps by mapping current assessments and identifying what content, skills, and depth of understanding are being emphasized, in terms of what is actually taught and assessed. Alignment tools are provided for local review of assessments in use and building a comprehensive assessment system.

A 4-stage workshop planning framework using the materials in each module

When I decided to organize the assessment toolkit as a guide for school leaders, I began to think about a practical framework to support users of the materials in designing their own professional learning activities. I decided to incorporate what I have been using for more than 30 years—a hybrid planning tool that integrates key ideas from David Kolb's experiential learning model (1984) with Bernice McCarthy's 4MAT® learning styles system for curricular planning (1987). McCarthy introduced me to Kolb's and her model while I was working at the New Jersey Department of Education. I had an in-depth opportunity while at the department to learn from McCarthy and then to provide training under her mentorship on how to use the 4MAT® system, which was built upon Kolb's experiential learning model. It is my hope that by synthesizing a few key ideas from these models into my work, their good ideas will remain relevant for future generations of educators.

Kolb's experiential learning cycle

David Kolb's research advanced a model of experiential learning that combined two key dimensions: how we PERCEIVE new or the reintroduction of information (along a vertical continuum from concrete to abstract) and how we then PROCESS that information (along an intersecting/horizontal continuum from reflection to experimentation).

One dimension of Kolb's model is how we PERCEIVE (take in) new or the reintroduction of information. At the top of the model is perceiving via *concrete experiences*. At the other end of the continuum is perceiving via *abstract conceptualization*. While two learners might have the same learning experience, such as taking a hike, how they perceive—or take in information about the experience of the hike—might be very different based on individual learning preferences. Concrete experiences are very individual and personalized, using senses, feelings, and prior knowledge to initially make sense of them. Abstract conceptualization is more generalized, with learners intellectually defining and categorizing what is being perceived. All learners use both ways to perceive or take in information at different times during learning.

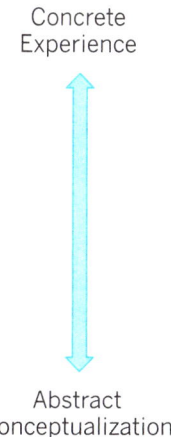

A second, intersecting dimension of Kolb's model is how we PROCESS information once we've taken it in.

At the far left of this axis is processing by *active experimentation*. At the other end of the continuum is processing by *reflective observation*. Combining the two axes yields four different learning style preferences as part of an ongoing experiential learning cycle.

Introduction 9

Kolb's experiential learning theory is typically represented by a four-part learning cycle in which the learner "touches all the bases." Effective learning is seen when a person progresses through a cycle of (1) having a concrete experience followed by (2) observation of and reflection on that experience which leads to (3) the formation of abstract concepts (analysis) and generalizations (conclusions) which are then (4) used to test hypotheses in future situations, resulting in new experiences (McLeod, 2013).

Kolb's Experiential Learning Cycle

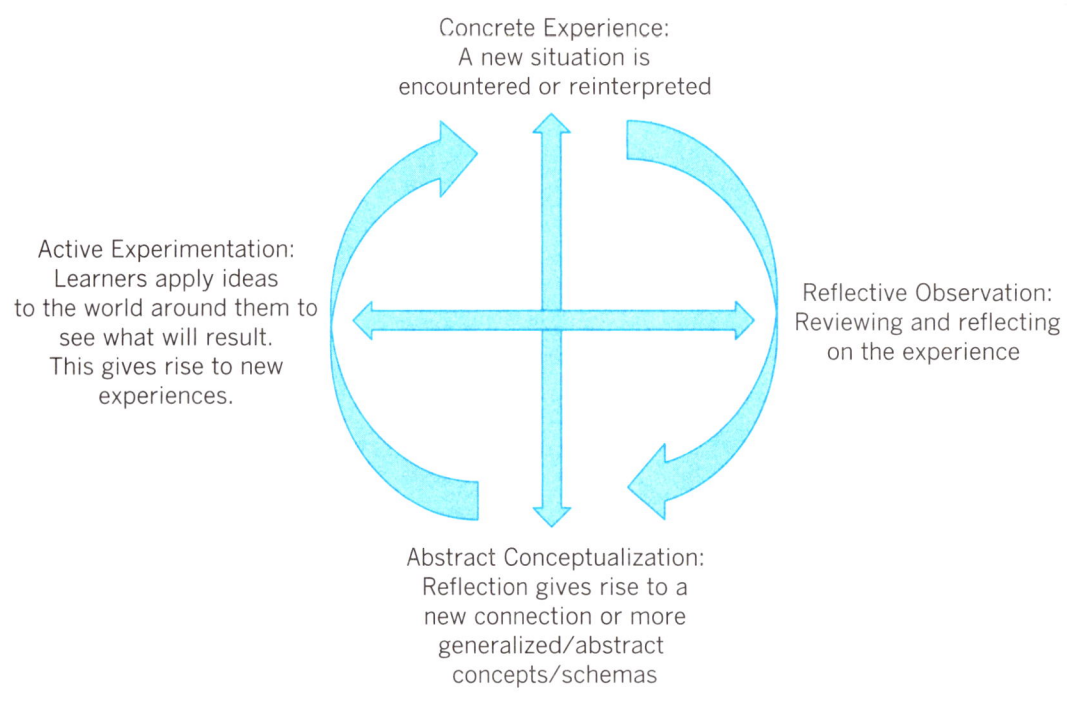

McCarthy's 4MAT® System

McCarthy employed Kolb's experiential learning model to identify four distinct learning style preferences, each one defined by the intersection of two adjacent dimensions. A type 1 learner (represented by the upper-right quadrant) prefers reflecting on concrete experiences. This is a learner who needs to know WHY the new learning is personally important. McCarthy's lesson and curricular planning begins with teachers designing a concrete experience for students to reflect on. A type 2 learner (represented by the lower-right quadrant) wants to know and reflect on WHAT the books, the experts, and the research say about this new concept or principle. These learners prefer to generalize what they are learning. A type 3 learner (represented by the lower-left quadrant) starts to get fidgety simply talking and reading about concepts. These learners are most interested in knowing HOW it works in the real word. Type 3 learners like to tinker and actively practice applying the new learning. The type 4 learner (represented by the upper-left quadrant) tends to be more interested in moving beyond what the experts say and how it typically works. These learners begin to ask, "WHAT IF I experiment with this concept or principle? What might happen? What will I learn from the next new experience?" The complete 4MAT® model is an integration of learning styles and left-right brain hemisphericity in a sequence that follows a natural and dynamic cycle of learning through eight stages (McCarthy, 1987).

McCarthy's work stresses that traditional instructional approaches are mostly supportive of type 2 and type 3 learners. Because all learners tend to have a preferred primary learning style (types 1–4), curriculum and instruction should be designed to continually honor all learners, and all learning styles. This is as true for adult learners as it is for our students.

My workshop planning frame does not add McCarthy's left-right brain components to each quadrant, but draws from Kolb and McCarthy to create a four-stage plan for designing professional learning. In part 2 of each module, tools and activities are suggested for each stage, beginning with a concrete and personal experience that can be shared and reflected upon.

Toolkit Workshop Planning Frame
Drawn from the work of Kolb (1984) and McCarthy (1987)

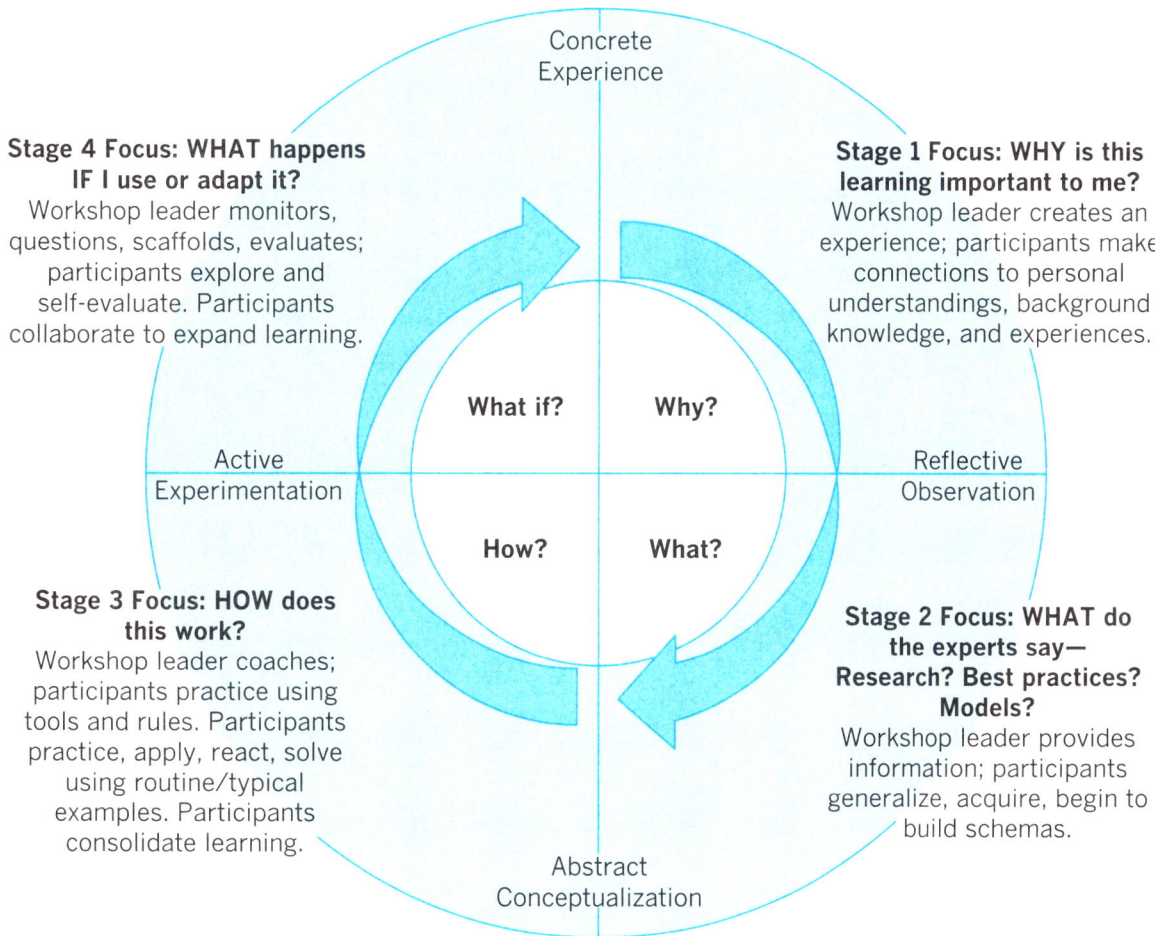

Introduction 11

Generally, this is how the suggested worksop activities might flow:

Stage 1—Moving From Concrete Experience to Reflective Observation:
Workshop leaders create an experience. Participants reflect on what they think and their prior knowledge and compare their ideas with others in small groups. Workshop leaders listen in, perhaps recording some ideas or identifying some common factors. Workshop leaders think about how to make conncetions with the next phase of the learning cycle—integrating 'expert' information. (In a personal email from Bernice, as I was preparing this manuscript, was a reminder that I stress that the experience the teacher or workshop leader creates in Stage One must be an experience that the teacher can use to connect the content—or the essence of the learning—with the students.)

Stage 2—Moving From Reflective Observation to Abstract Conceptualization:
Workshop leaders introduce definitions, show models and examples, and may provide a short reading or video that ties ideas together with concepts. During this stage, guided practice might be used with some of the tools or strategies in order to generalize ideas and begin to build broader conceptual schemas.

Stage 3—Moving From Abstract Conceptualization to Active Experimentation:
In pairs or small groups, participants now practice using tools with some of their own examples, such as a local performance task, unit of study, or common assessment. Participants compare earlier impressions (from stage 1) with new observations and insights, based on collaborative analyses and discussion.

Stage 4—Moving From Abstract Conceptualization to *New* Concrete Experiences:
Teams brainstorm ways to apply or expand new learnings with instruction and assessment in their own curriculum. They create action plans and try using new strategies, reflecting once again how things worked.

| KOLB'S EXPERIENTIAL LEARNING CYCLE | A WORKSHOP PLAN WITH SUGGESTED ACTIVITIES |

Stage 1: WHY is this new learning important to me? And what do I already know?

Moving From Concrete Experience to Reflective Observation

- Create a common concrete experience, asking participants to make connections, drawing on personal knowledge and experience.
- Small groups compare and reflect on common ideas.

Stage 2: WHAT do the research and experts say?

Moving From Reflective Observation to Abstract Conceptualization

- Help participants connect their personal reflections to broader, more abstract generalizations.
- Provide expert advice and review the research via interactive lecture, readings, and video clips.
- Use models and examples or nonexamples to further develop concepts and build schemas. Stop frequently to allow participants to consolidate the new learning.

Stage 3: HOW does this work? How can I apply this?

Moving From Abstract Conceptualization to Active Experimentation

- Provide guided practice using tools and protocols to examine examples and strategies.
- Suggest revising or updating a current assessment, lesson plan, or unit of study.

Stage 4: WHAT IF I experimented with this? What might work in my classroom or school?

Moving From Active Experimentation Back to Concrete Experiences

- Encourage participants to apply use of tools or protocols in their own work.
- Structure review and reflection activities.
- Give "homework"—experiment with a new strategy in your classroom. Reflect on how it worked and what you might do next.

Source: Stages adapted from Kolb (1984) and McCarthy (1987).

MODULE 1: ARE MY STUDENTS THINKING DEEPLY OR JUST WORKING HARDER?

Infusing Rigor Into Instruction and Assessment: Laying the Groundwork for Deeper Learning for All Students

1.1 What Is Cognitive Rigor?

Rigor. These days, everyone seems to have something to say about it. Policymakers want standards and testing to include it; administrators want their schools to strive for it; publishers promote materials oozing with it; researchers look for but often can't find it; and most teachers end up getting mixed messages about what exactly everyone means when they are asked to produce results of it. Does increasing the level of rigor simply mean doing more homework, reading harder books, taking advanced courses, or just memorizing more stuff?

I frequently introduce the concept of rigor by sharing a favorite *Sally Forth* comic strip (Howard, 1991).

Panel 1:

We see a scene at the breakfast table with Mom saying to Dad, *"Hilary's spelling test is today, Ted. Can you give her one last run through?"*

Dad responds, *"Sure."*

Panel 2:

Dad begins with the spelling list: *"Ready? Erosion"*

"That's not the first word, Dad. How can I spell them if you jumble them up?"

Panel 3:

Dad looks surprised. *"You only know them in order?"*

"I don't know them—I memorized them. Nobody said anything about having to know them!"

For too many years, we have equated being a good memorizer with being smart. Students knew that if they could memorize something quickly, they usually got a good grade. Class participation was praised if you were the first one with your hand up, and that made you feel really smart, smarter than most of the other kids. It felt good to be a good memorizer. Sadly, in some classrooms today, this is still the case.

The most effective teachers know that when they start to probe those "canned answers" a bit, they quickly discover that the good memorizers don't always know what they are talking about. Most of the time, memorization doesn't take learners very far or very deep. Memorization may be efficient if you're good at it, but it is not effective if deeper understanding is the intended learning outcome. That is why I care about rigor. Specifically I am talking about *cognitive* rigor. **Cognitive rigor** encompasses the complexity of the content, the cognitive engagement with that content, and the depth and scope of the planned learning activities. Cognitive rigor begins and ends with the student. In an ideal world, teachers orchestrate access to, time for, and engagement with the content so that students can move from foundational to conceptual to deeper layers of meaning.

When I was in the classroom, I found that my students were more engaged when lessons weren't about memorizing content, but about digging into the content and doing something interesting or novel with it. As a matter of fact, I knew I had achieved success when my students entered the classroom one day and one of them asked, "What are we going to do today?"

Before I could answer, another student smiled and responded, "You know she's not going to tell us. We're going to have to figure it out on our own."

I took that as a sign that my students knew that this was a "thinking" classroom—a classroom with rigorous learning activities leading to deeper understanding, a classroom where learning required mental effort and engagement. The specifics of what my students were going to learn on any given day may not have been all that obvious at the start of a lesson, but the questions and tasks I asked them to engage with were interesting enough for them to be willing to go on that journey with me. In the end, they could always articulate that they had learned—not memorized—something. That is not to say that every student loved doing homework or always got high grades. What they all learned was how to struggle together in order to figure something out that might have initially confused them. In other words, they all learned *how* to learn. At first, this proved to be especially hard for my highest-performing students who had always relied on knowing the right answer without having to explain *why* it was the right answer or how they had figured it out. They never had to really "know" the content. Good memorizers are not generally willing to move out of their comfort zone to become flexible thinkers, at least not at first. Students learn to value what adults value. It's time to let our students know that we value thinking and that we believe that all students can do this, given the appropriate time and supports.

1.2 Developing a Common Understanding of What Cognitive Rigor Is and What It Is Not

When we infuse cognitive rigor across the curriculum, it's not only about deciding what we teach, but how we teach it, how we assess it, and what we believe about our students' abilities to successfully work through challenging material. Rigorous curriculum that is not accessible to every student results in only some students developing the college- and career-readiness skills of reasoning, problem solving, critical thinking, and self-regulation. If we truly believe in equity, then we need to ensure that all students leave high school with the confidence and skills to make sense of increasingly complex (and unfamiliar) content.

College- and career-readiness (CCR) standards set expectations for all students to demonstrate deep conceptual understanding through the application of content knowledge and skills in new situations. However, content standards provide little or no guidance as to how, when, or to what degree specific concepts and skills should be emphasized by educators in the classroom. Without a clear direction and use of rich, engaging learning tasks, important college- and career-readiness skills and dispositions will be, at best, inconsistently or randomly addressed by teachers, or forgotten in the design of local assessment systems. We know that what gets tested is what gets instructional attention. If assessments of CCR standards only test acquisition and basic application of academic skills and concepts, there is little incentive for schools to focus instruction and assessment on deeper understanding and transfer of learning to new and authentic (real-world) contexts (Hess & Gong, 2014).

What Immediately Comes to Mind When You Think of Cognitive Rigor?

Take a minute to jot down some of the words and phrases that immediately come to your mind when you think of cognitive rigor as it relates to instruction, learning, or assessment. Then think about what each phrase on your list has to do with the complexity of the content, the cognitive engagement with that content, or the depth and scope of the planned learning activities. Perhaps some of the things on your list are related to your belief system about how you support learners or some of the challenges you've faced when you tried to make your instruction and assessments more rigorous.

In my workshops, I ask participants to make their personal lists and then compare them in small groups to see what is similar and what is different on their lists. As they share with the larger group why they've agreed to include certain words and phrases, I unpack some of the related research. What follows is a typical discussion of the key research ideas that almost always surface during these workshops.

 View a video clip of a similar workshop discussion, *Karin Hess Linking Research and Rigor* (2015), at http://www.karin-hess.com/free-resources.

1.2a Cognitive Rigor Is Making Connections to Consolidate the Learning

Making connections is critical to understanding cognitive rigor and the mental processing of information. This is related to short-term or working memory and long-term memory and how we mentally organize new information so it can be retrieved later to solve problems and perform complex tasks. Cognitive scientists agree that short-term memory is limited. Think back to a time when you've been introduced to a new group of people. Once you've met the fifth or sixth person, you realize that you don't remember the first person's name—unless you were able to make some personal connection to them.

 View a video clip of Robert Bjork (2012) discussing strategies for slowing down learning to increase long-term memory and transfer at https://www.youtube.com/watch?v=gtmMMR7SJKw&feature=youtu.be.

Research studies in the 1950s through the 1970s suggested that most children and adults could hold only about five unrelated things (plus or minus two) at any given time in their working memory. More recent studies suggest that "it is less than previously thought and may now be three to five items for adults. . . . [T]he actual number varies with the learner's age and type of input (factual information, visual, auditory, etc.) and the nature of the cognitive processing" (Sousa, p. 23, 2015).

The functional implications are obvious: When your working memory is full, you have to either let go of something in order to add a new piece of information or make a connection in order to hold onto it. In the classroom, we introduce our students to fact after fact after fact. It must feel like "drive-by" teaching to many students, as we strive to cover the curriculum. The problem is that if students are not making meaningful connections, there is little chance that new information will ever be connected and remembered. This becomes a case of use it or lose it (Brown, Roediger, & McDaniel, 2014; Gregory & Kaufeldt, 2015; Sousa, 2015).

Two important conditions have to be present to move information from short-term or working memory into long-term memory—making sense and having meaning for the learner.

- *The first step is called "consolidation," which is the process of allowing the brain to reorganize and stabilize the memory.* The new information has to connect to something you already know, even if it challenges something you think you know. (That's sometimes called cognitive dissonance.) "Prior knowledge is a prerequisite for making sense of new learning, and forming those connections is an important task of consolidation" (Brown et al., 2014, p. 73). Without making some kind of connection, the new information simply doesn't have a place to live in your memory. Your brain must decide if it makes sense. Does this fit into my understanding—or schema—of how the world works based on my background knowledge, my experiences, and my perceptions?

- *There also has to be relevance or personal usefulness to the new information.* When a student asks, "How will I ever use this?" it's an indicator that the student has not had sufficient time to establish meaning. "If both sense and meaning are present, the likelihood of the new information getting encoded into long-term memory is very high" (Sousa, 2015, p. 28).

What is in your long-term memory is there because you connected it to something you already knew, you expanded upon something you knew, and you were able to internalize and use (transfer) it in ways that were meaningful to you. Information remains in long-term memory only when you periodically practice retrieving and using it. Interestingly, "the more effort you have to expend to retrieve knowledge or skill, the more the practice of retrieval will entrench it" (Brown et al., 2014, p. 79). This means that practicing simple retrieval of a skill or fact is less beneficial to retaining and being able to access it later than when you contextualize practice of the skill or fact. Context, such as the use of a skill or procedure in a problem-solving situation, tends to bring overall performance to an even higher level than will routine practice drills of the same skills (p. 81). Additionally, we've learned that when trying to unlock a memory, more connections can be made to the stored information by using multi-sensory processing (e.g., related visual, auditory, or kinesthetic memories).

Instructional Implications for Making Connections: Research by the psychologists Chris S. Hulleman of the University of Virginia and Judith Harackiewicz of the University of Wisconsin suggests that for most of us, whether we find something interesting is largely a matter of whether we find it personally valuable. For many students, science is boring because they don't think it's relevant to their lives (O'Keefe, 2014). In one study, a group of high school science students was randomly selected to write summaries of what they had learned in their class. Another group wrote about the usefulness of science in their own lives. At the end of the semester, the researchers found that, compared with those who simply summarized the material, the ones who reflected on its personal relevance reported more interest in science—as well as significantly higher grades, on average by almost a full grade point. This was particularly true for those with the lowest expectations for performing well in their class.

Throughout a lesson, as well as over the course of a unit of study, teachers need to stop periodically—with intent—to allow all students to consolidate the learning. My general rule of thumb is that during a lesson, this should happen about every 10 to 15 minutes. This can be as brief as 1 minute and as simple as turning and talking with a peer to paraphrase three key ideas, check understanding of a rule or definition, provide one example, or locate a piece of supporting evidence for a stated claim or conclusion. These types of formative assessment are often called quick checks for understanding, and they tend to be spontaneous, happening in the moment. It would be good for teachers to remember that a check for understanding should benefit the students as much as it might benefit the teacher.[1]

A second kind of formative assessment used to consolidate the learning is an activity designed with a specific purpose and learning target in mind. These include such things as exit cards (e.g., What do you remember from the lesson?), preassessments (e.g., What prior knowledge can you build upon?), and short tasks structured to encourage students to find personal meaning in information presented (such as completing pre- and post-anticipation guides[2] to see if personal perceptions or understandings have changed).

One example of a formative assessment I've used over the years to help students to consolidate and make meaning of new learning was to ask them to complete a "one-pager"[3] based on a reading assignment. I tried this approach one day when I had several students—okay, a lot of students—come to class unprepared for discussion of a text that had been assigned for homework. Because responses are not expected to be longer than one page, it was not threatening to students who struggle to read or write. At the top of the page, students selected and copied a quote from the text—that was easy even for my most struggling readers. And yes, some students simply copied the first line in the article, while others were more selective and skimmed for a particular line. It didn't matter what line they started with and was actually very motivating for students to choose where they wanted to start. In the middle of the page, students explained why they chose that quote and how it connected to the main idea of the text or topic. Now they had to make a connection. At the bottom of the page, students created a visual which gives personal meaning to the quote.

> View a video clip, *Studying and Designing for Transfer*, at http://blogs.elon.edu/issotl13/studying-and-designing-for-transfer.

All in all it's pretty simple: Students have to read a little to answer the second part, then think and reread a little more to make the visual. When they share their impressions with another student, they are starting to have a discussion about different interpretations of the text. They can now join others who have chosen the same quote but have different reasons and different visuals. I will tell you in all honesty, you will probably have a more genuine class discussion when there is a vehicle like the one-pager to help students to make connections and get deeper into what the text means to them.

1.2b Cognitive Rigor Is Applying What You've Learned, Also Known as Transfer

There are actually two kinds of "apply"—both are important to learning, but only one leads to the deepest understanding. Let's call the lower-level type of application "practice." Learn it and practice it! Practice is important, but there is also another way to apply—this happens when you apply what you know to a new situation or use it for a new purpose. The latter type of application is often referred to in the literature as transfer. Transfer happens when you see some similarity in the situation presented and you say to yourself, "Wait a minute; maybe there is something I've done before that will work here." So, you apply what you have learned in a new context. Maybe it

---

1. Sample turn and talk frames are included in Part 2 of this module.
2. A sample anticipation guide can be found at the beginning of Module 4.
3. A sample template for the one-pager can be found at the end of this module.

doesn't work the first time, but you are willing to explore different possibilities and in the process, begin to construct new knowledge, new meaning.

"In cognitive theory, knowing means more than the accumulation of factual information and routine procedures; it means being able to integrate knowledge, skills, and procedures in ways that are useful for interpreting situations and solving problems" (National Research Council [NRC], 2001, p. 62). The ability to transfer our knowledge and skill effectively involves the capacity to take what we know and use it creatively, flexibly, fluently, in different settings or problems, on our own (Wiggins & McTighe, 2005). When a student is able to understand concepts and apply skills beyond what is considered to be "routine understanding" (DOK 1–DOK 2),[4] this is what I mean when I say "transfer." Transferability of learning has probably been best operationalized in the Understanding by Design framework of McTighe and Wiggins, who defined it as "the ability to use knowledge appropriately and fruitfully in a new or different context from that [in] which it was initially learned" (1999, p. 283).

I was in a weeklong workshop with Grant Wiggins in 1990 when he shared a great metaphor for understanding the concept of transfer. He began the story saying, "Coming to school is like being on the team. You get to come to practice every day and do the drills; but you don't get to play many games." Wiggins then recounted a story about transfer (playing the game) when coaching his daughter's soccer team. Below is an excerpt from an article published by Edutopia (2006) with the story in his own words:

> When I was a soccer coach, I learned the hard way about transfer and the need to better assess for it. The practice drills did not seem to transfer into fluid, flexible, and fluent game performance. It often appeared, in fact, as if all the work in practice were for naught, as players either wandered around purposelessly or reacted only to the most obvious immediate needs.
>
> The epiphany came during a game, from the mouth of a player. In my increasing frustration, I started yelling, "Give and go!" "Three on two!" "Use it, use it—all the drills we worked on!" At that point, the player stopped dribbling in the middle of the field and yelled back, "I can't see it now! The other team won't line up like the (practice) drill for me!"
>
> That's both a clear picture of the problem and the road to the solution: too many sideline drills of an isolated skill, and not enough testing of it; too great a gap between what the simplified drill was teaching and testing and what the performance demands.

> **Suggested Resource**
>
> For more instructional examples to support near and far transfer, see Fisher, Frey, and Hattie (2016, pp. 107–115).

Let's be honest. Who would want to be on a team where you practice drills every day but rarely get to play the game? *Transfer is playing the game.* **Transfer** is taking the lower-level skills and putting them into play, deciding whether this is a time to use a particular skill; it is testing to see what will work in this situation and reflecting on how well it worked. Sometimes we ask our students to do all of the daily practice of skills in isolation. Then we get to the end of the unit of study and give them a rigorous assessment, only to find that they don't know how to apply what we thought we'd taught them. Maybe it's because they haven't had enough time to "scrimmage" before playing the game. Scrimmages are the bridge between the practice drills and the game. Scrimmages tell us whether students are making progress in preparing to take on more complex tasks.

Consider for a moment how a scrimmage is different from a game. First of all, it doesn't count; there is no score. It's a practice game guided by the coach. It's not a full game but selected

---

4. DOK stands for Depth-of-Knowledge. More detailed examples of DOK levels are provided in Table 1.1

scenarios of possible game situations. The coach can stop the scrimmage, tell everyone to look at where they are and ask what they should be doing or thinking, and then rewind, so to speak, and let them try it again. In a scrimmage, players are practicing transfer.

Instructional Implications for Teaching for and Assessing Transfer: Look at one of your units of study and identify the parts of lessons that look mostly like practice drills. This is when students practice applying foundational skills and concepts in a situation very much like how it was modeled during instruction. This type of learning activity was called "near" transfer by Perkins and Salomon (1988) to describe when students apply a skill or concept in a routine or typical way (e.g., decoding words in connected text, practicing word attack strategies, crafting a summary, identifying key words and information in math word problems, determining an appropriate strategy for solving a problem, writing equations and expressions). Near transfer—or "low-road transfer—reflects the automatic triggering of well-practiced routines in circumstances where there is considerable perceptual similarity to the original context. High-road transfer is not as dependent on superficial stimulus similarities, since through reflective abstraction a person can often 'see through' superficial differences to deeper analogies" (Perkins & Salomon, p. 29). Examples of high-road transfer (DOK 3–DOK 4) might include developing a chain of logic or analyzing evidence in support of a claim, interpreting the underlying theme or use of a metaphor, or looking across multiple **data** sources to determine why there may be differing perspectives on an event.

Turning back to your unit of study, locate the games, also known as summative assessments. Probably, they are near the end of the instructional sequence and include more complex tasks than the (low-road) routine skills students have practiced in isolation. Do the questions and tasks in the summative assessments simply include more opportunities for students to demonstrate near transfer? Or have you asked them to stretch their thinking to application in a new or unfamiliar context or text? "Far" transfer happens only when a deeper level of understanding is achieved. The evidence we look for in student work is revealed in the thinking, reasoning, and strategizing used to complete open-ended, complex tasks. It is not about "having some evidence" but what students do with the evidence in support of their solutions or final products.

Finally, have you also designed any scrimmages for this unit of study? Even the best athletes in the world scrimmage. Players refine their skills by scrimmaging over and over again and improve performance by reflecting on how well they played the game. Transfer doesn't happen by chance and often doesn't happen at all if we don't design learning opportunities for it. Scrimmages—tasks designed to move student thinking toward generalizing to bigger ideas and deepening understanding—are used to teach students how to engage with more complex tasks. This means learning how to solve problems with, and later without coaching (scaffolding). Providing opportunities for students to practice transfer should happen regularly before we ask them to do it more formally in a summative assessment. Teaching for transfer will greatly enhance instructional planning and progress monitoring.

1.2c Cognitive Rigor Is Challenge With Support

If students need multiple opportunities to successfully engage with complex tasks, then educators must be intentional about how they "balance" the complexity of the content with the ways that students will engage with it. Bloom (1968) made reference to this need for balance in his classic article, "Learning for Mastery." "We are expressing the view that, given sufficient time and appropriate types of help, 95% of students . . . can learn a subject up to a high level of mastery. We are convinced that the grade of 'A' as an index of mastery of a subject can, under appropriate conditions, be achieved by up to 95% of the students in a class" (p. 4).

I've heard Dr. John Hattie refer to this as "Goldilocks support"—meaning not too much support, not too little support, but just the right amount of support. I call this strategic scaffolding. **Scaffolding** is the purposeful use of supports to achieve a balance between cognitive complexity and student autonomy, as the overall cognitive demand of the task increases. Strategic scaffolding means designing intentional steps into the instruction (or assessment) to ensure that all students can eventually complete the same complex task independently.

Instructional Implications for Designing Challenge With Support: Rather than saying, "My students could never do this," we should ask, "What can I do so all of my students *can* be successful?" The key to strategic scaffolding is providing just enough of a challenge that students will have to dig a bit deeper into the content without becoming too frustrated and give up before completing the task. Teachers need to ask themselves (a) what makes this content or task complex, (b) how will my students engage with the content, and (c) what can I do to encourage less reliance on me (the teacher) in completing the task successfully? The goal of "just right" scaffolding is to gradually reduce it as students increase their capacity to work with more complex material. Here are four simple scaffolding examples that create a balance between content complexity and the cognitive demands of mental processing:

- *Hint Cards:* This scaffolding idea comes from the Teaching Channel (www.teachingchannel.org). In this math lesson, a teacher anticipates what her students might struggle with and creates several "hint" cards that students can use if they get stuck while solving the problems. One card includes a reminder of the steps that could be used. Another has similar (low-road) illustrated examples. A third card has a few questions to think about when solving the problems. While the learning tasks shown in the video are more focused on near transfer, the concept of hint cards could work effectively in different content areas with more complex tasks. This strategy supports students with limited **executive functioning**, by helping to trigger recall of how to complete a similar multistep task.

- *Partner Collaborations/Dyads:* This is so obvious that it might be overlooked as a scaffolding strategy. Working in the smallest of groups—especially in pairs—encourages full engagement, individual accountability, and flexible thinking through focused dialogue. For example, each partner could have a different role related to the larger task using paired texts. Each student locates information from a different text before collaboratively integrating or contrasting the ideas presented. This strategy lessens the reading load for individual students while still expecting them to integrate ideas from multiple sources.

- *Character Emojis:* I saw this scaffolding strategy being used in a high school English class in Delaware. Students were reading *Macbeth*—or should I say the teacher was reading *Macbeth*—and students were interpreting character interactions using text evidence to create character emojis depicting what each character was feeling. Pairs of students followed along during the read aloud, discussed what was just read while referring back to the text to locate supporting evidence, and then created faces for each character to express what they were feeling in that scene. This strategy also lessens the reading load, while focusing attention on interpreting the text, using text evidence.

- *EKGs for Characters, Events, or Interactions:* Similar to character emojis, the "EKG" visually represents an interpretation of rising and falling emotions, interactions, or conflicts brought on by a series of events. Students visually create the EKG and annotate the reasons for the rising and falling actions, based on (text) evidence. For example, imagine asking your science students to create an EKG depicting what happens when two chemicals meet.

1.2d Cognitive Rigor Is Higher-Order Thinking, Which Usually Means Analyzing, Evaluating, and Creating

Higher-order thinking is a concept we often associate with learning classifications or taxonomies, the most familiar of these to educators in the United States being Bloom's Taxonomy. Learning tasks involving analysis, evaluation, and synthesis (creation of new knowledge) are generally thought to be of a *higher order*, requiring different learning and teaching methods than the learning of *lower-order* facts and concepts. We frequently use these verbs without really thinking about what each type of thinking requires. As with the verb *apply*, there can be less rigorous versions and deeper versions of how these high-order thinking verbs play out in the assignments we give our students. Deeper analysis, critical evaluation, and creative productive thinking require far transfer when developing conclusions, solutions, or complex products.

Instructional Implications for Higher-Order Thinking: Let's unpack each of the so-called higher-order verbs to examine what students might be expected to be doing when they are analyzing, evaluating, or creating. (See Table 1.1.) I've provided some examples of task prompts for analyzing, evaluating, and creating at each Depth-of-Knowledge (DOK) level (DOK 1–DOK 4) just to show that we sometimes have a limited understanding of true "higher"-order thinking.

Table 1.1 Unpacking Higher-Order Thinking Verbs

THE "VERB"	WHAT THE STUDENT IS EXPECTED TO DO	EXAMPLES OF PROMPTS AT EACH DOK LEVEL
Analyzing	Analyzing is most closely associated with critical thinking. It means taking things apart to understand how the parts relate and work together as a whole. The primary purpose of analysis is to build an understanding of schemas in each content domain. We take a novel apart to understand how literary elements interact to achieve an intended purpose. We take science investigations apart to understand how the experimental design leads to control of variables, data collection, and valid interpretations based on evidence. Comparing/contrasting or distinguishing fact/opinion are at the lower end (DOK 2) of the analysis continuum—"analysis lite." Analyzing discourse styles of authors or how different data displays can influence interpretations require deeper and more generalized understandings—"analysis deep."	**DOK 1** Is this story realistic fiction? **DOK 2** Compare how the wolf character and Red Riding Hood are alike/different. **DOK 3** Is this realistic fiction or a fantasy story? Justify your interpretation by analyzing text evidence. **DOK 4** Are all wolves (in literature) like the wolf in this story? Support your response by analyzing evidence from this and other texts.

(Continued)

Table 1.1 (Continued)

THE "VERB"	WHAT THE STUDENT IS EXPECTED TO DO	EXAMPLES OF PROMPTS AT EACH DOK LEVEL
Evaluating	Evaluating begins with analysis in order to make an evidence-based judgment. Evaluation also requires the use of "established" criteria to guide analysis of the kind of evidence that *should be* used to support a claim or thesis in a particular context. For example, judging the effectiveness of a musical performance requires different criteria than evaluating flaws in an experimental design. Each content domain has organizational schemas, terms and principles, and ways of thinking about how to judge "expert" performances or products. The methodologies and set of agreed-upon criteria for evaluation are unique to each domain, such as using criteria for evaluating character archetypes (e.g., who really is the hero?) or critiquing the reasoning and models used to arrive at a solution in mathematics (e.g., who is correct or are they both correct?).	**DOK 1, 2** Did you like the story? **DOK 3** What is your opinion about the cleverness of the wolf? Justify your opinion by analyzing text evidence. **DOK 4** Which version's ending has the most emotional impact? (Establish criteria first; then locate and analyze text evidence.)
Creating	In the original Bloom's Taxonomy (1956), this higher-order level was called "Synthesis" and it was not placed at the top of the taxonomy. In the Revised Bloom's Taxonomy (Anderson et al., 2001), this level was moved to represent the highest order of thinking and the word *synthesis* was changed to *create* which seems to better represent the intent—producing something new. Creating is in some ways the opposite of analysis/critical thinking (Hess & Gong, 2014). When we think critically, we take things apart to build an understanding of schemas. When we create, we put parts together in different or innovative ways to reframe how to look at ideas or to find alternative solutions. Don't be fooled into thinking that every fun and engaging learning activity that results in students creating something is at the deepest level of thinking! Fun and engaging assignments are a means to deeper understanding, not an end.	**DOK 1** Brainstorm other ways the wolf might have fooled Red. **DOK 2** Write the text messages between Red and her mother explaining the wolf incident. **DOK 3** Write a new ending to this story. **DOK 4** Apply the theme of this story to compose a new fairy tale with different characters and a different story line.

Source: Hess (2013a).

1.2e Cognitive Rigor Is Engagement, Collaboration, and Discourse That Makes Thinking Visible

Putting students into groups can end up looking like either pure chaos or a high-energy exploration of complex ideas. While some educators believe that individual work is more manageable and perhaps a more efficient use of class time, let's consider what is most effective in terms of all students achieving deeper understanding. From the early work of researchers like Robert Slavin and educators like Spencer Kagan through to today, we find compelling research and strategies in support of thoughtfully designed small-group work.

In a 1991 article, Slavin describes "team learning" as supplementing a teacher's instruction by giving students the opportunity to discuss information or practice skills introduced by the teacher. He summarizes several important findings:

- For enhancing student achievement, the most successful approaches have incorporated two key elements: group goals and individual accountability of all group members.

- When group goals and individual accountability are employed, achievement effects are consistently positive.

- Achievement effects of cooperative learning have been found to be about the same (equally positive): at all grade levels (2–12); in all major subject areas; for high, average, and low achievers; and in urban, rural, and suburban schools.

- Positive effects of cooperative learning have been consistently found on diverse outcomes, such as self-esteem, intergroup relations, acceptance of students with varying academic abilities, attitudes toward school, and the ability to work cooperatively. (p. 71)

In a week-long workshop in 1990 with Spencer Kagan, I learned an acronym—PIGS—to remember the keys to designing successful group collaborations: *Positive interdependence* (group members depend on each other to accomplish a shared goal; each member has a role); *individual* **accountability** (each member is held responsible for his or her contributions); *group processing* (groups set goals and reflect on group interactions to achieve shared goals); and *simultaneous engagement* (all students learn the social skills that enable them to be engaged all the time, face to face). "What group goals and individual accountability do is to motivate students to give explanations and to take one another's learning seriously, instead of simply giving answers" (Slavin, 1991, p. 80).

If you've ever used strategies like Think-Pair-Share and 4 Corners then you know Spencer Kagan's work (1992). Kagan provided teachers with a plethora of practical strategies (structures) to facilitate the "PIGS doctrine" of effective group work. Each structure is used for an intended purpose, such as team building or concept development. Kagan stressed that we need to begin by teaching students the appropriate social skills of *how* to interact in groups by unpacking what it looks like and sounds like to be an active listener (e.g., how to ask clarifying questions, how to paraphrase) or how to take on a role in the group, such as team facilitator or materials manager. Teachers often skip this step only to find that students don't know how to share responsibilities, talk in respectful ways, or critique and give productive **feedback** to their peers. I still employ or have adapted many of the Kagan structures for my own work. Even though it's been updated, that 1992 seminal book by Kagan has had a very long shelf life in my office. Descriptions of some of my favorite collaborative structures are included in this module, under instructional implications.

> **Suggested Resources**
>
> For more examples to support dialogue or group work see
>
> - Frey, Fisher, and Everlove (2009)
> - Hammond and Nessel (2011)
> - Nottingham, Nottingham, and Renton (2017)
> - Wiggins (2017)

"Collaboration and teamwork can be powerful instructional vehicles for learning . . . research suggests that these skills support creative and deeper thinking" (Hess & Gong, 2014, p. 14). Here is one way to sum up what we know about deeper thinking and putting students into groups to take on a challenging task: They can learn more complex material; they can learn content more deeply; and they can learn more quickly when they are working with someone else (meaning a peer) than when working or studying alone. Study groups organized to learn large amounts of complex college course content are a prime example of this.

It's not simply collaboration that leads to deeper thinking. It's what drives the thinking within groups, large or small. Let's further refine what we know about effective collaboration—adding the research about how classroom discussion and discourse can have a major effect on student learning. "Dialogue is one of the best vehicles for learning how to think, how to be reasonable, how to make moral decisions, and how understand another person's point of view. Research also indicates that most teachers talk too much in the classroom and don't wait long enough for students to respond. It is supremely flexible, instructional, collaborative, and rigorous. At its very best, dialogue is one of the best ways for participants to learn good habits of thinking" (Nottingham, Nottingham, & Renton, 2017, p. 5). According to these authors, here are just a few important reasons to support high-quality dialogue:

- Dialogue can develop a climate of trust.
- Dialogue gives teachers valuable insights into their students' beliefs, questions, and misconceptions.
- All students benefit from being taught *how* to think and how to develop language skills to express their ideas and understanding.
- Dialogue helps students to move from surface-level knowledge to deeper understanding of concepts. (pp. 6–12)

To this list, I would also add that meaningful discourse—especially in small, face-to-face groups—provides students with practice and models of what reasoning, giving critical feedback, and "showing your thinking" can actually look or sound like. Discourse is great prewriting strategy when depth of thinking is the goal of the assignment!

Instructional Implications for Structuring Collaboration, Engagement, and Meaningful Discourse:

    Start with a task worth doing. If we are going to put our students into groups, they shouldn't simply be working on low-level tasks (near transfer). Most likely, students can do many familiar routine tasks (DOK 1–DOK 2) quite efficiently on their own. When you want students to do something challenging, perhaps more challenging than individual students are able to accomplish independently, this is an opportunity to allow them to take some risks, struggle through a problem, and learn together as they construct meaning.

    Everyone needs to have a job. We can maximize simultaneous engagement and support deeper understanding especially when we structure group work for the scrimmages, the practice games intended to integrate multiple skills and concepts (far transfer). To do this well, we need to answer two questions: (1) What is the purpose of the task? (2) How many people will it take to successfully complete the task? Think about what happens when you have four students doing a task that two could easily complete. Two students may decide to take the day off! To provide some added structure for completing a collaborative task, consider the specific roles needed, and all students will have individual accountability for doing their job. At first, you may want to assign roles, providing a short description of each one. Later on, shift this responsibility to students. Ask groups to plan how they will accomplish the task and who is taking responsibility for each aspect. Some role examples might include the following: task manager (keeps track of time, makes sure everyone contributes), recorder (records and presents the group's ideas), artist (creates the labeled diagrams, illustrations, visuals), fact checker (double-checks accuracy of information, edits spelling), materials manager (sets up/takes down the equipment), and passage picker (selects key quotes that support the team's findings). I've developed a group planning tool, the Collaborative Inquiry Plan,[5] to assist student teams in thinking through the first phase of completing a longer, more complex task. Thinking through the task requirements together helps students to clarify and take responsibility for answering these questions: What are we supposed to do, and how will we accomplish it together successfully?

<u>Establish parameters for completing the task.</u> Sometimes, we give students too much time and too little direction as to what we expect them to do. Saying "discuss this with the person next to you" is not as clear as "you have 1 minute to discuss and write three reasons why_____." Whether it is a short, informal group sharing (e.g., Turn and Talk,[6] complete an exit card) or a longer performance or project-based task taking several days to complete, giving students a set amount of time and clear success criteria holds everyone accountable for getting it done and staying on task. Remember, you can always give groups more time if they need it; giving them too much time initially is usually a recipe for impending chaos.

Here are several strategies that can effectively structure classroom or small group discourse at different levels of rigor. For each one, I've suggested the intended purposes and potential DOK levels that might be tapped.

- *Paraphrase Passport* is a Spencer Kagan strategy (1992) that promotes active listening and speaking. This can be used when students work in pairs, such as to study together or to facilitate making connections in larger group discussions. Basically, when a student wants to add information or make a comment, he must first paraphrase what the last person just said ("What I think I heard you say is _____."). Then he adds or extends the idea ("I think this is important because _____." or "Another reason might be _____."). Since students are bringing in prior knowledge and making connections using this strategy, it is likely to elicit DOK 1 or 2 thinking, encouraging near transfer.

- *Improving Participation With Talk Moves:* This idea comes from the Teaching Channel (www.teachingchannel.org). In this math lesson video, a fourth-grade teacher has taught her students to use four different "talk moves" during class discussions: *Repeating* (DOK 1, keeps all students engaged and ready to go deeper); *Adding on* (DOK 2, students are making connections and drawing on what they already know); *Silent Signal*—I'm thinking what you're thinking. (The only way to know DOK levels for silent agreement is to prompt students to share their thinking. A DOK 3–type prompt might be "Can you share your reasoning for why you agree/disagree?" or "I see that you disagreed. What evidence did you find that suggests a different perspective?"); and *Changing your minds when given new information*—Since reasoning is required for explaining what evidence changed your mind or your thinking, it is at minimum a DOK 3–type talk move.

- *Value Lines—Where do I stand?* This is another Spencer Kagan strategy (1992) that I've adapted several ways to promote team building and exploration of the deeper reasoning underlying diverse views. Students are given a provocative statement or claim and must decide to what degree they agree or disagree with it. In a 1990s workshop with Kagan

---

5. A sample template for the Collaborative Inquiry Plan can be found in Part 2 at the end of this module.
6. Sample Turn and Talk frames can be found in Part 2 at the end of this module.

where I learned this strategy, we wrote a percentage on an index card to show our levels of agreement: Complete agreement = 100%; no agreement = 0%. As you can imagine, most people wrote something in between 0% and 100%. Then we formed a line from 0% to 100% to see class differences and discuss our reasoning. First we talked with those near us; then we "bent the line" to talk with those at the other end to hear opposing views. Exploring perspective in this way is an excellent precursor to argument writing or mock trials. (Exploring diverse perspectives and providing supporting evidence for them is at minimum able to elicit DOK 3–, and perhaps DOK 4–type responses.) [Note: As far as I know, this is the original version of this cooperative structure; however, I've seen similar strategies to this one over the years called opinion lines or agree/disagree lines. I think having degrees of "in-between" sparks richer and more nuanced discussions.]

- *Carousel—Rotating Through Geometry Stations:* This idea comes from the Teaching Channel (www.teachingchannel.org). In this lesson, a geometry teacher heterogeneously groups students. Groups rotate from one problem to another when time is called by the teacher, checking the work of others until all problems have been fully completed. The teacher begins by clearly setting parameters for how students will rotate and what they will do at each station. Groups begin at a station with a multistep problem on large chart paper and begin to solve it (DOK 2—solving a routine problem involving more than one decision point). Time is called shortly after they begin working, and teams move to the next station where another group has begun to solve a different problem. Each group discusses what they see in their peers' work and decides if the last group was or was not correct up to that point (DOK 1—checking calculations, graphing; DOK 2—solving a routine problem). They continue the task if it is correct or make corrections if not. In the last round, groups develop a justification for the correct solution (DOK 3—critiquing the reasoning of others). The carousel strategy can be used with many different content areas (e.g., building upon ideas of others through "progressive" group writing; Hess, 1987, p. 55). Strategies such as these promote deeper discussions and collaborative reasoning even when assignments begin with a very basic task, such as solving a routine mathematics problem or developing a summary of a text.

- *Thesis Throwdown:* This idea comes from a 2015 blog post by Catlin Tucker, author of *Blended Learning in Action*. The ten-minute strategy begins with the teacher writing an essay prompt on the board. Small groups are given five minutes to discuss and construct a solid thesis statement in response to the essay question (DOK 3). Two groups are then randomly selected to "compete" by writing their thesis statements on the whiteboard. The teacher then uses a "think out loud" with each thesis statement to respond in a positive way—noting strong vocabulary (DOK 2), parallel language (DOK 1–DOK 2), and clearly stated assertion—and to suggest what needs to be added, removed, or edited (DOK 1–DOK 3). Tucker says this approach models the process of thinking like an editor and greatly improves the quality of her students' thesis writing. Finally, a winner is declared!

- *Stand and Deliver:* This is my variation of a Spencer Kagan structure, "stand up and share" (1992), that builds discussion, friendly competition, and active listening skills. Small groups are presented with a rigorous, open-ended question (DOK 3–DOK 4) with multiple possible responses (e.g., What are some possible effects/causes of . . . ?; How many ways can this be solved?; What is the strongest text evidence that reveals this character's motivations?). Groups are given a short amount of time to "put their heads together" to brainstorm possible responses. When time is called, all members of each group stand. The teacher samples responses one by one from each group until all possible responses have been heard. Groups are not allowed to repeat an answer already stated, so they must listen carefully; and the teacher or groups can challenge the reasoning behind any group's response

(DOK 3). Groups remain standing as long as they have new ideas to add. The added bonus of this review/prewriting strategy is that students begin to compete to generate multiple responses and get to move while they are thinking and sharing.

1.2f Cognitive Rigor Is Triggered by Asking a Different Kind of Question That Shifts Teacher–Student Roles

There are many excellent books and articles on developing effective questions. I'd like to focus my discussion on (a) analyzing *the kind of thinking* behind developing different types of questions; (b) matching the right question with the learning intent—clarifying your purpose, especially if it involves moving to deeper understanding; and (c) considering how the questions we pose can shift the students' role from question answerer to question generator in pursuit of self-directed inquiry, reflection, and learning. The ultimate goal of modeling how to ask and answer deeper-thinking questions is to teach our students how to become more engaged in their own learning. They will not become true critical and creative thinkers simply by answering *our* questions!

In my workshops, I provide a prompt like the one below to begin the discussion about questioning.

Turn & Talk:

Your class has just read some version of *Little Red Riding Hood*.

- What is a **basic comprehension** question you might ask?
- What is **a more rigorous** question you might ask?

Record your questions.

Then discuss: *What must you consider when developing each type of question?*

What do "basic questions" have in common? Basic questions are sometimes called "closed" questions because they have one right answer, which doesn't necessarily mean that they are easy questions for students to answer. Closed questions tend to be either DOK 1 "right there" foundational recall questions or DOK 2 "think and search" conceptual questions. Basic questions are easy to develop and easy to correct. The information needed to answer them is stated explicitly somewhere in the text, derived by applying a routine rule, formula, or procedure, or by recalling a fact, term, or principle. Basic questions don't take much time for students to answer because either they know the answer or they don't. There is not much time spent on "figuring it out" with basic questions. Over the course of our careers, we've seen thousands of these kinds of questions, so we know what they look like and how to generate them. We've learned how to ask for basic information in many different ways (fill in the blank, label the diagram, multiple choice, matching, etc.).

Basic questions have high scoring reliability (because there is only one right answer) and are a quick and efficient way to find out if students are acquiring the knowledge needed for learning activities involving near transfer. Dylan Wiliam (2015) suggests that teachers plan their lessons to purposely include "hinge" questions to get on-the-spot evidence about what students do and do not understand (e.g., key conceptual understandings) in order to determine whether all students are ready to move on or if they still may need additional review and practice.

Basic questions do have an important purpose in lesson planning and assessment. Nevertheless, basic questions can only tap into foundational, procedural, and conceptual knowledge (DOK 1–DOK 2). The greatest limitation of closed or basic questions is that even when we see correct answers, we do not find out that a student might know more than what was asked for. For example, we may learn that the student can count; but can the student also use counting to solve a nonroutine math problem? We should not be satisfied with simply asking different kinds of basic questions. Basic questions can be thought of as the first step to deeper explorations of interesting and relevant problems, issues, or themes; they should not be used as a barrier to be crossed before we allow for deeper thinking about those issues or topics. It is often the open-ended deeper or more rigorous questions that uncover important misconceptions along the learning trajectory.

Below are a variety of basic questions about erosion. Consider what the student knows if these are answered correctly and what deeper understandings about erosion (through collaborative construction of knowledge) we did not begin to ask. In other words, where could the learning go next?

- *Can you define erosion?* (DOK 1, recall a term, fact, or definition)
- *Which is the best word to go in this sentence? Erosion can be caused by _____.* (DOK 1, recall a definition)
- *Sort these pictures to show examples and nonexamples of erosion.* (DOK 2, conceptual understanding, comparing/contrasting)
- *Complete the Venn diagram to compare and contrast what you know about wind and water erosion.* (DOK 2, conceptual understanding, comparing/contrasting)
- *Can you demonstrate or explain what happens during erosion?* (DOK 1, recall, describe; DOK 2, procedural, explaining cause–effect, summarizing)

What do "deeper or more rigorous questions" have in common? Unfortunately, we probably have not seen as many strong models for these types of questions as we have for basic questions. Deeper questions are open-ended and have more than one possible right answer or more than one possible approach to finding the answer. They take more time to develop, more time for students to answer, and certainly more time to correct. Scoring guides for these types of questions[7] must consider the possible appropriate strategies or approaches that might be used, the credibility and accuracy of supporting evidence, and the reasoning (understanding, analysis, or evaluation) of the evidence used to support a solution or conclusion. What makes these types of questions correct is not simply having accurate calculations, correct use of terms, or including supporting evidence. Responses to deeper questions require overt evidence of *how* students are supporting their analyses, inferences, conclusions, or perspectives. Therefore, in order to develop questions and tasks that will uncover how students figured out an answer, there is more for us to consider when developing deeper questions, such as what prior knowledge or experience they will bring to the question or task (what might transfer from earlier lessons) and what might transfer from this lesson to future lessons. In other words, these questions are part of a learning trajectory intended to deepen understanding over time.

Now, consider the sample questions below related to a deeper understanding of erosion. How might a basic understanding of erosion be extended in answering these questions? How does more divergent thinking combine with basic knowledge to help students to answer these questions?

---

7. Tools and guidelines for developing high-quality scoring guides and rubrics are included in Module 3.

- *Use the data to identify a trend and predict some possible effects of erosion on this land mass over the next five years. Support your reasoning with data analysis.* (DOK 2—analyze data, identify a trend, and make a prediction; DOK 3—use data analysis and criteria to describe possible positive and negative effects of erosion; DOK 4—if supporting evidence is drawn from multiple sources).

- *After viewing the news footage and analyzing what is happening in this scenario, your team will develop a proposal to reverse the effects of erosion on the local stream banks.* (DOK 2—summarize the issue; DOK 3–DOK 4—use planning, strategic thinking, and multiple sources to devise a real-world solution).

- *What did the author mean when he said, "After that, her popularity began to erode"? Use your interpretation of the text to explain your thinking* (DOK 2—summarize the story line of the text; DOK 3—use contextual analysis of supporting evidence before and after a key event or turning point to interpret the author's intent behind word choice).

The Right Type of Question for the Intended Learning

Different types of questions are appropriate for different purposes—whether it be building a foundation, conceptualization of ideas, or deeper thinking and creative problem solving. Construction of knowledge, **disciplined inquiry**, creative or productive thinking, and deeper learning are only triggered when we set the stage for transfer—far transfer. "For most students, these (skills) will not develop by chance, but they can be nurtured. Studies of authentic intellectual work in Grades 3–12 found that, across the content areas and regardless of race, gender, or socioeconomic status, students who experienced instruction that promoted these skills demonstrated higher achievement than students who experienced more traditional curricular approaches (Newmann, King, & Carmichael, 2007)" (Hess & Gong, 2014, p. 13).

> **Suggested Resources**
>
> For more on questioning strategies, see
>
> - Francis (2016)
> - Walsh and Sattes (2015)
> - Walsh and Sattes (2017)
> - Wiliam and Leahy (2015)

Rigorous questions not only spark deeper understanding but can lead to both metacognitive thinking (strategizing while engaged in a task) and reflective thinking (evaluating effectiveness of learning processes afterward). The person who generates the question is actually thinking at a deep enough level not only to answer the question but to understand why it's being asked in the first place—the questioner has clarity of purpose even if the question is meant to clear up some confusion. Different kinds of questions shift not only the thinking but the roles of teachers and students during the learning process. At one end of the spectrum, teachers are using questions to focus, guide, and model while students are acquiring, explaining, and practicing. At the other end, teachers are probing for reasoning and promoting reflective discourse and extended thinking, while students are uncovering what is or is not relevant, initiating their own goals and questions, and constructing meaning.

Instructional Implications of Asking a Different Kind of Question: My younger son spent a week at soccer camp when he was in middle school. I asked him one night what he'd been learning and he told me that the way to tell the best players was to watch their "first touch" on the ball. Not being a soccer player, I was confused and asked him to explain. "When the ball is coming toward you, you quickly need to decide whether to trap (stop) and redirect it, head it, use your chest, left foot instead of right foot, pass it, etc."

His explanation made me think about what great teachers do—they decide in the moment how to "handle" the responses they get when they ask a question—basic or rigorous. I often say it's the *second question* you ask which really determines how deeply you are going to push your students to explore the content. Let's say you've asked an open-ended question and your students give you a variety of responses, maybe not exactly what you were hoping for. What are you going to do next?

What will your "first touch" be on the response? Are you going to tell them the correct answer and move on? Keep asking students till someone gets it right? Or are you going to delve deeper? Are you going to ask, "Can you say a little more? Would you elaborate on connections you're making to that idea? Can you find some examples of that? Is there any evidence in the text to support your reasoning? What model might support your thinking about that? Can you turn to the person next to you and ask them what they are thinking?"

> Marie Dickey, music teacher and district curriculum facilitator in Gillette, Wyoming, shared this reflection with me on asking "the second question" during a recent lesson. She told me it made her realize that she was sometimes guilty of doing the thinking *for* her students, instead of *with* them. She had constructed a music staff with treble clef and key signature on the board and asked, *"What key is this?"*
>
> When she got blank stares from her students, she was tempted to explain how to answer her own question. Instead, she decided to say, *"What do you know that might help you figure this out?"*
>
> As students began to suggest things they knew about key signatures, Marie wrote them on the board: It's a treble clef, the notes in the spaces are F-A-C-E, that symbol means sharp, and so on. None of these little facts and details alone was enough to answer the questions, but when students looked at the list of things that they knew about key signatures, they began to connect the information and figure it out together. For Marie, it was confirmation that they could figure it out if she gave them time to access stored information that would help.

Encouraging students to further clarify what they mean and to locate supporting evidence is a good strategy for getting them to go deeper, without having to do a lot of preplanning before the lesson. The first question asked and the responses to it can become the springboard to the teachable moment. Below are a few of my favorite strategies for teaching students how to frame a range of questions that require deeper thinking and broader explorations of ideas.

- *Send a Question:* This is another Spencer Kagan strategy (1992) that I've adapted in a variety of ways. It promotes team building and a review of what has been learned, as well as explorations that are more open-ended. Each team "puts their heads together" for a few minutes to develop a question or problem for another team to answer, solve, or respond to. Before they send it to the next team, they must draft an acceptable response to their question. Teams switch questions, develop answers to them, and, when time is called, send them back to the originators for feedback. Teaching students how to ask a range of question types strengthens the use of this strategy. Teams would be expected not only to answer the questions they've generated, but to teach another team how to find the answer if they get stuck or arrive at an incorrect solution. An adaptation of this strategy was generated spontaneously during a workshop when I was co-presenting with Lucy Calkins. We were discussing ways to get students to be more selective about the text evidence they located in support of their responses. In this approach, students send "evidence" to support a stated claim. The receiving group must judge the quality of the suggested evidence in supporting the stated claim and provide feedback.

- *Photo/Picture Search:* When I was teaching middle school, I purchased a kit of famous historical photographs, each with an inquiry question to get students started on researching the answer. Sometimes students needed to identify the date of the photo, other times the people in the photo, or the event depicted. For example, "When was this photo taken?" might be the only question that came with the photograph; however, the answers were never obvious and required some research and supporting evidence. Students needed to use some prior knowledge and some investigative work to determine which clues in the photo would lead them to an eventual answer. What was most interesting was how many new questions were generated by the students to get to the final answer. Questions that came with the photos were never as obvious as "Who is this president?" but more like "Who is standing with this president and what is the likely occasion?" This is an excellent way to introduce how to use research skills to triangulate information from multiple sources.

> View a video clip of a Socratic Seminar, *Students Cite Evidence from Informational and Literary Text*, posted by EL Education (2013) at https://vimeo.com/54871334.

- *The Art of Questioning—A Sequencing Strategy:* This idea comes from the Teaching Channel (www.teachingchannel.org). In this lesson, a high school ELA teacher poses a sequence of three types of questions to help students understand informational texts: (a) react personally (connect) to the content (DOK 2); (b) interpret the big picture, the underlying meaning, or theme (DOK 3); and (c) explore the way the text is structured (DOK 2) to deliver the author's message. The teacher explains that starting with a personal reaction to content, rather than with a few basic recall questions about content, engages all students in the discussion right from the start. When students begin to elaborate on their responses using both text-based and personal evidence, they are utilizing deeper thinking.

- *Socratic Questioning:* The Socratic Questioning technique involves teaching students to ask a range of different types of questions that move from clarification (What do you mean by that?) to assumption-based questions (What is the underlying assumption in this message? What does the speaker seem to believe?) to questions asking for supporting evidence, credibility of sources, implications and consequences (What would be the possible effects?), or differing viewpoints. Socratic questioning can be used in all content areas and grade levels. Student-led Socratic seminars are designed to shift teacher and student roles, putting students in greater control of the direction of their own learning.

- *SQS—Students Questioning Students:* I first heard about this peer-to-peer questioning strategy in 1988 from Judy Engle, a mathematics teacher at Bronx High School of Science. I had invited her to make a presentation at the Fifth Annual Forum on Gifted Education, held at Rutgers University. As in Socratic questioning, a variety of questions are asked by students of their peers' work and to probe their peers' explanations and thinking in arriving at solutions. "Using SQS, students stimulate their classmates to think. Since students are involved in questioning, they become more attentive listeners to other students and to me (the teacher) during the lesson. . . . Students are taught strategies for asking questions and strategies for providing specific feedback to their peers" (Engle, 1988, p. 1). Even decades after Judy's students graduate, she tells me that they still return to tell her that they hold this strategy in highest regard for keeping them engaged with learning while in high school. SQS shifts the role of students so that they are actively directing their learning.

Classroom visitations allow school leaders and teachers a window for observing the degree to which *all* students are actively engaged in the learning process and what the teacher is doing to initiate and sustain that engagement (e.g., asking probing follow-up questions, questioning to consolidate the learning). I begin my walk-throughs by noting the questions posed by both the teacher and especially those asked by the students. Are students' questions clarifying what they are supposed to do next, or have they begun to strategize how to complete the task at hand? Table 1.2 on the next page summarizes some of the teacher–student role shifts as the purpose and focus of questions and tasks become more challenging. I encourage teachers to work with their peers to observe and better understand how a shift in the way they ask questions can promote greater student ownership of learning.[8]

---

8. A walk-through tool, based on Table 1.2 (**TOOL #26**—Shifting Teacher–Student Roles), is included at the end of Module 4.

Table 1.2 Shifting Roles: Moving From Teacher-Directed to Student-Directed Learning

DOK LEVELS	TEACHER ROLES	STUDENT ROLES
1 Acquires a Foundation	Ask questions to focus attention (*Who? What? Where? How? When?*) Directs, leads, demonstrates, defines, provides practice Scaffolds for access and focus	Acquires vocabulary, facts, rules Memorizes, recites, quotes, restates Retrieves information Practices and self-monitors basic skills Clarifies procedures, asks for support in using resources, tools
2 Uses, Connects, Conceptualizes	Asks questions to build schemas: differentiate parts/whole, classify, draw out inferences Models/thinks aloud to uncover relationships Scaffolds to build conceptual understanding (Why does this work? Under what conditions?). Provides examples/nonexamples	Explains relationships; sorts, classifies, compares, organizes information Makes predictions based on estimates, observations, prior knowledge Proposes problems or issues/questions to be investigated Raises conceptual or strategy-based questions
3 Deepens and Constructs Meaning	Asks questions to probe reasoning and promote peer discourse and self-reflection Links Big Ideas (Where else would this apply? What concepts/principles could be used to solve this?) Designs tasks requiring proof, justification, and analysis of evidence quality and accuracy	Uncovers relevant, accurate, credible information, flaws in a design, or proposed solution and links with "Big Ideas" Plans how to develop supporting (hard) evidence for conclusions or claims Researches/tests ideas, solves nonroutine problems; perseveres Self-assesses; uses feedback to improve performance
4 Extends, Transfers, Broadens Meaning	Asks questions to extend thinking, explore sources, broaden perspectives/Big Idea (*Are there potential biases? Can you propose an alternative model?*) Encourages and scaffolds use of relevant and valid resources, peer-to-peer discourse and self-reflection	Initiates, transfers, and *constructs new* knowledge/insights linked to "Big Ideas" Modifies, creates, elaborates based on analysis and interpretation of multiple sources Investigates real-world problems and issues; perseveres; manages time and task Self-assesses; uses feedback to improve performance

Source: Hess (2013a).

Before going on, let's summarize the underpinnings of cognitive rigor and mental processing of information.

Cognitive Rigor Is . . .

Making connections to consolidate the learning

Applying what you've learned to new situations, also known as (far) transfer

Challenge with "just right" support (also known as "productive struggle")

(Sometimes) Higher-order thinking: analyzing, evaluating, and creating

Engagement, collaboration, and discourse that make thinking visible

Triggered by asking a different kind of question that shifts teacher–student roles

Now that we're moving toward building a common understanding of the many facets of cognitive rigor, we should also address some common misconceptions that I frequently hear.

1.3 Seven Common Misconceptions About Rigor

Rigor Misconception #1

All kids aren't able to think deeply, or kids shouldn't need scaffolding and support in order to think deeply.

Have you ever gone to the amusement park and seen the measuring stick that says you have to be *this tall* to be allowed to go on the ride? Well, there is no such thing as "you have to be this tall"—or this age, this grade level, or this ability level—to think deeply! All students can think deeply; it is really up to us to find ways to support the move from recall to deeper thinking and using information in more complex ways. Over the years, I have worked on designs of state assessments for the general population and on assessments for students with significant cognitive disabilities. What I've learned is that there are ways to design deeper thinking tasks for different populations of students. For example, in a 2008 pilot study in Georgia (Hess, McDivitt, & Fincher) with more than 2,000 special education students, Grades 5 through 8, we explored various ways to structure reading and mathematics questions with scaffolding that made the items more accessible while not changing the constructs being assessed. The questions were drawn from the state's grade-level assessment test items and reading passages, but looked different in the ways they were presented. For example, reading questions were reordered from basic questions to more complex and embedded within the passages (chunking the text), rather than all questions listed at the end of the passage; mathematics test questions were grouped by content domain (e.g., all of the operations questions, then data questions, then geometry questions). Both of these strategies were found to support students in accessing what they actually had learned without taxing their executive functioning to the point of them giving up and not completing the test. In one-on-one interviews with students after finishing the tests, an overwhelming number of the students said they felt they did well. These students may not have gotten all questions correct, but when students have confidence, they are more likely to access what is stored in their memories and attempt to answer all of the questions. Thus, the structure of tasks and test questions can have a positive effect on students demonstrating what they have learned.

The second idea that refutes misconception #1 is that anyone taking on a complex challenge—students and adults alike—benefits from some form of scaffolding (e.g., using a model, discussing/planning with others to get feedback, seeking out a mentor). Think of the most challenging thing you have accomplished recently. Did you just go out by yourself, do it all, and then say, "It's done"? Probably not. You most likely asked someone for advice, consulted the Internet to do some research, examined a similar finished model, or sought feedback along the way that led to improving the final product. Adults who are highly creative and productive usually seek some form of support through social interaction, such as talking or working through their ideas with others. It's useful to be reminded of Lev Vygotsky's idea of the zone of proximal development (ZPD). Vygotsky (1978) conceived the ZPD as representing a challenge just beyond a student's current level of mastery. Through social interaction—working with others, getting feedback, and thinking through a complex problem together—the gaps in understanding can be bridged and learning moves forward.

As a matter of fact, working on a complex task with others first is especially important to developing a high-quality product before producing similar products independently. I'm sometimes asked, "Is it really a DOK 3 or DOK 4 task if students don't complete the task on their own?" Well, have you ever been in a canoe? Have you ever ridden a tandem bike? How did you learn how to drive a car? Have you ever developed a curriculum guide with someone? Does one person do all the work? Of course not. When people work on something together, they all get credit for accomplishing whatever the thing is that they have produced or accomplished. Collaboration is one of the best ways to help students learn how to eventually do those same things independently.

In summary, several key things are needed for all students to think deeply and accomplish complex tasks: first and foremost, a belief system that all students *can* do this; tasks structured for optimal access and responding; collaboration, working though ideas with others first; and oral language, discourse, listening to what thinking actually looks and sounds like. When we structure classroom discourse so that our students can explore reasoning from different perspectives, they are better able to formulate their own reasoning. Having students talk about their thinking and understanding before we actually ask them to take on a complex assignment is not cheating. It is helping them to remain engaged as they work to integrate and refine their ideas.

Rigor Misconception #2

Webb's Depth-of-Knowledge Framework is a taxonomy
(meaning that DOK 4 is more desirable than DOK 1, 2, or 3 thinking).

Bloom's original taxonomy (Bloom, Englehardt, Furst, Hill, & Krathwohl, 1956) and the revised Bloom's Taxonomy (Anderson et al., 2001) were both conceived to be a hierarchy describing lower to higher levels of thinking. The goal was to get students thinking at the highest levels. In a taxonomy, "lower-order" thinking is often devalued.

If Webb's DOK levels composed a taxonomy, then our goal would be to have students working at DOK 3 and DOK 4 most of the time. The assumption is that extended thinking (DOK 4) is better (more valued) than strategic thinking (DOK 3), strategic thinking is better than conceptual understanding (DOK 2), and that is better than recall of foundational or surface knowledge (DOK 1). This devalues the role of foundational and conceptual understanding in laying the groundwork for deeper thinking. Norman Webb never intended his DOK levels to become a taxonomy. Depth-of-Knowledge levels are nominative; they name how you work and interact with the content. Sometimes you are working at a foundational level to acquire terms, rules, and principles. Sometimes you are building conceptual understanding or applying what you've learned to novel situations. Cognitive rigor and DOK are a balance of how you acquire and use what you've learned in increasingly more complex ways.

A useful rule of thumb for achieving balance, especially when designing summative assessments, is to designate about half of the score points in an assessment to DOK 2 types of questions. This means that in a reading assessment, half of the points are for questions related to identifying the main idea, sequencing events, summarizing the text, making predictions, comparing and contrasting information presented, or determining cause–effect. Yes, those would all be DOK 2—essential knowledge to draw upon for a more complex task, such as determining the theme, understanding the author's perspective or use of language, developing a text-based argument, or analyzing information across texts. In a mathematics assessment, students would be assessed on the ability to work through routine word problems requiring an appropriate strategy, decision making, and accuracy; organizing and interpreting data; or constructing models and representations. Again, all of these are DOK 2 types of tasks needed to tackle and solve more complex, nonroutine (DOK 3) mathematics problems requiring reasoning and proof.

If half of the summative test score points are applied to conceptual understanding (DOK 2), on what should the other half focus? Instead of low-level recall items, I recommend including at least one or two DOK 3 or DOK 4 type of tasks. Because these open-ended performance tasks will take longer for students to complete, there does not need to be many of them; however, the number of score points given to tasks requiring deeper understanding should "balance" the score to reflect that deeper thinking has value.

DOK was never intended to be used as a taxonomy. Every DOK level has a purpose and, therefore, has value. That is not to say that DOK levels are linear—that students cannot achieve DOK 3 or DOK 4 thinking unless they have first mastered all the of the basic skills and concepts. Think about your first year teaching. Did you have all the basics of teaching before you began to teach? Not likely. As we learn, we try things which are challenging to us (scrimmages), reflecting on and learning from both our failures and successes. We sometimes find that we need to go back and build a more solid foundation in order to be more successful with more rigorous tasks. In your classrooms, some students will be motivated by first knowing the goal—the challenging task or final product. They become invested in the need to learn the basics because they want to complete a more complex and interesting task (e.g., developing a website or podcast). Other students might require smaller steps at first in order to feel confident enough to take on a more complex task. In a classroom, you will always have a combination of students who are and are not ready for that cognitively rigorous task right from the start. Different entry points mean that students will have different pathways for how to get to deeper understanding. There is not one approach that will always work for all students.

Rigor Misconception #3

Verbs and levels in Bloom's Taxonomy can be equated with Depth-of-Knowledge levels.

Have you seen the visual of a wheel divided into 4 DOK levels? Each section is filled with a list of verbs. I've come to call this "The DOK Wheel of Misfortune" because it implies that if you spin the wheel and pick a verb, voila! Your students will be thinking deeply. In fact, if you examine this wheel carefully, you will see many of the same verbs recurring in multiple sections of the wheel. That should be your first red flag about verbs determining complexity levels. I am frequently asked about the wheel, so it's worth stating here that neither Norman Webb nor I created it. It may have been derived from a Bloom's Taxonomy wheel that long ago appeared in Barbara Clark's book, *Growing Up Gifted* (1983, p. 222). In Clark's book, the wheel also had verbs in each of the sections that represented levels of Bloom's Taxonomy. Clark used the Bloom wheel to make the case that rather than seeing Bloom's Taxonomy as a linear hierarchy, it should be viewed as a repeating cycle: The highest levels of thinking produce new insights and products that lead to a need to go back and expand upon the original knowledge base. That in turn leads to much deeper understanding in the next cycle. The same could be said of how to view Depth-of-Knowledge levels—guiding a continuous cycle of learning.

The DOK wheel implies a connection that really doesn't exist. Here is what we know about using "verbs" as the primary indicator of task complexity and deeper thinking:

1. Verbs are generic, void of content. Thinking and accessing information stored in long-term memory is domain specific, not simply generic mental processing. To analyze a literary text requires a different schema and thought process than analyzing an experimental design or analyzing a work of art. "Teaching for transfer within each discipline aims to increase transfer within that discipline. Research to date provides little guidance about how to help learners aggregate transferable competencies across disciplines. This may be a shortcoming in the research or a reflection of the domain-specific nature of transfer" (NRC, 2012, p. 7).

2. Verbs describe a type of thinking, not the depth of understanding.
3. The same verbs sometimes appear at multiple levels in taxonomies, making them less meaningful and more subjective when coming to consensus on determining the level of cognitive complexity of a given test item or task.
4. It's actually what comes after the verb—the content—and the engagement with that content that helps us to determine the complexity of the task—not the verb.

Rigor Misconception #4

Depth of Knowledge is about greater difficulty, things getting harder.

If you look up the word *rigor* in the dictionary, you'd see the synonyms *inflexible*, *hard*, *rigid*, and *strict*. Cognitive rigor is the opposite; it's flexible thinking, seeing multiple possibilities, multiple approaches, and different possible perspectives. Consider how many of us used to teach argument writing. We would say, "First state a claim. Then go and find some facts to support it." That's an ineffective way to teach argument writing and does not require very rigorous thinking. As a matter of fact, it was hard for students to produce a solid piece of writing using this approach.

What we've learned is to say, "Get into the topic deeply enough so you can start to see different perspectives emerging. Now decide which side you are going to defend and begin to locate the most compelling evidence to support that position." This approach is more cognitively rigorous than the first example because to uncover multiple perspectives means to understand the topic in a much deeper and broader way. Debate coaches often require students to fully prepare for either side of the debate. Debaters have to be flexible enough to know and use the evidence on each side so they can argue for either the claim or counterclaim at a moment's notice. That's cognitive rigor.

Is cognitive rigor about difficulty, things being harder and harder to do? Not really. **Cognitive demand** is about the complexity of the task and the mental processing required to complete it. Learning how to ski is usually hard at first, but with practice, the routine act of skiing becomes easier. Many things we learn are difficult to do at first, but once we memorize the rules and routines they become easier, more automatic. Learning to decode words may be a hard task that becomes easier with practice because it is routine. You use the same rules and strategies every time. Determining an author's purpose, theme, or potential bias is more complex because with each new text, the application of reading skills leads to both near and far transfer and deeper understanding than simply calling words.

Rigor Misconception #5

All Depth-of-Knowledge levels can be assessed with a multiple-choice question.

Let me begin by saying, "that's just dumb."

This misconception doesn't make any sense when you consider the level of engagement with content that is required by DOK 3 and DOK 4 tasks, which in my opinion are best assessed using **constructed-response** questions, performance tasks, and extended projects. To be clear, DOK 3 questions that focus on strategic thinking and reasoning can be assessed with multiple-choice items. These items typically include such things as determining the author's purpose, identifying text evidence or data that support a claim, interpreting a complex graph or data set, or identifying flaws in an experimental design. When a student is selecting the "best" option, such as locating supporting text evidence for a stated theme, the response yields a correct or incorrect answer; but this provides little insight to the teacher as to how a student applied concepts and reasoning to arrive at the answer or if the response is a result of guessing or skipping the item completely. Usability of test data, especially formative use, relies on the teacher being able to determine what students don't understand and therefore, what instruction should occur next.

Both the processing and the product of constructing an answer to a deeper or more rigorous question or task (DOK 3 or DOK 4) uncovers understanding; and we've learned that students remember what they construct better than what they simply memorize. Additionally, DOK 4–type tasks often require extended time, as well as extended thinking and reasoning to process multiple sources of information. Because there is more content to analyze and more perspectives or possible solutions to consider, selected-response items would need to have distractors that are quite lengthy to read. Excessive reading load can become a "source of challenge" in the test item that may not be related to what is actually being assessed, especially in mathematics assessments.

Combinations of multiple-choice items on large-scale assessments are designed to address the additional processing of ideas required for deeper thinking (DOK 3) as an alternative to using constructed-response items. Evidence-based questions like the Grade 10 reading "item set" below (PARCC Sample Items for ELA in 2012) illustrate item interdependence between Part A and Part B. Getting the second part correct depends on also getting the first part correct.

Associated Text: "Daedalus and Icarus" by Ovid

Part A
Which of the following sentences best states an important theme about human behavior as described in Ovid's "Daedalus and Icarus"?
a. Striving to achieve one's dreams is a worthwhile endeavor.
b. The thoughtlessness of youth can have tragic results.*
c. Imagination and creativity bring their own rewards.
d. Everyone should learn from his or her mistakes.

Part B
Select three pieces of evidence from Ovid's "Daedalus and Icarus" that support the answer to Part A.
a. "and by his playfulness retard the work / his anxious father planned" (lines 310–311)*
b. "But when at last / the father finished it, he poised himself" (lines 312–313)
c. "he fitted on his son the plumed wings / with trembling hands, while down his withered cheeks / the tears were falling" (lines 327–329)
d. "Proud of his success / the foolish Icarus forsook his guide" (lines 348–349)*
e. "and, bold in vanity, began to soar / rising above his wings to touch the skies" (lines 350–351)*
f. "and as the years went by the gifted youth / began to rival his instructor's art" (lines 376–377)
g. "Wherefore Daedalus / enraged and envious, sought to slay the youth" (lines 384–385)
h. "The Partridge hides / in shaded places by the leafy trees . . . for it is mindful of its former fall" (lines 395–396, 399)

This approach to selected response item design clearly works best for students who select the correct option for the first question. However, if a student gets the first part wrong, she is now looking for the wrong supporting details or evidence. Does the student decide to go back and change the first answer? Does the student take a guess and go on? In theory, a combination of selected response items may efficiently provide assessment information but may also trip up some students, especially those with limited executive functioning skills. A student might get both question parts wrong, perhaps for the wrong reasons. Using the same question (analyze evidence to support conclusions) without providing options to select results in responses will provide greater insights into the student's depth of thinking and conceptual understanding. Currently, there are online assessments that ask students to locate (highlight) supporting evidence within the text, rather than by choosing from options provided. If nothing else, this approach forces students to go back into the text and perhaps read some of it again to derive meaning.

This discussion is not intended to imply that multiple-choice test items should never be used. In many cases, they can be the best option for testing specific learning objectives. Selected-response (multiple choice, matching, true/false, etc.) and short-answer questions are an efficient means for assessing most foundational (DOK 1) and conceptual knowledge and skills (DOK 2). However, they should not be the only vehicle for collecting formative and summative evidence of learning, nor should there be an excessive use of multiple-choice practice tests for test preparation. Roediger and Marsh (2005) studied the positive and negative effects of multiple-choice testing. The authors examined the consequences of taking a multiple-choice test on a later general knowledge test. A large positive testing effect was obtained: Prior testing of facts aided final cued-recall performance. However, prior testing also had negative consequences: Prior readings of a greater number of multiple-choice options decreased the positive testing effect and increased production of multiple-choice lures as incorrect answers on the final test. Thus, overuse of multiple-choice testing may inadvertently lead to the creation of false knowledge. Frequently seeing too many incorrect responses can muddy the waters of memory and overall learning. Seeing too many wrong answers can cause some students to remember them as correct answers!

Because DOK 3 and DOK 4 tasks tend to be open-ended, I prefer to ask students to construct more insightful responses, rather than simply select "right" answers. As a matter of fact, when students begin to explain their reasoning, you may discover that students who did not get the correct answer actually have a deeper understanding and fewer misconceptions than some students who did answer correctly.

Rigor Misconception #6

Higher-order thinking always leads to deeper understanding.

Have you ever heard statements like this? "I'm using higher-order thinking questions in my lesson. That means students are learning at deeper levels."

This is a very common misconception. What we have generally thought of as "higher-order" thinking (Bloom's higher levels of analyzing, evaluating, and creating) might only be an engaging or fun activity for students and may not always lead to deeper understanding. Fun and engaging is not a bad thing, but it is not the same as deeper. Take the example of thinking critically. The essence of critical thinking is the ability to analyze, or take something apart—a primary source document, a science investigation, a solution to a math problem—in order to better understand how the parts work together or to determine where there might be flaws in the reasoning presented. Critical thinking activities can be used to build a conceptual foundation (DOK 2–type activities) or to interact with the content in order to deepen understanding and transfer learning to new or novel contexts (DOK 3– or DOK 4–type learning activities).

I've found that many "higher-order thinking," activities ask students to analyze, evaluate, or be creative with content without ever deepening their knowledge or asking them to work with more complex content. For example, "What if?" questions can be fun, draw upon prior knowledge, and provide engagement that helps students to build foundational knowledge. Still, the products of learning activities like these don't necessarily translate to evidence of deeper or insightful thinking. The curricular examples found in the Hess Cognitive Rigor Matrices (CRMs) for DOK 3 or 4 are meant to provide examples of the many ways to spur students not only to interpret content but also to convincingly justify and support their interpretations.

> Keeping with the theme of *"It's what comes after the verb,"* try this simple exercise: Take the same verb and show how it can be used to describe progressively deeper understanding of the same content. Table 1.3 illustrates task examples using the verb *describe*, which is often associated with lower-level thinking. Explanations of the mental processing required to complete each task are also included in the table. If you were to cover up the verb and focus only on the complexity of the content and the student's engagement with the content, it's easy to see how cognitive demand increases with each DOK level. DOK is not affected by the verb being used.

Table 1.3 Examples of Increasing Task Complexity Using the Same Verb

VERB	SAMPLE TASK	DOK	EXPLANATION OF MENTAL PROCESSING REQUIRED
Describe	Describe the information presented in this graph or a table.	1	This requires recalling how graphs and tables are constructed and reading the title and axes. Students are not working with the data but simply describing what the data represent. There is a correct answer.
Describe	Describe how these situations or scenarios are alike or different.	2	Students make connections by reading the entire text and looking for explicit relevant examples that can be compared and contrasted. There is a correct answer, although different examples may be used.
Describe	Describe the data or text evidence that supports your solution, your reasoning, or your conclusions about the effects of this phenomenon.	3	This requires articulating how the analysis of evidence influenced reasoning to arrive at a solution or conclusion, or to justify that a solution is viable. Different evidence, different approaches to the task, and the degree to which the analysis of evidence is of high quality are used to evaluate the "correctness" of the student's response.
Describe	Describe varying perspectives on this phenomenon using supporting scientific evidence and identify the most significant effects it might have on the planet in 100 years.	4	This requires not only an analysis of relevant evidence, but evidence coming from multiple sources. It also requires a deep understanding of the phenomenon and justification of criteria used to determine and predict "significant" effects. There is no correct answer. As with DOK 3, the credibility of evidence and the degree to which the analysis of evidence is of high quality and is used to explain differing perspectives contribute to evaluating the "correctness" of the student's response.

🚫 *Rigor Misconception #7*

*Multistep tasks, using multiple texts and resources,
or using complex texts will always lead to deeper thinking.*

I've sometimes heard people describe DOK levels in this way: One step means DOK 1, two steps means DOK 2, three steps means DOK 3, and so on. All multistep tasks are not created equal; many are actually learned routines with multiple steps. These include applying skills and rules that are important to know but are still considered foundational learning (DOK 1). Think about long division. It can have many steps and can be hard to do at first, but it is still a routine operation done the same way every time. Now, contrast the long division assignment with researching a topic, which also has multiple steps. Here, students might begin by building some foundational knowledge (e.g., brainstorming what they know about a topic; learning new terms and vocabulary; conducting a key word search—all DOK 1) and making connections between terms and concepts or begin examining cause–effect relationships (DOK 2). Then they might move to gathering data to help answer an issue-based question. The steps of this process may begin as routine but later involve planning and strategic thinking to determine relevance and accuracy of information and to evaluate the credibility of sources used. The number of steps is NOT the determining factor of cognitive rigor; it is the nonroutine nature of how one step might lead to decisions made about other steps in the process that deepens complexity, and ultimately learning.

Does the number of texts read or the complexity of a text always lead to deeper understanding and higher DOK levels? I would say that the task expectations and the level of engagement needed with the text to complete the task are as important as the complexity of the text.[9] We can ask lower-level, basic comprehension questions (DOK 1 or DOK 2) using a very complex text. We can ask lower-level, basic comprehension questions using two texts (e.g., compare the settings in these stories). Questions like these would only be DOK 2 because the information needed to answer the question is most likely *stated explicitly* in the texts. We can ask deeper, more rigorous questions using a wordless text. One of my favorite nonprint texts is the 2014 Caldecott Honor Book, *Journey* (Becker, 2013). Asking students to draw and support inferences using evidence from illustrations or nonprint texts can be just as mentally challenging as reading and interpreting words in a print text. (Both require justification, so both are DOK 3.)

If we were to ask students to read *Journey* and *Quest* (the second wordless text in this trilogy by Becker) in order to examine aspects of the author's craft across the texts, we set the stage for greater mental challenge and higher cognitive demand (DOK 4). Likewise, when we ask students to use two print texts to analyze the author's craft or the themes in two poems or stories, it becomes a DOK 4 task because the information needed to answer the question is not stated explicitly in the texts and must be interpreted using a deeper level of analysis and broader knowledge base.

Having tasks requiring multiple steps, asking students to read more texts, or using complex data or texts in routine ways doesn't lead to depth of thought. Deeper understanding is achieved when students dive into the concept, the scenario, the model, or the text(s) and come away with new understandings and insights, making connections that transfer to future learning.

---

9. In Module 2, we'll examine eight factors that make a text more or less complex.

Christy Mathes, secondary science teacher and district science curriculum facilitator in Gillette, Wyoming, shared this reflection with me on how a shift in her teaching affected her students' awareness of their own learning:

"I have, in personal practice, used your ideas on connecting the whys for the kids. Prior to this, my students were doing great activities that applied to the curriculum, but they didn't know that. Over the last two years, I have made a conscious effort to make the connections. What I am absolute about is that the kids have more engagement simply by seeing the connections. I had a principal observing in my classroom this week and he asked them the three questions you suggested (what are you doing, why are you doing it, and what are you learning). All of my students could clearly answer him. In fact one student said to him, 'We don't do any busy work in here; it is all to get to our Big Idea.'

Truly a moment of pride in my teaching career and really a small shift in my instruction."

Reflecting on the common misconceptions about rigor . . .
What surprises you? What is validated in your own practice?
What new questions have been raised?

Rigor Misconception #1 All kids aren't able to think deeply, or kids shouldn't need scaffolding and support in order to think deeply.

Rigor Misconception #2 Webb's Depth-of-Knowledge Framework is a taxonomy (meaning that DOK 4 is more desirable than DOK 1, 2, or 3 thinking).

Rigor Misconception #3 Verbs and levels in Bloom's Taxonomy can be equated with Depth-of-Knowledge levels.

Rigor Misconception #4 Depth of Knowledge is about greater difficulty, things getting harder.

Rigor Misconception #5 All Depth-of-Knowledge levels can be assessed with a multiple-choice question.

Rigor Misconception #6 Higher-order thinking always leads to deeper understanding.

Rigor Misconception #7 Multistep tasks, using multiple texts and resources, or using complex texts will always lead to deeper thinking.

1.4 Bloom Meets Webb: Origins of the Hess Cognitive Rigor Matrix

Creating the Matrix

The Hess Cognitive Rigor Matrices (CRMs) assist teachers in applying what cognitive demand might look like in the classroom and guide test developers in designing and aligning test items and performance tasks. Content-specific descriptors in each of the CRMs are used to categorize and plan for various levels of abstraction—meaning an analysis of the mental processing required of assessment questions and learning tasks. Today many schools, states, and testing companies use these tools for professional development, curriculum work, and test item development. So where did the Cognitive Rigor Matrix come from?

The CRM began to emerge in 2005, sparked by a thoughtful question from members of a state-level committee working with me on the design of their state's new large-scale assessment blueprint. Like many other states, this state and their testing contractor had been using Bloom's Taxonomy to describe test item difficulty. "Isn't Webb's DOK model just another way to describe the same thing as what Bloom's six levels do?" teachers asked me when I introduced and suggested a shift to using Depth-of-Knowledge level descriptors instead of Bloom's taxonomy as the frame of reference for determining the complexity of test items and standards they were aligned with.

I struggled at the time to clearly articulate the key differences between the two models, even though I knew they were not specifically addressing the same characteristics of complexity. On the plane home, I began to examine each model in greater depth and experimented with where the two models might intersect. Although related through their natural ties to the complexity of thought, I could see that Bloom's thinking levels and Webb's Depth-of-Knowledge levels differed in scope, application, and possibly intent. The result of my attempt to show where there was overlap was a model that superimposed Bloom's Taxonomy with Webb's Depth-of-Knowledge levels.

I started with a blank matrix template, putting Bloom's thinking levels along the vertical axis and DOK levels across the top (Table 1.4). At first, I thought maybe Bloom's levels of "Remember" and "Understand" might line up nicely with DOK 1; and descriptors for "Apply" might equate with DOK 2 examples. My assumption was wrong. I began to populate the cells of the matrix with specific examples, using reading and writing DOK-level descriptors that I'd developed earlier (Hess, 2004a). I soon realized that I was able to identify curricular examples in language arts at every DOK level for almost every cell in the new matrix. When this approach seemed to work well for language arts, I tried applying mathematics examples, science examples, and social studies examples at each DOK level. Eureka! My idea of a cognitive rigor matrix was born. It was becoming clear to me that higher-order verbs or thinking levels did not always result in learning tasks requiring deeper understanding or strategic thinking.

Table 1.4 Building a Cognitive Rigor Matrix to Describe Increasing Levels of Complexity

BLOOM	DOK 1	DOK 2	DOK 3	DOK 4
Remember	Recall a fact, detail, or term			
Understand	Identify literary elements	Summarize a text	Identify a theme	
Apply	Apply rules of editing	Use context to determine meaning		Illustrate how multiple themes are interrelated
Analyze	Identify information in a text feature	Compare characters		
Evaluate	UGs = opinions that have no valid supporting evidence; unsubstantiated generalizations		Citing evidence, develop a logical argument for conjectures	
Create	Brainstorm ideas on a topic			Synthesize ideas across sources

As I worked on the evolving matrix, I still had to resolve what to put in the cells at the lower DOK levels for "Evaluate" and at the upper DOK levels for "Remember." As I thought more about describing "Remember" in terms of *depth*, it made no sense to put anything under DOK 2, 3, or 4. You know or remember something or you don't. It's as simple as that. Those cells were purposely left blank.

Deciding what to put next to "Evaluate" under DOK 1 and DOK 2 was a bit more perplexing. What do you call it when you evaluate something—state an opinion or try to make an argument—and have no relevant supporting evidence, no elaboration, and cite no sources? Then it came to me as a flashback into my own past. These were "UGs." I frequently saw this notation on the early papers that I wrote while in graduate school. If Professor Bud Meyers put an UG in the margin, it meant that you had an unsubstantiated generalization: You stated an opinion, claim, or a "truth" but provided no credible support for it. An UG sent you back to find a source to back up your idea.

We often give students prompts that can elicit unsupported opinions: Did you like the book? Is he evil? Was this a good decision? We ask open-ended questions and then find ourselves giving the student credit for completing the assignment mostly because the handwriting was neat and it was handed in on time, not because their ideas and opinions were supported in a relevant or meaningful way. Either these essays have not used criteria in making a judgment,[10] or the reasons used would not be ones we would generally agree are the criteria that should be used to evaluate a character archetype (e.g., Who is the real hero?) or a viable mathematical solution to a real-world problem. UGs, therefore, are "low-level" (DOK 1–DOK 2) opinions—opinions without credible, justifiable support. Opinions supported by valid criteria and credible evidence rise to the levels of DOK 3 and 4.

Throughout this CRM development process, I came to better understand that deeper learning or thinking was not simply about verbs, taxonomies, complex texts, or what we have generally accepted as "higher-order" thinking. There was a significant difference between "analysis lite" (DOK 1 or DOK 2) and deeper analysis of a topic or concept (DOK 3 or DOK 4).

BLOOM'S TAXONOMY (1956)	BLOOM'S COGNITIVE PROCESS DIMENSIONS (2001)
Knowledge: Define, duplicate, label, list, name, order, recognize, relate, recall	Remember: Retrieve knowledge from long-term memory, recognize, recall, locate, identify
Comprehension: Classify, describe, discuss, explain, express, identify, indicate, locate, recognize, report, review, select, translate	Understand: Construct meaning, clarify, paraphrase, represent, translate, illustrate, give examples, classify, categorize, summarize, generalize, predict
Application: Apply, choose, demonstrate, dramatize, employ, illustrate, interpret, practice, write	Apply: Carry out or use a procedure in a given situation; carry out or use and apply to an unfamiliar task
Analysis: Analyze, appraise, explain, calculate, categorize, compare, criticize, discriminate, examine	Analyze: Break into constituent parts; determine how parts relate
Synthesis: Rearrange, assemble, collect, compose, create, design, develop, formulate, manage, write	Evaluate: Make judgments based on criteria, check, detect inconsistencies or fallacies, critique
Evaluation: Appraise, argue, assess, choose, compare, defend, estimate, explain, judge, predict, rate, core, select, support, value	Create: Put elements together to form a coherent whole; reorganize elements into new patterns or structures

---

10. A discussion of judgement-based opinions and arguments is presented in Module 3, in "Writing Better Prompts."

The two Hess CRM tools developed for ELA–social studies and mathematics–science in 2005 integrated the original wording and levels in Bloom's Taxonomy (1956). In 2006, I updated the matrices to reflect the revised wording and levels of Bloom's Taxonomy, renamed in 2001 as Bloom's Cognitive Process Dimensions (Anderson et al., 2001).

Proof of Concept and Final Steps in the Development of the Cognitive Rigor Matrix

In 2007–2008, the updated CRMs were used by The Standards Company to conduct a large-scale analysis of assignments given to students in Oklahoma and Nevada over a three-month time period (Hess, Carlock, Jones, & Walkup, 2009). Work samples of homework assignments, tests, and quizzes, for example, were collected and analyzed using the Hess CRMs in ELA–social studies and math–science to develop density plots that visually described the level of complexity (or lack of it) in most work assigned to students. This study confirmed that the Hess CRM tools could be useful in enhancing assessment planning and instructional practices at the classroom level.

Over time and with use, the CRMs have provided educators with a more sophisticated lens to systematically guide the creation of cognitively engaging and challenging assessment tasks while offering a range of choices when planning for increasing the rigor of instruction. Descriptors in the Hess CRMs offer a common language for analyzing the levels of rigor (cognitive demand) in assessments, units of study, and learning tasks. Often these analyses have led to refinements in classroom questioning, the design of learning tasks, and development of high-quality assessments. The strongest validation for use of the Hess CRM to examine rigor alignment and item quality of large-scale assessments is described in a June 2016 report, published by Understanding Language/Stanford Center for Assessment, Learning, and Equity (pp. 21–47).

The Thinking Behind the Tools in Module 1

Content domains matter when describing increasing complexity and teaching for transfer. The eight content-specific CRM tools included in Module 1 (**TOOLS #1–#5D**) were developed with this in mind. Each CRM superimposes a cognitive complexity framework with the concept of Depth of Knowledge in order to produce a vehicle for analyzing the emphasis placed on curriculum, instruction, and assessment. You may notice that not all of the Hess CRMs integrate Bloom levels with DOK levels. During development, I found that some content areas did not readily lend themselves to using Bloom; however, all content areas did work well using DOK. As I expanded my work from Webb's earlier DOK descriptions in reading, writing, mathematics, science, and social studies (2002), I consulted with content experts and teachers to help me think about what increasing rigor and complexity might look like in fine arts, world languages, health and physical education, or career and technology education (CTE) classrooms. Table 1.5 in the Part 2 Support Materials at the end of Module 1 describes the content-specific CRM **TOOLS #1–#5D**.

Summarizing Key Ideas: Bloom's Taxonomy and Depth of Knowledge

- Bloom's Taxonomy categorizes the cognitive skills required of the brain to perform a task, describing the "type of thinking processes" necessary to answer a question or complete a task.
- Most complex tasks require many different "types" of thinking.

- The types of thinking identified in Bloom's Taxonomy CAN lead to deeper learning when matched with increasingly more complex content: deeper understanding, deeper application, or deeper analysis.

- Verbs alone do not determine the complexity level of a task. It is what comes after the verb that indicates complexity.

- **Depth of Knowledge** focuses on how deeply students need to know and interact with content to be able to generate a specific type of response. DOK levels relate more closely to the depth of content understanding and scope of a learning activity, which manifests in the skills required to complete a task from inception to finale (e.g., planning, researching, and drawing conclusions based on research).

- DOK levels are *not* sequential or linear. Students need not fully master content with Level 1 tasks before doing Level 2 tasks. In fact, giving students an intriguing Level 3 or 4 task prompt can provide context and motivation for engaging in the more routine learning at DOK Levels 1 and 2 needed to be successful with the more complex task.

- DOK levels are *not* developmental. All students, including the youngest preschoolers, are capable of strategic and extended thinking. The questions or tasks may differ, as will the context, content, and scaffolding strategies used in a kindergarten classroom or for middle schoolers. All students should have opportunities and support to use strategic and complex reasoning every day.

- An activity that aligns to a particular DOK level is not always "easier" than an activity that aligns to a DOK level above it. Complexity and difficulty are NOT the same. Difficulty refers to how easy or hard something is. For example, once someone learns the "rules" of addition, they should be able to add any numbers. Adding 4 + 4 is DOK 1 and is also easy to do. Adding 4,678,895 + 9,578,885 is still DOK 1, but it is more "difficult" for most students. A task where students recite a simple fact or a much more complex abstract theory are both DOK 1, even though the abstract theory is much more difficult to memorize and restate. Neither task asks for depth of understanding of the content.

- The complexity of both the content (e.g., text complexity, number of texts, theory vs. terms) and the task expectations (processes and products) are used to determine the intended DOK levels, not the grade level or innate ability of students.

- If there is a question regarding which of two DOK levels a standard addresses, such as Level 1 versus Level 2, or Level 2 versus Level 3, it is appropriate to assign the highest level as the "DOK ceiling" for the task but also provide opportunities at the lower DOK levels as an instructional progression (e.g., summarizing a text/DOK 2 before analyzing a text/DOK 3; making observations/DOK 2 before drawing conclusions using data from an investigation/DOK 3) (Hess, 2004a, 2004b, 2008a).

Reflections

On your own or with colleagues, take a minute to reflect on the topics covered in this module. Then identify a useful takeaway, something to try next.

Ways I am refining my thinking about DOK/rigor/deeper learning...
- It's not about doing more.
- ?
- ?

Strategic scaffolding strategies for getting students to deeper thinking...
- Small groups, pairs
- Chunking text
- ?
- ?
- ?

R My personal prescription for infusing rigor...

1.5 Getting Started Applying Your Understanding of Rigor and Deeper Learning

Here are some ways to collaboratively expand your school community's understanding of how to support deeper learning for all students. Some of the general ideas are followed with specific support materials included at the end of Module 1 and at **resources.corwin.com/HessToolkit**. These resources are referenced in bold print under the bullets that follow.

- Become more knowledgeable of Depth of Knowledge (DOK) as a framework for thinking and engaging with content. Explore with your staff how various learning and assessment tasks may be "hard" for students to do but do not reach the complexity of DOK 3 or DOK 4.

  o To have some fun discussing differences among DOK levels, use the workshop activity **What's TV Got to Do With DOK?** I ask participants to come up with another DOK 4 TV show and justify their thinking. This activity is also a way to introduce deeper and more complex thinking to students.

  o Take the **DOK "IQ" Test.** I developed this collaborative workshop activity for educators who have already been using DOK but may need to fine-tune their collective understandings of the levels of thinking that different learning activities are intended to elicit.

- Shift the professional discourse in your school from saying "higher-order thinking" to "deeper learning" when planning lessons and developing assessments. This should include deeper understanding (e.g., drawing from multiple sources to understand a topic from different perspectives) and deeper analysis through solving nonroutine, real-world tasks utilizing a combination of approaches. Ask teachers to collect classroom examples of assignments and assessments intended to elicit deeper thinking.

    o The eight content-specific Hess Cognitive Rigor Matrices/CRM (**TOOLS #1–#5D**) can be used to guide collaborative analysis of samples collected across content areas and grade levels. Digital versions of these tools can be downloaded from **www.karin-hess.com** as well as from **corwin.resources.com/HessToolkit**.

- Grade-level or PLC teams can examine ways to tweak current learning and assessment tasks or prompts used in each lesson. Determine what mental processing is actually required to complete specific tasks. For example, if the prompt asks students to interpret or solve _____, then encourage teachers to have students delve deeper into content or concepts by adding words such as "*. . . and justify your claim or solution by providing evidence to explain your thinking.*"

    o The Hess Cognitive Rigor Matrices (**TOOLS #1–#5D**) and Hess CRM **Question-Planning Worksheets** can be used to support these PLC activities.

    o See also Module 3 PLC **TOOL #9** (summative and performance task development), PLC **TOOL #10** (formative task development), and PLC **TOOL #11** (rubric development guide) and additional examples of classroom assessments of deeper thinking included in Modules 2 and 3.

- Have teachers collaboratively review unit questions and evaluate them for promoting a progression from foundational to conceptual to deeper and broader understanding. A blank Hess CRM template can be useful for examining or creating a range of unit or lesson questions and formative assessment tasks.

    o The Hess CRM **Question-Planning Worksheets** can be used to analyze unit or lesson questions and assessment tasks, or to develop kid-friendly examples of expectations for increasing rigor.

    o The "I Can Rock the Rigor Kid Tool" was inspired by students in Utah who wanted to create their own CRMs. This tool is available for downloading from **resources.corwin.com/HessToolkit.**

- Plan professional development opportunities that provide teachers with time to codevelop or revise tasks or questioning strategies to deepen the thinking processes used by students.

- Ask teachers to experiment with a strategy that they think will get to deeper thinking and understanding. Then ask them to share reflections with colleagues on what worked and what might work better next time.

- Collaboratively analyze student work products that "uncover" evidence of critical thinking.

    o See Module 3, PLC **TOOL #12** (student-work analysis) for a protocol to analyze student work products and plan next steps for differentiating instruction based on evidence seen in the work.

- Above all else, stay the course. A schoolwide shift to deeper thinking takes time. In my long-term work with schools, I find it takes 3+ years for a true systemic shift in practice to take hold. Don't underestimate the importance of slowly building a critical mass with the early adopters in your building who can share their examples, their successes, and their reflections with colleagues.

PART 2: SUPPORT MATERIALS FOR MODULE 1

I. A Workshop Plan for Module 1

Kolb's Experiential Learning Cycle

Suggested Activities

Stage 1: WHY is this new learning important to me? And what do I already know?

Moving from Concrete Experience to Reflective Observation

Create a concrete experience, asking participants to make connections, drawing on personal knowledge and experience. Small groups compare and reflect on common ideas.

- Activity: *What comes to mind when you think of cognitive rigor?* Validate connections made and begin to link ideas with research and classroom examples.
- Activity: Collaboratively develop questions that are basic versus rigorous. (I use *Little Red Riding Hood* as the context.) Hold questions for review later in the workshop using the Hess CRM.
- Select a small number of video examples to discuss: *How might I/we use this strategy?*

Stage 2: WHAT do the research and experts say?

Moving from Reflective Observation to Abstract Conceptualization

Help participants connect their personal reflections to broader, more abstract generalizations.

- Provide expert advice and review the research via interactive lectures, readings, and video clips.
- Use models and classroom examples and nonexamples to further develop concepts and build schemas. Stop frequently (every 15–20 min.) to consolidate the new learning.
- Discuss 7 Common Misconceptions About Rigor. Reflect: What was validated? What surprised you? What questions do you have?
- Review Activity: *What's TV got to do with DOK?*

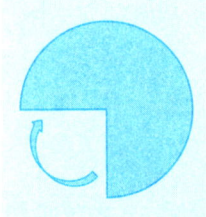

Stage 3: HOW does this work? How can I apply this?

Moving from Abstract Conceptualization to Active Experimentation

Use tools and protocols to examine examples and strategies.

- Provide background on development of Hess CRM.
- Activity: Examine the CRM closest to your content area. Discuss observations and questions. Use the CRM **TOOLS #1–#5D** to develop parallel "Kid Language" for specific grade level and content or topic you teach.
- Activity: Collaboratively analyze your own classroom assessments and questioning examples.

50   A Local Assessment Toolkit to Promote Deeper Learning

Stage 4: WHAT IF I experimented with this? What might work in my classroom or school?
Moving from Active Experimentation back to Concrete Experiences

- Activity: Apply CRM Planning Tools to new learnings in your own work. Develop or revise a current unit of study. Brainstorm deeper questions and strategic scaffolding strategies to add to lessons.
- Review Activity: Take the DOK IQ Test. Use Hess CRM **TOOLS #1–#5D** to check understanding.
- T-Chart Reflections: In what ways are you refining your ideas about rigor? And about strategic scaffolding?
- Experiment with a new strategy in your classroom. Reflect on how it worked and what you might do next.

Source: Stages adapted from Kolb (1984) and McCarthy (1987).

II. The Hess Cognitive Rigor Matrix Tools

About the Tools in This Module

Tools #1–#4 Core Subject CRMs

These tools are on pages 53–56, and available for download from **resources.corwin.com/HessToolkit** and **karin-hess.com/free-resources**.

Tools #5A–#5D Special Subject CRMs

These tools are on pages 57–60, and available for download from **resources.corwin.com/HessToolkit** and **karin-hess.com/free-resources**.

Table 1.5 Overview of the Hess Cognitive Rigor Matrix Tools

TOOL	DEVELOPMENT AND POSSIBLE USES FOR EACH HESS COGNITIVE RIGOR MATRIX TOOL
1 Close Reading and Listening CRM	**TOOL #1** identifies many ways that close reading of texts might be demonstrated across content areas, grade levels, and text types. It is also useful in thinking about tasks that require students to listen to or view nonprint texts (film, drama, podcasts, etc.). I've expanded upon Webb's original DOK descriptors (2002) for reading, drawing from my alignment study and test development work over the years.
2 Mathematics and Science CRM	**TOOL #2** identifies how mathematics and science skills and concepts might be demonstrated across grade levels, domains, or problem-solving situations. Math and science were combined in this matrix to illustrate the complementary nature of mathematics, science, and STEM activities. I've expanded upon Webb's original DOK descriptors for math and science (1997) drawing from my alignment study and test development work over the years.

(Continued)

Table 1.5 (Continued)

TOOL	DEVELOPMENT AND POSSIBLE USES FOR EACH HESS COGNITIVE RIGOR MATRIX TOOL
3 Writing and Speaking CRM	**TOOL #3** identifies many ways that written and oral communication might be demonstrated across content areas, grade levels, text genres, and communication formats (plays, speeches, graphic novels, etc.). I've expanded upon Webb's original DOK descriptors for writing (2002), drawing from my alignment study and test development work over the years.
4 Social Studies and Humanities CRM	**TOOL #4** identifies ways that social studies (which can include history, civics, economics, and geography) and humanities skills and concepts might be demonstrated across units of study and in-depth inquiry activities. I've expanded upon Webb's original DOK descriptors for social studies (2002), drawing from my alignment study and test development work over the years and my work with humanities assessments.
5A Fine Arts CRM	**TOOL #5A** was created and refined during my work with several states' development of standards and assessments for visual arts, music, dance, and theater. This tool represents my interpretation of DOK when applied to the fine arts. To my knowledge Norman Webb has not worked with DOK in the fine arts. You will notice right away that in this matrix, Bloom's Taxonomy is not integrated with DOK. Instead, I worked with arts educators to identify common "arts practices" that could integrate with DOK descriptors. The result is the many ways that the fine arts might be demonstrated across arts disciplines and grade levels.
5B Health and Physical Education CRM	**TOOL #5B** was created and refined through my work with whole-school faculties. As with fine arts and world language CRMs, HPE teachers struggled to see how DOK or Bloom applied to their curriculum and assessments. Tool #5B represents my interpretation of how DOK could apply to the National HPE standards. For this tool, I drew from Porter and Smithson's Cognitive Demand Categories (2001) rather than Bloom. To my knowledge neither Webb nor Porter and Smithson have specifically described cognitive demand in health or physical education.
5C World Languages CRM	**TOOL #5C** With the help of Rachel Gilbert, world language instructional coach, and Amy Flynn, world language coordinator, we explored content used in world language courses, identifying five broad practices and modes of communication consistent with national standards. Then I developed curricular examples specific to world language content and expectations for ELLs for each DOK level.
5D Career and Technical Education CRM	**TOOL #5D** closely resembles **TOOL #2**, identifying how mathematics and science skills and concepts might be demonstrated across grade levels, domains, or problem-solving. Many CTE teachers were already using Tool #2 but were looking for more specific examples that would more closely apply to courses they were teaching, such as building trades, health science, and auto mechanics. With the help of Kirsten Soroko, who helped me gather CTE assessment examples and feedback from CTE teachers in New Hampshire, we refined **TOOL #2** to be more CTE specific.

HESS COGNITIVE RIGOR MATRIX (READING CRM):
Applying Webb's Depth-of-Knowledge Levels to Bloom's Cognitive Process Dimensions

Revised Bloom's Taxonomy	Webb's DOK Level 1 Recall and Reproduction	Webb's DOK Level 2 Skills and Concepts	Webb's DOK Level 3 Strategic Thinking/Reasoning	Webb's DOK Level 4 Extended Thinking
Remember Retrieve knowledge from long-term memory, recognize, recall, locate, identify	o Recall, recognize, or locate basic facts, terms, details, events, or ideas explicit in texts o Read words orally in connected text with fluency and accuracy	Use these Hess CRM curricular examples with most close reading or listening assignments or assessments in any content area.		
Understand Construct meaning, clarify, paraphrase, represent, translate, illustrate, give examples, classify, categorize, summarize, generalize, infer a logical conclusion, predict, compare-contrast, match like ideas, explain, construct models	o Identify or describe literary elements (characters, setting, sequence, etc.) o Select appropriate words when intended meaning or definition is clearly evident o Describe or explain who, what, where, when, or how o Define or describe facts, details, terms, principles o Write simple sentences	o Specify, explain, show relationships; explain why (e.g., cause-effect) o Give nonexamples or examples o Summarize results, concepts, ideas o Make basic inferences or logical predictions from data or texts o Identify main ideas or accurate generalizations of texts o Locate information to support explicit-implicit central ideas	o Explain, generalize, or connect ideas using supporting evidence (quote, example, text reference) o Identify or make inferences about explicit or implicit themes o Describe how word choice, point of view, or bias may affect the readers' interpretation of a text o Write multiparagraph composition for specific purpose, focus, voice, tone, and audience	o Explain how concepts or ideas specifically relate to other content domains (e.g., social, political, historical) or concepts o Develop generalizations of the results obtained or strategies used and apply them to new problem-based situations
Apply Carry out or use a procedure in a given situation; carry out (apply to a familiar task), or use (apply) to an unfamiliar task	o Use language structure (pre- or suffix) or word relationships (synonym/antonym) to determine meaning of words o Apply rules or resources to edit spelling, grammar, punctuation, conventions, word use o Apply basic formats for documenting sources	o Use context to identify the meaning of words or phrases o Obtain and interpret information using text features o Develop a text that may be limited to one paragraph o Apply simple organizational structures (paragraph, sentence types) in writing	o Apply a concept in a new context o Revise final draft for meaning or progression of ideas o Apply internal consistency of text organization and structure to composing a full composition o Apply word choice, point of view, style to impact readers' or viewers' interpretation of a text	o Illustrate how multiple themes (historical, geographic, social, artistic, literary) may be interrelated o Select or devise an approach among many alternatives to research a novel problem
Analyze Break into constituent parts, determine how parts relate, differentiate between relevant-irrelevant, distinguish, focus, select, organize, outline, find coherence, deconstruct (e.g., for bias or point of view)	o Identify whether specific information is contained in graphic representations (e.g., map, chart, table, graph, T-chart, diagram) or text features (e.g., headings, subheadings, captions) o Decide which text structure is appropriate to audience and purpose	o Categorize or compare literary elements, terms, facts or details, events o Identify use of literary devices o Analyze format, organization, and internal text structure (signal words, transitions, semantic cues) of different texts o Distinguish: relevant-irrelevant information; fact-opinion o Identify characteristic text features; distinguish between texts, genres	o Analyze information within data sets or texts o Analyze interrelationships among concepts, issues, problems o Analyze or interpret author's craft (literary devices, viewpoint, or potential bias) to create or critique a text o Use reasoning, planning, and evidence to support inferences	o Analyze multiple sources of evidence, or multiple works by the same author, or across genres, time periods, themes o Analyze complex or abstract themes, perspectives, concepts o Gather, analyze, and organize multiple information sources o Analyze discourse styles
Evaluate Make judgments based on criteria, check, detect inconsistencies or fallacies, judge, critique	"UG"—unsubstantiated generalizations = stating an opinion without providing any support for it!		o Cite evidence and develop a logical argument for conjectures o Describe, compare, and contrast solution methods o Verify reasonableness of results o Justify or critique conclusions drawn	o Evaluate relevancy, accuracy, and completeness of information from multiple sources o Apply understanding in a novel way, provide argument or justification for the application
Create Reorganize elements into new patterns or structures, generate, hypothesize, design, plan, produce	o Brainstorm ideas, concepts, problems, or perspectives related to a topic, principle, or concept	o Generate conjectures or hypotheses based on observations or prior knowledge and experience	o Synthesize information within one source or text o Develop a complex model for a given situation o Develop an alternative solution	o Synthesize information across multiple sources or texts o Articulate a new voice, alternate theme, new knowledge or perspective

© Karin Hess (2009, updated 2017). Available for download at resources.corwin.com/HessToolkit and www.karin-hess.com. *A local assessment toolkit to support deeper learning: Guiding school leaders in linking research with classroom practice.* Permission to reproduce is given only when authorship is fully cited [karinhessvt@gmail.com]

HESS COGNITIVE RIGOR MATRIX (MATH–SCIENCE CRM):
Applying Webb's Depth-of-Knowledge Levels to Bloom's Cognitive Process Dimensions

Revised Bloom's Taxonomy	Webb's DOK Level 1 Recall and Reproduction	Webb's DOK Level 2 Skills and Concepts	Webb's DOK Level 3 Strategic Thinking/Reasoning	Webb's DOK Level 4 Extended Thinking
Remember Retrieve knowledge from long-term memory, recognize, recall, locate, identify	o Recall, observe, and recognize facts, principles, properties o Recall/identify conversions among representations or numbers (e.g., customary and metric measures)	Use these Hess CRM curricular examples with most mathematics or science assignments or assessments.		
Understand Construct meaning, clarify, paraphrase, represent, translate, illustrate, give examples, classify, categorize, summarize, generalize, infer a logical conclusion, predict, compare or contrast, match like ideas, explain, construct models	o Evaluate an expression o Locate points on a grid or number on number line o Solve a one-step problem o Represent math relationships in words, pictures, or symbols o Read, write, compare decimals in scientific notation	o Specify and explain relationships (e.g., nonexamples or examples; cause-effect) o Make and record observations o Explain steps followed o Summarize results or concepts o Make basic inferences or logical predictions from data or observations o Use models or diagrams to represent or explain mathematical concepts o Make and explain estimates	o Use concepts to solve nonroutine problems o Explain, generalize, or connect ideas using supporting evidence o Make and justify conjectures o Explain thinking or reasoning when more than one solution or approach is possible o Explain phenomena in terms of concepts	o Relate mathematical or scientific concepts to other content areas, other domains, or other concepts o Develop generalizations of the results obtained and the strategies used (from investigation or readings) and apply them to new problem situations
Apply Carry out or use a procedure in a given situation; carry out (apply to a familiar task) or use (apply) to an unfamiliar task	o Follow simple procedures (recipe-type directions) o Calculate, measure, apply a rule (e.g., rounding) o Apply algorithm or formula (e.g., area, perimeter) o Solve linear equations o Make conversions among representations or numbers, or within and between customary and metric measures	o Select a procedure according to criteria and perform it o Solve a routine problem applying multiple concepts or decision points o Retrieve information from a table, graph, or figure and use it to solve a problem requiring multiple steps o Translate between tables, graphs, words, and symbolic notations (e.g., graph data from a table) o Construct models given criteria	o Design an investigation for a specific purpose or research question o Conduct a designed investigation o Use concepts to solve nonroutine problems o Use and show reasoning, planning, and evidence o Translate between problem and symbolic notation when not a direct translation	o Select or devise an approach among many alternatives to solve a problem o Conduct a project that specifies a problem, identifies solution paths, solves the problem, and reports results
Analyze Break into constituent parts, determine how parts relate, differentiate between relevant-irrelevant, distinguish, focus, select, organize, outline, find coherence, deconstruct	o Retrieve information from a table or graph to answer a question o Identify whether specific information is contained in graphic representations (e.g., table, graph, T-chart, diagram) o Identify a pattern or trend	o Categorize, classify materials, data, figures based on characteristics o Organize or order data o Compare-contrast figures or data o Select an appropriate graph and organize and display data o Interpret data from a simple graph o Extend a pattern	o Compare information within or across data sets or texts o Analyze and draw conclusions from data, citing evidence o Generalize a pattern o Interpret data from complex a graph o Analyze similarities-differences between procedures or solutions	o Analyze multiple sources of evidence o Analyze complex or abstract themes o Gather, analyze, and evaluate information
Evaluate Make judgments based on criteria, check, detect inconsistencies or fallacies, judge, critique		"UG"—unsubstantiated generalizations = stating an opinion without providing any support for it!	o Cite evidence and develop a logical argument for concepts or solutions o Describe, compare, and contrast solution methods o Verify reasonableness of results	o Gather, analyze, and evaluate information to draw conclusions o Apply understanding in a novel way, provide argument or justification for the application
Create Reorganize elements into new patterns or structures, generate, hypothesize, design, plan, produce	o Brainstorm ideas, concepts, or perspectives related to a topic	o Generate conjectures or hypotheses based on observations or prior knowledge and experience	o Synthesize information within one data set, source, or text o Formulate an original problem given a situation o Develop a scientific or mathematical model for a complex situation	o Synthesize information across multiple sources or texts o Design a mathematical model to inform and solve a practical or abstract situation

© Karin Hess (2009, updated 2017). Available for download at resources.corwin.com/HessToolkit and www.karin-hess.com/free-resources *A local assessment toolkit to support deeper learning: Guiding school leaders in linking research with classroom practice.* Permission to reproduce is given only when authorship is fully cited [karinhessvt@gmail.com]

HESS COGNITIVE RIGOR MATRIX (WRITING/SPEAKING CRM):
Applying Webb's Depth-of-Knowledge Levels to Bloom's Cognitive Process Dimensions

Revised Bloom's Taxonomy	Webb's DOK Level 1 Recall and Reproduction	Webb's DOK Level 2 Skills and Concepts	Webb's DOK Level 3 Strategic Thinking/Reasoning	Webb's DOK Level 4 Extended Thinking
		Use these Hess CRM curricular examples with most writing and oral communication assignments or assessments in any content area.		
Remember Retrieve knowledge from long-term memory, recognize, recall, locate, identify	o Complete short answer questions with facts, details, terms, principles, etc. (e.g., label parts of diagram)			
Understand Construct meaning, clarify, paraphrase, represent, translate, illustrate, give examples, classify, categorize, summarize, generalize, infer a logical conclusion, predict, compare-contrast, match like ideas, explain, construct models	o Describe or define facts, details, terms, principles, etc. o Select appropriate word or phrase to use when intended meaning or definition is clearly evident o Write simple complete sentences o Add an appropriate caption to a photo or illustration o Write "fact statements" on a topic (e.g., spiders build webs)	o Specify, explain, show relationships; explain why, cause-effect o Provide and explain nonexamples and examples o Take notes; organize ideas or data (e.g., relevance, trends, perspectives) o Summarize results, key concepts, ideas o Add an explain key concepts, ideas o Explain central ideas or accurate generalizations of texts or topics o Describe steps in a process (e.g., science procedure, how to and why control variables)	o Write a multiparagraph composition for specific purpose, focus, voice, tone, and audience o Develop and explain opposing perspectives or connect ideas, principles, or concepts using supporting evidence (quote, example, text reference, etc.) o Develop arguments of fact (e.g., Are these criticisms supported by the historical facts? Is this claim or equation true?)	o Use multiple sources to elaborate on how concepts or ideas specifically draw from other content domains or differing concepts (e.g., research paper, arguments of policy—should this law be passed? What will be the impact of this change?) o Develop generalizations about the results obtained or strategies used and apply them to a new problem or contextual scenario
Apply Carry out or use a procedure in a given situation; carry out (apply to a familiar task) or use (apply) to an unfamiliar task	o Apply rules or use resources to edit specific spelling, grammar, punctuation, conventions, or word use o Apply basic formats for documenting sources	o Use context to identify or infer the intended meaning of words or phrases o Obtain, interpret, and explain information using text features (table, diagram, etc.) o Develop a (brief) text that may be limited to one paragraph, précis o Apply basic organizational structures (paragraph, sentence types, topic sentence, introduction, etc.) in writing	o Revise final draft for meaning, progression of ideas, or logic chain o Apply internal consistency of text organization and structure to a full composition or oral communication o Apply a concept in a new context o Apply word choice, point of view, style, rhetorical devices to impact readers' interpretation of a text	o Select or devise an approach among many alternatives to research and present a novel problem or issue o Illustrate how multiple themes (historical, geographic, social) may be interrelated within a text or topic
Analyze Break into constituent parts, determine how parts relate, differentiate between relevant-irrelevant, distinguish, focus, select, organize, outline, find coherence, deconstruct (e.g., for bias or point of view)	o Decide which text structure is appropriate to audience and purpose (e.g., compare-contrast, proposition/support) o Determine appropriate, relevant key words for conducting an Internet search or researching a topic	o Compare-contrast perspectives, events, characters, etc. o Analyze-revise format, organization, and internal text structure (signal words, transitions, semantic cues) of different print and nonprint texts o Distinguish: relevant-irrelevant information; fact-opinion (e.g., What are the characteristics of a hero's journey?) o Locate evidence that supports a perspective-differing perspectives	o Analyze interrelationships among concepts, issues, and problems in a text o Analyze impact or use of author's craft (literary devices, viewpoint, dialogue) in a single text o Use reasoning and evidence to generate criteria for making and supporting an argument of judgment (Was FDR a great president? Who was the greatest ball player?) o Support conclusions with evidence	o Analyze multiple sources of evidence, or multiple works by the same author, or across genres, or time periods o Analyze complex or abstract themes, perspectives, concepts o Gather, analyze, and organize multiple information sources o Compare and contrast conflicting judgments or policies (e.g., Supreme Court decisions)
Evaluate Make judgments based on criteria, check, detect inconsistencies or fallacies, judge, critique	"UG"—unsubstantiated generalizations = stating an opinion without providing any support for it!		o Evaluate validity and relevance of evidence used to develop an argument or support a perspective o Describe, compare, and contrast solution methods o Verify or critique the accuracy, logic, and reasonableness of stated conclusions or assumptions	o Evaluate relevancy, accuracy, and completeness of information across multiple sources o Apply understanding in a novel way, provide argument or justification for the application o Critique the historical impact (policy, writings, discoveries, etc.)
Create Reorganize elements into new patterns or structures, generate, hypothesize, design, plan, produce	o Brainstorm facts, ideas, concepts, problems, or perspectives related to a topic, text, idea, issue, or concept	o Generate conjectures, hypotheses, or predictions based on facts, observations, evidence/observations, or prior knowledge and experience o Generate believable "grounds" (reasons) for an opinion-argument	o Develop a complex model for a given situation of problem o Develop an alternative solution or perspective to one proposed (e.g., debate)	o Synthesize information across multiple sources or texts in order to articulate a new voice, alternate theme, new knowledge or nuanced perspective

© Karin Hess (2009, updated 2017). Available for download at resources.corwin.com/HessToolkit and www.karin-hess.com/free-resources A local assessment toolkit to support deeper learning: Guiding school leaders in linking research with classroom practice. Permission to reproduce is given only when authorship is fully cited [karinhessvt@gmail.com]

HESS COGNITIVE RIGOR MATRIX (SOCIAL STUDIES/HUMANITIES CRM):
Applying Webb's Depth-of-Knowledge Levels to Bloom's Cognitive Process Dimensions

Revised Bloom's Taxonomy	Webb's DOK Level 1 Recall and Reproduction	Webb's DOK Level 2 Skills and Concepts	Webb's DOK Level 3 Strategic Thinking/Reasoning	Webb's DOK Level 4 Extended Thinking
		Use these Hess CRM curricular examples with most assignments, assessments, or inquiry activities in social studies, history, civics, geography, economics, or humanities.		
Remember Retrieve knowledge from long-term memory, recognize, recall, locate, identify	o Recall or locate key facts, dates, terms, details, events, or ideas explicit in texts			
Understand Construct meaning, clarify, paraphrase, represent, translate, illustrate, give examples, classify, categorize, summarize, generalize, infer a logical conclusion, predict, observe, compare-contrast, match like ideas, explain, construct models	o Select appropriate words or terms when intended meaning is clearly evident o Describe or explain who, what, where, when, or how o Define facts, details, terms, principles o Locate or identify symbols that represent . . . o Raise related questions for possible investigation	o Specify, explain, illustrate relationships; explain why (e.g., cause-effect) o Provide and explain nonexamples and examples o Summarize results, concepts, main ideas, generalizations o Make basic inferences or logical predictions (using data or text) o Locate relevant information to support explicit-implicit central ideas	o Explain, generalize, or connect ideas using supporting evidence (quote, example, text reference, data) o Support inferences about explicit or implicit themes o Describe how word choice, point of view, or bias may affect the reader's or viewer's interpretation o Write multi-paragraph composition or essay for specific purpose, focus, voice, tone, and audience	o Explain how concepts or ideas specifically relate to other content domains or concepts (social, political, historical, cultural) o Apply generalizations to new problem-based situations o Use multiple sources to elaborate on how concepts or ideas specifically draw from other content domains or differing concepts (e.g., research paper, arguments of policy: Should this law be passed? What will be the impact of this change?)
Apply Carry out or use a procedure in a given situation; carry out (apply to a familiar task), or use (transfer) to an unfamiliar or nonroutine task	o Apply basic formats for documenting sources o Apply use of reference materials and tools for gathering information (e.g., key word searches)	o Use context to identify the meaning of words or phrases o Interpret information using text features (diagrams, data tables, captions, etc.) o Apply simple organizational structures (paragraph outline)	o Investigate to determine how a historical, cultural, or political context may be the source of an underlying theme, central idea, or unresolved issue or crisis	o Integrate or juxtapose multiple (historical, cultural) contexts drawn from source materials (e.g., literature, music, historical events, media) with intent to develop a complex or multimedia product and personal viewpoint
Analyze Break into constituent parts, determine how parts relate, differentiate between relevant-irrelevant, distinguish, focus, select, organize, outline, find coherence, deconstruct (e.g., for bias, point of view, approach/strategy used)	o Identify causes or effects o Describe processes or tools used to research ideas, artifacts, or images reflecting history, culture, tradition, etc. o Identify ways symbols and metaphors are used to represent universal ideas o Identify specific information given in graphics (e.g., map, T-chart, diagram) or text features (e.g., heading, subheading, captions)	o Compare similarities or differences in processes, methods, styles due to influences of time period, politics, or culture o Distinguish relevant-irrelevant information, fact or opinion; primary from a secondary source o Draw inferences about social, historical, cultural contexts portrayed in (literature, arts, film, political cartoons, primary sources) o Explain, categorize events or ideas in the evolution of _____ across time periods	o Analyze information within data sets or a text (e.g., interrelationships among concepts, issues, problems) o Analyze an author's viewpoint or potential bias (e.g., political cartoon) o Use reasoning, planning, and evidence to support or refute inferences in policy or speech o Use reasoning and evidence to generate criteria for making and supporting an "argument of judgment" (e.g., Was FDR a great president? Is this a fair law?)	o Analyze multiple sources of evidence across time periods, themes, issues o Analyze diverse, complex, or abstract perspectives o Gather, analyze, and organize information from multiple sources o Analyze discourse styles or bias in speeches, legal briefs, etc., across time or authors o Compare and contrast conflicting judgments or policies (e.g., Supreme Court decisions)
Evaluate Make judgments based on criteria, check, detect inconsistencies or fallacies, judge, critique	"UG"—unsubstantiated generalizations = stating an opinion without providing any support for it!		o Develop a logical argument for conjectures, citing evidence o Verify reasonableness of results of others o Critique conclusions drawn, evidence used, credibility of sources	o Evaluate relevancy, accuracy, and completeness of information using multiple sources o Apply understanding in a novel way, provide argument or justification for the application o Critique the historical impact on policy, writings, advances
Create Reorganize elements into new patterns, structures, or schemas, generate, hypothesize, design, plan, produce	o Brainstorm ideas, concepts, problems, or perspectives related to a topic, principle, or concept	o Generate testable conjectures or hypotheses based on observations, prior knowledge, and/or artifacts	o Synthesize information within one source or text o Develop a complex model or symbol for a given issue o Develop and support an alternative solution	o Synthesize information across multiple sources of texts o Articulate a new voice, alternate theme, new knowledge, or new perspective o Create historical fiction drawing on sources

© Karin Hess (2009, updated 2017). Available for download at resources.corwin.com/HessToolkit and www.karin-hess.com/free-resources A local assessment toolkit to support deeper learning: Guiding school leaders in linking research with classroom practice. Permission to reproduce is given only when authorship is fully cited [karinhessvt@gmail.com]

HESS COGNITIVE RIGOR MATRIX (FINE ARTS CRM):
Applying (Hess's Interpretation of) DOK to Artistic Practices

Artistic Practice	DOK Level 1 Recall and Reproduction *Having the knowledge required; do not need to "figure it out"*	DOK Level 2 Connect or Apply Skills and Concepts *Making connections among skills or concepts or decisions (e.g., about approach, tools)*	DOK Level 3 Strategic Thinking/Abstract Reasoning *Complex and Abstract; Exploring multiple solution paths; Justifying with evidence*	DOK Level 4 Extended Thinking *Relating/developing complex ideas using multisources and evidence*
Perceiving, Performing, and Responding	o Identify or describe ways art represents what people see, hear, feel, believe o Recall or describe a variety of instruments, forms, symbols, rhythms, conventions of music o Describe how artists or dancers might represent . . . o Identify or describe narrative conventions depicted in the arts	o Show relationships between (dance, music, film, etc.) and other art forms o Make observations or compare similarities or differences: styles, forms, techniques, etc. o Explain possible reasons for selecting tools, medium, elements, principles, images, etc. o Select a familiar artistic work to perform o Explain the artist's central message	o Analyze or find evidence of how a combination of elements or principles are used to achieve a desired effect or theme o Analyze narrative artwork, using supporting evidence to interpret setting, characters, action, conflict, etc. o Develop personal response to or interpretation of a work of art	o Analyze more than one performance or product (same composer, time period, theme, etc.) drawing from multiple source materials for the analyses (e.g., different treatments of same theme) o Perform an "old" idea in a new way
Historical, Social, and Cultural Contexts	o Describe processes used by artists to select or create ideas, images that reflect history, culture, tradition, etc. o Identify ways symbols and metaphors are used to represent universal ideas o Locate symbols that represent . . . o Identify or describe characteristics and origins of dance, art, or music genres	o Draw inferences about social, historical, or cultural contexts portrayed in art, music, dance, theater, or film o Explain or compare how different art forms communicate culture, time period, issues o Compare similarities or differences in processes, methods, styles due to influences of time period, politics, or culture o Explain or trace the evolution of art forms across time periods	o Analyze how historical or cultural context is applied to develop theme in a performance or product o Plan artworks based on historical, social, political, or cultural theme, concept, or representative style o Apply problem solving strategies used among the arts, humanities, and sciences to solve visual "problems"	o Integrate or juxtapose multiple (historical, cultural) contexts drawn from source materials (e.g., literature, music, historical events, media) with intent to develop a complex or multifaceted performance or product and personal viewpoint
Creative Expression, Exploration, and Production	o Explore ideas and techniques by manipulating media, materials, tools for different effects (e.g., how color, rhythm, or camera angles create various moods) o Demonstrate a variety of movements, methods, techniques o Locate or compile examples illustrating different approaches (e.g., camera angles; use of white space)	o Select or use tools for specific artistic purposes by combining elements, aesthetic principles, and/or forms, etc. o Develop a study of o Use or apply choreographic forms to communicate ideas, feelings, concepts o Improvise simple rhythmic variations o Create examples or models that represent the same topic, concept, idea, etc.	o Combine elements of (dance, art, music) to create _____ that conveys an intended point of view or specific idea, mood, or theme o Create or compose for a specific purpose, using appropriate processes, tools, techniques o Create narrative artwork depicting setting, characters, action, conflict, etc. o Research a given style and develop personal interpretation of it	o Apply *multiple sets of criteria* to develop and present a complex or multifaceted performance or product (e.g., consistent application of awareness of space, physical discipline, concentration, and projection from rehearsals to performance; development of portfolio showing evolution of ideas/personal style)
Aesthetics, Criticism, and Reflection	o Recognize or describe choreographic forms, elements of art or music, principles of design, etc., when presented in isolation o Describe criteria used for executing technical or artistic quality	o Explain ways in which artistic choices (choreographic forms, etc.) might affect performance or audience response o Critique examples and nonexamples of a given technique, style, etc.	o Defend the selection of criteria and evidence used to critique the quality or develop a performance or product (e.g., compose a melody, perform improvisation, direct a scene, solve a visual "problem")	o Formulate or use *multiple sets of criteria* and evidence to critique a complex or multifaceted performance or final product o Compile and defend exemplars chosen to depict a theme or style

© Karin Hess (2009, updated 2017). *A local assessment toolkit to support deeper learning: Guiding school leaders in linking research with classroom practice.* Permission to reproduce is given only when authorship is fully cited [karinhessvt@gmail.com]

Available for download at **resources.corwin.com/HessToolkit** and **www.karin-hess.com/free-resources**

HESS COGNITIVE RIGOR MATRIX (HEALTH AND PHYSICAL EDUCATION):
Applying (Hess's Interpretation of) Depth of Knowledge to Porter's Cognitive Demand Categories

Porter's Cognitive Demand Categories	DOK Level 1 Recall and Reproduction — Having the knowledge required; do not need to "figure it out"	DOK Level 2 Connect or Apply Skills and Concepts — Making connections among skills or concepts or decisions (e.g., about approach, tools)	DOK Level 3 Strategic Thinking/Abstract Reasoning — Complex and Abstract; Exploring multiple solution paths; Justifying *with evidence*	DOK Level 4 Extended Thinking — Relating or developing complex ideas using multi sources *and evidence*
Memorize	o Recall or identify basic facts, terms, definitions, skills, rules, principles, concepts, symbols o Acquire new terms, vocabulary, etc.	Use these Hess CRM Curricular Examples with most assignments, assessments, or learning activities for Health and Physical Education. See also the Hess CRM for Fine Arts with examples for dance.		
Communicate Understanding	o Define terms, principles, concepts o Describe how to perform a routine skill or task o Use words, visuals, or symbols to represent basic ideas, movements, procedures, etc.	o Explain concepts: show or predict relationships (if-then, cause-effect); provide examples and non-examples o Observe and interpret teacher or student demonstrations o Summarize a concept, series of events, movements, or a result	o Use evidence (data, examples, source, observations) to justify an interpretation of a result or performance o Locate or reproduce supporting evidence for results of effectiveness of a plan (e.g., exercise or diet routine) o Create a personal plan when given criteria	o Share results of comparing different plans (e.g., compare exercise or diet routines) using data and evidence from multiple sources or data sets o Explain how a concept relates across content domains or to "big ideas" (e.g., systems, patterns)
Perform Procedures	o Safely demonstrate or use appropriate tools or equipment o Execute or repeat basic skills or procedures (e.g., follow step-by-step directions or pattern) o Demonstrate a basic skill sequence, movement pattern, etc., with smooth transitions	o Make observations; collect and record data and observations (e.g., health diary, skills progress) o Select and use appropriate tool or equipment for a given task o Complete routine tasks in a fitness assessment	o Plan, execute, and evaluate multistep procedures (a dance routine, football play, rules of a new game, etc.). o Test effects and trends of using different activities by observing and collecting data (e.g., exercise or diet routines) o Select and plan how to use a combination of movements to achieve a desired effect	o Design and conduct a performance (e.g., exercise or dance routine) using multiple sources or resources, and/or given constraints (e.g., use of space) o Test effects of different variables on performance (e.g., applied to a new situation)
Apply Concepts/ Make Connections	o Apply rules or score-keeping of a game or simple routine o Apply appropriate content-specific vocabulary or terms to tasks o Brainstorm ideas, problems, or perspectives related to a situation, scenario, or observation	o Create an infographic or visual to show connections or to summarize key ideas (e.g., cause-effect, heart rate-activity type, warm up-cool down, healthy or unhealthy) o Explain connections among concepts or skills in a given context (e.g., movement or open space concepts, health benefits)	o Revise a plan (self, peer) based on feedback and evidence o Use concepts to explain phenomena or research or medical advances (e.g., use of steroids, drugs, food choices) o Investigate how an event or advancement led to a new perspective or outcome	o Apply and adapt information and concepts to real-world situations o Integrate ideas from multiple sources to extend an idea or solve a problem with an alternative solution o Trace the evolution of (game, drug, etc.) from past to present, citing sources used
Analyze Information	o Identify, describe, match, or name parts in a diagram or visual (e.g. muscle groups or skeletal system) or patterns o Determine which skill, rule, or principle applies to a given situation o Record performance data	o Compare-contrast routines, skill sets, or qualities (e.g., use T-chart, graphic organizer for locomotor-nonlocomotor) o Generate questions and make predictions based on observations or information o Classify types of … (movements, sports, symptoms, examples, etc.)	o Analyze data in order to recognize patterns or draw conclusions based on evidence (e.g., batting averages, areas needing remediation) o Identify faulty arguments, strategies, or misrepresentations of data or media message o Defend the selection of criteria used to critique or develop a performance or product	o Research a topic in-depth, evaluating relevancy, accuracy, and completeness of information from multiple sources or perspectives o Analyze evidence and recommend the most effective course of action for intended purpose (e.g., food, fitness)

Available for download at **resources.corwin.com/HessToolkit** and **www.karin-hess.com/free-resources**

© Karin Hess (2009, updated 2017). *A local assessment toolkit to support deeper learning: Guiding school leaders in linking research with classroom practice.* Permission to reproduce is given only when authorship is fully cited [karinhessvt@gmail.com]

HESS WORLD LANGUAGE COGNITIVE RIGOR MATRIX

Tool 5C

World Language Practices and Modes of Communication	DOK Level 1 Recall and Reproduction — Having the knowledge required; do not need to "figure it out"	DOK Level 2 Skills and Concepts — Making connections among skills/concepts or decisions (e.g., about approach, tools)	DOK Level 3 Strategic Thinking/Reasoning — Complex and Abstract; Exploring multiple solution paths; Justifying *with evidence*	DOK Level 4 Extended Thinking — Relating/developing complex ideas using multisources *and evidence*
Memorize and Recall	o Reproduce, recall, and repeat vocabulary, grammar rules, facts, definitions, dictated statements, etc. o Describe cultural conventions o Recite in sequence (e.g., alphabet, counting, songs, rhymes)	Use these World Language CRM curricular examples for designing most language and communication assignments or assessment tasks.		
Interpersonal Communication Understand, Perceive, and Respond	o Understand simple, familiar messages in social settings o Identify everyday objects o Follow simple oral directions or written procedures (recipe, etc.) o Convey simple messages, express feelings (e.g., I'm sad because . . .) o Ask or answer literal questions after reading, listening, or viewing	o Explain how or why alternative responses may be correct (where do you live?) for different situations o Carry on a short conversation using familiar vocabulary and grammar o Paraphrase, summarize, or retell what was said, read, viewed (with cues) o Make logical predictions (e.g., what might happen next . . .); describe event	o Prepare for an interview or develop survey on topic of interest anticipating audience questions or possible responses o Initiate and extend a conversation about an unfamiliar topic, appropriately using language mechanics and tense throughout o Create a theme-based photo essay o Justify interpretation of purpose or tone (in media message, photo essay, etc.)	o Carry on an extended conversation responding appropriately to multiple speakers (e.g., using multiple tenses, asking and answering, elaborating on ideas, raising questions) o Deepen knowledge of a topic using multiple (oral, visual, textual) sources for an informational communication (e.g., "by the numbers" infographic)
Interpret and Apply	o Match vocabulary (e.g., picture-word; synonyms); locate details o Apply a spelling or grammar rule (e.g., conjugate a verb, make plural) o Use resources to translate literally o Use nouns or verbs in familiar contexts	o Infer and explain meaning using context, cognates, or structure in a familiar situation o Translate to identify use of nonliteral, figurative, or idiomatic language o Sequence events for given text or visual	o Explain inferences or colloquial expressions using supporting evidence o Interpret symbolic or abstract meaning (from music, video, reading, art, etc.) o Interpret idiomatic or figurative language in context (poem, song lyric, media, etc.)	o Make and justify conclusions based on 2+ ads for the same product or two political cartoons about the same event or person o Write, draw, perform in the style of a known author, artist, or cartoonist
Compare, Analyze, Critique, Evaluate, and Reflect	o Edit a sentence or phrase o Select appropriate word or phrase for intended meaning o Answer what, when, and where questions using a source (map, calendar, schedule, visual, photo) o Connect words or phrases between languages (origins, meanings, etc.)	o Categorize or compare (objects, foods, tools, people, etc.) using oral/physical/textual stimuli o Self-correct when speaking or reading o Evaluate message or cultural nuances (e.g., gestures, language) using listening and observational skills	o Evaluate and correct inaccuracy of a message in print or nonprint text (e.g., facts, sequence, cultural nuances) o Support an opinion, argument, or disagreement with evidence, reasoning o Determine if source can or cannot answer specific questions and why (e.g., websites)	o Critique authentic literature, arts, or historical events from multiple sources: authors/perspectives/time periods o Evaluate relevancy, accuracy, and completeness of information o Keep a journal and use it to reflect on or evaluate personal progress
Presentational Communication Produce or Create	o Represent vocabulary or common phrases in pictures, symbols, visuals, gestures, pantomime o Brainstorm related words, ideas, images, possible responses o Label information on a diagram, map, visual o Tell or select phrases as thumbnail sketch for a narrative text or story line	o Perform a memorized dialog o Choose which tense to use in a less familiar context o Create an ABC book connecting entries by central or organizing topic (e.g., animals, foods) o Create text messages or description (narration or voice-over) for a visual stimuli or "muted" video scene o Make or label a timeline of key events	o Develop a vocabulary-based game to teach about geography, culture, etc. o Develop a new scene or ending, consistent with the original text o Create or perform a dialog based on visual stimuli or a current or cultural event (integrating academic vocabulary) o Co-plan website or event highlighting target culture (foods, traditions, places to visit)	o Produce an "old" idea in a new way (e.g., multimedia, podcast) o Integrate ideas from several sources o Research a topic with evidence pro and con for debate, essay, or cartoon o Research and present performance or presentation using multiple sources o Design a theme-based café, including the menu, location, and décor and develop an ad for targeted clientele

Available for download at **resources.corwin.com/HessToolkit** and **www.karin-hess.com/free-resources**

© Karin Hess (2009, updated 2017). *A local assessment toolkit to support deeper learning: Guiding school leaders in linking research with classroom practice.* Permission to reproduce is given only when authorship is fully cited [karinhessvt@gmail.com]

HESS COGNITIVE RIGOR MATRIX | Career and Technical Education (CTE CRM):
Hess's Interpretation Applying Webb's Depth-of-Knowledge Levels to Bloom's Cognitive Process Dimensions

Revised Bloom's Taxonomy	Webb's DOK Level 1 Recall and Reproduction	Webb's DOK Level 2 Skills and Concepts	Webb's DOK Level 3 Strategic Thinking/Reasoning	Webb's DOK Level 4 Extended Thinking
Remember Memorize, recognize, recall, locate, identify	o Recall or locate key facts, terms, details, procedures (e.g., explicit in a technical manual)	Use these Hess CRM curricular examples with most assignments, assessments, or inquiry activities for Career and Technical Education		
Understand Construct meaning, clarify, paraphrase, represent, translate, illustrate, give examples, summarize, generalize, infer a logical conclusion, predict, observe, match like ideas, explain, construct models	o Select correct terms or graphics for intended meaning o Describe or explain who, what, where, when, or how o Define terms, principles, concepts o Represent relationships with words, diagrams, symbols o Solve routine problems	o Specify and explain relationships (e.g., non-examples/examples; cause-effect; if-then) o Summarize procedures, results, concepts, key ideas (paragraph) o Make and explain estimates, basic inferences, or predictions o Use models to explain concepts o Make and record observations	o Explain, generalize, or connect ideas using supporting evidence (quote, example, text reference, data) o Justify your interpretation when more than one is plausible o Explain how a concept can be used to solve a nonroutine problem o Develop a multiparagraph manual or infographic for specific purpose or focus	o Use multiple sources to outline varying perspectives on a problem or issue o Explain how a concept relates across content domains or to "big ideas" (e.g., patterns in the human or designed world; structure-function) o Apply generalizations from one investigation to new problem-based situations, using evidence or data
Apply Carry out or use a procedure in a given situation; carry out (apply to a familiar task), or use with (transfer to) an unfamiliar or nonroutine task	o Apply basic formulas, algorithms, conversion rules o Calculate; measure o Use reference materials and tools to gather information o Demo safe procedures	o Select and use appropriate tool or procedure for specified task o Use context to identify the meaning of terms or phrases o Interpret information using diagrams, data tables, etc.	o Build or revise a plan for investigation using (new) evidence or data o Use and show reasoning, planning, and evidence to support conclusions or to identify design flaws o Conduct a designed investigation	o Draw from source materials with intent to develop a complex or multimedia product with personal viewpoint o Conduct a project that specifies a problem, identifies solution paths, tests the solution, and reports results
Analyze Break into constituent parts, determine how parts relate, compare-contrast, differentiate between relevant-irrelevant, distinguish, focus, select, organize, outline, find coherence, deconstruct (e.g., for potential bias, point of view, technique or strategy used)	o Identify trend, pattern, possible cause, or effect o Describe processes or tools used to research ideas o Identify ways symbols or metaphors are used to represent universal ideas o Retrieve data to answer a question (e.g., diagram, graph)	o Compare similarities or differences or draw inferences about _____ due to influences of _____ o Distinguish relevant-irrelevant information; fact or opinion; primary from a secondary source o Extend a pattern o Organize and represent data o Categorize materials, data, etc., based on characteristics	o Interpret information from a complex graph or model (e.g., interrelationships among variables, concepts) o Use reasoning, planning, and evidence to support or refute inferences or results stated o Use reasoning and evidence to generate criteria for making and supporting an argument o Generalize and support a pattern/trend	o Analyze multiple sources of evidence (e.g., compare-contrast various plans, solution methods) o Analyze and compare diverse, complex, abstract perspectives, models, etc. o Gather, organize, and analyze information from multiple sources to answer a research question
Evaluate Make judgments based on specified criteria, detect inconsistencies, flaws, or fallacies, judge, critique	"UG"—unsubstantiated generalizations = stating an opinion without providing any support for it!		o Develop a logical argument for conjectures, citing evidence o Verify reasonableness of results or conjectures (e.g., of others) o Critique conclusions drawn or evidence used or credibility of sources	o Evaluate relevancy, accuracy, and completeness of sources used o Apply understanding in a novel way, provide argument or justification for the application o Critique the historical impact of _____ on _____
Create Reorganize into new patterns or schemas, design, plan, produce	o Brainstorm ideas, concepts, problems, or perspectives related to a given scenario, observation, question posed	o Generate testable conjectures or hypotheses based on observations, prior knowledge, and/or artifacts	o Develop a complex model for a given concept and justify your reasoning o Develop an alternative solution and justify your reasoning	o Synthesize information across multiple models, sources, or texts o Articulate new knowledge or new perspectives

Available for download at resources.corwin.com/HessToolkit and www.karin-hess.com/free-resources

© Karin Hess (2009, updated 2017). *A local assessment toolkit to support deeper learning: Guiding school leaders in linking research with classroom practice.* Permission to reproduce is given only when authorship is fully cited [karinhessvt@gmail.com]

III. Strategies and Tools for Professional Developers and Teacher Planning

a. *The eight content-specific Hess Cognitive Rigor Matrices/CRMs (**TOOLS #1–#5D**) can be used to guide collaborative analysis of sample assessment tasks collected across content areas and grade levels, as well as for future lesson and unit development.* Digital versions of these tools can be downloaded from **resources.corwin.com/HessToolkit** or **http://www.karin-hess.com/free-resources.**

b. *What's TV got to do with DOK?* Inspired by professional development providers in Ohio, this activity can be used as a review or to introduce differences among DOK levels. After sharing my TV examples, I ask table groups to come up with another DOK 4 TV show and, of course, justify their reasoning. This activity is also a fun way to introduce deeper and more complex thinking to students.

c. *The DOK "IQ" Test:* I developed this collaborative workshop activity for teachers at the American School in Nicaragua who had already been using DOK, but needed to fine-tune their collective understandings of the levels of thinking that different learning activities are intended to elicit. There are enough different content examples to divide the list so that each table group analyzes about three to five examples. A blank form and a "cheat sheet" are included. Some examples in this workshop have been adapted from Brulles, Brown, and Winebrenner, 2016.

d. *The Hess Cognitive Rigor Matrix Question-Planning Worksheets* can be used to analyze unit or lesson questions and assessment tasks; or to develop kid-friendly expectations for increasing rigor. Included at the end of Module I are four worksheets: a blank CRM template that I like to use for analyzing units of study, a sample template using text-based examples from *Little Red Riding Hood*, a template with examples of prompts and questions, and a student version (kid tool) with examples. <u>The goal is never to fill all cells in the CRM</u> but to explore a variety of ways to reach deeper thinking using a text, topic, unit of study, or project.

e. *A visual display of work produced at each DOK level over a given period of time provides concrete examples of what deeper thinking looks like.* While working with teachers in Hawaii, learning progressions[11] were codeveloped for grade levels K–8 to show increased understanding in mathematics and ELA. Evelyn Ibonia and Margeaux Ikuma, fifth-grade math teachers at Mililani Uka Elementary School, came up with the idea of displaying descriptors of the week's learning targets they were working on and then posting student work samples to illustrate how the work was becoming more sophisticated. The learning targets (large white squares seen in the first photo) were worded similarly to the general DOK descriptions in the Hess CRMs, for DOK 1, DOK 2, and DOK 3. The numbered sticky notes (on the bulletin board) represent each student in the class and were moved from "just starting" (on Monday) to match the descriptors as they made progress to "got it" (later in the week). Students work together daily to get everyone to the "high end" of the progression by the end of the unit of study.

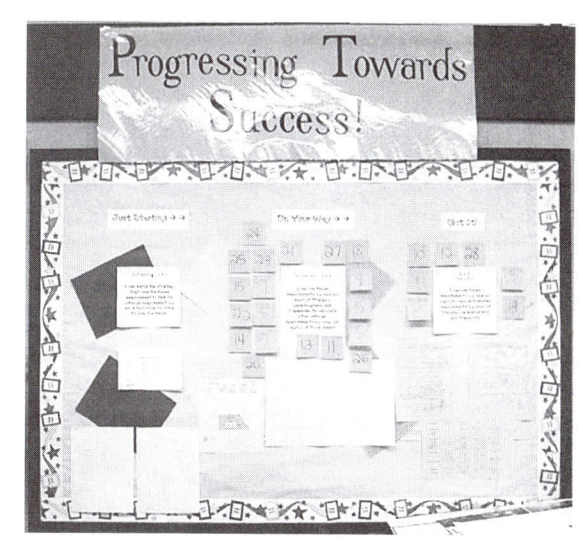

Source: Margeaux Ikuma (2010).

---

11. Learning progressions are discussed in greater detail in Module 4.

A second visual example is seen in the photo below where individual student photos indicate how each student is progressing during the week. Margeaux explained to me in an email, "The sections of paper on my board are a 'progressional' rubric—and I found it to work great! I took the same indicators as the progress map[12] and put it into a rubric format. The kids assessed themselves each day and I also gave them feedback based upon their work in class and exit passes. They could self-assess their own skills, and I was able to give them quick feedback after each lesson."

Source: Margeaux Ikuma (2010).

---

12. "Progress map" is another name for learning progression.

What's TV Got to Do With DOK?

While working in Ohio, professional development providers Barb Cockroft and Tom Rounds shared that they had identified TV game shows for each DOK Level. I loved the idea, and of course that got me thinking about which shows I'd use to illustrate the differences among DOK levels.

I've always used *Jeopardy* as an example to illustrate DOK 1—quick recall of unrelated facts, locations, and names. But do we ever hear host Alex Trebek follow up with "Let's talk about the theme of that play?" or "What has been the impact of that world leader?"

Nope.

DOK 1 is just the facts! There is always a right answer—you either know it or you don't.

What are your examples? Here are TV shows I would use for DOK 2, 3, and 4.

I think *The Price Is Right* works well for DOK 2. To play that game, you apply basic prior knowledge of pricing to estimate and compare prices. There is still a right answer, but you need to make some decisions along the way as you do some mental arithmetic. You play this (routine) game pretty much the same way every time.

And what about *NCIS* or those *CSI* shows for DOK 3? Rich DOK 3 performance tasks are kind of like solving a mystery—looking for compelling evidence to support conclusions or to build a defensible argument to support a claim. Each episode presents a nonroutine case, and solving it requires answering more complex questions than those posed on shows like *Jeopardy* or *The Price Is Right*.

Finally, there is DOK 4. Extended thinking and integrating multiple, relevant sources is required at DOK 4, sometimes to understand a topic in greater depth, or from multiple perspectives, or to create a new product or model. For me, it's got to be all of those Ken Burns documentaries: *Baseball*, *The Civil War*, *The Roosevelts*, *Viet Nam* . . . and the list goes on. To produce a documentary takes more than the speed of IBM's Watson at uncovering facts. Checking credibility of sources and determining relevance of information is only the first step to integrating or synthesizing information, making connections among Bigger Ideas, and producing a message that is compelling. Now, that's DOK 4!

Test Your DOK "IQ" (IQ = I May Still Have Some Questions)

Individually, read each sample assignment and circle some key words to help you decide whether you think it taps into DOK 1, 2, 3, or 4 thinking. Refer to the Hess CRMs for support. Then discuss each one with your group and provide your agreed-upon reasoning for the intended DOK levels.

INSTRUCTIONAL EXAMPLES	INTENDED DOK	YOUR GROUP'S REASONING: WHAT MENTAL PROCESSING IS CALLED UPON TO COMPLETE THE TASK?
1. Listen to or read an article about holidays and then present information describing some of the customs and traditions of the place you read about.	1	The product for "presenting" is not specified, so it may not be a full summary (DOK 2). It is likely to be a list of explicit facts or bullet points or perhaps a drawing = DOK 1; little or no analysis required.
2. Create a "Who am I?" wanted poster for a story character or real person. Include key information of what he or she did, traits, and the motivation behind his or her actions.		
3. Read a picture book that illustrates cause and effect. Select key sentences and diagram the cause and the effect in each sentence.		
4. Prepare a timeline of a historical time period you are studying. Identify the most important people, places, and events to include.		
5. Identify six or more character traits that represent characters in plays we've read. List the traits. Then select a specific character and provide a description of the character. Include the name of the play, the character, and some of the traits.		
6. Compare and contrast two novels written in about the same time period and determine which version is the most historically accurate. Use evidence cited in the texts and other sources to support your conclusions.		
7. Evaluate the historical accuracy of a novel you read. Compare evidence in the text to historical facts from the same place and time period to support your conclusions.		
8. Invent a new word. Include its definition, root word, affix, part of speech, synonyms, antonyms, an example, a sentence using the word, and the context in which you believe the word would be understood.		
9. Compose an original poem using one of the forms or genres we have studied. Include an analysis using the appropriate terminology and domain-specific language.		

INSTRUCTIONAL EXAMPLES	INTENDED DOK	YOUR GROUP'S REASONING: WHAT MENTAL PROCESSING IS CALLED UPON TO COMPLETE THE TASK?
10. Read two or three biographies of authors who have written in a specific category. Illustrate or report on what elements they have in common.		
11. Write or tell this story from another character's point of view.		
12. View several videos of "The Star-Spangled Banner" from educationally respected websites (e.g., History Channel, Smithsonian Institute, or *History Detectives* on PBS). Identify what depictions are more and less prevalent among the sites' videos. Describe how the videos differ. Draw conclusions as to why the different organizations might highlight different aspects of our national anthem.		
13. Create a booklet of _____. Include illustrations, a description of attributes, and other identifiable information for each example.		
14. Select one of the paintings at http://www.byrdseed.com/wp-content/uploads/Portrait_of_Dr._Gachet.jpg. Create an implicit statement about what you see, such as describing the style or mood. Then use visual evidence to support your interpretations, such as how you know what the person feels (peaceful, sad, upset, lonely, etc.).		
15. Make a table showing the advantages and disadvantages of _____.		
16. Create a presentation to demonstrate the relationships between data, sample, and statistics.		
17. Create a presentation using a real-world context to discuss the relationships among data, sample, and statistics when designing an investigation.		
18. Explain the difference between a ratio and a proportion. Give both examples and nonexamples of each to support your explanation.		
19. Construct a "place" (city, neighborhood, amusement park, etc.) using all unit geometric shapes and terminology. Label your location.		

(Continued)

(Continued)

INSTRUCTIONAL EXAMPLES	INTENDED DOK	YOUR GROUP'S REASONING: WHAT MENTAL PROCESSING IS CALLED UPON TO COMPLETE THE TASK?
20. Redesign a "place" (city, neighborhood, amusement park, etc.) for a specific purpose, using all unit geometric shapes in innovative ways. Label the name of your place and your display using math terminology.		
21. Two friends were arguing about the best seat in the movie theater. One of them had heard that it is best to sit so that the angle formed by the line of sight between the left and right sides of the screen is 30 degrees. John believes there is only one seat in the theater that meets these criteria. Amy argues there is more than one place where the viewing angle is also 30 degrees. Decide and then prove who is correct.		
22. Create step-by-step instructions on how to draw a particular figure using only a protractor. You must include the angles and the exact measurement of the lines in millimeters and centimeters. Make sure to use proper math terminology in your instructions.		
23. Create a game that will teach your classmates about a particular body system. Include facts about the body system, its organs, their functions, and how they work together. Provide a set of directions with your game.		
24. Create a model of one system of the human body. Label each organ or part of the body system describing how the parts of the system work together. Be prepared to answer questions about what might be the short- and longer-term result if a particular part malfunctions or there is an injury to the system.		
25. How does water pollution affect the fishing industry? Which states are most significantly impacted? Locate these states on a map or globe and provide examples to show the impact of pollution on fishing. Create a presentation to share your findings.		
26. Create your own example for another group to analyze OR revise one of the DOK 1 to 3 examples to require deeper thinking. For example, turn a DOK 2 task into a DOK 3 task, or a DOK 3 task into a DOK 4 task.		

Test Your DOK "IQ" Test "Cheat Sheet"

Individually, read each sample assignment and circle some key words to help you decide whether you think it taps into DOK 1, 2, 3, or 4 thinking. Refer to the Hess CRMs for support. Then discuss each one with your group and provide your agreed-upon reasoning for the intended DOK levels.

INSTRUCTIONAL EXAMPLES	INTENDED DOK	YOUR GROUP'S REASONING: WHAT MENTAL PROCESSING IS CALLED UPON TO COMPLETE THE TASK?
1. Listen to or read an article about holidays and then present information describing some of the customs and traditions of the place you read about.	1	The product for "presenting" is not specified, so it may not be a full summary (DOK 2). It is likely to be a list of explicit facts or bullet points or perhaps a drawing = DOK 1; little or no analysis required.
2. Create a "Who am I?" wanted poster for a story character or real person. Include key information of what he or she did, traits, and the motivation behind his or her actions.	2	Some analysis required to make connections among actions and motivations. Mostly a summary of what is explicitly known.
3. Read a picture book that illustrates cause and effect. Select key sentences and diagram the cause and the effect in each sentence.	2	Making connections and basic inferences.
4. Prepare a timeline of a historical time period you are studying. Identify the most important people, places, and events to include.	2	Sequencing events; making connections, although the information is likely only explicit information, some decisions will be made about who or what is most important.
5. Identify six or more character traits that represent characters in plays we've read. List the traits. Then select a specific character and provide a description of the character. Include the name of the play, the character, and some of the traits.	2	Listing traits might be a DOK 1; making some basic inferences about a character's actions, words, and motivations to determine traits is a DOK 2. No real reasoning or evidence to back up your description is asked for.
6. Compare and contrast two novels written in about the same time period and determine which version is the most historically accurate. Use evidence cited in the texts and other sources to support your conclusions.	4	Use of multiple sources for locating evidence. Requires support for conclusions drawn.
7. Evaluate the historical accuracy of a novel read. Compare evidence in the text to historical facts from the same place and time period to support your conclusions.	4	Use of multiple sources for locating evidence. Requires support for conclusions drawn.

(Continued)

(Continued)

INSTRUCTIONAL EXAMPLES	INTENDED DOK	YOUR GROUP'S REASONING: WHAT MENTAL PROCESSING IS CALLED UPON TO COMPLETE THE TASK?
8. Invent a new word. Include its definition, root word, affix, part of speech, synonyms, antonyms, an example, a sentence using the word, and the context in which you believe the word would be understood.	2	Making connections; creative, but not deep
9. Compose an original poem using one of the forms or genres we have studied. Include an analysis using the appropriate terminology and domain-specific language.	3	Deep analysis of one source, style, or genre
10. Read two or three biographies of authors who have written in a specific category. Illustrate or report on what elements they have in common.	2	Making connections using explicit information; compare/contrast; does not require figuring anything out or drawing conclusions that need to be supported with reasoning or evidence.
11. Write or tell this story from another character's point of view.	3	Same storyline, same characters, same events, just change POV
12. View several videos of "The Star-Spangled Banner" from educationally respected websites (e.g., History Channel, Smithsonian Institute, or *History Detectives* on PBS). Identify what depictions are more and less prevalent among the sites' videos. Describe how the videos differ. Draw conclusions as to why the different organizations might highlight different aspects of our national anthem.	4	Analyze multiple representations and focus of the same information and make connections to perspectives or themes of each organization. This might also require some investigation as to the organization's mission.
13. Create a booklet of _____. Include illustrations, a description of attributes, and other identifiable information for each example.	1	A bunch of facts; fun and engaging and creativity to make the book, but not deep
14. Select one of the paintings at http://www.byrdseed.com/wp-content/uploads/Portrait_of_Dr._Gachet.jpg. Create an implicit statement about what you see, such as describing the style or mood. Then use visual evidence to support your interpretations, such as how you know what the person feels (peaceful, sad, upset, lonely, etc.).	3	Deep analysis of one source; applying elements of art principles or design, etc.

INSTRUCTIONAL EXAMPLES	INTENDED DOK	YOUR GROUP'S REASONING: WHAT MENTAL PROCESSING IS CALLED UPON TO COMPLETE THE TASK?
15. Make a table showing the advantages and disadvantages of _____.	2	Compare/contrast mostly explicit information, even if coming from multiple sources
16. Create a presentation to demonstrate the relationships between data, sample, and statistics.	2	This is likely to be a summary with definitions and perhaps some examples, but not requiring any analysis; making connections.
17. Create a presentation using a real-world context to discuss the relationships among data, sample, and statistics when designing an investigation.	3	Requires strategic thinking and planning
18. Explain the difference between a ratio and a proportion. Give both examples and nonexamples of each to support your explanation.	2	Providing examples and nonexamples is always DOK 2; requires conceptual understanding and showing relationships.
19. Construct a "place" (city, neighborhood, amusement park, etc.) using all unit geometric shapes and terminology. Label your location.	2	Fun and time-consuming, but requiring much analysis.
20. Redesign a "place" (city, neighborhood, amusement park, etc.) for a specific purpose, using all unit geometric shapes in innovative ways. Label the name of your place and your display using math terminology.	3	Requires strategic thinking, reasoning, and planning
21. Two friends were arguing about the best seat in the movie theater. One of them had heard that it is best to sit so that the angle formed by the line of sight between the left and right sides of the screen is 30 degrees. John believes there is only one seat in the theater that meets these criteria. Amy argues there is more than one place where the viewing angle is also 30 degrees. Decide and then prove who is correct.	3	One context to analyze from two perspectives; supporting evidence (calculations, measurements, diagrams, words) required
22. Create step-by-step instructions on how to draw a particular figure using only a protractor. You must include the angles and the exact measurement of the lines in millimeters and centimeters. Make sure to use proper math terminology in your instructions.	2	Summarizing steps is generally not deep thinking. Saying WHY the steps work would be DOK 3.

(Continued)

(Continued)

INSTRUCTIONAL EXAMPLES	INTENDED DOK	YOUR GROUP'S REASONING: WHAT MENTAL PROCESSING IS CALLED UPON TO COMPLETE THE TASK?
23. Create a game that will teach your classmates about a particular body system. Include facts about the body system, its organs, their functions, and how they work together. Provide a set of directions with your game.	2	Most games tend to be fact based and concept based; they do not require much, if any, analysis.
24. Create a model of one system of the human body. Label each organ or part of the body system describing how the parts of the system work together. Be prepared to answer questions about what might be the short- and longer-term result if a particular part malfunctions or there is an injury to the system.	3	Display is DOK 1, maybe 2; but must know one system in depth for malfunctioning questions
25. How does water pollution affect the fishing industry? Which states are most significantly impacted? Locate these states on a map or globe and provide examples to show the impact of pollution on fishing. Create a presentation to share your findings.	2	Making connections, cause-effect examples; summarizing factual information
26. Create your own example for another group to analyze OR revise one of the DOK 1 to 3 examples to require deeper thinking. For example, turn a DOK 2 task into a DOK 3 task, or a DOK 3 task into a DOK 4 task.		

Hess Cognitive Rigor Matrix Question-Planning Worksheets

Analyze or develop unit or text-based questions requiring a range of rigor and supporting evidence.

Unit of Study/Topic/Text(s):

Standard(s):

REVISED BLOOM	DOK LEVEL 1 RECALL/ REPRODUCTION FOUNDATIONAL	DOK LEVEL 2 SKILLS AND CONCEPTS CONCEPTUAL	DOK LEVEL 3 STRATEGIC THINKING DEEPER – NEAR TRANSFER	DOK LEVEL 4 EXTENDED THINKING BROAD + DEEPER FAR TRANSFER
Remember What terms, principles, and facts are located, recalled, or defined?				
Understand What do students do to build conceptual understanding?				
Apply What rules, procedures, formulas, and so forth will be used?				
Analyze = taking apart What will be taken apart to see how the parts work together? How will students build schemas?				
Evaluate What will be judged? What agreed-upon criteria will be used?	UGs = opinions that have no valid supporting evidence; unsubstantiated generalizations			
Create = putting parts together in a new way Will a new model, story, solution, or visual display, be created?				

Module 1: Are My Students Thinking Deeply or Just Working Harder?

Hess CRM Question-Planning Worksheet—Little Red Riding Hood (Text-Based Example)

REVISED BLOOM	DOK LEVEL 1 RECALL/ REPRODUCTION FOUNDATIONAL	DOK LEVEL 2 SKILLS AND CONCEPTS CONCEPTUAL	DOK LEVEL 3 STRATEGIC THINKING DEEPER – NEAR TRANSFER	DOK LEVEL 4 EXTENDED THINKING BROAD + DEEPER FAR TRANSFER
Remember What terms, principles, and facts are located, recalled, or defined?	What color was Red's cape? Where was Red going? How did the wolf trick Little Red Riding Hood? How did the story end?			
Understand What do students do to build conceptual understanding?	Who is the main character? What was the story's setting?	Retell or summarize the story in your own words. Sequence or make a timeline of the key events.	Was there a lesson or message in this story? Use details and examples from the story to support your interpretation.	
Apply What rules, procedures, formulas, and so forth will be used?		Identify transitional words and phrases that help you to know the sequence of events in the story.		Given when this was written, what social context is applied by the author? Provide support by analyzing multisource evidence.
Analyze = taking apart What will be taken apart to see how the parts work together? How will students build schemas?	Is this a realistic or fantasy story?	What are some examples of personification used in the story? How are the characters of the wolf and Little Red Riding Hood alike and different?	Is this a realistic or fantasy story? Justify your interpretation analyzing text evidence.	Are all wolves (in literature) like the wolf in this story? Support your response analyzing evidence from this and other texts.

(Continued)

REVISED BLOOM	DOK LEVEL 1 RECALL/ REPRODUCTION FOUNDATIONAL	DOK LEVEL 2 SKILLS AND CONCEPTS CONCEPTUAL	DOK LEVEL 3 STRATEGIC THINKING DEEPER – NEAR TRANSFER	DOK LEVEL 4 EXTENDED THINKING BROAD + DEEPER FAR TRANSFER
Evaluate What will be judged? What agreed-upon criteria will be used?	UGs = opinions that have no valid supporting evidence; unsubstantiated generalizations		What is your opinion about the intelligence or cleverness of the wolf? Provide reasoning for your opinion, analyzing text-based details and evidence.	Which version's ending has the most emotional impact on readers? (Establish criteria for how to evaluate emotional impact; then locate and analyze evidence.)
Create = putting parts together in a new way. Will a new model, story, solution, or visual display be created?		Create text messages between Little Red Riding Hood and her mother to explain the wolf incident. (This is a creative summary.)	Write a new ending to the story. Draw from the original version to build your story line.	

Hess CRM Question-Planning Worksheet (Sample Prompts and Questions)

REVISED BLOOM	DOK LEVEL 1 RECALL/ REPRODUCTION FOUNDATIONAL	DOK LEVEL 2 SKILLS AND CONCEPTS CONCEPTUAL	DOK LEVEL 3 STRATEGIC THINKING DEEPER – NEAR TRANSFER	DOK LEVEL 4 EXTENDED THINKING BROAD + DEEPER FAR TRANSFER
Remember — What terms, principles, and facts are located, recalled, or defined?	What new strategy did you learn and practice? Is this a factor tree? Name some odd and even numbers.			
Understand — What do students do to build conceptual understanding?	What does it mean for a number to be odd or even? How can a factor tree be used to solve a problem?	Why is it good to have different strategies? Describe your observations about the pattern. Are these equivalent?	What concept(s) will help solve this? How do you know? (Use specific examples to provide your reasoning.)	What are different perspectives on this topic? Is some of the same evidence used to support different claims? Analyze multiple sources of evidence to support your response.
Apply — What rules, procedures, formulas, and so forth will be used?	Can you solve or read this? Convert this fraction to a decimal. What are the steps of this technique?	What strategies to use to understand what I read? (give specific examples) Locate and organize data to answer this.	Identify and give examples of rhetorical devices used in presenting the author's ideas or perspective. Conduct the investigation, interpret results, and support conclusions with data.	Apply or adapt an approach you've learned to a real-world situation or phenomenon.

(Continued)

74 A Local Assessment Toolkit to Promote Deeper Learning

REVISED BLOOM	DOK LEVEL 1 RECALL/ REPRODUCTION FOUNDATIONAL	DOK LEVEL 2 SKILLS AND CONCEPTS CONCEPTUAL	DOK LEVEL 3 STRATEGIC THINKING DEEPER – NEAR TRANSFER	DOK LEVEL 4 EXTENDED THINKING BROAD + DEEPER FAR TRANSFER
Analyze = taking apart What will be taken apart to see how the parts work together? How will students build schemas?	Is this a cause or an effect? What does this symbol stand for? Is anything missing?	Is there a book you can read now that you couldn't read easily before? Describe what helped. How could you organize, sort, or compare these?	Which guidelines for conducting a "fair test" are or are not being followed in this procedure?	How do I put ideas in two texts together to make my reading and learning more meaningful? Can you design and conduct an investigation to test your idea?
Evaluate What will be judged? What agreed-upon criteria will be used?	UGs = opinions that have no valid supporting evidence; unsubstantiated generalizations		What does the author do to make the book "come alive" for the reader? Which solution is correct? Which design has flaws? Which is the most efficient strategy?	Analyze multiple sources of evidence (based on agreed-upon criteria) in order to . . . (e.g., evaluate historical accuracy; critique the style used).
Create = putting parts together in a new way Will a new model, story, solution, or visual display be created?	What other ways are there to approach this problem? Brainstorm what you know about this topic.	How could you teach a friend a strategy you learned? How can you use what you know to solve this problem?	Create a way to share your new knowledge or a new perspective. Develop an alternative solution or model.	

"Kid Friendly" Hess CRM Question-Planning Worksheet (Examples)
"I can . . . rock the rigor!"

REVISED BLOOM	DOK LEVEL 1 RECALL/ REPRODUCTION FOUNDATIONAL	DOK LEVEL 2 SKILLS AND CONCEPTS CONCEPTUAL	DOK LEVEL 3 STRATEGIC THINKING DEEPER – NEAR TRANSFER	DOK LEVEL 4 EXTENDED THINKING BROAD + DEEPER FAR TRANSFER
Remember Locate, recall, define.	I can . . .			
Understand Show what you know.	I can . . . explain who, what, where, when, or how after reading, viewing, or listening.	The main idea is . . . I'd summarize the important ideas this way: _____. My (timeline, flowchart, etc.) shows the order (steps/events).	I think one lesson learned or a possible theme is _____ and this is my supporting evidence.	These sources say something different about . . . (topic). The sources interpret the same facts (_____) in different ways . . . I put these ideas together: . . .
Apply Use it.	I can . . . calculate, measure, or apply a rule.	I used (words in the text, visuals) to figure out . . . I think this might mean . . . because . . .	I can . . .	I can . . .
Analyze = taking apart Take it apart.	A pattern I see is . . .	I sorted these this way because . . . I organized my data to show . . .	I can . . .	I can . . .
Evaluate Support a judgement.	UGs = opinions that have no valid supporting evidence; unsubstantiated generalizations		I can justify how I ranked _____ using _____ as my evidence-based criteria.	I can . . .
Create = putting parts together in a new way Put it together in a new way.	I can . . .	I can . . .	I can develop a model to show . . .	I can . . .

IV. Kid Tools: Resources for Use With Students to Support Deeper Thinking

Several kid tools are included in Module 1. These examples have been field-tested for classroom success, but they are really meant to spark your thinking about how to support all students in getting to deeper understanding. Below is a description of each strategy.

STRATEGY 1: "I Can Rock the Rigor" Kid Tool

Inspired by students in Utah, this tool can be used by students to develop learning goals and track their own weekly progress. If your students begin to get interested in DOK, they might enjoy creating their own versions of "I can . . ." or "we can . . ." statements for each week or each unit of study. *This tool is not included in this book, but an interactive version of this tool can be downloaded from* **resources.corwin.com/HessToolkit.**

STRATEGY 2: Collaborative Inquiry Plan

I developed this planning tool to help my students figure out how they would accomplish group inquiry activities in science. Giving students the responsibility of organizing *how* they will work and establishing group goals and roles is essential to developing independent learners and supports executive functioning. A template is on page 81 and available for download from **resources.corwin.com/HessToolkit.**

STRATEGY 3: The One-Pager

I developed this idea for guiding text-based discussions when teaching middle school. My seventh graders were reading novels, but as is the reality of school, not every student was coming to class having read the assigned homework. I wanted all of my students to be more engaged in the discussions, so one day I told them, "Today you will be completing a one-pager." If you know middle school students, then you know they immediately think this will be easy because it only has to fill one page. At the top of the page, students select and copy a quote—any quote. In the middle of page, they connect it the central idea of the text and explain why they chose that quote. At the bottom, they create a visual that gives meaning to the quote. I've even used this strategy when teaching graduate courses and in workshops. The one-pager helps students of any age to make personal connections to the text that they really are interested in sharing with others. A template is on page 82 and available for download from **resources.corwin.com/HessToolkit.**

STRATEGY 4: TBEAR and Kid TBEAR

I came across TBEAR in 2010 when I was searching for graphic organizers that did more than ask students to simply list words and phrases without making connections among ideas or applying deeper analysis. I discovered quite a few teachers using some version of TBEAR, including a middle school teacher whose master's thesis analyzed how using TBEAR as a prewriting activity could improve student writing. I liked that TBEAR effortlessly scaffolds students to move from DOK 1 to DOK 3 or 4:

- **T:** Writing a **T**opic sentence/**T**hesis (DOK 1);
- **B: B**riefly summarizing the text as a **B**ridge to evidence (DOK 2);
- **E:** Locating text **E**vidence/**E**xamples (DOK 2);
- **A:** Analyzing text evidence/**A**dding more to elaborate (DOK 3); and
- **R:** Stating **R**eflections that may go beyond DOK 3 to DOK 4 (e.g., making text-to-world connections).

The first TBEAR example on page 83 illustrates using a text-based prompt after reading *Little Red Riding Hood*. I frequently use this example in workshops and with students to help them learn how to analyze text evidence starting with a familiar and accessible text. In my field-testing of TBEAR, I've found that when students leave the "A" (analysis/add more) box blank, they generally end up writing a summary rather than an opinion or argument with supporting evidence. Teachers have used or adapted TBEAR for all grade levels and told me it works especially well for students with limited language proficiency skills. Working as a whole class or with a partner, students use TBEAR as a guide to locate text evidence and prepare for class discussions or writing.

While presenting TBEAR to educators in Connecticut a few years ago, I was asked if it could be used in other content areas, such as mathematics. That inquiry led to the second TBEAR vocabulary example on pages 84–85, using the mathematics term "line of symmetry." I've seen middle school teachers introduce new vocabulary for a unit of study by giving small groups a different term to analyze using TBEAR. Then students create wall or anchor charts for each new term. Finally, a third version—Kid TBEAR—was inspired by kindergarten teachers in Utah for use in shared literacy activities. For this one, we "start with the heart" of the book—What's the **B**ook about? Then we move to **T**—What does this make you think about? Can you find some **E**xamples? **A**dd or say more about the examples? And what will you **R**emember? A Kid TBEAR template is on page 86 and available for download from **resources.corwin.com/HessToolkit.**

STRATEGY 5: Multi-sensory Clustering

This graphic organizer (on page 87 and available for download from **resources.corwin.com/HessToolkit**) is designed to help students build vocabulary, draw upon prior experiences, and make connections using all parts of their brain (adapted from Hess, 1987) as they prepare to write. To introduce this tool, I use a collection of photographs. Students choose a photo and list words and phrases to describe things they could see (in the top section) if they were there observing the scene. Next they list things they might hear if they were in this place. For the section labeled "Feel," students can list both feelings and tactile impressions. Finally they list things they might smell or taste there. During this first round of brainstorming, students can ask for help to identify specific words or vocabulary they may want to include.

In round two, students close their eyes and imagine actually being there as an observer or participant in the scene. They are prompted to think about what they are doing in this place. [*Notice why you are here . . . and what you are doing in this place . . .*] With gentle teacher prompting during the creative visualization—phrased as statements, NOT questions—students again look [*look to your left . . . and to the right . . . noticing things you had not seen before*], hear [*listen to new sounds and describe them in your mind . . .*], feel [*now pay closer attention to things you're feeling . . . or touching . . . , notice textures, shapes . . .*], and so on. [*Continue as if you are a camera panning the scene.*] Finally, after a few minutes, students are asked to get a general impression of this place—such as creepy, relaxing, gloomy, or tense. The visualization always generates new impressions to add to the clustering of ideas.

Students are directed to open their eyes and write the general impression about this place—a word or phrase—in the center of the circle. Then they circle or add new words from the brainstorming and visualizing that support this key idea. Words and phrases that are not useful in the description are crossed out. Now the prewriting clustering is used to compose a text.

- The words in the center of the cluster become or are adapted to create a title.
- The first line begins with "I am . . ." so writing will be in the first person and in present tense.

- Students select circled words and phrases to develop and add lines that strongly help to describe the scene.
- The final line emphasizes the idea in the title in some way: as a question, a restatement, or perhaps an exclamation of insight.

Final editing is used to decide ordering and organizing ideas. These short writings can be turned into poems or paragraphs used to introduce a topic or describe phenomena. Below is an example used as the introductory hook to a biography of Cesar Chavez, an assignment given to students in a middle school I visited.

> *I am in a large and noisy crowd gathering at the edge of town. It's nearly sundown and many are still in well-worn work clothes, sweaty and tired from a long day in the fields. They say they want better wages. They want fair working conditions. I hear their frustration and anger when they mumble to each other. As a farm worker and activist steps onto the stage, the noise of the crowd begins to get quiet. Will a riot break out? Who is this leader we've come to listen to? We listen intently to what he has to say.*

STRATEGY 6: Sample Turn and Talk Frames

Every 12 to 15 minutes, students should be given a short amount of time to consolidate their learning. At the end of Module 1, I've included a few examples of frames teachers can use.

STRATEGY 7: Jigsaw to Develop Schemas

This idea comes from a middle school lesson posted on the Teaching Channel, "Jigsaw: A Strategy for Understanding Texts" (www.teachingchannel.org). The teacher engages students and scaffolds learning by giving different groups of students only one aspect of the argument to analyze. In other words, the jigsaw structure is not for dividing up content to read and understand, but for examining components of an argument in order to build schemas about the genre of persuasive or argument writing. While one group is looking at rhetorical strategies used, another may be searching for a claim or counterclaim. Of course, they all have to read the entire text to determine how their part supports or interacts with the rest of the text; but the jigsaw structure encourages discussion and deeper thinking while students focus attention on how smaller parts relate to the whole. All students benefit from hearing the examples of their peers and may even want to challenge them. This strategy can begin by using mentor texts and move to more complex texts as students develop a deeper understanding of how to establish a logic chain and use narrative strategies and literary devices, among other things. In the video clip, most of the responses only identify examples (DOK 2), but the teacher could be probing for reasoning as to why those examples were chosen, moving it to DOK 3 thinking.

STRATEGY 8: Text Decks: A Close Reading Strategy

A few years ago, I came across examples of "text decks" on the website of Steve Peha.[13] It's hard to describe what a text deck is without showing you one, but I'll try. Think of how PowerPoint

---

13. Steve Peha has posted many teacher-friendly instructional materials ("Teaching That Makes Sense") on his website (https://www.ttms.org/), which are free for downloading. Now you can review them through a "DOK-intended rigor lens."

slides are designed to allow you to type text and insert photos or clip art onto each slide. That's essentially the way a text deck can be created. When I saw the examples, I thought about how I might use close reading and text decks to get to deeper thinking. This is basically the process for creating the slides or text deck:

1. Small groups of students are given a short text to read and analyze. The text examples I've seen used include poems (including those authored by students) and short historical texts (e.g., the Preamble of the U.S. Constitution).

2. Students read and discuss its meaning. Then they write the first line on the first slide. For lengthy sentences, such as in the Preamble of the U.S. Constitution, phrases would be used instead of the whole sentence; so students need to decide where to break the text for each slide.

> "We the People of the United States, in Order to form a more perfect Union, establish Justice, insure domestic Tranquility, provide for the common defence, promote the general Welfare, and secure the Blessings of Liberty to ourselves and our Posterity, do ordain and establish this Constitution for the United States of America."
> Preamble of the U.S. Constitution

3. Once students decide which part of the text goes on the first slide, they have to determine which word or phrase is most important in that line. For example, if students choose to write, "We the people of the United States, in order to form a more perfect Union," as their first line, they need to decide the most important word—*People*? *United States*? *Perfect*? *Union*? (There is no "single right answer" for which word to choose.)

4. After choosing what they believe to be the most important word in that line, they illustrate it visually using a drawing, photo, clip art, symbol, or physical object. As you can imagine, this is a good way to engage students in interpreting the meaning of the text; *and* there is not only one correct answer as long as they can justify choices made.

5. Once that slide is completed, they move to the next line and continue the process. A completed text deck should have overall coherence; so for this particular text, they might choose to research and use historical objects, documents, and monuments for many of the phrases. For words or phrases that might not be as familiar (e.g., *Posterity*, *Welfare*), they will have to decide what visual image is in keeping with the theme of the text and the other visuals used.

The final text deck assessment should include a group or personal refection on the reasoning for choices made, making this at least a DOK 3 task. This is also a good opportunity for providing peer feedback, team to team.

Collaborative Inquiry Plan

Task Description

?   ?

Concepts/Skills/Reasoning

Team Roles and Responsibilities

Resource Materials

Our Plan for Investigating

Success Criteria

Available for download at **resources.corwin.com/HessToolkit**

The One-Pager

Select and copy a quote from the speech or text (with page reference):

Be ready to explain WHY you chose this quote and HOW IT CONNECTS with the central idea of the text.

Create a VISUAL that gives meaning to the quote for you.

TBEAR—Planning for Discussion or Writing

Sample Writing Prompt: After reading the story *Little Red Riding Hood*, what is your opinion about the intelligence or cleverness of the wolf? Support your opinion by analyzing evidence from the text.

TBEAR LETTER AND WHAT IT REPRESENTS	HELPFUL WAYS TO BEGIN . . . (SENTENCE FRAMES)	YOUR TOPIC OR TEXT AND NOTES (E.G., EVIDENCE FROM TEXT, FACTS, DETAILS, EXAMPLES, PAGE NUMBERS)
T = Topic Sentence or Thesis (focus or opinion) Clearly and directly respond to the prompt. This establishes the purpose.	In the story *Little Red Riding Hood*, the author creates a character that clearly is or is not very intelligent or clever.	
B = Brief explanation or Bridge to evidence (context) Briefly explain and/or set the scene for those who do not know the topic or text. This should not retell the whole story, but focus on the aspect of the story that is important for your response.	This story is about a girl named Little Red Riding Hood who . . . Meanwhile, the wolf character tries many things to . . .	
E = Examples Support the writer's stance OR your opinion with specific textual references. Include quotation marks for direct quotes and page numbers, section, or chapter.	For example, when _____ _____, the wolf says, "_____" Also, the wolf tries to _____ _____.	
A = Analysis Analyzes the examples or evidence. Writer digs deep to uncover meaning. Consider the meaning or implications of word choice, tone, imagery, or author's purpose.	This part of the story shows that . . . The author uses the words "_____" and "_____" to describe the wolf as . . . Also, the illustrations show the reader that . . .	
R = Relate or Reflect Establish a connection to another literary text, historical occurrence, society, universal human behavior, etc. OR Reflect on the main idea or a lesson OR State a conclusion related to your stated opinion.	This kind of character is also in _____. This idea or lesson is similar to _____. Therefore, _____. Overall, _____. All of these examples show that _____.	

Available for download at **resources.corwin.com/HessToolkit**

Copyright © 2018 by Corwin. All rights reserved. Reprinted from *A Local Assessment Toolkit to Promote Deeper Learning: Transforming Research into Practice* by Karin Hess. Thousand Oaks, CA: Corwin, www.corwin.com. Reproduction authorized only for the local school site or nonprofit organization that has purchased this book.

TBEAR—Vocabulary Development (from Definitional to Conceptual)

TBEAR LETTER AND WHAT IT REPRESENTS	HELPFUL WAYS TO BEGIN . . .	YOUR TOPIC OR TEXT AND NOTES (E.G., EVIDENCE FROM TEXT, FACTS, DETAILS, EXAMPLES, VISUALS, ETC.)
T = Topic Sentence/Term/ Principle This establishes the focus and purpose of your paragraph, poster, or illustration. State the term, principle, or concept with a brief definition.	A line of symmetry is . . . [a line that divides a figure into two congruent parts, each of which is the mirror image of the other].	
B = Brief explanation or Bridge to evidence (context) Briefly explain or add context for those who do not know the term or concept. This should focus on aspects that further elaborate on the concept and bridge to some examples and nonexamples.	When a figure having a line of symmetry is folded along the line . . . [the two parts should coincide or match exactly. That means that two parts are the same size and same shape].	
E = Examples Provide examples and nonexamples *and illustrate them* visually or graphically. If referencing a source, include quotation marks for direct quotes and page numbers, section, chapter, or website, where located.	For example, www.amathsdictionaryforkids.com shows that a line of symmetry can be drawn down the middle of a capital letter A; but cannot be drawn down the middle of the letters P or F to divide the parts into mirror images. Some figures can even have more than one line of symmetry such as this one does:	
A = Analysis Analyze the examples or evidence *and tell why this concept is important or useful to math-science* or applied in the real world. Consider the meaning or implications of not having or using the concept = *so what?*	The concept of symmetry is applied in geometry . . . It is also important to the design of . . .	

TBEAR LETTER AND WHAT IT REPRESENTS	HELPFUL WAYS TO BEGIN . . .	YOUR TOPIC OR TEXT AND NOTES (E.G., EVIDENCE FROM TEXT, FACTS, DETAILS, EXAMPLES, VISUALS, ETC.)
R = Relate or Reflect Establish a connection to another term or concept (math/science/social studies/arts). OR Reflect on a key idea. OR State a conclusion related to your focus.	These examples show . . . The concept of symmetry is related to or important to an understanding of . . . Therefore, . . . Overall, . . .	

Available for download at **resources.corwin.com/HessToolkit**

Copyright © 2018 by Corwin. All rights reserved. Reprinted from *A Local Assessment Toolkit to Promote Deeper Learning: Transforming Research into Practice* by Karin Hess. Thousand Oaks, CA: Corwin, www.corwin.com. Reproduction authorized only for the local school site or nonprofit organization that has purchased this book.

Kid T–B–E–A–R

Thinking: This book makes me see or think about . . .

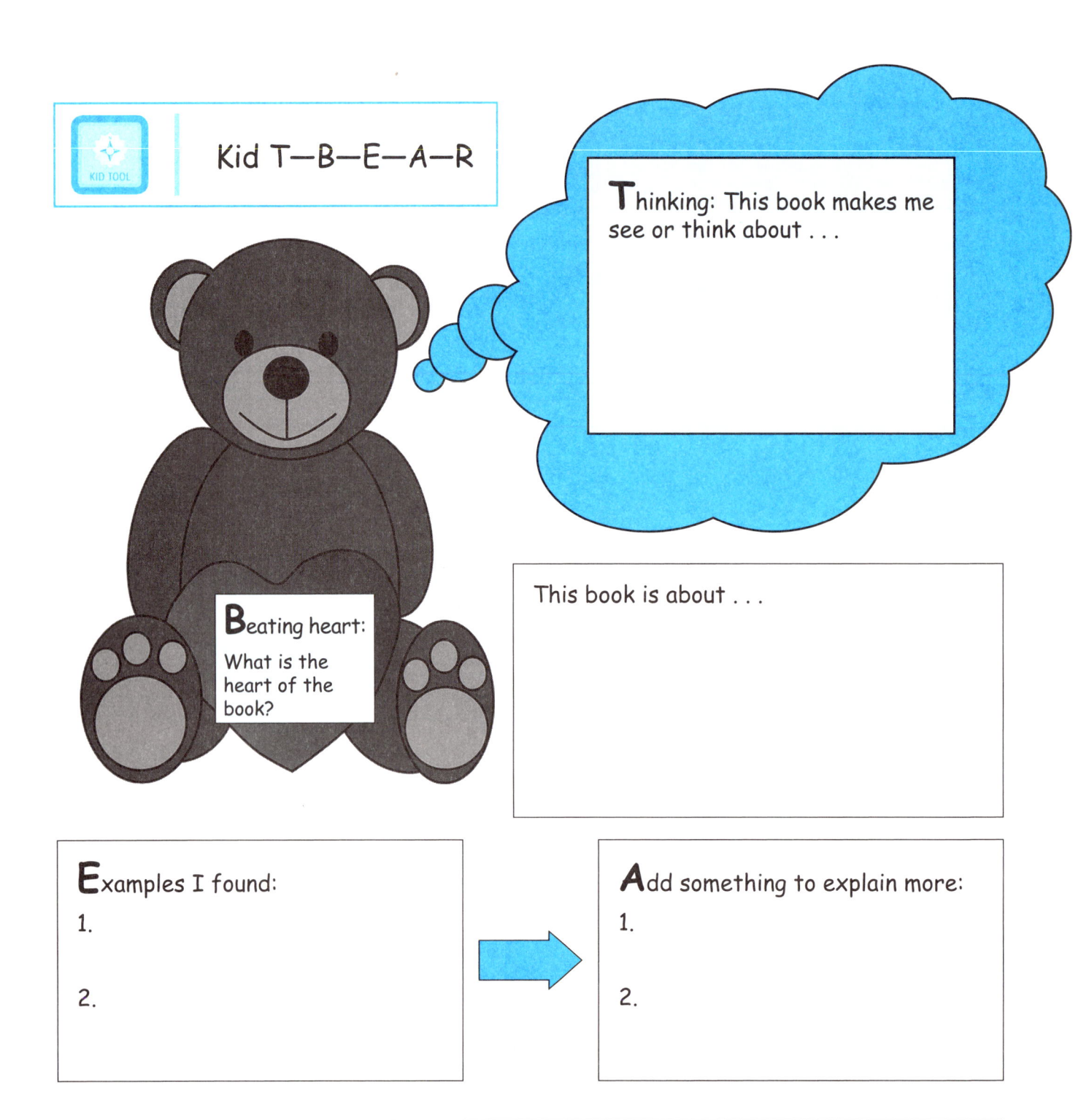

Beating heart: What is the heart of the book?

This book is about . . .

Examples I found:
1.
2.

Add something to explain more:
1.
2.

Remember: A lesson I learned or a question I wonder about is . . .

Available for download at **resources.corwin.com/HessToolkit**

Copyright © 2018 by Corwin. All rights reserved. Reprinted from *A Local Assessment Toolkit to Promote Deeper Learning: Transforming Research into Practice* by Karin Hess. Thousand Oaks, CA: Corwin, www.corwin.com. Reproduction authorized only for the local school site or nonprofit organization that has purchased this book.

Multi-sensory Clustering

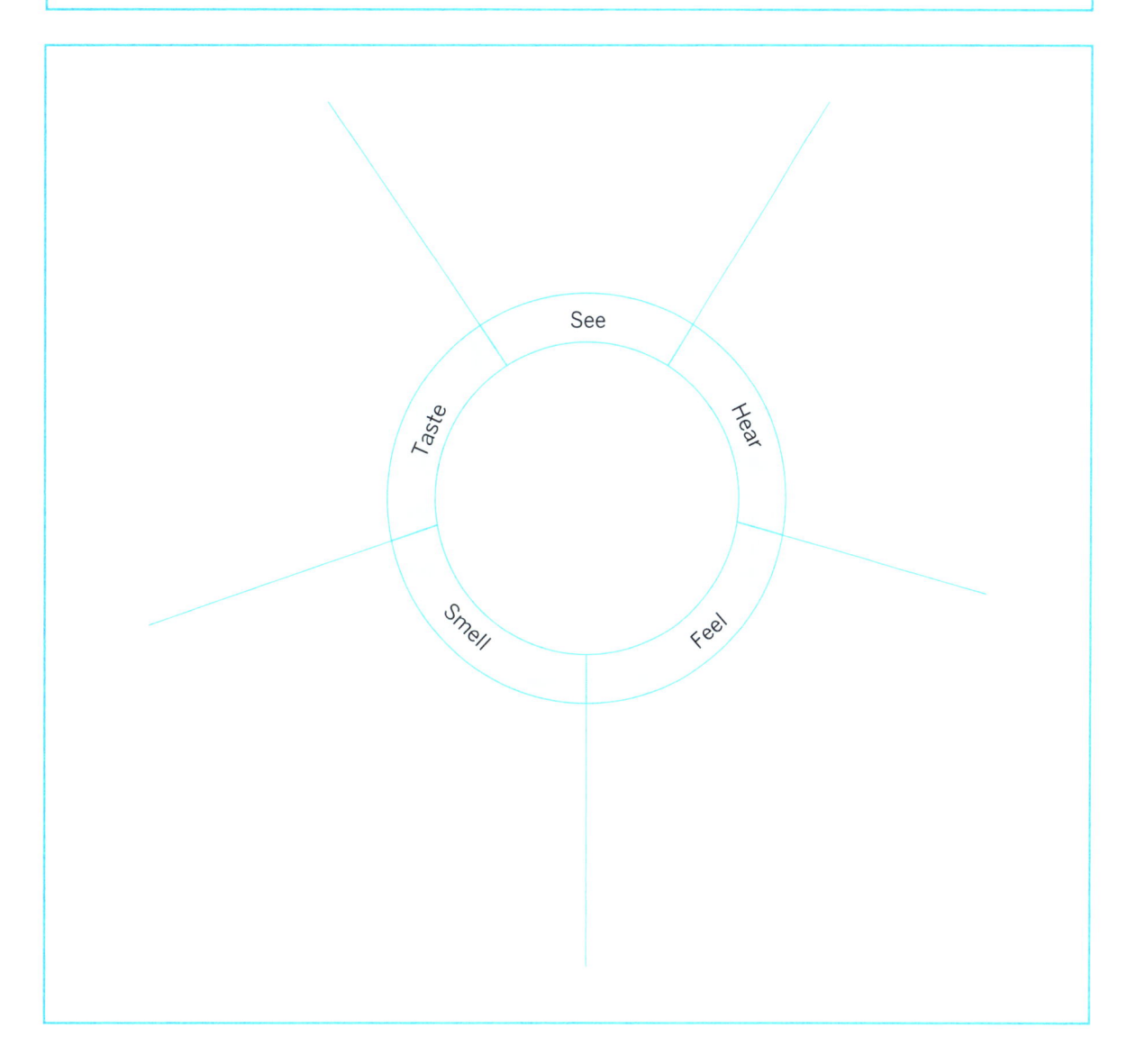

See

Taste

Hear

Smell

Feel

source: Adapted from Hess (1987).

Available for download at **resources.corwin.com/HessToolkit**

Copyright © 2018 by Corwin. All rights reserved. Reprinted from *A Local Assessment Toolkit to Promote Deeper Learning: Transforming Research into Practice* by Karin Hess. Thousand Oaks, CA: Corwin, www.corwin.com. Reproduction authorized only for the local school site or nonprofit organization that has purchased this book.

Sample Turn and Talk Frames

Name: _____

5 Things I know about _____

1.

2.

3.

4.

5.

Name: _____

Question of the day:
_____
_____

My response (with references/pages that helped me)

Name: _____

Locate evidence for this claim:

1.

2.

3.

Name: _____

Today's Text(s) or Topic:

A Text-to-Self Connection:

A Text-to-Text Connection:

A Text-to-World Connection:

Available for download at **resources.corwin.com/HessToolkit**

Copyright © 2018 by Corwin. All rights reserved. Reprinted from *A Local Assessment Toolkit to Promote Deeper Learning: Transforming Research into Practice* by Karin Hess. Thousand Oaks, CA: Corwin, www.corwin.com. Reproduction authorized only for the local school site or nonprofit organization that has purchased this book.

88 A Local Assessment Toolkit to Promote Deeper Learning

MODULE 2: IS THE TASK APPROPRIATE TO THE TEXT?

Examining and Using Increasingly Complex Texts

2.1 What Makes Texts Complex, and Why Should *Every* Teacher Care?

Over the past decades, much has been written about the importance of students' ability to not only comprehend, but to analyze increasingly complex texts as they advance across the grades. While much of the literature has focused on instructional strategies, lesson or unit design, and supports provided to struggling readers, we've also begun to see an emergence of research pointing to the importance of understanding the types of texts we ask our students to read, as well as what makes a specific text more or less complex than another. One such report, *Reading Between the Lines*, was released by ACT, Inc. in 2006. The findings in this report stated that what chiefly distinguished the performance of those students who had earned the benchmark score or better (on ACT exams) from those who had not was <u>not</u> their relative ability to make inferences while reading or to answer questions related to particular cognitive processes, such as determining main ideas or the meaning of words and phrases in context. Instead, the clearest differentiator was which texts students could read and understand, in terms of the complexity of the text. In other words, *what* students could read was at least as important as *what they could do* with what they read. These findings held for male and female students, students from all racial and ethnic groups, and students from families with widely varying incomes. The results of the ACT study have been borne out in years of results on other state assessments (National Governors Association, 2010a, p. 2).

On any given day, teachers at all grade levels ask students to read and interpret something—pictures, stories, informational or technical articles, textbooks, website or mixed media postings, their own writing, and even mathematics word problems. While the focus of Module 1 was on helping educators design questions and tasks that increase in depth and complexity across the school year, Module 2 is intended to support teachers in how to best match tasks with texts that are also increasing in complexity. For those teachers who have had little or no formal training in reading instruction, Module 2 lays the groundwork for understanding what factors might make a particular text more or less complex and provides insights into how to make that text accessible to students with a range of reading abilities. For school leaders and instructional coaches, Module 2 provides practical tools for collaborative assessment planning and supporting instruction. For some educators, this might be a shift in how you approach instructional or assessment planning. Let me just say that what I know now that I did not know as a beginning teacher is that we need to spend as much time thinking about the texts we use as we do about the text-based questions we pose to students. Both can provide critical evidence of learning progress over time.

So what actually makes a text complex? While Lexile measures, readability levels, or other quantitative measures are readily available from publishers, they only target a small number of factors that can make texts complex (Foorman, 2009; Hess & Biggam, 2004; Hiebert, 2013). A single readability score cannot fully reveal the complexity of a text because texts are not uniformly simple or complex across all dimensions that might make them complex.

2.2 The Thinking Behind the Tools in Module 2

The tools and protocols in Module 2 are designed to help teachers go beyond simply choosing texts based on quantitative scales that rate the relative complexity of texts. Using both qualitative and quantitative information about a text is important for several reasons:

- Nearly all readability formulas include two main features of text as measures of complexity: syntax and vocabulary use. These scales can provide a general look at text complexity, but not a full understanding of the demands of a text (Hiebert, 2013, p. 461).

- Readability formulas use different ways to mathematically analyze complexity factors (average sentence length, average number of syllables per word, word frequency, etc.). "Given such different approaches to measuring text difficulty, it is not surprising that scores for passage difficulty can vary widely, depending on which formula is used" (Foorman, 2009, p. 237). This is why many large-scale reading assessments (e.g., NAEP Reading, ACT, SAT) require that passage selection be based on both expert judgement and the use of at least two research-based readability formulas.

- Readability formulas are often used to assign passages to grade levels; the assigned grade passages are then used to determine grade-level equivalencies for texts or grade-level performance on tests. By exchanging words in a passage, writers can manipulate text difficulty, which in turn possibly distorts estimates of grade equivalencies and can invalidate predictions relating to the comprehension of authentic text (Foorman, 2009, p. 239).

- Quantitative scales are not practical or reliable for many specialized text types: poetry (short texts that employ use of figurative language, literary devices, etc.), texts used for beginning readers, plays and novels (with extensive dialogue, short sentences, or high-frequency vocabulary), and nonprint texts (digital, visual, auditory, or graphic). Hiebert (2013) provides many examples illustrating how less complex vocabulary and short sentences can underestimate the overall readability when the ideas presented can be quite complex. One such text is the 1997 Newberry Medal winner, *Roll of Thunder* (Taylor, 1976), which has the same Lexile as picture books, such as *Bat Loves Night* (Davies, 2001).

- Longer texts tend to be very complex in some ways (e.g., requiring deeper reasoning or more background knowledge), while less complex in other ways (e.g., format and layout may support reader understanding; simplified language facilitates decoding).

Finally, consider a favorite novel read by many middle school students over the years, the 1994 Newbery Medal winner, *The Giver* by Lois Lowry. This text utilizes simplistic sentence structure and language while exploring compelling and complex themes influenced by underlying societal and political issues. The same is true of John Steinbeck's *The Grapes of Wrath*, read by most middle and high school students. This novel actually falls into suggested quantitative complexity bands for elementary students. While younger students may be able to read and cope with the vocabulary in *The Grapes of Wrath*, they would be unlikely to unlock and fully understand the overall complexity of the text's message, which lies within a historical context and intertwines multiple themes running through the text (Hess & Biggam, 2004; Hess et al., 2012; Hess & Gong, 2015; Hess & Hervey, 2010). *The overall complexity of texts becomes evident only when qualitative measures are interpreted along with the formulaic readability levels.*

In my curriculum and assessment work over the years, I've found that when teachers are equipped to easily "unpack" the complexity of texts, they are better able to design instruction and assessments that support *all students* in getting to deeper levels of meaning. To that end, this module lays out how school leaders might approach professional development and PLC activities that build a shared understanding of how to examine and effectively use texts of increasing complexity for instruction and assessment.

Included in this module are the following:

- Definitions of quantitative measures and qualitative factors that make texts complex
- A research-based overview of ten increasingly complex text structures
- Tools and protocols for conducting *qualitative analyses* of texts
- Sample strategies for using text analysis to develop a range of text-based questions and tasks (DOK 1, 2, 3, and 4) or to determine what supports or strategic scaffolding might be needed for all students to successfully *access and use* texts of varying complexity
- Strategies for collaboratively creating a local list of mentor and benchmark texts or for the design of common assessments

Text Complexity TOOLS #6, #7, and #8 and the related protocols for the text complexity analyses were originally developed by Hess and Hervey (2010) working with educators in New York City schools. Teachers met regularly over the course of a school year to collaboratively analyze and then describe what made their texts more or less complex. This study included literary, informational, and some nonprint and digital texts in use. Later, the draft tools were piloted in schools in more than dozen states and refined to reflect both the research base and educator-friendly descriptors (Hess, 2013a).

Table 2.1   Overview of the Hess Text Complexity Tools

TOOL	USES FOR EACH TEXT COMPLEXITY TOOL
6 Qualitative Text Analysis Planning Worksheet	**TOOL #6:** This worksheet is useful for making notes on initial analyses and impressions about a text. After making notes about each qualitative factor, TOOLS #7 or #8 can be used to rate each factor and to determine which factors are generally most complex. Finally, alignment to standards, text-based questions, and strategic scaffolding strategies are developed.
7 Gradients of Complexity—Informational Texts	**TOOL #7:** This analytic rubric describes how **informational texts** can increase in complexity across multiple qualitative dimensions. What you will find is that most texts are complex in many different ways. Overall ratings are given for each qualitative factor based on the majority of indicators checked.
8 Gradients of Complexity—Literary Texts	**TOOL #8:** This analytic rubric describes how **literary texts** can increase in complexity across multiple qualitative dimensions. What you will find is that most texts are complex in many different ways. Overall ratings are given for each qualitative factor based on the majority of indicators checked.
32 Text Complexity Analyses Summary	**TOOL #32 (included in Module 5):** This tool is used to analyze current high-priority literacy assessments to determine and summarize the complexity of texts used in each assessment. This compiles information from Text Complexity TOOLS #7 and #8.

2.3 Five Key Learnings From a Text Complexity Analysis Process

We took away several key learnings from this text complexity analysis process with teachers:

1. *A continuum of complexity descriptors was most useful in analyzing texts.* While most teachers could easily agree on which texts were the least or the most complex, finding agreement on where texts fell along a continuum of complexity (between the least and most complex) was essential, since that's where most texts lie. Previous use of dichotomous analysis tools—those having only descriptions of very simple texts at one end versus very complex texts at the other end—were of little use to most teachers. Every text seemed to end up in the "middle" of the dichotomous scales. An analytical continuum offered opportunities for objectively differentiating texts along that scale, and across multiple text factors.

2. *Two descriptive continua were developed—one for literary and one for informational texts.* It was critical to use a variety of authentic (published) literary and informational texts to develop the complexity descriptors. Literary texts do not necessarily increase in complexity in the same ways that informational texts do. For example, text features, such as captioned photos, graphics, footnotes, and subheadings in informational texts provide unique ways of organizing information that generally are not found in literary texts. Text structures used in literary texts (e.g., chronology, description, problem–solution) also vary from those structures typically used in informational texts (e.g., sequence–procedures, definition, compare–contrast, critique, inductive–deductive).

3. *Teachers needed tools that were both efficient and effective.* Tools that take too long to use will never become embedded in instructional or assessment planning practices. The analysis tools were fine-tuned with teacher input to maintain fidelity with the underlying research base while remaining "teacher friendly" in terms of ease of use in analyzing and planning how to use texts.

4. *Qualitative analysis deepened teacher understanding of both text complexity and instructional supports.* Even when teachers were very familiar with the texts prior to doing qualitative analyses, they noticed new factors they had been unaware of, in terms of defining the text's potential complexity. New insights about the texts led to new instructional strategies for unlocking text meanings, supporting readers, and creating text-based questions.

5. *Collaboratively using the analysis tools and protocols (in PLC or curriculum work sessions) helped to build a common understanding of what made different text types complex and how they compared with other texts.* Talking through and assigning ratings to texts used at different grade levels can guide schools to establish a set of benchmark texts. Just as benchmark student work illustrates how student writing varies at different performance levels, benchmark texts illustrate varying levels of complexity and provide models—or anchors—for matching other texts. "The identification and use of benchmark texts is an ideal way for teachers within a school or district to begin to look at texts with a critical eye on what it means to be a proficient reader at different points within a grade and across grades" (Hiebert, 2013, p. 463).

2.4 Understanding Quantitative and Qualitative Complexity Measures

Quantitative text dimensions refer to those aspects of texts that are difficult, if not impossible, for a human reader to evaluate efficiently, especially in longer texts. Quantitative text dimensions are measured by computer software, using proprietary formulas based on factors such as word length, word frequency, sentence length, and text cohesion, for example. The "chief weakness [of qualitative scales] is that longer words, less familiar words, and longer sentences are not inherently hard to read. In fact, series of short, choppy sentences can pose problems for readers precisely because these sentences lack the cohesive devices, such as transitional words and phrases, that help establish logical links among ideas and thereby reduce the inference load on readers" (National Governors Association, 2010a, p. 7).

Qualitative text dimensions refer to those characteristics of texts that are best (collaboratively) evaluated by human readers. These factors interact to affect the relative difficulty of texts, such as author's purpose, levels of intended meaning and reasoning required, discourse style, language use, and background knowledge demands. In 2004, Hess and Biggam's review of the research identified eight specific qualitative factors influencing overall text complexity. These factors[1] were incorporated into test specifications of the New England Common Assessment Program (NECAP), influenced the development of Appendix A of the *Common Core State Standards for English/Language Arts and Literacy* (National Governors Association, 2010a, p. 6), and were later used by the Smarter Balanced Assessment Consortium (SBAC) to qualitatively analyze and select passages, as well as to write text-based questions for reading assessments.

View a video clip of Karin Hess (2013b) describing eight qualitative factors of text complexity, "Text Complexity Toolkit" at **http://www.karin-hess.com/free-resources**.

Eight Qualitative Measures Affecting Text Complexity

1. *Length of Text*: The length and density of a text can affect a student's sustained engagement with that text.

2. *Format and Layout of Text*: The physical layout and format of a text can provide support to readers or actually make a text more challenging for them to locate what's most important to pay attention to.

3. *Genre and Characteristic Features of the Text*: When students are building schemas about what to expect from different text genres, they can make semantic predictions about how information is likely to be organized. "Transfer" is evidenced when a student knows what to expect of a particular text, even before beginning to read it.

4. *Purpose, Levels of Meaning, and Reasoning Required*: Many texts with simplistic sentences and familiar vocabulary can actually be very complex in their purpose, themes, and underlying meanings.

5. *Text Structures (and their related signal words and semantic cues)*: When students begin to recognize *how* information is organized and presented (e.g., compare–contrast versus chronology cues), they are better able to create mental models of it. Longer texts generally use combinations of structures, some being more complex than others.

6. *Discourse Style*: An author's discourse style (e.g., humor, satire, irony) and use of rhetorical devices can influence misinterpretations of the intended message, even when students are able to fluently decode most words in the text. This is especially true for English language learners.

7. *Word Difficulty and Language Structure*: Readability formulas use mathematical analyses to examine syntax and vocabulary; however, knowing *which words* in a text might be most important to understand is critical to instructional approaches when using a text.

8. *Background Knowledge and/or Degree of Familiarity With Content*: Texts with literary allusions and content-based texts, such as historical and technical passages, sometimes require that for full understanding, a student must "bring" certain background knowledge of the content to the text.

Source: Hess and Biggam (2004).

---

[1]. A detailed discussion of what to look for with each of the eight qualitative factors can be found in section 2.6 of this module.

2.5 Unpacking Overall Text Complexity Using a Qualitative Analysis Approach

Before beginning to qualitatively analyze a text or passage, I ask educators to read the entire text all the way through, noting how long they estimate that it will take for most of their students to read the text. During the second reading of the text, we begin to examine and discuss each qualitative dimension, one at a time.

STEP 1: Use the Instructional and Assessment Planning Worksheet

Using **TOOL #6**, the Qualitative Text Analysis Planning Worksheet, enter the title, author, text genre, approximate reading time, and Lexile or text level (if known) at the top of the form. Raters then skim the text for the first feature (length and density of the text), discussing and making notes in the center column, "Characteristics of this Text." This review continues for each of the qualitative factors listed. Facilitators may want to set estimated times for evaluating and discussing each of the text dimensions.

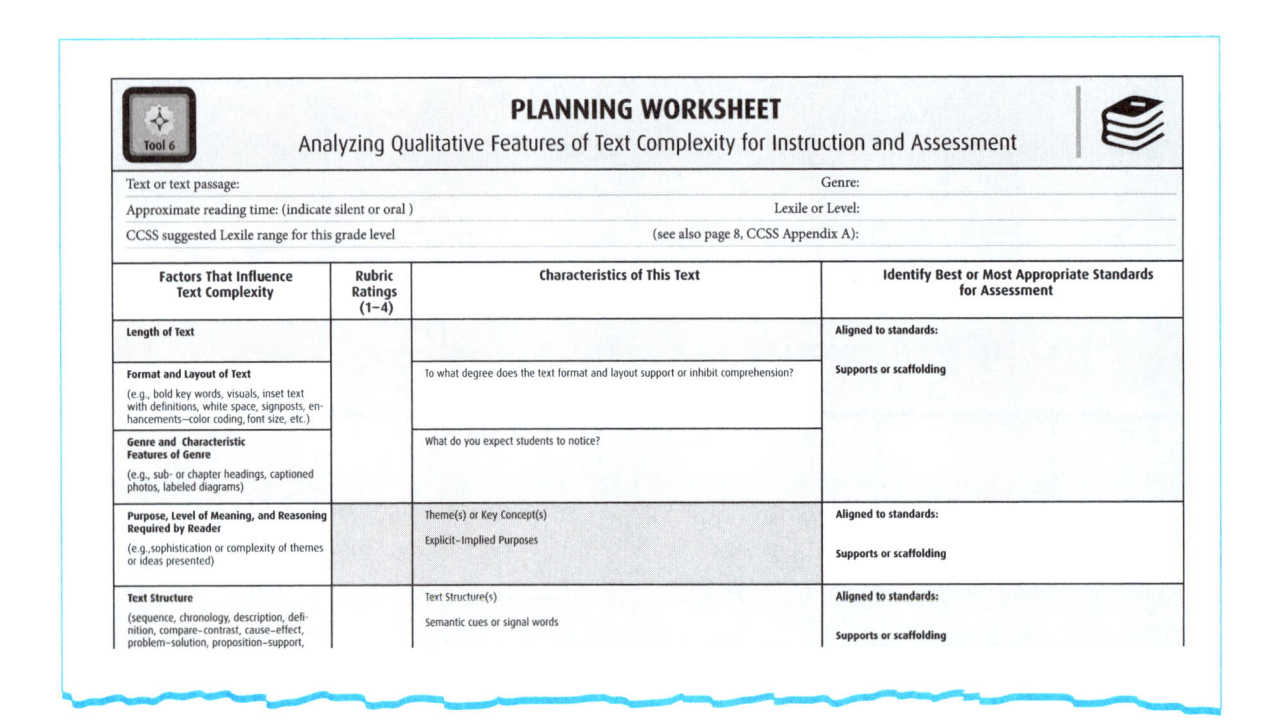

PLANNING WORKSHEET
Analyzing Qualitative Features of Text Complexity for Instruction and Assessment

Text or text passage: _____ Genre: _____
Approximate reading time: (indicate silent or oral) _____ Lexile or Level: _____
CCSS suggested Lexile range for this grade level _____ (see also page 8, CCSS Appendix A):

Factors That Influence Text Complexity	Rubric Ratings (1–4)	Characteristics of This Text	Identify Best or Most Appropriate Standards for Assessment
Length of Text			Aligned to standards:
Format and Layout of Text (e.g., bold key words, visuals, inset text with definitions, white space, signposts, enhancements—color coding, font size, etc.)		To what degree does the text format and layout support or inhibit comprehension?	Supports or scaffolding
Genre and Characteristic Features of Genre (e.g., sub- or chapter headings, captioned photos, labeled diagrams)		What do you expect students to notice?	
Purpose, Level of Meaning, and Reasoning Required by Reader (e.g., sophistication or complexity of themes or ideas presented)		Theme(s) or Key Concept(s) Explicit–Implied Purposes	Aligned to standards: Supports or scaffolding
Text Structure (sequence, chronology, description, definition, compare-contrast, cause-effect, problem-solution, proposition-support,		Text Structure(s) Semantic cues or signal words	Aligned to standards: Supports or scaffolding

STEP 2: Determine Rubric Ratings

Use team notes and descriptions with either TOOL #7 (informational texts) or TOOL #8 (literary texts) to determine rubric ratings (1–4) for each set of factors.

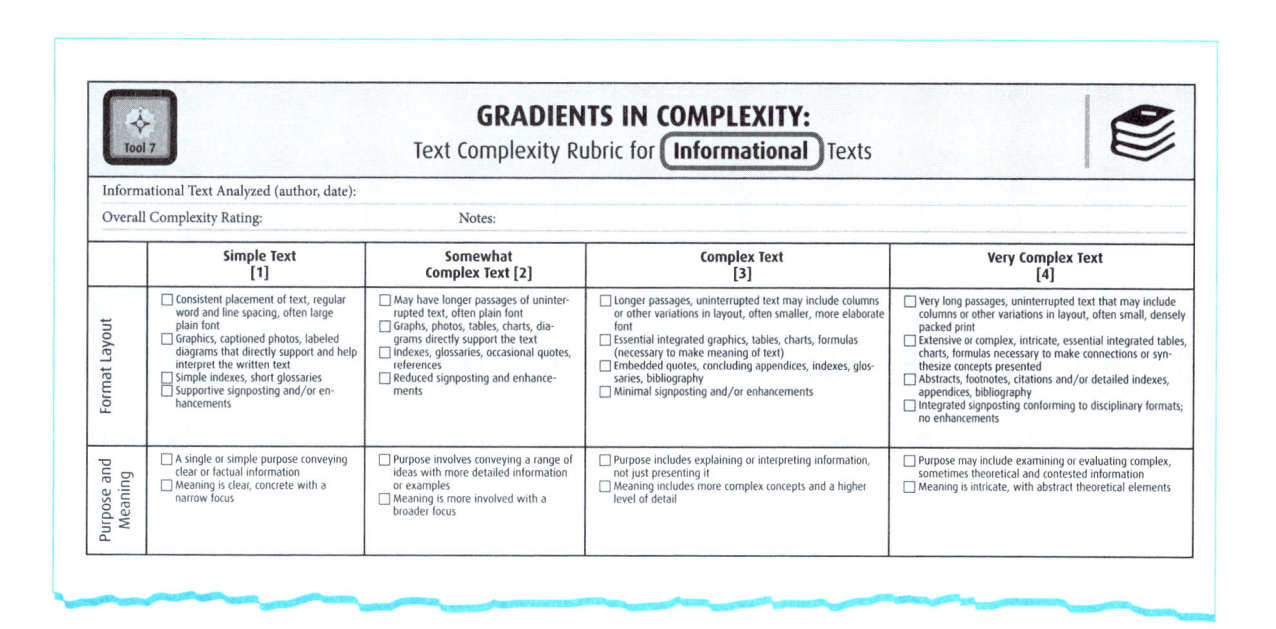

GRADIENTS IN COMPLEXITY:
Text Complexity Rubric for Informational Texts

Tool 7

Informational Text Analyzed (author, date):
Overall Complexity Rating: _____ Notes:

	Simple Text [1]	Somewhat Complex Text [2]	Complex Text [3]	Very Complex Text [4]
Format Layout	☐ Consistent placement of text, regular word and line spacing, often large plain font ☐ Graphics, captioned photos, labeled diagrams that directly support and help interpret the written text ☐ Simple indexes, short glossaries ☐ Supportive signposting and/or enhancements	☐ May have longer passages of uninterrupted text, often plain font ☐ Graphs, photos, tables, charts, diagrams directly support the text ☐ Indexes, glossaries, occasional quotes, references ☐ Reduced signposting and enhancements	☐ Longer passages, uninterrupted text may include columns or other variations in layout, often smaller, more elaborate font ☐ Essential integrated graphics, tables, charts, formulas (necessary to make meaning of text) ☐ Embedded quotes, concluding appendices, indexes, glossaries, bibliography ☐ Minimal signposting and/or enhancements	☐ Very long passages, uninterrupted text that may include columns or other variations in layout, often small, densely packed print ☐ Extensive or complex, intricate, essential integrated tables, charts, formulas necessary to make connections or synthesize concepts presented ☐ Abstracts, footnotes, citations and/or detailed indexes, appendices, bibliography ☐ Integrated signposting conforming to disciplinary formats; no enhancements
Purpose and Meaning	☐ A single or simple purpose conveying clear or factual information ☐ Meaning is clear, concrete with a narrow focus	☐ Purpose involves conveying a range of ideas with more detailed information or examples ☐ Meaning is more involved with a broader focus	☐ Purpose includes explaining or interpreting information, not just presenting it ☐ Meaning includes more complex concepts and a higher level of detail	☐ Purpose may include examining or evaluating complex, sometimes theoretical and contested information ☐ Meaning is intricate, with abstract theoretical elements

STEP 3: Brainstorm Instructional Strategies and Scaffolding

Brainstorm instructional strategies and scaffolding that might make the text more accessible. If the purpose of the text analysis is to use texts for instruction or unit planning, individuals or PLC teams can now brainstorm instructional strategies and strategic scaffolding, such as adding a visual of a cliff house. (See sample analysis notes on the next page for the article "The Lost People of Mesa Verde" by Elisa Marston, 2005.) This information is entered in the column to the far right on TOOL #6.

Text-based questions with a range of cognitive demand can also be developed for instruction or assessment purposes using the notes about text complexity.

> *Interactive digital versions of TOOLS #7 and #8 make STEP 2 easy to complete.* Descriptors matching team notes are checked in the analytic rubrics. Additional indicators may also be included at this point. Rubric scores are recorded for each complexity grouping.
>
> Tools can be downloaded at **http://www.karin-hess.com/free-resources** and **resources.corwin.com/HessToolkit**

- The least complex text structures used in this article were description and chronology. This suggests less complex questions, such as

  - *Chronology: Use the information from the text to create a timeline.* **(DOK 2)**

  - *Description: Describe how the life of the Anasazi changed. Use information from the article to support your summary.* **(DOK 2)**

- The most complex text structure used in this article was cause–effect. This suggests a deeper question might be asked, such as "*Based on the information in the article, what most likely caused the mesa top to wash away? Use textual evidence to support your thinking.*" **(DOK 3)**

Purpose, Level of Meaning and Reasoning Required by Reader (sophistication or complexity of themes or ideas presented)	Theme(s)/Key Concept(s) Explicit-implied Purposes "lost people" "reasons are not quite clear"—facts and possibilities given to support propositions	CC standards Supports/scaffolding
Text Structure (sequence, chronology, description, definition, compare—contrast, cause–effect, problem—solution, proposition—support, judgment—critique, inductive—deductive) **and Discourse Style** (sarcasm, satire, irony, humor, etc.)	Text Structure(s) description, chronology, cause-effect, proposition-support? Semantic cues/signal words Dates, time sequences Discourse style (employs use of literary devices)	CC standards Supports/scaffolding
Words, Language Features, and Structure • Word length, word frequency • Sentence length; transitions • Potential levels of meaning (single or multiple; explicit or implicit; literal or figurative) • Precise or nuanced meaning • Domain specific	Tier 2 words-academic words (precise, contextual, literal or figurative, archaic) plateau, "wore out," mingled, lost Tier 3 words (technical, content or domain specific) mesa, cliff houses, erosion	CC standards Supports/scaffolding (before and after reading) -Add a visual of cliff house -Add a footnote to define erosion
Background Knowledge Demands or Degree of Familiarity With Content Required (prior knowledge, multiple perspectives, embedded citations)	Embedded references (literary, historical, cultural, economic, political, etc.) Intro sentence provides context	CC standards Supports/scaffolding (before and after reading)

- Worksheet notes for the "Purpose, Levels of Meaning, and Reasoning" section also suggest creating deeper questions requiring text support, such as

  ○ *Explain the meaning of the title. Use information from the article to support your interpretation.* **(DOK 3)**

  ○ *For which information about the Anasazi are there opposing points presented in the article? Analyze text evidence to explain why you think so.* **(DOK 3)**

  ○ *Locate and use a second source to verify or refute claims stated in this article.* **(DOK 4)**

STEP 4: Develop a Local Bibliography of Benchmark Texts

If the purpose of the text analysis is to develop a local bibliography of benchmark texts, PLC teams may want to split up by grade level or grade spans to do this work, which can be added to over time. Teams collaboratively analyze and record information about each text reviewed in a table similar to the one below, codeveloped with educators in Alaska. In this 2011 workshop, K–12 classroom teachers and library media specialists from across the state gathered in Anchorage to analyze texts from their own schools and classrooms. They arrived with large bags filled with books by Alaskan authors and books reflecting Alaskan culture. The texts included novels, short stories, graphic novels, and a variety of informational texts. After a one-hour overview of text complexity and guided practice in how to use **TOOLS #6, #7, and #8** to examine a text together, teams were ready to begin. They spent the rest of the day in small groups documenting their analyses. Approximately 100 texts were collaboratively reviewed that day, with many teachers returning to their schools to continue the process with colleagues.

A sample format for creating a local text bibliography based on text complexity analyses is shown in Figure 2.1.

Figure 2.1 Sample Format for a Local Text Bibliography

Sample *Preliminary* Bibliography of Texts Analyzed by (Alaska) Educators for Range of Complexity and Classroom Use										
Author Publisher & Pub Date	**Title**	**Genre**	**Suggested Grade Level(s)**	**Lexile**	**Complexity Ratings (using Hess & Hervey rubric descriptors)**					**Other Comments**	**Overall Low- Mid- High for Grade(s)**
					Format & Layout	Purpose & Meaning	Text Structures/ Discourse	Language Features	Knowledge Demands		
Wade, P., & Macheras, D. (publisher unknown)	*Luk' ae*	Graphic novel	Gr 4	?	1 Easy to follow visuals and text	2 Salmon, effects of pollution	1	2 Domain-Specific	1	Use to introduce science concept —human impact on environment	L
Wallis, V. (1993) Harper Perennial	*Two Old Women*	Historical fiction	Gr 7–8	870	2–3 Longer passages of uninterrupted text; a few illustrations support the text	2 Theme is clear, levels of complexity clearly distinguished	1–2 Text is clear, chronological, easy to predict Different text types	1–2 Simple and compound sentences, with some complex constructions A few unfamiliar words (Gwitchin names)	1 Some assumed cultural knowledge	Presented as a traditional Native story	L–M
Huntington, S. (1993). Alaska Northwest Books	*Shadows on the Koyukuk*	Auto-biography (historical reflection and recollection)	Gr 9–10	1050	3 Longer passages of uninterrupted text; chapter headings; minimal signposts; maps	3 Explain and interpret some information; complex subjects	3 Time shift, complex characters, connections are subtle	2 Simple and compound sentences; some unfamiliar vocabulary	3 Much assumed personal experience and cultural knowledge	Well-written, complex biography	M–H

2.6 A Detailed Discussion of What to Look for—Eight Qualitative Complexity Factors

To begin STEP 1, the following detailed discussion of what to look for with each of the eight qualitative factors might be useful.

STEP 1: Using **TOOL #6**, the Qualitative Text Analysis Planning Worksheet, enter the title, author, text genre, approximate reading time, and Lexile or text level (if known) at the top of the form. Raters then skim the text for the first feature (length and density of the text), discussing and making notes in the center column, "Characteristics of This Text." This review continues for each of the eight qualitative factors listed.

1. Length and density of text

The first complexity factor, probably not a surprise, is the *length of the text*. If I were to give you an article to read right now, what is the first thing you would do? Probably you'd flip through it to see how long it is. Next you might look for illustrations or other graphics that break up the print text and add meaning. We know that the length of text is directly related to student engagement. This is especially true when the text is both long and "dense," meaning that there is little to break up the text, such as with use of white space or subheadings. Students—especially poor readers—often give up before they even try to read a text if it looks like there is too much to read in the time they have been given. We also know that if a text is introduced by "chunking it" into smaller parts (which may or may not be single paragraphs) and asking different questions for each section, students tend to sustain engagement with the text all the way to the end. Therefore, if you could change one thing to make texts more accessible, it would be to chunk the text and order your questions from surface level to deeper levels of meaning as students get closer to the end of the passage (Hess, McDivitt, & Fincher, 2008). Each question draws students deeper into the text, allowing them to process key ideas as they read and reread each part. This type of strategic scaffolding can lead to teaching students how to annotate texts as they read, such as underlining a key sentence in each paragraph and using margin notes to paraphrase each key idea (Fisher, Frey, & Hattie, 2016). Examples of using chunking can be found in the work of Lucy Calkins and colleagues at the Teachers College Reading Writing Project (TCRWP). Sample questions for each chunk might progress in this way:

- What do you know now about (character)?
- What new information is provided about (character)?
- What does the author want you to picture in your mind right now? Draw it using text details.
- What might happen next? What evidence makes you think so?
- What can (you/this character) learn from this experience? Support your thinking using text evidence.

Key Ideas

Chunking longer texts builds reader confidence and stamina.

- Break up dense text to sustain reader engagement.
- Provide a few questions after each chunk.
- Move from explicit to implicit to interpretive and inferential.

2. Format and layout of text

The second qualitative factor of text complexity which is fairly easy to get agreement on is describing the *format and layout* of the text, meaning how information is organized and presented visually and how text features break up an otherwise dense text. Things to look for are the size, color, and location of print and white space; use of numbering or bullets; headings and subheadings; graphics and visual displays (charts, tables, diagrams); and other features that provide support to readers when their intended purpose is known. For example, the purpose of numbering is often to indicate steps in a procedure or a prioritized list. In digital texts, such things as drop-down menus and interactive tools and links are part of the layout and format. Sometimes a very "busy" text layout can actually become a challenge to readers with limited executive functioning. These students are not always sure what information to pay attention to. Another way to provide instructional scaffolding without changing any of the vocabulary or syntax that affects Lexiles or text levels is to select text layouts that support students' understanding as they read the first of two paired texts on the same topic. For visually busy texts, you might cover some of the distracting features of text with numbered sticky notes that can be revealed one at a time, and asking, "How does this (new) information help you to understand the key ideas?"

3. Genre and characteristic features of the text

The third complexity factor is really important because it relates to students building and generalizing schemas about what to expect from various text types (historical fiction vs. historical documents, poems vs. plays, etc.). What we know from the literature on reading comprehension is that when readers start to develop schemas about different text genres, they are already anticipating the text purpose and what to expect to be presented in the text. If they know a text is not likely to be a story, they will not be looking for the characters, the setting, or the plot. Instead, they'll expect to see facts or information about events, people, or concepts. You can test this out by holding up a book and asking your students, "What kind of a text do you think this is?"

Let's say that the students respond, "It's an informational article."

Rather than confirm or praise their assumption, ask a few more probing questions that will help them to verify or refute their thinking. "Why do you think it's informational? What do you see or expect to see that would tell you this is an article?"

When students suggest that there may be a glossary of terms, facts in bold print, timelines and dates, or captions under photographs, you know they are developing schemas for the kind of information that might be included and how it is likely to be organized even before they start to read. In your preview of texts, note whether there are characteristic features of this text genre—texts that are typical examples of the genre or ones that are not as obvious. Strong genre models offer instructional opportunities for students to differentiate: for example, how an illustration is used in a short story and how that is different from why a labeled diagram is included in a science or mathematics text; how an editorial is structured differently from a short story or an article.

Building schemas advances the ability of students to transfer, to say "I've seen this type of text before and I know how this is going to be similar to or different from other texts I've read."

Key Ideas

- Students need to develop a schema for each genre type:
  - What kind of text is this?
  - How is the information organized?
  - What can I expect in a text like this?
- Schemas help with both reading comprehension and writing.

A second related idea where typical genre features can support comprehension is when students make semantic predictions about texts. For example, they think this is going to be a mystery story because they see cues that are similar to what they've come across in other mystery stories. This is in contrast to making an episodic connection, where students are asked if anything like this ever happened to them—whether there ever was an episode in their lives like this. Usually episodic connections take students away from the text evidence, rather than deeper into the text. I like to suggest that while making personal connections to a text can be very important to increasing engagement, those connections are best incorporated into text-to-self conclusions when writing or speaking about a text read.

Key Ideas

- **Semantic predictions**: Take students back into the text and help them to build schemas about characteristic features of each text genre.
- **Episodic connections**: Often take students away from the text evidence.

4. Levels of meaning and reasoning required

Interpreting the author's purpose and message can be quite complex even when the actual words and sentence structure appear on the surface to be simplistic. For determining this factor, consider the sophistication of themes and ideas presented, as well as the use of abstract metaphors and other literary devices. Complex visual, metaphoric, or symbolic images in multimodal texts (e.g., repeated images, called motifs) may require deeper analysis to get at their significance or to determine how they are connected to themes. Consider whether there are embedded iconic images of historical significance that require understanding of their context or whether there are juxtapositions of text and images that reveal humorous irony or contradictions.

5. Text structures

Text structures are the *internal organizational structures* used within paragraphs or longer texts, appropriate to genre and purpose. This is different from genre characteristics that help students to determine whether a text is a fable, fairy tale, or myth based on how it is structured. Research in literacy learning indicates that (a) an understanding of various text structures and their purposes enhances students' ability to comprehend what is read, and (b) some text structures are more easily learned and understood before other more complex structures. Increasingly complex structures tend to follow this general progression: sequence (procedure), chronology (time order), description, definition, compare–contrast, cause–effect, problem–solution, proposition–support, critique, and inductive–deductive (Hess, 2008c).

Each text structure has associated semantic cues and signal words or phrases that help readers understand how the information is organized and connected, as well as to compose their own texts with greater coherence and clarity. The analytical review uses signal words and semantic cues to identify text structures used. Longer texts have multiple structures, with some being easier to use and understand than others. For example, locating embedded definitions or dates that help to establish chronology are much easier to understand than determining cause–effect structures. Qualitative analyses can uncover which text structures will be the most complex for students to use and which will best support understanding. Your job is to decide what to focus on *in this text* at any given time during the instructional process.

> ### Key Ideas
>
> - Texts are structured for meaning and effect, and if you don't notice and unpack how the structuring works on both the global and local levels, you'll miss much of the meaning and effect.
> - Nonfiction texts embed many different text structures into their superstructure, so readers have to be vigilant, following the overall flow of the text, while being alert to shifts in text structure at particular moments that help organize information in sections of the text.

One instructional approach to teaching text structures is to codevelop classroom anchor charts throughout the year that identify sample texts used in the class, locating signal words and semantic cues used in each text. (Examples for each text structure are described in Module 2, STRATEGY 5.)

Another instructional strategy is to provide a "frame" for applying a structure in writing, such as compare–contrast. (A sample instructional frame is shown in Module 2, STRATEGY 1.)

6. Discourse style

Discourse style (e.g., sarcasm, satire, humor, dramatic irony) can add a more complex dimension of language use for readers to interpret by providing an implicit view into an author's perspective, voice, meaning, and sometimes potential biases. Consider the popular and funny Amelia Bedelia stories that most elementary students enjoy. Using humor results in the literal interpretation of words not being what the reader is supposed to be understanding. Fluent decoding of words is not sufficient to understand these texts. More sophisticated discourse styles can change the complexity of texts, simply due to the style used by the author, especially if it is a style unfamiliar to readers at this point in their education.

7. Word difficulty and language structure

Vocabulary, sentence type, and complexity of words or structure are usually expressed through the use of readability formulas, such as Lexiles. A deeper qualitative analysis includes identification of Tier 1, Tier 2, and Tier 3 words to determine whether some words might need extra instructional attention. Beck, McKeown, and Kucan (2002) define the kinds of words in each tier and suggest that the greatest instructional emphasis should be given to Tier 2 words—words that may be generally familiar to most students, but not really understood in the context used.

- *Tier 1*: Words that rarely require instructional attention in school; familiar words with high frequency, everyday use. These words are generally of Anglo-Saxon origin and not considered a challenge for native speakers of English.

- *Tier 2*: Words with high utility; considered high-frequency use for mature language users; found across a variety of domains and texts; vary according to age and development; words we assume students know, but often they have only "heard" the word, (e.g., glance, confident, commotion, regret, relative, faltered). These include words that the Common Core State Standards refer to as "academic words."

- *Tier 3*: Low frequency words, often limited to content-specific domains; important to learn when the specific need arises; critical for content area learning; found most often in informational texts. These are words the Common Core State Standards refer to as "domain-specific words" (e.g., lava, legislature, circumference).

Key Ideas

- Limit the number of words to preteach. Determine which words and concepts are essential to understanding the text but do not have any cues in the text to support figuring out their meanings.

- Do not preteach words that have embedded definitions, words illustrated by examples or visuals, or words that might be nice to know but are not essential to understanding the text.

- The best way to build depth and breadth of vocabulary is not by use of vocabulary lists. Deeper understandings come with successive readings and focused discussions.

8. Background knowledge and/or degree of familiarity with content

Building background and world knowledge depends on both the degree to which students have read widely and discussed texts in the past and how well prepared they are to read a text that might require additional context (outside of the text) for deeper or nuanced understanding. This doesn't mean knowing everything about the topic prior to reading, but identifying essential background. Look for historical, geographical, or literary references that may greatly inhibit or enhance reading comprehension. For example, Martin Luther King Jr.'s 1963 "Letter from a Birmingham Jail" includes both historical and biblical references that not all students have been exposed to. Text analyses can determine what is essential background knowledge and ways to provide it.

Placing a short introductory summary before the text is an easy way to provide background context for the piece. For text above, it might look like this:

> "Written in April 1963, Martin Luther King Jr.'s 'Letter from Birmingham Jail' delivered an important statement on civil rights and civil disobedience. The 1963 racial crisis in Birmingham, Alabama, was a critical turning point in the struggle for African American civil rights. Although King's letter was not published until after the Birmingham crisis was resolved, it is widely regarded as the most important written document of the modern civil rights movement and a classic text on civil disobedience."
>
> *Source:* http://www.mlkonline.net/jail.html

Other ways to provide critical background knowledge prior to reading a text would be to use a short video showing the historical or geographical context for the text, adding several captioned photos as an introduction to the text, or pairing a second, less complex introductory text with the more complex text.

Reflections

On your own or with colleagues, take a minute to reflect on the topics covered in this module. Then identify a useful takeaway, something to try next.

Ways I am refining my thinking about what makes texts more or less complex:

- There's more than one way for a text to be complex
-
-
-

Strategies for getting students to deeper thinking with text-based questions:

- Chunking text
-
-

℞ My personal prescription for using texts more effectively:

PART 2: SUPPORT MATERIALS FOR MODULE 2

I. A Workshop Plan for Module 2

Kolb's Experiential Learning Cycle

Suggested Activities

Stage 1: WHY is this new learning important to me? And what do I already know?

Moving from Concrete Experience to Reflective Observation

Create a concrete experience, asking participants to make connections, drawing on personal knowledge and experience. Small groups compare and reflect on common ideas.

- Activity: Ask participants to bring some of their own texts or provide a small number of texts to be sorted from less to most complex. Table groups collaboratively discuss common features of less to more complex texts.
- Show Hess video describing eight factors that make texts complex. Ask participants to reflect on how their sorting of texts compares with the qualitative factors identified.
- Reflections: *What was validated? What surprised you? What questions do you have?*

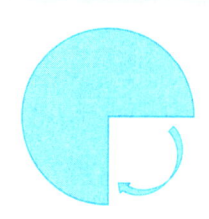

Stage 2: WHAT do the research and experts say?

Moving from Reflective Observation to Abstract Conceptualization

Help participants connect their personal reflections to broader, more abstract generalizations.

- Provide expert advice and review the research via interactive lecture.
- Use (informational, literary, and nonprint) mentor texts as examples and nonexamples for each qualitative factor (layout, genre characteristics, text structures, meaning, etc.) to further develop concepts and build schemas. Stop frequently (every 15–20 min.) to consolidate the new learning.

Stage 3: HOW does this work? How can I apply this?

Moving from Abstract Conceptualization to Active Experimentation

Use tools and protocols to examine examples and strategies.

- Provide brief background on development of Hess Text Complexity **TOOLS #6, #7, and #8**.
- Activity: Guided practice using **TOOL #6** with a short (informational) text. Introduce each factor, allowing time for table groups to complete each analysis before moving to the next factor.
- Activity: Use **TOOL #6** with **TOOL #7 or #8** to collaboratively analyze classroom texts and develop a range of questions DOK 1 to 4 for each one; or review existing text-based questions provided by book publishers.
- Activity: Guided practice using **TOOL #6** with assessment targets planning templates[2] to develop a range of text-based questions for one or more texts.

---

2. See Strategy 13 in Module 2 for examples of predetermined assessment targets.

Stage 4: WHAT IF I experimented with this? What might work in my classroom or school?

Moving from Active Experimentation back to Concrete Experiences

- Activity: Revisit current texts and text-based questions used in your curriculum or units of study. Develop or revise a current unit of study, pairing texts of varying complexity. Brainstorm deeper questions and strategic scaffolding strategies to add to lessons (e.g., teaching students to identify and use signal words for different text structures).

- Revisit current texts and text-based questions used in your curriculum or units of study. Use **TOOL #32**[3] to develop a school-based bibliography of texts for each grade level.

- Use assessment targets planning templates for unit planning.

- Experiment with a new strategy in your classroom. Reflect on how it worked and what you might do next.

Source: Stages adapted from Kolb (1984) and McCarthy (1987).

II. The Hess Text Complexity Tools

About the Tools in This Module

TOOL #6: Analyzing Qualitative Features Worksheet

Use this Planning Worksheet during the first step in your qualitative analysis. Then use your notes about the text to consider ways to support instruction and assessment tasks and questions.

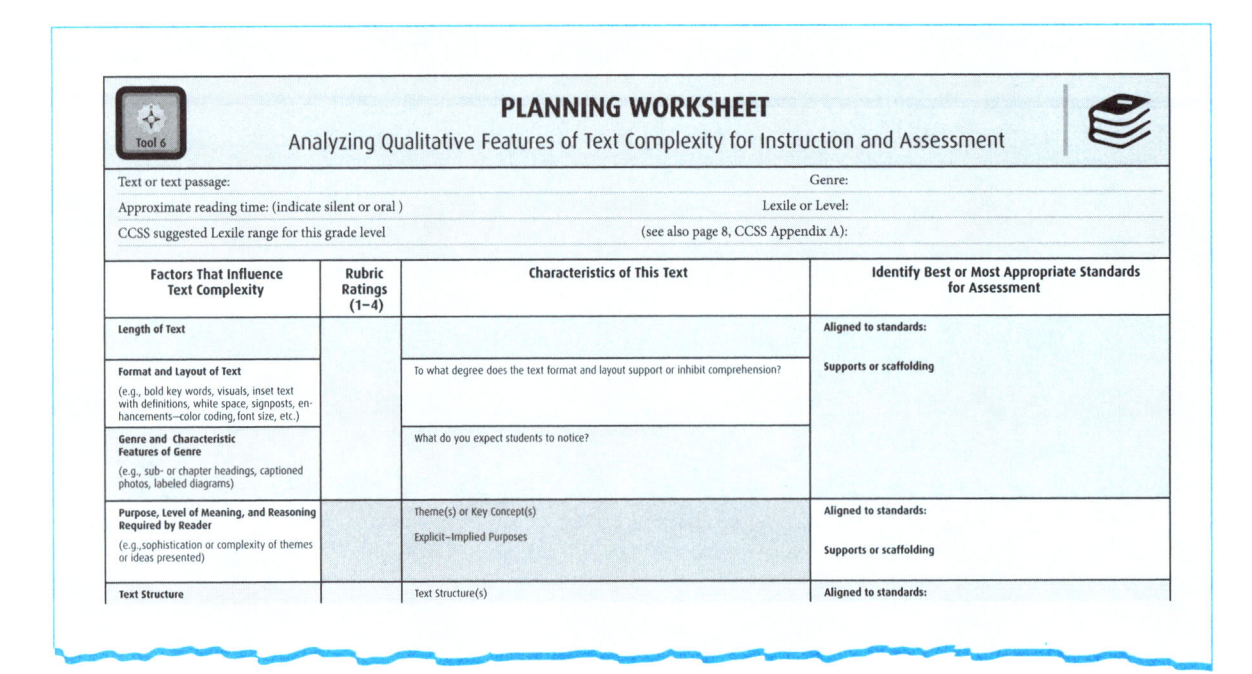

A full version of this tool can be found on page 107. It is also available for download from **resources.corwin.com/HessToolkit** and **www.karin-hess.com/free-resources.**

---

3. Use of **TOOL #32** is explained in Module 5.

104   A Local Assessment Toolkit to Promote Deeper Learning

TOOL #7: **Analytic Rubric for Informational Texts**
Use this Rubric with your notes about the text to rate each dimension of text complexity.

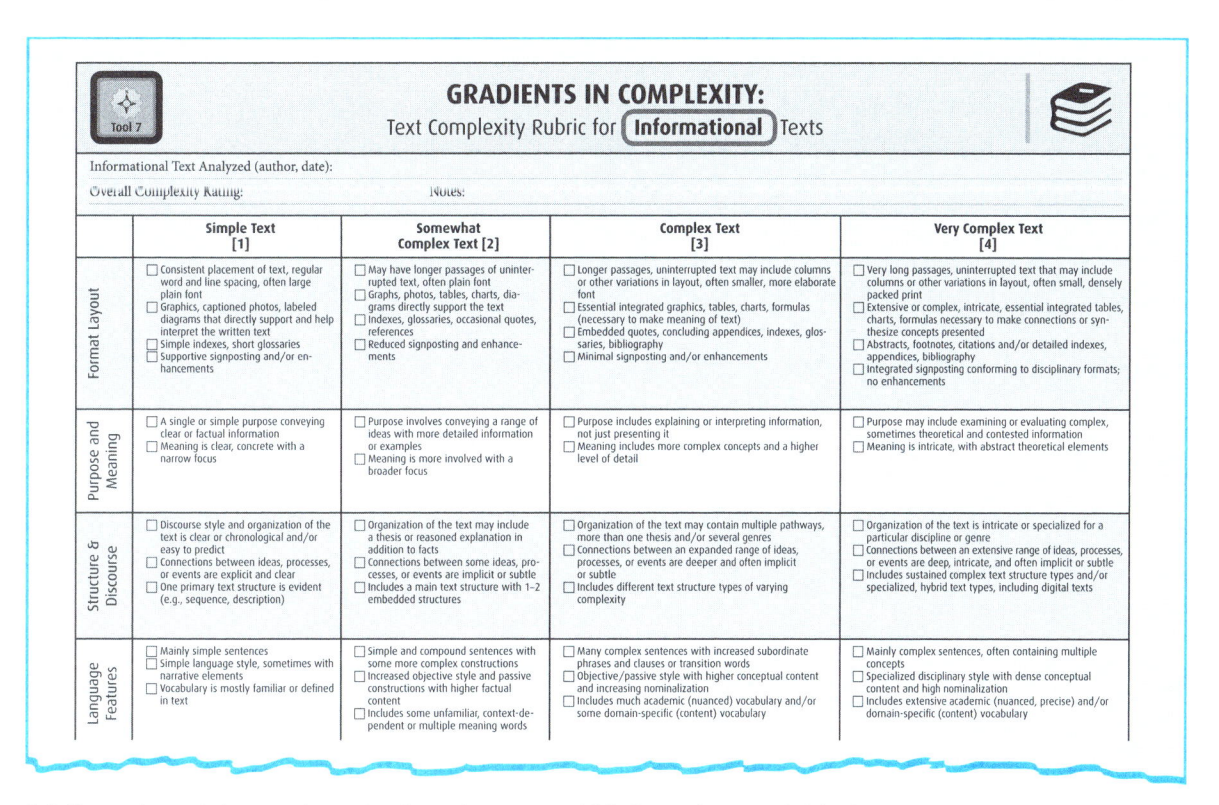

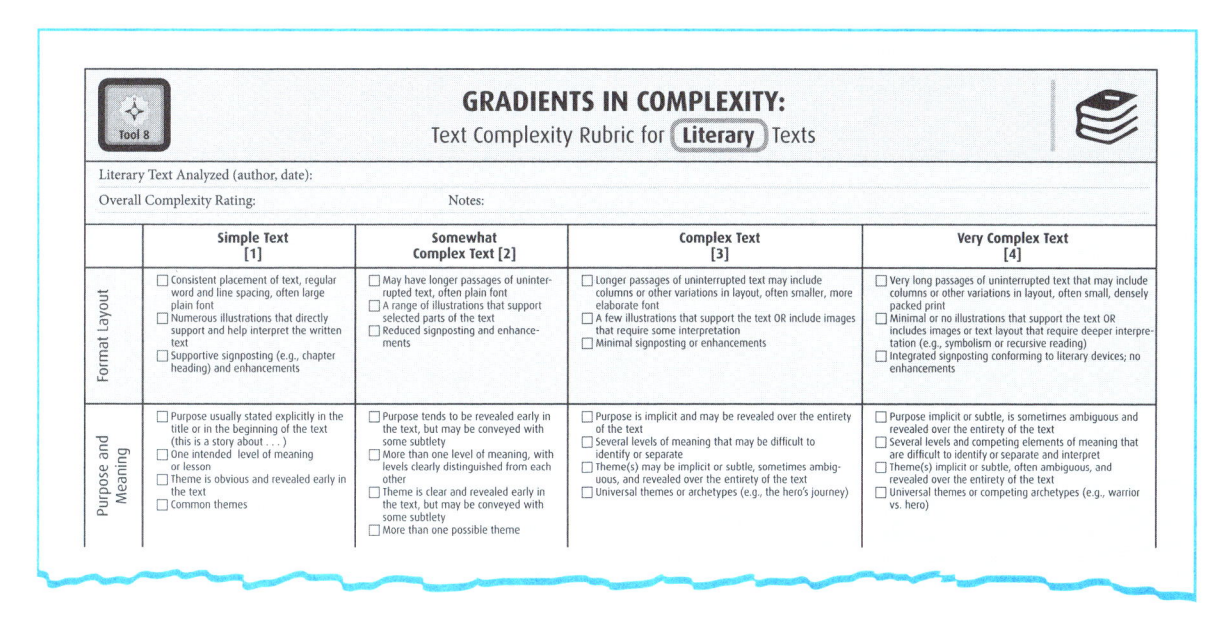

GRADIENTS IN COMPLEXITY:
Text Complexity Rubric for **Informational** Texts

Informational Text Analyzed (author, date): _____
Overall Complexity Rating: _____   Notes: _____

	Simple Text [1]	Somewhat Complex Text [2]	Complex Text [3]	Very Complex Text [4]
Format Layout	☐ Consistent placement of text, regular word and line spacing, often large plain font ☐ Graphics, captioned photos, labeled diagrams that directly support and help interpret the written text ☐ Simple indexes, short glossaries ☐ Supportive signposting and/or enhancements	☐ May have longer passages of uninterrupted text, often plain font ☐ Graphs, photos, tables, charts, diagrams directly support the text ☐ Indexes, glossaries, occasional quotes, references ☐ Reduced signposting and enhancements	☐ Longer passages, uninterrupted text may include columns or other variations in layout, often smaller, more elaborate font ☐ Essential integrated graphics, tables, charts, formulas (necessary to make meaning of text) ☐ Embedded quotes, concluding appendices, indexes, glossaries, bibliography ☐ Minimal signposting and/or enhancements	☐ Very long passages, uninterrupted text that may include columns or other variations in layout, often small, densely packed print ☐ Extensive or complex, intricate, essential integrated tables, charts, formulas necessary to make connections or synthesize concepts presented ☐ Abstracts, footnotes, citations and/or detailed indexes, appendices, bibliography ☐ Integrated signposting conforming to disciplinary formats; no enhancements
Purpose and Meaning	☐ A single or simple purpose conveying clear or factual information ☐ Meaning is clear, concrete with a narrow focus	☐ Purpose involves conveying a range of ideas with more detailed information or examples ☐ Meaning is more involved with a broader focus	☐ Purpose includes explaining or interpreting information, not just presenting it ☐ Meaning includes more complex concepts and a higher level of detail	☐ Purpose may include examining or evaluating complex, sometimes theoretical and contested information ☐ Meaning is intricate, with abstract theoretical elements
Structure & Discourse	☐ Discourse style and organization of the text is clear or chronological and/or easy to predict ☐ Connections between ideas, processes, or events are explicit and clear ☐ One primary text structure is evident (e.g., sequence, description)	☐ Organization of the text may include a thesis or reasoned explanation in addition to facts ☐ Connections between some ideas, processes, or events are implicit or subtle ☐ Includes a main text structure with 1–2 embedded structures	☐ Organization of the text may contain multiple pathways, more than one thesis and/or several genres ☐ Connections between an expanded range of ideas, processes, or events are deeper and often implicit or subtle ☐ Includes different text structure types of varying complexity	☐ Organization of the text is intricate or specialized for a particular discipline or genre ☐ Connections between an extensive range of ideas, processes, or events are deep, intricate, and often implicit or subtle ☐ Includes sustained complex text structure types and/or specialized, hybrid text types, including digital texts
Language Features	☐ Mainly simple sentences ☐ Simple language style, sometimes with narrative elements ☐ Vocabulary is mostly familiar or defined in text	☐ Simple and compound sentences with some more complex constructions ☐ Increased objective style and passive constructions with higher factual content ☐ Includes some unfamiliar, context-dependent or multiple meaning words	☐ Many complex sentences with increased subordinate phrases and clauses or transition words ☐ Objective/passive style with higher conceptual content and increasing nominalization ☐ Includes much academic (nuanced) vocabulary and/or some domain-specific (content) vocabulary	☐ Mainly complex sentences, often containing multiple concepts ☐ Specialized disciplinary style with dense conceptual content and high nominalization ☐ Includes extensive academic (nuanced, precise) and/or domain-specific (content) vocabulary

A full version of this tool can be found on page 108. It is also available for download from **resources.corwin.com/HessToolkit** and **www.karin-hess.com/free-resources**.

TOOL #8: **Analytic Rubric for Literary Texts**
Use this Rubric with your notes about the text to rate each dimension of text complexity.

GRADIENTS IN COMPLEXITY:
Text Complexity Rubric for **Literary** Texts

Literary Text Analyzed (author, date): _____
Overall Complexity Rating: _____   Notes: _____

	Simple Text [1]	Somewhat Complex Text [2]	Complex Text [3]	Very Complex Text [4]
Format Layout	☐ Consistent placement of text, regular word and line spacing, often large plain font ☐ Numerous illustrations that directly support and help interpret the written text ☐ Supportive signposting (e.g., chapter heading) and enhancements	☐ May have longer passages of uninterrupted text, often plain font ☐ A range of illustrations that support selected parts of the text ☐ Reduced signposting and enhancements	☐ Longer passages of uninterrupted text may include columns or other variations in layout, often smaller, more elaborate font ☐ A few illustrations that support the text OR include images that require some interpretation ☐ Minimal signposting or enhancements	☐ Very long passages of uninterrupted text that may include columns or other variations in layout, often small, densely packed print ☐ Minimal or no illustrations that support the text OR includes images or text layout that require deeper interpretation (e.g., symbolism or recursive reading) ☐ Integrated signposting conforming to literary devices; no enhancements
Purpose and Meaning	☐ Purpose usually stated explicitly in the title or in the beginning of the text (this is a story about . . .) ☐ One intended level of meaning or lesson ☐ Theme is obvious and revealed early in the text ☐ Common themes	☐ Purpose tends to be revealed early in the text, but may be conveyed with some subtlety ☐ More than one level of meaning, with levels clearly distinguished from each other ☐ Theme is clear and revealed early in the text, but may be conveyed with some subtlety ☐ More than one possible theme	☐ Purpose is implicit and may be revealed over the entirety of the text ☐ Several levels of meaning that may be difficult to identify or separate ☐ Theme(s) may be implicit or subtle, sometimes ambiguous, and revealed over the entirety of the text ☐ Universal themes or archetypes (e.g., the hero's journey)	☐ Purpose implicit or subtle, is sometimes ambiguous and revealed over the entirety of the text ☐ Several levels and competing elements of meaning that are difficult to identify or separate and interpret ☐ Theme(s) implicit or subtle, often ambiguous, and revealed over the entirety of the text ☐ Universal themes or competing archetypes (e.g., warrior vs. hero)

A full version of this tool can be found on page 109. It is also available for download from **resources.corwin.com/HessToolkit** and **www.karin-hess.com/free-resources**.

Using the information from **TOOL #6, TOOL #7,** *and* **TOOL #8**[4]

- Transfer text complexity rubric scores from **TOOL #7** or **Tool #8** onto **TOOL #6**.
- Generate ideas for instruction or assessment by completing the far right column on **TOOL #6**.
- You may also want to transfer text complexity rubric scores to a spreadsheet as you build a set of benchmark texts for each grade level or grade span, as seen in Figure 2.1.

---

4. **TOOL #7** and **TOOL #8** are used again in Module 5 (with **TOOL #32**) during alignment studies, when examining text-based assessments and summarizing the range of complexity of texts used.

PLANNING WORKSHEET

Analyzing Qualitative Features of Text Complexity for Instruction and Assessment

Text or text passage: _____ Genre: _____

Approximate reading time: (indicate silent or oral) _____ Lexile or Level: _____

CCSS suggested Lexile range for this grade level _____ (see also page 8, CCSS Appendix A):

Factors That Influence Text Complexity	Rubric Ratings (1–4)	Characteristics of This Text	Identify Best or Most Appropriate Standards for Assessment
Length of Text			Aligned to standards: Supports or scaffolding
Format and Layout of Text (e.g., bold key words, visuals, inset text with definitions, white space, signposts, enhancements—color coding, font size, etc.)		To what degree does the text format and layout support or inhibit comprehension?	
Genre and Characteristic Features of Genre (e.g., sub- or chapter headings, captioned photos, labeled diagrams)		What do you expect students to notice?	
Purpose, Level of Meaning, and Reasoning Required by Reader (e.g., sophistication or complexity of themes or ideas presented)		Theme(s) or Key Concept(s) Explicit–Implied Purposes	Aligned to standards: Supports or scaffolding
Text Structure (sequence, chronology, description, definition, compare–contrast, cause–effect, problem–solution, proposition–support, judgment–critique, inductive–deductive) **Discourse Style** (sarcasm, satire, irony, humor, etc.)		Text Structure(s) Semantic cues or signal words Discourse style (e.g., employs use of literary devices)	Aligned to standards: Supports or scaffolding
Words, Language Features • Word length, frequency • Sentence length; simple–complex with transitions • Potential levels of meaning (single–multiple; explicit–implicit) • Precise-nuanced meaning • Domain-specific meaning		Tier 2 words–academic words (precise, contextual, literal, figurative, archaic) Tier 3 words (technical, content- or domain-specific)	Aligned to standards: Supports or scaffolding
Background Knowledge Demands or Degree of Familiarity with Content Required (e.g., prior knowledge, multiple perspectives, embedded citations)		Embedded references (literary, historical, cultural, economical, political, etc.)	Aligned to standards: Supports or scaffolding

© Hess & Hervey (2010). Tools for Examining Text Complexity, in Hess, K. (2017). *A local assessment toolkit to support deeper learning: Guiding school leaders in linking research with classroom practice.* Permission to reproduce is given only when authorship is fully cited [karinhessvt@gmail.com].

Available for download at **resources.corwin.com/HessToolkit** and **www.karin-hess.com/free-resources**

Copyright © 2018 by Corwin. All rights reserved. Reprinted from *A Local Assessment Toolkit to Promote Deeper Learning: Transforming Research into Practice* by Karin Hess. Thousand Oaks, CA: Corwin, www.corwin.com. Reproduction authorized only for the local school site or nonprofit organization that has purchased this book.

GRADIENTS IN COMPLEXITY:
Text Complexity Rubric for Informational Texts

Informational Text Analyzed (author, date):

Overall Complexity Rating:

Notes:

	Simple Text [1]	Somewhat Complex Text [2]	Complex Text [3]	Very Complex Text [4]
Format Layout	☐ Consistent placement of text, regular word and line spacing, often large plain font ☐ Graphics, captioned photos, labeled diagrams that directly support and help interpret the written text ☐ Simple indexes, short glossaries ☐ Supportive signposting and/or enhancements	☐ May have longer passages of uninterrupted text, often plain font ☐ Graphs, photos, tables, charts, diagrams directly support the text ☐ Indexes, glossaries, occasional quotes, references ☐ Reduced signposting and enhancements	☐ Longer passages, uninterrupted text may include columns or other variations in layout, often smaller, more elaborate font ☐ Essential integrated graphics, tables, charts, formulas (necessary to make meaning of text) ☐ Embedded quotes, concluding appendices, indexes, glossaries, bibliography ☐ Minimal signposting and/or enhancements	☐ Very long passages, uninterrupted text that may include columns or other variations in layout, often small, densely packed print ☐ Extensive or complex, intricate, essential integrated tables, charts, formulas necessary to make connections or synthesize concepts presented ☐ Abstracts, footnotes, citations and/or detailed indexes, appendices, bibliography ☐ Integrated signposting conforming to disciplinary formats; no enhancements
Purpose and Meaning	☐ A single or simple purpose conveying clear or factual information ☐ Meaning is clear, concrete with a narrow focus	☐ Purpose involves conveying a range of ideas with more detailed information or examples ☐ Meaning is more involved with a broader focus	☐ Purpose includes explaining or interpreting information, not just presenting it ☐ Meaning includes more complex concepts and a higher level of detail	☐ Purpose may include examining or evaluating complex, sometimes theoretical and contested information ☐ Meaning is intricate, with abstract theoretical elements
Structure & Discourse	☐ Discourse style and organization of the text is clear or chronological and/or easy to predict ☐ Connections between ideas, processes, or events are explicit and clear ☐ One primary text structure is evident (e.g., sequence, description)	☐ Organization of the text may include a thesis or reasoned explanation in addition to facts ☐ Connections between some ideas, processes, or events are implicit or subtle ☐ Includes a main text structure with 1–2 embedded structures	☐ Organization of the text may contain multiple pathways, more than one thesis and/or several genres ☐ Connections between an expanded range of ideas, processes, or events are deeper and often implicit or subtle ☐ Includes different text structure types of varying complexity	☐ Organization of the text is intricate or specialized for a particular discipline or genre ☐ Connections between an extensive range of ideas, processes, or events are deep, intricate, and often implicit or subtle ☐ Includes sustained complex text structure types and/or specialized, hybrid text types, including digital texts
Language Features	☐ Mainly simple sentences ☐ Simple language style, sometimes with narrative elements ☐ Vocabulary is mostly familiar or defined in text	☐ Simple and compound sentences with some more complex constructions ☐ Increased objective style and passive constructions with higher factual content ☐ Includes some unfamiliar, context-dependent or multiple meaning words	☐ Many complex sentences with increased subordinate phrases and clauses or transition words ☐ Objective/passive style with higher conceptual content and increasing nominalization ☐ Includes much academic (nuanced) vocabulary and/or some domain-specific (content) vocabulary	☐ Mainly complex sentences, often containing multiple concepts ☐ Specialized disciplinary style with dense conceptual content and high nominalization ☐ Includes extensive academic (nuanced, precise) and/or domain-specific (content) vocabulary
BK Knowledge Demands	☐ General topic is familiar, with some details known by reader ☐ Simple, concrete ideas	☐ General topic is familiar, with some details new to reader (cultural, historical, literary, political, legal, etc.) ☐ Both simple and more complicated, abstract ideas	☐ General topic is somewhat familiar but with many details unknown to reader (cultural, historical, literary, political, legal, etc.) ☐ A range of recognizable ideas and challenging abstract concepts	☐ General topic is mostly unfamiliar with most details unknown to reader (cultural, historical, literary, political, legal, etc.) ☐ Many new ideas, perspectives, and/or complex, challenging, abstract, and theoretical concepts

© Hess & Hervey (2010). Tools for Examining Text Complexity, in Hess, K. (2017). *A local assessment toolkit to support deeper learning: Guiding school leaders in linking research with classroom practice.* Permission to reproduce is given only when authorship is fully cited [karinhessvt@gmail.com].

Available for download at **resources.corwin.com/HessToolkit** and **www.karin-hess.com/free-resources**

Copyright © 2018 by Corwin. All rights reserved. Reprinted from *A Local Assessment Toolkit to Promote Deeper Learning: Transforming Research into Practice* by Karin Hess. Thousand Oaks, CA: Corwin, www.corwin.com. Reproduction authorized only for the local school site or nonprofit organization that has purchased this book.

GRADIENTS IN COMPLEXITY:
Text Complexity Rubric for (Literary) Texts

Literary Text Analyzed (author, date):

Overall Complexity Rating:

Notes:

	Simple Text [1]	Somewhat Complex Text [2]	Complex Text [3]	Very Complex Text [4]
Format Layout	☐ Consistent placement of text, regular word and line spacing, and/or large plain font ☐ Numerous illustrations that directly support and help interpret the written text ☐ Supportive signposting (e.g., chapter heading) and enhancements	☐ May have longer passages of uninterrupted text, often plain font ☐ A range of illustrations that support selected parts of the text ☐ Reduced signposting and enhancements	☐ Longer passages of uninterrupted text may include columns or other variations in layout, often smaller, more elaborate font ☐ A few illustrations that support the text OR include images that require some interpretation ☐ Minimal signposting or enhancements	☐ Very long passages of uninterrupted text that may include columns or other variations in layout, often small, densely packed print ☐ Minimal or no illustrations that support the text OR includes images or text layout that require deeper interpretation (e.g., symbolism or recursive reading) ☐ Integrated signposting conforming to literary devices; no enhancements
Purpose and Meaning	☐ Purpose usually stated explicitly in the title or in the beginning of the text (this is a story about . . .) ☐ One intended level of meaning or lesson ☐ Theme is obvious and revealed early in the text ☐ Common themes	☐ Purpose tends to be revealed early in the text, but may be conveyed with some subtlety ☐ More than one level of meaning, with levels clearly distinguished from each other ☐ Theme is clear and revealed early in the text, but may be conveyed with some subtlety ☐ More than one possible theme	☐ Purpose is implicit and may be revealed over the entirety of the text ☐ Several levels of meaning that may be difficult to identify or separate ☐ Theme(s) may be implicit or subtle, sometimes ambiguous, and revealed over the entirety of the text ☐ Universal themes or archetypes (e.g., the hero's journey)	☐ Purpose implicit or subtle, is sometimes ambiguous and revealed over the entirety of the text ☐ Several levels and competing elements of meaning that are difficult to identify or separate and interpret ☐ Theme(s) implicit or subtle, often ambiguous, and revealed over the entirety of the text ☐ Universal themes or competing archetypes (e.g., warrior vs. hero)
Structure & Discourse	☐ Discourse style and organization of the text is clear, chronological, and/or easy to predict or follow ☐ Connections between events or ideas are explicit and clear ☐ One primary text structure is evident (e.g., chronology)	☐ Organization of text may have two or more story lines or additional characters and is occasionally difficult to predict ☐ Connections among events or ideas are sometimes implicit or subtle ☐ Includes a main text structure with 1–2 embedded structures	☐ Organization of text may include subplots, time shifts, and more complex characters ☐ Connections among events or ideas are often implicit or subtle (e.g., flashback establishes chronology) ☐ Includes different text types (diary entry or news story within narrative) of varying complexity	☐ Organization of text is intricate with regard to elements (e.g., narrative viewpoint, time shifts, multiple characters, story lines/subplots, detail) ☐ Connections among events or ideas are implicit or subtle throughout the text ☐ Includes sustained complex text types and hybrid or nonlinear texts (story within a story)
Language Features	☐ Mainly short, simple sentences ☐ Simple, literal language; predictable ☐ Vocabulary is mostly familiar for grade level; frequently appearing words	☐ Simple and compound sentences with some more complex constructions ☐ Mainly literal, common-use language ☐ Some unfamiliar or context-dependent, multiple meaning or precise words	☐ Many complex sentences with increased subordinate phrases and clauses ☐ Some figurative language or literary devices ☐ Includes much academic vocabulary and some domain-specific (content) vocabulary, precise language	☐ Many complex sentences, often containing nuanced details or concepts ☐ Much figurative language–or use of literary devices (metaphor, analogy, connotative language, literary allusion, etc.) ☐ Includes extensive academic and domain-specific (content) vocabulary, and possibly archaic language
Bk Knowledge Demands	☐ Minimal assumed personal experience or background knowledge needed ☐ Simple, straightforward ideas	☐ Some assumed personal experience and/or knowledge (e.g., cultural or historical) or ideas ☐ Both simple and more complex ideas	☐ Much assumed personal experience and/or explicit references to cultural, historical, literary, or political knowledge ☐ A range of recognizable ideas and challenging concepts or themes	☐ Extensive, demanding, assumed personal experience and implied cultural, historical, literary, or political knowledge ☐ Many new ideas, perspectives, and/or complex, challenging concepts

© Hess & Hervey (2010). Tools for Examining Text Complexity, in Hess, K. (2017). *A local assessment toolkit to support deeper learning: Guiding school leaders in linking research with classroom practice.* Permission to reproduce is given only when authorship is fully cited [karinhessvt@gmail.com].

Available for download at **resources.corwin.com/HessToolkit** and **www.karin-hess.com/free-resources**

Copyright © 2018 by Corwin. All rights reserved. Reprinted from *A Local Assessment Toolkit to Promote Deeper Learning: Transforming Research into Practice* by Karin Hess. Thousand Oaks, CA: Corwin, www.corwin.com. Reproduction authorized only for the local school site or nonprofit organization that has purchased this book.

III. The Importance of Teaching About Text Structures

Text Structures are the internal organizational structures used within paragraphs or longer texts, appropriate to genre and purpose. Research in literacy learning over the past two decades indicates that (a) an understanding of various text structures and their purposes enhances students' ability to comprehend what is read, and (b) some text structures are more easily learned and understood before other more complex structures (Hess, 2008c).

> *The benefits of text structure instruction for reading comprehension have strong empirical support. Research also supports the causal relationship between text structure instruction and improvement in composition skills.*
> –Dickson, Simmons, and Kame'enui, 1998

What the research says about text structure . . .

- Knowledge about the ways different types of text are structured and the ways these structures reveal the organization and interweaving of the author's ideas have been shown to influence *comprehension, memory, and writing and composition skills*.

- *Proficient readers* use awareness of text structures to understand key points of the text. When they are asked to recall what they have read, their summaries reflect the text organization.

- *Less experienced (novice) readers*, apparently unaware of text structures, have difficulty organizing and prioritizing text information. Often, students who can follow a typical narrative are bewildered by expository text structures.

- *Expository texts* often rely on scientific discourse, characterized by (a) complex sentences containing multiple embedded clauses, (b) verbs that have been turned into nouns representing large disciplinary concepts, and (c) Latin and Greek derived vocabularies.

- When students are taught to identify text structures, through use of such supports as graphic organizers, writing frames, text pattern signals, or text previewing, their *comprehension* increases.

- *Use of graphic organizers and writing templates or frames* help readers to identify relationships between and among ideas: to organize information, to identify how facts relate to main ideas, and to retain information.

- When retelling stories in narrative texts, *diverse learners* (students with learning disabilities) appear to recall less information than their normally achieving counterparts. They display difficulty understanding characters in stories (e.g., interactions, motivations) and making inferences.

- When reading content area texts, *diverse learners* have difficulty distinguishing between relevant and irrelevant information, identifying interrelationships between main ideas, organizing information, and memorizing and retaining isolated facts.

- *Explicit text structure* facilitates reading comprehension, yet many textbooks are poorly organized or fail to be explicit. Well-presented text enables readers to identify relevant information, including main ideas and relations between and among ideas. General education students (elementary through college) demonstrate difficulty analyzing main ideas of textbooks, especially when main ideas are implied rather than clearly stated.

- Well-structured expository text facilitates *understanding of main ideas* rather than facts.

Types of paragraphs and text structures

Generally speaking, the text structures below are *presented in order of increasing complexity*, although this is NOT meant to be a linear sequence. Other factors, such as explicitness of ideas presented, structural and semantic cues in text, length of text, vocabulary "load," level of reasoning required to understand ideas presented, and the reader's "knowledge of the world" also influence overall complexity and comprehension of text.

1. *Sequence (Process) Structure*—In this pattern, steps or phases of a process or project are specified without cause–effect relationships being implied. A recipe or procedure for a science investigation would be examples of differing complexity.

2. *Time Order–Chronology*—This pattern is found in most narrative texts, where the plot unfolds over time. More complex texts use literary devices such as flashback and foreshadowing to implicitly establish time order or chronology.

3. *Events–Enumeration–Description Structure*—This pattern usually covers a larger piece of writing rather than a single paragraph. An introductory paragraph is provided which states the topic and facilitates the listing or elaboration of important descriptions, characteristics, or attributes.

4. *Definition Structure*—Typically this pattern includes a "definition" and examples of class membership or type, attributes, and functions. It may also include the parts and the relationship between the parts or structure and function. In some instances, it will include ways something is similar to or different from other things.

5. *Compare–Contrast Structure*—This pattern shows similarities and dissimilarities between objects, actions, ideas, or processes. Headings and subheadings generally provide extra support and signals to readers about this structure. Often one paragraph is dedicated to similarities and another to differences.

"Top-level Structures" require a more holistic understanding of ideas presented.

6. *Cause–Effect (Antecedent–Consequence) Structure*—Unlike the sequence pattern, this pattern carries the implication that the effect is produced by a specific cause or that the consequences follow from the specified antecedents. This might be found in a discussion of science investigation results or historical articles linking multiple causes and effects.

7. *Problem–Solution (Hypothetical) Structure*—This pattern may follow a number of different forms. At one extreme, the problem and solution are labeled as such. At the other extreme, the pattern is a series of questions and answers that may or may not lead to a resolution of the problem or issue.

8. *Proposition–Support (Persuasion)*—This is similar to problem–solution, although arguments and counterarguments are both presented in support of a thesis statement.

9. *Judgment–Critique Structure*—This pattern uses a set of topic-specific criteria to evaluate information or ideas that have been presented. Often discourse style (e.g., humor, satire) affects the complexity and understanding of this type of text.

10. *Inductive–Deductive Structure*—There are subtle differences between these two structures, which apply elements of enumeration and definition structures. A deductive structure first presents a generalization or definition and then follows it with specific examples; conversely, an inductive structure presents illustrations and examples and then moves the reader to draw a conclusion from the examples presented. These structures are often embedded within cause–effect, proposition–support, and judgment–critique structures.

IV. Sample Instructional Strategies for Teaching About Text Structures

STRATEGY 1: Providing Frames to Build a Schema for Each Text Structure

A simple way to introduce each text structure is to have students use common signal words for a structure and a "frame" (see example below, also available for download from **resources.corwin.com/HessToolkit**) to create short texts. Over time, students will be able to create their own text structure examples and revise first drafts, expanding their use of appropriate signal words and semantic cues.

Writing Practice With Compare–Contrast Structure

SIGNAL WORDS FOR COMPARE-CONTRAST TEXT STRUCTURE

although	but	If . . . then	same as
as opposed to	conversely	in contrast	similar to
as well as	different from, differ	in fact	whereas
alike	Either/or	instead of	while
also	for example	not only . . . but also	yet
both	however	on the other hand	

Sample frame for writing using a compare–contrast structure:

_____ and _____ are similar, but also different in several ways. First, they are both _____

_____, as well as _____.

Also, they both _____.

Although there are alike, they are also different in some ways. For example, _____ _____, while _____ _____. Another way they are different is _____ _____.

My conclusion is that they are more (different or similar) because _____

STRATEGY 2: Using Graphic Organizers to Analyze or Compose Texts

- *Instructional Support:* How could you graphically depict the different text structures? When introducing a graphic organizer, "match" the specifics of the graphic to the text or passage example you are using. For example, if there are four steps in the process, don't give students a generic graphic organizer with five boxes. Begin with text-specific organizers, next move to helping students adapt the organizer for different situations and texts, and later encourage students to generalize and transfer use of graphic organizers for note-taking when reading or as a prewriting activity for planning ideas for written responses.

- *Assessment:* Ask students to graphically organize central ideas and supporting information in a text passage to assess their understanding of how information is connected. Ask students to use information from the text to "fill in" graphic organizers to assess their comprehension. A key to conceptual understanding when using graphic organizers is to write how or why they are connected (e.g., this "leads to" or this "was caused by" or this "describes" that).

STRATEGY 3: Using Text Signals to Analyze and Interpret Intended Meanings

- *Instructional Support:* Take some time to find different text passage types that can be used for instructional purposes to illustrate text signals and text structures. Newspapers are a good source for event and proposition–support texts (editorials). Short magazine articles are often good sources of text examples for events, proposition–support, cause–effect, and problem–solution text structures. Instruction manuals, game rules, and science experiments and procedures provide good models for sequence text structures. Subject-specific texts are filled with examples of description, event, enumeration, compare–contrast, and problem–solution text passages.

- *Assessment:* Ask students to identify the text structure of a passage and provide text-based support for their determination of that structure. Support for responses would include text signals used, transitional devices (numbering, bullets, white space, etc.), and the organizational patterns of the text.

STRATEGY 4: Examining How Text Features and Text Structures Support Meaning

- *Instructional Support:* Take some time to find different text types that can be used for instructional purposes to illustrate text features and their purposes within text structures. Identify texts with pictures that have captions that ADD new information to the written text. Identify semantic cues that signal text structures.

- *Assessment:* Ask students to identify the text structure of a passage and provide text-based support for their determination of that structure. Support for responses would include text signals, transitional devices and their purposes (numbering, bullets, white space, etc.), text features (headings, bold text, etc.), the organizational patterns of the text, and semantic cues. Have students use sticky notes to annotate a text's features and describe each feature's use or purpose in supporting that text's meaning.

STRATEGY 5: Building Anchor Charts With Students for Each Structure Studied

As seen in the completed text structure charts on the following pages, text structures are defined with students using classroom examples of text types, text features, signal words, and semantic cues (phrases found in key sentences, such as explicit topic sentences and thesis statements). Ten text structures, generally ordered by increasing complexity, are listed in the charts. Anchor charts such as these provide informal scaffolding in the classroom throughout the school year in support of both reading and writing. The examples can also guide development of discussion and test questions.

10 INCREASINGLY COMPLEX TEXT STRUCTURES

SEQUENCE–PROCEDURE	TIME ORDER–CHRONOLOGY	ENUMERATION–DESCRIPTION–EVENT	DEFINITION	COMPARE–CONTRAST
Describes a rule, procedure, or recipe. Lists steps to follow in specific order to complete a task or to make something. EXAMPLES: rules to follow (e.g., math, decoding) to more complex tasks, such as science data collection or research steps.	An event or plot unfolds over time. More complex texts use literary devices, such as flashback foreshadowing, or dates, visual timelines, or graphs to establish or imply time order. EXAMPLES: Narrative and historical texts and articles to inform.	An object, person, place, concept, or event is described using data, sensory features, and precise characteristics. Longer texts also apply chronology, definition. EXAMPLES: Story settings, paragraphs that introduce topic, elaborate on ideas, summarize or conclude.	A definition is followed by uses, description, or examples based on attributes or functions (types, groupings). More narrow and specific than description. May include domain-specific word relationships, synonym–antonym.	Describes how two or more objects, actions, or processes, for example, are alike and different. Each paragraph or section applies less complex structures to illustrate similar, contrasting, or summary ideas.

SIGNAL WORDS, TEXT FEATURES, AND SEMANTIC CUES TYPICALLY USED WITH EACH TEXT STRUCTURE

After, At the same time, Before, Finally, First, Following that step, Last, Next, Now, Second, Then, Third, Simultaneously "This is how to . . ." **Look for** bullets, numbering, outlining, white space, arrows, diagrams, for example.	Afterward, As, At last, Before, Earlier, Finally, Following that, Initially, Later on, Meanwhile, Much later, Next, Then, Not long after, Now, On (date), Previously, Soon after, Suddenly, The next day, When **Look for** white space, subheadings, chapter titles, dates.	Also, Besides, First of all, For instance, For one thing, In fact, Such as . . . , To begin with, An example of this, To illustrate this "This article describes . . ." **Look for** the topic subheadings, visuals.	Also called . . . , An example is, Another word for this is . . . , Belongs to this . . . group, Characteristics include . . . , For instance, In fact, Such as . . . , Is illustrated or used when, Is the opposite of, Means . . . **Look for** definitions embedded in text after bolded terms, inset text, footnotes, diagram, or glossary.	Alike, Also, Although, As opposed to, As well as, Both, But, Conversely, Different from, Either . . . or . . . , For example, However, In contrast, In fact, Instead, On the other hand, Same as, Similar to, Not only . . . but also, Yet **Look for** T-charts, subheadings.

PROMPTS FOR UNDERSTANDING INFORMATION IN THE TEXT

What do you have to do first? Next? Do you need special materials or equipment? Do the steps always happen in this order? Are there specific things to be careful of?	What led up to . . . ? What helped you to develop a timeline of events? Which event was the turning point?	What is being described? How is it being described (what does it look like, how does it work, what does it do, etc.)? What is most important to remember about it?	Is there more than one meaning for this? What in the text helped you to determine the intended meaning? Is the meaning literal or figurative as it is used?	What is being compared and why? In what ways are they alike or different? Are they more alike than different? Which is more . . . ?

"TOP-LEVEL" STRUCTURES REQUIRE MORE TEXT AND A DEEPER, MORE HOLISTIC UNDERSTANDING OF IDEAS PRESENTED.				
CAUSE–EFFECT	**PROBLEM–SOLUTION**	**PROPOSITION–SUPPORT**	**JUDGEMENT–CRITIQUE**	**DEDUCTIVE–INDUCTIVE**
More complex than sequence or chronology. Cause is why something happens. Effect is what happens—the consequence. Sometimes multiple effects or causes are possible.	Narrative texts introduce problem or conflict facing the characters. Informational texts and articles explain why there is a problem, then offer one or more possible solutions.	Informational texts (e.g., speech, editorial) similar to problem–solution, although these include a thesis or claim to frame the side supported. An argument and counter-argument are developed or elaborated on using hard facts and evidence.	Uses a set of agreed-upon criteria to evaluate data, sources, or issues that have been presented (e.g., Is this food healthy? How do you rank these? Who is a great leader? Is there bias?).	Deductive: presents a generalization and follows it with examples. Inductive: gives examples and illustrations and asks the reader to draw conclusions or generalizations from them.
SIGNAL WORDS, TEXT FEATURES, AND SEMANTIC CUES TYPICALLY USED WITH EACH TEXT STRUCTURE				
According to, As a result, Because, Consequently, Effects of, For this reason, Furthermore, May be due to, Possible reason why, Since, So, Therefore, This led to, Thus Often include data, graphs, timelines, flowcharts.	According to, Consequently, May be due to, Raises the question . . . , The dilemma or puzzle is . . . , To solve this . . . One possible answer is . . . , One reason for the problem is . . . , Since, So, Therefore, Thus Often begins with a scenario, shocking facts, a question, or quote.	Although, As opposed to, As well as, Both . . . but, Consequently, Conversely, Either . . . or . . . , For example, However, If . . . then, In contrast, In fact, Instead, On the other hand, Similar to, Not only . . . but also, While, Unless, The facts show, To begin with, If . . . then, Yet	Although, As opposed to, As well as, Both . . . but, Conversely, Either . . . or, For example, However, If . . . then, In contrast, In fact, Instead, On the other hand, Similar to, Not only . . . but also, While, The facts show, Thus, Therefore, Unless, Yet	Alike, Also, Although, Another example, Conversely, Different from, For example, For instance, In contrast, In fact, Instead, Most members . . . , Similar Look for labeled diagrams, captions, flowcharts, subheadings.
PROMPTS FOR UNDERSTANDING INFORMATION IN THE TEXT				
What event happened first? What were the possible causes or results of . . . ? Can you find another source that supports this?	What is the problem? Why is this a problem? What is being done or can be done to solve the problem? What will happen if it is not solved?	What is the author claiming? Are the facts accurate? Are sources credible and valid? Can you find other sources that support either side?	What criteria are used? Are the criteria appropriate to content? Would most agree on using these criteria to make this judgment?	What do these have in common? Can you provide other examples? Can you show this visually (chart it)?

Available for download at **resources.corwin.com/HessToolkit**

Copyright © 2018 by Corwin. All rights reserved. Reprinted from *A Local Assessment Toolkit to Promote Deeper Learning: Transforming Research into Practice* by Karin Hess. Thousand Oaks, CA: Corwin, www.corwin.com. Reproduction authorized only for the local school site or nonprofit organization that has purchased this book.

V. Sample Text-Based Assessment Strategies

Several informal pre-, post-, or self-assessment strategies are included in this final section of Module 2. They are intended to encourage students to think, discuss, reflect on, and revise their thinking as they build depth and breadth of vocabulary or strategy use over time.

STRATEGY 6: Word Splash (pre-, post-, self-assessment)

A word splash presents several new (and perhaps unfamiliar) vocabulary words and phrases randomly across the page. A "question box" appears at the bottom of the page with a prompt.

As a preassessment, I like to ask: *What do you know NOW about . . . ? Answer this question using some or all of these words, making connections among them.*

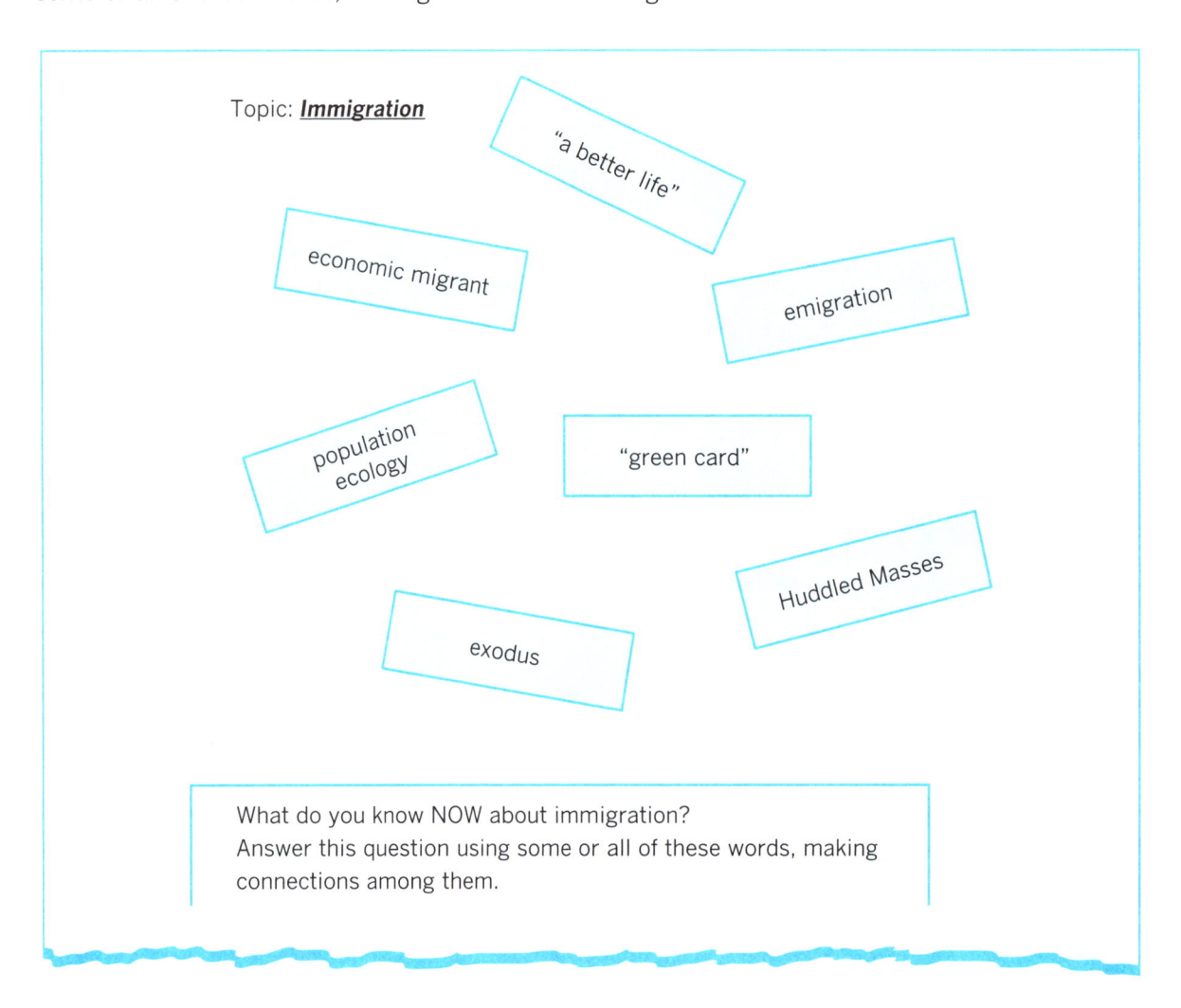

Topic: **Immigration**

"a better life"

economic migrant

emigration

population ecology

"green card"

Huddled Masses

exodus

What do you know NOW about immigration?
Answer this question using some or all of these words, making connections among them.

A full version of this tool can be found on page 127. It is also available for download from **resources.corwin.com/HessToolkit.**

As an informal preassessment, the teacher can easily determine common misconceptions the class has about the topic. This helps the teacher to decide on which terms to preteach and on which terms to focus readings, role plays, and discussions. During the unit of study, as students read, view, and discuss the topic (e.g., immigration), they revisit earlier responses and self-assess their progress as they deepen their understanding.

STRATEGY 7: What Do I Know About These Words? (pre-, post-, self-assessment)

This preassessment–self-assessment strategy is adapted from the work of Janet Allen (1999). As with the Word Splash (STRATEGY 6), this formative assessment asks students to begin by sorting words and phrases into (A) those they have never heard or don't know; (B) those they have heard, but are not sure of any meaning; (C) those for which they think they know at least one meaning; and (D) those for which they are sure they have a meaning in the context of the topic or text being studied. Using the same word list for immigration in the example below, this is what this peer- or self-assessment might look like.

What Do I Know About These Words?

Text/Topic: Immigration

1. Silently read the words listed below. Which column **A, B, C, or D** best describes <u>what you know now</u> about each word, phrase, or term. **Put an A, B, C, or D after each word, phrase, or term in the word list below.**
2. Next, discuss with a partner the meaning of each word, phrase, or term within the context of this topic or text. **Then list the words or phrases under the column that best describers your current understanding.**
3. Finally, share responses with your table group. Check your understanding after reading or using a dictionary or thesaurus. **Move words or phrases to a new column if you feel you now have a better understanding.**

A. Don't know at all—totally new to me; I need help!	B. Have seen or heard this—but not sure of the meaning	C. I think I know at least one definition—<u>provide a definition or take a guess</u>	D. I know the meaning for this context—<u>explain meaning of each word or phrase as use</u>

Word list:
"a better life"   escape
potato famine   emigration
economic migrant   population ecology
Hitler   "green card"
disparaging   exodus
Underground Railroad
huddled masses

Source: Adapted from Allen (1999).

Through several rounds of thinking and discussing with peers, students will typically "move" several terms from the left to the right columns. This allows the teachers to determine which, if any, words require preteaching and which words and phrases can best be acquired through further reading and viewing of sources and discussion. Students can also use a dictionary or thesaurus to check understanding.

STRATEGY 8: Bookmark—As-You-Read (formative assessment)

Codeveloped in 2005 with my Vermont colleague, Sue Biggam, for the VT Reads Summer Literacy Institute, this formative assessment is quite simple. Two examples are provided (see page 128) to illustrate different DOK levels for differing instructional purposes. On the left, an "as-you-read" bookmark at DOK 1, locating text features and describing the information that is contained in them. This might be used to scaffold to a later lesson. On the right is an open-ended template for use with a range of questions. (DOK 2 and DOK 3 questions are suggested.) This simple tool is an excellent way to help students to keep track of text evidence as they read and prepares them for discussion or writing.

STRATEGY 9: Card Pyramid (orally summarizing before writing)

I learned this research-based strategy when it was modeled in a 2011 workshop sponsored by the Neuhaus Center, in Austin, Texas. It's used to teach students how to summarize orally before they begin to write. Index cards are used to pull out key details from a text. The order of the cards links each subtopic with supporting details. Once cards have been created, students orally summarize key ideas from the text with a partner and then write their summaries. I've adapted it for units of study like the example below. A tool for planning for writing a summary or précis can be found on page 129. It is also available for download from **resources.corwin.com/HessToolkit**.

An example of modeling the creation of a card pyramid

1. The teacher reads the text, "Winter," as students follow along.

2. The teacher asks questions after reading the text together and fills in index cards with main idea, subtopics, and details. Together, they create a card pyramid as described here:

   What is this text about? Teacher writes "winter" on card #1 and places it at the top of the pyramid they are building.

   What interesting fact is in the introductory paragraph? Let's read it again [different hemispheres have different winter times]. Teacher draws a little globe on card #1 as a reminder of the interesting fact.

   What is the second paragraph talking about? [cold/weather] Teacher writes the subtopic on card #2 and places card under card #1 and to the left. "Let's put a '2' on the card."

   What are some supporting details for the second paragraph? What words can you find that are about cold or weather? [Write facts or words on card #3: *blizzard, ice fog, ice crystals, temperature*, etc.] Place card #3 under card #2.

   What is the third paragraph talking about? [winter activities] Teacher writes the subtopic on card #4 and places card under card #1 and to the right of card #2. "Let's put a '4' on that card."

   What are some supporting details for the third paragraph? What descriptions can you find that are about winter activities? [Write facts or words on card #5: *skiing, bobsledding*, for example.] Place card #5 under card #4.

3. Continue the same way with other with paragraphs.

4. The teacher says, *"Let's ORALLY summarize the passage about winter. Start with card 1, 2, 3, and so forth and see if we can recall the information."* (Oral summarizing can be done again in pairs. This repetition reinforces the underlying structure and involves EVERY student.)

1 MAIN IDEA OR TOPIC: WINTER			
2 winter weather	**4** winter activities	**6** what animals do	**8** plants in winter
3 blizzard, ice fog, ice crystals, temperature	**5** skiing, bobsledding	**7** migrate, hibernate, change fur color, store food	**9** adapt, some die, roots are protected

5. The teacher asks, *"If I wanted to write a report about why I think winter is the best season, could I use some of this information on the cards? Should I use all of this information? How would I decide what information to use?"*

6. Discuss how they have been selecting information to support a focus and how <u>all facts</u> would not be good to include. Identify some facts that they could elaborate on—what they could tell more about, such as a few activities they enjoy or an animal they observed.

STRATEGY 10: Pattern Folders—Emerging Themes (organizing text evidence)

This idea comes from the Teaching Channel, "Pattern Folders—A Literary Analysis Tool" (www.teachingchannel.org). In this lesson, a high school ELA teacher uses a strategy for helping students (a) gather text evidence, (b) organize the evidence into pockets on their pattern folders in order to see patterns or themes emerge, and (c) draw conclusions based on the text. When patterns are identified during reading (e.g., political, social), they are listed on "pockets." Inside each pocket are index cards with text-based notes and quotes. This is an excellent scaffolding strategy to help students organize their text evidence (DOK 2) to support conclusions about themes (DOK 3).

STRATEGY 11: Reading Strategy Use (self-monitoring while reading)

This is another self-monitoring assessment co-developed in 2004 with my Vermont colleague, Sue Biggam. Students document a variety of strategies used while reading and use notes during peer conferencing. A template can be found on page 130. It is also available for download from **resources.corwin.com/HessToolkit**.

STRATEGY 12: Sample Frames for Text-Based Questions (discussion and writing prompts)

Sometimes, we can get bogged down asking the same kinds of questions over and over. The table below provides a variety of ways to ask a DOK 3 or DOK 4 text-based question, all of which require analysis of text-based evidence. Consider providing several prompts as options for students to choose from to answer.

Table 2.2 Sample Frames for Prompts for Responding to Texts (With Intended DOK Levels)

Interpretive	Why do you think (character) felt (emotion) when (action/event)?
	Analyze evidence from the text (actions, interactions, dialogue) to support your response.
	(DOK 3)
Thematic	What can this (story/character/event) teach us about _____ (possible themes: conflict, kindness, gratitude)?
	Analyze evidence from the text to support your ideas.
	(DOK 3)
Visual and Imaginative	What did you find especially vivid? Analyze evidence from the text (use of imagery, word choice, figurative language) to describe what you imagined or pictured and how senses were evoked.
	(DOK 3)

(Continued)

Table 2.2 Sample Frames for Prompts for Responding to Texts (With Intended DOK Levels) (Continued)

Author's Craft	What are some interesting words or techniques used by the author to (e.g., develop characters, illustrate contrasts or comparisons, create suspense, lay out a chain of reasoning, advance the story or action)? Analyze evidence from the text to support your interpretations. (DOK 3)
Metacognitive	Did your opinion, awareness, or understanding (of character/event/history, etc.) change from the beginning to the end of the text? How? Why? Analyze evidence from the text to support your interpretations. (DOK 3)
Moral and Ethical	Was it right for (character/person) to _____ (action)? Why or why not? OR Who is the real hero or villain in this story? Why or why not? Analyze evidence from the text to support your interpretation. (DOK 3)
Intertextual (text to text)	Does this story or event remind you of another story or event? In what ways are they alike and different? Analyze evidence <u>from both texts</u> to support your comparisons. (DOK 4)
Analogical (text to self or text to world)	Can you describe or remember a similar situation in which the result or effect was different? Analyze evidence from <u>2 or more sources</u> to support your response. (DOK 4)
Elaborative	This character (character name) describes herself or himself as _____ (trait). After reading the story, poem, or play, how else would you describe her or him? Analyze evidence from the text (words/actions/interactions/motivations) to support your thinking. (DOK 3)

Source: Adapted from Hammond and Nessel (2011).

STRATEGY 13: Using Predetermined Assessment Targets to Develop Comparable Text-Based Questions

Tracking student progress over time relies heavily on maintaining consistency in what is being assessed, while asking for greater breadth and sophistication in the types of texts read, the reading strategies employed, and the increasing complexity of analyses used. In designing large-scale assessments, test specifications are written to identify the types of items that will be used (multiple choice, constructed response, short answer, performance tasks, etc.), as well as how test questions and prompts will be written. Assessment targets and task shells[5]

---

5. Using task shells for designing performance assessments is explained with examples in Module 3.

identify the content (standards) and intended rigor of the assessment items so that, for example, Grade 3 reading tests will test comparable content year after year. This strategy can also be applied to designing classroom assessments and will greatly enhance progress monitoring within one grade level and across school years.

On the following pages, I've included an example of how predetermined assessment targets for reading can be used to consistently assess the same standards and intended DOK levels. I've used these planning templates[6] with school-based teams to analyze text-based questions in their current curricula and to ensure that a range of questions will be used to assess deeper thinking. Because there are seven assessment targets for literary and seven "parallel" assessment targets for informational texts, the targets can be used in any content area where text-based questions are included for instruction and assessment. Targets are comparable across grade levels, even though standards identify slightly different specifics to be assessed. Using comparable targets across grade levels makes progress monitoring more efficient and useful.

A short summary of how the assessment targets can be used to track progress and target instruction is shown in Table 2.3.

Table 2.3 Using Consistent Assessment Targets to Track Progress and Target Instructional Needs

ASSESSMENT TARGETS	WHAT THEY ASSESS	WHAT YOUR ANALYSIS OF ASSESSMENT RESULTS MIGHT TELL YOU
1–3 (literary texts) Or 8–10 (informational texts)	Basic understanding of the text (key details, facts), ability to summarize the text, make basic inferences, and determine intended meaning of unfamiliar words and phrases used in context (Tier 2 words)	Students who do not do well with these questions might need strategic scaffolding supports, practice with decoding, work on expanding word and vocabulary analysis skills, or identifying which reading strategy works best for this kind of question or text. Students who do well on these types of questions are ready to read more complex texts, applying the same skills (applying assessment targets 1–3 or 8–10).
4–7 (literary texts) Or 11–14 (informational texts)	Deeper understanding and interpretations of texts: point of view, potential bias, use of text structures. Cross-text analyses, evaluating author's craft (e.g., determine intended meaning of literary devices and narrative strategies used) or message (e.g., discourse style, rhetorical devices)	Students who can read or get the gist of the text (targets 1–3) but are struggling with these questions would benefit from more small group discussion and developing depth and breadth of vocabulary. Students who do well on these types of questions are ready to read more complex texts or multiple texts, applying the same skills (assessment targets 4–7 or 11–14).

---

6. I originally developed the assessment target templates concept for the SBAC assessments (Hess et al., 2012).

To use the assessment targets planning templates for developing a range of text-based questions:

STEP 1: Begin by listing one or more texts at the top right side of the template.

STEP 2: Read or skim the text(s) and analyze key features you want to emphasize in the class discussion or assessment questions. Text complexity **TOOL #6** is useful for completing this step.

STEP 3: Review both the intended DOK levels and the content standards aligned with each assessment target, selecting your focus. Assessment targets align with and can assess several different standards, so it is important to decide which standard (or part) you will focus on for each question. CRM **TOOLS #1–#5D** can help when completing this step.

STEP 4: Generate possible questions. Determine if all seven targets will be used; or focus on only a few of them. For example, there may not be any text features, such as illustrations, subheadings, or captions (assessment targets 6 and 13) for writing questions. Decide which questions will be open-ended (constructed response, performance tasks) and how many score points you will give each question. Open-ended questions usually get more points than short-answer questions and assess deeper thinking (literary assessment targets 4–7 or informational assessment targets 11–14).

USING PREDETERMINED ASSESSMENT TARGETS: GRADE 3 LITERARY TEXT		
GRADE 3 READING LITERARY TEXTS—TYPES OF QUESTIONS	**UNDERLINED CONTENT (RELATED CC STANDARDS) SHOWS WHAT EACH ASSESSMENT QUESTION COULD ASSESS**	**SAMPLE TEXT-BASED QUESTIONS**
1. KEY DETAILS: Use explicit details and information from the text to support answers or basic inferences. Standards: RL-1, RL-3 (DOK 1, DOK 2)	Key Ideas and Details RL-1: Ask and answer questions to demonstrate understanding of a text, referring explicitly to the text as the basis for the answers. RL-3: Describe characters in a story (e.g., their traits, motivations, or feelings) and explain how their actions contribute to the sequence of events.	(DOK 1: locate or recall details) – Where does this story take place? – Which of these phrases best describes Sarah? (DOK 2: make inference) Why did _____ worry when _____?
2. CENTRAL IDEAS: Identify or summarize central ideas, key events, or the sequence of events presented in a text. Standards: RL-2 (DOK 2)	Key Ideas and Details RL-2: Recount stories, including fables, folktales, and myths from diverse cultures; determine the central message, lesson, or moral and explain how it is conveyed through key details in the text.	(DOK 2: show relationships) – Put these story events into correct sequence. – Which event (or action) led to _____ being rescued?

122 A Local Assessment Toolkit to Promote Deeper Learning

USING PREDETERMINED ASSESSMENT TARGETS: GRADE 3 LITERARY TEXT		
GRADE 3 READING LITERARY TEXTS—TYPES OF QUESTIONS	**UNDERLINED CONTENT (RELATED CC STANDARDS) SHOWS WHAT EACH ASSESSMENT QUESTION COULD ASSESS**	**SAMPLE TEXT-BASED QUESTIONS**
3. WORD MEANINGS: Determine intended meaning of words, including words with shades of meaning and words with multiple meanings, based on context, word relationships, word structure (e.g., common roots, affixes), or use of resources (e.g., beginning dictionary). Standards: RL-4; L-4, L-5c (DOK 1, DOK 2)	Craft and Structure RL-4: Determine the meaning of words and phrases as they are used in a text, distinguishing literal from nonliteral language. Vocabulary Acquisition and Use L-4: Determine or clarify the meaning of unknown and multiple-meaning words and phrases based on Grade 3 reading and content, choosing flexibly from a range of strategies. a. Use sentence-level context as a clue to the meaning of a word or phrase. b. Determine the meaning of the new word formed when a known affix is added to a known word (e.g., agreeable–disagreeable, comfortable–uncomfortable, heat–preheat). c. Use a known root word as a clue to the meaning of an unknown word with the same root (e.g., company, companion). d. Use glossaries or beginning dictionaries, both print and digital, to determine or clarify the precise meaning of key words and phrases. L-5c: Distinguish shades of meaning among related words that describe states of mind or degrees of certainty (e.g., knew, believed, suspected, heard, wondered).	(DOK 2: using context and definitions to determine meanings) – The word _____ has different meanings. Use the dictionary definitions (below) to choose the meaning of the word _____ as it is used in the sentence.
4. REASONING and EVALUATION: Use supporting evidence to interpret and explain inferences about character traits, motivations, feelings; point of view, author's lesson or message. Standards: RL-2, 3, 6 (DOK 3)	Key Ideas and Details RL-2: Recount stories, including fables, folktales, and myths from diverse cultures; determine the central message, lesson, or moral and explain how it is conveyed through key details in the text. RL-3: Describe characters in a story (e.g., their traits, motivations, or feelings) and explain how their actions contribute to the sequence of events. Craft and Structure RL-6: Distinguish their own point of view from that of the narrator or those of the characters	(DOK 3: support interpretation with explanation and text evidence) – What lesson did _____ learn as a result of _____? Use details and evidence from the text to support your response. – What kind of person was _____? Use details and evidence from the text to support your response. – Who is telling the story? Use details and evidence from the text to explain how you know.

(Continued)

(Continued)

USING PREDETERMINED ASSESSMENT TARGETS: GRADE 3 LITERARY TEXT		
GRADE 3 READING LITERARY TEXTS—TYPES OF QUESTIONS	**UNDERLINED CONTENT (RELATED CC STANDARDS) SHOWS WHAT EACH ASSESSMENT QUESTION COULD ASSESS**	**SAMPLE TEXT-BASED QUESTIONS**
5. ANALYSIS WITHIN OR ACROSS TEXTS: Specify or compare relationships across texts (e.g., literary elements, problem-solution, theme). Standards: RL-9[7] (DOK 2 or DOK 4)	Integration of Knowledge and Ideas RL-9: Compare and contrast the themes, settings, and plots of stories written by the same author about the same or similar characters (e.g., in books from a series).	**NOTE:** Students may be asked to read excerpts from two texts (e.g., paragraphs with character or setting descriptions taken from each text—DOK 2), rather than two full texts in the on-demand assessment. Comparing theme or plot would require reading the full or longer texts (DOK 4).
6. TEXT STRUCTURES AND FEATURES: Relate knowledge of text structures or text features (e.g., illustrations) to gain, interpret, explain, or connect information. Standards: RL-5, 7 (DOK 2)	Craft and Structure RL-5: Refer to parts of stories, dramas, and poems when writing or speaking about a text, using terms such as chapter, scene, and stanza; describe how each successive part builds on earlier sections. Integration of Knowledge and Ideas RL-7: Explain how specific aspects of a text's illustrations contribute to what is conveyed by the words in a story (e.g., create mood, emphasize aspects of a character or setting).	(DOK 2) What clue to solving the problem is provided in the illustration?
7. LANGUAGE USE: Interpret use of language by distinguishing literal from nonliteral meanings of words and phrases used in context. Standards: RL-4; L-5a (DOK 2)	Craft and Structure RL-4: Determine the meaning of words and phrases as they are used in a text, distinguishing literal from nonliteral language. Vocabulary Acquisition and Use L-5a: Distinguish the literal and nonliteral meanings of words and phrases in context (e.g., take steps).	(DOK 2) – When the author says _____ in the story or poem, what does she mean?
8. KEY DETAILS: Use explicit details and implicit information from the text to support answers or inferences about information presented. Standards: RI-1, RI-3 (DOK 1, DOK 2)	Key Ideas and Details RI-1: Ask and answer questions to demonstrate understanding of a text, referring explicitly to the text as the basis for the answers. RI-3: Describe the relationship between a series of historical events, scientific ideas or concepts, or steps in technical procedures in a text, using language that pertains to time, sequence, and cause-effect.	(DOK 2: explaining relationships) – Why is it important to _____ before doing this step? (procedure) – What is likely to happen if you don't remember to _____? – What caused _____ to happen? (news article)

---

7. When the standard requires reading more than one text, the assessment item is sometimes at DOK 2 and sometimes at a DOK 4 level.

USING PREDETERMINED ASSESSMENT TARGETS: GRADE 3 LITERARY TEXT

GRADE 3 READING LITERARY TEXTS—TYPES OF QUESTIONS	UNDERLINED CONTENT (RELATED CC STANDARDS) SHOWS WHAT EACH ASSESSMENT QUESTION COULD ASSESS	SAMPLE TEXT-BASED QUESTIONS
9. CENTRAL IDEAS: Identify or summarize central ideas, key events, or procedures and details that support them. Standards: RI-2 (DOK 2)	Key Ideas and Details RI-2: Determine the main idea of a text; recount the key details and explain how they support the main idea.	(DOK 2: identify central idea) — What is the main idea of this paragraph? (SR item with choices that include both details in the paragraph and at least two broader statements, one of which is the main idea, perhaps a paraphrase of the topic sentence)
10. WORD MEANINGS: Determine intended meaning of words, including domain-specific words and words with multiple meanings, based on context, word relationships, word structure (e.g., common roots, affixes), or use of resources (e.g., beginning dictionary, glossary). Standards: RI-4; L-4 (DOK 1, DOK 2)	Craft and Structure RI-4: Determine the meaning of general academic and domain-specific words and phrases in a text relevant to a Grade 3 topic or subject area. Vocabulary Acquisition and Use L-4: Determine or clarify the meaning of unknown and multiple-meaning words and phrases based on Grade 3 reading and content, choosing flexibly from a range of strategies. a. Use sentence-level context as a clue to the meaning of a word or phrase. b. Determine the meaning of the new word formed when a known affix is added to a known word (e.g., agreeable–disagreeable, comfortable–uncomfortable, care–careless). c. Use a known root word as a clue to the meaning of an unknown word with the same root (e.g., company, companion). d. Use glossaries or beginning dictionaries, both print and digital, to determine or clarify the precise meaning of key words and phrases.	DOK 1: word structure — How does adding "un" to the beginning of the word _____ change its meaning? DOK 1: word relationships—synonyms or antonyms — Which pair of words in this article means almost the same thing?
11. REASONING AND EVALUATION: Use supporting evidence to interpret and explain how information is presented or connected within or across texts (author's point of view, ideas and supporting details, relationships). Standards: RI-6, RI-8, RI-9 (DOK 3, DOK 4)	Craft and Structure RI-6: Distinguish their own point of view from that of the author of a text. Integration of Knowledge and Ideas RI-8: Describe the logical connection between particular sentences and paragraphs in a text (e.g., comparison, cause–effect, first/second/third in a sequence). RI-9: Compare and contrast the most important points and key details presented in two texts on the same topic.	(DOK 3: determine point of view using evidence from text) – Does the author support or agree with this claim: _____? Use details and evidence from the text to explain your response. (DOK 4: using multiple sources) – Which facts are supported in both texts?

(Continued)

(Continued)

USING PREDETERMINED ASSESSMENT TARGETS: GRADE 3 LITERARY TEXT		
GRADE 3 READING LITERARY TEXTS—TYPES OF QUESTIONS	**UNDERLINED CONTENT (RELATED CC STANDARDS) SHOWS WHAT EACH ASSESSMENT QUESTION COULD ASSESS**	**SAMPLE TEXT-BASED QUESTIONS**
12. ANALYSIS WITHIN OR ACROSS TEXTS: Specify, integrate, or compare information within or across texts (e.g., cause-effect, integrate information). Standards: RI-9 (DOK 2, DOK 3)	Integration of Knowledge and Ideas RI-9: Compare and contrast the most important points and key details presented in two texts on the same topic.	(DOK 2: compare information presented, locating details from text) – Use the fact sheet about frogs and the fact sheet about toads to complete the T-chart showing how they are alike and how they are different. (DOK 3: compare claims made on differing sides of an issue)
13. TEXT STRUCTURES AND FEATURES: Relate knowledge of text structures or text features (e.g., graphics, bold text, headings) to obtain, interpret, or explain information. Standards: RI-5, RI-7 (DOK 2)	Craft and Structure RI-5: Use text features and search tools (e.g., key words, sidebars, hyperlinks) to locate information relevant to a given topic efficiently. Integration of Knowledge and Ideas RI-7: Use information gained from illustrations (e.g., maps, photographs) and the words in a text to demonstrate understanding of the text (e.g., where, when, why, and how key events occur).	(DOK 2: interpret or compare visual information) – What information is provided in the caption, photo, or diagram that was NOT described in the text? (DOK 2: interpret visual or graphic information) – Use the timeline or table to answer this question: _____?
14. LANGUAGE USE: Interpret use of language by distinguishing literal from nonliteral meanings of words and phrases used in context. Standards: L-5a, L-5b (DOK 2, DOK 3)	Vocabulary Acquisition and Use L-5: Distinguish the literal and nonliteral meanings of words and phrases in context (e.g., take steps). L-5b: Identify real-life connections between words and their use (e.g., describe people who are friendly or helpful).	(DOK 3: interpret language use) – According to this article, what does "underground railroad" really mean? Use details and evidence from the text to support your response.

Source: Hess (2011c).

Additional grade-level planning worksheets for reading assessment targets can be found at **resources.corwin.com/HessToolkit**.

Word Splash

Topic: _____

_____?

Answer the question above using some or all of these words, making connections among them. What sources helped you to develop your answer?

AS-YOU-READ BOOKMARK ASSESSMENT

Name: _____

Text: _____

Author: _____

Text Type: _____

As you read, please note the following text features <u>and describe the information the features provide</u> (include page references).

☐ Headings/Subheadings
_____
_____
_____

☐ Graphs and Tables
_____
_____
_____

☐ Photos and Captions
_____
_____
_____

☐ Vocabulary and Terms (e.g., bold or italicized print)
_____
_____

☐ _____
_____
_____
_____

AS-YOU-READ BOOKMARK ASSESSMENT

Name: _____

Text: _____

Author: _____

Text Type: _____

As you read this text, please note text references (including page and paragraph) that will help you to answer this question:

_____
_____
_____
_____
_____
_____
_____
_____
_____
_____
_____
_____
_____
_____

Available for download at **resources.corwin.com/HessToolkit**

Copyright © 2018 by Corwin. All rights reserved. Reprinted from *A Local Assessment Toolkit to Promote Deeper Learning: Transforming Research into Practice* by Karin Hess. Thousand Oaks, CA: Corwin, www.corwin.com. Reproduction authorized only for the local school site or nonprofit organization that has purchased this book.

Card Pyramid
Planning for Writing a Summary or Précis

1. Main idea or topic:

   Interesting fact ("grabber"):

2. New idea–Subtopic	4. New idea–Subtopic	6. New idea–Subtopic	8. New idea–Subtopic
3. **Details, facts, examples** that support the idea above	5. **Details, facts, examples** that support the idea above	7. **Details, facts, examples** that support the idea above	9. **Details, facts, examples** that support the idea above
Which details will I elaborate on? Cross out details that will NOT be used in my summary.	Which details will I elaborate on? Cross out details that will NOT be used in my summary.	Which details will I elaborate on? Cross out details that will NOT be used in my summary.	Which details will I elaborate on? Cross out details that will NOT be used in my summary.

10. Conclusions

Available for download at **resources.corwin.com/HessToolkit**

Copyright © 2018 by Corwin. All rights reserved. Reprinted from *A Local Assessment Toolkit to Promote Deeper Learning: Transforming Research into Practice* by Karin Hess. Thousand Oaks, CA: Corwin, www.corwin.com. Reproduction authorized only for the local school site or nonprofit organization that has purchased this book.

Response to Text With Strategy Use

STRATEGIES THAT HELPED WHILE READING	PAGE(S) OF QUOTE OR EVIDENCE USED:
❑ Visualizing ❑ Breaking unfamiliar words apart; using a glossary ❑ Making and using a graphic organizer ❑ Determining the central idea ❑ Annotating parts: summarizing, noting details ❑ Rereading ❑ Connecting information in the text (compare–contrast, cause–effect, fact–opinion) ❑ Making personal connections ❑ Making connections to another text, broader ideas, and themes ❑ Another strategy?	The question or my focus: My response, with quote or evidence:

Available for download at **resources.corwin.com/HessToolkit**

Copyright © 2018 by Corwin. All rights reserved. Reprinted from *A Local Assessment Toolkit to Promote Deeper Learning: Transforming Research into Practice* by Karin Hess. Thousand Oaks, CA: Corwin, www.corwin.com. Reproduction authorized only for the local school site or nonprofit organization that has purchased this book.

MODULE 3: WHAT DOES THIS TEST REALLY MEASURE?

Designing and Refining High-Quality Assessments for Deeper Learning

3.1 What Is a High-Quality Assessment?

When I recently visited The New York Performance Standards Consortium website, this quote caught my eye: *"Learning is complex. Assessments should be, too."* There is a lot of meaning packed into those two little sentences. For me, it confirmed two key beliefs: First, traditional paper and pencil assessments have never really captured the depth, breadth, or complexity of what students might actually be able to learn if we provide the opportunity. And second, because they can be scored efficiently and reliably, we've settled for using (or perhaps overusing) a less complex approach to testing, instead of taking the time needed to teach and assess true depth of understanding. I explored the site further because I wanted to find out what performance assessment looked like in these schools. What were the expectations for students and what was their underlying philosophy about assessment and their assessment systems? In a related article about one school in the Consortium, I found this scenario describing one student's assessment experience.

> Brittany, an 18-year-old senior at the Urban Academy Laboratory High School in Manhattan, is sitting in a room with three teachers and a scientist unaffiliated with the school. She looks and sounds confident as she describes an aroma chemistry experiment that she recently completed.
>
> "I was interested in learning how the ratio of ethanol and water impacts the scent, color, and consistency of a frankincense extract," she begins. She then explains her methods—the measurements, the movement of substances from vial to vial, the evaporation and distillation processes. This is followed by questions and it is quickly evident that Brittany understands the scientific method. Her openness, poise, and maturity are impressive. "I got results I did not expect," she admits. She then zooms in on a possible glitch. "I should have used purified or distilled water rather than tap water since there may have been contaminants in the tap water. Next time, I will know that."
>
> After her presentation, the committee reviews her write-up of the experiment—complete with numerous charts and graphs—and several revisions are suggested. "You need to add the 'why,'" one teacher recommends. "Is there some bigger meaning to your study? That is, beyond just learning the subject, is this information important for other people?"
>
> Brittany's hands move rapidly as she jots down her assessors' ideas and she leaves the room as soon as the meeting is over. She then sits at a computer and starts to input changes. But the typing does not suppress her joy: She is grinning from ear to ear, visibly proud of her successful defense and the critical reception it received.
>
> "Were you nervous?" I ask. "No, I'm used to speaking in public and defending my ideas," she says. "That was my sixth defense. I completed my math, literature, creative arts, social studies and criticism defenses earlier."

Source: Bader, 2014. Reproduced with permission.

> I know what you might be thinking: Our students *would* never—*could* never—do assessments like those. Before you dismiss this as a possibility in your school, read the scenario again and try to identify anything embedded in the example that you think is a feature of a high-quality assessment.

I'm sure you've included some things on your list that are also cited on the Consortium website as part of their assessment philosophy. A partial list of Consortium components is shown below. Compare them to your brainstorm. You may also be making connections with what's been discussed in Module 1 about characteristics of cognitive rigor. (A complete list of the Consortium's seven components for a performance-based assessment system can be found at performanceassessment.org/performance/pcomponents.html.)

How do the NY Performance Standards Consortium Schools assess their students?

Active learning

- Discussion-based classrooms
- Project-based assignments
- Original research and experiment design
- Student choice embedded in course work

Strategies for corrective action

- Feedback on written work
- Student–teacher conferences

Multiple ways for students to express and exhibit learning

- Writing—literary essays, research papers, playwriting, poetry, lyrics
- Oral presentations—discussions, debate, poetry reading, dramatic presentation, external presentations
- Artistic renderings—sculpture, painting, drawing, photography

Graduation-level performance-based tasks aligned with Learning Standards

- Analytic literary essay
- Social studies research paper
- Original science experiment
- Application of higher-level mathematics

External evaluators of student work

- Experts in various disciplines (such as writers, scientists, historians)

Clearly there is a continuum of what a high-quality performance assessment can look like, from least complex to much more complex. Brittany's chemistry example would be placed at the far right end on this continuum—a student-initiated performance assessment requiring in-depth engagement with content, extended time, and related instruction embedded in courses to help prepare her for designing and carrying out her assessment. So what else is along this continuum of performance assessment? Probably many assessment-related terms and types begin to come to mind, including the following:

- *Short diagnostic tasks* and formative assessments such as running records in reading, "free writes" during a literacy block, or theater games that demonstrate acting techniques
- *Course-embedded performance tasks* that require one or more class periods to complete, such as mathematics problem-solving activities, open-ended writing or research prompts, arts-based explorations, scenario role-plays, and science investigations
- *Extended multistage assessments* that may take as long as a semester to research and develop, such as culminating group projects at the end of a unit of study, student-designed expeditionary learning activities, community service projects, and in-depth analyses of case studies in science or social studies.

| Short, diagnostic, formative tasks | Course-embedded formative, interim, and summative performance tasks | Extended, multistage interim and summative assessments |

These are just a few examples of performance assessments we can find in classrooms. In the real world, our lives are filled with them—"authentic" performance assessments like learning to ride a bike, getting a driver's license, developing a resume, interviewing for a job, planning logistics for a family reunion, or diagnosing a student's learning needs and delivering an intervention.

I like to introduce the concept of performance assessment this way:

> Quickly brainstorm a variety of performance assessments that happen in or outside of the classroom.
>
> Table groups then select one of the examples on their list and collaboratively answer several questions:
>
> - What skills and concepts are being measured with this assessment task?
> - How can best or excellent performance be differentiated from poor performance?
> - What makes this a performance assessment?
>
> Use the examples generated to derive what the research says about what all high-quality assessments have in common.
>
> Let's generalize. No matter what performance-based example you chose, how would you complete or respond to the following?
>
> - With regard to skills and concepts assessed in any performance assessment, _____.
> - What makes something a performance assessment?
> - The kind of evidence that will distinguish poor from exemplary performances is determined by _____.
> - What makes any task a "good" (high-quality) performance assessment?

The discussion about high-quality assessment can generally be summarized this way:

With regard to skills and concepts assessed,

- the assessment task requires application of multiple skills and concepts in a new or novel context (transfer);
- the skills and concepts have been taught and practiced prior to this assessment (practice drills *and* scrimmages);
- the task requires an authentic, focused application of the skills and concepts, and is not intended to assess other unrelated skills.

What makes something a performance assessment?

- There are usually multiple steps or parts to completing the task, which result in producing a product or observable performance (e.g., gathering and processing information, deciding how to deliver the final product or performance, self-monitoring progress).
- The task requires the student to actually *do* something, not simply describe how to do it (e.g., swimming the length of the pool versus telling you "I know how to swim").
- The student understands the relevance of applying these skills or concepts in a real-world situation (**validity**).
- The task engages the student in making decisions as to how skills and concepts should be applied (while playing the game).
- Performance assessments can assess varying levels of cognitive demand (DOK) and may be used formatively or summatively.
- The task is designed to be "**authentic,**" having a real-world context and authentic audience.

The kind of evidence that will distinguish poor from exemplary performances:

- There is a shared understanding (by teacher and students) about what an exemplary performance or product would, or could, look like (validity).
- A scoring guide or rubric articulates the criteria and indicators that will be used consistently to evaluate this and similar performances or products (reliability).
- Multiple performance levels in a scoring rubric illustrate how a student might progress from being a beginner (novice) to being proficient at completing tasks like these.
- Both the content knowledge (skills/concepts) and performance expectations (cognitive demand) are articulated in the task directions and illustrated by examples seen in student work. The use of a scoring rubric with benchmarked work samples ensures both reliability and agreement in scoring and task validity (assesses what it is intended to assess).
- Common performance assessments, used across different classrooms and schools, provide administration guidelines to teachers in order to maintain fidelity as to how assessments are intended to be implemented. PLC teams use student work analysis and calibration practice with common assessments to learn how to consistently interpret how students are doing and how to best support their learning needs.

> **What We Know (from the research) About High-Quality Assessment**
>
> It is defined by agreed-upon standards and expectations.
>
> It measures the individual's learning and can take different forms or use different formats.
>
> It measures the effectiveness of instruction and appropriateness of curriculum.
>
> It is transparent.
>
> - Students know what is expected of them and how they will be assessed.
> - Assessment criteria are clear and training is provided to educators and reviewers or raters.
> - It communicates information effectively to students, teachers, parents, administration, and the public at large.

Simply stated, a "good" (high-quality) performance assessment has these characteristics:

1. Clarity of expectations in completing the task and how the results will be used
2. Alignment to the intended content expectations (skills and concepts)
3. Reliability of scoring leading to valid interpretation of results
4. Attention to the intended rigor (in task directions and scoring guides)
5. Opportunities for student engagement and decision making
6. Flexible enough to provide opportunities to make the assessment "fair" and unbiased for all students to demonstrate what they have learned
7. Linked to ongoing instruction (opportunity to learn)

In designing PLC **TOOLS #9 and #10**—used for developing and analyzing assessment quality—I took into account what the research says about high-quality assessment and turned it into teacher-friendly language to create two useable protocols. These tools have been piloted and refined across many states to make them as efficient as possible when developing new assessments or reviewing assessments currently in use. Later in Module 3, I provide guidance about how to create validation teams, an ongoing review process for examining and giving feedback on locally designed assessments. PLC **TOOLS #9 and #10** are often combined with PLC **TOOL #11** (Rubric Quality Review) and PLC **TOOL #12** (Analyzing Student Work) when developing and piloting new assessments, especially performance assessments.

3.2 Assessment Purposes and Use: Formative, Interim, and Summative

At this point in our exploration of assessments of deeper learning, I'd like to clarify some of the terms[1] that have already been mentioned, beginning with formative, interim, and summative uses of assessment. It's important to understand that performance assessments can be used

---

1. Additional information about assessment-related terminology can be found in Appendix I.

formatively, summatively, or as an interim assessment, depending on where students are in the learning cycle. For example, a less complex performance task might be used as a preassessment to identify the prerequisite skills and understandings students already have acquired that they can build upon and which skills will need to be explicitly taught. A more complex performance task, assessing the same core content and skills (e.g., how to write an argument, collecting and interpreting data) can be used summatively at the end of the unit of study as a postassessment. Yes, I've just claimed that a preassessment does not look exactly like the postassessment, especially if you are measuring progress on multi-dimensional tasks, such as using a combination of complex skills applied to a new context. To prove my point, think back to preassessments you've taken or given to your students. If they were very complex tasks, probably no one knew much of anything before instruction. For a preassessment to be useful, you need to get results that you can build upon or react to as a teacher. Pre- and postassessments that assess exactly the same content work best when assessing a more narrow scope—unidimensional skills or knowledge—such as spelling words, vocabulary terms, and number facts. My approach to designing better pre- and postassessments will be discussed later in the Module, using task shells to create increasingly more complex tasks as pre-, mid-, and postassessments.

Now to clarify some assessment terminology . . .

> **Formative Assessment:** Formative assessment is as much a process or instructional strategy as it is a measurement tool. Also known as "short-cycle" assessment, formative assessment practices are embedded in instruction and used frequently during a teaching–learning cycle (e.g., to preassess readiness, to target mastery of specific skills, to check conceptual understanding).
>
> **Benchmark/Interim Assessment:** Benchmark (also called interim) assessments are generally standards-based and designed to align with a pacing calendar and grade-level content standards. They are typically used to measure progress on large units of district curriculums and to determine which students are "on track" to meet specified annual academic goals. Interim assessments are designed to inform decisions at both the classroom level and beyond, such as at the school, grade, or district level. Thus, they may be given at the classroom level to provide information for the teacher; but the results can also be meaningfully aggregated and reported at a broader level.
>
> **Summative Assessment:** A summative assessment is given at the end of a period of learning (e.g., unit of study, end of semester) and generalizes how well a student has performed. Summative assessments are typically used for grading and making high-stakes decisions.

We often simply use the assessments that come with a particular curricular program or what's been used in the past without examining it for the content and cognitive demand being measured and how the test results will be used. Before deciding to adopt or create assessments, first consider how the assessment results will be used and how each particular assessment can contribute to a larger **body of evidence**—work samples that will show to what degree a student is making progress toward achieving proficiency. Below are common purposes for the assessments.

> *Screening all students*—generally include standardized assessments with a broad scope of lower-level (DOK 1, 2) skills or tasks; intended to determine if further diagnostic testing or observation may be needed
>
> *Diagnosing individual student needs*—typically used after a screening tool identifies potential learning needs; generally diagnostic tools have many items with a narrow focus (e.g., identifying letters and sounds); strongest examples include eliciting student explanations that uncover thinking and reasoning related to skills demonstrated (DOK 3), as well as acquisition of basic skills and concepts (DOK 1, 2)

Monitoring progress—may be used both formatively and summatively; best examples are aligned with ongoing instruction and have a mix of item types, tasks, and range of cognitive demand (DOK 1–4); usually include common benchmark/interim assessments at specified periodic times during the school year (e.g., performance tasks each quarter, monthly running records)

Informing instruction—most closely aligned with current instruction and used formatively, not for grading; best examples are embedded in ongoing instruction and have a mix of item types, tasks, and range of cognitive demand (DOK 1–4); most useful when student work analysis is used to examine misconceptions, common errors, conceptual reasoning, or transfer of learning to new contexts

Communicating student or program outcomes—disaggregated data from these assessments is generally used summatively; include interpretations of performance from a combination of assessments (DOK 2–4), given over time to develop individual learning profiles, to determine and report on student or group progress (proficiency), or to evaluate program effectiveness

Many states and school districts have attempted to illustrate the differences among assessment uses and purposes by creating visuals along a continuum. In 2016, the Wisconsin Department of Public Instruction published Wisconsin's Strategic Assessment Systems Foundational Charts, which includes assessment types broken out by several features of all assessments: purposes for which they are designed; focus and scope; where in the system data are generated; and use of assessment data. Figure 3.1 illustrates the Wisconsin version of how to think about differences among assessment types in the local assessment system (Wisconsin, 2016, p. 4).

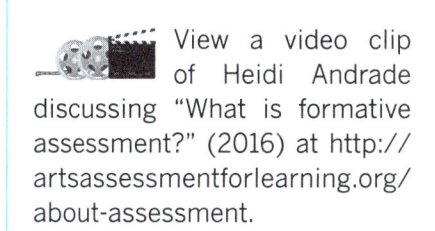

> View a video clip of Heidi Andrade discussing "What is formative assessment?" (2016) at http://artsassessmentforlearning.org/about-assessment.

Figure 3.1 What Are the Differences Among Assessments in a Comprehensive Local Assessment System?

Comprehensive Assessment System

By Type: What are the differences between assessment types within a comprehensive system?

FORMATIVE	INTERIM	SUMMATIVE
...ASSESSMENTS ARE DESIGNED TO...		
Quickly inform instruction	Benchmark and monitor progress	Evaluate learning
...BY PROVIDING...		
Specific, immediate, actionable feedback	Multiple data points across time	Cumulative snapshots
...THROUGH...		
Daily, ongoing instructional strategies	Periodic diagnostic/common assessments	Standardized assessments
...THAT ARE...		
Student/Classroom-centered	Grade-level/School-centered	School/District/State-centered
...AND THAT ANSWER...		
What comes next for student learning?	What progress are students making? Is the program working?	Are our students meeting the standards?

Source: Excerpted from Wisconsin's Strategic Assessment Systems (2016, p. 4) with permission from the Wisconsin Department of Public Instruction, 125 South Weber Street, Madison, WI 53703, 1-800-243-8782.

> A fun workshop activity is to create your own distinctions among formative-interim-summative assessments with visuals for each feature (e.g., visuals of arrows and targets to show scope and focus, calendars to show frequency, emojis to show low to high stakes uses). Then locate specific examples currently being used in your system for each purpose (e.g., quizzes, performance tasks, unit tests, projects, state assessments). Don't forget to include peer- and self-assessments! Are there any gaps to fill?

3.3 Developing and Refining Rubrics and Scoring Guides

The third tool in every local assessment toolkit is a scoring guide or rubric. Before you tell me you were "rubricized" many years ago and have nothing more to learn, let's unpack some terms, types, and best practices when using scoring guides. Like many of you, I began paying attention to rubrics when I began using performance tasks and projects to assess my students. Most of my rubrics were "task-specific" rubrics, designed for one-time use. While they worked well to spell out expectations for my students, they did not provide data (scores) that I could aggregate with scores or grades from other assignments. My task-specific rubrics were different, assessed different things, and I was creating a ton of them. When I began to collect work samples for student portfolios, I realized there was a role for generalized rubrics—rubrics that could be used to assess some of the same skills and knowledge across the school year. In science, this included the ability to make observations and support conclusions with data; in writing, I could now track students' ability to support interpretations of text by analyzing evidence.

My understanding of rubrics and types of criteria for different assessment tasks deepened when I spent a week in the late 1980s at one of Grant Wiggins's assessment institutes. At the same time, I was communicating with Jay McTighe at the Maryland Department of Education about how to design better performance tasks. I know now that what I was learning from each of them was some of the early thinking that led to the concept of "understanding by design" co-developed by Wiggins and McTighe (2005, 2012). Since that time, I have been able to connect their seminal work to many good ideas I've read about or developed in support of local assessment practice.

So let me clarify some terms and make connections to cognitive rigor/DOK, rubric scoring criteria, and assessment types and tasks. If this were a workshop, I'd start by announcing we're about to begin the "Great American Chocolate Chip Cookie Taste Test."[2] I adapted this activity from the original 1989 version created by Alysa Cummings and me while we were working at the New Jersey Department of Education. It's been used with students and educators alike for many years to introduce types of scoring criteria and to provide a rationale for considering weighting certain criteria (taste) over others (the number of chips, perhaps). Participants develop rubrics to score two cookies—Cookie A and Cookie B. Rating the cookies is a common experience that explains differences in what we measure and what we value most in a cookie or other work produced by students.

Rubrics and scoring guides provide a set of rules or guidelines for assigning scores to test takers. Rubrics are often used to elaborate on how to score longer constructed response items, performance tasks, and extended projects. More simplified scoring guides tend to be used for shorter open-ended test items. Scoring criteria fall into several types: **Form criteria** (e.g., following

---

2. This activity is explained in more detail at the end of Module 3 and can be used with students or teachers.

formatting guidelines for documenting sources, editing grammar use, turning in work on time—DOK 1); **Accuracy of Content criteria** (e.g., calculations, definitions, applying concepts or terms appropriately—DOK 1, DOK 2); **Process criteria** (e.g., gathering and organizing information, identifying trends, graphing data—DOK 2); **Impact criteria** (e.g., effectiveness in solving a problem or convincing an audience—DOK 3 or DOK 4); and **Knowledge Production criteria** (e.g., generating new questions for investigation or new insights, reflections on new learning—DOK 3 or DOK 4).

There are also several different types of scoring rubrics, each with unique strengths and weaknesses.

- **Analytic rubrics** apply several different, distinct criteria to evaluate products (e.g., process skills, content accuracy, editing skills). A score is given for each separate criterion, thus providing multiple scores and specific feedback to students on strengths and weaknesses of the performance. Analytic rubrics offer opportunities to yield "weighted scoring" such as giving more scoring weight to reasoning and justification (Knowledge production) than to steps being followed to solve the problem (Process).

- **Holistic rubrics** combine several criteria to yield one generalized or holistic score. While these scores can be used to describe overall performance, they are not as useful in providing specific feedback to students on strengths and weaknesses of the performance. Holistic rubrics are frequently used for scoring performance tasks in large-scale assessments because they may be seen as more efficient (taking less time) and tend to be easier to get scoring agreement across raters (interrater reliability) than are analytic rubrics.

- **Task-specific rubrics** are typically designed to score one specific constructed response item or performance task (e.g., essay, open-ended questions on state assessments) and therefore include examples of specific text evidence from a passage or a particular mathematical representation or method expected in the student response. Task-specific scoring rubrics are most useful when scoring large numbers of student work products with very particular success criteria or when defining what partial credit looks like.

- **Generalized rubrics** are typically designed to score multiple, similar (comparable) performance tasks at different times during the learning process (e.g., argumentative essay, scientific investigation). Because these are generalized for use with many tasks, it is highly recommended that annotated student work samples include explanations of specific scoring evidence that help to interpret rubric criteria. Generalized scoring rubrics are especially useful when building student understanding of success criteria and learning goals and are most useful when scoring student work products over time with similar success criteria, such as in an electronic portfolio.

Holistic rubrics combine several criteria to yield one generalized or holistic score. While these scores can be used to describe overall performance, they are not as useful in providing specific feedback to students on strengths and weaknesses of the performance when using performance tasks or project-based assessments. Using holistic scoring guides for open-ended questions and prompts that can be evaluated using minimal criteria make the most sense for classroom use. For example, a short essay question on a language arts test might only be scored on how well the student supported an interpretation of the text. Language use, grammar, and mechanics are not part of the scoring.

A Sample Holistic Rubric: Each performance level includes multiple criteria to consider (e.g., accuracy, insights, text-based support, connecting ideas, organization and general completion of the task). Scorers begin by comparing the "proficient" level descriptions (for a score of 3) with the student work. If all components for "proficiency" are not clearly evident, scorers move to the performance level below (for a score of 2) for comparison. Conversely, if all components for "proficient" are clearly evident, scorers move to the performance level above for comparison. A score of 4 ("advanced performance") cannot be given unless the work demonstrates the combination of all level 4 criteria. Partial credit is generally not given when papers fall "on the line" between two score points.

Sample 1   Holistic Rubric

SCORE	PERFORMANCE DESCRIPTORS
4 Advanced	The student provides a complete and accurate response that meets all of the requirements of the task. The response shows thorough and insightful understanding, includes comprehensive and detailed text-based support, connects ideas and elaborates, is well organized with clear focus, addresses all parts of the prompt, and provides a strong introduction and conclusion.
3 Proficient	The student provides a **thorough** and mostly **accurate** response that meets most of the requirements of the task. The response shows less **insight**, includes **ample and relevant text-based support, connects ideas, is well organized, and addresses** most of the prompt.
2 Approaching	The student provides an adequate and partially accurate response that meets some of the requirements of the task. The response shows a literal understanding of the text, possesses some organization, includes modest text-based support, and addresses part of the prompt.
1 Basic	The student provides an incomplete and less-than-accurate response that only superficially touches on the requirements of the task. The response shows little, if any, understanding, lacks focus, and includes little text-based support.
0	The student fails to provide a relevant response to the task.

> Multiple criteria are included in each performance level of holistic rubrics. Criteria are scored together. All must be present.

Source: Adapted from an early draft Grade 4 Unit, "John Muir," NYC Department of Education (2010).

A Sample Analytic Rubric: We could start with the holistic rubric in the previous example and create an analytic rubric by identifying the different criteria and then describing levels of performance for each. Note that you probably don't need to explicitly include a score of zero in your rubric. Personally, I favor using analytic rubrics for most classroom and common assessments that are designed to integrate multiple skills and concepts, such as with performance tasks and projects.

Sample 2 Analytic Rubric

SCORING CRITERIA	1 BASIC	2 APPROACHING	3 PROFICIENT	4 ADVANCED
Accuracy			**thorough** and mostly **accurate** response	
Organization			addresses most of the prompt well organized connects ideas	
Text-Based Support	includes little text-based support	includes modest text-based support	includes ample and relevant text-based support	includes comprehensive and detailed text-based support
Insights			response shows less **insight**	

> Criteria are scored separately for each performance level of analytic rubrics. This results in multiple scores, one for each criterion.

Source: Adapted from Grade 4 Unit, "John Muir," NYC Department of Education (2010).

Examining Rubric Quality

To be honest, I see a lot of poorly constructed rubrics, so many that I decided to develop a tool (Hess PLC **TOOL #11**) to help educators examine the quality of their rubrics from eight different dimensions.

✓ Odd versus Even—Determining the number of performance levels

I'm often asked for guidance as to the number of performance levels to use in a rubric—4? 5? Or even 6? I have two simple rules of thumb, plus one caveat:

- *Rule 1* Most scorers tend to gravitate to the middle score point of an odd-numbered scale. If a 3-point scale includes "partial" completion as a score of 2 and "full" as a score of 3, most educators will find something missing in the work and use a "2" to describe performance. In my experience, the same is usually true of a 5-point rubric scale. Even numbers of performance levels (when the lowest level is not simply "0") usually force some decision making between two critical score points (e.g., Is this just getting started or is the student making progress? Is the student getting close or are they actually there or proficient?).

- *Rule 2* My second rule of thumb for overall rubric design is to ask if there really is a way to describe *X* levels of performance. The best scoring guide for any task is the one with clearly distinctive *adjacent* performance levels that reflect REAL student learning and performance. This means that you will likely have to tweak some language in your rubric descriptors AFTER piloting a new performance task. As a matter of fact, this is exactly what you should do. Performance-level descriptions should not simply reflect our best guess of what students might do, but what we see students actually doing as they learn to improve performance.

A caveat to my two rules of thumb: I never really liked the idea of assigning score points between performance levels. It seemed to me that if your performance-level descriptions were clear, then it was or was not scored as a 2 or a 3. Score points between levels seemed to me like a cop-out on making a scoring decision. Often the "in-between" points had no accompanying descriptors. So, anything perceived by a scorer to be better than a 2, but not quite a 3 could be given a score of 2.5, while the collection of work scoring 2.5 may have looked very different.

As performance tasks and project-based assessments have become deeper, broader, and in my opinion much richer in demonstrating complex learning, I've come to believe that in some cases, "in between" score points should be used. My best example is when describing what it looks like between the "advanced" and "proficient" levels of performance. Let's say that a student has demonstrated a solid command of the material to be learned (is clearly proficient) and then attempts to go beyond by trying something more complex or novel with the solution or product. The student falls short, but clearly shows some thinking and understanding beyond proficient. If students like these received a score of "3.5" instead of a score of "3" I think it might honor their efforts to think more deeply and encourage them to try again. *If we present tasks of greater complexity and deeper thinking to our students and can describe the 3.5 or the 2.5 score point in clear, descriptive language, then some in-between scoring makes perfect sense.* I've used this approach with developing performance scales for proficiency-based learning. With proficiency-based assessment tasks, the 2.5 and 3.5 are described generally so that they can be applied consistently to different rubrics and tasks across different classrooms and teachers.

- ✓ Using descriptive versus judgmental language

You may have noticed that the above rubric example uses words such as *thorough, ample, less, mostly, superficially,* and *modest*. In my experience, the use of subjective language in rubrics is one of the reasons that scorers lack agreement. What really is the difference between a "thorough" response and one that is not quite thorough? Are there really four different levels ranging from not thorough to fully thorough? Minimizing vague and subjective descriptors is one way to gain greater clarity of expectations and justifiable scoring interpretations. Sometimes we can use student work products to better describe what degrees of performance quality actually look like. Analyzing student work is an important step to refining rubric language, as well as identifying and annotating work that exemplifies each performance level.

- ✓ Focusing on quality over quantity

Let's face it, it's easier to count sources cited than to evaluate a student's use of credible and reliable sources. As with the example of the chocolate chip cookie rubric, the number of chips in each cookie might not be as important to overall taste as the quality of the chocolate used in the chips! Try to eliminate as much quantitative language as possible when quality is really what you're looking for in the work. Instead of saying "used 3 sources," say something like, "more than 2 credible sources used."

✓ Stating performance in the positive—what IS happening, rather than what is NOT happening

I see many rubrics with language in the lower levels of performance that mostly describe what the student is not doing (e.g., lacks a focus, incomplete, no text evidence used). While these (more negative descriptions) may accurately reflect what we don't see in the work, ask yourself what *do* we see? Students who don't have a beginning, middle, and end to their stories usually have something, probably a beginning. Stating that the student has identified a main character or drafted a beginning to the story is what you actually see. Rather than saying "no illustration" or "illustration lacks details," why not try, "has an illustration that would be improved by adding more details." Think of the lower levels of the rubric as describing what "just getting started" might look like and what "making progress" actually means.

Rubric levels should describe a progression of performance from novice work to expert work. The progression should offer guidance to both the teacher and the students as to what comes next along the learning continuum and suggest how to get there.

✓ Perfection is not the same as excellence. Focus on describing excellent performance.

Perfection is great, but excellence is so much better. For example, a student who can be completely accurate when solving a less complex routine mathematics problem might make a calculation error when completing a more complex task. That small error might be carried throughout as the student uses an appropriate approach to solve the problem, develops a well-constructed representation to analyze the data, and provides reasoning and a justifiable solution. What is "taste" in this cookie—calculation or reasoning? Don't get me wrong, calculation is important, but it might not be the thing that you look for in student work that tells you the student has acquired deeper understanding or the ability to transfer learning.

✓ Matching rubric language and criteria to intended cognitive demands/DOK of the task

Consider the task demands and how you describe differing levels of thinking for each criterion. Does your rubric reflect the most important and demanding aspects of the task(s)? Should you consider giving more scoring weight to some criteria at this point in the school year?

✓ Using kid-friendly rubric language leads to kid-friendly self-assessment.

The purpose of the success criteria, or "What we are looking for?" is to make students understand what the teacher is using as criteria for judging their work, and, of course, to ensure that the teacher is clear about the criteria that will determine if learning intentions have been successfully achieved. Too often students may know the learning intention, but not know how the teacher is going to judge their performance, or when or whether they have been successful. (Hattie, 2009, pp. 169–179)

If the primary purpose of assessment is to help students learn, then performance expectations should be descriptive, focus on increasing quality and excellence, and be stated in the positive. I like to use the stem, "I can . . ." for designing student self-assessment rubrics. You can see how a negatively worded descriptor like these might not work for most students: I cannot develop ideas for a three-paragraph essay; I do not have any sources; I lack creativity and focus.

One approach I used effectively with my own students was to design a "What I Need to Do" rubric. Unlike rubrics with multiple performance levels, I focused only on the proficient level descriptors. This was not a checklist where students could simply check off boxes. I designed it so that students would have to interact with it (self-assess) both during the development of the product and when identifying evidence of quality at the final stage of the work. Note that peers are included in providing critical feedback.

Sample 3   Analytic Rubric for Student Self-Assessment of "Proficiency"[3]

SCORING CRITERIA	"WHAT I NEED TO DO" RUBRIC [PROFICIENT]	EVIDENCE OF WHAT I DID AND EXPLAIN HOW I MIGHT HAVE GONE BEYOND PROFICIENT . . .
Accuracy	I checked **accuracy** of facts and sources by doing this:	
Organization	_____ (peer sign off) has checked to see that my response fully **addressees all parts of the prompt.** I've organized my information using ❏ tables, visuals, diagrams, etc. ❏ subheadings, inset text ❏ other: This is (my logic chain) how I connected key ideas:	
Text-Based Support	I know my text-based evidence is relevant because . . .	
Insights	I've included one new **insight** or a learning that I now have by doing this project: ❏ Connected to a big idea ❏ Extended my thinking to past experiences ❏ Extended my thinking to other texts, world events, or _____?	

> Students are guided to self-identify evidence for each criterion in this type of analytic rubric.

---

3. Appendix D includes three content-specific examples of "What I Need to Do" rubrics, plus a blank planning template.

✓ Designing rubrics with purpose and use in mind

Form follows function. Remember that not all rubrics will or should use the same format. Performance tasks that require students to make a multimedia presentation or demonstrate a combination of complex skills (e.g., a dance routine, play, musical performance), or those that require real-time observation can be videotaped and scored at a later time. Initial observational notes can be quickly captured by peers, as well as teachers, using a format like the one below. This science performance task called "Giants of Science" required students to research and deliver a three-minute presentation about key scientists (giants of science), the importance of their discoveries, and their lasting impact on the world of science.

Sample 4 Format for Observation Rubric With Multiple Criteria

Task Expectations for Giants of Science: Provide information about background and career, identify major discovery in the field, discuss impact of the discovery, use your science knowledge to elaborate and make connections to relevant scientific concepts and terms, use media to enhance message, and . . . ?

PERFORMANCE TASK REQUIREMENTS	YES? NO?	DOCUMENT EVIDENCE FOR EACH CRITERION
WHO: Background information about scientist's interests and career		
WHAT: Major discovery in field*		
SO WHAT: Impact of discovery on later science/scientists*		(provides impact context, links with later discoveries)
MY CONNECTIONS: Relevant scientific concepts and knowledge*		(demonstrates content understanding: elaborates on science principles, concepts, terms, examples, uses)
Additional "points of interest"		(explains connection to self, other domains of science)
Other: Use of prop/visuals/pamphlet/media to enhance message		
ADDITIONAL SCORING NOTES		

*Most important to include and elaborate on = double score points

A Quick Guide to Rubric Development

A well-written rubric provides direction to both the teacher and student as to what to do next to advance the learning. You may end up creating a teacher- and a student-friendly version of your rubrics. This will encourage student self-assessment.

When developed collaboratively, rubrics reflect common understandings of expectations; and the quality and use of rubrics is vastly improved. Try codeveloping rubrics with your students by showing exemplars of student work (for example from a previous school year) and guide them to derive criteria and performance indicators based on the examples.

Some reminders for rubric development:

1. Be descriptive, not judgmental or vague with language.
2. Quantity does not equal quality. Emphasize quality!
3. Keep wording positive! Describe what IS there not what is missing, if possible (e.g., one of the three sections is complete).
4. Excellence is not the same as perfection.
5. Criteria should include both basic or foundational understandings and deeper thinking.
6. Describe a specific progression of development moving from less to more complex understanding and performance.
7. Be kid friendly, especially if you use "headings" rather than numbers for each performance level. Students would probably not want to self-assess with headings like "Below Basic" which is quite negative. "Beginning" or "Novice" means the same thing, but says it in a more positive way. After all, we've been a novice at everything we've ever learned how to do.

Step 1: Articulate a continuum of increasingly complex learning.

Begin by writing the desired learning outcomes for the proficient level in observable, measurable, and descriptive language. Consider how students will develop understanding and expertise to get to the desired performance. Emphasize skills in lower levels that move from foundational to conceptual to transfer and deeper understanding at the Advanced/Expert level. Don't worry if you can't clearly describe Advanced performance before seeing student work samples. Your early descriptions may actually limit what students will try to do. It's OK to say "meets all criteria at the Proficient level, plus provides a more sophisticated or deeper understanding of the concepts and skills." You can fill in examples to describe Advanced work, after analyzing what you saw in the student work. Finally, don't assume every cell in the rubric needs to be filled in. There is not always a way to describe advanced levels of skills such as editing or calculating or citing sources.

Step 2: Focus on the quality of student work at all performance levels.

Criteria at Proficient and Advanced levels should explicitly describe the knowledge, skills, and performance expected. Scoring criteria for levels below Proficient will not include all elements but should consider what might be completed first, such as drafting a plan and collecting data at the lower-performance levels and analyzing data collected at the upper-performance levels.

Step 3: Review criteria and performance indicators to see if they can apply to a variety of performances and products.

When scoring criteria can be used to assess multiple artifacts of student work, rather than for only one specific task, students have the opportunity to demonstrate their knowledge and skills in a variety of ways, and over time. Criteria that are "task neutral" help teachers to meet diverse learning needs of students and to integrate assessment data more meaningfully.

Step 4: Use PLC **TOOL #11** to get feedback on your draft rubric.

RUBRIC QUALITY REVIEW WORKSHEET

Tool 11

Assessment/Task:
Date: Reviewer(s):

Questions for Evaluating Rubric Quality	Comments or Feedback for Each Review Question
1. Do the number of performance levels and rubric format make sense? ☐ Format matches purpose and use ☐ Adjacent performance levels are qualitatively different ☐ Levels reflect how completion of the task might naturally progress with instruction	
2. Is descriptive language maximized? ☐ Little or no judgmental language ☐ Avoids use of subjective language (poor, neat, ample, etc.) and frequency indicators (rarely, often, etc.)	
3. Do descriptors emphasize quality over quantity? (e.g., relevant, descriptive details or sources versus three details or sources)	
4. Do descriptors state performance in the positive—what IS happening, rather than what is NOT happening? ☐ Lowest levels focus on beginning stages ☐ Describes a (real) progression of learning ☐ Have student work samples or piloting informed performance descriptions?	
5. Do descriptors describe excellent *rather than* perfect performance? ☐ Describes a progression from Novice to Expert performance ☐ Performance descriptors increase with depth, complexity, and/or breadth of knowledge ☐ Minor errors not weighted more than quality of ideas or thinking	
6. Do rubric language and criteria match rigor expectations of task?	

3.4 What Can You Learn From Analyzing Student Work Products?

Over the past decades, a variety of tools and protocols have been designed to analyze the work products of students. Most staff developers and practitioners alike seem to agree that when teachers collaboratively analyze student work—whether it be in formal scoring groups or at informal team meetings—they build a common understanding of what "good enough" looks like and are better able to determine what students might need in order to progress with their learning. A common use of student work analysis (SWA) has typically been to inform next steps for instruction by uncovering what students know and can do. A second use has been as an effective strategy for embedded professional development around what quality work looks like, especially when using rubrics to determine how to score work at different performance levels. I'd like to expand on these two generally accepted purposes of SWA: to use assessment results to inform instruction and to develop common understandings of progress and proficiency in scoring.

The focus of my most recent work with schools and states has been primarily on cognitive rigor or deeper thinking and assessment design. This includes everything from large-scale state assessments to implementing common local performance tasks to formative uses of classroom assessments that track student progress over time. While the assessment purposes and scope have differed, each of these projects has included a SWA component. Sometimes, SWA was used to inform the task design and refinement stages; at other times, SWA was used to identify anchor papers that illustrate benchmarks of student progress across a school year. For all of these projects, SWA was used to analyze the quality of the task itself in eliciting deeper understanding.

Over time, this work has validated two things for me: The quality of the assessment task is critical to what it will uncover for the test developer, the teacher, or the student; and the SWA process must be manageable for educators or it will not become embedded in practice. At the end of the day, if you are going to take the time to analyze and use what you find in student work, then you should take the time to strategically design or choose designed tasks that will not only assess recall and application of basic skills or concepts, but also uncover thinking, reasoning, and possible misconceptions when skills are transferred to novel situations or scenarios.

What Are Strategically Designed Performance Tasks?

Strategically designed performance tasks can include a variety of forms and formats, such as short lesson-based formative probes that produce an oral or written response (e.g., Keely, 2008), single or multiday performance tasks that measure student competencies across grade levels and content areas (e.g., Center for Collaborative Education, 2012), or project-based tasks aimed to produce real-world, student-initiated products. To my thinking, strategically designed performance tasks are multistep tasks requiring integration of basic skills and concepts with more complex skills, such as problem solving, abstract thinking, reasoning, and justification using analysis of evidence.

In order to complete these nonroutine tasks, students must make decisions along the way as they work to find and justify a solution or develop a final product. Designers of these tasks strategize how the task prompts might increase with complexity over the school year or across a unit of study. In other words, a benchmark opinion-writing task given in November will likely be less complex than an opinion-writing assessment given later in the school year. Both tasks assess the same core writing skills (organization of ideas, use of elaboration, grammar, and word usage); but a benchmark writing task administered in the spring will demand greater levels of sophistication or depth of thinking in the student response. One such example can be illustrated in a pair of pre/post tasks[4] piloted in New York City schools at Grade 3 for an introductory unit on opinion writing. The earlier prompt—used as a preassessment for the unit—asked students to write about a favorite or not-so-favorite holiday and provide (personal) reasons to support their opinions. This task was designed to find out if students knew how to state and support an opinion, maintaining that focus throughout the piece. An analysis of the student work revealed that most students at the start of the unit could not differentiate writing an opinion from writing an informational summary about holidays. The results of the SWA from the preassessment led teachers to design lessons that built schemas about opinion writing (What are key parts of an opinion piece and how do they differ from parts of an informational summary?), as well as lessons on how to locate relevant text evidence to support opinions.

---

4. Additional discussions of pre/post testing are included later in this module (Student Work Analysis and using task shells) and in Module 4.

The postassessment for the unit was more complex than the preassessment. This task asked students to read about a shark scientist, examine facts about two different kinds of sharks, and then state and support an opinion about which shark they would want to study if they were shark scientists. Both tasks assessed the same core writing skills; the postassessment also included the integration of more complex skills, such as using text-based evidence as support. The "proficient" student work from the preassessment was much less complex than the proficient work from the postassessment; however, both tasks were appropriately designed to uncover what students were able to do and what students were ready to learn next, at each point in the learning cycle.

> View a video clip of Karin Hess (2016) discussing what we can learn from looking at student work at http://www.karin-hess.com/free-resources.

These types of performance tasks, designed for thinking and doing, will always yield many different levels of information because they "uncover" student thinking, reveal any lack of clarity or accessibility in the task prompts, and provide for a range of possible responses.

I've discovered that SWA can be used for six distinctly different purposes. Each purpose requires a different lens when analyzing the student work and acting on what was first *Described, Interpreted,* and then *Evaluated* before taking next steps. I call this evidence from student work "Student work to D-I-E for" and use the acronym DIE in this way: Describe first only what you actually see (or hear students tell you about) in the work, Interpret what that evidence might mean (specific to your intended purpose), and then Evaluate next steps to be taken. Will you revise the prompt for better clarity? Will you add scaffolding to make the task accessible to all students? Will you target specific lessons to address a common misconception? Will you be able to use these results from multiple tasks to show progress over time? And if not, should you design other assessment tasks to be given after more instruction and before the postassessment is given?

Table 3.1 summarizes the differences among six purposes and uses of SWA with some guiding "D-I-E questions" to frame individual teacher or group analyses of work samples.

Table 3.1   Six Purposes of Student Work Analysis: D-I-E

PURPOSE	WHAT TO DESCRIBE	WHAT TO INTERPRET	WHAT TO EVALUATE
1 Review quality and effectiveness of tasks or prompts and scoring rubrics.	• Did the task elicit what we expected or wanted to see? • Did we see a range of possible responses for this task—such as a range of depth of thinking and range of content knowledge? • Were there any surprises in what students did or showed in their work?	• Was the task prompt clear and accessible to all students? • Is less or greater scaffolding of this task needed (e.g., providing graphic organizers, breaking up the task into several parts, group versus individual responsibilities)?	• Do our rubrics and scoring guides capture the nuances in what students can demonstrate on this task across a range of performance levels from low to high? • Can we identify anchor papers and annotate work that reflects learning at various performance levels that will assist others in better interpreting results? • Is weighting or emphasis needed in the scoring guide?

(Continued)

Table 3.1 Six Purposes of Student Work Analysis: D-I-E (Continued)

PURPOSE	WHAT TO DESCRIBE	WHAT TO INTERPRET	WHAT TO EVALUATE
2 Make key instructional decisions; target support or differentiate instruction.	• What can students do right now? • Where did students get "stuck"?	• What do they need (or not need) next? • What are the possible misconceptions or overgeneralizations I need to address next?	• Is strategic scaffolding needed? • Are flexible groupings with targeted instruction needed?
3 Monitor student progress over time.	• How do I describe what each grouping of students can do or cannot do?	• How has the class shown progress from pre- to mid- to postassessment?	• Benchmark tasks across a unit or school year
4 Engage students in meaningful peer- and self-assessment.	• Describe what each of the students knows and understands well and where they each might improve. • Can you locate some areas of improvement from sample 1 to sample 2?	• What does the student know now that she or he did not know how to do as well in the first task? • Which work comes closest to the expectations for the task?	• Which responses can be used for peer or student analysis? • Which responses are most instructive (e.g., uncover common misconceptions)?
5 Better understand how learning progresses over time.	• What does novice work look like? • What does expert work look like? • Are there interim stages of learning that I did not anticipate?	• Where are they on the learning continuum?	• What is not explicit in the standards, but an essential stage in the learning?
6 Build content and pedagogical expertise.	• What does deeper thinking look like in this content area? • Does this task elicit or uncover deeper understanding? Common misconceptions?	• Is this quality work?	• Does this evidence cause me or us to reflect on current practice; change perceptions about what all students can do? • Are rich tasks and SWA worth the time? • How can we use common assessments more effectively?

Six Purposes and Uses of Student Work Analysis

Purpose 1: Review quality and effectiveness of tasks or prompts and scoring rubrics.

First and foremost is establishing the quality of the assessment task, whether it be a formative probe, performance task, or extended project. Piloting tasks and refining them based on SWA leads to clarifying prompts, making tasks accessible and engaging for all students, modifying wording in scoring rubrics, and ensuring that questions posed will result in evidence of deeper thinking. Some of the evidence from SWA at this stage in the task development process has resulted in reducing the overall number of items so that students have time to generate thoughtful responses or clarifying or eliminating unnecessary vocabulary in prompts. Tasks that have not worked as effectively as intended are revised and repiloted with another group of students. PLC **TOOLS #13–#15** are designed for identifying and annotating anchor papers from revised assessments that can be used for calibration and scoring.

SWA also stresses the need to scribe (record exact words and observations) for younger and language-delayed students who cannot always express their ideas with words and symbols on paper. Consider what we learned from analyzing work for the student samples below. This task, Boots and Hats (an adapted Exemplars task), was given as a fall benchmark task assessing kindergarten students' ability to apply counting in a problem-solving situation:

> I saw 4 kindergarten students lined up to go outside to play in the snow.
>
> Everyone was wearing boots and a hat. How many boots and hats did I see in all?
>
> Show and tell how you know.

© Exemplars.com

What makes this assessment a strategically designed task? The choice of the number "4" allows teachers to uncover whether students can count to 4, to 8, or above 10. Using a larger number early in the school year might not provide results for all children in the class. Using a smaller number than 4 makes this task minimally challenging for most students. A task like this will also show whether students have a counting strategy that works, and an appropriate way to represent the problem visually. Finally, it will elicit reasoning when students "show and tell" how they know their answer is correct. Note how the teacher scribing notes in the three samples really helps us to understand exactly what each student knows and can do.

Student work samples with teacher annotations (based on a Vermont pilot, 2015)

Can you identify some instructional implications for each student?

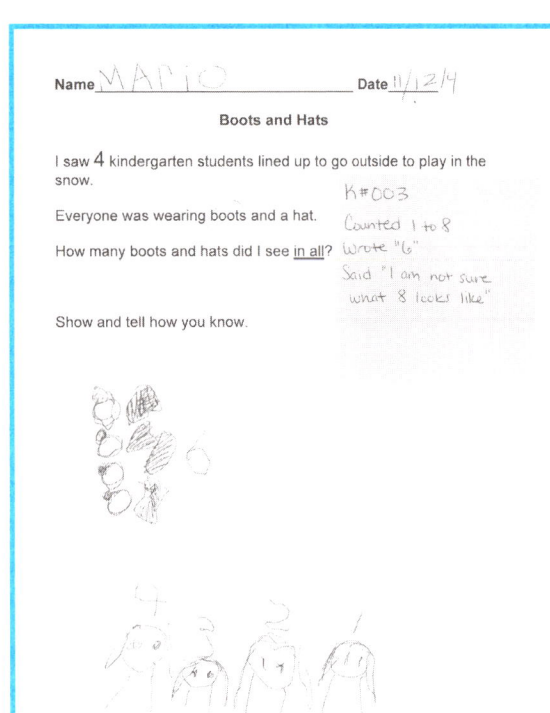

Student #K-003

Knows how to write numbers 1–4; Can use mental counting to get from 4 to 8; Uses 1–1 correspondence

Knows how to count 1 to 8, but does not know how to make an 8, so wrote a 6 instead

Appropriately represents the problem—only key parts are included: heads and feet, not entire bodies

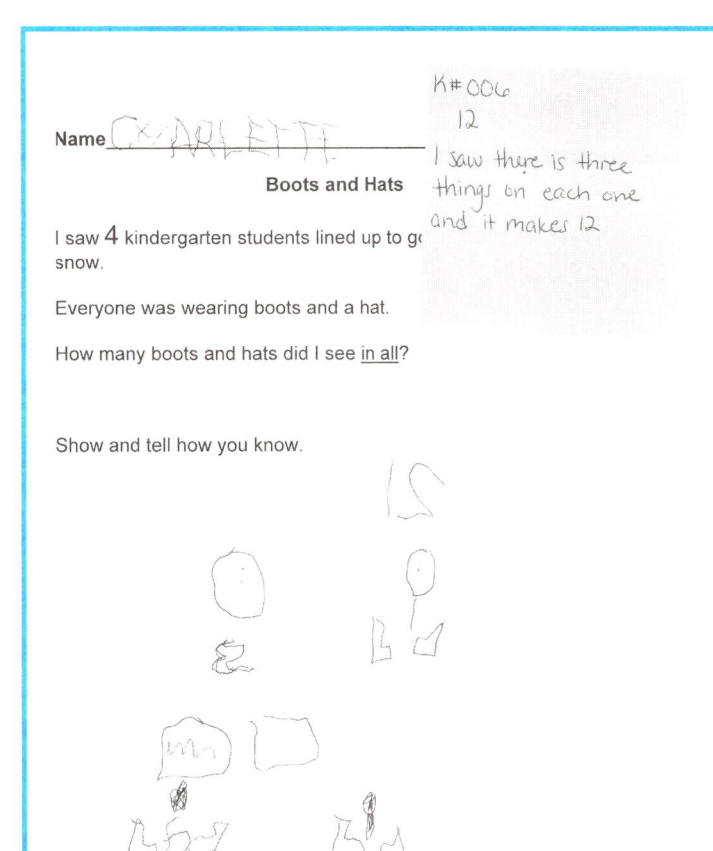

Student #K-006

Knows how to write some numbers

Attempts to represent the problem—only boots and heads, not entire bodies or people

Is not adding, but instead using "emergent" multiplicative reasoning to solve the problem: "I saw there is 3 things on each one and it makes 12."

Is appropriately using mental math and abstract reasoning

152   A Local Assessment Toolkit to Promote Deeper Learning

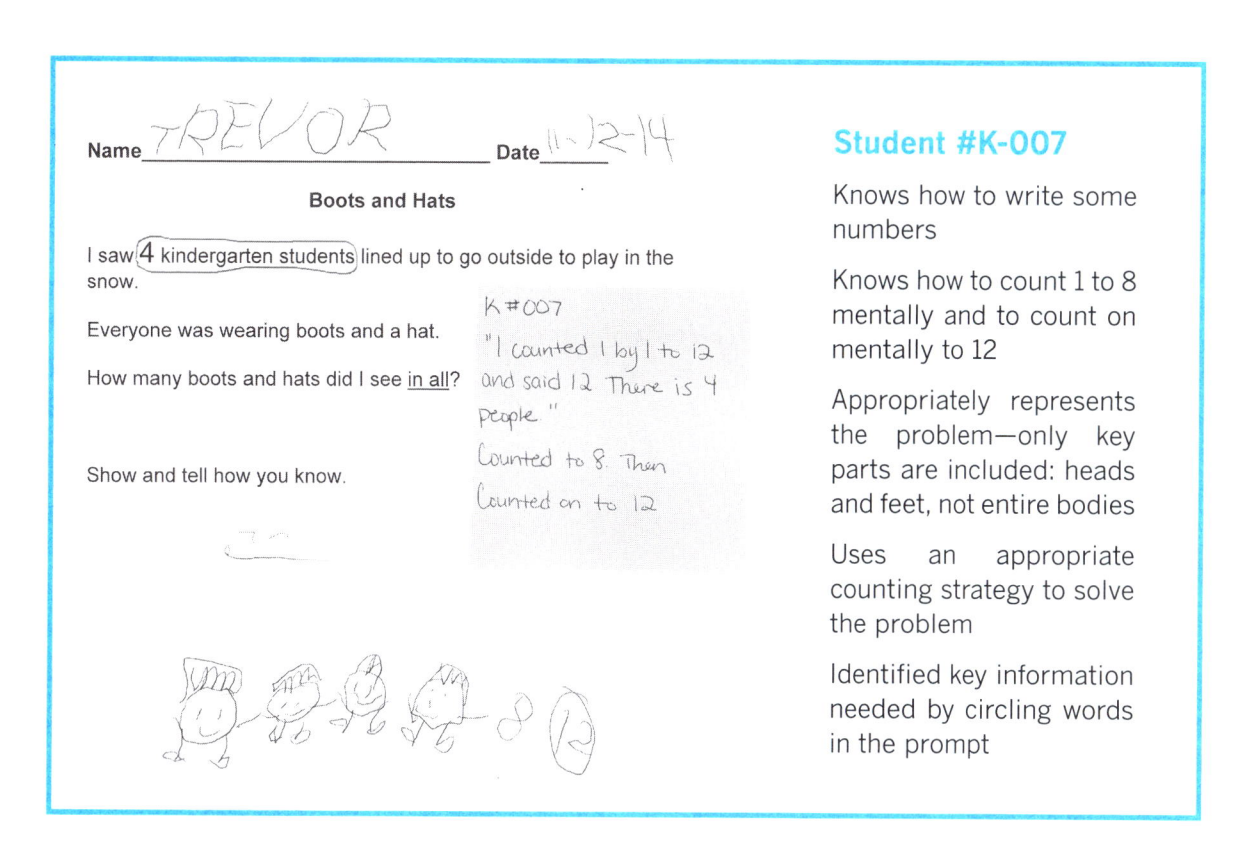

> Name _TREVOR_ Date _11-12-14_
>
> **Boots and Hats**
>
> I saw (4 kindergarten students) lined up to go outside to play in the snow.
>
> Everyone was wearing boots and a hat.
>
> How many boots and hats did I see <u>in all</u>?
>
> Show and tell how you know.
>
> K #007
> "I counted 1 by 1 to 12 and said 12. There is 4 people."
> Counted to 8. Then counted on to 12.
>
> **Student #K-007**
>
> Knows how to write some numbers
>
> Knows how to count 1 to 8 mentally and to count on mentally to 12
>
> Appropriately represents the problem—only key parts are included: heads and feet, not entire bodies
>
> Uses an appropriate counting strategy to solve the problem
>
> Identified key information needed by circling words in the prompt

Purpose 2: Make key instructional decisions; target support and/or differentiate instruction.

From piloting the task above in several kindergarten classrooms, teachers learned several things that informed their next steps for instruction. First of all, they learned that the phrase "show and tell how you know" had never been modeled by teachers before. Many students had no idea what that phrase meant, but picked up on it when teachers began to use or model it daily in math think-alouds. Scribing made it clear that what the teacher sees on the page is not the limit of what students know and can do. As a matter of fact, teachers were quite surprised that students could do as much as they did with this task. SWA of this first benchmark task changed perceptions of the most skeptical teachers as to what was possible in a kindergarten classroom early in the year.

Purpose 3: Monitor student progress over time.

Traditional uses of pre- and posttesting—which was fine for unidimensional skills, such as learning math terms or dates in social studies—must give way to a new approach when complex performance tasks are used. In the model I've found most effective (Hess, 2013a), the preassessment focuses on the core learning or prerequisite skills that students will need to build upon, not the most complex applications that will be expected at the end of the unit. Using PLC **TOOL #12** (Hess, 2013a), teachers administer a preassessment and "sort" student work based on evidence in the work. This first step in the SWA process of sorting (not scoring) the work makes it clear where individual students and the entire class are on a pre-, mid-, or postassessment. Sandy, a third-grade teacher from Connecticut, had these results from her postassessment, Opinion on Studying a Shark. The sorting of her preassessment, My Favorite Holiday,[5] was the reverse of these results seen below, with most student names listed under the two columns at the left. With each assessment, Sandy could identify what students did or did not understand and document individual and class progress with each new benchmark assessment.

---

5. The "My Favorite Holiday" performance assessment is included in Module 4 as a sample preassessment.

Module 3: What Does This Test Really Measure? 153

Using PLC **TOOL #12**—SWA Step 1: "Sort" students' work by degree of objectives met (list student names or percentage of class in each category so you can track their progress with each assessment administered).

STUDENT WORK ANALYSIS
Analyzing and Acting on Evidence

Subject Area: _____   Grade Level: _____

Unit/Topic: _____   Performance Task: _____

How used?   ☐ Pre/formative   ☐ Mid/Interim   ☐ Post/Summative

Date administered: _____

Content Standards Assessed: _____

Intended Depth-of-Knowledge (DOK) Level(s):   ☐ DOK 1   ☐ DOK 2   ☐ DOK 3   ☐ DOK 4

1. **Using district or classroom assessment or rubric, describe expectations for performance.**
   (See wording of prompt, standards-specific rubric, Hess CRM, and/or standards to determine desired expectations.)

2. Quickly "sort" students' work by degree of objectives met. List student names or % in each category so you can track progress over time with each major assessment. (a) **Start by sorting two larger piles: met or not met.** You may also need a "not sure" pile at this point.
   (b) **Re-sort each pile**: not met = partially met but close vs. minimal; met = met vs. met plus more. (c) **Distribute any remaining work samples** by matching them to typical work from each set.
   This is not scoring!

Objectives not met	Objectives partially met	Objectives fully met	Objectives fully met and exceeded
_% of class	_% of class	_% of class	_% of class

154   A Local Assessment Toolkit to Promote Deeper Learning

Note that four general performance levels are used in PLC **TOOL #12** for sorting work, not three, not high-middle-low. Three levels result in most students being in the middle, which is less useful for making instructional decisions.

Objectives not met	Objectives partially met	Objectives fully met	Objectives fully met and exceeded
5% OF CLASS	5% OF CLASS	52% OF CLASS	38% OF CLASS
Andrew	Olivia	Broad reasons with supporting details. Imply or have counter but lack connection to reasons to study. Donovan, Lana, Nolan, Christina, David-strong voice!, Cathie, Madison, Jada, Anthony, Gage, Dakota-no qualifier/counter claim suggested	Stronger-have stated a clear "qualifier" (beginning of a counter claim) with explicit connection WHY (e.g., you could not get close). Emily, Peter, Mackenzie, Colin, Robert, Victoria, +Emma, +Matt

Purpose 4: Engage students in meaningful peer- and self-assessment.

Active involvement in formative assessment means that students use assessment evidence to set and monitor progress toward learning goals, reflect on themselves as learners, and evaluate the quality of their performance. Valuing both one's struggles and successes accomplishing smaller learning targets over time has been proven to have a profound influence on deepening motivation, developing independence as a learner, and building what we have come to know as "a growth mindset" (Hess, 2015). One easy self- or peer-SWA strategy is what I call "Student Side-by-Side SWA." Students are given two pieces of student work (side-by-side) and asked to collaboratively discuss any of the following:

- Identify what each of the students knows and understands well, and where they each might improve.

- If sample work is from the same student (e.g., pre and post), what does the student know now that he or she did not know how to do as well in the first task? Can you locate some areas of improvement from sample 1 to sample 2?

- If work samples show an obvious lower and higher example, which work comes closest to the expectations for the task? Locate evidence to support your reasoning.

Purpose 5: Better understand how learning progresses over time.

An alternative to score or data analysis is using SWA to uncover how learning evolves over time. Comparing how various student groups have performed on a task helps to better understand how novice performers differ from expert performers. Again, in Sandy's Grade 3 writing example, she describes typical evidence for each group of students in step 2 of the SWA process, giving her a sense of how to move each grouping of students forward in step 3. Sandy is using evidence in student work to build descriptors in a learning trajectory. This is very different from simply "unpacking standards" because there are many skills or concepts and common misconceptions in student evidence that are not explicitly addressed in most standards. Learning trajectories include the interim stages of learning, as well as some of the common stumbling blocks along the learning pathway.[6]

> View a video clip of Ron Berger guiding students to give feedback using analysis of student work: "Austin's Butterfly" at https://vimeo.com/search?q=Austin%E2%80%99s+Butterfly.

Using PLC **TOOL #12**—SWA Step 2: Choose samples from each group or category and DESCRIBE "typical" performance, or specific performance of selected students.

Objectives not met	Objectives partially met	Objectives fully met	Objectives fully met and exceeded
- Is somewhat choppy as the writing jumps from one fact to another with few or no transitions - Basic use of vocabulary - Basic sentence structure - Visual not labeled to provide information or support ideas	- More of a summary of facts without general reasons - Some use of transitions - Little use of elaboration - Simple sentence structure throughout - Basic use of vocabulary - Visual labeled to provide information	- Related ideas are grouped together and connected to focus (opinion) - General or broad ideas that are supported by facts - Use of transitions - Have counter argument-lack connections to WHY facts make it the one to study OR what they want to learn - Visual labeled to support ideas	- Related ideas are grouped together and connected to focus (opinion) - General or broad ideas that are supported by facts - Use of transitions - Have counter argument-stated connections as to WHY facts make it the one to study OR what they want to learn

---

6. Module 4 explores learning progressions and learning trajectories in greater depth.

Using PLC **TOOL #12**—SWA Step 3: INTERPRET learning needs of identified students (or students in each targeted group).

Objectives not met	Objectives partially met	Objectives fully met	Objectives fully met and exceeded
- Grouping ideas - Transitions - Basic conventions- capitals at start of sentences - Selecting and using visuals labeled to provide information	- Adding specific reasons that are supported by facts - Variety of sentence structure - Add WHY these facts support what I could learn - Visual labeled to support ideas	- Adding Compelling intro or "hook" and conclusion - Variety of sentence structure - Elaboration of details and facts to support focus - Adding a clear WHY these facts support or expand-what I could learn - Visual labeled to support SPECIFIC ideas	- Compelling intro or "hook" and conclusion - Elaboration!! - Adding a clear WHY these facts support or expand-what I could learn - Visual labeled to support SPECIFIC ideas

Moss and Brookhart (2012) explain learning trajectories in this way: "Consider where the (next) lesson resides in the larger learning trajectory. . . . The right learning target for today's lesson builds upon the learning targets from previous lessons in the unit and connects to learning targets in future lessons to advance student understanding of important skills and concepts" (p. 2).

Purpose 6: Build content and pedagogical expertise.

Teachers give assignments and grade them daily; but it is analyzing evidence in student work that causes teachers to reflect on *how* students learn and how to make their instructional and assessment practices more effective. Working collaboratively, teachers can establish common understandings of what "good enough" looks like and how to measure progress over time that involves more than counting score points going up or down. Teachers who use SWA to design and refine **assessments of thinking and doing** learn more about student understanding than they will ever learn from questions with only one right answer. By the same token, students who engage with rich, strategically designed tasks on a regular basis learn that finding the answer is not as personally meaningful as knowing how to apply their knowledge in new situations and explain the reasoning that supports their thinking.

3.5 Developing Anchor Papers for Performance Tasks and Anchor Sets for Calibration

Benchmarking is a term frequently used to describe the process of identifying assessment anchors for a given assessment task or question. If you are using common assessments in any content area, you should also be developing annotated assessment anchors at each performance level for responses to open-ended questions and for performance tasks. **Anchor papers** or **exemplars** are comprised of student work samples usually collected and analyzed when piloting new assessments. Often it can take more than one administration of an assessment to identify clear examples at each performance level (representing beginning to advanced performance). Frequently some anchor papers are replaced with better models as time goes on and performance (and instruction) improves. If a performance task is being piloted for the first time, you can expect to get several anchor papers for the lower-performance levels; but you may not get strong exemplars at the proficient and advanced levels. In my experience, as teachers use tasks, they become better skilled at teaching students how to express their reasoning. By the second or third administration, you should be able to identify and annotate examples for all performance levels. If you continue to struggle with getting high-end exemplars, you need to examine both the assessment task and your instructional approach.

During calibration and scoring practice, annotated assessment anchors are used to interpret the rubric criteria and illustrate what student work products at different performance levels are expected to look like. Collaborative student work analysis protocols are used to identify the best set of training examples, which should include

(a) at least one unambiguous sample (exemplar) at each performance level;

(b) more than one way to achieve a proficient or advanced level; and

(c) a few examples that provide guidance for how to score "line" papers—those papers that seem to fall between almost proficient and proficient.

Many teachers also use anchor papers without annotations to help students understand expectations for performance, by asking peers to collaboratively analyze and score work samples. I recommend beginning with the extreme examples (lowest versus highest) when asking students "what do you see in this example?" or "what can be improved upon?"

Benchmarking: The Big Picture

The goal of identifying anchor papers is to locate enough samples to create "anchor sets"— multiple examples at different performance levels for the same assessment task. Anchor sets are used for scoring practice and for calibration purposes. Practice sets include annotations and justifications, while calibration sets do not. Figure 3.2 provides a visual and explanation of each set of papers.

Once exemplar papers are identified, scoring and discussion notes are used to develop both the annotations and "justifications," which are brief rationales for why each score was given.

Figure 3.2 Creating Anchor Papers for Scoring Practice

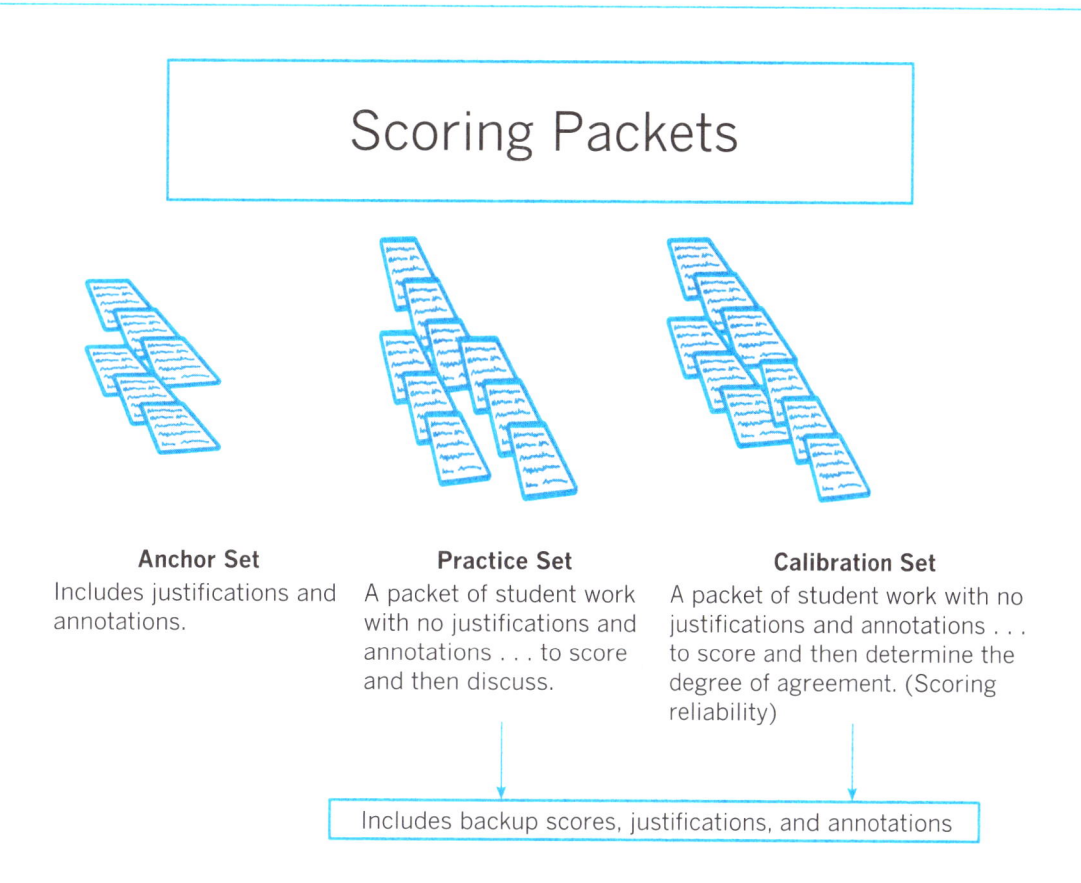

Scoring Packets

Anchor Set
Includes justifications and annotations.

Practice Set
A packet of student work with no justifications and annotations . . . to score and then discuss.

Calibration Set
A packet of student work with no justifications and annotations . . . to score and then determine the degree of agreement. (Scoring reliability)

Includes backup scores, justifications, and annotations

Annotations are usually written as side notes near the "observable evidence" on a piece of student work, and are most useful when they include the rubric scoring criterion being addressed. Sometimes they include an arrow pointing to the actual evidence, or evidence may be underlined (in a text) to call attention to it. Figure 3.3 illustrates an annotation on Grade 3 student work scored as "Expert" using the Exemplars science rubric (available at www.exemplars.com/assets/files/science_rubric.pdf). This science performance task, "Can You Design a Marble Mover?" was developed and piloted for Exemplars.com in 2007. Note that rubric criteria (Scientific Procedures and Reasoning, Scientific Communication/Using Data, and Scientific Concepts and Related Content) are linked in the annotations.

For more examples of annotated student work at each performance level, see the following sources:

http://www.karin-hess.com/formative-and-performance-assessments

www.exemplars.com

www.weteachnyc.org

Figure 3.3 Sample Annotation (Grade 3 Science)

Exemplars

Expert

Question: How can you design a marble mover to make a marble go 5ft 3 sec

Parameters to this problem: marble table, 3sec to travel 5ft

PICTURE: desk, ball track, dictionary

Materials: A couple track and tape unit

Test	design	RESULTS	time	Did it work
#1	5 ft		3½ sec	
#2	5 ft		3 sec	It did work because we put tape on the curves at track that slow it down.
#3	5 ft		3 sec	
#4	5 ft		5 sec	
#5	5 ft		4 sec	

Conclusion: I learned that curves make it go slower and also tape on the track.

What Improved: I had to change nothing on my marble mover.

Inertia, gravity, friction, my Iversion is the Height and the track. My gravity was that I had a drop off the end. It was kind of steep. My friction was that I put tape sticking up and curves that made it go slower.

> Conclusions are related to both the design and scientific concepts. Explanations of gravity, inertia, and friction are correct, but could be expanded upon more for expert level.

> The initial design worked—evidence of use of prior knowledge and experience in the development stage.

> A testable question is stated, as are the parameters for the task. The diagram is clearly labeled and data is organized in a table.

Source: Exemplars, https://www.exemplars.com/

Checklist for writing annotations:

General

- ❏ Be selective—don't have too many; use the most illustrative examples
- ❏ Address all criteria in rubrics

Specific

- ❏ Criterion identified
- ❏ Linked to rationale

- Specific evidence in student work underlined or identified (e.g., arrow, highlighting, boxed)
- Concise, descriptive, and precise wording; link to rubric wording if possible

Justifications summarize evidence (groups of annotations) used to arrive at a score point. Figure 3.4 illustrates an example of how a justification might be written. I developed this training example for a statewide performance assessment project conducted in Wyoming, from 2002 to 2004.

Figure 3.4 Sample Justification (HS Science)

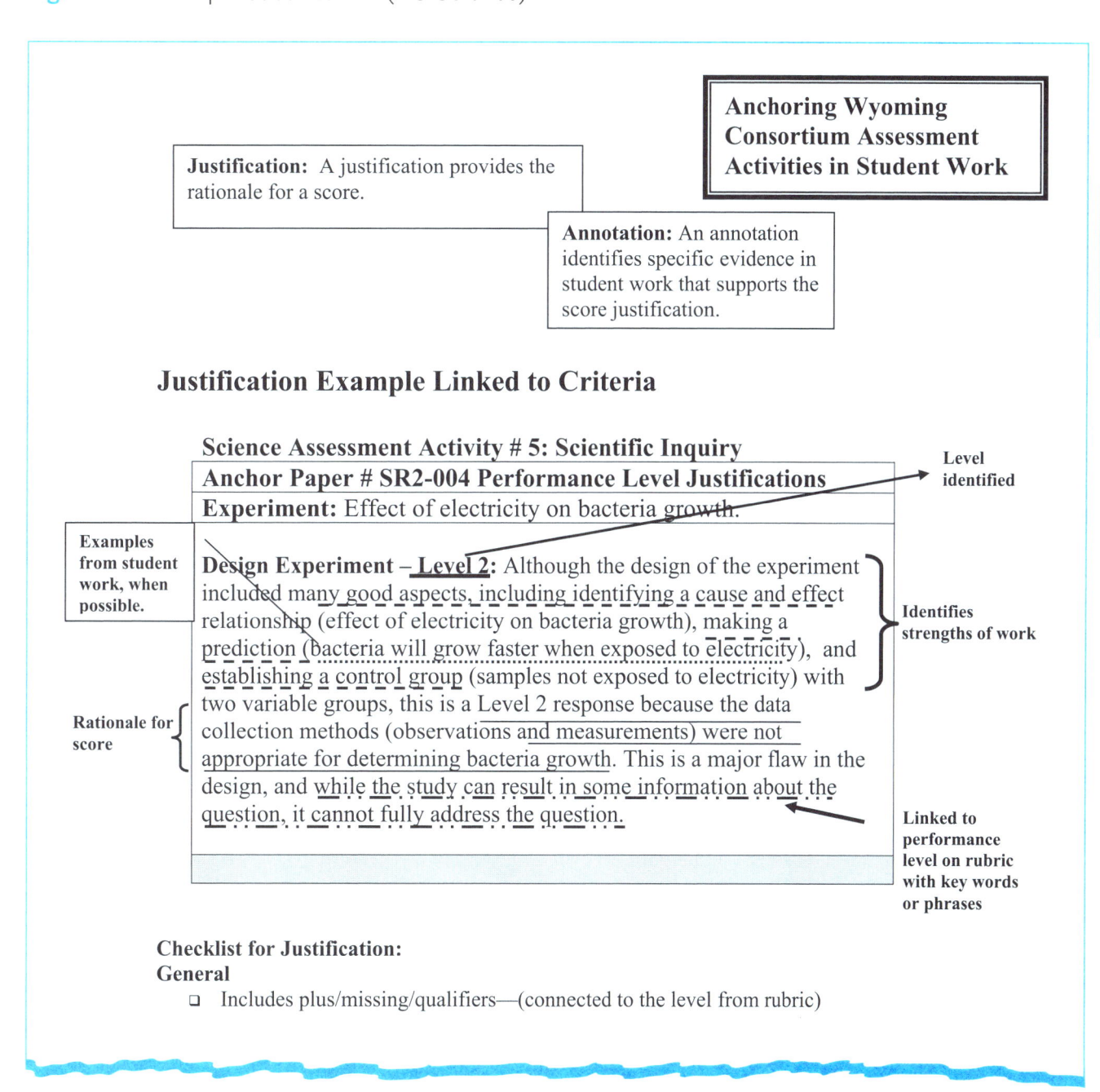

Anchoring Wyoming Consortium Assessment Activities in Student Work

Justification: A justification provides the rationale for a score.

Annotation: An annotation identifies specific evidence in student work that supports the score justification.

Justification Example Linked to Criteria

Science Assessment Activity # 5: Scientific Inquiry

Anchor Paper # SR2-004 Performance Level Justifications — Level identified

Experiment: Effect of electricity on bacteria growth.

Examples from student work, when possible.

Design Experiment – Level 2: Although the design of the experiment included many good aspects, including identifying a cause and effect relationship (effect of electricity on bacteria growth), making a prediction (bacteria will grow faster when exposed to electricity), and establishing a control group (samples not exposed to electricity) with two variable groups, this is a Level 2 response because the data collection methods (observations and measurements) were not appropriate for determining bacteria growth. This is a major flaw in the design, and while the study can result in some information about the question, it cannot fully address the question.

Identifies strengths of work

Rationale for score

Linked to performance level on rubric with key words or phrases

Checklist for Justification:
General
- Includes plus/missing/qualifiers—(connected to the level from rubric)

Selecting Anchor Papers: PLC TOOLS #13, #14, and #15

For six years, I wrote the annotations for all of the K–8 student work published in Science Exemplars (www.exemplars.com). In doing so, I developed a variety of ways to begin the process of identifying and annotating student work samples. Here are some suggestions. When new assessments are piloted, teachers or grade-level teams can use PLC TOOL #12 to "sort" work from their classrooms and identify three to five examples from each "pile" (getting started/getting close/meets or exceeds) without doing any actual scoring. This smaller sample of student work can then be scored by multiple reviewers to see if some samples would make good anchor papers.

PLC TOOLS #13, #14, and #15 are designed to walk teams through this process without initially having to score every piece of student work. Directions for how to use each tool are included on the tool and summarized below.

PLC TOOL #13 Calibration Tool: What Is the Evidence?

You can use this tool for developing annotations to go with specific evidence in the student work. Each worksheet should include these notes: name of the assessment, student ID (not name), how the annotation might be written for the evidence identified, and the score for the particular related rubric criterion (indicated on the tool as A-B-C-etc.). I recommend that reviewers use sticky notes while analyzing work so they can place it right on the work samples. Those notes are transferred to this worksheet.

WHAT IS THE EVIDENCE?
Locating Examples in Student Work for Writing Annotations

Student ID#	Describe Evidence With Possible Annotation Assessment Task or Open-Ended Question:	✓ Criterion & Score
		A____ B____ C____ D____ E____ F____
		A____ B____ C____ D____ E____ F____
		A____ B____ C____ D____ E____ F____

PLC TOOL #14 Calibration Tool: Individual Reviewer Rubric Score Sheet

This tool can be used as "step 1" in developing annotated assessment anchors. Individual reviewers use the task rubric to score each paper listed on the summary score sheet. These examples might be papers drawn from the smaller sample after using SWA TOOL #12, or selected after scoring all papers from an entire class or grade level. ONLY potential anchor papers are listed on this worksheet, along with coding about your reason for thinking it would make a good training or calibration paper.

Anchor sets should include examples that represent solid scores at each performance level, papers with unique or alternative solutions, and examples that are "on the line" between score points that might need discussion as to how to decide a score. This is when we can again talk about "taste" or what, if anything, might put a paper over the line between two scores.

INDIVIDUAL REVIEWER RUBRIC SCORE SHEET

Reviewer ID#:
Date:

Assessment Task Name/Number:

List Student ID #s

Letters Below Correspond to Each Rubric Criterion
(E.g., In a math assessment, A = Appropriate Strategy; B = Representations; C = Computation and Use of Symbols and Terms; D = Justification and Reasoning. E and F are left blank if there are no other criteria to score.)

	A	B	C	D	E	F

Scoring Notes/Comments

S = Solid at This Score
A = Alternative Solution
UF = Unique Feature/Approach
BT = Between Score Points
Other?

PLC TOOL #15 Calibration Tool: Team Rubric Score Sheet

This matrix is used for identifying consensus scores and assessment anchors. Think of this as "step 2" in the process, compiling scores from individual reviewers. When there is consensus or agreement across raters, anchor papers can be chosen to illustrate a variety of ways to achieve each score point. One Team Rubric Score Sheet is used for *four different pieces* of student work.

At least three people must score each piece of work <u>before</u> compiling scores. (To save time, you can sort samples of scored work from your SWA or pre-score examples before meeting and using PLC **TOOL #14**.) Table leaders are chosen to record each reviewer's scores by criterion.

1. Record all individual reviewer scores for a given piece of student work. (A, B, C, etc. are for <u>each rubric criterion</u>.)

2. Indicate (X) where all reviewers at the table had consensus on the assigned scores.

3. Decide if the work sample should be used for training or as an anchor paper. (Anchor papers can be scored by multiple scorers with high level of exact agreement or can be useful for training discussions if there are unique features in the solution or product.)

TEAM RUBRIC SCORE SHEET

Tool 15

Content Area: **Assessment Task:**   **Table Leader:**   **Date:**

Use one Team Rubric Score Sheet form for *4 different pieces* of student work. Have at least three people score each piece of work before you compile scores. (To save time, you can sort samples of scored work from your SWA.)
List each reviewer's scores by criterion (e.g., in art, A = Use of Space; B = Applying Principles of Design, etc.).

1. Record all individual reviewer scores for a given piece of student work. (A, B, C, etc., are for <u>each rubric criterion</u>).
2. Indicate *X* where all reviewers at the table had consensus on the assigned scores.
3. Decide if the work should be used for training or as an anchor paper. (Anchor papers can be scored by multiple scorers with high level of exact agreement, or can be useful for training if there are unique features.)

	List Each Reviewer	Record Score for Each Rubric Criterion						Causes of Discrepancies in Individual Scores?	Developing Scoring Packets for Training	
	Reviewer Name or ID # Scoring the same work	A	B	C	D	E	F	Scoring Notes/Discrepancies	Use as anchor paper yes/no?	Reason for Selection S = Solid score point A = Alternative solution UF = Unique feature BT = Between score points Other?
Student ID #1										
	Team Consensus?									
Student ID #2										

164   A Local Assessment Toolkit to Promote Deeper Learning

3.6 Cognitive Labs: An Effective and Efficient Alternative to Piloting New Assessments

You've developed some performance assessments and scoring rubrics, but what happens if you give it to students and they don't do very well because the task itself was not as clear as it could have been? You have three choices to get an assessment ready for "prime time" (meaning administration to a large number of students): field testing, piloting, or conducting a cognitive lab.

Field testing is one of three common strategies used for determining how well a new or draft assessment will "perform"—meaning how effective is this assessment (test items, reading passages, overall difficulty, and tasks) in eliciting the intended evidence of learning? Field testing requires that a large representative sample of students (across gender, income, ability, race/ethnicity, etc.) take an assessment—such as a state reading or science assessment—before it is administered to all students at that grade level in the following year. Student responses from the field test are disaggregated by subgroup and analyzed to determine which test items and tasks can be used as currently written, which items or tasks need to be revised and field tested a second time before they can be used, and which ones should not be used at all in the operational test. This strategy is used most often by testing companies, either by embedding new (field test) items into an existing test at that grade level, or administering the test to students at the intended or an adjacent grade level who will not be taking this assessment in the future. Sometimes testing companies will field-test a new assessment in a state where those students will not be taking this particular test.

Because this approach is costly and time-consuming, it is not ideal for schools to employ. That said, one way I have seen larger schools or consortia of schools successfully use field testing is with development of performance tasks, such as "testing" new writing prompts. A representative sample of at least 100 students at the intended grade level (across multiple schools or districts) is given the task to complete. Work samples are collected and collaboratively analyzed by teachers. The goal is NOT to score every paper, but to see if a large enough number of samples exhibit the intended assessment evidence. If you find that after looking at the first twenty-five papers, for example, the prompt was unclear or students did not provide enough evidence to be scored, then you might assume that some revision will be needed before the task can be widely used. If most student samples are scorable, but fall into the lower performance levels, the committee may determine that instruction was not adequate or expectations were unreasonable for this grade level. Either way, this assessment task probably needs some work.

Piloting is a second common strategy used for determining how well a new or draft assessment will "perform." An assessment piloting process requires fewer students than does field testing a new assessment and is therefore a more time-efficient strategy for "trying out" new assessments. In a locally designed pilot, students from a minimum of two or three representative classrooms (within or across schools) will take an assessment. Then educators collect and collaboratively review the results (student work, scoring rubrics, administration guidelines, etc.) to determine whether or not this assessment elicited the intended evidence and can be reliably scored. Student work analysis (PLC **TOOL #12**) is used to refine both task prompts and rubrics. For strong assessments, scoring anchors may also be identified during the piloting phase.

A **cognitive laboratory—or cognitive lab**—is a method of studying the mental processes one uses when completing a task, such as solving a mathematics problem, interpreting a text passage when reading, or uncovering potential flaws of a designed science investigation. The idea of someone revealing his or her own mental processes by talking about how he or she performs a task is actually quite common. People often "think out loud" in everyday life, such as when a teacher asks a student to solve and explain a mathematics problem for the rest of the class or when a leader is asked to justify the reasoning used to make his or her policy decision.

Cognitive labs are used by researchers and test writers in the development of surveys, questionnaires, and a variety of assessment types from diagnostic to performance tasks used in large-scale assessments. Sometimes cognitive labs are used to better understand why students chose particular distractors in multiple-choice items. Federal agencies involved in the collection of survey data (e.g., Bureau of the Census, Bureau of Labor Statistics) regularly use this approach to assist in understanding how to interpret respondents' thought processes as they respond to survey questions. I've personally been involved in using cognitive labs to develop and refine performance tasks for the Vermont state science assessments, to conduct research regarding accessibility of test items, and to help fine-tune teacher-developed performance tasks in proficiency-based assessment systems in New Hampshire.

Why Might Educators Use Cognitive Labs?

We generally tend to assume that when a student answers a test question correctly, the student has mastery of the concept or skills being measured. Conversely, it is assumed that when a student answers a question incorrectly, it is because the student does not have mastery of the concept. In reality, we cannot always discern between those students who actually have mastery, those students who answered the item correctly because there was a "clue" hidden somewhere in the question, or those students who answer questions incorrectly for the wrong reasons, such as getting it wrong because of some confusion in reading the test question or understanding the graphics displayed.

Cognitive labs capture information about the reasons behind student performance, thereby enabling test developers and educators to determine whether students are using the knowledge and skills intended for a given item. Such information facilitates further refinement of test items, and ultimately enhances the reliability and validity of achievement tests. When used as formative assessment probes in the classroom, the teacher can act immediately to correct or reteach a misconception that has been uncovered during the cognitive lab.

What Does a Cognitive Lab Look Like?

Cognitive labs are conducted with either small groups or individual students, focusing on directly observable behavior while students are working (e.g., how they use manipulatives, how long it takes to solve a problem or task, did they struggle with reading some words) and then questioning students immediately after the testing (e.g., what was clear or unclear, what was challenging for them, how did they approach the problem).

Using cognitive labs as formative assessment probes in the classroom

In addition to using cognitive labs to make decisions about the usefulness and validity of assessments by analyzing data from observations or surveys, cognitive labs can also be used to make instructional decisions based on what students know and can do during the learning process.

Teachers may want to *intentionally* do any or all of the following when conducting a cognitive lab in their classrooms in order to make instructional decisions, or to refine current assessment practices:

- Listen to students "thinking out loud" while working
- Make observations
- Ask students to explain approaches or solutions
- Ask students about their perceptions of the problems or passages (e.g., "Why was this question difficult or easy?" "Did you like this passage?" "Why or why not?");
- Ask student to keep journals where they can reflect on their own learning

General Cognitive Lab Protocols

There are actually three parts to conducting a cognitive lab:

- *Parts #1 and #2 (data collection)* may be done by individuals or pairs of facilitators. Different teachers can collect data on the same tasks or assessments with different students. It does not have to be the classroom teacher who collects the data for draft common assessments that will be used by many teachers across classrooms or schools. Identify any staff member to pull a few students out of class to take the assessment.

- *Part #3 (interpret data and revise tasks)* is best done through collaborative discussions and analysis of student work (e.g., content committee members or teachers who teach the same course and plan to use the assessment).

Preparing for the cognitive lab

Identify a small representative sample of students: The ideal is to use a small number of students with a range of abilities. This will give you a better idea of how the general population of students will respond to the assessment. It's important to include lower- to higher-performing students and to include at least one student with special needs that is representative of your population (e.g., ELL student, student with an IEP). A minimum of three to six students with differing abilities taking the same assessment will provide a wealth of information in a short amount of time. To facilitate scheduling, different teachers in different schools can each conduct labs for the same assessment task with a few students.

For longer assessments, such as interim or benchmark assessments with multiple sections or tasks, consider breaking the assessment into parts. Different students can take different parts of the assessment, as long as you are sure to include students with varying abilities for each part. Assign a unique ID number to each student, rather than using the student's name.

Helpful hints for conducting cognitive labs

I've worked long term with several school districts to help them develop new performance assessment tasks for K–12 and then conduct cognitive labs to refine them. Many thanks go to district and school leaders in districts I've worked with—Chris Rashleigh (Gillette, WY), Bob Stanton (Stowe, VT), and Bill

> View a video clip of Karin Hess (2017) conducting a cognitive lab with CTE students in New Hampshire at http://www.karin-hess.com/free-resources.

Demers (Littleton, NH)—for providing feedback that has enhanced my helpful hints for conducting cognitive labs.

1. Find a quiet place and estimate time needed for the slowest student to finish. (Rough estimates: 1 min/multiple-choice item; 5–8 min/constructed response item; 20–55 minutes for performance tasks; longer tasks may require two sessions)
2. Set up data collection worksheets ahead of time for each assessment. Fill in rubric criteria as in the example for analyzing observations and student work.
3. Use a clipboard for taking notes while walking around the room as it makes it easy to jot down ideas while on the move, from student to student.
4. Photocopy the task or assessment and reduce size, so you will have adequate room for jotting down margin notes as students offer their feedback.
5. Have a copy of the scoring rubric handy in case you want to refer to it.
6. Use sticky notes for flagging some "potential" anchor papers or benchmarks in student work collected (e.g., parts of tasks that worked well in eliciting evidence).

Preparing students for what to expect

Provide a little introduction to tell students what you are doing and why you are doing it. (You want to know if the problems are clearly written, if they are not too easy or not too difficult, and the thinking strategies used to complete the tasks.) Tell them you'll be making some notes while they work; and after they all finish, you'll ask them some questions about the tasks or problems they completed and how they solved them. You'll also ask them if they have some suggestions about how to improve aspects of the problems (clarify student directions, enlarge the print, provide additional tools, etc.). I usually model a brief "think aloud" for students, so they get the idea, such as doing a math problem or mentally visualizing and counting how many windows are in my house. Most of all, be sure to thank students when you finish.

Cognitive Lab Part 1: Observe and Document—Done While Students Are Working

Take notes in a systematic way—such as using margin notes directly on the assessment task or using sticky notes with student questions.

Record the starting and ending times for each student to determine estimates for all students who might take the assessment in the future. Older students can record the starting and ending times on their own papers.

Circulate around the room:

- Record questions students ask—are they clarifying terms, procedural questions, or related to task content?
- Engagement—note where the struggles are (texts, use of specific tools, etc.)
- Identify specific things that several students mentioned or asked you about
- DECIDE what things you'd like to know or ask about, such as the complexity of a text
    - ✓ Listening to students thinking out loud while they work

Sometimes, students are asked to verbalize thoughts while remaining focused on completing the task. For example, in multiplying 24 by 36, a student might say out loud "36 times 24" . . . "4 times 6" . . . "24" . . . "write down 4" . . . "carry the 2" . . . "2 times 3" . . . and so on, until arriving at the answer, 864.

$$36 \times 24 = ?$$

In reading a text passage and then responding to questions, a teacher might make notes about accuracy (e.g., *key words* read or pronounced incorrectly, key words a student might ask for the meaning of) or fluency in order to interpret how well she or he understood the passage or test question.

✓ Making observations

Two students doing the same mathematics problem might approach the problem in different ways. One might reach for a calculator, press some buttons, and arrive at the answer, 864; another might rewrite the problem vertically before solving it using mental math.

In reading, the interviewer might be able to observe reading strategies used, such as tracking text, rereading a section, making side notes, or subvocalizing. After reading the passage, the interviewer might ask directly which strategies the student used, or say something like "It looked like you went back to reread that part. Can you tell me about whether that was helpful?" Of course, fluency and accuracy can also be observed if the student is reading orally.

✓ Asking students to explain solutions or responses

After students complete the task, they then describe their thought process for solving the problem or constructing the response. This can be done as a small group or individually. Students might also be asked for their perception of the difficulty of a text or a mathematics problem, whether or not it held their interest, or what they thought the most challenging aspect was. We also might ask a student how he or she knew this was the correct response or how or why he or she eliminated the other responses.

COGNITIVE LAB PART 2
Small Group Interview

After students finish, ask them a few questions, such as the ones below. Print out your questions ahead of time with enough room for taking notes. You may want to ask questions based on your notes and observations (e.g., I noticed when some of you were working on this part . . . ; can you tell me about your thinking when you were solving this one?)

Thinking Aloud With Students After They Complete the Assessment

When students have completed the assessment, take about 10 minutes to ask them questions like these (large group, small groups, or ask a few individuals that represent your high to low performing students). Also add your own observations and recommendations.

"I'd like to ask you some questions about the task: _____"

1. Were the directions clear? Did you know what you were supposed to do? Did you understand all parts of the task?

2. Was the [planning sheet, graphic organizer, checklist, manipulative] helpful?

3. What was the easiest part? Why?

4. What was the hardest or most confusing part? Why?

5. Have you done tasks like this before in your classroom? How did this one compare—Easier? Harder? About the same?

6. Can you suggest ways to improve this task for use next year?

7. Other?

For the full version of **TOOL 17**, see page 203.

COGNITIVE LAB PART 3A
Interpret Student Work Samples and Make Decisions

Collaboratively review and discusses observations/notes (be sure notes are clear—it may be a while before you get together to do this!)

Collectively review all samples of student work. Look at evidence across different facilitators and populations—what was the same? What was different?

Determine Next Steps—What needs fixing?

☐ Revise student directions, prompts, visuals, texts, for clarity

☐ Delete items/parts—due to excessive time needed, developmental appropriateness

---

COGNITIVE LAB PART 3B
Collaboratively Interpreting Evidence in Student Work

Performance Task _____ Grade /Course _____
Total Number of Students Assessed ___
Estimated Time Needed _____ (*based on cog lab times: slowest _____ fastest _____*)

(Notes below are drawn from across *all assessment tasks/parts and rubric criteria*)

What did you <u>expect to see</u> in student work? What does "proficient" look like? [e.g., Skills—apply formula for area]	What evidence <u>did you see</u> in the student work? Is it the same as described in the scoring rubric? [Use student ID #s if useful for referring back to the work]
Process Criteria: Applying skills/procedures, use of formulas, strategies, approach, gathering and organizing data or evidence	

For the full version of **TOOL 18**, see page 204. For the full version of **TOOL 19**, see page 205.

3.7 Guidelines for Creating Task Validation Teams: Analyzing the Technical Quality of Assessments

There really isn't one right way to design an assessment; but having a thoughtful, iterative, and collaborative process is critical in developing high-quality assessments for your local assessment system. Even if your school district purchases its assessments, many protocols in this toolkit can and should be used to ensure that all assessments are of high quality and administered with fidelity. I've provided several strategies for getting started with developing and refining draft assessments to ensure that they have a high degree of technical quality before making high-stakes decisions using the results. Different assessments will benefit from using different strategies, which include the following:

(a) using CRM **TOOLS #1–#5D** to develop questions and task prompts for deeper thinking;

(b) using Text Complexity **TOOLS #6–#8** to select a range of texts and a variety of text-based question prompts for assessment;

(c) using sample assessment targets to develop a range of text-based questions and prompts (Module 2);

(d) using PLC **TOOL #9 or #10** to codevelop assessments that are engaging and uncover thinking and deeper reasoning;

(e) using PLC **TOOL #11** to develop and get feedback on rubric quality;

(f) using PLC **TOOL #12** to collect and analyze student work samples; or

(g) using PLC **TOOLS #17–#19** to conduct cognitive labs to fine-tune directions or parts of the assessment prior to wider administration.

Over the years, I have found that high-priority summative assessments (e.g., final exams, unit tests, exhibitions, project-based assessments) and performance assessments used as common formative, interim, or summative assessments improve greatly when there is a formal review of their technical quality. A review of this kind answers several questions: Is the assessment valid (aligned to both the intended content and rigor); do scoring guides and support materials such as annotated student work ensure that the assessment will be scored reliably (the same) by different teachers; will it engage students in authentic applications of skills and concepts (transfer); and is it free of bias and designed to be flexible enough for all students to show what they have learned? My term for conducting a formal, collaborative assessment review is *task validation*.

- Task validations are part of an ongoing process, not one-time events.

- Task validations are not necessary for all assessments, so start with the ones used for making high-stakes decisions, such as determining whether a student has met a district proficiency requirement.

- A *validated assessment* is one that has gone through a critical revision process and has been determined to measure what it was intended to measure. Therefore, users of the assessment can make valid interpretations about student learning based on scores given.

During a task validation, a school- or district-based team meets to analyze assessments developed by their peers. The overall goals of task validation are developing a common language for assessment quality or calibration and providing constructive advice for improving both assessment and instructional practice across all content areas. Teams often review the same assessment more than once using a validation process guided by criteria and questions in PLC **TOOL #9**.

Validation criteria—clarity, alignment to content and rigor, scoring reliability, student engagement, and fairness are systematically reviewed, discussed, and documented. Validation team members then give their peers feedback in the form of descriptive comments and questions. Teacher teams who developed the assessment reflect on the feedback, decide what should be revised, and at some point may resubmit their assessment for a second review. Two things I can say for sure about using this task validation process over more than a decade in many states: No assessment ever gets by with "flying colors" on the first review; and the resulting quality of the revised assessment always improves. Collaboration works!

Preparing to Have an Assessment Formally Reviewed

Several important things need to happen before conducting a task validation. Decisions must be made about which teachers will make up each validation team and when time will be allowed for guided practice and calibration and for the actual validation meetings. Most schools try to use existing structures, such as their scheduled professional development days or during PLC or grade-level team time to conduct the validations. Once time structures are determined, the assessments to be reviewed are put on a schedule and prepared for review. Don't be overambitious with scheduling; completing one round (one assessment/team) each month is a good way to begin. Estimate at least 1 to 1 ½ hours for a task validation review to be completed. We have typically organized several different teams to work simultaneously, so that several assessments can be reviewed on the same day. For example, if a middle school has three instructional teams, each team might validate an assessment developed by another team, so that three assessments go through the process at the same time. Then allow at least three more weeks for task feedback and revisions before scheduling your next session.

Determining the Makeup of Validation Teams

While working over several school years with the K–12 staff and administrators in Park County School District #1 (Powell, WY), a valuable lesson was reinforced: EVERY staff member needs to be involved in the assessment development and validation process. This work began with the district superintendent making it clear that every teacher would codevelop, refine, and implement at least two performance tasks of DOK 3 or 4 each school year. This included all special subject teachers (fine arts, Health/PE, world languages, etc.) as well as all classroom teachers. All special education teachers and instructional coaches joined a grade-level or content team to work with on-task design and were assigned to validation teams accordingly. All building principals were members of a validation team.

Once the task design and validation processes had been practiced for two school years, I queried the administrative team to see if they wanted me to try to streamline the validation process a bit. The immediate response from the administrators was, "No! We've never before had such rich discussions about assessment quality and assessment practices in our district. We've never had discussions like this at the high school across departments and never really included our special education staff in assessment design."

When I've asked teachers about their participation in the task design and validation processes, typically I hear something like this: "It wasn't so much the feedback from peers about my assessments, but looking at the assessments of my peers that really made me think differently about how to improve my own assessments."

Each school district will need to consider the best configurations for creating validation teams that will involve every staff member at each school. Often elementary teams are structured differently than middle and high school teams. Here are some ideas to guide your thinking about team makeup.

VALIDATION PRINCIPLE 1: Each local validation team represents the diversity of the school or district.

- Involve everyone on a team, including administrators, curriculum leaders, teachers, and instructional coaches.

- All content areas and grade levels or grade spans are represented (decisions may differ depending on school configurations and staffing, but diversity in teams is critical, especially including special educators and special-subject teachers on every team).

- Elementary teams may configure by grade spans, middle schools by instructional teams (e.g., each team with an ELA, math, science, and social studies teacher), and high schools with one department member on EACH team. I do not recommend content-based teams for validations. Content teams develop the assessments; cross-content teams validate the assessments.

- Have representation from special subjects, such as fine arts, HPE, CTE, foreign language, ELL, on each validation team (divide members of this group across teams in the most meaningful ways you can).

- Consider team size. Teams with more than six to eight members are generally too large and become unproductive. Consider having one member representing each of the core content areas (ELA, math, science, social studies) + one special subject teacher + one special educator/resource teacher/ELL teacher + administrator or instructional coach on each team.

VALIDATION PRINCIPLE 2: Provide guided practice in task design and task validation.

It's important to educate and engage all staff in processes for developing, validating, and eventually scoring common assessments and analyzing student work products. Yes, this takes time at the start, but it will increase the consistency of schoolwide expectations and build a common language for describing the quality of student work. The first rounds are for calibrating these understandings and processes. Later rounds are for improving assessment quality and interpreting assessment results. I begin each new process first by modeling (using a less-than-perfect assessment that I provide), then by providing guided practice with debriefing, and finally by letting teams take the lead.

VALIDATION PRINCIPLE 3: Frequency and involvement will vary or be determined by the intended uses of the assessment task validation tools and protocols.

First, identify your short- and long-term purpose(s):

- Develop new assessments; smaller teams work on new assessments.

- Analyze existing assessments; larger, more representative teams review draft assessments.

- Validate a revised assessment or new assessments prior to broader administration or purchase (e.g., tasks available from existing task banks).

- Provide OBJECTIVE feedback to assessment developers—whole school or district.

- Promote collaboration and a shared understanding of high-quality assessment—whole school or district.

- Assemble (or update) a "collection" (task bank) of validated common performance assessments. As common performance assessments achieve validation with analysis of student work, create electronic files of agreed-upon proficient work samples—whole school or district working in smaller teams.

Then determine frequency and staff involvement:

- Initially, learning and debriefing the process together serves as calibration—so everyone is on the same page—"developing a shared understanding" of what high-quality assessment looks like.

- School teams set up their schedules—once each month, every other month, as needed—identified by highest priority (time and semester to be given, for making high-stakes decisions).

- Team members may eventually rotate on and off so more (all) staff are regularly involved over time, but NOT before all staff have been engaged with the process.

Prepare assessments for validation panels:

- Grade-level or department teams develop the assessments using (a) the CRM **TOOLS #1–#5D** for the content area; (b) PLC **TOOL #9**, the Basic Validation Protocol; and (c) a scoring rubric or guide using PLC **TOOL #11** (e.g., a Grade 2 team might develop a common mathematics assessment for all Grade 2 classes or schools). The team might also decide to pilot the task with one or two classrooms or conduct a cognitive lab with a small number of students prior to bringing the task to the validation panel. This will help to streamline what might need more revision later and allow developers to collect some student work samples.

- Developers create brief administration guidelines[7] for the task, providing general instructions to any teacher who might want to use the assessment in his or her classes. This is very important for all commonly administered assessments.

- Developers put the assessment on the local (school or district) validation calendar.

---

7. Examples of Assessment Administration Guidelines and an assessment administration template are included in the Module 3 Support Materials.

- Developers complete a task cover sheet describing the assessment parts or what will be reviewed by the panel. When we began to run validation panels, we did not require a cover sheet from developers but soon found that panels were spending too much time searching for parts that were not included or not well organized. The cover page simply lets the validation panel know what to look for (e.g., rubric, texts used, and student work samples with indicators of scores given).

- Developers make multiple copies of the assessment or provide a link to where it can be downloaded. Support materials such as texts or text passages or student work do not need to be duplicated, but <u>at least one set</u> should be available to the validation team.

- Developers also provide scoring rubrics and answer keys, if appropriate.

- Validation panels prioritize the order of validations: for example, common assessments, major assessments reviewed first, second round review after getting feedback.

Local Assessment Cover Page for Task Validation

First submission (date)

Re-submission (date)

Subject Area:

Grade Level/Department: Developer(s):

Title of Assessment:

Alignment Information:

- List (parts or combinations of) Content Standard(s) Assessed:

- List Essential Skills/Content Assessed (what is the focus?):

- Identify intended rigor assessed (list DOK levels with descriptors):

- Describe what this assessment is intended to accomplish (purpose):

(Continued)

(Continued)

When is this assessment administered?

Grade level___

Time of year/MP_____

Course/Unit of Study_____

Type of Assessment/Item Types: Check all that apply.

- ❏ *Selected Response* (multiple choice, true/false, matching, etc.)
- ❏ *Short answer* (short constructed response; fill in a graphic organizer or diagram, explain or justify your reasoning or solution, make and complete a table, etc.)
- ❏ *Product* (essay, research paper, editorial, log, journal, play, poem, model, multimedia, art products, script, musical score, portfolio pieces, etc.)
- ❏ *Performance* (demonstration, presentation, science lab, dance or music performance, athletic performance, debate, etc.)
- ❏ Other?

Scoring Guide: Check all that apply and please attach.

- ❏ Answer key, scoring template, computerized or machine scored
- ❏ *Generalized Rubric* (e.g., for text-based writing, for all science labs)
- ❏ *Task-Specific Rubric* (only used for this task)
- ❏ *Checklist* (e.g., with score points for each part)
- ❏ Teacher Observation Sheet or Observation Checklist

Identify possible allowable accommodations for this assessment:

DESCRIPTION OF ACCOMMODATIONS CATEGORIES

Accommodations are commonly categorized in four ways—presentation, response, setting, and timing and scheduling. Check all that apply:

- ❏ *Presentation Accommodations*—Allow students to access information in ways that do not require them to visually read standard print. These alternate modes of access are auditory, multisensory, tactile, and visual.
- ❏ *Response Accommodations*—Allow students to complete activities, assignments, and assessments in different ways or to solve or organize problems using some type of assistive device or organizer.
- ❏ *Setting Accommodations*—Change the location in which a test or assignment is given or the conditions of the assessment setting.
- ❏ *Timing and Scheduling Accommodations*—Increase the allowable length of time to complete an assessment or assignment and perhaps change the way the time is organized.

Has this assessment been field tested or piloted? If yes, when?

If no, when will it be field tested or piloted?

Are there student anchor papers to illustrate <u>proficient</u> work? (Please describe what's included.)

Are there student anchor papers to illustrate other performance levels (low to highest)? (Please describe what's included; use sticky notes on student work samples, if helpful.)

This submission includes (indicate all that apply) the following:

- ❑ Teacher directions for administration or scoring
- ❑ Administration Guide is attached
- ❑ Includes prerequisites or description of instruction before giving the assessment (e.g., this assessment should be given after students have learned . . .)
- ❑ Scoring guides or rubrics and answer keys for multiple-choice questions, short-answer items, constructed response or performance-based tasks
- ❑ Sample anchor papers to show what student performance might look like at the "proficient" level _____ other performance levels _____
- ❑ Materials (if needed to complete the assessment, such as text passages)
- ❑ Estimated time for administration

Other

- ❑ Student Directions and Assessment Task or Prompt—what the student sees or uses

Analyzing Assessments for Technical Quality: Conducting a Task Validation

Materials for the Validation Panel

- Each panel member needs (electronic or hard copy) validation protocol (PLC **TOOL #9**).

- Each person needs a copy of the cover pages with the assessment and scoring rubric or answer key attached.

- There may be additional materials, such as anchor papers or examples of student work that do not need to be copied for everyone but may be helpful to see during the review.

- Each person needs a content specific DOK reference sheet (Module 1, Hess CRM **TOOLS #1-#5D** as appropriate to content of assessment).

- One copy of Task Validation Summary and Recommendations (PLC **TOOL #16A OR #16B**)

Validation Protocols

A task validation session takes about 75 to 90 minutes. The process helps the panel of four to six people ascertain whether the assessment presented has achieved technical quality for each criterion. It may help to have one of the task developers briefly (5 minutes) provide an overview of the assessment submitted for review and answer any clarifying questions right at the start of the session. We have not found it helpful for developers to remain as observers to the review panel discussions—this is especially true when you are just starting out with task reviews.

STEP 1: Start by determining who on the panel will act in the roles of the facilitator and recorder. Two key jobs of the facilitator are to be sure everyone on the panel has a chance to provide input and to keep the group moving along. Sometimes a timekeeper can also be helpful (5 minutes).

STEP 2: Next, quickly review and update the group's norms. It's helpful to get agreement on norms and to add, delete, or revise some of them before beginning. Agreed-upon norms allow members to hold each other accountable while working. Below is an example of group norms (Figure 3.5), a draft used in Powell, Wyoming (5 minutes).

STEP 3: One of the developers briefly walks the panel through the materials and explains the context of the assessment. Then, panel members skim the assessment materials silently and ask a limited number of clarifying questions about the materials. If the developer is not there to present the assessment, the panel does a quick skimming of the assessment materials to clarify what they are to review. This time is not for depth of understanding the assessment or for analysis (5–10 minutes).

STEP 4: Individuals now silently review each part of the assessment and make their own notes. Facilitators may need to remind panels this is for initial impressions or questions (15–20 minutes).

STEP 5: After each member has had time to look more closely at the assessment, the facilitator leads the group through each section of the Validation Checklist/PLC **TOOL #9**. Decide on a process to reach consensus (fist 5, thumbs up, etc.). Be sure to involve each person! Once there is consensus on each section, the recorder documents key points, including positive points, to be used for summarizing feedback to developers (30–50 minutes).

Figure 3.5 Example of Group Norms

I AM	I AM NOT
• Keeping electronic devices on vibrate or off	• Using killer phrases
• Listening to understand other points of view	• Preparing my next remark instead of listening
• Respecting everyone as a professional	• Sounding apologetic
• Focusing on the issues	• Engaging in unrelated activities
• Avoiding side conversations	• Using negative gestures or body language
• Encouraging everyone having a turn to speak	• Others?
• Refraining from judgmental statements	
• Representing the best interests of all students	
• Asking clarifying questions	
• Demonstrating a commitment to the process (attending meetings, on time, etc.)	
• Others?	

When the review is completed, there will be summary notes for each section of the Validation Checklist/PLC **TOOL #9** that can now be clarified and transferred to PLC **TOOL #16A OR #16B**.

- Clarity and Focus
- Content Alignment
- Rigor Alignment
- Scoring Reliability
- Student Engagement
- Fairness and Principles of Universal Design for Learning (UDL)
- And the overarching question: What makes this a high-quality assessment?

  STEP 6: Summarize final recommendations and choose two panel members to share feedback with the developers. It may sound silly, but they should "rehearse" what they plan to say. Why have two panel members deliver feedback? It's easy to forget what to say or to feel a bit uncomfortable saying it. A second person provides moral support and makes scheduling the brief feedback meeting easier. More than two panel members can make developers feel a bit overwhelmed. So, I suggest starting with two and meeting in person (10 minutes).

Remember that being a "critical friend" means not being too critical (harsh and negative), and also not being too friendly (afraid to be honest with your feedback).

Suggestions for giving feedback

- Use descriptive language, NOT judgmental language.

- While you may wonder about instructional aspects, comments or suggestions about instruction are probably not appropriate.

- Your job is NOT to redo or rewrite the assessment! Keep feedback crisp and to the point (e.g., pose a question: "We are wondering if students can work with a partner on this step?"). It is the developers' job to decide what to do next to strengthen the assessment tasks.

- Well-written, clear feedback guides assessment developers to make a stronger assessment in the end. See feedback examples below.

- Place your most positive (and descriptive) comments under the feedback section at the bottom of PLC **TOOL #16A**: What makes this a HQ (high-quality) assessment? If you decide to use PLC **TOOL #16B**, it will require more detailed feedback.

Examples of How to Say "It" in Descriptive, NOT Judgmental, Words

1. "The rubric assesses all key aspects of the task."
2. "Teacher instructions and support materials are very helpful."
3. "We were unable to locate. . . . Did you forget to include it?"
4. "We think this might be DOK 2, not DOK 3, because. . . . What do you think?"
5. "We were not clear what the student is expected to do or to produce. Did you mean . . . ?"
6. "This might be better aligned to this content standard . . . because. . . ."
7. As hard as it will be, avoid saying "We liked. . . ." This implies you did not like other things and your job is NOT to like the assessment.
8. Don't tell them WHAT to do—"You have to revise this rubric" feels a bit preachy.
9. Suggest what might be missing—"Have you considered adding a criterion for representations? It seems that it is a required component to this task that has not been included in the rubric."
10. Include some "HQ" positives at the end! "The student directions are clear; students have authentic choices," for example.

STEP 7: Don't skip the DEBRIEF! (5 minutes)

- Did the validation team honor the norms at all times?
- Do we need to modify or revise norms?
- What went well?
- What could have gone better?
- What will we do differently next time?
- Who will meet with authors to give feedback?

STEP 8: You may be tempted to slip your feedback into a mailbox or to email it. I suggest meeting in person with developers to share feedback—it's the "friendly" part of being a critical friend. It is the developers' job to review feedback and determine their next steps.

An ongoing validation process helps the school or district maintain a consistent high level of instructional and assessment practice. Many teachers make comments like this after using the protocol: "Even when we teach the same grade, we can have different interpretations of the same rubrics. This helps us to build consistency across content areas and make expectations clear for us and our students."

TASK VALIDATION SUMMARY
(Use notes from PLC Tool #9 to develop your summary)

Tool 16A

Assessment:
Date of Review: Validation Team:

Feedback Summary: Comments and Questions From Validation Team

Clarity and Focus	
Validity: Content Alignment	
Validity: Rigor Alignment	
Scoring Reliability	
Student Engagement	

Module 3: What Does This Test Really Measure?

Reflections

On your own or with colleagues, take a minute to reflect on the topics covered in this module. Then identify a useful takeaway, something to try next.

Ways I am refining my thinking about what makes something a high-quality assessment

- Must be designed for all learners to show what they know
- ?

Strategies for assessing deeper thinking with formative-interim-summative assessments

- Build (formative) probing questions into each lesson
- ?

℞ *My personal prescription for improving the technical quality and use of my assessments...*

PART 2: SUPPORT MATERIALS FOR MODULE 3

I. A Workshop Plan for Module 3

Kolb's Experiential Learning Cycle

Suggested Activities

Stage 1: WHY is this new learning important to me? And what do I already know?

Moving from Concrete Experience to Reflective Observation

Create a concrete experience, asking participants to make connections, drawing on personal knowledge and experience. Small groups compare and reflect on common ideas.

- Activity: Analyze an assessment scenario and identify components that make it an effective (high-quality) assessment.

- Activity: Ask participants to quickly brainstorm a variety of performance assessments. Then select one example and collaboratively answer several questions: *What skills and concepts are being measured with this assessment? How can best or excellent performance be differentiated from poor performance? What makes this a performance assessment?* Use the examples generated to derive the research about all high-quality assessment.

Stage 2: WHAT do the research and experts say?

Moving from Reflective Observation to Abstract Conceptualization

Help participants connect their personal reflections to broader, more abstract generalizations and research on characteristics of high-quality assessment.

- Provide expert advice or research via interactive lecture, short readings, or suggested video clips.

- Use formative and summative assessment exemplars to illustrate features of high-quality assessments and to further develop concepts and build schemas. Stop frequently (every 15–20 min.) to consolidate the new learning.

- Activity: Create a visual display illustrating differences among assessment types, purposes, and uses.

(Continued)

(Continued)

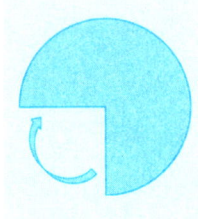

Stage 3: HOW does this work? How can I apply this?

Moving from Abstract Conceptualization to Active Experimentation

Use tools and protocols to examine assessment examples and strategies.

- Introduce Hess PLC **TOOLS #9 and #10**, making connections to research-based indicators of high-quality formative and performance assessment. Use criteria in the Tools to self-assess current strengths and challenges in developing assessments of high quality.

- Activity: Provide guided practice using **TOOL #10** to collaboratively examine a formative assessment. Ask participants to then examine some of their own formative assessments. They may want to refer to the content-specific Hess CRM **TOOLS (#1–#5D)** as well.

- Activity: Model using PLC **TOOL #9** with a sample performance task. Introduce each factor, allowing time for table groups to complete each analysis before moving to the next factor.

- Page 3 of PLC **TOOL #9** addresses "fairness" and accessibility. After sharing concrete examples, analyze a poorly designed assessment and collaboratively revise the assessment for fairness. Summarize findings using PLC **TOOL #16A**.

Stage 4: WHAT IF I experimented with this? What might work in my classroom or school?

Moving from Active Experimentation back to Concrete Experiences

- Activity: Revisit current assessments used in your curriculum or units of study. Develop or revise locally used performance assessments, using PLC **TOOLS #9 or #10**.

- Activity: Do the Chocolate Chip Cookie Taste Test. Then discuss rubric criteria and various scoring formats. Use PLC **TOOL #11** to examine and provide feedback on current scoring rubrics. Develop a kid-friendly version of a rubric for self-assessment.

- Try out a new performance assessment in your classroom. Collect samples of student work and analyze them using PLC **TOOL #12**.

- Co-analyze results of a common assessment with your peers: Review, reflect, revise (task prompt, administration guide, and rubric), and maybe repilot.

- Create a plan for conducting a cognitive lab with a new assessment. Use PLC **TOOLS # 17–#19** to conduct a cognitive lab with a new performance assessment.

- Set up a process for local validation teams to meet regularly to review assessment quality and assessment results.

- Use PLC **TOOLS #13–#15** to develop anchor papers for future calibration activities using student work that has been sorted, scored, and analyzed. Develop annotations for exemplars.

Source: Stages adapted from Kolb (1984) and McCarthy (1987).

II. The Hess PLC Tools

About the Tools in This Module

The tools in Module 3 have been used by instructional coaches and school leadership teams to develop high-quality assessments and rubrics, pilot and refine new assessments, and create a variety of local training and calibration resources. They are often used in conjunction with the CRM Tools (Module 1) and Text Complexity Tools (Module 2). Most common uses for these PLC tools include the following:

- Developing and refining new performance assessments
- Analyzing existing assessments, including more traditional summative assessments (e.g., final exams, unit tests) and course program–based assessments
- Validating a revised or new assessment prior to broader administration (or purchase)
- Providing OBJECTIVE feedback to assessment developers and colleagues
- Promoting collaboration and a shared understanding of high-quality assessment

Table 3.2 Overview of the Hess PLC Tools

TOOL	POSSIBLE USES FOR EACH HESS PLC TOOL
9 Task Quality Validation Protocol	Developing new assessments or analyzing and revising existing assessments; best for summative and performance assessments.
10 Analyzing Formative Assessments	Analyzing what is being assessed with formative assessments and planning potential next steps for instruction.
11 Rubric Quality Review Worksheet	Providing feedback on seven criteria related to scoring rubric language and format.
12 Student Work Analysis	Revising assessments and rubrics, planning next steps for instruction, identifying assessment anchors and annotation, monitoring progress. FOUR levels are used to force thinking about what might be close to "got it" and what work might reflect just getting started.
13 What Is the Evidence?	Making preliminary notes before developing annotations for assessment anchors; locating evidence in student work.
14 Individual Reviewer Rubric Score Sheet	Doing preliminary scoring by individuals before compiling consensus scores and developing annotated assessment anchors.

(Continued)

Table 3.2 (Continued)

TOOL	POSSIBLE USES FOR EACH HESS PLC TOOL
15 Team Rubric Score Sheet	Compiling team consensus scores and selecting annotated assessment anchors.
16A Task Validation Summary: Short Version	Summarizing feedback from validation panels to development teams; use with PLC TOOL #9. This tool is good for when you are just getting started with validations. It is the "streamlined" version for giving feedback on draft assessments.
16B Task Validation Summary: In-Depth Version	Summarizing feedback from validation panels to development teams; use with PLC TOOL #9. This tool is more detailed for giving validation feedback. It can also be used as a conferencing tool during development of performance assessments.
17 Cognitive Labs Part 2	Thinking Aloud With Students After They Complete the Assessment—small group interview template; can also be used as a teacher–student conferencing tool.
18 Cognitive Labs Part 3A	Interpreting Student Work Samples From Cognitive Labs—some students may have taken different parts of the assessments.
19 Cognitive Labs Part 3B	Collaboratively Interpreting Evidence in Student Work—using student work from Cognitive Labs to validate evidence elicited by the assessment task(s) and to refine rubric language.
20 A Guide to Performance Assessment Development	A Guide to Performance Assessment Development—unpacks the process of developing and designing performance assessments.
21 Performance Assessment Overview: Purpose and Use	Where will the performance assessment be embedded? Use this planning tool to provide an overview of when the assessment will be used and what it is intended to assess.

TASK QUALITY VALIDATION PROTOCOL:
Purpose, Alignment, Engagement, and Fairness | Use for Assessment *Development* or *Analysis of Performance Tasks*

Title of Assessment/Task: Grade Level/Dept/Course/Subject:

Author(s):   or   Reviewer(s):

How will the assessment results be used?

(e.g., screening for placement; diagnostic to inform instruction or to provide targeted additional support; formative or interim for progress monitoring; summative for grading/report card; or other?)

Analyze and discuss each of the assessment components. Check "YES" if there is evidence of each indicator of high-quality assessment listed. Then add any additional notes.

Clarity and Focus

☐ 1. Addresses an **essential issue, big idea, or key concept or skill** of the unit, course, or discipline:

☐ 2. Directions or prompts clearly indicate what the student is being asked to do or produce:

☐ 3. If parts are completed within a group: Specifies what will be assessed **individually** (e.g., projects, multimedia presentations)

☐ 4. **Assesses what is intended to be assessed**—will elicit what the student knows and can do related to the chosen standards and benchmarks. **Any scaffolding** provided (e.g., task broken into smaller steps; graphic organizer to preplan) does not change what is actually being assessed.

☐ 5. Is clearly linked to **ongoing instruction or opportunity to learn** (e.g., assessed within or at the end of a unit of study or course)

Clarity and Focus Notes

Content Alignment

☐ 6. Items or tasks are clearly **aligned with specific or identified content standards** (or intended parts or combinations of content standards)

☐ 7. Appropriate **rubric(s) or scoring guide(s)** assess all intended parts of content standards assessed. Scoring guides are useful in determining what the student knows or does not know, not simply yield a score (e.g., What does a score of 25 really mean? What additional or next steps in instruction does the student need? Are some rubric criteria "weighted" reflecting greater instructional emphasis for this time of year?).

☐ 8. **Exemplars or anchor papers** illustrate expectations aligned to standards at proficient level and performance levels above or below proficient. **Qualitative distinctions between performance levels are evident.**

Content Alignment Notes

(Continued)

continued...

TASK QUALITY VALIDATION PROTOCOL:
Purpose, Alignment, Engagement, and Fairness | Use for Assessment *Development* or *Analysis of Performance Tasks*

Tool 9

Rigor Alignment or Cognitive Demand

☐ 9. Identify Depth-of-Knowledge/DOK levels assessed or emphasized (e.g., number of score points given, weighting in the rubric). For example, an essay would mostly assess DOK 3 (full multiparagraph composition), but also have some DOK 2 items or parts (text organization, structure) and DOK 1 (grammar, conventions) also assessed. You would check "most of the test/task" for DOK 3 and "some of the test/task" for DOK 2 and DOK 1. (See Hess Cognitive Rigor Matrix /CRM Tools for content-specific descriptors of each DOK level.)

DOK 1: Students recall, locate, and reproduce: words, terms, facts; basic application of rules, procedures, which may be routine and multistep

(☐ most of the test/task ☐ some of the test/task ☐ none of the test/task)

DOK 2: Students apply level 1 within the ability to paraphrase, summarize, interpret, infer, classify, organize, compare; determine fact from fiction; solve, as in routine word problems; determine meanings in context. There is a correct answer, but may involve multiple concepts or decision points.

(☐ most of the test/task ☐ some of the test/task ☐ none of the test/task)

DOK 3: Students must support their thinking by citing evidence (e.g., text, data, calculations, models). Students are asked to go beyond the text or data collection to analyze, generalize, or connect to bigger ideas. Requires "uncovering" and interpreting less explicit knowledge. Items may require abstract reasoning, alternate approaches, inferences that connect information, application of prior knowledge, or text support for an analytical judgment.

(☐ most of the test/task ☐ some of the test/task ☐ none of the test/task)

DOK 4: Students use deeper knowledge of content, and evidence of complex reasoning, planning, and developing new ideas, insights, or products **from multiple sources**. Usually applies to an extended task or project. Examples: evaluate works by the same author; critique an issue across time periods or research topic or issue from different perspectives; longer science, math, or arts investigations or research projects involving all phases of design, testing, and refining.

(☐ most of the test/task ☐ some of the test/task ☐ none of the test/task)

☐ 10. Has alignment with the **intended rigor** of the content standards (or parts or combinations of the content standards). Scaffolding does not significantly reduce cognitive demand.

Rigor Alignment Notes

Student Engagement

☐ 11. The situation or scenario or application is **authentic.** Reflects a meaningful, real-world problem, issue, or theme worth exploring.

☐ 12. Provides for student ownership, **choice, and/or decision making**; requires the student to be actively engaged in solution finding.

☐ 13. Is administered after students have had adequate time to learn, practice, and expand their understanding of skills or concepts assessed.

Student Engagement Notes

(Continued)

continued...

TASK QUALITY VALIDATION PROTOCOL:
Purpose, Alignment, Engagement, and Fairness | Use for Assessment *Development* or *Analysis of Performance Tasks*

Tool 9

Fairness: Universal Access and Design Features

- [ ] 14. **Is fair and unbiased in language and design.**
  - [ ] Material is familiar to students from identifiable cultural, gender, linguistic, and other groups
  - [ ] The task stimulus or prompt and materials (context/texts used) are free of stereotypes
  - [ ] All students (e.g., all ability levels) are on a level playing field and have had opportunity to learn
  - [ ] All students have access to necessary resources (e.g., Internet, calculators, spellcheck, etc.)
  - [ ] Assessment conditions are the same for all students or flexible enough not to change what's actually being assessed (e.g., reading a passage aloud may be fine for interpreting overall meaning, but not for assessing ability to decode words)
  - [ ] The task can be reasonably completed under the specified conditions; extended time is allowable
  - [ ] The rubric or scoring guide allows for different response modes (oral, written, etc.)

- [ ] 15. **Adheres to the principles of Universal Design for Learning (UDL)**
  - [ ] Instructions are free of excessive wordiness or irrelevant (unnecessary) information
  - [ ] Instructions are free of unusual words (unusual spellings or unfamiliar word use) that the student may not understand or have been exposed to
  - [ ] Low frequency words (words not used in other content areas, such as technical terms) are only used when explicitly needed or when the assessment is explicitly testing understanding of terms
  - [ ] Instructions are free of ambiguous words
  - [ ] Irregularly spelled words have been avoided whenever possible
  - [ ] There are no proper names that students may not understand (e.g., students have never seen them before in instruction)
  - [ ] Multiple words, symbols, or pronouns intended to mean the same thing are NOT used in the same sentence or stimulus or prompt (e.g., inches and the symbol " for inches; phrases such as the boys, they, the friends)
  - [ ] The format or layout conveys the focus of the expected tasks and products and allows adequate space for responding
  - [ ] The format clearly indicates what the actual questions to answer or prompts are (e.g., each question or prompt is clearly separated from the introductory stimulus or problem context)
  - [ ] Questions or prompts are consistently marked with graphic or visual cues (bullets, numbers, in a text box, etc.)
  - [ ] The test format (spacing, presentation, etc.) is familiar, consistent, and predictable as to what students will be expected to do

- [ ] 16. **Allows for accommodations for students with IEPs or 504 Plans.**
  - [ ] **Presentation**—Students may access information in ways that do not require them to visually read standard print (auditory, multisensory, tactile, and visual).
  - [ ] **Response**—Students may complete activities in different ways or use some type of assistive device or organizer to assist them in responding.
  - [ ] **Setting**—Location in which a test is given or the conditions of the assessment setting are flexible.
  - [ ] **Timing or Scheduling**—The length of time to complete an assessment may be increased and/or the way the time is organized may be changed.

Fairness: Universal Access and Design Notes

Available for download at resources.corwin.com/HessToolkit and www.karin-hess.com/free-resources

© Karin Hess (2009, updated 2013). *Linking research with practice: A local assessment toolkit to guide school leaders.* Permission to reproduce is given when authorship is fully cited [karinhessvt@gmail.com]

ANALYZING FORMATIVE ASSESSMENTS
Strategic Planning Tool

What (thinking or learning) will this formative assessment uncover?

List formative assessment task(s) or probing question(s):

Content Standard(s) Assessed:

Intended Depth-of-Knowledge (DOK) Level(s): ☐ DOK 1   ☐ DOK 2   ☐ DOK 3   ☐ DOK 4

Expected Understandings		Possible Misunderstandings	
Concepts and Reasoning	**Skills and Procedures**	**Common Errors**	**Overgeneralizations**
If I see evidence of this . . . how will it inform my instruction?	If I see evidence of this . . . how will it inform my instruction?	If I see evidence of this . . . how will it inform my instruction?	

Available for download at resources.corwin.com/HessToolkit and www.karin-hess.com/free-resources

© Karin Hess (2009, updated 2013 and 2017). *Linking research with practice: A local assessment toolkit to guide school leaders.* Permission to reproduce is given when authorship is fully cited [karinhessvt@gmail.com]

RUBRIC QUALITY REVIEW WORKSHEET

Tool 11

Assessment/Task:

Date: Reviewer(s):

Questions for Evaluating Rubric Quality	Comments or Feedback for Each Review Question
1. Do the number of performance levels and rubric format make sense? ☐ Format matches purpose and use ☐ Adjacent performance levels are qualitatively different ☐ Levels reflect how completion of the task might naturally progress with instruction	
2. Is descriptive language maximized? ☐ Little or no judgmental language ☐ Avoids use of subjective language (poor, neat, ample, etc.) and frequency indicators (rarely, often, etc.)	
3. Do descriptors emphasize quality over quantity? (e.g., relevant, descriptive details or sources versus three details or sources)	
4. Do descriptors state performance in the positive—what IS happening, rather than what is NOT happening? ☐ Lowest levels focus on beginning stages ☐ Describes a (real) progression of learning ☐ Have student work samples or piloting informed performance descriptions?	
5. Do descriptors describe excellent *rather than* perfect performance? ☐ Describes a progression from Novice to Expert performance ☐ Performance descriptors increase with depth, complexity, and/or breadth of knowledge ☐ Minor errors not weighted more than quality of ideas or thinking	
6. Do rubric language and criteria match rigor expectations of task? ☐ A range of criteria align with task expectations (form, accuracy, process, impact, construction of knowledge) ☐ Not limited to basic skills and concepts or only routine tasks ☐ At least one criterion builds to transfer and construction of knowledge or deeper understanding	
7. Is the language kid friendly? ☐ Could this be used for peer- and self-assessment? ☐ Have students had input into the writing or refinement of performance level descriptions?	
ADDITIONAL NOTES	

Available for download at resources.corwin.com/HessToolkit and www.karin-hess.com/free-resources

© Karin Hess (2009, updated 2017). *A local assessment toolkit to support deeper learning: Guiding school leaders in linking research with classroom practice.* Permission to reproduce is given only when authorship is fully cited [karinhessvt@gmail.com]

STUDENT WORK ANALYSIS
Analyzing and Acting on Evidence

Tool 12

Subject Area: _____ Grade Level: _____

Unit/Topic: _____ Performance Task: _____

How used? ☐ Pre/formative   ☐ Mid/Interim   ☐ Post/Summative

Date administered: _____

Content Standards Assessed: _____

Intended Depth-of-Knowledge (DOK) Level(s):   ☐ DOK 1   ☐ DOK 2   ☐ DOK 3   ☐ DOK 4

1. **Using district or classroom assessment or rubric, describe expectations for performance.**
   (See wording of prompt, standards-specific rubric, Hess CRM, and/or standards to determine desired expectations.)

2. Quickly "sort" students' work by degree of objectives met. List student names or % in each category so you can track progress over time with each major assessment. (a) **Start by sorting two larger piles: met or not met.** You may also need a "not sure" pile at this point.
   (b) **Re-sort each pile**: not met = partially met but close vs. minimal; met = met vs. met plus more. (c) **Distribute any remaining work samples** by matching them to typical work from each set.

   This is not scoring!

Objectives not met	Objectives partially met	Objectives fully met	Objectives fully met and exceeded
_____ % of class	_____ % of class	_____ % of class	_____ % of class

(Continued)

continued...

STUDENT WORK ANALYSIS
Analyzing and Acting on Evidence

Tool 12

3. **DESCRIBE:** Choose a few work samples from each group or category and **describe** "typical" performance for most of these students or describe the specific performance of selected students in each group.

Objectives not met	Objectives partially met	Objectives fully met	Objectives fully met and exceeded

4. **INTERPRET:** Consider the next steps for instruction based on your **interpretation of the learning needs** of students in each targeted group and the overarching learning goals. **List learning needs below**.

Objectives not met	Objectives partially met	Objectives fully met	Objectives fully met and exceeded

5. **EVALUATE and PLAN:** Identify differentiated tasks or strategic scaffolding strategies to move **targeted groups or ALL** students forward. Note any whole-class or small-group patterns or trends.

Instruction for all students:

Targeted instruction for some students:

Available for download at resources.corwin.com/HessToolkit

© Karin K. Hess (2009, updated 2013 and 2017). *Linking research with practice: A local assessment toolkit to guide school leaders.* Permission to reproduce is given when authorship is fully cited [karinhessvt@gmail.com]

WHAT IS THE EVIDENCE?
Locating Examples in Student Work for Writing Annotations

Tool 13

Student ID#	Describe Evidence With Possible Annotation Assessment Task or Open-Ended Question:	✓ Criterion & Score
		A____ B____ C____ D____ E____ F____
		A____ B____ C____ D____ E____ F____
		A____ B____ C____ D____ E____ F____
		A____ B____ C____ D____ E____ F____
		A____ B____ C____ D____ E____ F____
		A____ B____ C____ D____ E____ F____

Available for download at **resources.corwin.com/HessToolkit**

Copyright © 2018 by Corwin. All rights reserved. Reprinted from *A Local Assessment Toolkit to Promote Deeper Learning: Transforming Research into Practice* by Karin Hess. Thousand Oaks, CA: Corwin, www.corwin.com. Reproduction authorized only for the local school site or nonprofit organization that has purchased this book.

196　A Local Assessment Toolkit to Promote Deeper Learning

INDIVIDUAL REVIEWER RUBRIC SCORE SHEET

Tool 14

Reviewer ID#:
Date:

Assessment Task Name/Number:							Scoring Notes/Comments
List Student ID #s	\multicolumn{6}{c|}{**Letters Below Correspond to Each Rubric Criterion** (E.g., In a math assessment, A = Appropriate Strategy; B = Representations; C = Computation and Use of Symbols and Terms; D = Justification and Reasoning. E and F are left blank if there are no other criteria to score.)}		**S** = Solid at This Score **A** = Alternative Solution **UF** = Unique Feature/Approach **BT** = Between Score Points Other?
	A	**B**	**C**	**D**	**E**	**F**	

Available for download at **resources.corwin.com/HessToolkit**

Copyright © 2018 by Corwin. All rights reserved. Reprinted from *A Local Assessment Toolkit to Promote Deeper Learning: Transforming Research into Practice* by Karin Hess. Thousand Oaks, CA: Corwin, www.corwin.com. Reproduction authorized only for the local school site or nonprofit organization that has purchased this book.

TEAM RUBRIC SCORE SHEET

Tool 15

| Content Area: | Assessment Task: | Table Leader: | Date: |

Use one Team Rubric Score Sheet form for *4 different pieces* of student work. Have at least three people score each piece of work before you compile scores. (To save time, you can sort samples of scored work from your SWA.)

List each reviewer's scores by criterion (e.g., in art, A = Use of Space; B = Applying Principles of Design, etc.).

1. Record all individual reviewer scores for a given piece of student work. (A, B, C, etc., are for each rubric criterion).
2. Indicate *X* where all reviewers at the table had consensus on the assigned scores.
3. Decide if the work should be used for training or as an anchor paper. (Anchor papers can be scored by multiple scorers with high level of exact agreement, or can be useful for training if there are unique features.)

	List Each Reviewer	Record Score for Each Rubric Criterion						Causes of Discrepancies in Individual Scores?	Developing Scoring Packets for Training	
	Reviewer Name or ID # Scoring the same work	A	B	C	D	E	F	Scoring Notes/Discrepancies	Use as anchor paper yes/no?	Reason for Selection S = Solid score point A = Alternative solution UF = Unique feature BT = Between score points Other?
Student ID #1										
	Team Consensus?									
Student ID #2										
	Team Consensus?									
Student ID #3										
	Team Consensus?									
Student ID #4										
	Team Consensus?									

Available for download at **resources.corwin.com/HessToolkit**

Copyright © 2018 by Corwin. All rights reserved. Reprinted from *A Local Assessment Toolkit to Promote Deeper Learning: Transforming Research into Practice* by Karin Hess. Thousand Oaks, CA: Corwin, www.corwin.com. Reproduction authorized only for the local school site or nonprofit organization that has purchased this book.

TASK VALIDATION SUMMARY
(Use notes from PLC Tool #9 to develop your summary)

Tool 16A

Assessment:
Date of Review: Validation Team:

	Feedback Summary: Comments and Questions From Validation Team
Clarity and Focus	
Validity: Content Alignment	
Validity: Rigor Alignment	
Scoring Reliability	
Student Engagement	
Fairness and UDL	
What makes this a HQ assessment?	

Validation Team Recommendation:

_____ Validation pending—please review feedback, make revisions, and schedule another review.

_____ Validation complete—please submit final edited version to team leader.

First submission (date) _____   Resubmission (date) _____

Available for download at **resources.corwin.com/HessToolkit**

Copyright © 2018 by Corwin. All rights reserved. Reprinted from *A Local Assessment Toolkit to Promote Deeper Learning: Transforming Research into Practice* by Karin Hess. Thousand Oaks, CA: Corwin, www.corwin.com. Reproduction authorized only for the local school site or nonprofit organization that has purchased this book.

TASK VALIDATION SUMMARY
In-Depth Feedback: Performance Assessments
Criteria for Opportunity to Learn

Tool 16B

Name of Task: _____

Developers: _____

Date of Review: _____

Content Area: _____

Review Team: _____

Assessment task validation: A high-quality performance assessment task should be...

VALID (Aligned)	Strengths/Suggestions
Is the assessment task aligned to the content and performance in the stated standards or proficiencies?	Does the assessment elicit clear evidence (performance, products, responses, etc.) of the stated concepts, skills, and thinking or reasoning expected? Provide evidence from the student work (if applicable).
Describe the content knowledge or concepts assessed. List the skills or performance assessed.	Suggestions for improved alignment?

RELIABLE	Strengths/Suggestions
Is the accompanying rubric or scoring guide clearly aligned among the performance and content demands of the assessment, stated standards or proficiencies, and student work collected?	Will the scoring result in comparable scores from different teachers? With different student groups? Why or why not?
Do the rubric or scoring criteria address all of the requirements (products, performances, responses) of the task? Are the performance criteria and descriptors in the rubric consistent across all performance levels?	Suggestions for improved reliability?

(Continued)

continued . . .

TASK VALIDATION SUMMARY
Tool 16B

Assessment task validation: A high-quality performance assessment task should be...

FAIR and UNBIASED	Strengths/Suggestions
Is the task design and format visually clear and uncluttered (e.g., use of while space, graphics, illustrations)?	Strengths?
Is the task presented in as straightforward a way as possible for a range of learners? Has all unnecessary and potentially distracting information been eliminated?	
Are the task language (vocabulary) and context(s) free from cultural or other references that might be unfamiliar to students or present potential unintended bias?	Suggestions for improved fairness?

ENGAGING AND AUTHENTIC/PERFORMANCE BASED	Strengths/Suggestions
Are the student directions, and all other supporting materials, clear, complete, and user friendly (e.g., student rubrics)?	Strengths?
Are there aspects of the assessment that help students to know what they are supposed to know and be able to do before they are assessed? (e.g., student rubrics, work samples to show expectations, prerequisite skills needed, opportunities for peer and self-assessment)	
Does the task require thinking applied to a real-world situation, new context, problem, or challenge?	Suggestions for improved engagement or student choice and voice?
Does the assessment require students to assume a perspective, determine an approach, address an audience,	
Are there aspects of the assessment or assessment practices that help students to set future goals for learning and tracking their own progress?	

(Continued)

continued . . .

TASK VALIDATION SUMMARY

Tool 16B

Assessment Development Team Self-Assessment Reflection Tool	
Used to Guide and Support Instruction	**Our Comments/Questions**
1. Is this assessment embedded in curriculum and instruction (or seen only as "an event" to judge degree of proficiency)? List unit of study or where in the curriculum this assessment is (best) used:	
2. Do teachers use expectations assessed in the summative assessments to teach prerequisite skills and monitor progress prior to this assessment being given?	
3. Do teachers use assessment results (scores and student work analysis) to impact their future instruction or the need for additional and targeted support to students? How does this happen?	
4. Do teachers know where the assessment evidence might fall along the broader learning continuum (learning progression), so that they can design usable pretests and formative assessments and use ongoing data collection to plan or change next steps in instruction?	

Available for download at **resources.corwin.com/HessToolkit**

Copyright © 2018 by Corwin. All rights reserved. Reprinted from *A Local Assessment Toolkit to Promote Deeper Learning: Transforming Research into Practice* by Karin Hess. Thousand Oaks, CA: Corwin, www.corwin.com. Reproduction authorized only for the local school site or nonprofit organization that has purchased this book.

COGNITIVE LAB PART 2
Small Group Interview

After students finish, ask them a few questions, such as the ones below. Print out your questions ahead of time with enough room for taking notes. You may want to ask questions based on your notes and observations (e.g., I noticed when some of you were working on this part . . . ; can you tell me about your thinking when you were solving this one?)

Thinking Aloud With Students After They Complete the Assessment

When students have completed the assessment, take about 10 minutes to ask them questions like these (large group, small groups, or ask a few individuals that represent your high to low performing students). Also add your own observations and recommendations.

"I'd like to ask you some questions about the task: _____

1. *Were the directions clear? Did you know what you were supposed to do? Did you understand all parts of the task?*

2. *Was the [planning sheet, graphic organizer, checklist, manipulative] helpful?*

3. *What was the easiest part? Why?*

4. *What was the hardest or most confusing part? Why?*

5. *Have you done tasks like this before in your classroom? How did this one compare— Easier? Harder? About the same?*

6. *Can you suggest ways to improve this task for use next year?*

7. *Other?*

Available for download at **resources.corwin.com/HessToolkit**

Copyright © 2018 by Corwin. All rights reserved. Reprinted from *A Local Assessment Toolkit to Promote Deeper Learning: Transforming Research into Practice* by Karin Hess. Thousand Oaks, CA: Corwin, www.corwin.com. Reproduction authorized only for the local school site or nonprofit organization that has purchased this book.

COGNITIVE LAB PART 3A
Interpret Student Work Samples and Make Decisions

Collaboratively review and discusses observations/notes (be sure notes are clear—it may be a while before you get together to do this!)

Collectively review all samples of student work. Look at evidence across different facilitators and populations—what was the same? What was different?

Determine Next Steps—What needs fixing?

☐ Revise student directions, prompts, visuals, texts, for clarity

☐ Delete items/parts—due to excessive time needed, developmental appropriateness

☐ Revise wording or criteria in rubrics—were there other possible acceptable solutions? **Write notes *directly on master copy* of scoring rubrics to be revised**

☐ Determine if you need to revise—develop administration guidelines

☐ Presentation—Formatting: Decide how to format and/or combine "parts"—consider time needed, number of sessions (administer in two sessions instead of one, for example)

☐ Add or revise something to make this assessment more accessible (e.g., larger print, reduce reading load, more white space)?

What worked well? Are there any potential anchor papers?

☐ **Use or keep these items or tasks as written:** _____

☐ **Student work for benchmark or anchor paper (list ID codes):** _____
  - Benchmarks can be at any performance level—note level of each annotation
  - Not all annotations must come from one student's work—sticky note each part with a short annotation as to why selected (e.g., unique solution, complex reasoning, typical or expected solution, etc.) and rubric performance level exhibited
  - Annotations should "match" rubric language for that criterion and include the criterion

Available for download at **resources.corwin.com/HessToolkit**

Copyright © 2018 by Corwin. All rights reserved. Reprinted from *A Local Assessment Toolkit to Promote Deeper Learning: Transforming Research into Practice* by Karin Hess. Thousand Oaks, CA: Corwin, www.corwin.com. Reproduction authorized only for the local school site or nonprofit organization that has purchased this book.

COGNITIVE LAB PART 3B
Collaboratively Interpreting Evidence in Student Work

Performance Task _____ **Grade/Course** _____

Total Number of Students Assessed ___

Estimated Time Needed _____ (*based on cog lab times: slowest* _____ *fastest* _____)

(Notes below are drawn from across *all assessment tasks/parts and rubric criteria*)

What did you <u>expect to see</u> in student work? What does "proficient" look like? [e.g., Skills—apply formula for area]	What evidence <u>did you see</u> in the student work? Is it the same as described in the scoring rubric? [Use student ID #s if useful for referring back to the work]
Process Criteria: Applying skills/procedures, use of formulas, strategies, approach, gathering and organizing data or evidence	
Accuracy Criteria: Calculations, measurements, use of terms, language, facts, data	
Accuracy Criteria: Visual representations or graphing, understanding of concepts and principles	
Knowledge Construction Criteria: Reasoning, interpreting, supporting with evidence, justifying	
Impact Criteria: effectively solved, created or composed, persuaded, presented, invented	

Available for download at **resources.corwin.com/HessToolkit**

Copyright © 2018 by Corwin. All rights reserved. Reprinted from *A Local Assessment Toolkit to Promote Deeper Learning: Transforming Research into Practice* by Karin Hess. Thousand Oaks, CA: Corwin, www.corwin.com. Reproduction authorized only for the local school site or nonprofit organization that has purchased this book.

A GUIDE TO PERFORMANCE ASSESSMENT DEVELOPMENT

Performance assessment design requires that you consider four key questions prior to actually developing an assessment task or scoring rubric:

- What (content + skills) will this assess;
- Within what (authentic) context;
- Using what assessment design format (case study analysis, role playing scenario, research project, performance task, etc.); and
- To what degree will students be given choices or be required to make decisions about the task design, approach, resources used, or presentation of learning?

Once these general questions have been explored, specific student and teacher directions and rubric development can be started. PLC Tool #20 can be used to examine existing assessments or to develop new ones. It is designed to walk you through a process to unpack the assessment purpose and to clarify the context, format, and task expectations.

STEP 1:

Use the five rubric criteria types (in this table) to identify what will be assessed. CRM Tools 1–5D will be useful in identifying specific performance indicators and intended DOK levels. All criteria do not need to be included in the final assessment, but they should be considered during the design phase. Only the last two criteria will allow you to assess far transfer of skills or concepts, so one of them SHOULD be included.

Criterion	Questions Typically Answered by Each Criterion
Process	Will the student follow or be expected to use particular processes (e.g., procedures for a science investigation; data collection; validate credibility of sources)? (Usually DOK 2 for more complex tasks)
Form	Are there formats or rules to be applied and assessed (e.g., correct citation format; organize parts of lab report; use required camera shots or visuals; edit for grammar and usage)? (Usually DOK 1)

(Continued)

continued . . .

A GUIDE TO PERFORMANCE ASSESSMENT DEVELOPMENT

Tool 20

Accuracy of Content	List essential domain-specific terms, calculations, concepts, or models to be applied and assessed. (Usually DOK 1 or 2)
Construction of New Knowledge	How will the student go beyond the accurate solution and correct processes to gain new insights, raise new questions? (Usually DOK 3 or 4)
Impact	How will the final product achieve its intended purpose (e.g., solve a complex problem, persuade the audience, synthesize information to create a new product or performance) (Usually DOK 3 or 4)

STEP 2:

Identify one or more authentic contexts or products created when applying these skills, concepts, and dispositions. Consider how real-world professionals employ these skills and concepts (scientists, artists, historians, researchers, choreographers, etc.).

STEP 3:

TASK DESIGN—What is an appropriate assessment format for demonstrating learning?

- case study analysis
- role playing scenario (e.g., GRASPS)
- research project
- science investigation
- performance task (e.g., using a task shell)
- performance or presentation
- develop a product
- other?

Once you decide on the design format, explore existing models and use one as a template for your assessment design.

(Continued)

continued...

A GUIDE TO PERFORMANCE ASSESSMENT DEVELOPMENT

STEP 4:

To what degree will students be given choices or be required to make decisions about the task design, approach to solution, resources used, or presentation or products of learning? Use this "Shifting Roles" table to consider and make notes about the student's role in assessment and what is emphasized.

Shifting Roles: Moving From Teacher-Directed to Student-Directed Learning

DOK Levels	Teacher Roles	Student Roles
1 **Acquires a Foundation**	Asks basic questions *(Who? What? Where? How? When?)* Scaffolds for access and focus	Recalls vocabulary, facts, rules Retrieves information Practices and self-monitors basic skills
	In this assessment:	In this assessment:
2 **Uses, Connects, Conceptualizes**	Asks questions to build schema: differentiate parts-whole, classify, draw out inferences Assesses conceptual understanding (*Why does this work? Under what conditions?*) Asks for or uses examples or non-examples	Explains relationships, sorts, classifies, compares, organizes information Makes predictions based on estimates, observations, prior knowledge Proposes problems or issues or questions to investigate Raises conceptual or strategy-based questions
	In this assessment:	In this assessment:

(Continued)

continued . . .

A GUIDE TO PERFORMANCE ASSESSMENT DEVELOPMENT

Tool 20

3 **Deepens & Constructs Meaning**	Asks questions to probe reasoning and promote peer discourse or self-reflection Links to Big Ideas Requires proof, justification, and analysis of evidence quality and accuracy	Uncovers relevant, accurate, credible information, flaws in a design, or proposed solution and links with "Big Ideas" Plans how to develop supporting (hard) evidence for conclusions or claims Researches or tests ideas, solves non-routine problems; perseveres
	In this assessment:	In this assessment:
4 **Extends, Transfers, Broadens Meaning**	Asks questions to extend thinking, explore sources, broaden perspectives or Big Idea *(Are there potential biases? Can you propose an alternative model?)* Encourages use of relevant and valid resources, peer-to-peer discourse or self-reflection	Initiates, transfers, and *constructs* new knowledge/insights linked to "Big Ideas" Modifies, creates, elaborates based on analysis and interpretation of multiple sources Investigates real-world problems and issues; perseveres; manages time-task
	In this assessment:	In this assessment:

STEP 5:

Use PLC Tool #9 or PLC Tool #16B to identify and align success criteria (standards/proficiency statements), develop student and teacher instructions, and check for accessibility (fairness) for all students.

STEP 6:

Use PLC Tool #11 to develop a reliable scoring guide/rubric.

Available for download at **resources.corwin.com/HessToolkit**

Copyright © 2018 by Corwin. All rights reserved. Reprinted from *A Local Assessment Toolkit to Promote Deeper Learning: Transforming Research into Practice* by Karin Hess. Thousand Oaks, CA: Corwin, www.corwin.com. Reproduction authorized only for the local school site or nonprofit organization that has purchased this book.

PERFORMANCE ASSESSMENT OVERVIEW: PURPOSE AND USE

Use this tool to provide an overview of when the assessment will be used and what it is intended to assess.

Unit of Study/Course	Grade Level

Enduring Understandings/Big Ideas

Essential Question(s) to Guide Inquiry/Learning

Performance Assessment Overview

In this assessment, students will . . .

Assessment Alignment to Learning Goals: List . . .	**Performance Indicators (in Student "Language")**
Competency/Proficiency Statement(s)	I can . . .
Standards	
Students will know (key terms, concepts, principles)	**Students will do or apply** (include intended DOK levels)
Assessment Success Criteria (and intended DOK)	**Allowable/Possible Accommodations/Supports**

How will results be used? Formative/Preassess ___ Interim /Progress Monitoring ___ Summative/Post ___

List other RELATED performance assessments <u>in this unit of study/course</u>:

Formative/Preassessment:

Interim /Progress Monitoring:

Summative/Postassessment:

(Continued)

continued . . .

PERFORMANCE ASSESSMENT OVERVIEW: PURPOSE AND USE

Tool 21

Describe Student's Role/Decisions/Engagement/Input Into Task Expectations or Task Design

o   Choices or decisions to be made *during* the assessment:

o   Group collaborations (*prior to* or *during* the assessment):

o   Student input into task design or presentation or product format:

o   Self-assessment, reflections:

o   Other:

Develop an Administration Guide

A common assessment requires a short administration guide to ensure fidelity of implementation across teachers and schools. Below are four essential things to include in the administration guide. Most schools create and store this information with each assessment in a digital task bank for easy access.

1. **Student Prompt or Stimulus**—What directions will the student see? (make this short, clear, and visually interesting)

2. **Teacher Instructions**—What directions will help the teacher to prepare for and use the assessment?

These are more detailed than what is given to students, including any important considerations, such as special set-up requirements, equipment or materials, or scribing guidelines. At minimum, include the following:

Name of Assessment Task: **Grade:**

Purpose:

Suggested Time to Administer:
(For example, time of year, part of a unit of study or course, after students have learned particular content or completed a specific activity, such as an investigation in science or viewing a play or video.)

Suggested Use: Formative _____ **Interim** _____ **Summative** _____

Estimated Time Needed:

Resources Needed to Complete the Assessment (e.g., equipment, texts, digital tools, data, case study)

Specific Skills, Concepts, or Practices <u>Emphasized</u> in Task:

Additional Allowable Accommodations:

3. **Scoring Guide or Rubric**

4. If possible, include a sample of annotated student work at the "proficient" level.

(Template content and format adapted from McTighe & Wiggins, 2004)

Available for download at **resources.corwin.com/HessToolkit**

Copyright © 2018 by Corwin. All rights reserved. Reprinted from *A Local Assessment Toolkit to Promote Deeper Learning: Transforming Research into Practice* by Karin Hess. Thousand Oaks, CA: Corwin, www.corwin.com. Reproduction authorized only for the local school site or nonprofit organization that has purchased this book.

III. Strategies and Tools for Professional Developers and Teacher Planning

ACTIVITY: The Great American Chocolate Chip Cookie Taste Test. This activity was cocreated by Alysa Cummings and me while working at the New Jersey Department of Education (1989). It's been revised several times and used with students and educators for many years to introduce types of scoring criteria and to provide a rationale for weighting some criteria over others. Any assessment task can have a "taste" criterion—the thing that is most important to the final product, and therefore gets more instructional attention and more scoring emphasis.

ACTIVITY: Anatomy of an Opinion/Argument/Critique: Planning Tools for Teachers and Students. I use this as both a workshop activity for teachers and an introductory lesson for students. Table 3.3, Unit Planning—Sample Prompts Informational vs. Argument Types, is used as guidance for developing better writing prompts which can lead to identifying more appropriate and stronger supporting evidence.

RESOURCE: General Guidelines for Administration of Progress-Monitoring Performance Assessments in Writing (with sample scribing of student work) and Mathematics

RESOURCE: Sample Template for Developing Administration Guidelines for a Performance Assessment

The Great American Chocolate Chip Cookie Taste Test

(AKA "Is Everything in the Rubric Equally Important to Assess?")

Context

The purpose of the activity is to introduce the concept of using a rubric with multiple and varied criteria as a tool for assessment. It provides teachers (and students) with a concrete experience in the development and use of an assessment tool and then transfers that learning to examination of rubrics currently in use.

What this task accomplishes

The universal appeal of chocolate chip cookies makes this task both accessible and enjoyable to teachers and students alike. The rubric development process helps participants to quantify the quality of "good" which they later apply to content-specific assessment work. The deeper examination of the criteria used in the rubric leads to two important key ideas when using rubrics with multiple criteria: (a) a common understanding of the purpose and intent of each criterion is needed before one begins to score student work; and (b) it is important to have an understanding that not all criteria are equally important and therefore, some criteria may need to be weighted to better describe "good enough" performance.

Source: pixabay.com/StevenGiacomelli.

What groups will do

Divide the large group into smaller groups of four to six people per group. Ask groups to brainstorm the qualities of a good chocolate chip cookie, recording ideas on chart paper. They then decide which qualities are related and may want to combine two into one category (e.g., taste, texture, number of chocolate chips, size).

Once groups have identified the categories (or criteria), they need to define performance levels for each criterion. I suggest breaking down each criterion into four different levels, starting with descriptions of the "proficient" level. Once proficient performance is defined by group consensus, the other three levels are described: from the optimum or expert level to the lower end or novice level of the range. These descriptors are written into a group rubric using chart paper or typed so they can be displayed for the whole group. Sometimes it's helpful to suggest they add specific examples of what they might be looking for at each level, such as the kind of chocolate used. (Remember, they will not see the two cookies to be rated until the rubric is completed.)

The workshop leader hands out cookies A and B, but does not reveal brands. Each group's rubric is then used with cookie A and cookie B to taste test two "blind" brands of chocolate chip cookies. (I try to find two very similar cookies—but, for example, one is crispy and one is chewy. Try to make the decision difficult for the raters.) After rating the two cookies, a spokesperson for each group must state conclusions using the data collected. Comparisons are made across groups about the criteria used, how criteria were defined, and what scores were given to each cookie for each criterion.

Time required for task

Approximately 40 minutes to an hour is needed for developing criteria, taste testing, and summarizing and comparing results.

Suggested materials

- Chart paper and markers
- Two different chocolate chip cookie varieties to sample (I prefer using several store brands sold by the same company.)
- Napkins or paper plates with A and B on them to keep things organized
- Rulers, scales, or any other measuring devices (e.g., size or weight of cookies)

Possible conclusions

These will vary depending on the group's criteria. It is important for the facilitator to compare criteria used by each group and descriptors for the same criteria.

Applying the chocolate chip cookie mindset

After the group sharing, ask, "Are all criteria equally important? What if a cookie has a high score in the number of chips or size, but a low score in taste? Does that matter? What are the implications for rubrics we use in our classes or courses?"

Generally speaking, there are five different types of criteria used in most rubrics and not all of them must be included all of the time. When creating a rubric, keep these criteria types in mind and consider whether some are more essential than others in evaluating the product or performance:

CRITERION	QUESTIONS TYPICALLY ANSWERED BY EACH CRITERION
Process	Did the student follow the correct or appropriate steps or processes (e.g., procedures for a science investigation; data collection, measuring, and recording; note-taking; developing an outline; following a routine or recipe; validating credibility of sources)? (Usually DOK 1 or 2)
Form	Did the student apply correct formats and rules (e.g., handed in on time, used correct citation format, organized parts of task properly, used required camera shots or visuals, edited for grammar and usage)? (Usually DOK 1)
Accuracy of Content	Is the answer, terminology, or calculation correct? Is the relationship explained in enough detail with elaboration or examples? Is the concept understood or accurately applied? Does the data representation align with appropriate content and intended purpose? Are diagrams or representations correctly constructed and labeled? (Usually DOK 1 or 2)
Construction of New Knowledge	Did the student go beyond the accurate solution and correct processes to gain new insights, raise new questions, or provide supporting evidence for claims or judgments made? Was an alternative solution presented with supporting evidence? (Usually DOK 3 or 4)
Impact	Did the final product achieve its intended purpose and provide supporting evidence for claims or judgments made (e.g., solved a problem, persuaded the audience, synthesized information to create a new product or performance) (Usually DOK 3 or 4)

Now, analyze your group's cookie rubric criteria using the above criteria types and determine if some criteria are more important, given the task. What weight or increased emphasis might you give to some specific criteria? What do you value the most in a cookie?

Analyze your classroom rubrics in the same way:

1. *Determine intent (what is uniquely being assessed), emphasis, and potential evidence for each criterion.*

    - Which types of criteria are included?

    - Do the types of criteria match the critical aspects of the assessment task(s)? Do all criteria apply? Or only some of them?

    - Should some criteria get greater scoring emphasis? For example, you might (at the start of the unit) place greater emphasis or only assess process skills (organization and data collection procedures) when introducing what will be required in the culminating activity. By the end of the unit, impact criteria may have greater weight than data collection.

2. *Do a "DOK check" of your rubrics, assessment tasks, and unit assignments: Does the wording of assessment prompts and rubric wording match the intended depth of knowledge[8] (DOK) expected to be observed in student work? Do the lessons build (scaffold) to the highest DOK expected by the end of the unit?*

    - *Process criteria*—following the correct steps is usually only a DOK 1 level. If students are designing their own process, such as in deciding which variables to control and how to collect and organize data, it would bump up to DOK 2 or DOK 3 depending on the task complexity.

    - *Form criteria*—applying correct formats and rules (e.g., what makes a good oral or visual presentation) is usually only DOK 1.

    - *Accuracy of content criteria*—locating or describing correct facts, details, definitions, or principles would generally be DOK 1; demonstrating conceptual understanding or accurate applications of concepts are generally DOK 2.

    - *New knowledge criteria*—providing support for insights, judgments, and synthesized ideas is DOK 3 or DOK 4 depending on the sources required.

    - *Impact criteria*—evaluation of whether the final product achieved its intended purpose looks at coherence and effectiveness across criteria and generally would be at DOK 3 or 4, since form, process, and accuracy are used to generate supporting or compelling evidence for ideas (new knowledge) for a particular purpose and intended audience.

---

8. You may want to refer to the Hess CRM Tools in Module 1 for examples.

Anatomy of an Opinion, Argument, or Critique: Planning Tools for Teachers and Students

The ability to write evidence-based opinions, arguments, or critiques is important in all content areas and at all grade levels; but how do we teach the schema of this genre? What I see in schools I've worked with are teachers using a variety of strategies and materials—some very good and some that might not promote transfer when students leave one classroom or grade level. If we teach the overall schema of what comprises components of any argument or opinion, then we can build expertise over time by adding refinements and greater sophistication of thinking within each content area.

I like to introduce the underlying schema of opinions and arguments with one of my very popular workshop activities: "What's an argument?"

(I hope you'll also notice how this workshop follows the flow of Kolb's Experiential Learning Cycle.)

Step 1: Ask small groups to generate a consensus definition of *opinion* and *argument*. Discuss how the definitions are alike and different.

Step 2: Next, provide examples to be sorted into three piles: opinions, arguments, and "UGs" (claims without support). My examples include many of the following: political ads; brochures; empty cereal boxes, chips or food bags, or food containers; editorials; short articles from issues of *Consumer Reports*; student writing samples; political cartoons; news or media articles. Building a schema means seeing the parts, no matter the context or format, not seeing parts of "cookie cutter" five-paragraph essays!

Each group gets more examples than can be analyzed in the time given, so they can choose what to discuss and sort. To get started, I provide an example of an UG—the cereal box for Lucky Charms™ states that they are "magically delicious"—a claim. Are there grounds for this claim? Well, there is a leprechaun and pot of gold at the end of the rainbow, clearly magical. Is there any hard evidence? No. It's an UG. Use sticky notes to label examples and be prepared to defend why you put them there (using DOK 3 thinking).

Step 3: After discussing (arguing) and sorting, ask participants to check understanding using definitions of opinions or arguments which I summarize from a short article, "Teaching Argument" (Marzano, 2012). These argument "parts" (Claims, Grounds, Backing [hard evidence], Qualifiers) are expanded upon in my planning tool, Anatomy of an Opinion/Argument. (NOTE: By introducing this information after the sorting activity, I am scaffolding strategically by providing information that now connects in a more meaningful way to their personal understandings. Giving them definitions at the start would not be as effective instructionally. Students remember what they create or construct.)

Step 4: Groups revisit their sorting and select one argument to further dissect using the Anatomy of an Opinion/Argument template. (I've also provided two examples of student work at the end of this section for guided analysis, using my template. The first is from a New York City assessment pilot; the second is work from an Exemplars performance task.)

Step 5: Create the missing parts of something that was almost, but not quite an argument. (The beauty of using authentic examples is that you can analyze and then revise them. Examples do not have to be "perfect" models and may be more engaging to use if they lack some aspect of arguments.)

Step 6: Discuss new insights and instructional and assessment implications. Collaboratively examine and build the continuum of moving from opinion writing to argument writing, rather than those being two distinctly different schemas. Think of the slide below as an anchor chart for the genre.

What's the difference?????

← **Continuum** →

Opinions
- **Claim**–opinion/focus (stated versus implied or inferred as in political cartoons)
- **Give Reasons**
- **Support claim and elaborate:** text evidence, facts, anecdotes for each reason
- **? Would make it stronger**
- **Conclusion**

Arguments and Critiques
- **Claim**–thesis
- **Grounds ("warrants")**–context, appeals
  - Why is this claim true or believable? (define criteria)
- **Backing**–analysis, elaboration, and reasoning
  - Support with "hard evidence" and analysis providing legitimacy for the claim
- **Qualifiers** (*not always true*)
  - Address counterclaims; exceptions/conditions
  - Provide rebuttal
- **Conclusions**–summary, text to word/text, call to action

To further refine your thinking about developing prompts for informational and argument writing, I apply the work of Hillocks (2011), *Teaching Argument Writing*, who defines three different types of arguments: fact based, judgment based, or policy based. I've summarized his approach on the next sample slide:

Teaching Argument Writing: Supporting Claims With Relevant Evidence and Clear Reasoning
George Hillocks Jr. (2011)

Teach simple to more complex arguments, starting with . . .

1. **Arguments of fact** – explore "the facts of the case"

2. **Arguments of judgment** – provide relevant evidence in support of rules or criteria used to make a judgment

3. **Arguments of policy** – make a case to establish, amend, or abolish a rule, procedure, etc., that affects people's lives – criteria (and evidence) used to examine impact

Provide Instructional Scaffolding – one type of argument builds to the next

- Examine facts of the topic deeply – read, discuss, interpret
- Identify perspectives
- Use evidence to build criteria or rules and reasoning for judgment

What the research tells us about teaching this genre of writing (Hess et al., 2012) is that first students need to know a topic deeply; then they can begin to see emerging and (possibly) competing claims or opinions about it. This implies that an informational prompt might come before an argument-based prompt. If your prompt implies making a judgement, then the evidence is based on broader criteria (e.g., "Is he a hero?" implies using the criteria of the hero archetype to make a determination).

I've found that when teachers understand the nuanced differences in the types of arguments to be written, their prompts and their teaching become more focused. The resulting student products are of higher quality, because students begin to recognize WHAT KIND of evidence is required to frame their logic chain. I've tested this "prompt planning" idea using examples of argument types in different content areas. Table 3.3 includes a few content-specific examples that have helped teachers refine the prompts that students write to and the types of evidence they need to support their claims (see headers in table for cues).

Table 3.3 Unit Planning—Sample Prompts Informational vs. Argument Types

Sample Units Major topic(s) and possible source materials	Informational writing prompts (exploring facts or concepts about the topic) [DOK 2–4]	Fact-based prompts (evidence is based on facts of the case or event: facts, research, data, sources) [DOK 3–4]	Judgment-based prompts (evidence is based on criteria <u>commonly agreed upon</u> for the content domain) [DOK 3–4]	Policy-based prompts (evidence is based on impact) What problem is being solved by the new rule? Who benefits? Who does not benefit if the rule is made? [DOK 3–4]
Communities and Local Foods (Grades 1–2)	Where does our food come from? What are products you can buy locally? What is produced locally? How far from here is local? What are some of the benefits of buying and eating local products?	How does serving local food in the school café help our community? (e.g., students might use a survey to get opinions; investigate or interview cafeteria workers to find out what is locally grown and how food costs compare)	Should the local village market sell more locally grown food? Do you think eating local food is important? (What criteria help us to evaluate healthy food?)	Should our principal make a rule that only locally grown food is served in the cafeteria?
Inventions (Grades 3–4) Resource Books: Then & Now Brilliantly Ridiculous Inventions	Who was _____? What did he or she invent? Why did he or she invent it? Why was it needed?	How would life be different if this had not been invented? (before/after)	Did this invention make life better or worse for people? Was this invention a good idea?	Some people say funding is needed to solve this problem. Will _____ invention solve or help this problem? Will it be worth the money invested?
Theme of Courage (Grades 5–6) Content: Five books, different levels in unit—read aloud + choice	What is courage (as seen through different books we're reading)?	What lesson about courage is learned in your book?	Who is the most courageous in this story? Across the books read? How have you shown courage? How has it changed or shaped your life?	Should a new law be written to protect people from going to jail for doing courageous acts?

218 A Local Assessment Toolkit to Promote Deeper Learning

The Outsiders (Grades 7–8) Background (1950s OK, rodeo culture) West Side Story, etc.	What are universal themes? How do some stories address social conflicts (family units) in their themes?	How does the author of The Outsiders use the (concept of) family unit (biological versus gang) to portray social conflict?	Which character is a hero? Is Johnny a hero? Did he get what he deserved? Which family was Johnny's true family?	How would a different policy or law change the story line or behaviors of the characters? (e.g., Minors taken away from families; gun control laws)
FDR (or other famous leaders) (MS/HS)	Who was he? What did he do (e.g., major initiatives)? What were the historical, social, and political contexts when he became president? How does history remember him?	FDR had tremendous support from the Jewish community throughout his presidency; however, critics say he did not do much to support them and their issues. Are these criticisms supported by the historical facts within the historical context?	Was FDR a great president? Should _____ be named as one of TIME magazine's 100 most influential people of the year?	What has been the historical impact of a major FDR policy?
Applying Statistics (HS)	What statistics are used for (describing a player's performance, Hall of Fame)? What do top earning players have in common in their performances?	Is _____ eligible to be voted into the Hall of Fame?	Who was the greatest ball player? Based on their lifetime careers, how should these five players be ranked?	
Habitats/Biomes (ES/MS/HS depending on topic)	Compare/contrast fresh- and saltwater habitats. What do organisms need to survive here? What laws currently exist to protect aquatic habitats?	What factors might be causing the (fish) population to decline?	Is this _____ (river/lake/ocean) healthy?	Do we need a new law to protect this habitat? What will be the likely impact of this change?
Your Unit of Study?				

Anatomy of an Opinion, Argument, or Critique

OPINION/CLAIM/THESIS Attempts to answer a question, respond to a conjecture (Is this true? Do we need . . . ?)	The Question: My Opinion/Thesis/Claim:		
CONTEXT/GROUNDS: Why is this claim true or believable?	Stated: Implied?		
KEY REASONS or criteria used in support of claim (e.g., for stated conjecture, judgment, or policy impact). These are <u>broad</u> categories, supported by facts, evidence, and analysis or justification.	Reason 1/Criterion 1	Reason 2/Criterion 2	Reason 3/Criterion 3
RELEVANT EVIDENCE: Backing—support using "hard evidence" —available facts, quotes, examples, data, observations, anecdotes, analyses of others—surveys/studies + evidence + <u>SOURCE</u>			
+ CLEAR REASONING: Analysis and elaboration of each set of evidence under the criterion, *providing justification* for the thesis or claim	How do facts or data illustrate relevant support for claim?	How do facts or data illustrate relevant support for claim?	How do facts or data illustrate relevant support for claim?
QUALIFIERS or COUNTER-CLAIMS Evidence + <u>SOURCE</u>	Exceptions, conditions, counterclaims—Who might disagree and why? When might this not be true?		
CONCLUSIONS/ CONNECTIONS: summarize, connect, extend, suggest consequences or new questions, or call to action	What is your main message? What have you learned or confirmed? What new questions might be raised? Can you make connections?		

Available for download at **resources.corwin.com/HessToolkit**

Copyright © 2018 by Corwin. All rights reserved. Reprinted from *A Local Assessment Toolkit to Promote Deeper Learning: Transforming Research into Practice* by Karin Hess. Thousand Oaks, CA: Corwin, www.corwin.com. Reproduction authorized only for the local school site or nonprofit organization that has purchased this book.

Anatomy of a Mathematical/Scientific Argument or Critique

OPINION/CLAIM/THESIS — Attempts to answer a question, respond to a conjecture (Is this true all of the time? Do we need . . . ?)	The Question: My Claim:		
CONTEXT/GROUNDS: Why is this claim true or believable?	Stated: Implied?		
KEY REASONS or criteria used in support of claim (e.g., for stated conjecture, judgment, or policy impact). These are broad categories, supported by facts, evidence, and analysis or justification.	Strategy or approach to solve problem and connection to concept, theory, or law applied	Calculations, equations, measurements, formulas	Representations, models, diagrams, data, or observations
RELEVANT EVIDENCE: Backing—support using "hard evidence"—available facts, quotes, examples, data, observations, anecdotes, analyses of others—surveys/studies + evidence + SOURCE			
+ CLEAR REASONING: Analysis and elaboration of each set of evidence under the criterion, *providing justification* for the thesis or claim	Why did it work? How does it illustrate a concept/theory/law?	How do they support accuracy/precision?	Why/how do they represent quantitative relationships or concepts?
QUALIFIERS or COUNTER CLAIMS Evidence + SOURCE	Exceptions, conditions, counterclaims—Who might disagree and why? When might this not be true?		
CONCLUSIONS/CONNECTIONS: summarize, connect, extend, suggest consequences or new questions, or call to action	What is your main message? What have you learned or confirmed? What new questions might be raised? Can you make connections?		

Available for download at **resources.corwin.com/HessToolkit**

Copyright © 2018 by Corwin. All rights reserved. Reprinted from *A Local Assessment Toolkit to Promote Deeper Learning: Transforming Research into Practice* by Karin Hess. Thousand Oaks, CA: Corwin, www.corwin.com. Reproduction authorized only for the local school site or nonprofit organization that has purchased this book.

Examples of Grade 3 Student Work (DOK 3) for Analysis Using the Anatomy of an Opinion/Argument Templates

Halloween!

My favorite holiday is Halloween for severl reasons. A few reasons are that I get to wear a costume, eat candy, stay up all night, watch scary movies and have fun with pumkins.

First, I like costumes because I get to pretend what I am dressed as. My most favorite costume that I have ever wore is my fairy costume.

Next, I like to eat candy because I can get a sweet tooth and because I get to go trick-or-treating.

After that, I like to stay all night because I get to build a haunted house and to tell scary stories in the haunted house.

Then, I like to watch scary stories because I get scared and I get into the Halloween spirit.

Finally, I like having fun with pumpkins because I get to carve them and I get to eat pumpkin pies. Clearly, these are reasons why Halloween is my favorite holiday.

Grade 3

P/S	R/P	Com	Con	Rep	AC/LV
P	P	P	P	P	P

Practitioner   Student 1

Ben's Apple Pie

Ben's mom made an apple pie. Ben's mom cut the pie into eight equal pieces. Ben and three friends each ate one piece. Ben said they ate one half of the pie. Brad said they ate four eighths of the pie. Who is correct? Show all your mathematical thinking.

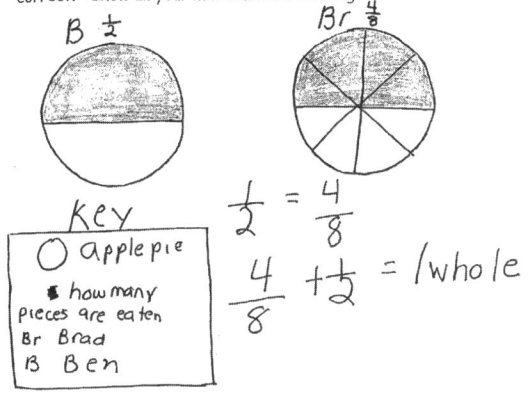

B $\frac{1}{2}$ Br $\frac{4}{8}$

Key
○ apple pie
✱ how many pieces are eaten
Br Brad
B Ben

$\frac{1}{2} = \frac{4}{8}$

$\frac{4}{8} + \frac{1}{2} = 1$ whole

I claim that they are both correct because $\frac{4}{8} = \frac{1}{2}$. I know this because I did a diagram and a equation. This is a fair share.

page 1 of 2

© Exemplars.com

My diagram says that there is 2 pies and that one pie is cut into $\frac{1}{2}$ and the other one is cut into 8 pieces. My equation says $\frac{1}{2} = \frac{4}{8}$ and $\frac{4}{8} + \frac{1}{2} = 1$ whole pie because mom only made one pie. There is $\frac{1}{2}$ pie left so they can all have 1 more piece.

page 2 of 2

General Guidelines for the Administration of Progress-Monitoring Performance Assessments in Writing

When administering progress-monitoring assessments across different classrooms, teachers, and schools, it is important to ensure the consistent and reliable administration and interpretation of results. Collectively, assessment portfolio tasks should provide the teacher with the most comprehensive amount of information possible as it relates to particular writing skills and concepts being taught during the school year.

Writing assessments should typically take several class periods for all students. If a teacher feels that additional time or scribing is needed in order to get an accurate understanding of a student's thinking beyond the regular testing session, then more time should be provided for the scribing to be completed. This should be done as soon as possible (within a day or two at most) after the assessment has been given to the class.

What is allowable during administration of progress-monitoring assessments?

Prewriting and planning

During the administration of the progress-monitoring writing assessments, students are encouraged to use graphic organizers or other prewriting tools and available classroom writing resources to help them communicate their ideas. For example, in the language arts classroom there may be a word wall or students may have personal writing journals with vocabulary terms that they have been learning. As long as the posted terms are not specific to one possible response for the assessment (prompt) being given (meaning that the word list accumulates over instructional time and will include many descriptive words and ideas to choose from), and the teacher does not cue students to use only particular terms in their responses (unless a student asks where a specific word is located or the student asks the teacher to read some of the listed words aloud), students can refer to the word list for spelling support when composing or responding to a writing prompt.

Providing additional time

All progress-monitoring assessments include an estimated administration time based on piloting data. However, these should NOT be considered timed tests! Students who need additional time to complete their compositions should be given that time as long as they are engaging with the writing tasks in meaningful ways.

Scribing to document demonstrations of learning

A student's assessment portfolio should be an accurate reflection of what the student knows and can do. Since many primary students and some upper-grade-level students (e.g., IEP students, ELL students, students unable to write or type due to an injury) are not always able to fully articulate written responses, scribing can be an appropriate accommodation. Therefore, during a progress-monitoring assessment, all students should be given the opportunity of having their work scribed if needed.

Scribing support means having someone translate a student's ideas, thoughts, and feelings as they are expressed orally or represented in the student's illustrations. This can be accomplished in several different ways:

(1) The student thinks aloud as she or he describes what is in an illustration and an adult or older student records the student's actual words.

(2) The teacher moves about the classroom to provide spelling support as requested (for descriptions or captions) and <u>documents students' actual words</u> on their work while students are working.

(3) Audio- or videotape the student's oral dictation and later transfer the student's actual words onto the actual work or illustrations. For example, a center could be set up in one corner of the classroom for students to audio record their stories.

(4) Explore technology that can be used to document how students solve problems and plan out their writing.

Providing generic prompts to clarify student ideas

It is appropriate to provide encouragement and <u>use a few generic prompts</u> to assist a student in clarifying his or her thinking while developing or elaborating on an idea. *"Can you tell me (more) about your picture?"* or *"Tell me what's happening here?"* or *"Can you add some more descriptive words?"* or *"Who is this?"* and *"What happened next?"* are all examples of generic prompts that can encourage students to better clarify their written or oral explanations.

Comments such as "You need to add some dialogue" or "Put a period here, at the end" are not appropriate and should <u>not</u> be used during these writing assessments.

Providing a generic self-monitoring checklist (see optional examples provided with writing prompts)

It is appropriate to provide a self-monitoring tool (such as a writing checklist) for students to use during the assessment <u>only if the teacher has been using the tool during instruction and students understand how to use it</u>. Self-monitoring checklists generally list the key parts of assessment tasks (e.g., I included a title, I checked my spelling, I used capital letters at the beginning of sentences) and help to promote metacognitive thinking by keeping students focused. My preference with checklists is to ask students to do more than simply check off each box. For example, I ask them to write in their title, rather than check that they have one. Writing checklists are optional and not part of the assessment. Additionally, a teacher or scribe can support students staying on task by providing ongoing encouragement (without an indication about whether what the student is writing is "correct").

Guidelines for scribing writing assessment tasks

1. When scribing student work, the scribe should <u>take dictation rather than paraphrasing</u> the student's response, even if the student's response is confusing. Vocabulary and sentence structure must be <u>exactly what the student says, even if it is grammatically incorrect</u>. Clearly indicate which information was student dictated, and which information was documented by the scribe. <u>Use quotation marks to indicate what the student orally stated in the writing or picture.</u>

2. <u>When a scribe provides a prompt</u> (e.g., asks a clarifying question), <u>it should be noted in brackets</u>—for example, [Tell me about your picture/TMAYP]. For efficiency, scribes may want to use a template with several generic prompts for all students taking the writing assessment. The student's responses are noted on the scribing template instead of on the student's illustrations and are simply attached to the student's work. (A sample scribing template for narrative writing is at the end of this section.)

3. <u>The scribe should always initial any writing put on a student's work</u>. If the person who is scoring the student's work is different from the scribe, she or he can contact the scribe if there are any questions. This is especially helpful in kindergarten classrooms where several different scribes (adults or older students) may be working with students.

Whenever you are not sure about the appropriateness of a scribing practice, ask yourself this question: "Does this accurately demonstrate what the student is expressing in the drawing?"

A scribing example for narrative writing

Scribes will develop procedures that are comfortable for their students and themselves. Below is an example of what scribing might sound and look like <u>at the primary level for writing</u>. Scribes need to record both THEIR prompts and student responses.

1. Start with a broad, open-ended question: *"Tell me about your picture."* (". . . *your story*," ". . . *your idea*"). *"Who is this story about and what's happening?*

2. *"What happened first?"* (or restate the specific writing prompt: *"Tell me about the exciting day you are writing about."*).

3. If the picture or ideas seem vague, a teacher may want to suggest that the student add some more details: *"Can you add some more details to your picture to show what he looked like or how he moved? I'll come back in a while to see what you have added."*

4. Scribes often ask primary students, *"How does your story end?"* This may not be evident in the student's picture, but a student may be able to describe the ending of the event or story or how the problem was solved.

5. End a scribing session by reading back what the student has dictated and then asking, *"Is there anything else you would like to add?"*

Scribing Template for _____ Date _____

Add any other prompts you asked particular students. You do not need to ask all questions. Students often offer the information freely and completely after you ask the first question. Attach this to student's work for analysis or scoring.

1. *"Tell me about your picture"* (or some variation on this question: tell me about your story, your idea; who this story is about and what's happening).

   _____
   _____

2. *"What happened first?"* (or restate the specific writing prompt):

   _____
   _____

3. *"What happened next/then?"*

   _____
   _____

4. *"Can you add some more details to your picture to show* _____
   (e.g., what he looked like). *I'll come back in a while to see what you have added."*

   _____
   _____

5. *"How does your story end?"* or *"How was the problem solved?"*

   _____
   _____

6. Read back what the student has dictated and ask: *"Is there anything else you would like to add or tell me?"*

   _____
   _____

Copyright © 2018 by Corwin. All rights reserved. Reprinted from *A Local Assessment Toolkit to Promote Deeper Learning: Transforming Research into Practice* by Karin Hess. Thousand Oaks, CA: Corwin, www.corwin.com. Reproduction authorized only for the local school site or nonprofit organization that has purchased this book.

Sample Student Work With Teacher Scribing (NYC, Grade K)

A Sample Scribing Template for _____ 2/7/11

Add any other prompts you asked particular students. You do not need to ask all questions if the student offers the information freely.

1. **Tell me about your picture.** (your story, your idea, who this story is about and what's happening, etc.)

   Me and my mom were going to the zoo. I was crying because the car was running out of gas. Then my mom went to the gas store then we were driving to the zoo.

2. **What happened first?** (or restate the specific writing prompt: _____)

   We're going to the zoo.

3. **What happened next/then?**

   Mommy was frozen because when she turned the keys we were driving and then it was broken.

4. **Can you add some more details to your picture to show** _____ _____. I'll come back in a while to see what you have added."

5. **How does your story end?**

   We were getting gas and then we went to the zoo.

6. Read back what the student has dictated and ask: **Is there anything else you would like to show or tell me?**

November 28, 2010 draft

General Guidelines for the Administration of Progress-Monitoring Performance Assessments in Mathematics

When piloting or administering progress-monitoring assessments across classrooms, teachers, and schools, it is important to ensure the consistent and reliable administration and interpretation of results. Collectively, assessment portfolio tasks should provide teachers with the most comprehensive amount of information about mathematical learning possible as it relates to particular skills and concepts being taught.

A student's assessment portfolio should be an accurate reflection of what the student knows and can do. Since many primary students and some upper-grade-level students (e.g., IEP students with language delays, ELL students, students unable to write or type due to an injury) are not always able to fully articulate a written response to a problem-solving task, scribing is an appropriate accommodation. Therefore, during a progress-monitoring assessment, all students should be given the opportunity of having their work scribed, if needed.

If a teacher feels that additional scribing is needed for complete understanding of a student's thinking beyond the regular testing session, then more time should be provided for the scribing to be completed. This should be done as soon as possible (within a day or two at most) after the assessment has been given.

What is allowable during administration of progress-monitoring assessments? During the administration of progress-monitoring mathematics assessments, students are encouraged to use diagrams or labels or ask for help with spelling to show their thinking. In the mathematics classroom, there may also be a word wall with math terms that students have been learning. As long as the posted terms are not specific to the assessment being given (meaning that the word wall accumulates over instructional time and will have many terms students have been learning), and the teacher does not cue students to use particular terms in their responses, students can refer to the word wall for spelling support when responding or explaining their reasoning.

Providing additional time

All progress-monitoring assessments should include an estimated administration time based on piloting data. However, these should NOT be considered timed tests! Students who may need additional time to complete their responses should be given that time as long as they are engaging with the tasks in meaningful ways.

Scribing to document learning

Scribing support means having someone translate a student's mathematical solution as it is expressed orally or observed by the teacher (such as how they use manipulatives or a number line to count). This can be accomplished in several different ways:

(1) The student thinks aloud as she or he solves the problem or presents the solution to the class (or small group) and an adult records the student's actual words (and perhaps actions).

(2) The teacher moves about the classroom to provide spelling support as requested (for terms or labels) and documents or writes students' exact words on their work while students are working.

(3) Audio- or videotape the student's presentation or explanation of his or her solution and later transfer the student's words onto the actual work. For example, a center could be set up in one corner of the classroom for students to audio record their explanations.

(4) Explore technology that can be used to document how students solve problems or talk through their process.

Providing generic prompts to clarify student thinking

It is appropriate to provide encouragement and use a few generic prompts to assist a student in clarifying his or her ideas while explaining or developing a solution. *"What is your plan?"* and *"Tell me how you did this part"* and *"How do you know your solution is correct?"* are examples of generic prompts that can encourage students to better clarify their written or oral explanations.

> Comments such as "You need to make a chart" or "Your solution is incorrect" are not appropriate and should not be used during assessments.

Providing a generic self-monitoring student checklist

It is appropriate to provide a self-monitoring tool, such as a student checklist during the assessment, <u>if the teacher has been using the tool during instruction and students understand how to use it</u>. Self-monitoring checklists generally list the key parts of assessment tasks (e.g., identified the important parts, answered the question, or showed my thinking) and help to keep students focused and promote metacognitive thinking. If you make checklists interactive, students will have to react to what is on the list, not simply check something off. For example, in math I might ask them to circle important words in the problem or provide a key to explain the information in the table or graph. These checklists are optional and usually are not part of the assessment.

Additionally, a teacher or scribe can support students staying on task, by providing encouragement for persevering with the problem (but with no indication about whether the student is correct or incorrect).

Guidelines for scribing mathematics assessment tasks

1. When scribing student work, the scribe should <u>take dictation rather than paraphrasing</u> the student's response, even if the student's response is incorrect or shows poor understanding of the task. Vocabulary and notation must be <u>exactly what the student says, even if it is incorrect.</u> Clearly indicate which information was student ("St") dictated, and which information was documented by the scribe. <u>Use quotation marks to indicate what the student orally stated about his or her solution.</u>

2. When a scribe provides a prompt (e.g., asks a clarifying question), it should be noted in brackets. For example: ["Tell me how you decided to make a triangle." or "Can you show me how you counted these?"]

3. For efficiency, scribes may want to use a template of a few generic prompts for all students taking the assessment. The student's responses are noted on the template instead of on the student's work and are attached to the student's work for interpretation or determining next steps in instruction.

4. Scribes also document student actions in parentheses. For example: (Sarah counted 1, 2, 3, . . . 10 correctly; John correctly pointed to the triangle, but missed the circle; student did not respond to the prompt.)

5. <u>The scribe should always initial any writing put on a student's work</u>. If the person scoring or interpreting the student's work is different from the scribe, she or he can contact the scribe if there are any questions. This is especially important in classrooms with multiple adults doing scribing.

> Whenever you are not sure about the appropriateness of a scribing practice, ask yourself this question: "Does this accurately demonstrate what the student knows and can do independently?"

A scribing example for mathematics

Scribes will develop procedures that are both manageable and comfortable for their students and themselves. Here is an example of what scribing might sound and look like <u>at the primary level</u>:

1. "Tell me your plan." (or "your thinking," "your idea," "what you did first," "what you did here," etc.).

2. "What is your answer?" (or state the specific question asked, "How many cookies were there?" "What was the tenth one?" "How many sides did you find?")

3. If the solution to the task asked for a particular number, it is suggested that you <u>ask the student to count to that number</u>. For example, if the answer is six shoes and the student only put the number 6 on his or her paper you would ask the student to count how many shoes she or he has on the paper. A student may count 1, 2, 3, 4, 5, 6. Another student may count 2, 4, 6 or another student might count 1, 3, 2, 5, 4, 6 or not be able to say any numbers. You want to document an answer that is completely accurate and not a numerical misunderstanding (or copying a number).

4. Scribes often ask primary students, *"How did you know when to stop?"* An example would be a pattern problem that asks what shape is the seventh one. Some students will continue the pattern until they reach the end of the paper and might indicate the correct answer without understanding that they were to find the seventh one. It just happened to be the last shape on the paper.

5. End a scribing session by reading back what was dictated and asking, "Is there anything else you would like to show or tell me?" or "Can you tell me anything else about the numbers you put on your paper or about your counting?"

Sample Template: Administration Guidelines for Common Assessment Tasks

Name of Assessment Task: Boots and Hats

Grade: K

Suggested Time: November/Fall (after completion of the first 3 units in math program)

Suggested Use: Formative ____ Interim _X_ Summative ___

Estimated Time Needed: Most students were able to complete this task in one class period during piloting. Added time may be needed to scribe student responses.

Prioritized Math Standards: K.CC4a

Math Skills & Concepts Emphasized: Counting (0-20; some students may count by 2s or notice the odd/even pattern of boots and hats), using representations and different strategies (e.g., diagrams, symbols), multiple decision points.

Mathematical Practices: Abstract reasoning; problem solving and perseverance (multistep problem).

Use of Manipulatives: Most piloting teachers used models or pictures of real boots and a hat counters, and word tents.

Additional accommodations/supports: Most teachers did some scribing or noted observations if a student "demonstrated" counting. (See Administration Guidelines for allowable accommodations and scribing.)

Clarifying task language: boots, hats, students, "in all." Teacher modeling was used during piloting to ensure that all students understood the words and the question they were expected to answer. Some teachers taught a similar lesson the day before, such as using the context of X number of kids with one helmet and bike (two wheels). Other teachers have used duck feet (two) and duck tail (one).

Scoring Guide: Currently piloting this task—No rubric yet. Teachers are asked to collect work samples and sort them for discussion and rubric development.

General Teacher Directions

1. [Distribute copies of the problem.] "Listen and follow along as I read the directions."

   [Read the directions to the problem aloud together with the students.]

2. *"Can you find the question you need to answer? Circle the question."* [Teacher models and allows time for students to circle the question. Check to see that students circled: *How many boots and hats did I see in all?*]

3. *"Now let's read the problem again to find the important information you need in order to solve the problem."* [Allow time for students to highlight or underline the important information. Guide students to locate <u>important</u> information: **Four students; everyone wearing boots and a hat. You may want to discuss how many boots each student will wear. For example,** *"How many boots will one student wear?"*]

4. "Think about how you will answer the question, and how you will show your math thinking. Remember, you can use many different ways to help you solve the problem. *"What simple shape could we use to make a hat? What shape could you use to make boots?* Begin when

you are ready." [Note: In mathematics, we try to stress that they are not "drawing pictures" but representing the problem . . . e.g., a triangle can mean one hat.]

5. [Circulate around the room as children work and scribe for individual students. Some teachers have used sticky notes for quick scribing or a master scribing template for capturing exact words of different students. See guidelines for allowable accommodations.]

6. While students work, generic prompts may be given to the whole class or individuals, such as "What is your plan?" "How are you showing your thinking?" "How do you know your answer is correct?" "Did you make any connections or notice something mathematical?"

7. You can have students share their solutions, as you do during instruction after you have seen their work and have been able to do a "quick sort" using the Student Work Analysis form. You do not want students to change their responses for this assessment before you can analyze what they were able to do. To review this task and solution with students, it is recommended that you solve it together on the board or in small groups after collecting the papers or make copies of their papers (saving originals) and then give them copies of their papers to add to or to present or share solutions.

Performance Task Administration Guidelines

Name of Assessment Task:

Grade:

Purpose:

Suggested Time to Administer:

(Describe when best to use: For example, time of year, part of a unit of study or course, after students have learned particular content or completed a specific activity, such as an investigation in science or viewing a play or video.)

Suggested Use: Formative ____ Interim ___ Summative ___

Estimated Time Needed:

Resources/Tools Needed:

Proficiency Statements/Standards Assessed:

Specific Skills, Concepts, or Practices Emphasized in Task:

Additional Accommodations Allowed:

Scoring Guide/Rubric:

General Teacher Directions:

Copyright © 2018 by Corwin. All rights reserved. Reprinted from *A Local Assessment Toolkit to Promote Deeper Learning: Transforming Research into Practice* by Karin Hess. Thousand Oaks, CA: Corwin, www.corwin.com. Reproduction authorized only for the local school site or nonprofit organization that has purchased this book.

IV. Sample Formative Assessment Strategies

5 Key Ideas Underlying Effective Formative Assessment

The practice of formative—or "informal"—classroom assessment has been around for years, but it was probably the research of Paul Black and Dylan Wiliam (1998) that made educators stop and think more deeply about what makes an assessment formative—more specifically, the purpose and potential impact that the use of assessment evidence can have on future learning. While there are a variety of definitions of formative assessment in the literature, most agree that formative assessment is assessment FOR learning—assessment that provides information about what students know now in relation to where they are going and used to help them get to the intended learning target. Black and Wiliam's research highlighted that students who learn in a formative way achieve significantly better than matched control groups receiving more traditional approaches to teaching and testing. Several key ideas emerge from the last two decades' research on effective uses of formative assessment.

Key Idea #1: *Authentic assessment is continuous. Formative assessment is both integral to the cycle of learning and part of a balanced assessment system.* The success of formative assessment use within a local assessment system (formative assessment + interim assessment + summative assessment) is highly related to the quality of student involvement and how effectively teachers plan for and use assessment data to adjust instruction.

Key Idea #2: *Formative assessment may take different forms but should always inform instruction and learning.* Feedback from formative assessment is based on different sources of observable evidence (written, oral, visual, kinesthetic, etc.) and used to guide next steps in instruction and learning. Formative assessment is constantly occurring. It may be (a) "in-the-moment" (e.g., quick checks for understanding, probing questions during instruction based on what was just heard or observed); (b) designed with a specific purpose and learning target in mind (exit card, preassessment, conferencing, planned formative "probe"); or (c) curriculum embedded, such as using common formative assessments or performance tasks as preassessments and interim assessments (sometimes less complex than post/summative assessments) to monitor student progress across the school year.

Key Idea #3: *Feedback is multi-faceted and used to gauge how close a student is to the intended learning target.* A balance of feedback coming from three key sources—from teachers, from peers (e.g., peer tutoring, peer editing, peer conferencing), and self-assessment tools (e.g., Hess's "What I need to do" rubrics)—has been proven to enhance effectiveness of formative assessment use.

- Assessment evidence can be based on a variety of observable artifacts (e.g., portfolios, works in progress, systematic observations of individual or group activities, classroom discourse, performance tasks coupled with scoring guide or rubric based on intended learning targets and success criteria).

> **Suggested Resources**
>
> For guidance on embedding formative assessments, see Wiliam and Leahy (2015).

- Feedback to the student is primarily descriptive. Feedback emphasizes strengths, identifies challenges, and points to possible next steps in learning based on intended learning targets.

Key Idea #4: *Students are actively involved in formative assessment.* Active involvement means students use assessment evidence to set goals for learning and monitor progress, reflect on themselves as learners, and evaluate the quality of their performance. Valuing both one's struggles and one's successes accomplishing smaller learning targets over time has been proven to have a profound influence on deepening motivation, developing independence as a learner, and building what we have come to know as "a growth mindset."

Key Idea #5: All high-quality assessment utilizes three key components—understanding how one learns, how one demonstrates what was learned, and how we interpret or measure the evidence observed. The concept of the Assessment Triangle (Figure 3.6), first presented by Pellegrino, Chudowsky, and Glaser in Knowing What Students Know (KWSK) (National Research Council [NRC], 2001), is shown below. "The assessment triangle explicates three key elements underlying assessment: 'a model of student cognition and learning in the domain, a set of beliefs about the kinds of observation that will provide evidence of students' competencies, and an interpretation process for making sense of the evidence' (NRC, 2001, p. 44)." KWSK uses the heuristic of an "assessment triangle to illustrate the relationships among learning models, assessment methods, and inferences one can draw from the observations made about what students truly know and can do" (Hess, Burdge, & Clayton, 2011, p. 184). Assessment design (formative/interim/summative) and planning should consider all three.

Figure 3.6 The Assessment Triangle

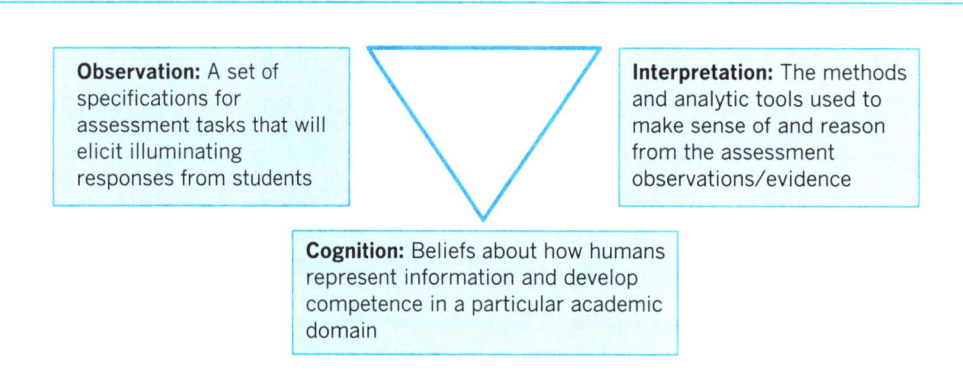

- **Observation:** A set of specifications for assessment tasks that will elicit illuminating responses from students
- **Interpretation:** The methods and analytic tools used to make sense of and reason from the assessment observations/evidence
- **Cognition:** Beliefs about how humans represent information and develop competence in a particular academic domain

Source: NRC (2001, pp. 44–51).

The formative assessment examples on the following pages are strategies addressing the following:

- *"in-the-moment"* (e.g., quick checks for understanding, asking probing questions during instruction based on what was just heard or observed); or
- *designed with a specific purpose and learning target in mind* (e.g., exit card, preassessment, conferencing, planned formative "probe").

The third category of formative assessments is included in the next section on performance assessment strategies:

- *curriculum embedded*, such as using common formative assessments (CFAs) and performance tasks as preassessments and interim assessments (sometimes less complex than post/summative assessments) to monitor student progress across the school year.

Sample Formative Assessment Strategies

FORMATIVE STRATEGY 1: Graphic Organizers Designed for Deeper Thinking—I've included two examples of graphic organizers intended for deeper understanding, usable as student prewriting tools or as formative assessments to help teachers see how students are drawing evidence from multiple texts and making connections (DOK 4).

Example 1: Differing perspectives on the same topic, requiring multiple text sources (adapted from Hess, 1987). This graphic organizer on page 238 visually supports executive functioning—helping students to keep track of text evidence from multiple texts so they can see and make connections among ideas or evidence. Use with multiple informational texts or media messages (DOK 4).

> **Suggested Resources**
>
> For guidance on developing common formative assessments (CFAs) see Ainsworth (2014).
>
> For more on performance task design, see McTighe and Wiggins (2012).

Example 2: Analyzing themes across texts (adapted from Hess, 1987). This graphic organizer on page 239 visually supports executive functioning—helping students to keep track of text evidence from multiple texts so they can see and make connections among ideas or evidence. Use with multiple literary texts (DOK 4).

FORMATIVE STRATEGY 2: Systematic Observation—This is a strategy for systematically documenting observations of student performance over extended time (e.g., fine art classes, literature circles) that might be difficult to capture with paper and pencil tests. It assists teachers in systematically documenting smaller numbers of student performances each time classes meet (DOK 1–4 is possible).

FORMATIVE STRATEGY 3: Probing Questions—I've included some math and science examples to show how a teacher might add a probing question to a lesson that requires deeper reasoning and justification. Probing questions spark greater student engagement and more meaningful discourse (DOK 3).

FORMATIVE STRATEGY 4: Interactive Student Self- and Peer-Assessment—The true goal of formative assessment is to involve students in assessment and reflection processes. I've included three examples that have been used for conferencing about writing in elementary classrooms (DOK 3).

FORMATIVE STRATEGY 5: Anticipation Guides—In the past, anticipation guides have probably been used more by reading teachers than in other content areas. Anticipation guides are excellent discussion starters and self- and peer-assessment tools that require supporting evidence for stating and supporting opinions or claims (DOK 3, DOK 4).

Introduction: Focus, Controlling Idea, or Thesis Statement—Respond to Prompt

Comparing perspectives on an event or issue or problem: Authors often have differing perspectives on the same issue, event, or problem. Select two print or nonprint texts read or viewed and discussed. Explain what each perspective is and analyze how each author supports the central idea of the piece. Show a clear relationship between the perspectives presented by each source. Upon which points or evidence do they agree or disagree?

Relevant Evidence From Text #1

- Perspective?
- Supporting evidence?
- Potential biases of source or interpretation of evidence used?

Relevant Evidence From Text #2

- Perspective?
- Supporting evidence?
- Potential biases of source or interpretation of evidence used?

Conclusion linked to focus or thesis: restate or recap, summarize key points, end with question, advice, insights to ponder

"Come full circle" concluding with how these texts or perspectives are related or differ in some way.

Available for download at **resources.corwin.com/HessToolkit**

Copyright © 2018 by Corwin. All rights reserved. Reprinted from *A Local Assessment Toolkit to Promote Deeper Learning: Transforming Research into Practice* by Karin Hess. Thousand Oaks, CA: Corwin, www.corwin.com. Reproduction authorized only for the local school site or nonprofit organization that has purchased this book.

Introduction: Focus, Controlling Idea, or Thesis Statement—Respond to Prompt

People make decisions that affect others. From texts read or viewed and discussed, select two. Provide some context, explain how the decision made by someone and why, and the effect it had on others or events or themes.

Show a clear relationship between texts or characters chosen and decisions made with themes or resulting effects.

Relevant Evidence From Text #1

- Literary work and character
- Decision made/why/motivation
- Resulting effect on others or event outcome?

Relevant Evidence From Text #2

- Literary work and character
- Decision made/why/motivation
- Resulting effect on others or event outcome?

Conclusion linked to focus or thesis: restate or recap, summarize key points, end with question, advice, insights to ponder—"Come full circle" concluding how these texts or characters are related in some way.

Available for download at **resources.corwin.com/HessToolkit**

Copyright © 2018 by Corwin. All rights reserved. Reprinted from *A Local Assessment Toolkit to Promote Deeper Learning: Transforming Research into Practice* by Karin Hess. Thousand Oaks, CA: Corwin, www.corwin.com. Reproduction authorized only for the local school site or nonprofit organization that has purchased this book.

FORMATIVE STRATEGY 2: Documenting systematic observation

What is systematic observation?

Systematic observation is an assessment strategy used to document knowledge and skills of a group of students over a period of time, rather than assessing all students at the same time (on demand). Generally, this approach works well for areas that are difficult to assess with pencil and paper tests or when multiple opportunities are provided for students to demonstrate acquisition of skills and knowledge over time. Systematic observation captures the often "missed opportunities" for collecting assessment data during an instructional activity and can document progress being made over time in meeting broader learning goals for the school year.

Data collection can be embedded in the instructional activity, such as during a class or group discussion, or done during small group or individual conferences with students. Brief notations are made including the date, student name, and key quotes or comments related to the focus of the learning goal(s). In a single lesson or activity, only a few specific notations might be made by the observer; however, eventually all students will be documented several times in the same areas of focus. Ongoing data collection provides information for making instructional decisions and for making evidence-based decisions about student learning.

How to use the Systematic Observation Documentation Template

1. *Identify two or three areas you will consistently (systematically) be able to document over time (such as throughout a unit of study)*—Although you *could* observe many different areas, limit the number of areas you will document through observation to ensure quality data collection and minimal instructional interruption as you make notes. Identify areas difficult to assess with pencil and paper assignments (e.g., open-ended discussion topics about text features or use of comprehension strategies).

2. *Do a quick "standards match" with areas selected for observation*—What standard or expectations are you assessing? What are some key components you'll focus on? Make a few notes at the bottom of the page to help you remember, since you won't ask for all of them in one lesson or learning activity. (For example, you might list the literary devices or text features that students will be asked about over several lessons.)

3. *Make systematic notes*—Date notes with student names and enough information to guide further instruction or to make evidence-based judgments about student learning.

4. *Use systematic notes to make informed decisions*—Some notes will be used to individualize support and instruction for particular students, some notes will inform general ongoing instructional practices for the group or entire class, and some notes will be used collectively to generalize how much progress each student is making.

Systematic Observation Documentation Template

TASK/ACTIVITY: GROUP/GRADE LEVEL:

(Remember to date each notation about student responses)

Standard(s):   Standard(s):

Standard(s):   OTHER COMMENTS and OBSERVATIONS:

TEACHER NOTES: (Key skills and understandings to look for in observations)

Source: Hess (2004).

Available for download at **resources.corwin.com/HessToolkit**

Copyright © 2018 by Corwin. All rights reserved. Reprinted from *A Local Assessment Toolkit to Promote Deeper Learning: Transforming Research into Practice* by Karin Hess. Thousand Oaks, CA: Corwin, www.corwin.com. Reproduction authorized only for the local school site or nonprofit organization that has purchased this book.

Sample Systematic Observation Documentation

Task/Activity: Discussion in Literature Circles—Poetry Unit Group/Grade Level: 3

Standard(s):

Identify characteristics of types of text

(CCSS RL.5: refer to parts of stories...)

3/17 Mandy: this poem is not rhyming like all the other ones—I sort of liked it cuz of that

3/17 Aaron: I like this story-kind of poetry more than the rhyming kind

3/19 Meg: The verses are shorter in this poem

Standard(s):

Identify literary devices

(CCSS RL.4: distinguish literal from nonliteral language)

3/17 Sarah: The words help me make a picture in my mind of what's happening

3/19 Joseph: noticed rhyme scheme!

3/20 Aaron: This part was cool—how they talked back and forth to each other—like in a play. Dialogue, right?

Standard(s):

Participating in discussions, offering comments and supporting evidence from text

(CCSS RL.1: refer explicitly to the text...)

3/20 Peter, Josie, Aaron, and Mandy: lots of participation, used text-based comments to support ideas

3/21 Joseph: beginning to do so, needs scaffolding—can locate evidence when given supporting statement or can make supporting statement if given two or three evidence or references from text

OTHER COMMENTS and OBSERVATIONS:

3/20 Joseph—remembered to bring Readers Notebook!

3/21 Aaron: may be interested in reading (or writing?) some plays?

TEACHER NOTES: (Key skills and understandings to look for in observations)

Rhyme, rhyme scheme

Narrative and lyric poems

Imagery, dialogue

Source: Hess (2004).

Copyright © 2018 by Corwin. All rights reserved. Reprinted from *A Local Assessment Toolkit to Promote Deeper Learning: Transforming Research into Practice* by Karin Hess. Thousand Oaks, CA: Corwin, www.corwin.com. Reproduction authorized only for the local school site or nonprofit organization that has purchased this book.

FORMATIVE STRATEGY 3: Probing questions

Table 3.4 includes examples of how a basic (DOK 1 or 2) question or scenario presented can be turned into deeper student thinking by adding a probing, evidence-based question. The math examples are inspired by Rose, Minton, and Arline (2007). The science probe is modeled after formative probes in Keeley, Eberle, and Farrin (2005).

Table 3.4 Sample Frames for Formative Probes

[Present several equations.] Decide which equations below are true and which ones are false. 4 + 2 = 7, 3 + 13 = 16, 5 = 5 [Then ask] For each one, how can you prove you are correct?	Study the graph below. Choose an explanation from the ones provided that best describes what happened with each runner in the race. [Provide a graph.] Runner A won the race. Runner B fell down. Runner C started slowly but finished first. [Then ask] Explain your reasoning using math terms, concepts, calculations, and interpretation of data.
[Prompt] Four friends observed a rotting apple along the road and disagreed with why it was rotting. [Present several different explanations that include common misconceptions.] Abby thinks . . . John says . . . Aria says . . . Tristan disagrees with Aria because . . . [Then ask] Which student do you most agree with? Describe your thinking. Provide a scientific explanation for your answer.	Your turn . . . start with a basic question or provide a context: [Then ask]

Module 3: What Does This Test Really Measure? 243

FORMATIVE STRATEGY 4: Student self- and peer-assessment example—genre-specific interactive conferencing tools

EXAMPLE #1 is designed to reinforce differences in schemas for composing persuasive/opinion-based texts.

MY WRITING CHECKLIST—OPINION

Name: _____ Date: _____

My Title: _____

What I Need to Do . . . when I persuade or sell my ideas to others.

❑ My opinion is: _____

❑ My opinion answers a question: _____
_____

❑ My beginning starts with: _____

❑ REASON #1 is: _____

❑ I say more about REASON #1 explaining __ actions __ facts __ images __ quote.

❑ REASON #2 is: _____

❑ I say more about REASON #2 explaining __ actions __ facts ___ images __ quote.

❑ These words connect my ideas: _____

❑ My writing makes sense – the ideas and details are grouped together. I have a conclusion

❑ My pictures, tables or diagrams **go with my writing __ have details __ add more information** __. Labels, titles, or captions point out what is most important.

❑ My ideas and facts are from these sources: __ book __ Internet __ person __ video

Partner Editing Checklist: I worked with _____

❑ All of my sentences begin with a capital letter. I have space between paragraphs (REASONS).

❑ Names of people and book titles start with capital letters.

❑ My sentences end with __ periods (.) __ question marks (?) __ exclamation marks (!).

❑ We used __ **work bank** __ **journal** __ **dictionary** __ **text** __ **glossary** to check spelling.

❑ I listed __ or included __ my sources in my final product.

Available for download at **resources.corwin.com/HessToolkit**

Copyright © 2018 by Corwin. All rights reserved. Reprinted from *A Local Assessment Toolkit to Promote Deeper Learning: Transforming Research into Practice* by Karin Hess. Thousand Oaks, CA: Corwin, www.corwin.com. Reproduction authorized only for the local school site or nonprofit organization that has purchased this book.

EXAMPLE #2 is designed to reinforce differences in schemas for composing literary or narrative texts.

MY WRITING CHECKLIST—NARRATIVES

Name: _____ Date: _____

My Title: _____

What I Need to Do . . . when I write a story, play, or poem.

❏ My focus is: _____

❏ My beginning starts with: _____

❏ The middle tells more about: _____
_____

❏ My end _____

❏ Descriptive words to show __ actions __ feelings __ images __ describe places.

❏ There is dialogue for characters: _____

❏ I used words to show the order of events __ next __ then __ later __ while __ after __ (other words) _____
_____

❏ My pictures go with my writing and add interesting ideas and details.

Partner Editing Checklist: I worked with _____

❏ All of my sentences begin with a capital letter.

❏ The word "I" and names start with capital letters.

❏ The sentences end with __ periods (.) __ question marks (?) __ exclamation points (!)

❏ I used "quotation marks" to show when someone is talking.

❏ We used __ word bank __ journal __ dictionary to check spelling.

❏ I have spaces between words and sentences.

Available for download at **resources.corwin.com/HessToolkit**

Copyright © 2018 by Corwin. All rights reserved. Reprinted from *A Local Assessment Toolkit to Promote Deeper Learning: Transforming Research into Practice* by Karin Hess. Thousand Oaks, CA: Corwin, www.corwin.com. Reproduction authorized only for the local school site or nonprofit organization that has purchased this book.

EXAMPLE #3 is designed to reinforce differences in schemas for composing informational texts.

MY WRITING CHECKLIST—INFORMATIONAL

Name: _____ **Date:** _____

My Title: _____

What I Need to Do . . . when I teach with my writing or speaking.

- ❏ This is my focus: _____

- ❏ My beginning starts with _____

- ❏ <u>BIG IDEA #1</u> answers a question _____

- ❏ <u>I say more</u> about IDEA #1 describing __ actions __ facts __ images __ details.

- ❏ <u>BIG IDEA #2</u> answers a question _____

- ❏ <u>I say more</u> about IDEA #2 describing __ actions __ facts __ images __ details.

- ❏ These words connect my ideas: _____

- ❏ My writing makes sense – the ideas and details are grouped together.

- ❏ My pictures or diagrams go with my writing and add interesting ideas.

- ❏ I have labels or captions that help to explain what is most important.

Partner Editing Checklist: I worked with _____

- ❏ All of my sentences begin with a capital letter.

- ❏ The word "I" and names of people and book titles start with capital letters.

- ❏ My sentences end with __ periods (.) __ question marks (?) __ exclamation marks (!).

- ❏ We used __ word bank __ journal __ dictionary __ book __ glossary to check spelling.

- ❏ I have spaces between words and sentences.

Available for download at **resources.corwin.com/HessToolkit**

Copyright © 2018 by Corwin. All rights reserved. Reprinted from *A Local Assessment Toolkit to Promote Deeper Learning: Transforming Research into Practice* by Karin Hess. Thousand Oaks, CA: Corwin, www.corwin.com. Reproduction authorized only for the local school site or nonprofit organization that has purchased this book.

FORMATIVE STRATEGY 5: Anticipation Guides

Prior to reading, researching, or viewing, decide if you:

Strongly Disagree (SD)—Disagree (D)—Agree (A)—Strongly Agree (SA) with each statement.

After reading, viewing, or discussing the topic, have your opinions changed? Explain why.

SD	D	A	SA	READ EACH STATEMENT BELOW DECIDE IF YOU AGREE OR DISAGREE BY PUTTING AN "X" IN THE COLUMN TO THE LEFT	AFTER? EXPLAIN WHY YOU AGREE OR DISAGREE. (CITE SUPPORTING EVIDENCE, SOURCES, ETC.)

Available for download at **resources.corwin.com/HessToolkit**

Copyright © 2018 by Corwin. All rights reserved. Reprinted from *A Local Assessment Toolkit to Promote Deeper Learning: Transforming Research into Practice* by Karin Hess. Thousand Oaks, CA: Corwin, www.corwin.com. Reproduction authorized only for the local school site or nonprofit organization that has purchased this book.

V. Sample Performance Assessment Design Strategies

Formative, interim, and summative performance assessments include learning activities and assessments that ask students to demonstrate the transfer of knowledge, skills, and dispositions in an authentic context, such as designing a mechanical structure for a specific purpose, creating a performance or product to express a theme, or investigating a natural phenomenon. Observable and measureable products or performances are used as evidence of learning across multiple dimensions. As stated earlier in this module, performance assessment encompasses a range of types and purposes.

- *Short diagnostic tasks* used formatively assess "near transfer" such as fluency checks in reading, asking probing questions to uncover misconceptions in science, or practicing how to do a key word search in preparation for gathering information for a research project.

- *Course-embedded performance tasks* require "far transfer" such as complex mathematics problem-solving activities, open-ended writing or research prompts, arts-based explorations, scenario role-plays, and STEM investigations.

- *Extended multistage assessments* also require "far transfer" and may take as long as a semester to research and develop, such as culminating group projects at the end of a unit of study, student-designed expeditionary learning activities, community service projects, and in-depth analyses of case studies in science or social studies.

⬅ Short, diagnostic, formative tasks | Course-embedded formative, interim, and summative performance tasks | Extended, multistage interim and summative assessments ➡

> To clarify the range of possibilities with performance assessments, gather and provide a collection of examples (diagnostic tasks, performance tasks, projects, student-designed exhibitions, etc.) asking participants to discuss and sort them along an imaginary assessment continuum. Discuss: What do all of them have in common? What differentiates these assessments along the continuum?

Performance assessment: Important to demonstrate a learning stretch, but difficult to design

For this last section, I'm focusing on course-embedded tasks and extended performance assessments, both of which are not as easy to design as you might think. This is partly because there generally is not one "right" answer or approach and because we probably have not seen as many strong models to guide us as we have for more traditional assessment item types and tasks. I suggest starting by modifying an existing performance assessment or using a task shell to design an assessment for your purposes, rather than starting from scratch to develop a new one. The more you do this, the better you'll get at it. The more you look critically at the assessments of your peers (during task development or task validations), the more confidence you'll have in creating your own.

Course-embedded tasks and extended performance-based assessments for and of deeper learning are framed by these common characteristics:

1. *Require (Far) Transfer*: Products and performances embed the use of basic skills and concepts in novel, authentic contexts. Although skills and concepts are being assessed, it is how (and how many) skills and concepts are applied that results in a learning stretch for students.

2. *Open-Ended*: Prompts or situations posed to (or designed by) students are open-ended. Varied approaches and use of multiple resources are expected. Solutions are not intended to result in only one correct solution path.

3. *Challenging*: Prompts cause students to actively grapple with concepts (e.g., apply multiple possible strategies and approaches), stretch their thinking, and explore alternative solutions and constraints.

4. *Uncover Thinking*: Products or performances require students to engage in substantive reasoning related to concepts or theories (e.g., research, justification, explaining thinking). Generating ideas, questions, propositions, alternative strategies, and representations, for example, are integral to completion of the task or project.

5. *Authentically Doing*: Products or performances reflect real-world skills and dispositions for the context presented. A health sciences assessment or arts assessment reflects what health or arts professionals actually do.

6. *Reflective and Metacognitive*: Unlike traditional tests that may ask for recall and near transfer of less to more complex skills and concepts, performance assessments require students to reflect on or be informed by what they have done in the past, self-monitor what they are doing now and how well it's working, and articulate what was learned and how they have extended their own knowledge.

Components of (Validated) Performance Assessments
For and of deeper learning

- *Embedded in Ongoing Learning or Curriculum*—Students have had the opportunity to learn and are "ready"

- *Student Directions*—Clear, focused, and engaging (options, decisions to be made by student)

- *Teacher Directions/Administration Guidelines*—Ensure consistency or fidelity of administration across teachers and schools; essential for common assessment tasks

- *Flexible for All Learners*—Attention to possible accommodations is built into the assessment design ahead of time

- *Scoring Guide/Rubric*—Student-friendly language clarifies success criteria for students and teachers

- *Annotated Student Work at Each Performance Level*—Used with scoring rubrics, ensures reliability and consistency of scoring across teachers and schools

- *If part of a larger task bank, use of a consistent presentation format* to make requirements and expectations predicable for students (e.g., rubrics use the same number of performance levels and consistent language in performance indicators; task prompts follow a similar format or use a similar template)

Beginning performance assessment design with "the end in mind"

Performance-based assessment design requires that you consider four key questions as you begin to develop a prompt or task description:

- What will this assess?
- Within what (authentic) context?

- Using what assessment format (case study analysis, role-playing scenario, research project, performance task, etc.)?
- To what degree will students be given choices or be required to make decisions about the task design, approach, resources used, or presentation of their learning?

Before deciding what format the assessment will take or the specifics of what students will "produce" or demonstrate, I suggest using the table below (Table 3.5) of rubric criteria types to identify what the assessment is intended to measure. This is only an initial brainstorm to clarify your assessment purpose and scope; the details will likely change as the task evolves. For each criterion, generate a list of the expected processes or skills, concepts, dispositions, and thinking strategies you plan to assess. All criteria do not need to be included in the final assessment, but all *should be* considered during this phase of the planning.

Table 3.5   Using Rubric Criteria Types to Plan Performance Assessments

CRITERION	QUESTIONS TYPICALLY ANSWERED BY EACH CRITERION
Process	Will the student follow particular processes (e.g., procedures for a science investigation, data collection, validating credibility of sources)? (usually DOK 2 for more complex tasks)
Form	Are there formats or rules to be applied (e.g., use correct citation format, organize parts of lab report, use required camera shots or visuals, edit for grammar and usage)? (usually DOK 1)
Accuracy of Content	List essential domain-specific terms, calculations, concepts to be applied. (usually DOK 1 or 2)
Construction of New Knowledge	How will the student go beyond the accurate solution and correct processes to gain new insights or raise new questions? (usually DOK 3 or 4)
Impact	How will the final product achieve its intended purpose (e.g., solve a complex problem, persuade the audience, synthesize information to create a new product or performance) (usually DOK 3 or 4)

PLC **TOOL #20** incorporates this table into step 1 of the design process and walks you through a protocol for assessment development. Listed below are my suggested steps for designing a performance-based assessment (PBA) task:

STEP 1: Use the rubric criteria types to identify what will be assessed in the PBA. CRM **TOOLS #1–#5D** may be useful in identifying specific performance indicators and intended DOK levels. All criteria types do not need to be included, but they should be considered in the design phase. Only the last two criteria will allow you to assess far transfer of skills or concepts.

STEP 2: Identify one or more authentic contexts for applying these skills, concepts, and dispositions. Consider how real-world professionals employ these skills and concepts (scientists, artists, historians, researchers, choreographers, etc.).

STEP 3: Identify an appropriate assessment format for demonstrating learning. Once you decide on format, explore existing models and use or modify one as a template for your PBA design.

- case study analysis
- role-playing scenario (e.g., GRASPS)
- research project
- science investigation

- performance task (e.g., using a task shell)
- performance or presentation
- develop a product
- other?

STEP 4: Determine to what degree students will be given choices or be required to make decisions about the PBA task design, approach to solution, resources used, or presentation of learning.

STEP 5: Use PLC **TOOL #9** or PLC **TOOL #16B** to identify and align success criteria (standards or proficiency statements), develop student and teacher instructions, and check accessibility (fairness).

STEP 6: Use PLC **TOOL #11** to develop a reliable scoring guide or rubric.

STEP 7: Use PLC **TOOL #21** to provide an overview of what this task assesses, where this will be embedded in curriculum (unit or course), how results will be used (formative vs. summative), and how it relates to other assessments in the unit of study or course (e.g., "relates" might mean that there is a unit preassessment and this is the post-assessment for the same unit).

Two general approaches are included to help get you started with PBA design. The examples I've included for each strategy will work with any content area and provide various options for format and product or performance. If you are creating PBAs as part of a larger task bank, use a consistent presentation format making requirements and expectations predicable for students (e.g., rubrics use the same number of performance levels and consistent language in performance indicators; task prompts follow a similar format or use a similar template to provide instructions to students). For example, if you are familiar with the mathematics assessments designed by Dan Meyer (http://blog.mrmeyer.com/category/3acts/), then you know that he uses the consistent format of "3 Acts." The first act is usually a stimulus in the form of a short video clip with a question to be answered (e.g., A faucet is dripping; water is rising. The question posed: How long will it take to fill the sink with water?). The second act poses questions to the student, such as "Which information will help you to solve this problem?" (e.g., the cost of water, the amount of water in a drop, the number of drops/minute). Usually more than one piece of information will be needed; students have to use reasoning to decide what is needed and how it will help them to solve the problem. The final act might provide a solution with which to compare their solutions or a solution for students to evaluate.

Some online sources for extended performance assessments and performance tasks:

- K–12 Performance Tasks Website: http://galileo.org/teachers/designing-learning/articles/what-is-inquiry
- Model Learning Exhibitions: https://eleducation.org/resources/model-learning-expedition-snapshots
- New York Performance Standards Consortium: http://democraticeducation.org/index.php/library/resource/nyc_performance_assessment_consortium
- Sample STEM Case Study Assessments: http://sciencecases.lib.buffalo.edu/cs/collection
- Jay McTighe's seven-part blog series on performance tasks: https://blog.performancetask.com
- New York City public schools have piloted and validated many performance tasks using my task validation process. You can find some of them posted at https://www.weteachnyc.org
- SCALE Performance Assessment Task Bank: https://www.performanceassessmentresourcebank.org
- Additional performance assessment examples and interactive PLC **TOOLS (#9, #10, and #12)** are posted at http://www.karin-hess.com/formative-and-performance-assessments

PERFORMANCE ASSESSMENT STRATEGY 1: Case Studies and Student-Designed Expeditionary Learning

If you are looking for a way to integrate multiple content areas into one rich PBA, then you might want to explore using case studies for science or social studies. High school science teachers in Springdale, Arkansas, that I've been working with came upon a resource through the University of Buffalo that is excellent for promoting in-depth thinking about science phenomena (sciencecases.lib.buffalo.edu/cs/collection). Teachers use the case studies as the stimulus for (a) collaborative close reading of the case to identify key aspects, either by annotating the text or completing a graphic organizer; (b) small and large group discussions to make connections with what they are currently learning in class or what they need to learn more about (in chemistry, biology, etc.) that helps to understand the case study; and then (c) researching and proposing a solution to the related problem presented in the case study.

Some large-scale science assessments currently use case studies as the stimulus to the prompt for their performance tasks. I have written some sample case studies for the test specifications of the New England Common Assessment Project (NECAP) in Science. I can tell you that case studies are not that easy to write from scratch; but you can often find scenarios of historical or current events that can be used as the basis for developing a case study. Case studies naturally address many of the bigger ideas that we want students to make connections with when they are learning.

PERFORMANCE ASSESSMENT STRATEGY 2: Task Shells

A second strategy for designing performance assessments is to use a task shell that frames the structure and limits how the task is designed. **Task shells** (also referred to as task models) provide general guidelines for what a performance task should include if it is to effectively measure the stated learning objective(s). For example, a template for science performance tasks might include the following components: (a) scenario or data related to a real-world phenomenon is used as the stimulus; (b) prompt asking students to state a hypothesis (or testable question) based on the data or scenario; (c) prompt asks students to develop steps to conduct an investigation to test their hypothesis; and (d) conduct the investigation, stating conclusions based on evidence collected.

Test developers use task shells to ensure that (parallel) PBAs will elicit comparable evidence of learning year to year and can be reliably scored using the same performance criteria. Currently, the Smarter Balanced Assessment Consortium (SBAC) uses task shells both to guide task development and to inform teachers about what to expect in the assessment. Figure 3.7 shows an excerpt from the SBAC task specifications (2017) for designing and aligning SBAC mathematics performance tasks.

Examples of task shells

Examples of several task shells are included on pages 258–280 to suggest the many ways that performance assessments can be structured. They should be self-explanatory as to how different teachers could use the same task shell to design different, but comparable assessments, or to increase the complexity of the task by keeping the general prompt the same but increasing the complexity or number of texts or changing the stimulus in some way. For example, I've included a place value assessment that works well at Grades K–4 when you change the magnitude of the numbers used in the prompt. I've also included a measurement task and social studies/STEM artifact analysis task that can easily be used with many different objects or artifacts.

Figure 3.6 Mathematics Performance Task Specifications

Smarter Balanced
Assessment Consortium

Aligned With Claims and Standard's	PTs should go to the heart of the key Smarter Balanced Claims and Common Core State Standards for Mathematics. In particular, they should elicit evidence of Claims 2, 3, and 4: • Students can solve a range of complex, well-posed problems in pure* and applied mathematics, making productive use of knowledge and problem solving strategies. (Claim 2) • Students can clearly and precisely construct viable arguments to support their own reasoning and to critique the reasoning of others. (Claim 3) • Students can analyze complex, real-world scenarios and can construct and use mathematical models to interpret and solve problems. (Claim 4) In addition, they should elicit evidence of student engagement in the Common Core Mathematical Practices.
Developmentally Appropriate	PT topics, tasks, and scoring should be appropriate for the age and developmental experience base of the students.
Engaging	Topics should be authentic and realistic, engaging students in solving a problem or making a decision they would find relevant.
Accessible	Topics and tasks should minimize sources of bias, allow for multiple pathways, and provide appropriate scaffolds or supports while keeping in mind that sources and response types need to allow access for students with different English language proficiency and students with disabilities.
Purposeful and Coherent	Tasks should have an authentic purpose, and all task components should be connected to achieving that goal.

*Note: PTs in particular aim to assess problem solving in applied mathematics.

Source: SBAC Mathematics Task Specifications Excerpt (2017, p. 4).

Most of the content-specific task shell examples were developed through piloting projects that I've worked on. These are performance tasks that we found to be flexible enough to use them at different grade levels for designing pre-, mid-, and postassessments. There are no scoring rubrics included with these tasks, although we did use rubrics to score and develop annotated anchor papers for most of them. If you think they might work for you, I suggest you develop and pilot or conduct cognitive labs for some of them. Then use student work samples to develop scoring rubrics for them.

Scenarios and simulations

Role-playing is a great way to get students involved in authentic assessment, applying a combination of real-world skills and concepts. The GRASPS model designed by McTighe and Wiggins (2012, pp. 77–85) is one of the easiest task shells to begin with. I've included a slight variation of the original model and follow it with a CTE example designed by health sciences teachers in New Hampshire for a cognitive labs videotaping session.

Task Shell Examples

#	GRADE LEVEL	CONTENT AREA	TASK SHELL EXAMPLES
1	any	any	GRASPS Role-Play Scenarios (Health sciences example)
2	any	Social studies, Arts, STEM	Artifact Analysis
3–4	K–1	ELA	Informational writing: We read a book about . . . Opinion writing: We read a book. My favorite part . . .
5, 6, 7	4–5	ELA	Opinion writing: Character analysis
8	K–5	Math	Measurement (Grade K example)
9	1–4	Math	Place Value (Grade 2 example)
10	4	Math	Multiplication Strategies (Grade 4 example)
11	MS/HS	Science	Giants of Science
12	MS/HS	Science	Scientific Inquiry
13	MS/HS	ELA	The Novel
14	MS/HS	Social studies	Turning Points in History

None of these task shells is "perfect" or complete. (I have not included teacher directions, scoring rubrics, or samples of annotated student work with them, just to make them more "discussion worthy.") They are intended to provide opportunities for examination and discussion, offering concrete ideas as to how to design multiple tasks using the same basic template. I use examples like these to introduce and provide guided practice for how to use PLC **TOOL #9**, or to use PLC **TOOL #11** to develop rubrics for them. All of these assessments have gone through a piloting process to select and develop anchor papers. With the exception of the Health Sciences GRASPS example, all of these (in their final versions) have been edited based on piloting or cognitive labs.

Some Useful Workshop Notes

- Place Value Task Shell: When we piloted this task at Grades K–4 (using different numbers), we found that we gave far too many examples to students to examine at first; and although we only asked for explanations for "False," students gave explanations for all of them—both the "True" and "False" ones. Therefore, we reduced the number of examples and tried to include both concrete and more abstract (symbolic) examples. We also discovered that students needed more room to write, so the actual assessment provides more space to explain their thinking.

- The Wyoming examples (11–14) are useful for seeing a consistent presentation format and simplified way to present student directions. Teacher directions will have more detail.

- For Scientific Inquiry, we discovered through piloting that we needed to add room for "teacher sign-off" on the experiment proposal page. By adding teacher approval, students who had not developed a useful design would not be able to proceed with their investigations before making corrections. This had happened during the first piloting administration and a lot of time was lost on poor designs—not a very good learning experience for students, but valuable for the task developers! Since there was a rubric for designing the experiment, that was scored before students began to set up equipment and collect data. This strategically scaffolded the task and greatly improved the ability of all students to complete the assessment.

- For the last two examples—The Novel (13) and Turning Points in History (14)—I like to have workshop participants examine and discuss the alternate tasks given to students for each assessment. Giving students a choice in products encourages student engagement; however, it's generally a good idea to provide COMPARABLE options. While the content may be similar, the intended rigor of the options in these tasks is not. This approach (providing options at differing DOK levels) was used so that students at all ability levels would be able to successfully complete one of the options. Today, I think we would work harder—using strategic scaffolding—to support all students in completing more rigorous assignments. These are tasks that provide opportunities for this discussion and to collaboratively revise them to be more equitable assessments.

Using GRASPS to Develop Simulations and Role-Play Scenarios as Performance Assessments

- **G**   Your Goal
- **R**   Your Role
- **A**   The Audience
- **S**   The Situation/Scenario
- **P**   Your Products or Performances
- **S**   Success Criteria (Based on Competencies/Proficiencies, Standards)

Source: Adapted from McTighe and Wiggins (2012, pp. 77–85). Used with permission.

Your Goal	Provide a statement of the task. Establish the goal, problem, challenge, or obstacle in the task. (*Your goal is to help foreign visitors to understand the history and culture of your geographic region.*)
Your Role	Define the student's role and what they must do. (*You are an intern working at the state Office of Tourism.*)
The Audience	Who is the (real-world) target audience in this scenario? Could be client, patient, or board members, for example. (*Your audience is a group of nine visitors from another country. They do speak English, but it is limited.*)
The Situation or Scenario	Set up the context. What is the situation? Is there a problem to solve? A multi-aspect task to complete? (*You have been asked to develop a plan for a three-day tour of your city. Decide what sites to see, how they will show important ideas about culture and history, and how visitors will find these sites.*)
Your Products or Performances	Clarify what the students will create and why they will create it. (*You need to prepare a written itinerary with map, visuals, and short descriptions about why you have chosen these sites—it must be clear as to how each site will show something of importance about history and culture. Since it is multiday, think about what to see first and why.*)
Success Criteria	Provide criteria, rubrics, examples (from past years) of what success will look like. It helps to list each separate product or component. (*Your plan will include (1) itinerary and map for each day with estimated time needed at each site—a museum might take all of one day, (2) at least six key sites with rationale for why each one is important to visit, (3) something fun for them to do along the way. The final product should be visually interesting, accurate, and clear.*)

GRASPS Template—page 2

Consider the following set of STEM statements as you construct a scenario for a PBA task. Refer to the table above to help you brainstorm possible scenarios. Note: These are idea starters. Resist the urge to fill in all of the blanks!

Your Goal:

- ❑ Your task is _____.
- ❑ Your goal is to _____.
- ❑ The problem or challenge is _____.
- ❑ The obstacle to overcome is _____.

Your Role:

- ❑ You are _____.
- ❑ You have been asked to _____.
- ❑ Your job is _____.

The Audience:

- ❑ Your clients are _____.
- ❑ The target audience is _____.
- ❑ You need to convince _____.

The Situation or Scenario:

- ❑ The context you find yourself in is _____.
- ❑ The challenge involves dealing with _____.

Your Product, Performance, and Purpose:

- ❑ You will create a _____ in order to _____.
- ❑ You need to develop _____ so that _____.

Success Criteria:

- ❑ Your performance or product needs to _____.
- ❑ Your work will be judged by _____.
- ❑ Your product must include the following _____.

Source: Adapted from McTighe and Wiggins (2012, pp. 77–85). Used with permission.

Copyright © 2018 by Corwin. All rights reserved. Reprinted from *A Local Assessment Toolkit to Promote Deeper Learning: Transforming Research into Practice* by Karin Hess. Thousand Oaks, CA: Corwin, www.corwin.com. Reproduction authorized only for the local school site or nonprofit organization that has purchased this book.

Task Shell Example 1—Hospital Discharge

YOUR GOAL:

The goal: Explain and demonstrate principle of infection control as it applies to classifying microorganisms, chain of infection, mode of transmission, and will differentiate methods of controlling the spread and growth of microorganisms.

The problem/challenge is: Your patient has a diagnosis and needs to understand the safety precautions.

The obstacle(s) to overcome are: Understand the diagnosis and teach it to the patient and family members.

Phase 1: Microorganism information campaign

Each student or group will be assigned a disease. Each participant will create a brochure using scholarly sources translated by the student into common language for an acute-care setting. Critical information will need to be "translated" from medical jargon to something the public can understand and perform.

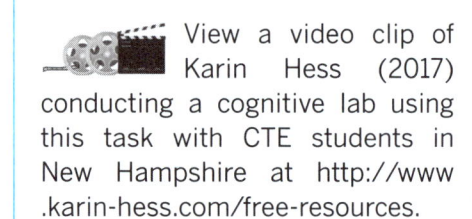

> View a video clip of Karin Hess (2017) conducting a cognitive lab using this task with CTE students in New Hampshire at http://www.karin-hess.com/free-resources.

- Criteria for information required in the brochure is as follows:
- mode of transmission
- method of controlling the spread of microorganism
- treatment
- proper use of PPE
- scholarly resources in common language

In addition, it must be well organized and contain relevant data in graphic such as a pie chart or graph.

Students will present the brochure to the class for feedback before the role-play.

Phase 2: Communicating infection control techniques to the patient

YOUR ROLE:

You are: a nurse

You have been asked to: teach your patient and family about the diagnosis as it applies to their scenario and demonstrate and teach your patient and family about precautions to prevent the spread of infection.

THE AUDIENCE:

Your client(s) is/are: the patient

The audience of the brochure will be patients and families being discharged from your facility.

The target audience for the role-play is the patient and his or her family.

THE SITUATION/SCENARIO:

As a nurse responsible for care of a postsurgical patient recently diagnosed with _____, your patient is being discharged and the family is present. You notice that the patient's family appears apprehensive, but you are unsure why. After questioning the family about what their concerns may be, you identify that the family has concerns about what their loved one "has" for a disease and is it "catchy." You then identify that this is an excellent opportunity to teach your patient and their family about the diagnosis as it applies to the chain of infection and the control of spread and growth of microorganisms, and demonstrate and teach your patient about applicable transmission-based precautions as required.

Diseases may include the following: MRSA, VRE, C-diff, staph, strep, TB, whooping cough, influenza, chicken pox, tetanus, HIV, hepatitis A, B, or C; or immunocompromised patient.

The challenge involves dealing with

1. Preparing the patient for discharge
2. Identifying family members' and patient's nonverbal cues for questions
3. Assessing the patient's and family's level of understanding

YOUR PRODUCTS/PERFORMANCE:

You will create a Patient Instructions Sheet/Brochure in part 1. In part 2, during a role-play, you will present information to the "family" for applying the proper PPE at home, have the family demonstrate the proper technique, and provide appropriate feedback to their questions.

SUCCESS CRITERIA:

Your product must meet the following standards: Safety Practices—Understand and identify existing and potential hazards to clients, coworkers, and self. Employ safe work practices and follow health and safety policies and procedures to prevent injury and illness.

A successful result will be demonstrated when the patient verbalizes understanding by reiterating back in his own words how he will protect himself at the time of discharge.

National Healthcare Foundations Standards in the State of New Hampshire

Foundation 1: 1, 2, 4

Foundation 2: 5, 6, 7

Foundation 3: 8

Foundation 4: 9

> This draft assessment was used to videotape how a cognitive lab would be administered to students. Try watching the video (30 minutes total) at http://www.karin-hess.com/free-resources as if you were the teacher. How would you modify the task? What would the (more streamlined) student directions look like? What would your scoring rubric include?

Source: High School CTE, Health Sciences (Littleton, NH) using GRASPS.

[This assessment was developed as a NH CTE PACE Common Performance Task (2017).]

Copyright © 2018 by Corwin. All rights reserved. Reprinted from *A Local Assessment Toolkit to Promote Deeper Learning: Transforming Research into Practice* by Karin Hess. Thousand Oaks, CA: Corwin, www.corwin.com. Reproduction authorized only for the local school site or nonprofit organization that has purchased this book.

Task Shell Example 2—Artifact Analysis

ARTIFACT ANALYSIS

Your Tasks

Your investigation:

Your team has been given an unfamiliar artifact to examine and investigate its origin and use. Your tasks are listed below. You may use any resources available to you and your team to complete your investigation.

1 TYPE OF ARTIFACT

Describe the material from which it was made: bone, pottery, metal, wood, stone, leather, glass, paper, cardboard, cotton, plastic, or other materials.

2 SPECIAL QUALITIES OF THE ARTIFACT

Describe how it looks and feels: shape, color, texture, size, weight, movable parts; anything printed, stamped, or written on it? What makes it unique or unusual?

3 YOUR HYPOTHESES ABOUT THE ARTIFACT

When might it have been used? What might it have been used for? Why do you think so? (Provide at least one source to support your thinking.)

4 PLAN AND CONDUCT RESEARCH

How will you investigate to confirm your hypothesis about the object? What resources might help? Are there mentors or experts you can ask? (Remember to document your sources!)

5 PRESENT YOUR FINDINGS

What have you learned about the artifact? What have you learned about the technology or culture of the time period and place it comes from?

Source: Adapted from educational materials developed by the Education Staff at the National Archives and Records Administration, Washington, D.C.

Available for download at **resources.corwin.com/HessToolkit**

Copyright © 2018 by Corwin. All rights reserved. Reprinted from *A Local Assessment Toolkit to Promote Deeper Learning: Transforming Research into Practice* by Karin Hess. Thousand Oaks, CA: Corwin, www.corwin.com. Reproduction authorized only for the local school site or nonprofit organization that has purchased this book.

Task Shell Example 3—Informational Writing

We read a book about _____.

This is what I learned:

_____

- -

_____

- -

_____

- -

_____

- -

_____

Source: Adapted from NYC Schools Performance Assessment Pilot—Grade K Informational Writing (2010).

Available for download at **resources.corwin.com/HessToolkit**

Copyright © 2018 by Corwin. All rights reserved. Reprinted from *A Local Assessment Toolkit to Promote Deeper Learning: Transforming Research into Practice* by Karin Hess. Thousand Oaks, CA: Corwin, www.corwin.com. Reproduction authorized only for the local school site or nonprofit organization that has purchased this book.

Task Shell Example 4—Opinion Writing

We read a book about _____.

My favorite part was

_____

_____

_____

_____

_____

because

_____

_____

_____

_____

_____

Source: Adapted from NYC Schools Performance Assessment Pilot—Grade K Informational Writing (2010).

Available for download at **resources.corwin.com/HessToolkit**

Copyright © 2018 by Corwin. All rights reserved. Reprinted from *A Local Assessment Toolkit to Promote Deeper Learning: Transforming Research into Practice* by Karin Hess. Thousand Oaks, CA: Corwin, www.corwin.com. Reproduction authorized only for the local school site or nonprofit organization that has purchased this book.

TASK SHELL EXAMPLES 5, 6, 7— CHARACTER ANALYSIS

Sample Task Shells for Developing Pre-, Mid-, or Postassessments: Literary Texts Character Study

Three "opinion-based" examples piloted previously at Grade 4 are on the following pages. These assessments introduce the concept of "text-based opinions"—also called literary analysis and critique. These task shells could be adapted for use at other grade levels with appropriately selected texts. Both print and nonprint texts can be read aloud, viewed, or read independently for instructional and assessment purposes.

- The first example is an opinion/critique of a self-selected text. This could be adapted for any independently read text as a pre-, mid-, or postassessment. Task complexity increases (over time) as the text's complexity increases.

- The second example uses a short text (chosen for students) and asks students to state and support an opinion about how a character changed during the story. Prewriting activities include a short class discussion using basic comprehension questions. A generic template for this prompt is provided. Before students move to analyzing multiple texts, they should "practice" with one text.

- The third example is designed for use with two short texts and asks students to compare main characters (traits, actions, motivations, etc.) from the stories. While these task shells are for examining characters, they could be used for exploring other aspects of author's craft (e.g., use of literary devices).

Each writing assessment should include prewriting discussions about texts read to help students generate ideas and to plan how to locate text evidence to use in their writing. This is to ensure that a student's writing ability is not negatively impacted because they have not been able to understand the text or generate ideas to get started.

Discussions may be as a whole class or a small group and do not need to be in-depth discussions. The purpose is to generate a basic understanding of the text (getting the gist of the text), in order to understand the intent of the prompt (explore author's craft—how the author develops characters, advances the action, uses descriptive language to create sensory images, etc.), and to begin to generate related vocabulary and text evidence that will help them to connect and explain their ideas.

Task Shell Example 5—Critique of Literary Texts: Character Study in a Self-Selected Text

Name _____   **Date** _____

Every story character, even animal characters, have personality traits that we learn about by what they say, think, want, and do, and by how other characters interact with them during the story. Authors use the characters and events in a story to develop themes and to teach lessons.

Select a text that you read earlier this year using a list provided by your teacher. Skim the story again and make some notes about the different characters in the story. Then select the character you think:

(a) *learned* the most during the story OR

(b) *taught* others an important lesson.

Write a response that states your opinion (a or b as your focus). Support your focus by analyzing and explaining how the character's traits, actions, and interactions with events and other characters during the story support your reasoning or opinion and focus.

You can use a graphic organizer to help you plan your response.

Be sure to

1. Have an introduction that sets the context. Include the title and author and a two- or three-sentence summary of the story (plot).
2. State a focus that includes your opinion about one of the characters (learning a lesson or teaching a lesson) and why you think this is so.
3. Have body paragraphs that have topic sentences and details from the text to support each reason that you identify.
4. Analyze your evidence from the text. Use descriptive words to elaborate on WHY your evidence supports your reasoning.
5. Use transitional words or phrases to connect your ideas.
6. Write a conclusion that connects to or summarizes your focus or opinion.
7. Use correct punctuation and spelling.

Source: Adapted from NYC Schools Performance Assessment Pilot—Grade 4 Opinion Writing (2010).

Available for download at **resources.corwin.com/HessToolkit**

Copyright © 2018 by Corwin. All rights reserved. Reprinted from *A Local Assessment Toolkit to Promote Deeper Learning: Transforming Research into Practice* by Karin Hess. Thousand Oaks, CA: Corwin, www.corwin.com. Reproduction authorized only for the local school site or nonprofit organization that has purchased this book.

My planning notes for _____

(text)

LIST KEY CHARACTERS IN THE STORY	DESCRIBE TRAITS, ACTIONS, MOTIVATION AT THE BEGINNING	DESCRIBE TRAITS, ACTIONS, MOTIVATION AT THE END	DID THIS CHARACTER **LEARN** OR **TEACH** A LESSON? LIST AND ANALYZE TEXT EVIDENCE.

Source: Adapted from NYC Schools Performance Assessment Pilot—Grade 4 Opinion Writing (2010).

Available for download at **resources.corwin.com/HessToolkit**

Copyright © 2018 by Corwin. All rights reserved. Reprinted from *A Local Assessment Toolkit to Promote Deeper Learning: Transforming Research into Practice* by Karin Hess. Thousand Oaks, CA: Corwin, www.corwin.com. Reproduction authorized only for the local school site or nonprofit organization that has purchased this book.

Task Shell Example 6—Analyzing Literary Texts —Character Study

Name _____   **Date** _____

Every story character has a personality and character traits. We learn about characters by what they say, think, and do, and by how other characters interact with them. Sometimes authors use events or problems in the story to show how characters can change.

Read _____. Then write a response that describes one character's traits at the beginning of the story. Also tell why or how this character changes attitude and actions by the end of the story. Use specific details from the story to support your opinion and analysis.

Use the notes from your graphic organizer to help you plan and write your response.

Be sure to

1. Have an introduction that sets the context. Include the title, the author, and two or three sentences describing key events in the story.
2. Have a focus that describes one character's traits at the beginning of the story.
3. Have body paragraphs with topic sentences and details to support each example you use to explain why you think this character changed during the story.
4. Use details from the text and descriptive words to elaborate on and explain your thinking.
5. Use simple and compound sentences.
6. Use transitional words to connect your ideas.
7. End with a conclusion that connects to your focus or tells a lesson learned by the character.
8. Use correct punctuation and spelling.

Source: Adapted from NYC Schools Performance Assessment Pilot—Grade 4 Opinion Writing (2010).

Available for download at **resources.corwin.com/HessToolkit**

Copyright © 2018 by Corwin. All rights reserved. Reprinted from *A Local Assessment Toolkit to Promote Deeper Learning: Transforming Research into Practice* by Karin Hess. Thousand Oaks, CA: Corwin, www.corwin.com. Reproduction authorized only for the local school site or nonprofit organization that has purchased this book.

Task Shell Example 7—Analyzing Literary Texts —Character Study: Comparing Characters

Name _____   Date _____

Every story character has a personality. We learn about a character's traits by what they say, think, and do, and by how other characters interact with them. Read or view these two short stories:

_____

_____

Then write an analysis that compares the main characters' traits. <u>Determine your focus</u>: Are the main characters **mostly alike** or **mostly different**? Use specific details from the stories to support your opinion. Be sure to <u>elaborate on how those text-based examples support your reasoning</u> (and focus).

Use the notes from your graphic organizers for each story to help you plan and write your response.

Be sure to

1. Have an introduction that sets the context: the story titles and authors and a one- or two-sentence summary of each story.
2. State a focus that compares the main characters' personality traits.
3. Have body paragraphs that have topic sentences and details to support each new trait that you are comparing.
4. Analyze your evidence from each text. Use descriptive words to elaborate on <u>WHY</u> your evidence supports your reasoning.
5. Use transitional words or phrases to connect your ideas.
6. Write a conclusion that connects to or summarizes your focus or opinion.
7. Use correct punctuation and spelling.

Source: Adapted from NYC Schools Performance Assessment Pilot—Grade 4 Opinion Writing (2010).

(Continued)

Available for download at **resources.corwin.com/HessToolkit**

Copyright © 2018 by Corwin. All rights reserved. Reprinted from *A Local Assessment Toolkit to Promote Deeper Learning: Transforming Research into Practice* by Karin Hess. Thousand Oaks, CA: Corwin, www.corwin.com. Reproduction authorized only for the local school site or nonprofit organization that has purchased this book.

(Continued)

After reading each story, analyze how the author develops the main character. What does the author reveal to the reader about this character (actions, interactions, motivations, what the character says, does, thinks, or feels) that supports your interpretations? Complete a table for each story's main character before you begin to compose your text-based opinion: Are the main characters **mostly alike** or **mostly different**?

NAME SEVERAL CHARACTER TRAITS THAT WOULD DESCRIBE THIS CHARACTER: _____ (LIST ONE TRAIT IN EACH ROW. NOT ALL ROWS MUST BE FILLED IN.)	WHAT EXAMPLES FROM THE TEXT SUPPORT YOUR REASONS FOR USING EACH TRAIT TO DESCRIBE THIS CHARACTER?	ANALYZE OR EXPLAIN YOUR INTERPRETATION. HOW DO THESE EXAMPLES SHOW THE TRAIT?

Source: NYC Schools Performance Assessment Pilot—Grade 4 Opinion Writing (2010).

Available for download at **resources.corwin.com/HessToolkit**

Copyright © 2018 by Corwin. All rights reserved. Reprinted from *A Local Assessment Toolkit to Promote Deeper Learning: Transforming Research into Practice* by Karin Hess. Thousand Oaks, CA: Corwin, www.corwin.com. Reproduction authorized only for the local school site or nonprofit organization that has purchased this book.

Task Shell Example 8—Measurement

Kindergarten: Measurement and Data (Winter Benchmark)

Cardboard Box

Look at this picture or object:

What can you measure about this object?

WHAT CAN YOU MEASURE?	HOW COULD YOU MEASURE IT?	USING WHAT TOOLS? UNITS?

Kindergarten teachers interview students and record or scribe their responses.

Grades 1–5 students are given different objects or photos and students record their own responses. After the initial pilot, teachers can begin to create checklists of expected responses for each object.

Source: Adapted from VT Schools Math Performance Assessment Pilot—Grade K (2015).

Copyright © 2018 by Corwin. All rights reserved. Reprinted from *A Local Assessment Toolkit to Promote Deeper Learning: Transforming Research into Practice* by Karin Hess. Thousand Oaks, CA: Corwin, www.corwin.com. Reproduction authorized only for the local school site or nonprofit organization that has purchased this book.

Task Shell Example 9—Place Value

Grade 2: Place Value—243?

(Fall Benchmark)

Think about the number 243.

Put T after all the true statements about 243.

Put F after all the false statements about 243.

Explain and show all of your mathematical thinking.

READ THESE.	T OR F?	EXPLAIN AND SHOW ALL OF YOUR THINKING.
2 tens and 43 ones		
243 ones		
2 hundreds and 403 ones		
24 tens and 3 ones		
2 hundreds and 43 ones		
1 hundred and 143 ones		

Write another true statement about the number 243.

At each grade level, the magnitude of numbers increases. Examples on the left side include concrete to more abstract representations of how to express quantities.

Source: Adapted from VT Schools Math Performance Assessment Pilot—Grade 2 (2015).

Copyright © 2018 by Corwin. All rights reserved. Reprinted from *A Local Assessment Toolkit to Promote Deeper Learning: Transforming Research into Practice* by Karin Hess. Thousand Oaks, CA: Corwin, www.corwin.com. Reproduction authorized only for the local school site or nonprofit organization that has purchased this book.

Task Shell Example 10—Multiplication Strategies

Grade 4: 17 x 4 (Fall)

Part I—Create Visual Representations

Using this multiplication expression given, create a representation of the problem that matches each of the labels in each of the four boxes below.

$$17 \times 4$$

Equal Groups:

Repeated Addition:

Array:

Area Model:

Part II—Create a Narrative Representation

Write a story problem that could be represented by this expression: 17×4.

At each grade level, the magnitude of numbers or the operation changes. Parallel assessments were developed for division, addition, and subtraction, reinforcing multiple use of strategies.

Source: Adapted from VT Schools Math Performance Assessment Pilot—Grade 4 (2015).

Copyright © 2018 by Corwin. All rights reserved. Reprinted from *A Local Assessment Toolkit to Promote Deeper Learning: Transforming Research into Practice* by Karin Hess. Thousand Oaks, CA: Corwin, www.corwin.com. Reproduction authorized only for the local school site or nonprofit organization that has purchased this book.

Task Shell Example 11—Giants of Science

Science Assessment Activity: Giants of Science

"You cannot hope to build a better world without improving the individuals. To that end, each of us must work for our own improvement and, at the same time, share a general responsibility for all humanity, our particular duty being to aid those to whom we can be most useful." Marie Curie (1867–1934)

"Two things inspire me to awe—the starry heavens above and the moral universe within." Albert Einstein (1879–1955)

Introduction: Marie Curie and Albert Einstein are among thousands of notable scientists who, through the ages, have advanced humankind through their work. There are chemists, biologists, physicists, environmentalists, astronomers, earth scientists, and many others who have played important roles in helping us understand our world and advance technology and medicine.

In this activity, you will

- choose and research a "giant of science" in a field of science that you are studying;
- present your findings in written form; and
- make an oral presentation about what you learned.

Science Assessed

- Research skills
- Historical development of science
- Distinguish among theories
- Communicate science concepts and information
- Make connections to social and political issues

Part I—The Research

After you have selected a scientist to study, research the following aspects about your scientist:

1. The major contribution or discovery of the scientist—Why is this person considered a "Giant of Science"?

    - Make a drawing(s) or model to represent one of the major ideas of the scientist.
    - What were political and social conditions like when this scientist made his or her major contributions? Did the political or social conditions influence his or her thinking or prevent the scientific ideas from developing? If yes, in what ways?
    - Does that science discovery still hold true today? Why or why not?

2. Include supporting biographical information.

    - Personal history
    - Educational background
    - Other relevant information of interest

3. *OPTIONAL*: Select a quote made by your scientist and then demonstrate how the scientist's actions are consistent or inconsistent with the chosen quote.

Part II—Present Your Findings in a Written Presentation

Select one of the following to present the information about your scientist. Include the information from your research in Part 1, and cite all references, regardless of the written form you select.

- Formal research paper
- Magazine article
- Newspaper article
- Brochure
- Poster
- PowerPoint presentation (must include a script)

Part III—Present Your Findings in an Oral Presentation[9]

Prepare and deliver a two- to three-minute oral report about your scientist. Your presentation should include the following:

- the most important and most interesting aspects of your scientist's life and contributions; and
- a prop—You must select or make a prop to use in your oral presentation that best characterizes your scientist and his or her work. The prop can be an object, model, or poster, but must be an essential part of the oral presentation.

Source: Adapted from assessment developed as part of the Wyoming Body of Evidence Consortium & Wyoming Department of Education Performance Assessment Project—Grade HS (2002–2004). Source of image of Albert Einstein: Pixabay.com/janeb13 Image of Marie Curie (photographer unknown) licensed under CC BY 4.0: https://creativecommons.org/licenses/by/4.0/deed.en

9. The observation rubric designed to record evidence for this assessment is included in this module, in the section discussing rubric formats.

Available for download at **resources.corwin.com/HessToolkit**

Copyright © 2018 by Corwin. All rights reserved. Reprinted from *A Local Assessment Toolkit to Promote Deeper Learning: Transforming Research into Practice* by Karin Hess. Thousand Oaks, CA: Corwin, www.corwin.com. Reproduction authorized only for the local school site or nonprofit organization that has purchased this book.

Task Shell Example 12—Scientific Inquiry

Science Assessment Activity: Scientific Inquiry—Your Turn and Your World

In this activity, you will

- propose, design, and carry out an experiment;
- present your findings in a laboratory report; and
- make a presentation to your peers about what you learned.

Part I—The Experiment and Laboratory Report of Your Experiment

In this part of the assessment activity, you will propose, design, and carry out an experiment and communicate the experiment and results in a laboratory report. To propose your experiment, you must have it approved by your teacher. Use the form, Experimental Approval Form, before you proceed.

Important Note: Follow appropriate safety precautions based upon your experiment.

Your experiment and laboratory report should include the following:

> **Science Assessed**
> - Ability to design and carry out an experiment
> - Ability to draw conclusions from evidence
> - Ability to represent and use data to make inferences and draw conclusions
> - Ability to communicate findings in a laboratory report and defend findings in a presentation to your peers

(A) Purpose

  (a) A title

  (b) A clearly stated problem

  (c) (Optional) Research of the problem

  (d) A hypothesis stated in terms of cause and effect and based on observations and research information (if . . . then)

(B) Experimental design and procedures

  (a) A safe experimental design that addresses the cause and effect relationship in your hypothesis, includes appropriate controls, and considers the sample size necessary to study your problem

  (b) A safe implementation of the experiment as designed (or changes made based upon data collected)

  (c) Observations or measurements sufficient to address the question being asked and that are reproducible

(C) Data

  (a) Data collected, organized, analyzed, and displayed with appropriate statistics, graphs, and tables

  (b) Measurements taken that are repeatable, including a discussion of procedures and an analysis of experimental error

(D) Conclusions

    (a) Conclusions drawn based upon the data and observations generated and that address all aspects of the hypothesis and original problem

    (b) Explanations provided for any experimental errors with suggestions for improved experimental design

    (c) Communication of your experiment and results

(E) Optional Analysis:

An analysis of the central tendencies of the data that includes any or all of the following: mean, median, standard deviation, range and interquartile ranges, and depending upon the nature of the experiment and data derived, a scatterplot with a line of best fit and the equation for that line, and the correlation coefficient. The analysis should include the meaning and implication of these findings.

Part II—Presenting Your Findings

Peer review of scientific findings has historically been an integral part of scientific research and the scientific community. Scientists present their findings to their peers through scientific journals, seminars, and conferences to name a few ways. Peers evaluate the experimental results in terms of the experimental design and consistency with other research methods and findings.

In this part of the activity, you will present your findings to your peers:

- Develop and complete a 5- to 8-minute presentation of your experiment and findings.
- Use visual aids, such as PowerPoint, overheads, or posters as part of the presentation. Visual aids should enhance understanding and meaning of the information being shared.
- Be prepared to field questions for an additional 3 to 5 minutes after your presentation.
- Consider other technologies to use in your presentations, such as video microscopes, digital cameras, spreadsheets, or databases.

Source: Adapted from assessment developed as part of the Wyoming Body of Evidence Consortium & Wyoming Department of Education Performance Assessment Project—Grade HS (2002–2004).

Available for download at **resources.corwin.com/HessToolkit**

Copyright © 2018 by Corwin. All rights reserved. Reprinted from *A Local Assessment Toolkit to Promote Deeper Learning: Transforming Research into Practice* by Karin Hess. Thousand Oaks, CA: Corwin, www.corwin.com. Reproduction authorized only for the local school site or nonprofit organization that has purchased this book.

Scientific Inquiry: Experimental Approval Form

Please fill out the following form and submit to your teacher for approval. Do not begin your experiment until you have received written permission from your teacher.

Name _____   Class _____

Grade _____   Date _____

Proposal:

Materials Needed:

Summary of Proposed Experimental Procedures

Title:

Purpose (Include hypothesis):

Procedures:

List of safety considerations:

Teacher's Signature _____   **Date** _____

Source: Adapted from assessment developed as part of the Wyoming Body of Evidence Consortium and Wyoming Department of Education Performance Assessment Project—Grade HS (2002–2004).

Available for download at **resources.corwin.com/HessToolkit**

Copyright © 2018 by Corwin. All rights reserved. Reprinted from *A Local Assessment Toolkit to Promote Deeper Learning: Transforming Research into Practice* by Karin Hess. Thousand Oaks, CA: Corwin, www.corwin.com. Reproduction authorized only for the local school site or nonprofit organization that has purchased this book.

Task Shell Example 13—The Novel

Language Arts Assessment Activity

Perspectives on a Novel

Title of Novel:

Author:

Did you know . . . that Stephen King was a high school English teacher in Hampden, Maine, before he sold his first book?

What interesting fact can you find out about your book's author?

"A classic is not a *classic* because it conforms to certain structural rules, but because of a certain eternal and irrepressible freshness."

–Ezra Pound

Introduction

In this assessment activity, you will select a novel from choices approved by your teacher.

These are your tasks:

- keep a chapter-by-chapter log of questions and brief notes;
- write a literary analysis paper, personal essay, or book review using your chapter questions and notes as a resource; and
- deliver a brief oral presentation about your book.

You will have various choices to make about what form your written work and your presentation will take. The details of the tasks and choices you have are provided below.

Language Arts Skills Assessed by This Activity:

- Trace the development of theme(s) or characters throughout the book
- Use effective oral communication skills in critiquing or reviewing the book
- Connect the experiences of the characters with current issues in our lives
- Analyze how the author uses literary elements or literary devices to develop a theme or plot

Part I: Keeping a Reading Log

(NOTE: Students will be assessed for the content of the log, but not for conventions, such as spelling, grammar, or punctuation.)

In your reading log, write:

1. One key question for each chapter that touches on a major theme you have identified running throughout the book, or about the development of characters, plot, or use of literary devices. (You will probably have to read several chapters before you are able to see themes beginning to emerge.)

    Brief notes—only two or three sentences, direct quotes, or examples—of essential reminders to you about developments you notice in the chapter that shape the direction of the story, characters, or theme. You will use these notes in development of Parts II and III.

Available for download at **resources.corwin.com/HessToolkit**

(Continued)

(Continued)

Part II—Writing About the Book (select one)

Your teacher may require that your paper be done on a word processor. (Effective essays examining pieces of literature are typically between 500 and 750 words.) Follow the writing process and address the guidelines described by the rubric criteria.

Your choices:

- **Write a formal literary analysis** related to character, setting, plot structure, point of view, theme, or literary devices or techniques used. The paper should present appropriate support for the thesis of the text, properly cited, drawing a conclusion and commenting on the significance of the book.

- **Write a personal essay** about how a character or theme in the book is connected to your own life or to your thoughts and values. Make direct references to specific details in the book that illustrate the significance of the character or the theme. Remember that your chapter notes will be your best resource for developing your ideas.

- **Write a book review** of the assigned or selected text. Follow the format of professional book reviewers, found in various sources, such as the *New York Times Book Review,* or other media sources. You may want to investigate several book review examples before you begin to write.

Part III—Your Oral Presentation

Prepare and deliver a five- to eight-minute oral presentation that accomplishes the following:

- analyzes the plot, characters, and theme; and
- comments on the novel's personal and cultural value.

Your oral presentation may be a formal commentary on the story, its characters, and themes; or it may be a collection of scenes or episodes that you present dramatically (possibly with the assistance of others); or it might be designed as a question–answer session in a character or author role that you adopt.

The oral presentation may be accompanied by audiovisual aides appropriate to your plan (such as a PowerPoint, props, and/or costume for a dramatization).

Did you know . . . that J. K. Rowling, the author of the Harry Potter books, was a divorced mother living on welfare in Edinburgh, Scotland?

She wrote the first book at a table in a cafe during her baby's nap times.

Image Source: iStock.com/carneadele

Source: This assessment was developed as part of the Wyoming Body of Evidence Consortium & Wyoming Department of Education Performance Assessment Project—Grade HS (2002–2004).

Available for download at **resources.corwin.com/HessToolkit**

Copyright © 2018 by Corwin. All rights reserved. Reprinted from *A Local Assessment Toolkit to Promote Deeper Learning: Transforming Research into Practice* by Karin Hess. Thousand Oaks, CA: Corwin, www.corwin.com. Reproduction authorized only for the local school site or nonprofit organization that has purchased this book.

Task Shell Example 14—Turning Points in History

Social Studies Assessment Activity

April 9–15, 1865: The Week That Changed America

WAR CASUALTIES	
Gulf War:	383
Vietnam:	55,000
Korean:	50,000
W.W. I:	100,000
W.W. II:	250,000
Civil War:	650,000

Introduction: One Turning Point in History

No war was more costly in lives lost, and no war had such a profound impact on the character of the United States as the Civil War of 1861–1865. In the spring of the final year of the war, public opinion and the angry voices of senators and congressmen in Abraham Lincoln's own party, the Republicans, were calling for revenge on the South and for the hanging of Southern political and military leaders as traitors. In the South, many generals and politicians wanted to continue the struggle, even if it meant years of guerrilla war, a prospect that would have prevented peaceful reunification of the nation.

On April 9, Confederate General Robert E. Lee and Union General Ulysses S. Grant met at the McLean home in Appomattox, Virginia, to sign the surrender of the Army of Northern Virginia. Lee was one of several generals in the field of battle across the South, and he did not have the authority to end the war. He was, however, the most respected man in the South.

Only a week later, Lincoln would be assassinated. Calls for a military takeover of the U.S. government and a bloodbath of revenge on the South were louder than ever. Although events of that week did result in harsher treatment of the South by the conquering North, the South did surrender; both sides accepted the reunification of the country and moved on.

What was the turning point in that fateful week in April 1865 that shaped the future of America and prevented the worst and likeliest outcomes? Historians still ponder the complex factors, but the power of leadership of the two generals and the terms they decided upon in a famous exchange of letters during the days just before the meeting at Appomattox may have decided the fate of the nation.

Other Turning Points in History:

"The week That Changed America" is just one of the many turning points in history. You are about to explore such a turning point.

In this assessment activity, you will

- write an essay on a historical period and a turning point in that period; and
- make an oral presentation exploring the role of leaders in historical turning points.

(Continued)

Available for download at **resources.corwin.com/HessToolkit**

(Continued)

> **Social Studies Assessed**
>
> - The causal influence of historical factors on future societal developments
> - The role of leadership in the dynamics of change
> - The significance of effective historical interpretation in shaping the direction of society
> - Integrating research into analytical writing and oral presentations

You and one or two partners will be assigned to explore a turning point in history.

In doing so, you are to do the following:

Part I—Write Your Essay

Research the historical moment in time and individually write an essay (approximately 500 words) including the following elements:

- The historical context
- Key factors
- The apparent turning point
- Key players involved
- Outcomes, both long and short term
- Bibliography of sources

Part II—Prepare a Group Oral Presentation on the Turning Point

Although your formal presentation should be only 5 to 10 minutes, the length of the class discussion could vary considerably. It is important to try to anticipate the questions likely to be asked by your classmates or your teacher.

- The oral presentation should be in outline form accompanied by supporting audiovisual materials.
- Include a brief biography of the person or persons you believe to be at the center of the forces of change. Only focus on biographical details that provide insight into their role in the moment in history under discussion.
- In addition to references to elements in your essay, also plan a discussion session for the class in which you encourage classmates to explore this question:

"What do you believe is one or more major lessons for leaders seeking to bring about change from this turning point in history?"

Source: Adapted from assessment developed as part of the Wyoming Body of Evidence Consortium & Wyoming Department of Education Performance Assessment Project—Grade HS (2002–2004). Image of Robert E. Lee (photographer unknown) from the Heritage Auction Archives. Image of Ulysses S. Grant by Edgar Guy Fawx from the Library of Congress.

Available for download at **resources.corwin.com/HessToolkit**

Copyright © 2018 by Corwin. All rights reserved. Reprinted from *A Local Assessment Toolkit to Promote Deeper Learning: Transforming Research into Practice* by Karin Hess. Thousand Oaks, CA: Corwin, www.corwin.com. Reproduction authorized only for the local school site or nonprofit organization that has purchased this book.

MODULE 4: WHERE DO I START, WHAT DO I TEACH NEXT, WHICH SUPPORTS WORK BEST?

Using Learning Progressions as a Schema for Planning Instruction and Measuring Progress

Consider where the lesson resides in the larger learning trajectory. . . . The right learning target for today's lesson builds upon the learning targets from previous lessons in the unit and connects to learning targets in future lessons to advance student understanding of important skills and concepts.

Moss and Brookhart, 2012, p. 2

4.1 What Are Learning Progressions (or Learning Trajectories) and How Can They Be Used to Scaffold Instruction and Guide the Design and Use of Assessments of Deeper Learning?

Think about how you might respond to the following questions: Are all students (in our school) expected to think deeply when engaging with grade-level content; or are some students simply expected to acquire basic skills and concepts? To what degree do grade-level standards (the destinations of learning) provide a coherent road map to plan meaningful instruction and assessment within each school year for all students? Do the learning destinations for one school year link logically with those of adjacent grade levels? Finally, what consistently guides instructional decisions when students fall behind or when students are ready to move on at a different pace? In other words, what guides your thinking about what "might come next" in the learning process?

This module is designed to offer ideas and examples about how a measure of progress within and across grades can be reframed with a new conceptual view of how to get all students from here (whatever the entry point) to there . . . and beyond. Some of the content in this module is based on my earlier writings and work with developing learning progressions frameworks (LPFs) in mathematics and language arts used to guide large-scale assessment design and developing instructional supports for teachers working with students with learning disabilities (Jabot & Hess, 2010; National Center and State Collaborative [NCSC], 2015). The examples and suggested classroom uses in Module 4 are drawn from various projects using progressions to develop pre-, mid-, and postassessments (with New York City [N.Y.C.] and Vermont schools), developing units of study for argument writing (with Connecticut schools), and developing K–12 competencies to guide performance-based assessments to meet competency-based graduation requirements (in New Hampshire). I'll use these examples to illustrate how learning progressions (LPs) might be employed to support student learning and enhance local instructional and assessment practices. It is not the intent of the module to suggest that you start from scratch to develop your very own learning progressions but to use existing resources to deepen your understanding of their usefulness with formative, interim, and summative assessments and lesson planning.

What a Learning Progression Is and What It Is Not—Building a Working Definition

In the United States, we have paid much more attention to developing content standards and specifying grade-level expectations than to using assessment data to discover how learning actually progresses *within a grade level* or researching how learning "connects and builds" from one grade to the next. Our state assessment results typically tell us who is and who is not proficient; each school is left to figure out how to improve those results. There are currently many state- and district-level initiatives seeking to provide guidance to teachers and schools about how to use formative classroom assessment more effectively to plan instruction and measure progress, how to "break down" content standards and benchmarks within grade levels in order to meet the diverse needs of learners, especially the lowest performing students in each classroom, and how to make content standards more accessible in order to provide meaningful academic instruction for students participating in alternate assessments. I believe that many instructional and assessment challenges can be informed by the use of thoughtfully constructed learning progressions. But beware—everything "advertised" as a learning progression may not actually be one!

The phrase "learning progressions" has been referenced throughout the education literature, especially since the Common Core State Standards were published in 2010. Similar phrases, such as curricular progressions, learning trajectories, developmental continuums, pacing guides, and scope and sequences have been used interchangeably when talking about learning progressions; however, all of these terms are not rooted in the same core meaning or purpose. Take a minute to identify your current thinking about learning progressions, using the anticipation guide below.

> *Using the Anticipation Guide:*[1] Background information for better understanding the statements in the anticipation guide is addressed throughout Module 4. You can use this anticipation guide as a self-assessment to reflect on your own learning as you build a deeper understanding of learning progressions and their uses. To complete the guide, first read each statement. Decide whether you agree (A) or disagree (D) with each statement based on your current background knowledge and experience. Indicate your opinion by using an *A* or *D* in the corresponding box to the left of each statement. As you work though the Module 4 activities, discussions, and readings, make notes (to the right) as to whether your opinion or understandings have changed or deepened and what (evidence) now supports your thinking.

What Exactly Are Learning Progressions?

First of all, there really isn't one simple definition for *learning progression*, although I do provide mine in Appendix I. What educational researchers and cognitive scientists agree on is that LPs are important enough for us to pay attention to when we think about guiding instruction to meet the needs of all learners. A unique aspect of learning progressions is being able to determine how

---

1. A full-page version of the anticipation guide is included in Part 2 with the Module 4 support materials. A blank template for an anticipation guide is included in Part 2 of Module 3 as a sample formative assessment.

Anticipation Guide: What Do I Know or Believe About Learning Progressions?

AGREE (A)? DISAGREE (D)?	READ EACH STATEMENT BELOW. DECIDE IF YOU AGREE OR DISAGREE AND INDICATE IN COLUMN TO THE LEFT.	EXPLAIN WHY YOU AGREE OR DISAGREE. HAVE YOU CHANGED YOUR MIND? WHY/WHY NOT?
	1. Learning progressions are the <u>same as a scope and sequence or pacing guide</u> that lists the order of what to teach next.	
	2. "<u>Big Ideas</u>" help to frame descriptors (progress indicators) in a learning progression.	
	3. An example of a "Big Idea" would be learning how to read.	
	4. To validate a learning progression, one would consult cognitive research, as well as teacher observations and analysis of student work collected over time *after* targeted instruction.	
	5. Students can use learning progressions as a <u>self-assessment</u> to monitor their own progress.	
	6. Learning progressions can be used to <u>diagnose</u> individual students' strengths and weaknesses.	
	7. Progress maps, developmental continuums, and learning continuums are qualitatively <u>different from learning progressions.</u>	
	8. <u>Other countries</u> have been using research-based learning progressions for many years to guide classroom assessment and instruction.	
	9. Learning progressions can guide development of <u>formative assessments</u> and formative uses of assessment data.	
	10. Learning progressions describe increasingly <u>more difficult content and skills.</u>	

Copyright © 2018 by Corwin. All rights reserved. Reprinted from *A Local Assessment Toolkit to Promote Deeper Learning: Transforming Research into Practice* by Karin Hess. Thousand Oaks, CA: Corwin, www.corwin.com. Reproduction authorized only for the local school site or nonprofit organization that has purchased this book.

close a student is getting to achieving the intended learning goal, something that standards are not able to do. As we examine various ways that LPs have been defined, you'll begin to clarify your own understanding and possible applications of LPs in your work.

First let me start with a personal story that I first shared at a conference in 2008 to illustrate a nonschool learning progression—a horse story (Hess, 2008b).

A Horse Story

When I purchased a 6-year-old, high-strung, Arabian mare, I had no idea what her past "education" and life experiences had been. As soon as I began to work with her, I knew that she was not the perfect horse I had imagined her to be. Leichda (a name that roughly translated means "lighten up" in ancient Bohemian) immediately let me know by her body language that she was head-shy. For those who are not familiar with the term, it means that she would jerk her head away from anything that came near her face, probably because she had been hit in the face as a young horse as punishment for misbehaving. This meant, in practical terms, that I could not easily touch her face or neck, brush or trim her mane, or put on a halter or a bridle. Since controlling a horse's head is the key to controlling a horse, I had my work cut out for me. I am a horse lover, not a horse trainer. So I set out to research available methods to address this problem.

I found an excellent video by a well-known horse trainer who explained that this problem would require something like moving from the first floor to the top floor of a building. Leaping from the ground to the top floor without a ladder or stairway was out of the question—this would be accomplished using many small steps in between, all of which might not look like the final goal of easily putting on a bridle. A variety of items were suggested as a starting point for this progression of learning in order to desensitize her face and head (e.g., different-textured materials and objects, large pieces of plastic and crinkly paper, leather items). I was to consider these as possible ladder steps (fewer for a steeper rise) or stairs (more steps for a gentler rise) and place them in order as to which progression might move Leichda forward toward the learning goal. In other words, I had to consider how each interim learning activity would be used to map the overall learning pathway and then provide ample time and opportunity to get there.

Ultimately, it took many months to consistently touch increasingly "scary" items to her face and head without a fearful or aggressive reaction. Each step along the way required that I use formative assessment data to determine what should come next—a new approach? different material? shorter duration? While I was following a typical learning progression for all head-shy horses, I could not assume that all horses learn exactly at the same rate or in identical ways. It was also important that I not lose sight of the ultimate learning goal or I might end up with a horse that could never be ridden (no bridle), but would happily wear all kinds of hats on her head! As an educator, it was hard not to make comparisons to what I'd done for many years in my classroom—planning, teaching, and then adjusting the teaching when needed.

How does my horse story connect with definitions that researchers and content specialists have used to define and operationalize the use of LPs for instruction and assessment purposes over the years? Wilson and Bertenthal (2005) define LPs in terms of "descriptions of the successively more sophisticated ways of thinking about an idea that follow one another as students learn," while Australian researchers Masters and Forster describe progress maps (their synonym for LPs) as "a picture of the path students typically follow as they learn . . . a description of skills, understandings, and knowledge in the sequence in which they typically develop" (1996).

- *These definitions also describe in general terms what I did with my horse's training. I began with an expert horse trainer's description of the "typical learning pathway" for overcoming being head-shy and was then able to develop, implement, and sometimes modify my training plan to get to each learning target along the progression.*

Duschl, Schweingruber, and Shouse (2007) describe LPs in science as "anchored on one end by what is known about the concepts and reasoning of students entering school . . . [for which] there now is a very extensive research base" (pp. 219–220). At the other end of the learning continuum are "societal expectations (values)" about what society wants students to know and be able to do in the given content area. Learning progressions propose the *intermediate* understandings between these anchor points that are "reasonably coherent networks of ideas and practices . . . that contribute to building a more mature understanding." Further, they explain that often, the "important precursor ideas may not look like the later ideas, yet crucially contribute to their construction."

- *This, too, was true in my horse story—the materials and strategies that I selected included some things that did not look like or function exactly like halters and bridles, but served as important precursors to what would be much more restrictive later on. It was the purposeful selection and use of these materials that gave me formative feedback to guide my next steps in instruction. This is similar to giving a preassessment to determine whether students already have the prerequisite skills to build upon to meet the learning targets along the progression.*

Another way to think about learning progressions is taken from the work of The National Alternate Assessment Center (NAAC; Flowers, Browder, Wakeman, & Karvonen, 2007) in which progress is described as students moving from generalizing their responses across people or settings to generalizing their understanding of concepts. The latter is a more sophisticated way of demonstrating understanding than simply generalizing across people or settings, in that "students eventually demonstrate responses across more than one task format, such as understanding the concept of the number 10 as applied in various contexts—time telling, bus numbers, math problem solving, etc."—in other words, near transfer.

- *With my horse, I had to consider the broader concept of how to desensitize her head and face with a variety of objects and materials, before she would readily accept and generalize that nothing coming toward her face or put on her head would hurt her. While this was not the initial and specific learning goal for her, it was clear to me that focusing on the essential underlying concept would take her much farther than the short-term objective.*

Clements and Sarama (2009), who have done extensive work researching how young children learn mathematics, identify three components of mathematics learning trajectories: (a) a mathematical goal; (b) a developmental path along which children develop to reach to that goal; and (c) a set of instructional activities or tasks, matched to each of the levels of thinking in that path that help children develop higher levels of thinking.

In a 2009 paper, Shin, Stevens, Short, and Krajcik also stress the importance of having coherence of instructional materials in support of using science learning progressions to guide conceptual development of critical science ideas:

> Coherence is a systematic approach to aligning and sequencing specific ideas and the depth to which those ideas are examined in order to help the development and integrated understanding in learners (AAAS, 2001; Schmidt, Wang, & McKnight, 2005; Shwartz, Weizman, Fortus, Krajcik, & Reiser, 2008). Researchers . . . have found that coherent curriculum is the primary predictor of student achievement in math and science

(Schmidt, Wang, & McKnight, 2005). However, in trying to address a multitude of standards (national, state, and local), the current U.S. science curriculum was not built to coherently help learners make connections between ideas within and among disciplines nor help develop meaningful structures for integrating knowledge. The U.S. curriculum approach has been referred to as the mile-wide and inch-deep approach because of its coverage of numerous topics at a superficial level. As a result, students lack foundational knowledge that can be applied to future learning and for solving problems that confront them in their lives (pp. 1–2).

Speaking in more general terms and in an attempt to clarify some terminology that I use throughout the module, here are a few working definitions that help us to clarify the meaning of the opening Moss and Brookhart quote:

- Broad **learning goals** (based on "Big Ideas" or enduring understandings) create the unifying thread around which each progression is built. A learning goal might be framed by a statement or a broad question, such as this learning goal for science inquiry (Conducting Investigations): *To what extent is the student developing skills of observing, measuring, recording, organizing, and summarizing data to make sense of science phenomena?*

- Smaller-grained **learning targets** are the "indicators" used to measure progress along the learning continuum to meet the learning goal. Learning targets frame short instructional cycles (e.g., one or more lessons with a specific focus); formative assessments target that learning and let the teacher know the students are ready to move on. Units of study and daily lessons are planned with the idea that one learning target leads to the next.

- **Coherence** is achieved when the learning targets and the instructional materials clearly support and align with the learning along an anticipated pathway, helping students to make connections that lead to deeper understanding. A test of a well-designed LP is seeing coherence among the learning goal, learning targets (aligned with content standards, increasing rigor/DOK, *and empirical research*), and instructional support materials (including formative assessments addressing specific learning targets).

Learning targets for the sample science learning goal above (Conducting Investigations) might look like the ones in Figure 4.1. The learning targets in this PreK–5 Science Profile[2] span several grade levels, providing guidance to teachers about how learning might simultaneously develop along several interrelated progressions: Formulating Questions (A), Planning/Critiquing Investigations (B), and Conducting Investigations (C). Seeing explicit learning targets across grades allows teachers to meet the needs of some students who may be performing below grade level, while others are at or above grade level. Teachers monitor progress by placing an X on each student's profile when a student has demonstrated sufficient evidence for each learning target. Student work samples are dated and saved with the science profile and used for student-led conferences.

4.2 Four Interrelated Guiding Principles of Learning Progressions

Drawing from the various definitions and examples of learning progressions that have been developed over the years, several unifying ideas emerge that can shape our thinking about what makes a well-constructed learning progression or how one might go about validating and using learning progressions for different purposes. The grain size and scope of different content-based progressions can vary greatly. Smaller-grained progressions are used by testing companies (e.g., Renaissance Learning, Educational Testing Service) to design individual test items or formative

---

2. The full sample PreK–5 Science Profile is included in Appendix E.

Figure 4.1 Excerpt From "Student Profile: Science Inquiry Learning Grades PreK–5"

SCIENCE INQUIRY GRADE LEVELS	A. IS THE STUDENT DEVELOPING AN AWARENESS AND CURIOSITY ABOUT OBJECTS, ORGANISMS, AND EVENTS IN THE ENVIRONMENT? **FORMULATING QUESTIONS AND HYPOTHESIZING**	B. IS THE STUDENT DEVELOPING THE ABILITY TO PLAN AND ANALYZE SIMPLE INVESTIGATIONS TO TEST PREDICTIONS/ANSWER QUESTIONS? **PLANNING AND CRITIQUING INVESTIGATIONS**	C. TO WHAT EXTENT IS THE STUDENT DEVELOPING SKILLS OF OBSERVING, MEASURING, RECORDING, ORGANIZING, AND SUMMARIZING DATA? **CONDUCTING INVESTIGATIONS**
Grades PreK-K	1. Sustains curiosity and focus during teacher-guided explorations 2. Sustains curiosity and focus during open-ended and self-guided explorations 3. Answers questions about things observed, manipulated, or predicted 4. Uses picture cues, prior knowledge, and observations to make predictions 5. Formulates questions about things observed or manipulated when cued (e.g., What do you wonder?) or on own	1. Selects materials and objects for open-ended explorations 2. Works with others to generate simple testable questions (Will it sink?) 3. Works with others to plan how to answer simple testable questions: What tools or materials to use How to "collect" data Where and how to record data Safety rules	1. Uses multiple senses to collect data and make observations *with teacher guidance* 2. Uses simple tools (e.g., magnifier, scale) to gather data *with teacher guidance* 3. Uses nonstandard units, numbers, words, drawings to record observations 4. Identifies differences in observable characteristics of materials or events 5. Identifies similarities in observable characteristics of materials or events 6. Drawings show some details (size, color)
Grade 1	6. Asks questions about things that can be observed or manipulated (how far . . .) 7. Connects prior knowledge and evidence to observations and predictions 8. Identifies variable to change or test (e.g., what if . . . more or less water?)	4. Works with others to generate simple testable questions 5. Identifies potential data to collect and tools and materials needed 6. Works with others to develop major steps to follow to collect and record data	7. Follows steps of a plan *with guidance* 8. Uses tools and senses to make observations 9. Drawings show detail of "target" features (size, color, shape, numbers, proportions) 10. Records similarities and differences in teacher-provided tables, charts, or templates
Grade 2	9. Poses observational questions (e.g., compare differences in speed) 10. Uses prior knowledge or evidence to explain logical predictions 11. Identifies variable to change or test 12. Generates new inquiry questions	7. Works with others to write a plan to answer observational questions 8. Identifies data to collect and tools and materials needed 9. Explains safety rules and (steps) procedure for data collection	11. Follows a plan to conduct investigations with peers 12. Uses tools and senses to collect data 13. Drawings show detail and completeness (relative proportions, key features, labels) 14. Explains similarities and differences 15. Organizes, labels, and titles drawings, graphs, and charts

Source: Hess (2009).

tasks for large task banks. Larger-grained progressions are more useful for local unit or lesson planning and performance task design. Whether the progressions are derived from research describing developmental stages of learning (e.g., early literacy or mathematics) or research initiatives (e.g., to uncover common misconceptions in science or integrating mathematical practices with mathematics content), all well-developed progressions embody four common interrelated guiding principles. A brief explanation of each guiding principle follows.

Four Interrelated Guiding Principles of Learning Progressions

Drawing from the various definitions and examples of learning progressions and learning trajectories, four unifying ideas can shape our thinking about what makes a well-constructed learning progression.

Learning progressions are different from standards and curriculum because they

- *are developed (and validated) using available* (empirical) *research*;
- *are organized around the "Big Ideas"* of each content domain that develop gradually over time and have clear binding threads that articulate development of essential/core concepts and processes as the learning becomes more sophisticated and complex;
- *articulate movement toward increased understanding* (deeper or broader or generalizable "far" transfer); and
- *go hand-in-hand with well-designed and well-aligned assessments, especially formative uses of assessment.*

Guiding Principle I—Validated by Research

Learning Progressions are developed (and validated) using available empirical research: Evidence of use of available research is essential in articulating learning progressions. Otherwise, it is simply a "best guess" about curriculum or standards, rather than how learning is expected to develop. Three common sources of research data can inform both the local development of LPs and refinements to existing learning progressions.

- *Cognitive science research* provides descriptions of how learning generally develops from novice to expert performance (e.g., Brown, Roediger, & McDaniel, 2014; National Research Council [NRC], 2001; Pellegrino, 2002; Willingham, 2009).

- *Content-specific empirical research* has uncovered indicators of how conceptual understanding typically develops for a content domain, such as Driver, Squires, Rushworth, and Wood-Robinson's (2002) synthesis of science learning and common misconceptions, or how learning develops when mathematical practices are interwoven with math concepts (Maloney, Confrey, & Nguyen, 2014).

- *Action research* at the classroom, school, or district levels offers possibilities for using formative assessment data to refine or "fill in gaps" in an existing "curricular" progression. Collaboratively analyzing data from ongoing classroom assessments provides a unique opportunity for teachers to develop a deeper understanding of how learning actually progresses. Teachers can "zoom in" for a closer look using formative assessment data with a much finer grain size and then "zoom out" again when using the larger-grained common interim and summative performance assessments that monitor progress over longer learning periods. This strategy can even be used by students as a formative assessment to examine their own progress over time. LP **TOOL #22** is specifically designed to analyze data and construct progressions through action research.

Guiding Principle II—Organized Around "Big Ideas"

Learning Progressions are organized around the "Big Ideas" of each content domain that develop gradually over time: These "binding threads" articulate the essential core concepts and processes that tie the learning targets to the progression. The "Big Ideas," meaning the "essence" of important concepts and essential processes, connect learning across grades or over instructional time. Measuring progress is only possible when these binding threads are clearly evident in the LP and describe increasingly more complex learning of core ideas and enduring understandings (Duschl, Schweingruber, & Shouse, 2007; Maloney & Confrey, 2013; Wiggins & McTighe, 2005, 2012; Wiliam & Leahy, 2015). For each content area, these essential threads interact to build greater understanding of the discipline. Identifying a small number of essential threads makes the LP manageable in terms of tracking ongoing progress in the classroom. For example, in reading, five core "unifying threads" might be (1) making meaning at the word level, (2) making meaning at the text level, (3) applying reading strategies, (4) developing breadth and depth of vocabulary, and (5) expanding independence through development of reading habits and dispositions. Each thread articulates increased understanding of the core idea. *Collectively, these threads weave the tapestry of what it means to become a proficient reader, while each thread develops both in isolation and in relation to the other threads*. And as with cloth, the whole of it will be stronger than any single strand of thread.

> View a video clip of teachers in Hawai'i (2010) discussing what they have learned from using progress maps (another name for learning progressions) at https://www.youtube.com/watch?v=8vltv2PaZVU&feature=youtu.be.

Table 4.1 shows an example of "a collection of reading concepts and skills" (on the left) and reading concepts and skills with a related "unifying thread," vocabulary development (on the right). The term *foundational* is used to mean foundational to the discipline or those basic emergent skills upon which all reading, mathematics, or science learning is built (Hess, 2008b).

Guiding Principle III—Describe Increasing Understanding

Learning Progressions articulate movement toward increased understanding: LPs are not linear or lockstep sequential routes to a learning goal; they articulate movement toward increased understanding in the way that a map provides both the network of interrelated routes with surrounding terrain and potential pit stops that might affect the journey. This movement toward increased understanding can be described in several possible ways:

- Greater depth of understanding

- Increased breadth of application or ability to generalize and transfer learning to new contexts

- Movement from "novice" or naive understanding of the content or concepts to more sophisticated "expert" thinking and reasoning

Through peer and self-assessment, student work samples provide an excellent means for "zooming in" to examine increased understanding, greater sophistication, and quality of work over time (such as in writing). Lucy Calkins and colleagues at the Teachers College Reading Writing Project (TCRWP) codevelop an understanding of progress and work quality with students as they look at writing samples that focus on different learning targets, such as developing theme or interpreting text.

> View a TCRWP video clip of students guided to discuss the progression they see in a range of student work samples (2013) at https://www.youtube.com/watch?v=8grZFus5OCo.

Module 4: Where Do I Start, What Do I Teach Next, Which Supports Work Best? 289

Table 4.1 Contrasting a Skills "List" With a Skills "Progression"

A "LIST" OF READING CONCEPTS AND SKILLS	ONE "THREAD" IN THE READING TAPESTRY: A SAMPLE LEARNING PROGRESSION FOR DEVELOPING BREADTH AND DEPTH OF VOCABULARY	

• Identify words that are nouns
• Identify words that are verbs
• Identify words that have same or different meanings
• Read high-frequency words with automaticity
• Determine meanings of words used in context
• Summarize key ideas using print or nonprint texts
• Locate facts and details in a print or nonprint text to answer basic comprehension questions
	Early/Foundational Skills for Developing Vocabulary
	
	• Identify vocabulary (pictures, symbols, objects, or words) that demonstrate knowledge of basic pragmatic functions (e.g., social words, asks questions, makes requests)
	• Generalize use of pictures, symbols, objects, and actions to identify their meaning
	• Use vocabulary to identify objects and events (e.g., apply vocabulary in a variety of settings)
		Developing and Expanding Depth and Breadth of Vocabulary
		
		• Expand vocabulary with words related to known words (e.g., words that sound the same, are spelled the same, are in the same category)
		• Use word structure or known parts of words to make sense of the whole word:
		  ○ Word parts (syllables, base words, word roots, affixes)
		  ○ Meanings of word parts
		  ○ Compound words, compound word families (e.g., everyone, everywhere, everything)
		• Determine word meanings in a single context (definitional meanings)
		• Determine connotative and figurative meanings of words and phrases used in different contexts (nonliteral and conceptual meanings)

*The above list of skills provides no obvious **conceptual** unifying thread, even though everything is related to reading in some way. The order is not useful for measuring progress or planning next steps for instruction.*	**A sample continuum of skills with a unifying thread—vocabulary development**	

Source: Hess (2008b).

Guiding Principle IV—Align With Formative Assessment

Learning Progressions go hand-in-hand with well-designed or aligned assessments, especially formative uses of assessment: Learning progressions of the appropriate grain size, used in conjunction with assessment data, can provide schemas for

- Planning and modifying instruction
- Developing assessments and interpreting assessment data—especially formative assessments
- Monitoring individual or group progress

When formative assessments are designed to uncover a range of thinking, teachers are better able to place students along a continuum of learning. "Zooming in" on a small number of progress indicators in the progression provides opportunities to examine the nuances of learning. The examples of student work (Figure 4.2) illustrate various stages of student understanding in mathematics that is moving from additive reasoning to multiplicative reasoning. Teachers can use student work analysis protocols (PLC **TOOL #12** or LP **TOOL #22**) to examine what they see in student work in order to determine how to differentiate next steps for instruction.

Problems like the ones in Figure 4.2 might be used formatively by a teacher to align with Progress Indicators (and highlighted parts of standards) as seen in the Mathematics Learning Progressions Framework/LPF (Hess, 2010b, p. 36) on the pages that follow.[3]

Figure 4.2 Formative Assessments Can Uncover Thinking to Show How Student Understanding Is Developing Along the Continuum of Learning or Learning Progression.

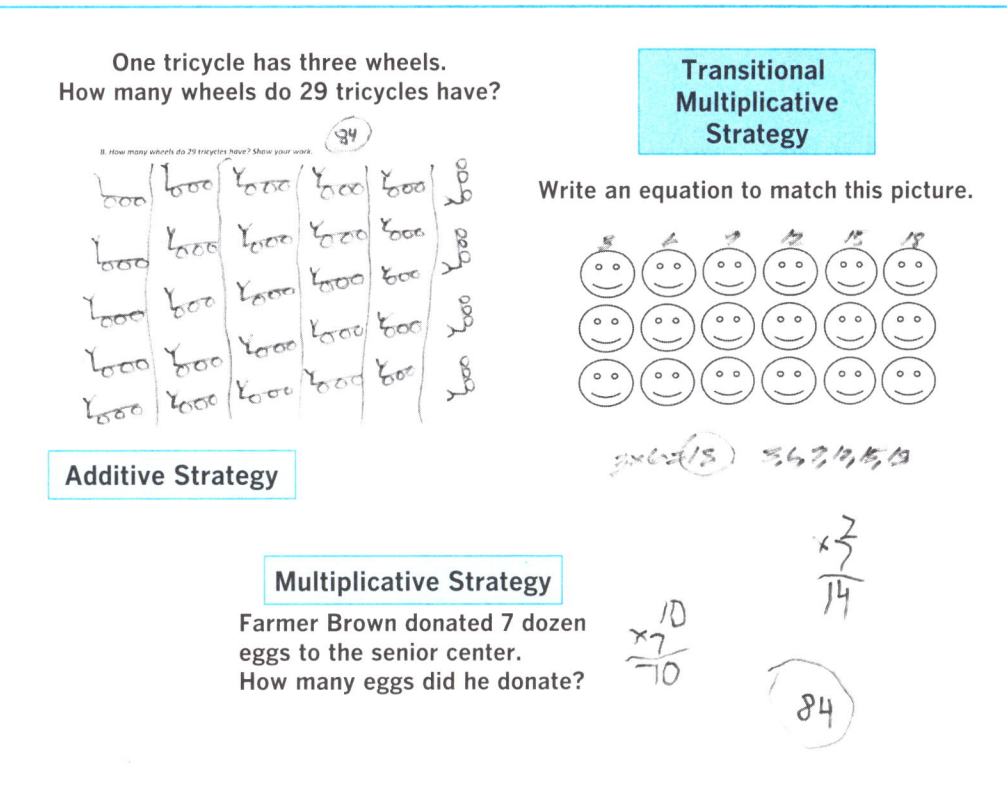

Formative assessments can uncover thinking to show how student understanding is developing along the continuum of learning/learning progression. Student work in the above examples is similar to work collected from formative assessments developed by Vermont's Ongoing Assessment Project [OGAP].

Source: OGAP, 2008: The Vermont Mathematics Partnership is funded by a grant provided by the U.S. Department of Education (Award Number S366A020002) and the National Science Foundation (Award Number EHR-0227057).

---

3. The full Learning Progressions Frameworks (LPFs) for ELA and Mathematics and expanded versions of the mathematics LPF (like the one pictured above) are posted at http://www.karin-hess.com/learning-progressions.

Elementary (K–4) School Learning Targets, Progress Indicators, and Common Core Standards

The Nature of Numbers and Operations (NO): Understandings of number—"how many" or "how much"—and number types extend applications of arithmetic properties, operations, and number systems and guide the use of computational strategies and algorithms.

E.NO-2 Build an understanding of computational strategies and algorithms: Fluently add, subtract, multiply, divide, and estimate; Perform and represent operations with whole numbers, fractions, and mixed numbers; Identify multiples and factors of whole numbers.

PROGRESS INDICATORS FOR GRADES 3–4	GRADE 3 CCSS STANDARDS	GRADE 4 CCSS STANDARDS
E.NO.2d modeling multiplication (equal-sized groups, arrays, area models, equal-sized jumps on number lines, multiplicative comparisons) and division (successive subtraction, partitioning, sharing) of whole numbers **3.OA-1, 2, 3, 4, 5** **4.OA-1, 2, 3** **4.NBT-5, 6**	**3.OA-1, 2, 3, 4, 5** 1. Interpret products of whole numbers, e.g., interpret 5×7 as the total number of objects in 5 groups of 7 objects each. *For example, describe a context in which a total number of objects can be expressed as 5×7.* 2. Interpret whole-number quotients of whole numbers, e.g., interpret $56 \div 8$ as the number of objects in each share when 56 objects are partitioned equally into 8 shares, or as a number of shares when 56 objects are partitioned into equal shares of 8 objects each. *For example, describe a context in which a number of shares or a number of groups can be expressed as $56 \div 8$.* 3. Use multiplication and division within 100 to solve word problems in situations involving equal groups, arrays, and measurement quantities, e.g., by using drawings and equations with a symbol for the unknown number to represent the problem.* *See Figure 4.2.	**4.OA-1, 2, 3** 1. Interpret a multiplication equation as a comparison, e.g., interpret $35 = 5 \times 7$ as a statement that 35 is 5 times as many as 7 and 7 times as many as 5. Represent verbal statements of multiplicative comparisons as multiplication equations. 2. Multiply or divide to solve word problems involving multiplicative comparison, e.g., by using drawings and equations with a symbol for the unknown number to represent the problem, distinguishing multiplicative comparison from additive comparison.* *See Figure 4.2. 3. Solve multistep word problems posed with whole numbers and having whole-number answers using the four operations, including problems in which remainders must be interpreted. Represent these problems using equations with a letter standing for the unknown quantity. Assess the reasonableness of answers using mental computation and estimation strategies including rounding. **4.NBT-5, 6** 5. Multiply a whole number of up to four digits by a one-digit whole number, and multiply two two-digit numbers, using strategies based on place value and the properties of operations. Illustrate and explain the calculation by using equations, rectangular arrays, and/or area models.

292   A Local Assessment Toolkit to Promote Deeper Learning

PROGRESS INDICATORS FOR GRADES 3–4	GRADE 3 CCSS STANDARDS	GRADE 4 CCSS STANDARDS
	4. Determine the unknown whole number in a multiplication or division equation relating three whole numbers. *For example, determine the unknown number that makes the equation true in each of the equations 8 × ? = 48, 5 = _ ÷ 3, 6 × 6 = ?* 5. Apply properties of operations as strategies to multiply and divide. *Examples: If 6 × 4 = 24 is known, then 4 × 6 = 24 is also known. (Commutative property of multiplication.) 3 × 5 × 2 can be found by 3 × 5 = 15, then 15 × 2 = 30, or by 5 × 2 = 10, then 3 × 10 = 30. (Associative property of multiplication.) Knowing that 8 × 5 = 40 and 8 × 2 = 16, one can find 8 × 7 as 8 × (5 + 2) = (8 × 5) + (8 × 2) = 40 + 16 = 56. (Distributive property.)*	6. Find whole-number quotients and remainders with up to four-digit dividends and one-digit divisors, using strategies based on place value, the properties of operations, and/or the relationship between multiplication and division. Illustrate and explain the calculation by using equations, rectangular arrays, and/or area models.
E.NO.2e describing relationships between addition-multiplication; multiplication-division; addition-subtraction; why commutativity does not apply to subtraction or division **3.OA-5, 7, 9** **3.NBT-2**	**3.OA-5, 7, 9** 5. Apply properties of operations as strategies to multiply and divide. *Examples: If 6 × 4 = 24 is known, then 4 × 6 = 24 is also known. (Commutative property of multiplication.) 3 × 5 × 2 can be found by 3 × 5 = 15, then 15 × 2 = 30, or by 5 × 2 = 10, then 3 × 10 = 30. (Associative property of multiplication.) Knowing that 8 × 5 = 40 and 8 × 2 = 16, one can find 8 × 7 as 8 × (5 + 2) = (8 × 5) + (8 × 2) = 40 + 16 = 56. (Distributive property.)* 7. Fluently multiply and divide within 100, using strategies such as the relationship between multiplication and division (e.g., knowing that 8 × 5 = 40, one knows 40 ÷ 5 = 8) or properties of operations. By the end of Grade 3, know from memory all products of two one-digit numbers.	**4.OA-2** 2. Multiply or divide to solve word problems involving multiplicative comparison, e.g., by using drawings and equations with a symbol for the unknown number to represent the problem, distinguishing multiplicative comparison from additive comparison.* *See Figure 4.2.

(Continued)

(Continued)

PROGRESS INDICATORS FOR GRADES 3–4	GRADE 3 CCSS STANDARDS	GRADE 4 CCSS STANDARDS
4.OA-2	9. Identify arithmetic patterns (including patterns in the addition table or multiplication table), and explain them using properties of operations. *For example, observe that 4 times a number is always even, and explain why 4 times a number can be decomposed into two equal addends.* **3.NBT-2** 2. Fluently add and subtract within 1000 using strategies and algorithms based on place value, properties of operations, and/or the relationship between addition and subtraction.	
E.NO.2f identifying factors and multiples of numbers 3.OA-6 4.OA-4	**3.OA-6** 6. Understand division as an unknown-factor problem. *For example, find 32 ÷ 8 by finding the number that makes 32 when multiplied by 8.*	**4.OA-4** 4. Find all factor pairs for a whole number in the range 1–100. Recognize that a whole number is a multiple of each of its factors. Determine whether a given whole number in the range 1–100 is a multiple of a given one-digit number. Determine whether a given whole number in the range 1–100 is prime or composite.
E.NO.2g recognizing fractions as one number (one quantity), rather than two numbers (numerator and denominator) and using number lines to represent magnitude of fractions 3.NF-1, 2, 3a, 3c	**3.NF-1, 2, 3a, c** 1. Understand a fraction 1/b as the quantity formed by 1 part when a whole is partitioned into b equal parts; understand a fraction a/b as the quantity formed by a parts of size 1/b. 2. Understand a fraction as a number on the number line; represent fractions on a number line diagram. a. Represent a fraction 1/b on a number line diagram by defining the interval from 0 to 1 as the whole and partitioning it into b equal parts. Recognize that each part has size 1/b and that the endpoint of the part based at 0 locates the number 1/b on the number line.	*No specific Common Core Standards have been linked to this Progress Indicator at this grade level; however, instruction should include these skills/concepts as part of the "hypothesized" learning continuum.*

PROGRESS INDICATORS FOR GRADES 3–4	GRADE 3 CCSS STANDARDS	GRADE 4 CCSS STANDARDS

	b. Represent a fraction *a/b* on a number line diagram by marking off *a* lengths 1/*b* from 0. Recognize that the resulting interval has size *a/b* and that its endpoint locates the number *a/b* on the number line.
	
	3. Explain equivalence of fractions in special cases, and compare fractions by reasoning about their size.
	
	   a. Understand two fractions as equivalent (equal) if they are the same size, or the same point on a number line.
	
	   c. Express whole numbers as fractions, and recognize fractions that are equivalent to whole numbers. *Examples: Express 3 in the form 3 = 3/1; recognize that 6/1 = 6; locate 4/4 and 1 at the same point of a number line diagram.*	

E.NO.2h adding, subtracting, and multiplying fractions, including mixed numbers
4-NF-3, 4
	No specific Common Core Standards have been linked to this Progress Indicator at this grade level.	**4-NF-3, 4**
		
		3. Understand a fraction *a/b* with *a* > 1 as a sum of fractions 1/*b*.
		
		   a. Understand addition and subtraction of fractions as joining and separating parts referring to the same whole.
		
		   b. Decompose a fraction into a sum of fractions with the same denominator in more than one way, recording each decomposition by an equation. Justify decompositions, e.g., by using a visual fraction model. *Examples: 3/8 = 1/8 + 1/8 + 1/8; 3/8 = 1/8 + 2/8; 2 1/8 = 1 + 1 + 1/8 = 8/8 + 8/8 + 1/8.*
		
		   c. Add and subtract mixed numbers with like denominators, e.g., by replacing each mixed number with an equivalent fraction, and/or by using properties of operations and the relationship between addition and subtraction.

(Continued)

(Continued)

PROGRESS INDICATORS FOR GRADES 3–4	GRADE 3 CCSS STANDARDS	GRADE 4 CCSS STANDARDS

		d. Solve word problems involving addition and subtraction of fractions referring to the same whole and having like denominators, e.g., by using visual fraction models and equations to represent the problem.
		
		4. Apply and extend previous understandings of multiplication to multiply a fraction by a whole number.
		
		   a. Understand a fraction a/b as a multiple of 1/b. *For example, use a visual fraction model to represent 5/4 as the product 5 × (1/4), recording the conclusion by the equation 5/4 = 5 × (1/4).*
		
		   b. Understand a multiple of a/b as a multiple of 1/b, and use this understanding to multiply a fraction by a whole number. *For example, use a visual fraction model to express 3 × (2/5) as 6 × (1/5), recognizing this product as 6/5. (In general, n × (a/b) = (n × a)/b.)*
		
		   c. Solve word problems involving multiplication of a fraction by a whole number, e.g., by using visual fraction models and equations to represent the problem. *For example, if each person at a party will eat 3/8 of a pound of roast beef, and there will be 5 people at the party, how many pounds of roast beef will be needed? Between what two whole numbers does your answer lie?*

> *Discuss what you see in the student work samples* (shown in Figure 4.2). If each sample represents typical work for several students in the class, what instructional strategies would be helpful in moving each group of students forward to deeper understanding?

Linking Learning Progressions to Assessment Purposes and Formative, Interim, and Summative Uses

My conceptual view of learning progressions is one of overlapping "learning zones" along a broader continuum of learning. The visual (Figure 4.3) applies Vygotsky's concept of zones of proximal development (1978), which is based on an understanding of what a child can do *today* with assistance. At the lower end of the learning progression are "novice" or beginning performers (at any grade level), who may (or may not) demonstrate the necessary prerequisite skills or understandings needed to be successful. For example, does the student have the essential skills or concepts (knows letters and sounds, demonstrates concepts of print, can make and check predictions while reading, etc.) that can be built upon over time to become a confident reader? At the other end of the continuum are "expert" performers who not only have acquired the essential

Figure 4.3 Learning Progressions Viewed as Overlapping "Learning Zones" Along a Broader Continuum of Learning

Learning Progressions
"Link" the Zones of Proximal Development of ALL Students

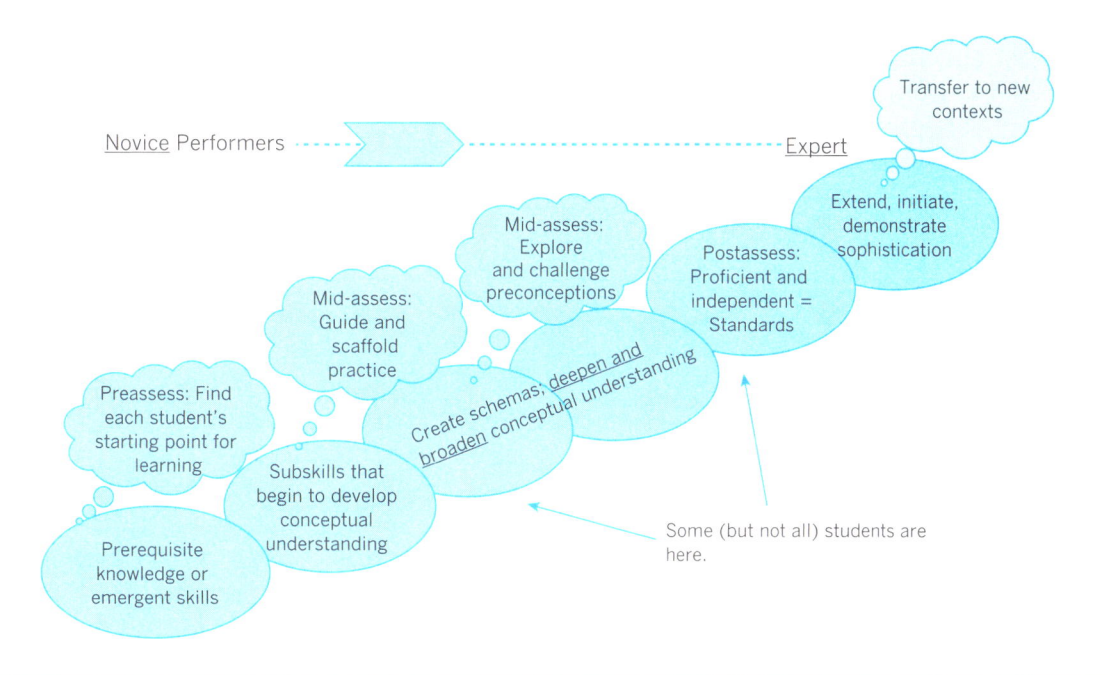

Novice Performers → ... → Expert

- Transfer to new contexts
- Extend, initiate, demonstrate sophistication
- Postassess: Proficient and independent = Standards
- Mid-assess: Explore and challenge preconceptions
- Mid-assess: Guide and scaffold practice
- Create schemas; deepen and broaden conceptual understanding
- Preassess: Find each student's starting point for learning
- Subskills that begin to develop conceptual understanding
- Prerequisite knowledge or emergent skills
- Some (but not all) students are here.

Source: Hess (2008b).

skills or concepts described in standards, but are able to transfer their learning to nonroutine and more complex learning tasks, such as comparing themes across texts or using mentor texts to inform their own writing. When planning for instruction or designing (pre-, mid-, and post-) assessments, it's essential to conceptualize a possible progression of learning and be able to place a student along that continuum: what a child can do independently now and how it connects with what a child should be able to do independently in the future. Learning progressions help teachers to find that zone of where to begin and how to "scaffold in" the instruction as a student advances along the progression.

I refer to the descriptors in the learning progressions as *"progress indicators."* Progress indicators help to unpack how learning might unfold for most students over time, moving from novice to expert. Progress indicators are used to frame the learning targets in your unit of study. They can also be used in the design of preassessments that uncover whether or not students already possess the critical prerequisite skills and knowledge that new learning can be built upon. Mid-assessments (comprised of ongoing formative assessments and performance tasks) are used after some instruction has occurred and may be less complex than the final summative or postassessment (the "game"), but assess the same core skills and concepts as does the postassessment. Mid-assessments are used to identify how well students are making progress toward achieving proficiency and integrating skills and concepts. Postassessments (such as end-of-unit tests, more complex performance tasks, and project-based assessments) are used to indicate to what degree students are able to make connections and work independently transferring skills and concepts to new situations. I like to think of the preassessments as the "tryouts" for the team and mid-assessments as the drills, short practices, and scrimmages that prepare students to "play the game" (summative assessments that require transfer and more sophisticated applications of the skills and concepts described in standards).

It's important to understand that "what distinguishes expert performers from beginner (novice) performers is not simply general mental abilities, such as memory or fluid intelligence, or even general problem-solving strategies. Experts have efficiently coded and organized (chunks of) information into well-connected schemas . . . which helps them to notice features and meaningful patterns . . . that might be overlooked by learners at the earlier stages" (NRC, 2001). Building schemas, therefore, is the true goal for learning over time. For example, if I understand how text genres are structured differently, then I'll be able to understand how the information presented in texts is likely to be organized, even if the complexity of the text increases. If I look for numerical patterns and mathematical structures when I solve problems, it will help me to solve similar problems, as well as know how I might approach future nonroutine problems applying the same concepts with greater sophistication.

4.3 Standards, Learning Progressions, and Curriculum: How Are They Related?

The terms *learning progressions, progress maps, developmental continuums,* and *learning trajectories* have been used in the literature to describe research-based, descriptive continuums of how students develop and demonstrate deeper, broader, or more sophisticated understanding over time. Learning progressions can visually and verbally articulate hypotheses about how most students will typically move toward increased understanding in a content domain. There is currently a growing body of knowledge surrounding purposes and uses of LPs, as well as ongoing research in identifying and empirically validating content-specific learning progressions (Hess, 2010a). Understanding typical steps along a progression can help teachers to target their instruction and use formative assessment more effectively.

I first stumbled upon the idea of learning progressions in the early 1990s when I was a curriculum director in Vermont. Part of my job was to work with curriculum teams in the district to develop and implement K–12 curriculum in each content area. As I searched for resources that we might use to guide our thinking in literacy, I discovered a series of guides researched and developed by the Education Department of Western Australia (1994), called *First Steps*. Unlike standards or curriculum documents I'd ever seen, these developmental continuums were based on the theoretical assumptions that learning means developing skills and knowledge along a (cross-grade) continuum; explicit indicators along the continua describe observable behaviors that can be used to guide instruction; individual children may exhibit a range of indicators from different phases of learning at any given time; and using a clustering of key indicators to describe each phase of learning allows teachers to map overall progress, while recognizing that learning and language does not develop in a linear sequence (pp. 2–3). Wow! It made so much sense to me that a developmental continuum (what LPs are often called in literacy and language arts), not standards, should be used to guide curriculum and classroom instruction during the school year. I wondered why countries such as Australia and New Zealand had taken such a different approach to designing instruction and formative assessment than we have in the United States.

To be honest, I'm still a bit perplexed that more schools are not thinking about LPs or systematically incorporating the concept of "empirically based progressions of learning" into their curriculum and assessment work. Thankfully, LP models continue to emerge that align with standards in mathematics, science, and literacy (Clements & Sarama, 2009; Corcoran, Mosher, & Rogat, 2009; Daro, Mosher, & Corcoran, 2011; Keeley, Eberle, & Farrin, 2005; Maloney et al., 2014; Pinnell & Fountas, 2007) and can guide educators to consider their benefits. The real shift in thinking will come when schools use LPs to provide a mapping of possible pathways to achieve the standards or demonstrate proficiency in a content domain.

How Are Learning Progressions Different From Standards?

Learning progressions are developed based on the pathways that learners generally take as they build deeper understanding in a content domain. Standards, and specifically the *Common Core State Standards Initiative* (National Governors Association, 2010b, 2010c), were developed "backward" from Grade 12, first identifying the skills and concepts that professors at U.S. colleges and universities said were needed for students to be college and career ready. The Common Core does not suggest any instructional sequencing (or learning) plan. As a matter of fact, the introduction to Common Core for mathematics states, "Just because topic A appears before topic B in the standards . . . does not necessarily mean that topic A must be taught before topic B. A teacher might prefer to teach topic B before A, or might choose to highlight connections . . . of her own choosing that leads to A or B" (National Governors Association, 2010c, p. 5). This implies that to reach the standards, any route will get you there. While that may be true, most people would prefer to study a map or use a GPS system when planning a yearlong trip to a designated destination. A well-thought-out plan can be more effective and probably help to avoid some bumps and detours in the road along the way.

Many people confuse "standards progressions" or curricular progressions with LEARNING progressions—however, they are not the same thing. The grade-level content standards do not show teachers how to get from one grade-level's content to the next grade level during a school year or across school years. Breaking down—or unpacking—a standard is not the same thing as considering what the earlier instructional building blocks might be for students to demonstrate mastery over time. For example, in my research synthesis (Hess, 2010b) examining how students develop expertise in mathematics, we found compelling studies that said it is essential for students to first conceptually understand the mathematical symbols used, before they apply procedures with them (e.g., students understand equivalence before using an equal sign; or "joining together" before using a plus sign for addition). While there may be standards about adding and standards about using mathematical symbols, the connections among standards is not explicit in terms of teaching or learning.

Regrettably, the adoption of standards is often a politically charged process. The beauty of learning progressions is that they allow us to peel back the political layer and get back to the business of teaching and learning. Standards will inevitably change, but how learning evolves over time tends to be fairly consistent.

Here are a few key differences that distinguish standards from learning progressions:

- Unlike content standards, learning progressions are based on empirical research describing how learning typically develops over time for most students. Some early stages of learning may not look like the later stages, but they include some important steps to get there. (Just as I hope my horse story illustrated.)

- Learning progressions sometimes include typical preconceptions along the learning pathway, something you will not see articulated in standards, but important to anticipating where students might struggle and need extra support.

- Learning progressions suggest an intentional mapping of how to teach and build upon concepts introduced earlier. They should not, however, be thought of as linear or lockstep sequencing of instruction. This is why the term *progress map* is sometimes used to mean learning progression. Conversely, pacing guides or scope and sequencing are used to ensure that all standards in the curriculum have been addressed during a given time frame (e.g., marking period). Sometimes pacing guides show the sequencing of what to teach that may be inconsistent with the optimal path most learning would take. For example, a school that wanted to stress argument writing might begin the school year with a unit to introduce this genre, which requires that students are able to describe (summarize key ideas), compare and contrast (to make a point), use chronology (to order events), and show cause–effect. These text structures are also central to informational writing and tend to be easier to teach first when they are embedded in informational writing. The genre of argument writing employs all of these structures plus the structure of proposition–support. Substructures (description, compare–contrast, chronology, cause–effect) are used in argument writing "in service of" proposition/support to develop a flow of ideas and a chain of logic.

Potential Benefits of Using a Learning Progressions Schema for Designing Instruction and Assessment

Learning progressions can help teachers to think about how to build on a student's prior learning by looking at the path students typically follow when they learn similar content. These pathways are not bound by grade level. Instructional decisions are constantly informed by examining student work products and reflecting on instructional practices. Remember that learning progressions, as well as standards, are just hypotheses about learning that will be confirmed or refuted with evidence demonstrated in student work *after* targeted instruction.

Corcoran, Mosher, and Rogat (2009) present a case for the use of learning progressions to inform teaching and learning:

> We are convinced that it is not possible for the reform goals with respect to "all students" to be met unless instruction in our schools becomes much more adaptive. That is, the norms of practice should shift in the direction in which teachers and other educators take responsibility for continually seeking evidence on whether their students are on track to learning what they need to if they are to reach the goals, along with tracking indicators of

what problems they may be having, and then for making pedagogical responses to that evidence designed to keep their students on track, or to get them back on track, moving toward meeting the goals. This, of course, is a description of a formative assessment process in action. We are additionally convinced that teachers will not be able to engage in such processes unless they have in their minds some idea about how students' learning in the subjects they are teaching develops over their time in school, as well as some idea of the ways of responding to evidence of their progress or problems that are likely to be effective. We have been looking for promising ideas about what this metaphor of "on track" (or its obverse—"off track") might mean in terms that could be accessible to and useful for teachers and their students. One such idea that has attracted growing attention in education reform circles is the concept of learning progressions. (p. 8)

Benefits of using a progressions mindset include the following:

- *Place greater emphasis on deeper understanding and complexity of learning*: We want students to demonstrate deeper conceptual understanding through the application of content knowledge and skills to new situations and sustained tasks (Hess, Carlock, Jones, & Walkup, 2009, p. 1). If we place equal emphasis on each standard, what we teach and assess in a deeper and more meaningful way will be limited. Learning progressions can show us where parts of standards belong along a continuum and where we might go next and stay longer to deepen understanding.

- *Maximize emphasis on foundational skills earlier in the learning process*: According to cognitive scientist Daniel Willingham (2009), basic processes that initially place demands on working memory become automatic with practice; this automaticity makes room for more complex levels of thinking. Willingham recommends that students acquire background knowledge—in other words, foundational skills—while practicing critical-thinking skills, noting that "critical thinking is not a set of procedures that can be practiced and perfected while divorced from background knowledge" (p. 37). While educators must offer students opportunities to acquire and demonstrate deeper, more complex learning, it's important to remember that doing so must begin on a solid foundation of basic skills—skills that require instruction, practice, and feedback.

- *Use assessment data to improve instruction*: Test items and assessment results inform curricular decisions that help ensure students are on track to college and career readiness. Assessment data supports teachers in taking the next steps after assessment to direct instruction to best support student achievement. This may be a new way to think about instructionally sensitive assessments.

- *Gather research-based growth data*: Assessments and instruction aligned with descriptors along a research-based progression offer a reliable and defensible interpretation and measurement of growth within and across academic years. Regularly examining student work with colleagues supports teachers' understanding of how students deepen conceptual understanding and to identify the "typical" intermediate understandings along the way.

- *Increase student achievement over time*: A key objective of assessments used for accountability and teacher effectiveness (e.g., measuring Student Learning Objectives/SLOs) is to examine whether or not students are proficient relative to agreed-upon standards at particular grade levels. In a more traditional design, the achievement of students at the highest and lowest levels usually cannot be accurately measured because there are not enough data points (test questions, aspects of more complex tasks) along a progression. Computer-adaptive assessments are designed to maximize interpretations of achievement along a continuum but often cannot assess depth and breadth of understanding the way performance tasks or project-based investigations do. In other words, if we design assessments for the full range of performance, we'll know more about how close students are to achieving or exceeding grade-level performance than we used to.

- *Identify where a student falls along a learning continuum* while also maintaining the ability to determine whether the student is proficient on a given grade-level standard. "Progress" can now be seen and interpreted as getting closer to the learning goal, rather than not meeting the goal.

If this visual of "nested dolls" represents a learning progression, . . .

can you imagine a "unifying thread" carried from the smallest doll to the next and the next that represents how the "Big Ideas" or core concepts are becoming more complex over time? Where are the foundational learning targets? Where are the most complex targets? What might represent the standards?

Source: Pixabay.com/Goshadron

4.4 Zooming "In" and Zooming "Out" of Learning Progressions: Two Sides to the Same Coin

I use the phrase *zoom in–zoom out* to describe ways that you might refocus your attention on parts or all of a learning progression. Zooming in and zooming out are complementary processes that support different instructional and assessment purposes and strategies.

Zooming "out" provides a panoramic view of one progression—or strand—across all grades, focusing on how the same core or "Big Ideas" develops over time in Grades K–12. This strand seen in Figure 4.4 is a learning progression for (Strand 7) writing persuasively, which is part of the Learning Progressions Framework for ELA[4] (Hess, 2011a). This wide-angle view is useful for establishing overall program coherence and curricular planning across adjacent grades, as well as for seeing how instructional materials might become more sophisticated and complex at each grade span. See Appendix G for the full K–12 progression for persuasive writing: writing opinions, arguments, and critiques.

In the LPF, multiple standards, including writing, reading, speaking–listening, and language standards are referenced to one or more progress indicators. The grain size of each progress

---

4. The full Learning Progressions Frameworks (LPFs) for ELA and Mathematics are posted at http://www.karin-hess.com/learning-progressions.

Figure 4.4 A View of One LP Writing Strand of the LPF Across All Grades

STRAND 7: <u>Writing Persuasively</u>/Communicating Opinions, Critiques, and Arguments (WP)—Different genres of persuasive writing (literary critiques, persuasive essays, speeches, editorials, etc.) are appropriate for different purposes and require use of genre-specific features, text structures, and strategic use of logic chains with compelling supporting evidence to produce a coherent unit of thought that persuades the intended audience.

(K–4) ELEMENTARY SCHOOL LEARNING TARGETS	(5–8) MIDDLE SCHOOL LEARNING TARGETS	(9–12) HIGH SCHOOL LEARNING TARGETS
E.WP Apply organizational strategies (e.g., description, definition, compare/contrast, cause/effect, proposition/support) and an understanding of topics or texts to develop and support opinions about them for authentic audiences.	**M.WP** Apply organizational strategies (e.g., cause/effect, problem/solution, proposition/support, critique), and use of multiple sources to analyze topics or texts in order to support a claim or thesis for authentic and varied audiences.	**H.WP** Apply organizational structures (e.g., proposition/support, critique, inductive and deductive reasoning), credible sources, and rhetorical strategies to the analysis and synthesis of complex ideas to present and support reasoned arguments/critiques of texts, issues, or problems for authentic and varied audiences.

GRADES K–2	GRADES 3–4	GRADES 5–6	GRADES 7–8	GRADES 9–12
Use a process approach to develop and communicate support for opinions . . . **E.WP.a** generating ideas about a topic, text, or stimulus shared (event, photo, video, peers, etc.) using a range of responses (e.g., discussion, dictation, drawing, letters/invented spelling, writing) K.W-1, 7; K.SL-4, 5; K.L-6 1.W-7, 8; 1.SL-1b, 2, 4, 5; 1.L-6 2.W-8; 2.SL-2, 4; 2.L-6 **E.WP.b** with prompting and **support**, connecting information or facts with personal opinions about a topic or text (e.g., I think it is an informational text because it has facts) using discussion, drawings with details, written words (labels, nouns) or completing statements (e.g., This is what I like about dogs . . . ; That character was funny because . . .) and "reading back" what they have written	Use a process approach to develop and communicate support for opinions . . . **E.WP.i** generating their own ideas for writing, using strategies to understand opinion writing (e.g., discuss possible reasons for/against with peers; analyze mentor texts—ads, book/movie reviews, letters to editor) 3.W-5; 3.SL-1d, 3; 3.L-3, 6 4.W-5; 4.SL-1d, 3; 4.L-3, 6 **E.WPj.** developing an understanding of a topic or text by locating evidence and using note-taking strategies to record and organize information relating to opposing sides of an issue (e.g., why people think/do not think dogs make good pets)	Use a process approach to develop and communicate support for claims or thesis . . . **M.WP.a** using strategies to better understand genres of persuasive writing (e.g., discuss opposing perspectives; analyze mentor texts—ads, essays, book/movie reviews, speeches, propaganda techniques)	Use a process approach to develop and communicate support for claims or thesis . . . **M.WP.i** using strategies to better understand genres of persuasive writing and their audiences (e.g., discuss opposing perspectives, analyze mentor texts—political cartoons, literary critiques, speeches, propaganda	Use a process approach to develop and communicate compelling and credible evidence to support reasoned arguments and critiques. . . **H.WP.a** using advanced searches and analyses to better understand genres and techniques associated with argument and critique and their intended audiences (e.g., discuss reasoning and rebuttals, analyze mentor texts—political commentaries, literary critiques, media messages, editorials, seminal historical and scientific documents) 9-10.W-7, 8, 9; 9-10.RI-6, 7, 8, 9 11-12.W-7, 8, 9; 11-12.RI-6, 7, 8 **H.WP.b** organizing, analyzing, and selectively integrating varied and complex information (facts, principles, examples, quotations, data), determining their significance to potential lines of reasoning (claims/counterclaims) either to support or refute the focus or thesis 9-10.W-1a, 1b, 1c, 7, 8, 9; 9-10.SL-2, 3 11-12.W-1a, 1b, 1c, 7, 8, 9; 11-12.SL-2, 3 **H.WP.c** establishing a critical stance and developing coherence among claims and evidence using nuanced transitions and varied syntax to link the focus or thesis with the major claims/counter claims as appropriate to intended audience

Source: Hess (2011a).

indicator in this progression is quite large and requires additional unpacking when designing specific assessments or units of study and identifying learning targets for individual lessons.

Zooming out can also provide a view of multiple LP strands for one grade level, such as you see in the excerpt below from Appendix F (Student Learning Progression Literacy Profile,[5] Grades 7–8) in Figure 4.5, showing three writing genre strands from the LPF. In this view, you again see persuasive writing (Strand 7), as well as strands for the other writing genre, each with a different essential question—one for narrative, one for informational, and one for persuasive (opinion/argument/critique). Progress indicators for each LP strand show how learning is likely

---

5. Literacy profiles, based on the Learning Progressions Frameworks (LPFs) for ELA, are posted at http://www.karin-hess.com/learning-progressions. Profiles were designed to apply the LPF descriptors in teacher-friendly progress-monitoring tools.

Figure 4.5 A View of Multiple LP Strands for Three Writing Genres (Grades 7–8), Based on the LPF

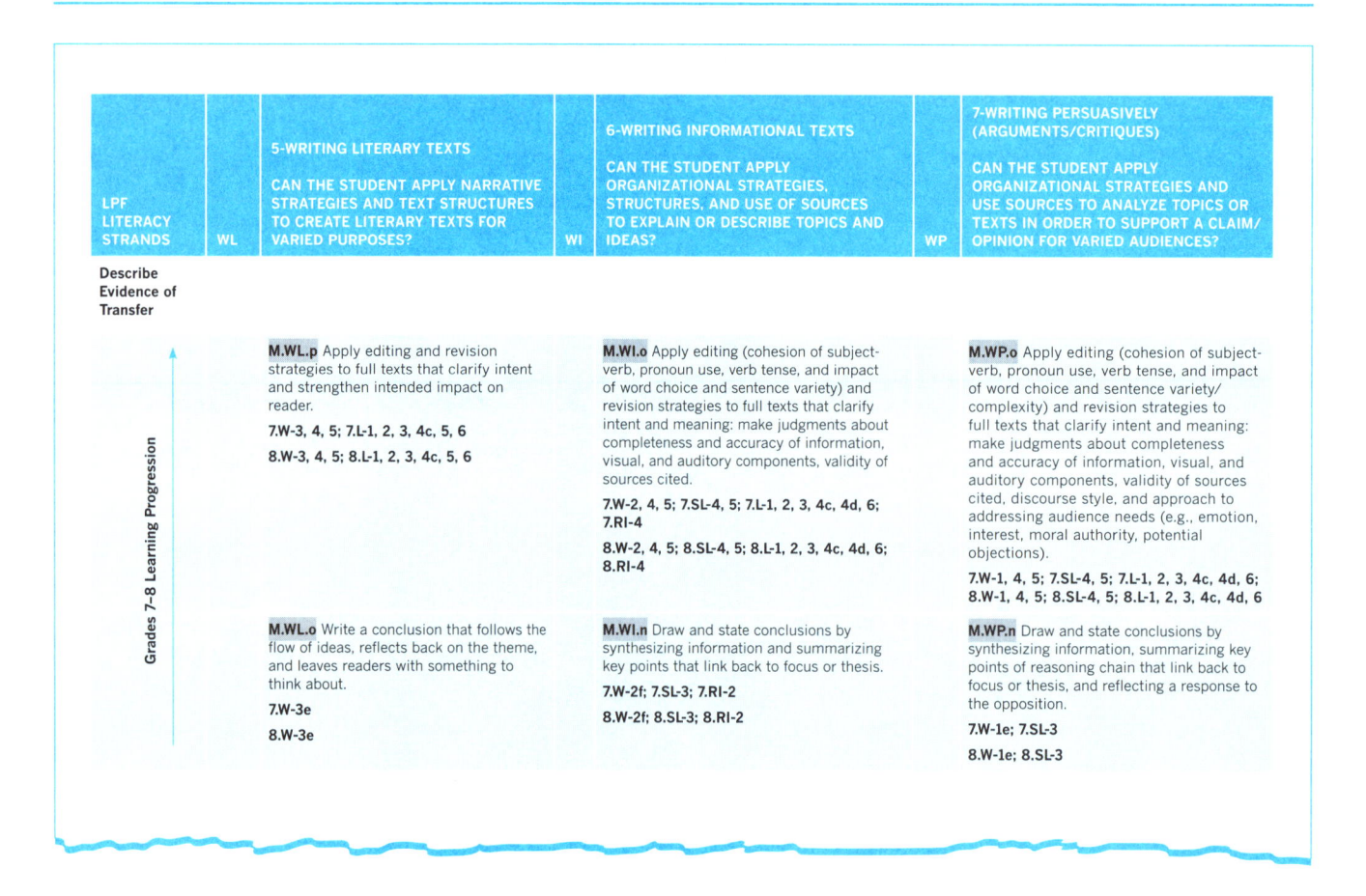

LPF LITERACY STRANDS	WL	5-WRITING LITERARY TEXTS CAN THE STUDENT APPLY NARRATIVE STRATEGIES AND TEXT STRUCTURES TO CREATE LITERARY TEXTS FOR VARIED PURPOSES?	WI	6-WRITING INFORMATIONAL TEXTS CAN THE STUDENT APPLY ORGANIZATIONAL STRATEGIES, STRUCTURES, AND USE OF SOURCES TO EXPLAIN OR DESCRIBE TOPICS AND IDEAS?	WP	7-WRITING PERSUASIVELY (ARGUMENTS/CRITIQUES) CAN THE STUDENT APPLY ORGANIZATIONAL STRATEGIES AND USE SOURCES TO ANALYZE TOPICS OR TEXTS IN ORDER TO SUPPORT A CLAIM/OPINION FOR VARIED AUDIENCES?
Describe Evidence of Transfer						
Grades 7–8 Learning Progression ↑		**M.WL.p** Apply editing and revision strategies to full texts that clarify intent and strengthen intended impact on reader. 7.W-3, 4, 5; 7.L-1, 2, 3, 4c, 5, 6 8.W-3, 4, 5; 8.L-1, 2, 3, 4c, 5, 6		**M.WI.o** Apply editing (cohesion of subject-verb, pronoun use, verb tense, and impact of word choice and sentence variety) and revision strategies to full texts that clarify intent and meaning: make judgments about completeness and accuracy of information, visual, and auditory components, validity of sources cited. 7.W-2, 4, 5; 7.SL-4, 5; 7.L-1, 2, 3, 4c, 4d, 6; 7.RI-4 8.W-2, 4, 5; 8.SL-4, 5; 8.L-1, 2, 3, 4c, 4d, 6; 8.RI-4		**M.WP.o** Apply editing (cohesion of subject-verb, pronoun use, verb tense, and impact of word choice and sentence variety/complexity) and revision strategies to full texts that clarify intent and meaning: make judgments about completeness and accuracy of information, visual, and auditory components, validity of sources cited, discourse style, and approach to addressing audience needs (e.g., emotion, interest, moral authority, potential objections). 7.W-1, 4, 5; 7.SL-4, 5; 7.L-1, 2, 3, 4c, 4d, 6; 8.W-1, 4, 5; 8.SL-4, 5; 8.L-1, 2, 3, 4c, 4d, 6
		M.WL.o Write a conclusion that follows the flow of ideas, reflects back on the theme, and leaves readers with something to think about. 7.W-3e 8.W-3e		**M.WI.n** Draw and state conclusions by synthesizing information and summarizing key points that link back to focus or thesis. 7.W-2f; 7.SL-3; 7.RI-2 8.W-2f; 8.SL-3; 8.RI-2		**M.WP.n** Draw and state conclusions by synthesizing information, summarizing key points of reasoning chain that link back to focus or thesis, and reflecting a response to the opposition. 7.W-1e; 7.SL-3 8.W-1e; 8.SL-3

Source: Hess (2011a).

to be enhanced with targeted instruction. Progress indicators are referenced to multiple standards or parts of standards in a way that allows teachers to

- examine particular *standards* or combinations of standards to focus on (in this unit),
- identify essential *instructional building blocks* (for this unit or this lesson),
- develop intended *learning targets for each lesson*, and
- create and use *formative assessments* to monitor learning.

Zooming out in this way is useful for thinking about the instructional sequencing of units of study across a school year, for a given grade level. It's also helpful for designing benchmark or interim assessments across a school year for each grade level. This example (using the three writing genres) might help in planning which performance assessments will be collected for each student's writing portfolio and how many opportunities they will have to produce them during the school year.

Zooming "in" for a close-up view allows teachers to focus on one or more progress indicators from one LP strand at one grade level. This view provides guidance for developing and sequencing lessons within a unit of study or creating pre-, mid-, or postassessments within a unit of study. Zooming in might also identify some potential trouble spots for students and lead to the creation of additional instructional tools to support the learning.

One example that illustrates this point—addressing trouble spots along the progression—comes from a writing project conducted during the 2010–2011 school year with teacher leaders from twenty N.Y.C. public schools (Hess, 2012a). The goal of the project was to develop, pilot, and refine performance assessments that were aligned with the Common Core and annotate student work samples for each task so that the assessments could be widely used as common assessments in the districts.[6] We were asked by the N.Y.C. Department of Education to design three performance-based assessments (PBAs) in mathematics and writing at each grade level that could be used by teachers across the district for monitoring progress on specific skills and concepts during the school year. All PBAs were required to be aligned with the *Common Core State Standards*; however, unique to this performance-based assessment project was that it also provided the opportunity to use a research-based learning progressions schema in mathematics (Hess, 2010b) and writing (Hess, 2011a) to

(a) formulate a thoughtful K–5 cross-grade assessment plan,

(b) design and field-test performance-based assessments that could potentially elicit evidence of more sophisticated learning and understanding over time, and

(c) interpret results and monitor individual and class progress in writing and mathematics at the K–5 grade levels.

Unlike much smaller grained learning progressions that are typically used to develop individual test items (e.g., for online item banks), the grain size of progress indicators in the Learning Progressions Frameworks (LPFs) are more suited to designing curriculum and more robust performance assessments. The LPFs were used not only to design the performance-based assessment tasks but also to develop a series of lessons whereby the PBAs could be embedded within an instructional unit of study, thus ensuring all students' potential opportunity to learn. The three PBAs were used as a preassessment, mid-assessment, and postassessment within each unit of study. Student work analysis (using PLC **TOOL #12**) was used after each assessment administration to analyze results, fine-tune the administration guide, develop instructional strategies for unit planning, and create annotations for work samples at each performance level.

During the development of the LPF K–2 grade span for informational writing (Strand 6), we found compelling research to indicate that organizing ideas for informational writing did not "typically" develop before the end of Grade 2. If you have ever examined writing of young children, you know that children can write and punctuate fact-based sentences; but often the sentences are not organized in a meaningful way, such as by categories of what things look like or how they are used. Our analysis of the Grade 2 preassessment results clearly supported what was expressed in the "early" progress indicators of the LPF for Strand 6. As a result, we designed a specific kid tool for organizing notes and teaching students how to use it, which was quite simple: (a) write your facts; (b) cut your facts apart; (c) think about how to group the facts, so that when you begin writing; (d) you can identify several key ideas (subtopics) using the facts as supporting details.

---

6. Many of the finalized writing and mathematics tasks with scoring rubrics and annotated student work from this project are available at www.weteachnyc.org.

Figure 4.6 Excerpt From the K–12 ELA Learning Progressions Framework, Informational Writing—Strand 6

STRAND 6: Writing Informative Texts/Communicating Information (WI)—Different genres of expository text provide information/explanations (science procedures, content-based articles, biographies, research reports, historical documents, etc.) for different purposes and require use of genre-specific features, text structures, and supporting evidence to produce a coherent unit of thought that informs or educates the intended audience.

(K–4) Elementary School Learning Targets

E.WI By the end of grade 4, students can . . . apply organizational strategies (e.g., sequence, description, definition, compare-contrast, cause-effect) to develop, summarize, and communicate factual information about topics and events for authentic audiences.

Grades K–2	Grades 3–4
Students use a process approach to compose informational texts . . .	Students use a process approach to compose informational texts . . .
E.WI.a generating ideas for using a range of responses (e.g., discussion, dictation, drawing, letters/invented spelling, writing), when responding to a topic, text, or stimulus (event, photo, video, peers, etc.)	E.WI.j generating their own ideas for writing; using strategies to clarify writing (e.g., conference with peers, find words for stronger descriptions)
E.WI.b describing information about a topic or text using drawings with details, written words (labels, names), and fact statements (e.g., "Spiders make webs") and 'reading back' what they have written	E.WI.k locating information from at least two reference sources (print/nonprint) to obtain information on a topic (e.g., sports); listing sources
E.WI.c representing facts and descriptions through a combination of illustrations, captions, and simple sentences that often connect two clauses; applying basic capitalization and end punctuation	E.WI.l using note-taking and organizational strategies (e.g., graphic organizers, notes, labeling, listing) to record and meaningfully organize information (e.g., showing sequence, compare/contrast, cause/effect, question/answer) relating topic/subtopics to evidence, facts
E.WI.d with support, using various information retrieval sources (e.g., word wall, book talks, visuals/images, Internet) to detail facts and compose information on a topic	E.WI.m writing an introduction of several sentences that sets the context and states a focus/controlling idea about a topic/subtopics (e.g., "Many sports can be played outside in winter.")
E.WI.e with support, using simple note-taking strategies to record and group facts (e.g., numbering, T-chart, graphic organizer) to plan writing	E.WI.n selecting *relevant* facts, details, or examples to support the controlling idea, including use of domain-specific vocabulary
E.WI.f selecting *and ordering* fact statements, using domain-specific vocabulary to describe a sequence of events or explain a procedure (e.g., list necessary materials and tell steps in logical order)	E.WI.o presenting factual information about subtopics of larger topics, grouping relevant details using several related and varied sentence types
E.WI.g presenting factual information describing subtopics of larger topics using sentences in *somewhat random order* (listing fact statements rather than connecting or relating ideas)	E.WI.p incorporating text features (e.g., numbers, labels, diagrams, charts, graphics) to enhance clarity and meaning of informational writing
	E.WI.q writing a conclusion or concluding statement that links back to the focus
	E.WI.r with support, editing informational text for clarity and meaning: grade-appropriate spelling (words that follow patterns/rules), end punctuation and capitalization, variety of sentence types

The Grade 2 informational writing PBA pre-assessment typically elicited this set of evidence. [pointing to E.WI.a–g]

Based on analysis of student work from the informational writing PBA pre-assessment, instruction and the mid- and post-assessment mainly targeted these more advanced skills: organizing information and selecting relevant supporting evidence for each subtopic.

Source: Hess (2011a).

Being able to anticipate a potential bump in the road and then seeing evidence in student work from the preassessment that confirmed it allowed us to create numerous learning activities in the unit that focused on ways to group ideas for writing. One example, "My Note Facts," is shown below and is also in the Module 4 Support Materials.

My Note Facts About _____

Name _____

Use the lines below to write your facts and details. Cut each fact apart.
Decide how to make groups of the facts, such as how things look or where they live. Use the **fact groups** to write about each key idea in your report.

✂--

_____
_____
_____
_____

4.5 Applying the Four Interrelated Guiding Principles to Better Understand a Learning Progression

A few simple questions related to the four guiding principles can be used to examine existing curricular, developmental, or even "draft" (in my head) learning progressions. Since the guiding principles are interrelated, there is not a linear sequence for using them to validate or refine the LP. One group of teachers might be starting with formative assessments and data collection in order to create a LP that will guide instruction; another group might be considering whether to "adopt" an existing LP and want to first examine its validity by checking the research base and identifying the unifying threads before determining which aligned assessments they will use to measure progress along that continuum. I've found these questions to be useful in examining whether existing curricular units of study and their assessments actually illustrate learning development over time, from novice to expert.

Guiding Questions for Developing, Refining, or Validating Learning Progressions[7]

1. Is this learning progression research based?

   - What does the research (or ours) say about learning this concept or skill?
   - What additional research or data collection might be needed to validate the progression?
   - How can we collect more data using our own action research?

2. What is the "essence" of learning in this progression or strand(s) of the progression?

   - What are the core ideas or the essence of concepts and processes for this content area?
   - Does the thread connect throughout the LP? And across grade levels?
   - Are different conceptual ideas—threads—getting tangled in ways that prohibit really measuring progress made?
   - What is a manageable number of core threads for this content area? (Is this essential learning an enduring understanding or simply a list of related facts/concepts to memorize?)

---

7. LP **TOOL #23** incorporates these guiding questions for reviewing draft progressions and progress indicators.

3. Does the learning progression describe a meaningful *range* of skills or concepts? How does understanding "grow" over time with instruction and learning experiences?

   - Depth? Breadth? Complexity? Generalize or transfer? (Check both the standards and intended DOK levels for increasing complexity across the progression.)
   - Does it describe novice (beginner) to expert (advanced/far transfer)?
   - Is there enough clarity to design or align assessments? (Check both the intended DOK and content standards.)

4. What do our assessment data (e.g., observations, student work samples) tell us?

   - Are there critical gaps in the LP? (Do we need to better describe earlier learning or thinking, something between levels, later levels, important "side trips" on the map, etc.?)
   - Are we getting enough or the right information from our assessments to track progress over time, see learning patterns, or locate where students are along the learning progression?
   - Do we need to modify or expand our use of formative assessment tools? (Are there tools or approaches that will better capture what students are thinking and doing at each progress indicator? Are there tools we can use more than once during the instructional cycle to measure deeper understanding over time?)

Practice examining a learning progression or unit of study (within a learning progression) using the guiding questions above (or LP **TOOL #23**). *Discuss how you might refine the progression or unit of study or create targeted assessments along the progression (e.g., adding a preassessment for assessing prefoundational skills, a midassessment performance of a task less complex than the postassessment or with more scaffolding than the postassessment).*

Considering refinements to learning progressions

Clarifying core concepts and "Big Ideas" in the (draft) LPs

- Are the MAJOR core concepts linked with the "Big Ideas" of this discipline? Remember that topics are not "Big Ideas" or concepts. Lists of facts are not core concepts. *Focus on the conceptual understanding that underlies the topics taught and why you teach them* (e.g., We teach counting and number sense so that students can reason abstractly using numbers).

- Consider whether progress indicators along the continuum are somewhat arbitrary. Have you simply made a best guess about what learning might be "halfway" between two grade-level benchmarks? (e.g., Do most students learn half of what they need to know about visual and numeric patterns simultaneously or do they need to master concepts using visual patterns before they transfer or generalize those ideas to understanding numeric patterns?) Formative assessment data and student work analysis **TOOL #12** will help to answer these questions.

- Check the coherence and range (from foundational to extending) of the core ideas or unifying threads.

Refining wording in progress indicators

- Is language clear enough for <u>identifying learning targets and designing formative assessments</u> that elicit differences (meaning a range of possibilities) of responses related to the same unifying thread?

- Is language clear enough for distinguishing "steps" along the learning continuum? For example, if a learning goal is about "making observations," a continuum of research-based progress indicators might include the following progression for most students:

- Distinguishes differences in physical characteristics
- Identifies similarities in physical characteristics
- Identifies both differences and similarities in physical characteristics
- Categorizes objects and materials by physical characteristics
- Explains why things belong to a specific group
- Distinguishes relevant differences from nonrelevant differences when trying to answer a specific question

Matching grain size of progress indicators to purpose

The grain size of progress indicators should match the purpose of the LP.

- Larger grain-size descriptors could be used across grades for program purposes or creating benchmark assessments.
- Descriptors used for within-grade monitoring might be of a finer grain size or are larger ones that can be unpacked for instruction and formative assessment development by zooming in on progress indicators.
- Very small grain-sized progress indicators are more narrow in scope and best for diagnostic testing.

4.6 Providing System Coherence: Using Learning Progressions for Instructional and Assessment Planning

In the past few years, I've been fortunate to have been involved with several interesting projects that applied a learning progressions mindset to improving teaching and learning for deeper understanding. In this last section, I'll share some of the highlights about what I've developed or learned about how learning progressions can enhance coherence in

- Unit or Lesson Planning and Progress Monitoring
- Developing Pre-, Mid-, and Postassessments
- Learning Progressions and Proficiency-Based Systems

First a Little Background About the Learning Progressions Frameworks (LPFs)

The short case study examples I'll be sharing in this section of the module used the LPF for mathematics or ELA to inform their work. While the LPF content was not simply adopted outright, having the LPF available made development of local tools and processes much easier than it would have been without it. I have found the planning tools in this module to be useful with any learning progression or trajectory that is of a larger grain size, such as those designed for curricular planning and performance assessment development.

To better understand the LPF documents, this is a brief history of how they were developed.

In 2010, as the *Common Core State Standards* were simultaneously being developed, I was charged to recruit researchers, content experts, and master teachers from both general and special education from across the United States to review research about how learning typically develops in mathematics, ELA, and science for all student populations. Three separate committees[8] worked on this project during 2010 in each content area—mathematics, language arts, and science. Committee members represented seventeen different states, eight colleges and universities, and seven state or national educational organizations. Their task was to review and synthesize the research literature about learning in the content

---

8. While there was a science committee working in parallel with the math and ELA groups, the science LPF document has not been shared widely, in part due to the timing with the release of the NGSS.

View a NCSC training video to learn how the LPF was used in the design of many state alternate assessments (2013) at https://www.youtube.com/watch?v=ss8fE1dBkE4&t=24s.

domain and collaboratively draft the conceptual learning progressions frameworks. This work began with the identification of enduring understandings (Wiggins & McTighe, 2005, 2012) for each content area and essential learning targets for the elementary (K–4), middle (5–8), and high school (9–12) grade spans. Later we broke down the grade spans further to K–2, 3–4, 5–6, 7–8, and 9–12. Grade spans, rather than grade levels, were chosen for a very good reason: Rarely did we ever come across a research study that specified learning at a particular grade level. Conversely, we found many studies that referenced such benchmarks as these: by the end of Grade 2, upper elementary grades, by the end of middle school, for example. A second very practical reason that we used grade spans is that we knew from personal experience that in any classroom and grade level, there is a range of learners at various developmental stages. It's our job to locate where they are on the progression and move their learning forward.

Once a framework had been established, committee tasks were to then (1) zoom in and break down specific targeted sections of the draft LPFs into what we called more detailed "mini progressions" for a smaller grade span, often adding some additional "interim steps" (progress indicators) to the mini progressions; (2) use the more detailed and focused mini progressions to design sample instructional modules (with a series of four to six detailed lessons) illustrating how a teacher in the general education classroom might move students along this smaller grain-sized learning progression using best practices in instruction; and (3) draw from best practices in instruction for students with significant cognitive disabilities to incorporate suggestions to each lesson plan for how to make the academic content more accessible for all students.

The final stage of development involved mapping progress indicators "back" to the *Common Core State Standards*. In most cases, we found that only parts of standards aligned to particular progress indicators. This was generally interpreted as "teach this part of the standard before that part of the standard," guidance that might be useful to most teachers. We also discovered that some learning stages uncovered by research were not included in any standard (e.g., acquiring a range of reading strategies for different text types). We chose to include them, even if not aligned, as they were indicators of important learning along the progressions.

Three Case Studies Applying Learning Progressions

LP Case Study #1: Unit/lesson planning and progress monitoring in Connecticut

I've worked on several projects that drew from the strands and progress indicators of the LPF to design units of study and develop assessments to monitor progress across the school year. I've found that the LPF can be overwhelming to teachers at first because of its comprehensiveness; so zooming in to focus on only one strand (and one grade span) at a time is much more useful and manageable as a starting point. One such project involved teams from several Connecticut schools that agreed to focus on Strand 7 of the LPF to develop a deeper understanding of how students develop expertise in opinion/argument/critique writing across K–12. The yearlong project was coordinated by Donna Drasch and Helen Weingart, literacy consultants at EASTCONN, a regional educational service center providing support to Connecticut schools.

School teams participated in a variety of workshop activities to develop a better understanding of the schema of this writing genre, such as sorting examples, grouping them as opinions, arguments, or "UGs" (unsubstantiated generalizations). They also used (and helped me to refine) some of my kid tools, such as "Anatomy of an Opinion/Argument."[9] One of the most helpful introductory activities was when teams at each grade span examined the alignment between LPF progress indicators (PIs) and the *Common Core State Standards* listed with them.

---

9. This kid tool is located in the support materials for Module 3.

Guided practice in getting familiar with the LPF strand looked something like this (see Figure 4.7):

1. *Begin by reading the first PI in the progression* for your grade span. This represents basic or foundational learning that will be built upon. It also might be used to develop a preassessment for the unit.
2. *Highlight key words* in the PI to determine the focus.
3. *Next review the standards or parts of standards* aligned with this PI. Since there are standards from more than one grade level, discuss what you might focus on at each grade level in the grade span, given what is embodied in each aligned standard.

Figure 4.7 Excerpt From the K–12 ELA Learning Progressions Framework, Persuasive Writing—Strand 7[10]

STRAND 7: Writing Persuasively/Communicating Opinions, Critiques, & Arguments (WP)—Different genres of persuasive writing (literary critiques, persuasive essays, speeches, editorials, etc.) are appropriate for different purposes and require use of genre-specific features, text structures, and strategic use of logic chains with compelling supporting evidence to produce a coherent unit of thought that persuades the intended audience.

(K–4) Elementary School Learning Targets

E.WP Apply organizational strategies (e.g., description, definition, compare-contrast, cause-effect, proposition-support) and an understanding of topics or texts to develop and support opinions about them for authentic audiences.

Grades K–2	CCSS focus	Possible Instructional Building Blocks & Lessons
Use a process approach to develop and communicate support for opinions . . . **E.WP.a** generating ideas about a topic, text, or stimulus shared (event, photo, video, peers, etc.) using a range of responses (e.g., discussion, dictation, drawing, letters/invented spelling, writing) K.W-1, 7; K.SL-4, 5; K.L-6 1.W-7, 8; 1.SL-1b, 2, 4, 5; 1.L-6 and 2.W-8; 2.SL-2, 4; 2.L-6 **E.WP.b** with prompting and support, connecting information/facts with personal opinions about a topic or text (e.g., I think it is an informational text because it has facts) using discussion, drawings with details, written words (labels, nouns) or completing statements (e.g., This is what I like about dogs . . . ; That character was funny because . . .) and 'reading back' what they have written K.W-1; K.SL-4, 5; K.L-1f, 6 1.W-1; 1.SL-4, 5, 6; 1.L-1j, 6 and 2.W-1; 2.SL-4, 6; 2.L-1f, 6 **E.WP.c** reading a variety of texts and distinguishing among text genres and their purposes (e.g., stories-entertain, texts that teach or give information, ads—convince you to buy, personal messages/letters—different purposes, include opinions) 1.RL-5 and 2.RI-6 **E.WP.d** with support, using simple note-taking strategies to record and distinguish facts-or opinions or reasons for-against a real-world topic (e.g., T-chart with reasons why people like/do not pizza) 1.W-8 and 2.W-8 **E.WP.e** locating facts to support stated opinions about a topic (e.g., survey peers) or text; collaboratively describing reasons for-against through illustrations, captions, and simple sentences that connect reasons with evidence; applying basic capitalization and end punctuation K.W-1; K.SL-4, 5; K.L-1f, 2, 6 1.W-1; 1.SL-4, 5, 6; 1.L-1j, 2, 6 and 2.W-1; 2.SL-2, 4, 6; 2.L-1f, 2, 6 **E.WP.f** selecting a topic or text of personal interest, finding accurate information about the topic/text, and generating statements (in *somewhat random order*) connecting opinion with reasons and supporting evidence (e.g., I like winter because . . .) K.W-1; K.SL-4, 5; K.L-1f, 2, 6 1.W-1; 1.SL-4, 5, 6; 1.L-1j, 2, 6 and 2.W-1; 2.SL-2, 4, 6; 2.L-1f, 2, 6 **E.WP.g** developing an opinion on a topic/text with statements that connect the stated opinion ("You will think/agree this story is funny . . .") in *several related sentences* with reasons and relevant details/supporting evidence for an authentic audience K.W-1; K.SL-4, 5; K.L-1f, 2, 6	Step 1: Highlight key words in each progress indicator of the learning progressions to get a general sense of how learning can develop with targeted instruction. Step 2: Review related standards for each progress indicator—make notes (in the middle column) about what parts of the CC standards your lessons will focus on. Note that you will likely have more than one unit addressing & assessing these standards during the school year.	Step 3: Identify what your instruction will focus on. We call that Instructional Building Blocks (Lesson learning targets) Step 4: Generate ideas for lessons/learning activities for each PI. This is the beginning of your Unit outline. You may decide to begin your unit part way along the progression if students have already demonstrated learning on the earlier skills in other units. Your pre-assessment will help to determine where to begin instruction.

Source: Hess (2011a).

---

10. A full-size version of this page can be found in Appendix H.

4. *Identify the instructional focus for the unit/lesson. We'll call those Instructional Building Blocks/IBBs (or learning targets). IBBs are not the same as learning activities; learning activities target the IBB content.*

5. *Continue this process with all of the PIs in the strand that will be covered in the unit of study.*

We found this approach to introducing the LPF strand and how to use it to be extremely meaningful for teachers. I recall a high school social studies teacher commenting that before doing this review, he had never really figured out how to integrate the ELA standards into his social studies curriculum, let alone how to decide what to teach first. Another "aha" came from two veteran high school debate team coaches who remarked that while they generally covered much of the content of the PIs at Grades 9 to 12, they also saw some gaps in their teaching and decided to try to integrate them. Since this project was designed as an "action research" project, teachers were asked to design and teach a unit, collecting work samples from their students. The debate teachers' reflections when they saw their students' work was that the overall quality increased dramatically (over what they had seen in prior years) by adding the "missing steps" they saw in the progression.

To make unit and lesson planning less cumbersome for teachers when referencing both the standards and the PIs in the LPF, Donna and Helen suggested embedding all of the standards into the LPF strand planning tools. It ended up being a worthwhile process copying the standards into our new planning template, because we ended up with an effective planning model for all of the LPF strands. Figure 4.8 shows how the "next generation" planning template was designed, this time for single grade levels. This format also helped to clarify the difference between a learning activity (what you plan to have students do in the lesson) and the learning target for the lesson—the Instructional Building Block that frames what they will learn by doing the activity.

Figure 4.8 Unit/Lesson Planning Template Using Strand 7, Persuasive Writing, ELA Learning Progressions Framework

	Learning Progressions aligned with
	**LPF STRAND 7:** <u>Writing Persuasively/Communicating Opinions, Critiques, & Arguments (WP)</u> - Different genres of persuasiv require use of genre-specific features, text structures, and strategic use of logic chains with compelling supporting evidence t
	(5–8) Middle School Lea M.WP Apply organizational strategies (e.g., cause-effect, problem-solution, proposition-support, critique), and use of mult
Use a process approach to develop and communicate support for claims/thesis . . .	**Aligned Common Core State Standards Grades 7-8**
M.WP.i using strategies to better understand genres of persuasive writing (e.g., discuss opposing perspectives; analyze mentor texts – political cartoons, literary critiques, speeches, propaganda techniques) 7.W-7, 8, 9; 7.SL-1d, 2, 3, 4; 7.RI-8	**Grade 7** **Writing** **Research to Build and Present Knowledge** 7. Conduct short research projects to answer a question, drawing on several sources and generating additional related, focused questions for further research and investigation. 8. Gather relevant information from multiple print and digital sources, using search terms effectively; assess the credibility and accuracy of each source; and quote or paraphrase the data and conclusions of others while avoiding plagiarism and following a standard format for citation. 9. Draw evidence from literary or informational texts to support analysis, reflection, and research. **Speaking and Listening** **Comprehension and Collaboration** 1. Engage effectively in a range of collaborative discussions (one-on-one, in groups, and teacher-led) with diverse partners on *grade 7 to pics, texts, and issues*, building on others' ideas and expressing their own clearly. d. Acknowledge new information expressed by others and, when warranted, modify their own views. 2. Analyze the main ideas and supporting details presented in diverse media and formats (e.g., visually, quantitatively, orally), and explain how the ideas clarify a topic, text or issue under study. 3. Delineate a speaker's argument and specific claims, evaluating the soundness of the reasoning and the relevance and sufficiency of the evidence. **Presentation of Knowledge and Ideas** 4. Present claims and findings, emphasizing salient points in a focused, coherent manner with pertinent descriptions, facts, details, and examples: use appropriate eye contact, adequate volume, and clear pronunciation. **Reading for Informational Text** **Integration of Knowledge and Ideas** 8. Trace and evaluate the argument and specific claims in a text, assessing whether the reasoning is sound and the evidence is relevant and sufficient to support the claims.
M.WP.j using varied (credible) sources and locating relevant evidence to analyze factual and contextual information on a topic or text to better understand possible perspectives/points of view 7.W-7, 8, 9; 7.SL-3; 7.RI-7, 8, 9	**Grade 7** **Writing** **Research to Build and Present Knowledge** 7. Conduct short research projects to answer a question, drawing on several sources and generating additional related, focused questions for further research and investigation. 8. Gather relevant information from multiple print and digital sources, using search terms effectively; assess the credibility and accuracy of each source; and quote or paraphrase the data and conclusions of others while avoiding plagiarism and following a standard format for citation. 9. Draw evidence from literary or informational texts to support analysis, reflection, and research. **Speaking and Listening** **Comprehension and Collaboration** 3. Delineate a speaker's argument and specific claims, evaluating the soundness of the reasoning and the relevance and sufficiency of the evidence. **Reading for Informational Text** **Integration of Knowledge and Ideas** 7. Compare and contrast a text to an audio, video, or multimedia version of the text, analyzing each medium's portrayal of the subject (e.g., how the delivery of a speech affects the impact of the words). 8. Trace and evaluate the argument and specific claims in a text, assessing whether the reasoning is sound and the evidence is relevant and sufficient to support the claims. 9. Analyze how two or more authors writing about the same topic shape their presentation of key information by emphasizing different evidence or advancing different interpretations of facts.
M.WP.k establishing a	Grade 7

Source: Hess (2014).

LP Case Study #2: Unit/lesson planning with pre-, mid-, postassessments

Assessment projects in several states made it clear to me that we need to rethink our approach to pre- and posttesting. As discussed in earlier modules, the concept of pre- and postassessments testing unidimensional, identical content (e.g., spelling words, math facts, vocabulary definitions) makes perfect sense. Trying that approach with multidimensional robust performance assessments does not work as well. When a preassessment yields little or no information about student learning or when students can do everything well in the preassessment, its value for monitoring progress is lost. Findings from research projects in Hawai'i (Hess, Kurizaki, & Holt, 2009; Hess, 2011b) and my work with N.Y.C. public schools confirmed that a better approach might be to

> **Suggested Resource**
>
> Sample planning tools for all grade spans for LPF Strand 7, Opinion and Argument Writing, can be downloaded at www.karin-hess.com/free-resources.

- Design a **preassessment of foundational/prerequisite skills** that are essential to build upon. The key is that the unifying idea will be built from earlier skills in the progression of learning.

- Analyze student work from the preassessment to determine what gaps, if any, need to be addressed through targeted instruction. Teach a few lessons moving to more complex content.

- Design a *mid-assessment that is more complex than the preassessment*, but may have more scaffolding than the final postassessment. The key is that the unifying idea is central to all of these assessments, and skills and concepts are being integrated to demonstrate deeper learning (near transfer).

- Analyze results of the mid-assessment to determine if students are ready to move on, without support.

- Design a *postassessment that is complex*, has little or no scaffolding, and integrates essential skills and core concepts with the unifying thread (far transfer).

Discuss the examples (included in Module 4 Support Materials) of a pre- and mid-assessment of opinion writing (Grade 3) and analyze them for how they "progress" in complexity. We first piloted the "Investigating Sharks" task in N.Y.C. schools as a preassessment and found that it was too difficult for most third graders at the beginning of the unit. Many students did not yet understand the difference between informational and opinion writing. (They did not have a schema for opinion writing.) Later in several Connecticut schools, we used the "Favorite Holiday" prompt as a (less complex) preassessment for a similar unit and got much better results when the "Investigating Sharks" task was given later in the unit, as a mid-assessment after some instruction. Actual results from the student work analysis for the "Investigating Sharks" task (using PLC **TOOL #12**) *are illustrated in Module 3.*

As you examine the two tasks, think about how you'd answer these questions:

1. *What core concepts and skills are being assessed in both assessments?* (framing and supporting opinions with evidence)

2. *How is the preassessment less complex than the mid-assessment?* (Evidence is required, but it is personal evidence so there is not any added reading load; this determines if students have the foundation or know how to state and support an opinion.)

3. *What scaffolding is provided in each assessment?* (Reading is added to the mid-assessment, but reading load is reduced due to using fact lists, rather than full texts being read; reminders and graphic organizers are provided in both.)

4. *What should or could the postassessment look like or assess?* (It might be expected that full texts be read and presented with fewer supports, such as graphic organizers. Paired texts of differing complexity might be used. It still assesses framing and supporting an opinion, looking for more elaboration and analysis of text-based examples.)

These questions can also be used to frame a review of other pre-, mid-, or postassessments used to monitor progress.

A second protocol for unit and assessment planning

A second protocol used in N.Y.C. schools to develop common progress-monitoring performance assessments was a bit more streamlined than the one used in the first case study. The primary difference with this protocol is that the summative (post) assessment is determined early in the planning process, using the PIs of the Learning Progressions Framework. This process works well with LP **TOOL #25**, which starts by connecting the learning goal of the unit to the summative assessment, and then begins to identify learning targets for lessons in the unit and ways to formatively assess them. Figure 4.9 shows a strand of the LPF with some guiding questions for unit planning. Answers to these questions (e.g., learning targets or assessments) can be transferred to LP **TOOL #25**. Having the steps next to the strand helps teachers to focus their collaborative discussions.

Figure 4.9 Using the Learning Progressions Frameworks to Plan Units of Study

STRAND 6: Writing Informative Texts/Communicating Information (WI)—Different genres of expository text provide information/explanations (science procedures, content-based articles, biographies, research reports, historical documents, etc.) for different purposes and require use of genre-specific features, text structures, and supporting evidence to produce a coherent unit of thought that informs or educates the intended audience.

(K–4) Elementary School Learning Targets

E.WI By the end of grade 4, students can . . . apply organizational strategies (e.g., sequence, description, definition, compare-contrast, cause-effect) to develop, summarize, and communicate factual information about topics and events for authentic audiences.

Grades K–2	Grades 3–4
Students use a process approach to compose informational texts . . .	Students use a process approach to compose informational texts . . .
E.WI.a generating ideas for using a range of responses (e.g., discussion, dictation, drawing, letters/invented spelling, writing), when responding to a topic, text, or stimulus (event, photo, video, peers, etc.)	E.WI.j generating their own ideas for writing; using strategies to clarify writing (e.g., conference with peers, find words for stronger descriptions)
E.WI.b describing information about a topic or text using drawings with details, written words (labels, names), and fact statements (e.g., "Spiders make webs") and 'reading back' what they have written	E.WI.k locating information from at least two reference sources (print/nonprint) to obtain information on a topic (e.g., sports); listing sources 3.W-7, 8; 3.SL-2; 3.RI- 5, 7, 9 4.W-7, 8, 9; 4.SL-2; 4.RI-1, 7, 9
E.WI.c representing facts and descriptions through a combination of illustrations, captions, and simple sentences that often connect two clauses; applying basic capitalization and end punctuation	E.WI.l using note-taking and organizational strategies (e.g., graphic organizers, notes, labeling, listing) to record and meaningfully organize information (e.g., showing sequence, compare/contrast, cause/effect, question/answer) relating topic/subtopics to evidence, facts
E.WI.d with support, using various information retrieval sources (e.g., word wall, book talks, visuals/images, Internet) to obtain facts and compose information on a topic	E.WI.m writing an introduction of several sentences that sets the context and states a focus/controlling idea about a topic/subtopics (e.g., "Many sports can be played outside in winter.")
E.WI.e with support, using simple note-taking strategies to record and group facts (e.g., numbering, T-chart, graphic organizer) to plan writing	E.WI.n selecting *relevant* facts, details, or examples to support the controlling idea, including use of domain-specific vocabulary
E.WI.f selecting *and ordering* fact statements, using domain-specific vocabulary to describe a sequence of events or explain a procedure (e.g., list necessary materials and tell steps in logical order)	E.WI.o presenting factual information about subtopics of larger topics, grouping relevant details using several related and varied sentence types
E.WI.g presenting factual information describing subtopics of larger topics using sentences in *somewhat random order* (listing fact statements rather than connecting or relating ideas)	E.WI.p incorporating text features (e.g., numbers, labels, diagrams, charts, graphics) to enhance clarity and meaning of informational writing
E.WI.h organizing factual information about subtopics of larger topics using relevant details in *several related sentences*	E.WI.q writing a conclusion or concluding statement that links back to the focus
E.WI.i with support, revising by adding concrete details, descriptions, and concluding statement/closure; editing using grade appropriate grammar, usage, spelling (high frequency words), and mechanics	E.WI.r with support, editing informational text for clarity and meaning: grade-appropriate spelling (words that follow patterns/rules), end punctuation and capitalization, variety of sentence types
	E.WI.s revising full texts from the reader's perspective: making judgments about clarity of message, intent of word choice, and overall continuity of text/visual/auditory components

Sample Unit Planning With the LPF

1. **Identify the unit focus**
   - End point/Essential Learning Goals
   - "Big Ideas"/Enduring Understandings?
2. **Review the Progress Indicators in the strand(s) of the progression** (e.g., E.WI.k – locating information)
3. **Review (focus of) related grade level CC standards**
4. **Determine a possible summative assessment**
5. **Look for critical skills and concepts** (prerequisites) needed to be successful at the end of the unit = lesson 1 (preassessment): Are they ready to learn? What do they already know?
6. **Consider possible learning activities for each step**—Instructional Building Blocks = each lesson's focus
7. **Analyze results after the preassessment and refine the Instructional Building Blocks/lesson learning targets**
8. **Select/create *strategic* formative assessments for each lesson**
9. **Build in increasing rigor** (text and/or skills) across the unit
10. **Build in a mid-assessment** (like the summative assessment, but might be less complex or scaffolded)

LP Case Study #3: Learning progressions and proficiency-based systems

In New Hampshire, as with many states, there has been a movement toward implementing competency-based (or proficiency-based) graduation systems. For many years, each New Hampshire school district developed its own graduation competencies for each content area. As you can imagine, they were different—not bad, but different enough that it was difficult to know whether schools had the same high expectations for their students. If a student went from school A to school B, would she or he still be on track for graduation? Were all students across the state getting a comparable education? Were all New Hampshire students expected to produce rigorous work and demonstrate deeper learning? The state decided to develop "model competencies" that districts were not required to use but could do so if they chose to. It was important the competencies be aligned with standards and have an underlying rationale for how to move from foundational to conceptual to deeper learning. Learning progressions offered schools in the state an opportunity to build their competencies around "Big Ideas," essential questions, and a research-based progression of learning.

This work was facilitated by me working with statewide content committees and the LPF research base and PIs in each strand. The result is that New Hampshire now has model competencies based on a learning progressions schema for measuring progress across grades.

You can view the NH Model Competencies in Mathematics, Grade K–8 at https://www.education.nh.gov/innovations/hs_redesign/documents/math-k-8-2016.pdf.

You can view the NH Model Competencies in Mathematics, Grade 9–12 at http://www.education.nh.gov/innovations/hs_redesign/documents/model_math_competencies.pdf.

You can view the NH Model Competencies in Science, Grade K–8 at http://www.education.nh.gov/innovations/hs_redesign/documents/science-k8-competencies.pdf.

You can view the NH Model Competencies in ELA, Grade K–8 at https://www.education.nh.gov/innovations/hs_redesign/documents/english-k-8-2016.pdf.

Since the adoption and posting of the New Hampshire Model competencies, I've begun to provide guidance to school districts in other states that are also interested in developing competency-based graduation systems. While some modifications are always employed to customize local competencies, school teams in other states have found the New Hampshire resources and the LPF extremely useful in building local models, grounded in research and aligned with standards.

4.7 Lessons Learned—Using Learning Progressions to Guide Instruction and Change Assessment Practices

The most extensive work I've done to date gathering evidence about how the use of learning progressions affects professional practice was in a three-year project with teachers in Hawai'i. The purpose of the project was to codevelop and implement K–8 progress maps in ELA and mathematics to guide within-grade-level instruction. These projects are detailed in two papers describing specific goals and protocols used to identify needs and support struggling learners in the general education classroom (Hess, Kurizaki, et al., 2009; Hess, 2012a). One of the most interesting unintended consequences was how teachers found value in adopting a learning progressions mindset to meet the learning needs of *all* learners in their classrooms. What follows is a summary of some of the key findings from those studies and similar projects described in the three case studies. (Teacher feedback comments are in quotation marks in italics.)

When teachers begin with a possible learning pathway in mind, they . . .

- begin to understand what a path to proficiency or "approaching proficiency" might actually look like, and where individual students are along that continuum.
- consider intermediate strategies for instructional scaffolding to get students to the next stage of learning, when they discover new ways to track progress.

  "Now I had a visual organizer of where students were and what I had to do next."

- adjust instruction according to what students CAN do, not what they CANNOT do.

Teachers change how they view and use assessment:

- Preassessments were used as "entry points" to differentiate instruction.
- Preassessments focused on the foundational skills needed to be successful, not on the "end point" of the continuum (the standards).
- Preassessments helped teachers to decide what NOT to teach.

  "Pretests allow me to skip over benchmarks students already know from previous years so I make up time that way. The preassessment is good to find out where they are now."

- Formative assessment data and student work analysis were new ways to flexibly group students for targeted instruction or support.

  "It was a real eye-opener. Some students I thought were proficient were actually below proficiency according to what they could and could not do."

- Use of formative assessment became "strategic" and was used more frequently. Assessments were designed to elicit specific evidence (e.g., level of reasoning).
- Short assessments, such as constructed response questions, worked most effectively because they were designed to "uncover" student thinking.
- Use of smaller, more targeted formative assessments and assessments of *prerequisite skills* at the start of a unit were used to gain more useful information about student background knowledge and the learning process.
- Teacher observations needed to be both ongoing and systematic.

Teachers' perceptions of students and the learning process

- Teachers began to shift perceptions, <u>especially of their lowest-performing students</u> and what to do next to support their learning.
- Many teachers told us that they had been using the grade-level benchmarks for years, but never really understood them in this way (how to get there from here).

  "I never really thought about each individual benchmark and generally taught and assessed many of them at the same time. So I never knew what the next steps might be when they didn't get it."

- Teachers learned that when assessments have greater focus and depth or rigor, assessment data are more useful.

"I don't just touch the surface of the benchmark now, but go more in depth."

- Teachers found they had to know the student better in order to "place them" on a learning continuum—they needed specific formative assessment data and designed assessments accordingly.

Professional practice, collaborations with colleagues, analyzing student work

- Teachers begin to better understand coherence as the alignment of standards, assessment, and instruction and the importance of assessment and scoring tool design being <u>driven by the purpose of an assessment</u>.

- Teachers noted that to be most effective, the work on assessments needs to be collaborative, and leads to new understandings about the importance of quality rubrics, exemplars, and scoring student work together.

- Many noted that they are making scoring rubrics more detailed, more explicit, with clearer language, and including depth of knowledge criteria. They are more conscious of identifying which level is proficient, and of identifying student work (anchor papers) at each performance level.

- There was a new awareness that student work analysis addressed all levels of achievement in terms of next steps for instruction.

"I never thought of sorting papers according to what students were able to do or not do. That really changed my thinking about next steps for instruction."

- Student work analysis uncovered "flaws" in assessments they had been using.

"When we looked at our first results and the assessment we used, we said, 'What were we thinking? This is an awful assessment!'"

- Collaboratively analyzing student work created a deeper understanding of how learning develops over time.

Involving students in understanding their own progress

- In some classrooms, students use progress maps for reflection and goal setting before and after testing—this change is a result of having specific information about performance and what the learning pathway looks like.

- Some teachers are using progress maps for student-led conferences and work sample collections for portfolios.

- Some teachers are including students more in designing and evaluating assessment tasks and products. They are designing rubrics and looking at student work with students.

- Some districts that have used cognitive labs or think-alouds[11] with students to design and refine new performance assessments also began to use the cognitive lab process as a formative assessment strategy in classrooms.

---

11. Module 3 includes a detailed description of how to implement a cognitive labs strategy.

Implications for Teacher Evaluation

Knowing what I know now about the power of having a learning progressions mindset, these are some questions I use when conferencing with teachers and grade-level teams:

- What is your sense of what the students know and understand at this point in the learning process (e.g., about this content)?

- What examples of student work (evidence) tells you this?

- Did you do anything specific to support your (struggling or advanced) learners during the lesson?

- What have you learned (about your instruction, your assessments, the learning process, etc.) from meeting with colleagues to discuss and analyze student work?

Of course, you could simply ask colleagues the three questions that I always ask students:

What are you doing?

Why are you doing it?

What are you learning?

4.8 Looking for Increasing Rigor—by Observing Shifts in Teacher and Student Roles

When I work with school leadership teams to analyze and refine their instructional and assessment practices, thoughts soon turn to ways that administrators and instructional coaches can support both teachers and students in the classroom. In this final segment of Module 4, we'll revisit some of the key ideas introduced earlier from the perspective of "How can I support and build a progression of deeper understanding in every classroom?" I think three things are central to providing support from a coaching perspective:

1. Understanding how the brain works and how memory and learning can be optimized

2. Clarifying what to look for and promote that indicate rigor and deeper thinking "in real time"

3. Having examples that match various instructional and assessment purposes linked with indicators of rigor

Keeping the focus of assessment on learning and deeper understanding for *all* students means that teachers must be willing to shift their role as the person who delivers instruction. In turn, this will shift the role of their students from acquiring information to producing knowledge.

When schools began to use my Cognitive Rigor Matrices (CRMs), I began to get questions about how to use the CRM for walk-throughs or as a tool for classroom observations and conferencing. To be honest, the CRM has so much information in it that while it is excellent for examining the variety of tasks that teachers develop for their students, it's a bit too busy for capturing nuanced observations made in the moment (unless, of course, you have most of it committed to memory as I do). One indicator of rigorous classrooms is the types of tasks teachers assign to their students; however, there is more to look for when you're looking for rigor in all the "right" places.

As a result of numerous inquiries from school administrators, I've experimented with developing user-friendly walk-through tools designed to capture the essence of deeper thinking while it's happening. Over the years, I've found that these tools can be "nested" in larger coaching and teacher evaluation systems (e.g., Danielson, 2013) to better clarify terms used in evaluation rubrics such as rigor, higher-order or quality of questions, knowledge of the learning process, and teacher interactions with students.

In Module 1, I introduced the idea that when the teacher shifts role, from the person who delivers and guides instruction to the person who gives more responsibility to students for their own learning, the result is that students have to shift their role and become more active in the learning process. Moving from DOK 1 and 2 questioning and tasks to DOK 3 and 4 questioning and tasks is a major shift and something I have found to be very easy to observe when you pay attention to teacher–student roles during the learning process. All DOK levels are important to the larger picture of supporting learning, so having a tool that allows the observer or the teacher to document how students react to particular tasks and supports at any given time can be useful for reflection.

My first version of Walk-Through **TOOL #26** (Hess, 2013a) included sample tasks for each DOK level which helped teachers and administrators to distinguish when students might be expected to apply foundational or conceptual thinking or when tasks required far transfer and deeper understanding. The descriptions of sample tasks came directly from the CRM **TOOLS #1, #2, #3, and #4** and were instructive in illustrating the following:

- what each DOK level could look like in terms of various assignments, not simply individual test questions;
- how the purpose of teacher questions shifts from a narrow focus to a more open-ended focus when moving from DOK 1 to DOK 4;
- how the scaffolding also shifts strategically when supporting learners at each level of thinking and engagement;
- how student questions also shift, to reveal their ability to take more control of their own learning; and
- a gentle "reality check" that what many educators were calling rigor was really just work that was more difficult, but did not really go very deep into the content.

That earlier walk-through tool is shown in Figure 4.10.

Figure 4.10 Shifting Teacher-Student Roles

SHIFTING ROLES: MOVING FROM TEACHER-DIRECTED TO STUDENT-DIRECTED LEARNING

DOK LEVELS	TEACHER ROLES ←	STUDENT ROLES →	SAMPLE LEARNING AND ASSESSMENT TASKS
1 Acquire Foundation	• Questions to focus attention (Who? What? Where? How? When?) • Directs, leads, demonstrates, defines, provides practice • Scaffolds for access and focus	• Acquires vocabulary, facts, rules • Memorizes, recites, quotes, restates • Retrieves information • Practices and self-monitors basic skills • Clarifies procedures, asks for support using resources, tools	– Reads orally, reads fluently – Draws/labels/acts to illustrate an event, parts of the whole, phases in a cycle – Writes a variety of sentences – Represents math/fine arts relationships with words, symbols, objects, visuals – Recalls math facts, terms, dates, formulas, rules – Calculates, measures, follows steps – Uses tools, records data – Reads or reproduces maps, diagrams – Highlights key words
2 Use, Connect, Conceptualize	• Questions to build schema: differentiate parts-whole, classify, draw out inferences • Models and scaffolds conceptual understanding (Why? Under what conditions? Gives example/ nonexample?)	• Explains relationships, sorts, classifies, compares, organizes information • Makes predictions based on estimates, observations, prior knowledge • Proposes problems, issues, or questions to be investigated • Raises conceptual or strategy questions	– Solves routine, multistep math word problems – Makes science observations, organizes data (graph, table, spreadsheet, etc.) – Writes a caption, paragraph, summary – Creates a timeline of events – Makes and uses models – Interprets simple graphics, tables, etc. – Retrieves information and uses it to answer a question or solve a problem – Creates survey to research a topic

SHIFTING ROLES: MOVING FROM TEACHER-DIRECTED TO STUDENT-DIRECTED LEARNING

DOK LEVELS	TEACHER ROLES ←	STUDENT ROLES →	SAMPLE LEARNING AND ASSESSMENT TASKS
3 Deepen and Construct Meaning	• Questions to probe reasoning and thinking, and to promote peer discourse/self-reflection; links "Big Ideas" (*How will you know/do this? Where is the evidence?*) • Designs tasks requiring proof, justification, analysis of evidence quality and accuracy	• Uncovers relevant, accurate, credible information, flaws in a design, or proposed solution and links with "Big Ideas" • Plans how to develop supporting (hard) evidence for conclusions or claims • Researches or tests ideas, solves nonroutine problems; perseveres • Self-assesses; uses feedback to improve	– Interprets complex graphics, tables – Sets up a database – Conducts a designed investigation – Develops both sides of a fact-based argument for debate or speech – Creates a website, podcast, multimedia presentation matched to purpose – Critiques an essay, performance, or novel, using discipline-based criteria – Analyzes theme, perspective, author's craft in a piece of work
4 Extend, Transfer, Broaden Meaning	• Questions to extend thinking, explore sources, broaden perspectives/"Big Ideas" (*Are there potential biases? Can you propose an alternative model?*) • Encourages and scaffolds use of relevant and valid resources, peer-to-peer discourse, and self-reflection	• Initiates, transfers, and *constructs* new knowledge or insights linked to "Big Ideas" • Modifies, creates, elaborates based on analysis and interpretation of multiple sources • Investigates real-world problems and issues; perseveres; manages time–task • Self-assesses; uses feedback to improve	– Produces a short film, play, or short story based on a theme, issue, style – Designs own research or investigation as an extension of concepts or issues studied – Critiques importance of policies or events from different perspectives (e.g., historical, social, economic, cultural) – Analyzes theme, perspectives, authors' craft across multiple pieces of work or time periods

Figure 4.11 Tool 26: Looking for Rigor

	LOOKING FOR RIGOR WALK-THROUGH TOOL: TEACHER-STUDENT ROLES			
DOK Levels	**Teacher Roles**	**Evidence Planned for or Observed**	**Student Roles**	**Evidence Planned for or Observed**
1 Acquire Foundation	○ Questions to focus attention *(Who? What? Where? How? When?)* ○ Directs, leads, demonstrates, defines, provides practice ○ Scaffolds for access and focus		○ Acquires vocabulary, facts, rules ○ Memorizes, recites, quotes, restates ○ Retrieves information ○ Practices and self-monitors basic skills ○ Clarifies procedures, asks for support using resources, tools	
2 Use, Connect, Conceptualize	○ Questions to build schema: differentiate parts from whole, classify, draw out inferences ○ Models and scaffolds conceptual understanding *(Why? Under what conditions? Gives example or nonexample?)*		○ Explains relationships, sorts, classifies, compares, organizes information ○ Makes predictions based on estimates, observations, prior knowledge ○ Proposes problems or issues or questions to be investigated ○ Raises conceptual or strategy questions	
3 Deepen & Construct Meaning	○ Questions to probe reasoning, thinking, and promote peer discourse or self-reflection; links "Big Ideas" *(How will you know or do this? Where is the evidence?)* ○ Designs tasks requiring proof, justification, analysis of evidence quality and accuracy		○ Uncovers relevant, accurate, credible information, flaws in a design, or proposed solution and links with "Big Ideas" ○ Plans how to develop supporting (hard) evidence for conclusions or claims ○ Researches or tests ideas, solves nonroutine problems; perseveres ○ Self-assesses; uses feedback to improve	

To use the descriptions of teacher–student roles as a walk-through tool for coaches or administrators, and to make it easy to capture observable evidence in real time, the final version of **TOOL #26** provides room for note taking (as seen in Figure 4.11). I cannot stress enough that a simple checklist is not useful to the person observed or to the observer. Supporting evidence of actual student questions or descriptions of a specific scaffolding strategy used by the teacher is what will promote reflection on practice. For example, high school science teachers in Springdale, Arkansas, found this tool to be useful in planning the flow of a lesson when using case study analyses with their students. Teachers identified several key questions they planned to use and how they expected students to work through the case when given different assignments as they moved from basic to deeper understanding (e.g., annotating the case study's key aspects).

4.9 Suggested Ways to Get Started
Using the "Looking for Rigor" Walk-Through Tool #26

The "Looking for Rigor" Walk-Through Tool creates a focus for structured conversations and reflections on practice. Observational descriptors are research-based indicators of deeper thinking and student engagement with a range of cognitively demanding tasks. **TOOL #26** is generally aligned with the DOK levels in the Hess Cognitive Rigor Matrices and designed to examine learning "in the moment" as it happens with students. This tool can be used to collect baseline data for current practice or to monitor "shifts" in practice over time. I suggest that you do not try to look for everything, but instead focus on specific aspects as you begin to document observations. Indicators in the walk-through tool are somewhat unique in that student roles as questioner, investigator, and self-evaluator are included as essential elements in documenting effective instructional practice. These descriptors of student behavior at different DOK levels are implied in the Hess CRMs examples, but not explicitly stated.

To introduce and provide practice using **TOOL #26**, I like to select and use short video clips from lessons that we can analyze and discuss together. Participants work in pairs—one looks at what students are doing and the other pays close attention to what the teacher is doing. Often when we watch the video several times, we begin to notice things we did not see the first time. Many of the suggested video segments included in the *Local Assessment Toolkit* are especially useful in calibrating how we look for shifting roles of teachers and students over time.

Begin by choosing a focus for your observational walk-throughs—here are a few ideas:

- Focus on teacher and student roles. Document WHAT students or teachers are doing (e.g., How does the teacher prompt certain responses? How do students respond? Are any strategic scaffolding strategies used by the teacher to engage all learners?)

- Identify or look for one or two specific teacher behaviors for engaging students in rigorous instruction, perhaps something teachers have been working on improving upon. Tools from earlier modules can be useful in analyzing the complexity and cognitive demand of assignments. Be sure to get a copy of instructions or tasks given to students during the lesson. Here are some teacher roles to make note of during your walk-though time:

    o Designing complex tasks

    o Using strategic scaffolding

    o Encouraging student discourse, peer or self-assessment or reflection (every 12–15 minutes)

    o Ability to use questioning to probe for deeper understanding. Don't forget to listen to the follow-up or second question teachers ask when student responses are too vague or superficial.

Reflections

On your own or with colleagues, take a minute to reflect on the topics covered in this module. Then identify a useful takeaway, something to try or apply.

Ways I am refining my thinking about what makes something a "progression" of learning, ...

- ?
-

Strategies for designing formative, interim, and summative assessments using learning progressions ...

- Use common misconceptions or stumbling blocks to create formative assessment probes
- ?

R My personal prescription for applying the concept of learning progressions to my instruction or assessment practices ...

Part 2: Support Materials for Module 4

I. A Workshop Plan for Module 4

Kolb's Experiential Learning Cycle　　　　　　**Suggested Activities**

Stage 1: WHY is this new learning important to me? And what do I already know?

Moving from Concrete Experience to Reflective Observation

Create a concrete experience, asking participants to make connections, drawing on personal knowledge and experience. Small groups compare and reflect on common ideas.

- Activity: Individually complete an anticipation guide with some common (true/false) statements about what learning progressions (LPs) are and how they can be used by teachers and students. Revisit these initial ideas throughout the workshop.

- Begin to build an understanding of LPs, by viewing a video of teachers in Hawai'i discussing how they use "progress maps" (another name for LPs). Discussion questions: What did you notice? What do you wonder about? Connect responses to some working definitions of LPs in Stage 2.

Stage 2: WHAT do the research and experts say?

Moving from Reflective Observation to Abstract Conceptualization

Help participants connect their personal reflections to broader, more abstract generalizations and research on characteristics of research-based learning progressions.

- Provide expert advice or research via interactive lecture, short readings: share several "working definitions" of learning progressions/learning trajectories. Use "A Horse Story" to deepen understanding of how progressions look at the novice versus expert ends of a learning continuum.

- Discuss what different definitions have in common (4 Interrelated Guiding Principles). Stop frequently (every 15–20 minutes) to consolidate the new learning.

- Review Activities: How can the "nested dolls" be a metaphor for a learning progression? Revisit understanding of statements in the anticipation guide. Discus new clarifications about LPs.

- Activity: Examine different content-based examples with some missing parts (unifying threads or correct order of progress indicators). Discuss what the parts could be.

(Continued)

(Continued)

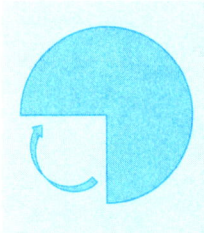

Stage 3: HOW does this work? How can I apply this?

Moving from Abstract Conceptualization to Active Experimentation

Use tools and protocols to examine assessment examples and strategies.

- Explore various ways to use LPs—Zooming In versus Zooming Out. Discuss uses and benefits of changing focus. (Appendices E, F, and G have concrete examples.)
- Introduce LP **TOOL #23** which applies the 4 Guiding Principles of LPs. Provide guided practice using LP **TOOL #23** to examine a sample LP or unit of study.
- Activity: Model using LP **TOOL #22** with student work samples or your own performance tasks.
- Activity: Model using LP **TOOL #24 or #25** to plan or unpack a unit of study and its assessments.

Stage 4: WHAT IF I experimented with this? What might work in my classroom or school?

Moving from Active Experimentation back to Concrete Experiences

- Activity: Revisit current assessments used within your curriculum or units of study. Use the LP **TOOLS #23, #24, or #25** to analyze potential gaps and refinements to units and assessments.
- Implement a series of pre-, mid-, and postperformance assessments for a unit of study. Collect samples of student work and analyze them using PLC **TOOL #12** and LP **TOOL #22**. Develop descriptions of a "mini" progression using student work and effective instructional supports at each stage in the mini progression.

Source: Stages adapted from Kolb (1984) and McCarthy (1987).

II. The Hess LP Tools

About the Tools in this Module

The tools in Module 4 have been used by instructional coaches and school leadership teams to align formative assessments within units of study to lesson learning targets (Instructional Building Blocks) and to unpack and better understand existing learning progressions. The tools are often used in conjunction with PLC **TOOLS #9, #10, and #11** (Module 3) for designing high-quality assessments. Most common uses for these LP tools include

- developing and refining pre- and mid-assessments;
- designing rubrics using LP language to describe *how* learning develops over time, rather than what students are not doing;
- analyzing the effectiveness of existing assessments or instructional strategies within units of study;
- validating a draft or an existing learning progression; and
- promoting collaboration and shared understanding of how learning actually develops and progress monitoring using learning progressions.

Table 4.2 Overview of the Hess LP Tools

TOOL	POSSIBLE USES FOR EACH HESS LP TOOL
22 Analyzing Learner Characteristics or Student Work Samples Along a Progression	Use this tool both to examine the characteristics of learners as they move along a learning continuum and to document the effectiveness of instructional supports at different stages of learning.
23 Guiding Questions for Developing, Refining, or Validating Learning Progressions	Use to review or revise draft learning progressions.
24 Planning Instruction Using a Learning Progressions Mindset	Use to unpack a learning progression or to analyze existing units of study along a progression.
25 Unit Planning Template: Using Learning Progression to Guide Formative, Interim, or Summative Assessment	Use to plan for or analyze assessments within units of study. A completed example of **TOOL #25** is also included.
26 Looking for Rigor: Shifting Teacher-Student Roles	Use for lesson planning or to provide a lesson overview of what a peer or instructional coaching tool will collect data and give feedback on. Use to collect baseline data, to look for trends over time, or to provide feedback and support to teachers.

ANALYZING LEARNER CHARACTERISTICS/STUDENT WORK SAMPLES ALONG A PROGRESSION

Tool 22

Teacher _____ Grade level _____ Date _____

Lesson/Unit/Assessment Task _____

Primary Learning Objective _____

For the purpose of better understanding how students demonstrate progress while moving through the activities you've designed, try to describe students you have "placed" in each general grouping along the learning continuum. To complete the table on the following page, think about how you would answer the three questions below for students who you have identified in each of these five general groupings:

Advanced—Students demonstrate additional depth, breadth, or creativity, for example

Proficient—Students successfully integrate multiple skills, solve complex problems

Just Below Proficient—Students lack some key skills, but are close to "proficient"

Somewhere in between Just Below and Emergent—Students demonstrate that they are building on foundational skills and beginning to combine skills or concepts

Emergent/Just Beginning—Students demonstrate foundational skills in isolation or with support

You may want to use PLC Tool #12 to analyze student work in conjunction with this tool to develop a learning progression for a specific assessment task or learning objective.

1. Describe the "typical" learning characteristics of students in each grouping. How would you typically describe them—when they read, write, or do mathematics, for example?

2. What tend to be the greatest challenges for students in each grouping? What do you anticipate they will struggle with, based on past experience?

3. What instructional strategies and/or scaffolding seem to best support their engagement and advance their learning?

List the scaffolding or instructional strategies you plan to use for this lesson, unit of study, or assessment task. Then analyze which groups respond best to each approach.

Developing "Typical" Learner Characteristics (What indicators best describe your students while engaging with the learning task or producing a product?)

Try to describe the learning characteristics of students you placed within each general grouping (for this lesson, unit of study, or assessment task).

(Continued)

continued . . .

ANALYZING LEARNER CHARACTERISTICS/STUDENT WORK SAMPLES ALONG A PROGRESSION

Tool 22

List specific instructional supports you've found helpful for any of these groups.

Groupings	Descriptions—What they can do and what seems to challenge them the most (at this point)?	Instructional supports they respond best to
Advanced		
Proficient		
Just Below Proficient		
Somewhere "in between"		
Emergent/Just Beginning		

Available for download at **resources.corwin.com/HessToolkit**

Copyright © 2018 by Corwin. All rights reserved. Reprinted from *A Local Assessment Toolkit to Promote Deeper Learning: Transforming Research into Practice* by Karin Hess. Thousand Oaks, CA: Corwin, www.corwin.com. Reproduction authorized only for the local school site or nonprofit organization that has purchased this book.

GUIDING QUESTIONS FOR DEVELOPING, REFINING, OR VALIDATING LEARNING PROGRESSIONS

Tool 23

I. Is this learning progression research based?
- What does our research say about learning this concept or skill?
- What additional research or data collection might be needed to validate the progression?
- How can we collect more data using our own action research?

Comments/Notes

II. What is the "essence" of learning in this progression or strand(s) of the progression?
- What are the core ideas or the essence of concepts and processes for this content area?
- Does the thread connect throughout the LP? And across grade levels?
- Are different conceptual ideas—threads—getting tangled in ways that prohibit really measuring progress made?
- What is a manageable number of core threads for this content area? (Is this essential learning an enduring understanding or simply a list of related facts or concepts to memorize?)

Comments/Notes

(Continued)

continued...

GUIDING QUESTIONS FOR DEVELOPING, REFINING, OR VALIDATING LEARNING PROGRESSIONS

Tool 23

III. Does the learning progression describe a meaningful *range* of skills or concepts? How does understanding "grow" over time with instruction and learning experiences?

- Depth? Breadth? Complexity? Generalize or Transfer? (check both standards and DOK levels for increasing complexity across the progression)
- Does it describe Novice (Beginner)-to-Expert (Advanced or Far Transfer)?
- Is there enough clarity to design/align assessments? (check intended DOK and standards)

Comments/Notes

IV. What do our assessment data (e.g., observations, student work samples) tell us?

- Are there critical gaps in the LP? (Do we need to better describe earlier learning or thinking, something between levels, later levels, important "side trips" on the map, etc.?)
- Are we getting enough or the right information from our assessments to track progress over time, see learning patterns, or locate where students are along the learning progression?
- Do we need to modify or expand our use of assessment tools? (Are there tools or approaches that will better capture what students are thinking and doing at each progress indicator? Are there tools we can use more than once during the instructional cycle to measure deeper understanding over time?)

Comments/Notes

(Continued)

continued . . .

GUIDING QUESTIONS FOR DEVELOPING, REFINING, OR VALIDATING LEARNING PROGRESSIONS

Tool 23

Ways to Refine Learning Progressions and Progress Indicators—Indicate Revisions Needed

Clarifying core concepts and big ideas in LPs

- Are the MAJOR core concepts linked with the "big ideas" of this discipline? Remember that topics are not big ideas or concepts. Lists of facts are not concepts. *Focus on the conceptual understanding that underlies the topics taught and why you teach them* (e.g., we teach counting and number sense so that students can reason abstractly using numbers).
- Consider whether progress indicators along the continuum are somewhat arbitrary. Have you simply made a best guess about what learning might be "halfway" between two grade level benchmarks? (e.g., do most students learn half of what they need to know about visual and numeric patterns simultaneously or do they need to master concepts using visual patterns before they transfer or generalize those ideas to understanding numeric patterns? Formative assessment data will help to answer these questions.)
- Check the coherence and range (from foundational to extending) of the core ideas or unifying threads.

Refining wording in progress indicators

- Is language clear enough for <u>identifying learning targets and designing formative assessments</u> that elicit differences (meaning a range of possibilities) of responses related to the same unifying thread?
- Is language clear enough for distinguishing "steps" along the learning continuum?

Matching grain size of progress indicators to purpose: <u>The grain size of progress indicators should match the purpose of the LP.</u>

- Larger grain size descriptors could be used across grades for program purposes or creating benchmark assessments.
- Descriptors used for within-grade monitoring might be of a finer grain size or are larger ones that can be unpacked for instruction and formative assessment development by "zooming in" on progress indicators.
- Very small grain-size progress indicators are more narrow in scope and best for diagnostic testing.

Available for download at **resources.corwin.com/HessToolkit**

Copyright © 2018 by Corwin. All rights reserved. Reprinted from *A Local Assessment Toolkit to Promote Deeper Learning: Transforming Research into Practice* by Karin Hess. Thousand Oaks, CA: Corwin, www.corwin.com. Reproduction authorized only for the local school site or nonprofit organization that has purchased this book.

PLANNING INSTRUCTION USING A LEARNING PROGRESSIONS MINDSET

Use this tool to "unpack" a learning progression or to analyze existing units of study.

Tool 24

Unit of Study

Content Area _____ **Grade Level** _____

	Unit Learning Targets Used for Lesson Planning—Key Instructional Building Blocks [Big Ideas, Essential Skills, Core Concepts]	List Unit Assessments
Purpose		
Find each student's starting point for learning List prerequisite knowledge or describe possible emergent skills and understandings		PREASSESS/Prerequisite Knowledge
Guide and scaffold practice Identify subskills that develop conceptual understanding		
Explore and challenge preconceptions Identify ways to build schemas; deepen and broaden conceptual understanding; challenge misconceptions		
Determine proficiency What will "good enough" look like? How will skills, concepts, dispositions be integrated?		POSTASSESS or Summative—Includes Opportunities to Extend Thinking
Transfer to new contexts How might students extend, initiate new learning, demonstrate greater sophistication, challenge		

online resources Available for download at **resources.corwin.com/HessToolkit**

Copyright © 2018 by Corwin. All rights reserved. Reprinted from *A Local Assessment Toolkit to Promote Deeper Learning: Transforming Research into Practice* by Karin Hess. Thousand Oaks, CA: Corwin, www.corwin.com. Reproduction authorized only for the local school site or nonprofit organization that has purchased this book.

MODULE 4
PART 2

UNIT PLANNING TEMPLATE: USING LEARNING PROGRESSIONS TO GUIDE FORMATIVE, INTERIM, OR SUMMATIVE ASSESSMENT

Step 1: Unit
Unit Overview (Learning Objective)

Step 3: Identify Lesson-Based Learning Targets (Instructional Building Blocks Along the Progression)	Step 4: Describe the Prerequisite or Mid-Formative Assessments How will you capture the observable evidence? Will you add scaffolding?	Step 2: Describe the Summative Assessment What's the Observable Evidence and DOK?
	Preassessment	Content (Big Ideas, Core Concepts, and Principles)
		Process or DOK (Essential Skills, Procedures)
		Product(s) or Assessment Task(s)
		Opportunities to Extend Learning?

Unit Resources and Texts

Available for download at **resources.corwin.com/HessToolkit**

Copyright © 2018 by Corwin. All rights reserved. Reprinted from *A Local Assessment Toolkit to Promote Deeper Learning: Transforming Research into Practice* by Karin Hess. Thousand Oaks, CA: Corwin, www.corwin.com. Reproduction authorized only for the ocal school site or nonprofit organization that has purchased this book.

SAMPLE UNIT PLANNING TEMPLATE: USING LEARNING PROGRESSIONS TO GUIDE FORMATIVE, INTERIM, OR SUMMATIVE ASSESSMENT

Tool 25A

Step 1: Unit—Argument Writing: Differentiating Argument Types

Unit Overview (Learning Objective)—Students will use relevant, credible evidence to develop and support arguments on a major topic, issue, or event studied in social studies.

Step 3: Identify Lesson-Based Learning Targets (Key Instructional Building Blocks Along the Progression)	Step 4: Describe the Prerequisite or Mid-Formative Assessments How will you capture the observable evidence? Will you add scaffolding?	Step 2: Describe the Summative Assessment What's the Observable Evidence and DOK?
Build schema—Generate ideas for writing arguments	**Preassessment** Write a personal op-ed piece about . . . (current topic) with use of supporting evidence	**Content (Big Ideas, Concepts, and Principles)** Choose prompt (Topic, Event, Issue) from list provided by teacher or generated by class
Build schema—understand unique features of argument types	Analyze class op-ed arguments by type: fact based, judgement based, and policy based and rhetorical devices used (ethos, logos, pathos)	**Process or DOK (Skills, Procedures)** Gather evidence from at least two sources to support your response; check reliability of sources (DOK 4)
Develop an understanding of a topic or issue—locate evidence; organize information relating to opposing sides of an issue	Gather and organize print and nonprint text evidence about topic or issue in "Multiple Perspectives" graphic organizer Analyze opposing ideas	Select and apply appropriate language and rhetorical devices for intended audience
Choose perspective or develop a claim or thesis—Frame introduction; select relevant evidence (facts, details, quotes, examples, etc.)	Distinguish fact from opinion, relevant from nonrelevant facts; credible sources Mid-assessment Use two short texts to develop opinion with supporting evidence	**Product(s) or Assessment Task(s)** Develop an argument, podcast, or speech responding to prompt and using supporting evidence from (at least) two credible sources
Develop logic chain and elaborate on each criterion: use transitions to connect ideas; link claim to conclusion	Mid-assessment Plan or analyze opinion pieces using graphic organizer (e.g., Hess's Anatomy of an Opinion)	**Opportunities to Extend Learning?** Select two+ sources presenting the same event, issue, or story (historical fiction, news story, biography, etc.) from differing perspectives. Analyze the varying perspectives and source credibility.
Revise and edit for clarity of message, word choice, and so on.	Peers edit and revise opinion pieces	
Unit Resources and Texts		

Available for download at **resources.corwin.com/HessToolkit**

Copyright © 2018 by Corwin. All rights reserved. Reprinted from *A Local Assessment Toolkit to Promote Deeper Learning: Transforming Research into Practice* by Karin Hess. Thousand Oaks, CA: Corwin, www.corwin.com. Reproduction authorized only for the local school site or nonprofit organization that has purchased this book.

LOOKING FOR RIGOR WALK-THROUGH TOOL: TEACHER-STUDENT ROLES

Tool 26

DOK Levels	Teacher Roles	Evidence Planned for or Observed	Student Roles	Evidence Planned for or Observed
1 Acquire Foundation	○ Questions to focus attention (Who? What? Where? How? When?) ○ Directs, leads, demonstrates, defines, provides practice ○ Scaffolds for access and focus		○ Acquires vocabulary, facts, rules ○ Memorizes, recites, quotes, restates ○ Retrieves information ○ Practices and self-monitors basic skills ○ Clarifies procedures, asks for support using resources, tools	
2 Use, Connect, Conceptualize	○ Questions to build schema: differentiate parts from whole, classify, draw out inferences ○ Models and scaffolds conceptual understanding (Why? Under what conditions? Gives example or nonexample?)		○ Explains relationships, sorts, classifies, compares, organizes information ○ Makes predictions based on estimates, observations, prior knowledge ○ Proposes problems or issues or questions to be investigated ○ Raises conceptual or strategy questions	
3 Deepen & Construct Meaning	○ Questions to probe reasoning, thinking, and promote peer discourse or self-reflection; links "Big Ideas" (How will you know or do this? Where is the evidence?) ○ Designs tasks requiring proof, justification, analysis of evidence quality and accuracy		○ Uncovers relevant, accurate, credible information, flaws in a design, or proposed solution and links with "Big Ideas" ○ Plans how to develop supporting (hard) evidence for conclusions or claims ○ Researches or tests ideas, solves nonroutine problems; perseveres ○ Self-assesses; uses feedback to improve	
4 Extend, Transfer, Broaden Meaning	○ Questions to extend thinking, explore sources, broaden perspectives or "Big Ideas" (Are there potential biases? Can you propose an alternative model?) ○ Encourages and scaffolds use of relevant and valid resources, peer-to-peer discourse, or self-reflection		○ Initiates, transfers, and *constructs* new knowledge or insights linked to "Big Ideas" ○ Modifies, creates, elaborates based on analysis and interpretation of multiple sources ○ Investigates real-world problems and issues; perseveres; manages time-task ○ Self-assesses; uses feedback to improve	

Available for download at **resources.corwin.com/HessToolkit**

Copyright © 2018 by Corwin. All rights reserved. Reprinted from *A Local Assessment Toolkit to Promote Deeper Learning: Transforming Research into Practice* by Karin Hess. Thousand Oaks, CA: Corwin, www.corwin.com. Reproduction authorized only for the local school site or nonprofit organization that has purchased this book.

III. Strategies and Tools for Professional Developers and Teacher Planning

Anticipation Guide: What Do I Know or Believe About Learning Progressions?

AGREE (A)? DISAGREE (D)?	READ EACH STATEMENT BELOW. DECIDE IF YOU AGREE OR DISAGREE AND INDICATE IN COLUMN TO THE LEFT.	EXPLAIN WHY YOU AGREE OR DISAGREE. HAVE YOU CHANGED YOUR MIND? WHY/WHY NOT?
	1. Learning progressions are the same as a scope and sequence or pacing guide that lists the order of what to teach next.	
	2. "Big Ideas" help to frame descriptors (progress indicators) in a learning progression.	
	3. An example of a "Big Idea" would be learning how to read.	
	4. To validate a learning progression, one would consult cognitive research, as well as teacher observations and analysis of student work collected over time *after* targeted instruction.	
	5. Students can use learning progressions as a self-assessment to monitor their own progress.	
	6. Learning progressions can be used to diagnose individual students' strengths and weaknesses.	
	7. Progress maps, developmental continuums, and learning continuums are qualitatively different from learning progressions.	
	8. Other countries have been using research-based learning progressions for many years to guide classroom assessment and instruction.	
	9. Learning progressions can guide development of formative assessments and formative uses of assessment data.	
	10. Learning progressions describe increasingly more difficult content and skills.	

Checking Understandings—Possible Responses: Learning Progressions Anticipation Guide

Anticipation Guide: What Do I Know or Believe About Learning Progressions?

AGREE (A)? DISAGREE (D)?	READ EACH STATEMENT BELOW. DECIDE IF YOU AGREE OR DISAGREE AND INDICATE IN COLUMN TO THE LEFT.	EXPLAIN WHY YOU AGREE OR DISAGREE. HAVE YOU CHANGED YOUR MIND? WHY/WHY NOT?
D	1. Learning progressions are the same as a scope and sequence or pacing guide that lists the order of what to teach next.	Scope and sequencing, pacing guides, and most content standards are not based in research about how children develop expertise in the content domain.
A	2. "Big Ideas" help to frame descriptors (progress indicators) in a learning progression.	This is true. I refer to these as the "unifying threads" of the progression.
D	3. An example of a "Big Idea" would be learning how to read.	This example is much too broad. To learn more about "Big Ideas", see Wiggins and McTighe's Understanding by Design work.
A	4. To validate a learning progression, one would consult cognitive research, as well as teacher observations and analysis of student work collected over time *after* targeted instruction.	See Hess LP Tool #23.
A	5. Students can use learning progressions as a self-assessment to monitor their own progress.	View video clips of Karin's project in Hawaii, or TCRWP videos of students discussing their progress and quality of their work.
A	6. Learning progressions can be used to diagnose individual students' strengths and weaknesses.	True. Most useful when you "zoom in" and focus on assessing a smaller grain size of indicators within a larger progression (e.g., Clements & Sarama, 2009).
D	7. Progress maps, developmental continuums, and learning continuums are qualitatively different from learning progressions.	All of these are based in research. Math tends to use the term "trajectory", science uses "progression", ELA often uses "continuum" or "progression". They are used to mean the same thing and are all research based.
A	8. Other countries have been using research-based learning progressions for many years to guide classroom assessment and instruction.	New Zealand was one of the first places to develop learning progressions in all content areas. Australia did the same, calling theirs "progress maps".
A	9. Learning progressions can guide development of formative assessments and formative uses of assessment data.	See Hess LP Tools #24 and #25, unit assessment planning.
D	10. Learning progressions describe increasingly more difficult content and skills.	While this might be partly true, it's not simply the difficulty of the tasks that increases. Progressions illustrate depth, breadth, and greater sophistication over time, with targeted instruction.

Two Sample Tasks Illustrating Pre- and Mid-assessments

Two "opinion" examples piloted at Grade 3 are on the following pages.

- The first example is an opinion on a familiar topic—holidays. This could be adapted for any familiar topic as a preassessment (e.g., favorite/not-so-favorite place to visit, pet, game, song).

- The second example uses fact sheets and asks students to state and support an opinion based on the facts provided in the texts. Fact sheets are used to reduce the reading load, while still expecting students to use text evidence to support their opinions.

- After reviewing these assessments, consider how they could be used as task shells[12] for other local progress-monitoring assessments.

- Consider how to design the postassessment for this unit of study that is more complex, but assesses the same "unifying thread" of learning along the same continuum.

Each writing assignment should include prewriting discussions about topics or texts to help students generate ideas from which to choose and use in their writing. This is to ensure that a student's writing ability is not negatively impacted because they have not been able to understand the text or generate ideas to get started. After all, these are writing assessments, not reading assessments!

Discussions may be as a whole class or a small group and do not need to be in-depth discussions. The purpose is to generate a basic understanding of the topic or text (getting the gist of the text) and to generate related vocabulary and ideas. The texts in the second assessment include some underlined words that students may not know. The task directions also include web links where students can locate additional information to use in their writing after the initial discussions.

---

12. Task shells are discussed in detail in Module 3.

My Favorite—or Not So Favorite—Holiday

Name _____ Date _____

Our families and friends celebrate lots of holidays each year. Do you have a favorite holiday? Write about <u>your favorite—or not-so-favorite—holiday</u>. Be sure to use facts and details to support why this is or is NOT your favorite holiday of the whole year.

You can use the graphic organizer to help you plan your writing.

Be sure to

1. Have an introduction that tells why this holiday is or is NOT your favorite holiday.

2. Have body paragraphs that have topic sentences and details to support each new idea.

3. Write a conclusion that connects to your focus or tells a lesson you have learned about holidays.

4. Use different kinds of sentences—statements, questions, and exclamations.

5. Use descriptive words to connect your ideas.

6. Use complete sentences and correct punctuation and spelling.

7. Add an illustration that supports your focus.

Available for download at **resources.corwin.com/HessToolkit**

Use the planning chart below to organize your reasons and supporting facts. Then use these details to write your opinion on this topic.

Details: Give specific reasons.	Elaborations: Explain, give examples, say more about why this supports your reason.

Investigating Sharks

Name _____ Date _____

Scientists like to study animals in their natural habitat. That means that a shark scientist has to study sharks in the oceans where they live. Shark scientists are scuba divers who go deep into the ocean to learn more about sharks.

Read and discuss "Facts About Sharks" by Susanna Batchelor. Think about how these two types of sharks are the same and also how they are different.

<u>Which shark would you study if you were a shark scientist and why?</u>

1. Decide which shark you would want to study.
2. Find the best shark facts to support your reasons.
3. Explain your reasons. Be sure to use facts about hammerhead sharks and whale sharks to explain why you would study the shark you chose and not the other shark.

You can use a graphic organizer to help you plan your writing.

Remember to <u>pick the best facts</u> to support your opinion, and not every detail you can find. You must <u>explain how the facts support your opinion and each of your reasons</u>.

Be sure to

- Have an introduction that tells <u>the topic and focus (opinion).</u>
- State your opinion: If I was a shark scientist, I would want to study (which shark) because (reasons).
- Have body paragraphs with topic sentences and details to support each new reason. Group your facts to <u>support and explain</u> each reason.
- Use linking words that connect your opinion with your reasons and facts.
- Use descriptive words to connect your ideas.
- Write a conclusion that connects to your focus (opinion) and reasons.
- Use different kinds of sentences—statements, questions, and exclamations to add interest.
- Use complete sentences. Check for correct punctuation and spelling.
- Add an illustration that supports your focus (opinion).

Available for download at **resources.corwin.com/HessToolkit**

Copyright © 2010 Karin Hess, The Local Assessment Toolkit: Persuasive Writing. Adapted from "About Sharks" by Susanna Batchelor, available online at http://www.childrenoftheearth.org. Permission to reproduce is given when authorship is fully cited. karinhessvt@gmail.com

Planning Your Writing

Use information from "Facts About Sharks" in your opinion piece. Pick some facts that will help you to compare the two kinds of sharks and then decide which shark you would want to study. You may also add new facts you have learned from other texts or sources on the Internet. Deciding and listing the reasons for your opinion (the shark you want to study) is an important step in your plan. A silly reason is given in the table to show you how to <u>connect your reasons with your opinion and facts</u>.

My opinion (the shark I would want to study or learn more about) is
_____

Because (my reasons for choosing this shark): _____

List <u>at least 2</u> Strong Reasons why you choose	<u>Explain</u> Hammerhead shark facts that support my reason	<u>Explain</u> Whale shark facts that support my reason
I like spots! (a silly reason—DO NOT use this reason)	Hammerhead sharks do not have spots <u>so they would be boring to study.</u>	Whale sharks do have spots <u>and I want to know more about animals with spots.</u>

Available for download at **resources.corwin.com/HessToolkit**

Copyright © 2018 by Corwin. All rights reserved. Reprinted from *A Local Assessment Toolkit to Promote Deeper Learning: Transforming Research into Practice* by Karin Hess. Thousand Oaks, CA: Corwin, www.corwin.com. Reproduction authorized only for the local school site or nonprofit organization that has purchased this book.

"Facts About Sharks" by Susanna Batchelor

My name is Susanna Batchelor and I am a veterinarian from England. I dive with sharks to learn more about them. I have dived with many different types of sharks all over the world.

Source: pixabay.com/skeeze

There are about 400 different types of sharks. Many of them are named after the way they look or where they live. For example, the hammerhead shark has a head shaped like a hammer; the whale shark is as big as a whale; and the reef shark lives on coral reefs. Sharks range from a few centimeters to many meters in length. And they eat all sorts of different foods—from tiny plankton, to fish, to larger mammals like seals.

I have collected some interesting facts about two different kinds of sharks – hammerhead sharks and whale sharks.

Interesting Facts About *Hammerhead Sharks*:

1. Have a head shaped like a hammer to help it detect electrical signals given off by its prey
2. Swing their heads from side to side like a metal detector
3. Their eyes and nostrils are at each end of the "hammer"
4. The position of the eyes allows it to look 360°—in a full circle
5. Hunt alone at night
6. Feed mainly on fish and squid
7. Grow up to 4 meters long
8. Get scared by the sound of divers' bubbles
9. Have been known to eat other sharks

Source: pixabay.com/skeeze

Interesting Facts About *Whale Sharks*:

Source: pixabay.com/JimmyDominico

1. Can grow to 18 meters long
2. Are the largest fish in the world
3. Feed on <u>plankton</u> that comes through their <u>massive</u> gills
4. Have 3,000 tiny teeth but they don't use them for chewing
5. Are very curious and will often slow down to inspect divers and even follow their bubbles
6. Make long <u>migrations</u> across the oceans to find food
7. Can live a long time
8. Have a pattern of spots on their sides (just behind the gills) like a <u>fingerprint</u> that is <u>unique</u> to each individual and can be used for <u>identification</u>

For more pictures and shark videos, you can go to http://www.childrenoftheearth.org/shark-information-kids/interesting-facts-about-sharks-for-kids.htm.

IV. Strategies and Resources for Use With Students

The Module 4 instructional/formative assessment strategies and kid tools have been tried in numerous classrooms with great success. They offer ways that units of study and lessons can be designed to formatively assess lesson learning targets along a continuum of learning. Below is a brief description of each strategy or kid tool, and how they might be used. In some cases, I've also included intended DOK levels.

STRATEGY 1: My Favorite No

This PREASSESSMENT lesson ("My Favorite No: Learning From Mistakes") idea comes from the Teaching Channel (www.teachingchannel.org) and provides an excellent formative assessment model. In this lesson, a middle school math teacher uses student mistakes as a teaching tool to begin her lesson. Students complete a math warm-up using index cards, a DOK 1 routine problem.

STRATEGY 2: Flipped Classrooms

Teachers are always concerned about how to DIFFERENTIATE and how to best use instructional time. Is there enough time for rich class discussions? Is there time for extended projects and time to correct the student work that comes from them? The list of concerns goes on and on and much of it is justified, given all of the content that must be covered. So how does a teacher meet the varying needs of students without having to be in ten different places at once? I suggest using a flipped-classroom approach to much of the basic teaching. Teachers record and post short videos of "direct teaching" that might have been taught in class—introducing a new mathematical procedure, demonstrating how to use a probe to collect data for a science investigation, or reminders about how to check sources or cite quotations. Students who need to see the lesson more than once can view it several times, such as for homework and again as a review for a test.

This is not simply about using technology. The key benefit of "flipping" the way you present lessons is so that lesson delivery can better meet the needs of all student ability levels. If students get the "basics" (by video) before they come to class, teachers are able to move the class ahead using the *found time* for richer tasks and deeper class discussions. A mathematics teacher in a high school I was working with in Delaware tried this approach and shared a reflection that actually surprised me. When I went back for a visit several months later, I asked her how the approach was working. This was her response: *"My students love it. They can come into class and get started right away on a more challenging group task than I ever had time for before. My problem is that I am so used to being up in front of them teaching, that I'm having trouble shifting my role to more of a coach."*

My guess is that if students like and benefit from a taped lesson being available to them prior to coming to class, then they are more able to go deeper into content than they used to do.

STRATEGY 3: Infographics

Infographics have become a common means of CONSOLIDATING LEARNING by summarizing and visually integrating information on a topic using a poster format. Students—especially those with limited language facility—can be successful in developing an infographic to show how they are connecting ideas from different sources. The visuals can integrate use of photos, structures like flowcharts and timelines, and other artifacts, such as part of a world or state map. If students are summarizing facts, it's a DOK 2 task; if they are looking for some common themes, it can rise to DOK 3.

STRATEGY 4: Assignment Menus—Quick Tips for Differentiation

I learned the "basics" of differentiation in a graduate course with Dr. Sandra Kaplan back in the 1970s. The essence of differentiation is this: differentiate the content, differentiate the process or thinking, or differentiate the product and give students a choice about which assignments they want to do. I tried this strategy—developing assignment menus—with my middle school students, first in mathematics and then in other subjects, such as ELA and science. This was long before anyone (even Norman Webb) was talking about DOK levels. I simply called the levels in the menu "challenge levels." Over the years, I found this strategy to work effectively in Grades 2 to 8 with my own students; and have worked with teachers in many states who have put their own interesting spin on it. Here I describe a few of the ways that have worked well, including my own templates and examples.

On a project in Wisconsin, first-grade teachers had been using something that looked like a Tic-Tac-Toe board that they called the "Nifty 9"—nine optional activities that students could choose to do when they completed their work. While it was a great concept, they discovered (with the aid of the Hess CRM during a workshop) that all of the options were only at a DOK 1 (e.g., read a book with a friend, practice your spelling words, color a picture). The teachers revised the choice activity options, using a current unit of study and the Hess CRM, making the revised Nifty 9s more effective in stretching learners with a mix of DOK 2 and DOK 3 activities, while still offering some choices.

Another example of assignment menus comes from Clint Mathews, a district ELA curriculum facilitator and high school teacher in Gillette, Wyoming. Clint created a deck of cards (as part of his assignment menu). Students could choose to do a given assignment or to pick five cards from the deck and do one of them. Each assignment has designated score points—an essay, or more complex task, might get 60 points, while a lower DOK-level task, such as an interview, might only get 25 points. Of the five cards they pull, students strategize how to choose an assignment, knowing that some "high-point" assignments had to be in the mix over the course of the unit. And, just to make it interesting, there was one wild card in the deck which said "free pass" that motivated his students to want to pick cards to get their assignments. Figure 4.12 below shows some of Clint's planning for creating the assignment cards.

The following examples of assignment menus that I've included in Module 4 include a sample menu for *To Kill a Mockingbird*, some blank planning pages for local planning, and an example created collaboratively during a workshop with N.Y.C. middle school teachers in about 20 minutes. When teachers begin to develop an assignment menu, I suggest they begin by filling in the cells of the menu with assessments they have already planned to use:

- *Appetizers* are shorter assignments used to provide an introduction to the topic or build background knowledge or a first step to understanding. Often the appetizers can be used to scaffold students to the next level. (DOK 1, 2)

- *Main courses* are used to build conceptual understanding and help students to make connections among some key ideas. (DOK 2, possibly DOK 3)

- *Desserts* are the rich tasks that will take longer and require transfer of skills and concepts in new contexts. (possibly DOK 3 or DOK 4)

Teachers generally have no trouble filling in the two lower "challenge levels" using what they already planned to assign to students. The menu approach pushes teachers' thinking about how students might go deeper—with dessert.

Figure 4.12 A Sample Assignment Menu for High School English

In order to complete this activity for Unit 6, you must complete a selection of the activities below. Each activity has an assigned point value. The only two stipulations are that the total number of activity points must add up to 200 and you must choose a minimum of one activity per row.

ROW 1 (Select at least one)	**DOK 2 20 pts** **A** Identify five major authors and their respective literary works. Explain how they represent this period of literature.	**DOK 3 40 pts** **B** Draw a Card Draw five cards from the "assessment deck" and review each card. Choose one card and complete the activity.	**DOK 2 20 pts** **C** Vocabulary: Select and define at least 10 words or terms that seem significant or vital to the work.	**DOK 4 80 pts** **D** Choose a poem from this unit and write a critical analysis essay using a specific approach to literature. Two-page minimum. Critics encouraged but not required. Visit with me regarding approaches.	____ pts
ROW 2 (Select at least one)	**DOK 3 40 pts** **E** Draw a Card Draw five cards from the "assessment deck" and review each card. Choose one card and complete the activity.	**DOK 2 20 pts** **F** Choose any poem from the period. Complete a detailed TPCASTT and include examples from the text.	**DOK 4 80 pts** **G** Choose any story from this period. Rewrite the ending taking the story in a different direction. Add at least 1 1/2 typed pages to this new narrative.	**DOK 3 40 pts** **H** Create a short poem, literary work, work of art, piece of music, etc. Write a detailed paragraph explaining how the work fits the period.	____ pts
ROW 3 (Select at least one)	**DOK 4 80 pts** **I** Close read Woolf: "Lady/Looking Glass" Develop a unique, original claim. Write a small essay proving your claim. Incorporate 3 sources plus evidence from the text. (pp.1190–1197)	**DOK 4 80 pts** **J** Close read Conrad's "The Lagoon" Develop a unique, original claim. Write a small essay proving your claim. Incorporate three sources plus evidence from the text. (p. 1220-1233)	**DOK 4 80 pts** **K** Close read "A Devoted Son" by A. Desai Develop a unique, original claim. Write a small essay proving your claim. Incorporate three sources plus evidence from the text. (p. 1419-1429)	**DOK 4 80 pts** **L** Close read Orwell's "Shooting/Elephant" Develop a unique, original claim. Write a small essay proving your claim. Incorporate three sources plus evidence from the text. (pp. 1318–1326)	____ pts
ROW 4 (Select at least one)	**DOK 3 40 pts** **M** In a short writing, (3/4 page) analyze the inter-relationship between text elements in the chosen work.	**DOK 4 80 pts** **N** Research a major trend, incident, or social issue from either period. Use at least 3 sources for this informative essay and include a works cited.	**DOK 3 40 pts** **O** Draw a Card Draw five cards from the "assessment deck" and review each card. Choose one card and complete the activity.	**DOK 2 20 pts** **P** Choose any story from either period. Complete a detailed SCASI and include details from the text.	____ pts

*Must add up to 200!   ____/200

My examples and template were developed before I was working with DOK. The numbers 1, 2, and 3 in my template represented increasing challenge, not DOK levels. In mathematics, a "1" was a set of routine calculation problems; a "2" was usually some type of routine word problems; and a challenge of "3" was what we now call performance tasks or projects. They could be DOK 3 or DOK 4. My rule for the challenge level of "3" was that you could work with a partner, thus building in an incentive (and scaffolding) to choose the most challenging assignments.

> View a video showing a sixth-grade teacher, "Differentiating With Learning Menus," at the Teaching Channel, https://www.teachingchannel.org/videos/differentiating-instruction-strategy.

I'm often asked how I "managed" students choosing all of these different assignments. First I created a few rules:

- You must do one assignment from each row and each column. This ensured that everyone did at least one high-challenge task. Or I required a certain number of total points so that students had to select a combination of appetizers, main courses, and at least one dessert.

- I decided if any assessments were required. For example, everyone might be required to summarize the chapter, but other assignments were optional as long as the minimum number were completed.

- Most importantly, I set due dates for each option—if students missed a due date, they had to select another option.

The most amazing thing that happened in my classrooms when I began using assignment menus was that most students completed more assignments than I would have given them. Choice was a motivator!

STRATEGY 5: Note Facts

This strategy (described earlier in Module 4) was developed after analyzing student writing at Grade 2. The Grade 2 preassessment results for informational writing commonly showed that students were not able to organize their ideas around common subtopics. As a result, we designed this tool for organizing notes and teaching students how to use it, which was quite simple: Write your facts, cut your facts apart, and think about how to group them before you begin writing. The act of cutting sentences apart was very freeing for most students; they were able to see more clearly how two facts might connect and were then able to join them using several sentences. Organizing ideas is a DOK 2–type scaffolding strategy. A template can be found on page 358 at the end of this Module. It is also available for download from **resources.corwin.com/HessToolkit.**

Quick Tips for Differentiation: Assignment Menus and DOK

Here are three ways to approach differentiating curriculum without creating completely different lessons; focus on <u>one aspect (content–concepts, process, or product) at a time</u>, or use combinations of the three components through an assessment menu (see sample below):

- **Content (texts or concepts)—different students get different—but related—content–texts** (e.g., different texts on same topic or by same author, with different levels of complexity; different texts that relate to topic, concept, theme, or same genre—different origins of myths, different subtopics or perspectives related to a study of cultures or time periods)

- **Process (Depth of Knowledge/DOK)—vary the DOK or process skills for the same text or content** (e.g., work independently or with others, analyze within one text or across multiple texts, compare and contrast versus deeper analysis). This differentiation can provide scaffolding for students who may need it before completing a more complex assignment.

- **Product—same content (text–concepts) and application of same process skills (DOK), but products may vary by choice or strengths and interest** (e.g., presentation, pamphlet, poster, letter, model, use of technology, illustration). Assess products with a "common" rubric.

Sample Uses of Assignment Menus: Describe multiple assignments that students choose to complete to get a total of 10 points ("10" is an arbitrary number used only as an illustration). For example, some students successfully complete fewer "3-point" assignments or more "1- and 2-point" challenge assignments to accomplish the required 10 points.

OR *"You must complete three assignments for this unit, one under each column and row (e.g., column headings could also be text-to-self/personal, text-to-text/making connections, and text-to-world/broader issue based). Choose a '1,' a '2,' and a level '3' challenge assignment."*

Text: To Kill a Mockingbird

Differentiated Challenge Levels	Initial Understanding (DOK 1 or 2)	Analysis and Interpretation (DOK 2, 3, or 4)	Opinion/Response to Text (DOK 2, 3, or 4)
3 **Desserts**	Create a 20-question quiz and answer key (true/false, matching, fill-in questions) that assesses sequence of major events, character motivations, for example. **OR** Create a graphic organizer with plot and subplot notes and facts. **(DOK 1, 2)**	Compare/contrast what happens to Boo Radley and Tom Robinson. Explain how each is related to the title of the novel. Analyze evidence from the text to support your response. **(DOK 3)** **OR** Also integrate another text's character(s) or theme with your analyses. **(DOK 4)**	Develop and conduct a class survey on your peers' perspective of at least one underlying theme in the novel (e.g., related to prejudice, human dignity, growing up). Present and discuss your results, comparing the class's perspective to a theme in the novel. What influences those perspectives? What conclusions can you draw? Use survey data and text references as support. **(DOK 4)**
2 **Main Courses**	Make a map of the neighborhood that shows where important events took place (Finch house, Radley house, school, etc.). Label places with their significance. **(DOK 2)**	In an essay, explain with text support why Atticus should or should not have taken the case. **(DOK 3)** **OR** Compare/contrast two main characters: traits, motivations, biases, changes over the plot. **(DOK 2)**	Write a letter to Harper Lee expressing your impressions of the book's theme(s), using text evidence to support your claims. **(DOK 3)**
1 **Appetizers**	Make a timeline of major events in the story. **(DOK 2)**	Chose a character and illustrate graphically what that character understands at the end that she or he did not understand in the beginning of the story. **(DOK 2)**	Create three journal entries of different days from (Calpurnia's) point of view. Entries should show how you think (Calpurnia) sees life. **(DOK 2)** **OR** Write to a character showing empathy with their perspective. **(DOK 2)**

Sample Planning Worksheet for the Differentiated Assignment Menu for Math

Topic Focus:

Skills:

Concept(s):

"Big Ideas":

Differentiated Challenge Levels	Process Skills/Use of Tools/Precision (DOK 1 or 2)	Concepts/ Mathematical Modeling (DOK 2)	Problem Solving/Reasoning/ Math Arguments/Critique (DOK 3 or 4)
3 **Desserts**	Work with a peer . . .	Work with a peer . . .	Work with a peer . . .
2 **Main Courses**			
1 **Appetizers**			

Sample Planning Worksheet for the Differentiated Assignment Menu for Science

Science Topic:

Concept(s):

"Big Ideas":

Differentiated Challenge Levels	Process Skills/Use of Tools (DOK 1 or 2)	Concepts (DOK 2) Science Argumentation (DOK 3 or 4)	Design/Critique/Conduct Investigations (DOK 3 or 4)
3 **Desserts**	*Work with a peer . . .*	*Work with a peer . . .*	*Work with a peer . . .*
2 **Main Courses**			
1 **Appetizers**			

**Assignment Menu Example
Collaboratively Created During a Workshop**

Text(s)/Context: Biographies/Autobiographies/Memoirs

Focus: Women's History—(e.g., across different time periods?)

Theme/"Big Ideas": Life stories and what shapes them (time period, social/cultural/political events of the day, challenges, decisions made, their contributions to history)

Essential question(s): How is a person's life story shaped by challenges, decisions made, paths taken or not taken?

Differentiated Challenge Levels	Basic Comprehension (DOK 1 or 2) [Who is this person and why should we care?]	Deeper Interpretation, Analysis, Critique (DOK 3 or 4) [How was the person's life story shaped by challenges... decisions made, paths taken or not taken?]	Vocabulary Development and Language Use (DOK 2 or 3) [What words and symbols help us to know more about and better understand this person?]
3 **Desserts**	Work with a peer... Make a presentation about a person or be in character as the person—props, dress as, share your contributions. Conduct an imaginary interview with person (DOK 2)	Work with a peer... Move this person into another time period. What would the person's perspective, impact be, or ??? (have the person converse or interact with someone or another famous person of that time period or with the same area of expertise or interest) (DOK 4) Compare/contrast two different interpretations of the same life story—e.g., memoir versus biography. How do the differing perspectives shape the way the story is told (and perhaps the details)? (DOK 4)	Work with a peer... Use of symbolic language, figurative language, and descriptive language—create a poem, rap, or graphic novel telling the life story, using descriptive and figurative language as well as symbolic visuals that relate to the time period (DOK 3)

2 **Main Courses**	Create a poster of this person's significance—use evidence from sources read; represent visually and in words (connect this assignment to the vocabulary terms column) (DOK 2)	Compare this person's life story with a person from another time period who contributed in a similar way. Create a collage of some type or print ad by person as to what they advocate—supported by sources (DOK 3 or 4)	Identify "time period words/phrases" that relate to this person's work/contributions/areas of interest (DOK 2)
1 **Appetizers**	Summarize the life story; make a timeline of important events in the person's life (DOK 2)	Create a timeline or life path visual—Connect important events that influenced their lives. Cite sources used (DOK 3 or DOK 4 "lite") (e.g., identify which five events were most critical; evaluate impact that those challenges or events had on the person's life path)	Focus: Understanding words in context; descriptive words/phrases, etc. Create a crossword puzzle with words or phrases used by others to describe this person (DOK 1 or 2)

My Note Facts About _____

Name _____

Use the lines below to write your facts and details. Cut each fact apart.

Decide how to make groups of the facts, such as how things look or where they live. Use the **fact groups** to write about each key idea in your report.

✂ --

_____
_____
_____
_____
_____
_____
_____
_____
_____
_____
_____
_____
_____
_____
_____

MODULE 5: IS THIS A COLLECTION OF TESTS OR AN ASSESSMENT SYSTEM?

Building and Sustaining a Comprehensive Local Assessment System for Deeper Learning

The assessment systems in high-achieving jurisdictions like Australia, Finland, Hong Kong, the Netherlands, and Singapore have long relied largely on open-ended items—essays and problem solutions—that require students to analyze, apply knowledge, and write extensively. Furthermore, a growing emphasis on inquiry-oriented learning has led to an increasing prominence for school-based tasks, which include research projects, science investigations, development of products, and presentations about these efforts. Because these assessments are embedded in the curriculum, they influence the day-to-day work of teaching and learning, focusing it on the use of knowledge to solve problems. Standardized performance tasks are incorporated into examination scores in systems as wide-ranging as the General Certificate of Secondary Education in Britain, the Singapore examinations system, the certification systems in Victoria and Queensland, Australia, and the International Baccalaureate program, which operates in more than 100 countries around the world.

Darling-Hammond, 2010, p. 2

When does a pile of bricks become a school building? And when does a collection of assessments become an assessment system? When I began my years as a building principal, I had the opportunity (and challenge) of working with colleagues, the community, and school boards to shepherd the merging of two school districts to form a new one and then plan and build a new school. Of course we needed a budget, architects to draw up blueprints, and the bond issue to pass; but we first had to clarify our philosophy of what this learning environment should encompass before anything could happen. If we felt that the arts were going to be an important part of the curriculum, then we needed to consider the design of and access to instrumental music practice rooms and music rehearsal and performance spaces. Would there be a visual arts work studio and dance area? Where should they be located? If we valued collaboration among teacher groups and within student groups, where should classrooms and common spaces be situated? In other words, we needed something more important than bricks to build our school. We needed an implementation plan for our educational philosophy. We needed to identify critical parts to the system and decide how they would interact and be maintained over time. We needed to identify the parts of the current school systems that were still relevant and useful (from playgrounds to policies) and the ones that needed to be upgraded or simply replaced.

The same is true for what makes a collection of assessments into an assessment system. The assessment system needs to reflect what you value and how best practices in assessment will be employed and supported by everyone at all levels of the system. An assessment system designed for deeper learning for all must go even further. It must be comprehensive and cohesive in order for all students to achieve a higher level of success than what exists in many schools today. The system needs to be designed to be proactive rather than reactive when students fail. The assessments in the system will look different from traditional assessments; and the students' role in the assessment process will also look different and thus be equitable and personalized.

5.1 Rethinking What It Means to Have a Comprehensive Local Assessment System

Stiggins (2017) makes the case for school leaders and teachers taking the time to rethink what we assess, why and how we assess it, and how we use the assessment results. While many books and resources have helped educators to design or select assessments for different purposes, few (if any) have guided a comprehensive review of *the system* they are housed in or provide ways to "fix" what isn't working. Stiggins states that "educational policy leaders . . . offer states guidelines for conducting audits of local assessment systems that focus almost exclusively on standardized accountability testing and provide little advice for monitoring the quality of classroom-level assessment, even though the classroom is where the vast majority of assessment takes place" (p. 2).

Clearly, teachers are the primary users of assessments and assessment results. And although they take numerous educational courses and attend in-service workshops throughout their careers, most teachers have not had in-depth and ongoing opportunities for codeveloping high-quality assessments or for examining assessment use within the larger system beyond their own classrooms or courses. Really good assessments used in isolated classrooms become islands of excellence, but rarely become part of the sea change toward building a cohesive assessment system.

> View an Edutopia video of Linda Darling-Hammond (2008) discussing 5 Keys to Comprehensive Assessment at https://www.edutopia.org/comprehensive-assessment-introduction.

For a variety of reasons, it's really difficult for a few great teachers to impact the system all by themselves. School leaders need to design the system from the ground up, creating mechanisms for collaboration and feedback loops when assessments of deeper learning are conceived, designed, and piloted. This approach creates a schoolwide assessment culture and may actually put student learning at the center of assessments in use.

When I begin to work with schools, I generally find that there is not a shared understanding of what deeper learning looks like at each grade level, how to support it, or how to assess it—formatively or summatively. The tools and protocols in Modules 1 to 4 of the *Local Assessment Toolkit* are designed to establish the foundation upon which the assessment culture and system can be built. In my experience, teachers need to begin this process by examining assessments they are currently using—Are they rigorous enough? Are they fair for all learners? How will I or we use the results? Next they need opportunities to create high-quality assessments with colleagues, especially common performance tasks so they can collaboratively reflect on and use assessment results. Are they valid (aligned to both content and intended rigor to provide accurate interpretations of learning)? Are they reliable so that each teacher using the same assessment gets the same score result? Do they engage students in their own learning while they are being assessed? How useful are they for student self-monitoring and reflection?

Of course, these questions are not expected to be used formally for each and every assessment a teacher uses. However, by regularly reviewing some "priority" assessments with colleagues (common assessments), teachers do develop an assessment literacy mindset and deeper

> **General Guiding Questions for Review of Individual Assessments**
>
> - What is its purpose? (What understandings—content or skills—are being assessed? Is there one "right" answer or multiple possible correct responses? Is the assessment intended to elicit thinking and reasoning or basic skills?)
>
> - How will the assessment results be used (screening, diagnostic, formative or interim for progress monitoring, summative for grading or determining proficiency reporting)?
>
> - Does the evidence elicited REALLY match the standards or proficiency being assessed? (intended content)
>
> - Does the evidence elicited REALLY match the intended rigor? (What mental processing do you expect students to engage in? *Use the Hess CRM* **TOOLS #1–#5D** *to identify descriptors.*)
>
> - Does the scoring guide or rubric match both intended content and rigor?
>
> - What would student responses tell a teacher if students could or could not do all or part of this assessment (open-ended tasks, reasoning used)? Will results clearly guide instructional decisions?
>
> - Can all students fully engage with this assessment to demonstrate what they know? (fairness)
>
> - What can students learn about themselves from taking this assessment (as learners, about building expertise, about their own perseverance with challenging tasks, etc.)?

awareness of how they use assessments and assessment results from day to day. Once teachers have acquired a comfort level with applying the technical criteria for high-quality assessments (described in PLC **TOOL #9** and **TOOL #10**), they are ready to think about where assessments fit in the system of assessments and how assessment results from one assessment can complement results from others. This is sometimes referred to in the literature as using multiple measures. Multiple assessment measures can include providing multiple opportunities for assessing the same constructs (content + rigor), such as using running records multiple times with different texts to assess reading fluency; or assessing the same constructs with different assessment formats (e.g., using constructed response items and performance tasks that assess some of the same skills or concepts in different contexts across the school year). Clarifying the intended purpose of assessments used is essential to using multiple assessment measures appropriately when combining or weighting scores.

Once teachers begin to acquire a foundation for understanding assessment purposes, quality, and use, they are ready to think about how a set of assessments—or a set of snapshots—can work together at multiple levels (classroom, district, and state) to create a more complete photo album of student learning and program effectiveness. Module 5 is designed to guide school leaders through a process of examining how cohesive and comprehensive the local assessment system really is or can be.

When I begin this work with teachers, we look at what assessments are already being used. Classroom teachers can begin documenting assessments used in <u>one content area</u>, while special subject teachers (art, music, physical education, etc.) might start with <u>one grade span</u> (e.g., K–2, Grades 6–8) or a course and organize the assessments used by the skills, concepts, or dispositions assessed. Most of these assessments are probably used formatively. Over time, summative assessments will also be added (e.g., unit tests, finished writing or math portfolio pieces, presentations, products). At first, data is gathered biweekly or monthly by simply recording what assessments were used and for what purpose. I've found that **TOOL #27**, Year-at-a-Glance, is an unobtrusive and teacher-friendly way to regularly document assessments in use without taking too much time (Figure 5.1). Typically several conclusions are drawn

Figure 5.1 Sample Tool #27, Year-at-a-Glance Used to Document Assessments in Use

YEAR-AT-A-GLANCE: PLANNING CLASSROOM-BASED ASSESSMENTS OVER THE SCHOOL YEAR

Teacher: _____ Content Area: _____ Grade: _____

Content Clusters/ Proficiency Areas	Aug.–Sept.	Oct.	Nov.–Dec.	Jan.	Feb.	March	April	May–June	When or how often

SAMPLE—YEAR-AT-A-GLANCE: PLANNING CLASSROOM-BASED ASSESSMENTS OVER THE SCHOOL YEAR

Teacher: _____ Content Area: ELA Grade: 4

Proficiency Areas + Others	Aug.–Sept.	Oct.	Nov.–Dec.	Jan.	Feb.	March	April	May–June	When or how often
1–Foundational Reading Skills	Screening Test Fluency Checks	Phonics assmt. targeted students	Fluency Checks	Conferencing	Fluency Checks	Conferencing	Fluency Checks	Conferencing	Periodic Targeted small groups, indiv
Vocabulary Development	vocab strategies	Knowledge rating scales	Knowledge rating scales	Vocab review assmt.	Knowledge rating scales	Knowledge rating scales	State assessment	Vocab review assmt.	Ongoing
2–Reading Lit 3–Reading Info	Short PTs; discussion	Literature circles	Literature circles	Content-based reading and discussion	Performance tasks; discussion	Content-based reading and discussion	Performance tasks; discussion	Performance tasks; discussion	Daily small-group guided reading
4–Narratives 5–Informational 6–Opinions	Free-writes, peer or self-assessed Narratives—2 units	Free-writes, peer or self-assessed Conferencing	Writing prompts—organization, idea development	Free-write, peer or self-assessed Informational—2 units	Soc Studies unit—Report Writing Conferencing	Writing prompts—organization, idea development	Free-write, peer or self-assessed Opinion—2 units	Portfolio, peer or self-assessed	Weekly—end of every ELA unit Conferencing

362 A Local Assessment Toolkit to Promote Deeper Learning

by most teachers: (a) Many assessments assess the same constructs over and over again, while some areas are completely left out or rarely assessed; (b) while many assessments are employed, there is so much data that teachers cannot possibly act on all of it in meaningful ways, such as to adjust instruction; or (c) rarely do results from multiple measures get combined in ways other than averaging scores—what I call the "meaningless" mean. Averaging scores from reading assessments that assess different constructs, for example, might yield a total reading score or grade for a report card, but the result does not reflect whether progress is being made. For example, later assessments may show improvement, but are averaged with earlier lower scores. The key ideas behind teachers completing **TOOL #27** are to raise awareness of what is being assessed and why and to consider which measures might be providing complementary information. Often teachers realize that using fewer targeted assessments can provide the same level of information about student learning as does using many assessments in a less organized or cohesive way.

School and district leadership teams begin by looking at what is already in place "systemwide" (philosophy, priority assessments, protocols/quality controls, etc.). Then they determine what is currently working well (the "Aces") and what is missing or needs to be eliminated or replaced (the "Spaces"). In 2010, I designed a set of questions for examining five indicators of a local assessment system that is *comprehensive*. Often, educators tell me that before seeing the list of these five indicators of comprehensive local assessment systems, they had not thought of all of them as being part of the system or had never clearly articulated them—such as their assessment philosophy. **TOOL #28** incorporates questions that can be used and revisited multiple times over several school years, while building the system and developing action plans for immediate and long-term development and refinement (Figure 5.2).

Figure 5.2 Tool #28: Discussion Questions for Examining Local Assessment Systems

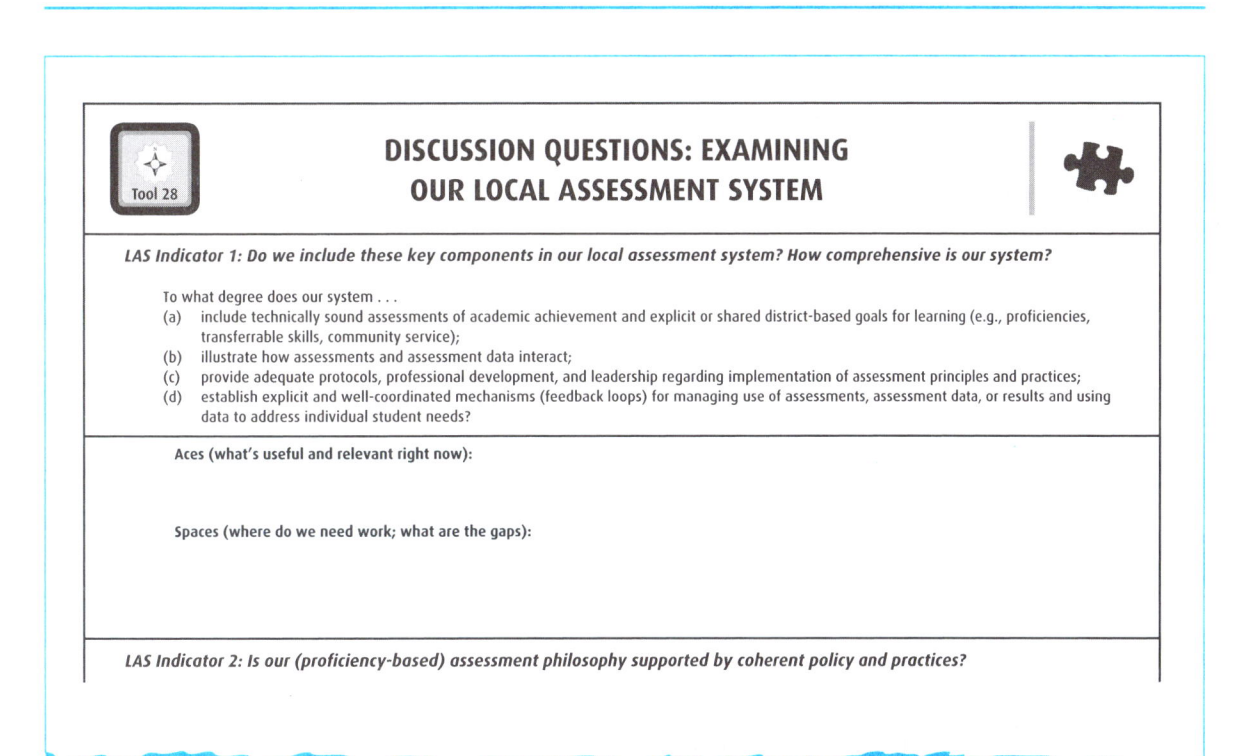

DISCUSSION QUESTIONS: EXAMINING OUR LOCAL ASSESSMENT SYSTEM

Tool 28

LAS Indicator 1: Do we include these key components in our local assessment system? How comprehensive is our system?

To what degree does our system . . .
(a) include technically sound assessments of academic achievement and explicit or shared district-based goals for learning (e.g., proficiencies, transferrable skills, community service);
(b) illustrate how assessments and assessment data interact;
(c) provide adequate protocols, professional development, and leadership regarding implementation of assessment principles and practices;
(d) establish explicit and well-coordinated mechanisms (feedback loops) for managing use of assessments, assessment data, or results and using data to address individual student needs?

Aces (what's useful and relevant right now):

Spaces (where do we need work; what are the gaps):

LAS Indicator 2: Is our (proficiency-based) assessment philosophy supported by coherent policy and practices?

Below is a summary of what constitutes a high-quality, comprehensive local assessment system (LAS).

5.2 Five Indicators of a Comprehensive Local Assessment System

LAS Indicator 1: Components of a comprehensive local assessment system: Varied assessment formats with high technical quality, professional learning and leadership, and well-coordinated mechanisms are for use and management of assessments and data.

If your local assessment system is more than a collection of tests, then it

(a) includes technically sound assessments of academic achievement and district-based goals for learning (e.g., proficiencies, transferrable skills, community service);

(b) illustrates how assessments and assessment data interact;

(c) provides adequate protocols, professional development, and leadership regarding implementation of assessment principles and practices; and

(d) establishes explicit and well-coordinated mechanisms (feedback loops) for managing use of assessments, assessment data, or results and using data to address individual student needs.

> What are some of the perceived benefits and challenges of including each of these key components (listed above) in your local assessment system? Divide the leadership team into four groups with each group creating a T-chart for recording ideas discussed for one area. A sample T-chart is shown below.

SOME CHALLENGES	SOME BENEFITS
Time needed to develop, pilot, and refine new assessments so that they are of high technical quality	*Knowing more about what students actually know and can do* *Assessing deeper thinking and learning*
Lack of resources or expertise to develop new assessments	*Perhaps more student engagement, more student choice in how to show what they know*
Learning how to combine scores or assessment data for grading, making critical decisions (placement, retention, etc.)	*Assessments that are better aligned to standards*
Common collaboration time to look at and score student work	*More rigorous assessments; more information about student learning*

LAS Indicator 2: The (proficiency-based) assessment philosophy is supported by coherent policies and practices.

Taking the time to discuss and collaboratively write a brief narrative to clarify what you assess, how you assess, and for what purposes you assess is well worth the time. It sets the course for all future assessment work, professional learning activities, and policy development related to use of assessments and assessment results. Your assessment philosophy should

- include a statement of purpose—What is the focus of your system (e.g., Are there "common" learning targets, expanded learning environments and pathways, student-centered or personalized learning?);

- establish a common language and perspective about assessing content, skills, and deeper understanding and the interpretation and use of data;
- describe how assessment use will improve curriculum, instruction, and student engagement;
- elevate expectations and learning opportunities for all students;
- strengthen communication about student performance with students and their families and within the educational community; and
- other?

LAS Indicator 3: Communications identify how learning expectations for all students relate to assessment types, purposes, and uses.

"Comprehensive" means more than using state assessment results for accountability. It means more than item analysis for some standardized or local measures or using an off-the-shelf formative assessment tool. Be honest as you examine this list of components. *Having* a variety of assessments and *using* assessment results to support student learning are not the same thing. Compiling examples from **TOOL #27**, Year-at-a-Glance for each grade level or subject area, can be useful in this discussion with staff.

> Rank these components as: <u>Fully</u> in place, <u>Partly</u> in place, or <u>Limited</u> needing updating or revision or replacement. Provide examples of what might be needed.
>
> - A range of assessment types and formats: observation, short answer, constructed response, unit assessments, performance tasks, and extended projects, for example.
> - Guidelines are provided for assessment purposes and users (audience): Formative, Interim, and Summative.
> - Alignment of curriculum and instruction with opportunities to learn (e.g., use of common or interim assessments with administration guidelines, and student work samples; progress monitoring)
> - Considerations for assessing young children and special populations
> - A Communication Plan: Communicating expectations and results to students, parents, and community

LAS Indicator 4: Processes ensure that assessments and bodies of evidence are of high quality.

Most of the Tools in the *Local Assessment Toolkit* were designed to support these processes. If you are using some or all of the tools, this component should be fairly easy to document.

> *Identify any tools in the Local Assessment Toolkit or local protocols and professional development activities that support each area of technical quality listed below.*
>
> How do we ensure
>
> - Clear agreed-upon learning expectations (proficiencies) and performance scales that guide assessment development, evidence-based grading, and interpreting and reporting results?

(Continued)

(Continued)

- Validity: content + performance or cognitive rigor alignment (standards, proficiencies)?
- Reliability: consistency of scoring and interpretations?
- Fairness and Engagement: All students are able to access and demonstrate authentic learning?
- Multiple Measures: a process for combining results from different assessments, comparability?
- Common Tools: Assessment system is articulated by content area and assessment blueprints (alignment), useful in determining proficiency (e.g., standard setting, student work analysis, Body of Evidence), validation protocols (e.g., cognitive labs, performance task review), classroom observations?
- Verification Methods: methods used for evaluating a Body of Evidence (Body of Evidence means each student's assessment evidence collected over time, such as in a portfolio)?

LAS Indicator 5: A comprehensive district implementation plan includes supports for short- and long-term goals.

- Multiyear implementation for each content area K–12: Developing, piloting, and refining assessments and curriculum that are proficiency based and responsive to established learning progressions
- Describes feedback loops and role of leadership (e.g., to document and support implementation in classrooms)
- Supports to teachers—Professional Development: Curriculum, PLCs, Student Work Analysis
- Processes for systematically collecting accreditation evidence

Discuss possible implementation issues, using a chart like the one below.

POSSIBLE DISTRICT IMPLEMENTATION ISSUE	CHALLENGE OR BENEFIT?	IMPORTANT TO US? WHY? WHY NOT?	IMPLICATIONS FOR ONGOING TECHNICAL SUPPORT, FURTHER READING, GATHERING INPUT FROM STAKEHOLDERS, ETC.

5.3 Multiple Measures and Common Assessments

The Use of Multiple Measures in Local Assessment Systems

Different assessment uses call for data collection at different points in time using a variety of assessment types and formats. For example, systematic observation is used for ongoing monitoring of individual progress, while more periodic assessments, such as common formative and interim performance tasks, can be used to monitor groups of students, as well as inform teaching and learning. Summative measures used for external accountability usually assess greater breadth of content, using several different assessment task types. Most importantly, different uses embody different technical requirements (e.g., degree of standardization, interrater reliability), thoughtful considerations for how assessments are chosen (or developed), and decisions about how results can be combined for interpretation and taking action (DePascale, 2011; Goertz, 2011). "As a matter of fact, the use of technically strong multiple measures is likely to improve overall performance of the entire system by providing more accurate and more complete information that better aligns with district goals and increases the reliability of measurement and validity of interpretations made. Having more robust information available (actionable assessment data) can also reduce potential corruption (misinterpretation or misuse of data) and heighten responsiveness, such as making program or instructional decisions based on student data; and providing targeted support to educators" (Hess, 2012b, p. 1).

When I began my teaching career, a simple checklist was used by my principal to evaluate teachers one to three times a year. Today, we have a much better understanding of the complexity of teaching and what it actually takes to be highly skilled. When we think about approaches to teacher evaluation in the 21st century, it's easy to understand the concept of multiple measures and why we use them. Data about teacher effectiveness comes from multiple sources (the ability to plan lessons, adjust or differentiate instruction, use assessment data, etc.) at different points in time. Data are used collectively to interpret consistency or patterns of performance. One assessment measure—like that old checklist—never provides the full picture of what it takes to be a highly effective teacher. Multiple assessment measures provide teachers with diverse opportunities to demonstrate their mastery of the art and science of teaching. The reliability of a composite score is increased by the number of data points assessing *relevant and related* skills, knowledge, and performance.

Likewise, the use of multiple assessment measures can provide diverse opportunities for students to demonstrate what they know, as well as providing educators with much finer nuances in performance along a continuum of learning than one assessment could ever do. The use of multiple measures also increases reliability by allowing users to collect data more often (e.g., more than one opportunity to pass the same test; more than one opportunity to apply the same learning in contexts from simple to more complex) and to triangulate evidence of learning across assessments (see Table 5.1). The strongest case for using multiple measures is what most educators and testing companies do agree on—one assessment never tells the whole story about learning. Other than for school accountability purposes, multiple assessment measures are used by teachers and schools to diagnose, to inform teaching or learning, or to evaluate. The guiding principle for decisions about what measures to use and how to combine and interpret results should be based on their intended purpose: what you need to know, why you need to know it, and how to collect actionable evidence for decision making (Brookhart, 2009; DePascale, 2011; Goertz, 2011).

Teacher Understanding of Purposes and Use of Multiple Assessment Measures

Effective teachers use student data at the individual and classroom levels to plan lessons and to align curriculum and instruction with standards—the skills, content, and dispositions assessed—to continually inform their teaching and student learning. This requires much more than a

Table 5.1 Three Primary Uses of Multiple Assessment Measures

PURPOSES	STUDENT-LEVEL DECISIONS	CLASSROOM-LEVEL DECISIONS	SCHOOL-LEVEL/ POLICY DECISIONS
1. **To Diagnose**	Screening or placement Allocation of specific educational services	Identify professional development needs or additional classroom supports	Resource allocation Professional development planning
2. **To Inform teaching and learning**	Differentiating instruction for individual students or small groups Help students set and monitor goals for learning	Plan or adjust instruction for a range of ability levels Set challenging goals for learning	Curriculum and assessment alignment or design School improvement planning
3. **To Evaluate**	Grading Certification of individual achievement (e.g., meeting proficiency-based graduation requirements)	Teacher effectiveness	Program evaluation Curriculum audit Principal evaluation

superficial understanding of the purposes and use of a range of assessments. Teachers need to select and use high-quality assessment tools to deepen their content knowledge to better understand how expertise develops in each discipline over time. *How teachers use formative, interim, and summative assessment results is probably as important, if not more important, than which assessments they use.* While valid and reliable assessments can measure student progress, teachers are the ones who will interpret results and make instructional decisions to (positively) affect learning. In turn, school leaders need to make decisions about how best to support teachers in achieving a high level of assessment literacy. If teachers are selecting and using assessments based mostly on their individual preferences, the job of the coach becomes more challenging. While some unique use of assessments by individual teachers is expected, common assessments included in the systemwide assessment bank will likely support more consistent implementation of best assessment practices. Common assessments are the high-priority assessments that have gone through a quality (validation) review; all teachers understand their purpose and collaboratively share assessment results. Common assessments become the optimal entry point for assessment coaching.

5.4 What Exactly Are "Common" Assessments and Where Do They Fit in the Local Assessment System?

Common assessments have three things in common: What they assess, how consistently they are administered, and how results are interpreted and used (e.g., diagnostic versus evaluative). The "commonness" of these assessments allows for standardized administration (e.g., explicitly stating what is allowed, such as calculators for some but not all math test items), shared understanding of when to embed the assessments during the learning cycle (e.g., preassessment for a unit of study vs. progress monitoring using benchmark assessments midyear), and reliable interpretations of assessment results across teachers or schools. Because the content assessed is the same and scoring criteria are "balanced" to emphasize particular learning goals (e.g., more emphasis on reasoning than on computation in a mathematics performance task), results can be compared more widely across similar demographic groups (ELL, low SES, etc.), classrooms, or grade levels to evaluate overall program and instructional effectiveness. This would not be possible if each teacher was primarily using different assessment tools or emphasizing different content.

Not all assessments need to be or should be designated as common assessments. Most "short-cycle" formative assessments will be teacher designed and uniquely used in particular lessons. Common assessments used across classrooms in the school or district will be the assessments identified as assessing essential, or highest priority—content, skills, and depth of understanding—during a school year or perhaps within courses or units of study. Common assessments should not be limited to assessing basic skills. When your system is designed to support deeper learning for all students, common assessments will require integration of skills and concepts with reasoning, problem solving, and deeper thinking, such as in common formative, interim, or summative performance tasks.

Common Assessments, Common Scoring Criteria

You may be wondering how open-ended assessments, such as student-designed expeditionary projects or capstone assessments required for graduation, fit in the comprehensive assessment system. These types of assessment will surely vary in terms of the specific content assessed or the products produced; but they can be standardized in the way they are scored or evaluated. For example, in one state I worked with to design success criteria for high school exhibitions at Grades 10 and 12, we identified several required common components: (1) a research question and approach appropriate to the content domain (e.g., a science field study requires different tools and procedures than are used for developing a research paper or participating in an internship), (2) a written component, (3) a public presentation, (4) content applied to a nonroutine problem or investigation of personal interest, and (5) a self-reflection on the learning experience. The collaborative scoring of the exhibitions is what becomes "common" to these assessments that are often included in proficiency-based learning systems.

Common assessments are useful for calibrating teachers' judgments about student work products, facilitating instructional feedback among teachers within and across schools and districts, and focusing on efficient improvement strategies for classroom practice in all classrooms. They *are not* intended to standardize teaching or limit local control over curriculum. Well-crafted common assessments (or common scoring) can be integrated into instructional programs and provide opportunities for students to produce rich, multifaceted projects that integrate "authentic" performance-based tasks. In nontested grades and subjects, common assessments, along with other student work products, can serve as a credible, defensible, and instructionally productive alternative to traditional standardized (e.g., off-the-shelf) tests. The purpose and the standards intended for assessment determine the grain size and time needed for completion of common assessments—from one or two class periods, to several days, to end-of-course projects that may take several weeks or a full semester.

Why Should Districts Develop Local Common Assessments?

The greatest strengths of common assessments are in providing consistency of teacher expectations and data collection about learning across courses, grade levels, and schools and helping to articulate growth and progress over time. Remember the high school exhibitions example that used similar criteria for both Grades 10 and 12? The consistent use of common scoring criteria led to making informed decisions about the overall quality, depth, and breadth of learning demonstrated by individual students during their high school years. Clarifying common expectations benefits both teachers and students and guides curriculum and scheduling decisions that will support deeper learning for all students. In one high school that I visited, tenth graders observed their older peers giving their capstone presentations in order to establish concrete models for what was expected for the senior high school exhibitions. Seniors participated in providing critical feedback to tenth graders when they gave their presentations, thus helping them to reflect on their own progress from Grades 10 to 12.

Districts that thoughtfully approach the development and use of common assessments receive multiple benefits. First, educators engage in sustained, collaborative activities—building deep understanding of technically sound assessment practices and expanding their capacity to use high-quality curricular and assessment materials. Second, if the work is supported by outside content and assessment experts and established protocols for review of technical quality, the final products will be customized to target locally agreed-upon skills and concepts, such as in proficiency-based systems. The role of outside experts is to objectively analyze and suggest ways to improve and refine locally developed materials and to locate, share, and codevelop exemplar models that can be used in district professional learning activities.

Factors to Consider During the Development of Common Assessments

Technical criteria used to judge the quality of assessments includes matching their intended use (clarity of purpose) with alignment to content standards and intended rigor, incorporation of accommodations for special populations (fairness and equity), and reliability in administration and scoring. Three other factors critical to common assessment development (or selection) are described below.

- Considerations of use of actionable assessment data for making instructional decisions and providing feedback

    Assessments can only be valued by teachers if the information from the assessments tells the teachers what they could not have known from other, less costly (in time and money) methods. In other words, when teachers use (common) assessments they should learn something they did not already know about teaching or learning. As most "national" tests often provide little beyond "ability" rather than calibrated achievement estimates, the information is of low quality to those people tasked with the responsibility of improving teaching and learning. The benefits for teachers accrue only if the feedback information is powerful, preferably oriented to the specific class of students (or individual student level) as to what learners can and cannot do, compared to similar students, and which indicate to teachers the next appropriate teaching actions in order to optimise the use of time and resources and to maximize the learning gains. In addition, the information needs to be powerful for improving future teaching and thereby enhancing teachers' knowledge of their students' (level of) proficiencies. (Hattie, 2006, p. 2)

Hattie's review of more than 600 meta-analyses (based on many millions of students) states that it is possible to identify the major influences on student achievement; and one factor in particular underlies many of the most powerful methods: feedback. Assessment feedback must answer three key questions for it to be powerful in informing instructional decisions:

  ○ Where are we going?—related to both the *rich* ideas (also called big ideas or enduring understandings) underlying the curricula and to the desired overarching levels of proficiency as expected;

- How are we doing relative to the target?—Is the current status of performance comparable to appropriate (similar sub-) groups and to expected performance?

AND

- Where do we go next?—provides direction related to future teaching, learning, curriculum innovations, and assessment system policies.

• Considerations of text complexity and the range and types of texts used in common ELA and text-based assessments

The assessment of reading comprehension and assessment of writing in response to texts read present unique challenges to classroom teachers and test developers alike; and the criteria used in selecting a variety and range of appropriate texts is essential to meeting those purposes. Over time, students who are exposed to a variety of text types with increasing complexity also develop schemas about how text features differ by genre, and they gain confidence in peeling back the layers of complexity for a deeper understanding of what is read (Hess & Biggam, 2004). It is therefore critical that common assessments chosen to measure progress in reading (or for text-based analyses) clearly include a range of both literary and informational text types, and that increasing text complexity is part of the underlying test design. Traditional reading assessments tend to rely solely on Lexiles related to word difficulty and language structures, while other qualitative factors affecting the complexity of texts should also be considered when selecting texts for assessment. The text complexity tools in Module 2 were designed to assist teams in developing common text-based assessments. **TOOLS #6**, **#7**, and **#8** (Module 2) and **TOOL #32** (Module 5) provide protocols for examining the types, genres, and complexity of texts used for assessment.

• Considerations of a range of cognitive complexity in common assessments, especially through the use of performance assessments

Ensuring that curriculum and assessments are aligned to "rigorous" content standards is, in itself, insufficient for preparing students for the challenges of the 21st century. Current research on the factors influencing student outcomes and contributing to academic richness supports the concept that learning is optimized when students are engaged in activities that require complex thinking and the application of knowledge. Expert teachers provide *all* students with challenging tasks and demanding goals, structure learning so that students can reach high goals, and know how to enhance both surface and deep learning of content (Darling-Hammond, 2010; Hattie, 2002; Hess & Gong, 2015).

Authors of *Knowing What Students Know* (National Research Council [NRC], 2001) state that students learn skills and acquire knowledge more readily when they understand concepts more deeply, recognize their relevance, and can transfer that learning to new or more complex situations. Transfer is more likely to occur when learners have developed deep understanding of content and when initial learning focuses on underlying principles and cause–effect relationships. Consequently, assessments that include difficult items but lack items that stretch students to think deeply about content fall short of measuring progress toward building expertise in reading, writing, and communication.

Assessments—or better yet, a combination of assessments (multiple measures)—must provide teachers with clear actionable data in order to address learning strengths and needs and engage all learners more fully in their own learning. The goal, therefore, is to identify or develop not only reliable and valid assessments, but assessments that can provide actionable data to teachers about deeper understanding.

5.5 Revisiting Alignment From a Systems Perspective

Good educational systems must have the capacity to evolve over time. Testing systems must also have this capacity, both in relation to their purposes and the actual assessment instruments that are created. Given the more rigorous demands on learning and teaching that have become accepted internationally, exemplified by recent Common Core State Standards, test validation requires a concomitant rigor with a broad range of strong evidence . . . not just testing those aspects that are easy to test.

ISDDE Working Group on Examinations and Policy, Black et al., 2011

What Makes Assessments Valid or Reliable?

In Module 3, you were introduced to several "validation" protocols for analyzing or developing common assessments, using PLC **TOOLS #9, #10, #16A,** and **#16B**. Embedded in those tools and throughout other discussions in the *Local Assessment Toolkit* related to the technical criteria of high-quality assessment, the terms *reliable* and *valid* continue to pop up. We hear them so often, we rarely think about what each one actually means—at least I know I did that until I came upon an analogy that helped me to remember and differentiate them. I have since put my spin on an explanation given by McKenna and Stahl (2003, p. 35).

What makes an assessment reliable? Think about McDonald's. McDonald's is reliable—same menu, same ingredients, same quality, same prices—same results every time, no matter which McDonald's you go to anywhere in the world. Reliable assessments are like McDonald's hamburgers. No matter who takes the assessment or who scores it, the score determination will be the same. The more an assessment is like a hamburger (with narrowly defined content being assessed, given under similar or standardized conditions, and using a clear scoring key), the easier it is to ensure that different raters will score them exactly the same. Relibiltiy is good thing, especially when we are talking about common assessments. We want teachers in my school to score assessments the way teachers in other schools would score them. We want our students to be scored by others, the way we would score them. Reliability—consistency of results—builds credibility and confidence in using the assessment and interpreting results. Very high reliability for an assessment is a ratio expressed as a decimal. The closer the reliability coefficient is to 1.0 (0.9 – 1.0 = excellent), the higher and more reliable the test. Between 0.9 and 0.8 is considered "good" reliability. Including more test questions or scoring points or triangulating scores across measures can sometimes increase reliability.

What makes an assessment valid? Imagine that I've come to town to work with your school and I ask where I can get a healthy meal? Or a meal that tastes great and reflects the culture of the region? My bet is that McDonald's does not even come to mind, even though it is highly reliable. McDonalds—and tests—can be reliable, but still not be valid for the intended purpose. A valid test is one that actually assesses what is proposed to be assessed and therefore accurate interpretations about learning can be made. There is no "number" that determines validity, as there is with reliability. Evidence, such as what is seen in student work samples, and professional judgments are used to decide if an assessment is valid, assessing the intended content or performance and producing results that lead to defensible interpretations about learning. An editing test in writing might be reliably scored but would not be valid if we wanted to know about a student's skills in developing a text-based argument. Both reliability and validity are harder to achieve—but not impossible—when assessments become more complex, such as when using open-ended performance tasks and student-designed projects scored with common rubrics. Increasing interrater reliability for performance-based assessments requires periodic calibration sessions using anchor sets for scoring practice, annotated student work at all performance levels, and clear descriptors in scoring rubrics. An assessment with a rubric is not enough to achieve high reliability.

Aligned Assessments, Aligned Systems

For many years, I worked with states to develop assessments and test specification, and to conduct alignment studies for large-scale assessments administered to both general education and special education students. **Alignment** has generally been defined as a measure of the extent to which a state's standards and assessments "agree" and the degree to which they work in conjunction with each other to guide and support student learning. It is not a question that yields a simple yes or no response; rather, alignment is a considered judgment based on a number of complex factors that collectively determine the degree to which the assessment tools used and evidence collected will gauge how well students are demonstrating achievement of the standards. *In other words, an alignment study tells you how effective the end-of-year summative assessment—and the assessment system as a whole—is in measuring the depth and breadth of knowledge and skills set forth in the content standards and the performance goals for each grade level.* This probably seems like a tall order for local assessment systems to undertake.

Actually, alignment studies used to be pretty straightforward: Analyze each test item for what content and depth of knowledge it assesses and use that data to determine what is emphasized and to what degree all content standards are covered in the assessment. Is this test too easy? Too hard? Too narrow in scope? Or, as with the story of Goldilocks, "Is it just right?"

College and career-ready (CCR) standards and assessments of proficiency-based learning place a greater burden on determining whether or not assessments and the assessment system are well aligned. By their nature, CCR assessments must be broader in scope than assessments have needed to be in the past. They are composed not only of test items but may also include performance tasks, open-ended prompts, scoring guides, and a range of text passages and text types. They may also assess the complex challenges laid out in CCR expectations (e.g., the ability to conduct short research projects and presentations, the ability to construct viable mathematical arguments). Let's face it, this cannot be done well in one on-demand test at the end of the school year. Given the purpose, scope, and challenges implementing today's college- and career-ready standards and assessments, a broader and deeper examination is now required than has been addressed with alignment studies of the past. I believe that a combination of mixed measures (e.g., complementary formative, interim, and summative assessments), rather than a single assessment provides the best data for making the overall determination of strong assessment system alignment. That requires looking at what is assessed over a school year, the assessments included in the system, and the assessment system as a whole.

Six Questions Alignment Studies Can Answer

Alignment studies are designed to examine how well an assessment design and the test items and tasks match the intent (standards to be assessed). Six central questions can be answered by the results of the alignment analyses of prioritized assessments in local assessment systems.

1. To what degree is there a strong *content match* between the test items or tasks (and the tests as a whole) and the standards (e.g., defined by eligible grade-level content or assessment targets)? Content alignment includes grade-level skills and concepts and the ways in which students are expected to demonstrate their understanding of them.

2. Are the test items or tasks (and the tests as a whole) more rigorous, less rigorous, or of comparable *rigor and complexity* to the intended rigor of the standards and performance expectations at each grade level? Rigor alignment may include an analysis of the complexity of content, DOK and processing demands (e.g., recall versus justification), and the degree to which assessment tasks reflect preparation for more challenging work in the next grade level or course.

3. Is the *source of challenge* for test items or tasks appropriate? That is, is the hardest thing about the test items or tasks that which the item or task is targeting for assessment; or is there an underlying factor making the item more difficult to access or comprehend than it should be? For example, is there an algebra demand embedded in items assessing other math content? Does the reader need particular background knowledge of the topic in order to answer some of the text-related questions? Is there an unnecessary or extensive linguistic or reading load (e.g., complex sentences) in mathematics items? Do math stimuli include unfamiliar and perhaps unnecessary or above-grade-level vocabulary or confusing graphics?

4. Are the *texts or stimuli* for reading, writing, and literacy assessments of appropriate length and complexity for this grade level? And does the balance between literary and informational texts appropriately reflect the intent of the CCR standards and have coherence with the state's test blueprint? This criterion is not meant to imply that local assessments need to replicate the state assessment. However, local assessments need to prepare students for assessments that are at least as rigorous as large-scale assessments students might be preparing to take (e.g., state assessment, ACT for college entrance).

5. To what degree does the content coverage and test design (of the assessment or combination of assessments) assess all of the *major strands or claims* (i.e., evidence-centered designed assessments) as described in eligible content (standards) in English language arts/literacy, mathematics, or science, for example, at corresponding grade levels?

6. To what degree does the test blueprint and *set of items* (test as a whole) *emphasize essential content and performance expectations* (e.g., application of mathematical practices to mathematics concepts and procedures; increasing text complexity) to elicit evidence that students are preparing to perform more sophisticated, college and career-type work in the future?

One-way alignment: Using test blueprints

One-way alignment compares what is assessed in a single assessment with the intended content and rigor of the standards for that grade level. In this alignment process, you look "one way" from the assessment to the standards to see if items or tasks in the assessment "match" some or all parts of the standards for the grade level. The findings from conducting a one-way alignment will tell you to what degree assessment items are aligned with standards. In some cases, you may find that some content being assessed is not grade-level content or not part of the standards at all; or

Figure 5.3 Degrees of Alignment: Visuals show from top left, moving clockwise: (1) a small or targeted amount of standards are assessed; (2) there is some overlap between what is in the standards and what is actually assessed, but a great deal of content outside of the standards is also being assessed; (3) all standards are assessed, but more content is on the assessment than is in the standards; and (4) a selection of standards, but not all standards, are being assessed—have these standards been intentionally prioritized for assessment?

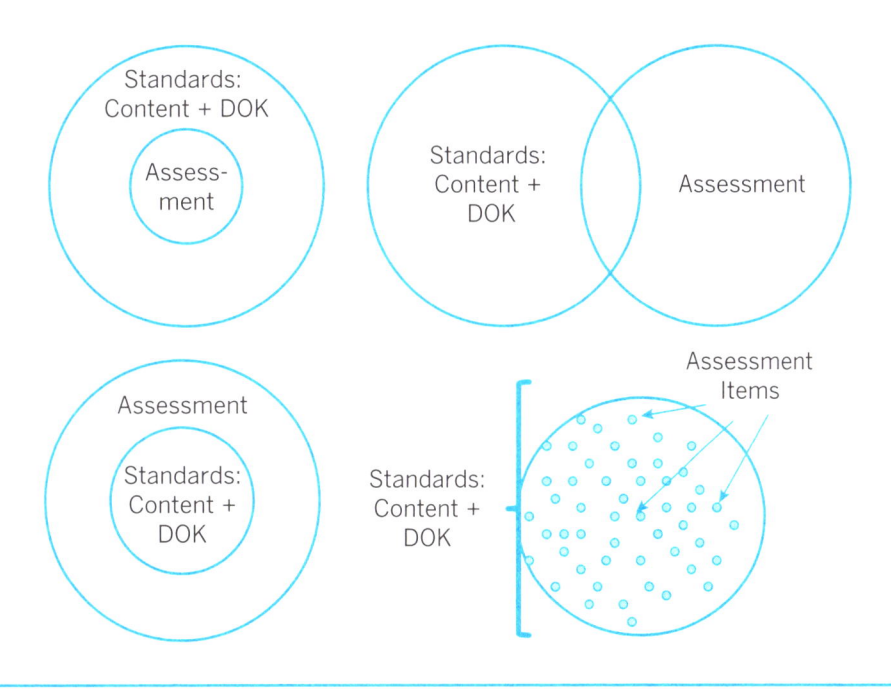

you might learn that while every test item and task is aligned to grade-level standards, only a very small number of standards are actually being assessed. Figure 5.3 illustrates differing degrees of alignment possible.

Alignment **TOOL #29** (Basic Individual Test Blueprint) can be used to identify basic information about what is being assessed with each item or task in an assessment—content, rigor, and balance of emphasis determined by how many score points each item will received. Alignment **TOOL #31** (Advanced Individual Test Blueprint) provides the same basic information as **TOOL #29** plus allows for a more sophisticated analysis of such things as application of math practices; balance of items assessing math concepts, math procedures, or math problem solving and reasoning; complexity and range of texts; and the type and quality of test items. Schools might begin with **TOOL #29** and later move to using **TOOL #31**, which takes longer to complete, but also provides much richer information about what content, skills, and dispositions are being assessed.

Two-way alignment: Using assessment system blueprints

Two-way alignment looks both at the assessments and at *all of* the standards. This alignment process takes the assessments determined to be aligned (using **TOOL #29** or **TOOL #31**) and builds the system by analyzing (a) whether all or most standards are being adequately assessed at some point in time; and (b) if the assessment emphasis (most of the test score points) represents the instructional emphasis (prioritizing what is most important to teach and learn). For example, if the writing standards expect students to write narratives, text-based informational pieces, and opinion pieces during the school year, as well as demonstrate the ability to edit for grammar, usage, and mechanics, then there should be multiple assessment tasks (and scoring rubrics) that address all of these components of writing. An assessment system blueprint (Alignment **TOOL #30**) for writing would list high-priority writing assessments given across the school year at each grade level (formative, interim, or summative) and indicate which writing content or skills and intended DOK levels are being emphasized by each one. Alignment **TOOL #30** includes two examples of what assessment system blueprints might look like when completed.

My recommendation in building an assessment system blueprint is to slowly add aligned assessments to a template (like Alignment **TOOL #30**) for one grade level and one content area as they are developed, piloted, and refined. Generally, a combination of existing assessments, along with new assessments will begin to populate the system blueprint. It will likely take one to two years to complete each content area K–12, but the results will be worth it. In my experience, as you add in aligned assessments, you begin to see assessment gaps that might have been initially overlooked. In one K–8 mathematics project that I worked on with two Vermont school districts, the first big aha was that, while every existing mathematics assessment clearly aligned to some math content in the standards, few or no math practices were being assessed and some content was never assessed. This ultimately led to new assessment development and piloting and a deeper understanding of high-quality assessments.

Alignment **TOOL #30** (Assessment System Blueprint) and **TOOL #31** (Advanced Individual Test Blueprint) have been designed not only to incorporate test item alignment to content and intended rigor, but also to reveal the dimensions that are often examined in formal alignment studies: categorical concurrence, depth of knowledge consistency, range of knowledge correspondence, balance of representation, and source of challenge. Webb (2005) describes each alignment criterion in this way:

- *Categorical Concurrence*—This criterion measures the extent to which the same or consistent categories of content appear in the standards and the assessments. The criterion is met for a given standard if there are more than five assessment items targeting that standard.
- *Depth-of-Knowledge Consistency*—This criterion measures the degree to which the knowledge elicited from students on the assessment is as complex within the content area as what students are expected to know and do as stated in the standards. The criterion is met if more than half of targeted objectives are hit by items of the appropriate complexity.
- *Range-of-Knowledge Correspondence*—This criterion determines whether the span of knowledge expected of students on the basis of a standard corresponds to the span of knowledge that students need in order to correctly answer the corresponding assessment items or activities. The criterion is met for a given standard if more than half of the objectives that fall under that standard are targeted by assessment items.
- *Balance of Representation*—This criterion measures whether objectives that fall under a specific standard are given relatively equal emphasis on the assessment.
- *Source of Challenge*—This criterion is met if the primary difficulty of the assessment items is significantly related to students' knowledge and skill in the content area as represented in the standards.

Applying Alignment Criteria

During a local review of the alignment dimensions (working with **TOOL #30** and **TOOL #31**), you may want to use the related guiding questions below. Note that source of challenge (SOC) has already been considered during the analysis of test items and assessment tasks and my tools apply balance of representation and range of knowledge a bit differently than Webb does. Rather than "equal" emphasis, I believe that the test design should designate greater or lesser emphasis on those test items and tasks that assess deeper understanding. This is the only way to ensure that test scores or results can be used to make interpretations about learning that go beyond basic skills and concepts. A high score should mean the student demonstrates the broader and deeper thinking required to be college and career ready—in other words, the student demonstrates the ability to transfer.

1. Categorical concurrence—Do the same "categories" of knowledge and skills appear in both the standards and the assessments in our system? For example, do the mathematics assessments include math skills, math concepts, and math problem solving, since all three "categories" are included in the state's mathematics standards? In literacy assessments, are all "categories" of writing genre assessed?

2. Depth-of-Knowledge (DOK)—Do the assessments reflect the cognitive complexity of the concepts and processes described in the CCR standards and/or proficiency-based system? In other words, are the assessments as cognitively challenging as the expectations for learning? This is often the most overlooked alignment component at the local (school) level. It requires both a careful analysis of the performance being targeted by the assessment tasks and a strong working knowledge of what rigor can look like and how it might be assessed in each content area. (CRM **TOOLS #1–#5D** can be helpful with this criterion.)

3. Balance of Representation—How are test items and score points distributed across content being assessed? Do the assessments reflect the instructional emphasis (e.g., college and career readiness) we have prioritized? (I take a different perspective from Webb's "rule" about equal emphasis for all standards. My suggestion is to predetermine what SHOULD be emphasized, especially if deeper understanding is your ultimate goal for learning.)

4. Range-of-Knowledge—Will the combination of assessments yield scores that reflect the full range of achievement implied by CCR standards and local priorities? This cannot be accomplished without combining standards or extending how they are applied in performance-based assessments.

> *Discuss*: How is one-way alignment different from two-way alignment? What new insights do you have about these concepts or about the quality of assessments in use? How could this understanding influence the refinement or further development of your local assessment system? Could this change how you prioritize content and intended rigor for assessments included in your local system?

5.6 Interpreting Results From Local Assessment Analyses

The Alignment Tools in Module 5 should prepare assessment teams for developing an assessment philosophy and analyzing local assessments. After using Alignment **TOOLS #29, #31, or #33,** your team will want to review the data and comments collected for each assessment and decide ways you might improve the quality of either individual assessments or the assessment system as a whole (Alignment **TOOL #30**). The following questions can be useful in determining whether or not revisions to specific assessments or scoring guides might be warranted before including them in the system as high-priority assessments:

1. *Content: Is the intended content assessed?* (Which standards are assessed? Which standards are emphasized?—based on more items or fewer items or score points.)

2. *Rigor: Is there a range of cognitive demand across the assessment?* A general rule of thumb is that about half of the test points should be conceptual (DOK 2): main idea, basic interpretations (e.g., word meaning in context), summarize text, sequence events; do routine math word problems where student must decide what strategy to use, and then perform it. Some DOK 3–type tasks should be included: interpret and use text evidence to support your interpretation, solve a math problem and provide reasoning or support as to why this solution or approach is reasonable (e.g., solve it a second way to show it is correct, explain why you did it this way and not another way).

3. *Balance: Does the test emphasis reflect the intent (such as described in the test blueprint or task shell)?* For example, what if the blueprint or task shell states that items require use of text evidence to interpret text meaning, but all items are lower DOK levels—these are questions that simply require locating explicit information. Some standards are not actually assessed, but were intended to be assessed. Replace some lower-level items with new items or tasks with greater complexity.

4. Comparability: When there are options for students or teachers to choose from different assessment tasks (e.g., select from a task bank or choose a prompt), are the resulting tasks of comparable quality and cognitive demand? If not, is the intent that assessments will assess differing content or be of varying complexity? This presents a validity concern: validity = testing what is intended to be assessed so you can make valid (accurate) inferences about student learning.

5. Scaffolding: When scaffolding is included in the assessment tasks, do the extra supports change what is actually being assessed? For example, "chunking text" to break it up and inset questions instead of all questions at the end still tests reading comprehension without changing the decoding skills needed to unlock meaning. On the other hand, giving students all of the steps to solve a complex math problem eliminates the ability to assess whether or not students can devise a plan to solve the problem. They are simply following a "recipe."

6. Source of Challenge (SOC): Are there any ill-constructed items or prompts within the assessment? They should be removed or revised and be piloted <u>again.</u> Additional sources of challenge (causing students not to be able to show what they know) may be due to test designers not applying principles of Universal Design (identified in PLC **TOOL #9** and in Appendix C). These items or tasks may not be accessible to all learners. <u>Piloting or using cognitive labs and item analysis are essential for all new assessment items or tasks. Determine: Which students are getting this right? And which students are getting this item wrong or are confused by what is expected?</u>

7. Scoring Guides: Are scoring guides provided for all open-ended tasks and constructed response items? Do they mirror content plus intended cognitive demand of standards or proficiencies being assessed?

8. Repiloting: After administering the assessment and reviewing results, are changes needed to the test items, performance tasks, or scoring guides? Every first administration should be seen as a pilot—to see if the format and content actually elicit evidence of what is intended to be assessed. You may need to revise and pilot again.

9. *Use of texts: For assessments requiring use of texts, examine the texts used*:

    a. For vocabulary items that require use of context, is the context actually there in the text? Or are you really testing prior knowledge of what words mean?

    b. Do the texts used for assessment represent high-quality (authentic) texts? Are they strong models of the genre, illustrating what a published text would look like (e.g., a news story, an informational article)?

c. When there are multiple texts required to answer or respond to, are they of varying complexity? Text complexity involves more than a simple Lexile number. Other complexity factors include predictable genre-specific features, the reasoning required to understand complex themes, and interpreting authors' discourse styles or more complex text structures (e.g., proposition–support, critique, deductive–inductive).

d. Are both print and nonprint texts used appropriate to the assessment task?

Reflections

With colleagues, take a minute to reflect on the topics covered in this module. Then identify a useful takeaway, something for your team to try or apply.

Ways we are refining our thinking about local assessment systems:
- ?
- ?

Strategies for evaluating local assessments:
- Consider the potential Source of Challenge in test items or tasks
- ?
- ?

℞ Our team prescription for improving the quality of our local assessment system:

PART 2: Support Materials for Module 5

I. A Workshop Plan for Module 5

Kolb's Experiential Learning Cycle **Suggested Activities**

Stage 1: WHY is this new learning important to me? And what do I already know?
Moving from Concrete Experience to Reflective Observation

Create a concrete experience, asking participants to make connections, drawing on personal knowledge and experience. Small groups compare and reflect on common ideas.

- Activity: In small groups, draft your assessment philosophy. *What are three to five key points you'd include?*
- Resource: View and discuss a video: "5 Keys to Comprehensive (classroom) Assessment" (https://www.edutopia.org/comprehensive-assessment-introduction). Compare these five ideas to the group's key ideas in their assessment philosophy.
- Activity: Individual teachers complete Alignment **TOOL #27**, Year-at-a-Glance for assessments used <u>during one month</u>. Share in small groups who teach the same content area or grade level. Are there any assessment trends in your classroom? Across classrooms at the same grade level and content area?

Stage 2: WHAT do the research and experts say?
Moving from Reflective Observation to Abstract Conceptualization

- Help participants connect their personal reflections to broader, more abstract generalizations. Stop frequently (every 15–20 minutes) to consolidate the new learning.
- Present the five indicators of local comprehensive assessment systems. Discuss or identify which tools in the *Local Assessment Toolkit* could be used to support the design of a comprehensive assessment system.
- Discuss: What's the difference between an assessment system and a <u>comprehensive</u> assessment system?
- Activity: Small groups brainstorm perceived benefits and challenges of developing a local assessment system that is comprehensive. Provide local examples to show where criteria are being met (the "Aces") and identify gaps (the "Spaces") using Alignment **Tool #28**.

380   A Local Assessment Toolkit to Promote Deeper Learning

Stage 3: HOW does this work? How can I apply this?

Moving from Abstract Conceptualization to Active Experimentation

Use tools and protocols to examine examples and strategies:

- Discuss potential usefulness of Alignment **TOOL #27**, Year-at-a-Glance, to gather baseline data on local assessment use.

- Activity: Provide guided practice using Alignment **TOOL #29** to analyze two high-priority summative assessments (exam vs. performance task). Compare the "balance of emphasis"—the focus of the most score points for each assessment. *Does emphasis reflect learning that you value most?*

- Activity: Provide guided practice using Alignment **TOOL #30** to map multiple high-priority assessments at one grade level. Using local assessments will reveal assessment gaps in the local system.

Stage 4: WHAT IF I experimented with this? What might work in my classroom or school?

Moving from Active Experimentation back to Concrete Experiences

- Activity: Collaboratively use the analysis of your assessment system (Alignment **TOOL #28**) to identify short- and long-term action steps.

- Activity: Draft an assessment philosophy for your school district.

- Activity: Have grade-level teams use Alignment **TOOL #33** to analyze items in an item or task bank.

- Activity: Choose several "high-priority assessments" (benchmark assessments, performance tasks, exams, etc.) currently in use and use them in a practice alignment study as a professional development activity for school staff. (Alignment **TOOL #29 or #31**)

Source: Stages adapted from Kolb (1984) and McCarthy (1987).

II. The Hess Alignment Tools

About the Tools in This Module

The tools in Module 5 (see Table 5.2) have been used by local assessment teams to examine the alignment of high-priority assessments and to examine the quality and comprehensiveness of the local assessment system.

Table 5.2 Overview of the Hess Alignment Tools

TOOL	POSSIBLE USES FOR EACH HESS ALIGNMENT TOOL
27 Year-at-a-Glance: Mapping Classroom-Based Assessments Over the School Year	Individual teachers or grade-level teams map use of existing classroom assessments as the first step to identifying potential assessment overlap and gaps. A completed ELA example is also included.
28 Discussion Questions: Examining Our Local Assessment System	Leadership teams can use the guiding questions to discuss and examine the current local assessment philosophy and system components and determine next steps for improving the quality and comprehensiveness of the local assessment system.
29 Basic Individual Test Blueprint Analysis Worksheet: One-Way Alignment, Mapping One Assessment Test or Performance Task to Standards and Intended DOK	Individual teachers or grade-level teams can analyze current assessments to determine the degree of alignment to intended content and rigor and identify what is being emphasized in the assessment, in terms of the potential number of score points for each item or task. Identifying specific assessment categories using this tool is optional. A completed math example is also included. PLC **TOOLS #9 and #10** (Module 3) can be used to analyze individual assessments, prior to compiling results.
30 Assessment System Blueprint—Mapping Content Standards or Proficiencies to Assessments	Grade-level or content teams analyze current high-priority assessments to determine the degree of alignment to intended content and rigor, range of knowledge and categories being assessed, and what is being emphasized in each assessment. This is done to build a system overview of assessments in use. Two completed examples are also included.
31 Advanced Individual Test Blueprint Analysis Worksheets: One-Way Alignment, With Additional Factors to Consider	Grade-level or content teams analyze current high-priority assessments to determine the degree of alignment to intended content and rigor, range of knowledge and categories being assessed, and determine what is being emphasized in each assessment. Two examples of content-specific templates are included. These should be customized by content area and intent. PLC **TOOLS #9 and #10** (Module 3) can be used to analyze individual assessments, prior to compiling results.

TOOL	POSSIBLE USES FOR EACH HESS ALIGNMENT TOOL
32 Text Complexity Analyses Summary	Grade-level or content teams analyze current high-priority literacy assessments to determine and summarize the complexity of texts used in each assessment. This template compiles information from Text Complexity **TOOLS #7 and #8**.
33 Item or Task Bank Review	Grade-level or content teams analyze item or task banks to determine the degree of alignment with local assessment priorities and a rationale for adopting the use of the assessments. PLC **TOOLS #9 and #10** (Module 3) can be used to analyze individual assessments, prior to compiling results.

YEAR-AT-A-GLANCE: PLANNING CLASSROOM-BASED ASSESSMENTS OVER THE SCHOOL YEAR

Teacher: _____   Content Area: _____   Grade: _____

Content Clusters/ Proficiency Areas	Aug.–Sept.	Oct.	Nov.–Dec.	Jan.	Feb.	March	April	May–June	When or how often

Tool 27

Available for download at **resources.corwin.com/HessToolkit**

Copyright © 2018 by Corwin. All rights reserved. Reprinted from *A Local Assessment Toolkit to Promote Deeper Learning: Transforming Research into Practice* by Karin Hess. Thousand Oaks, CA: Corwin, www.corwin.com. Reproduction authorized only for the local school site or nonprofit organization that has purchased this book.

SAMPLE—YEAR-AT-A-GLANCE: PLANNING CLASSROOM-BASED ASSESSMENTS OVER THE SCHOOL YEAR

Tool 27

Teacher: _____ Content Area: <u>ELA</u> Grade: <u>4</u>

Proficiency Areas + Others	Aug.–Sept.	Oct.	Nov.–Dec.	Jan.	Feb.	March	April	May–June	When or how often
1–Foundational Reading Skills	Screening Test Fluency Checks	Phonics assmt. targeted students	Fluency Checks	Conferencing	Fluency Checks	Conferencing	Fluency Checks	Conferencing	Periodic Targeted small groups, indiv
Vocabulary Development	vocab strategies	Knowledge rating scales	Knowledge rating scales	Vocab review assmt.	Knowledge rating scales	Knowledge rating scales	State assessment	Vocab review assmt	Ongoing
2–Reading Lit 3–Reading Info	Short PTs; discussion	Literature circles	Literature circles	Content-based reading and discussion	Performance tasks; discussion	Content-based reading and discussion	Performance tasks; discussion	Performance tasks; discussion	Daily small-group guided reading
4–Narratives 5–Informational 6–Opinions	Free-writes, peer or self-assessed Narratives—2 units	Free-writes, peer or self-assessed Conferencing	Writing prompts—organization, idea development	Free-write, peer or self-assessed Informational—2 units	Soc Studies unit—Report Writing Conferencing	Writing prompts—organization, idea development	Free-write, peer or self-assessed Opinion—2 units	Portfolio, peer or self-assessed	Weekly—end of every ELA unit Conferencing
Writing Conventions, Usage, Spelling	DSA spelling survey and Feature inventories	Writing scored for conventions	Writing scored for conventions	DSA spelling survey and Feature inventories		Writing scored for conventions		Writing scored for conventions	Weekly—spelling + writing
7–Speaking or Listening	Peer conferencing	Literature circles	Literature circles	Group-work presentation	Group-work presentation	Peer conferencing	Science Unit presentation	Peer conferencing	Informal—daily Formal—2
8–Inquiry and Research				Soc Studies unit	Soc Studies unit	Science Unit	Science Unit		
Reading and Writing Habits, Dispositions	Individual Book log and Writing attitude survey	Reading attitude survey Conferencing Individual Book log	Individual Book log and goal setting	Individual Book log Conferencing	Individual Book log	Individual Book log and goal monitoring Conferencing	Individual Book log	Reading and Writing attitude survey Conferencing Book log and goal evaluation	Weekly—part of every ELA unit

Available for download at **resources.corwin.com/HessToolkit**

Copyright © 2018 by Corwin. All rights reserved. Reprinted from *A Local Assessment Toolkit to Promote Deeper Learning: Transforming Research into Practice* by Karin Hess. Thousand Oaks, CA: Corwin, www.corwin.com. Reproduction authorized only for the local school site or nonprofit organization that has purchased this book.

DISCUSSION QUESTIONS: EXAMINING OUR LOCAL ASSESSMENT SYSTEM

Tool 28

LAS Indicator 1: *Do we include these key components in our local assessment system? How comprehensive is our system?*

To what degree does our system . . .
(a) include technically sound assessments of academic achievement and explicit or shared district-based goals for learning (e.g., proficiencies, transferrable skills, community service);
(b) illustrate how assessments and assessment data interact;
(c) provide adequate protocols, professional development, and leadership regarding implementation of assessment principles and practices;
(d) establish explicit and well-coordinated mechanisms (feedback loops) for managing use of assessments, assessment data, or results and using data to address individual student needs?

Aces (what's useful and relevant right now):

Spaces (where do we need work; what are the gaps):

LAS Indicator 2: *Is our (proficiency-based) assessment philosophy supported by coherent policy and practices?*

Do we have a clear statement of purpose? What is the focus (e.g., "common" learning targets, learning environments and pathways, student-centered or personalized learning)?

Does the (proficiency-based) assessment system . . .
- establish a common language and perspective about assessing content, skills, and deeper understanding and the interpretation and use of data?
- improve curriculum, instruction, and student engagement?
- elevate expectations and learning opportunities for all students?
- strengthen communication about student performance with students and their families and within the educational community?
- Other?

Aces (what's useful and relevant right now):

Spaces (where do we need work; what are the gaps):

LAS Indicator 3: *Do we communicate how learning expectations for all students relate to assessment types, purposes, and uses?*

Start by ranking these components as follows: <u>Fully</u> in place, <u>Partly</u> in place, or <u>Limited</u> needing updating or revision or replacement. Then decide what's working well and potential gaps.

How comprehensive is our assessment system? Does it include . . .

- a range of assessment types and formats—observation, short answer, constructed response, unit assessments, performance tasks, or extended projects, for example?
- guidelines for assessment purposes and users (audience)—Formative, Interim, Summative?
- alignment with opportunity to learn or curriculum and instruction (e.g., use of common or interim assessments with administration guidelines, and student work samples; progress monitoring)?
- considerations for assessing young children, special populations?
- a communication plan—Communicating expectations and results to students, parents, and the community?

Aces (what's useful and relevant right now):

Spaces (where do we need work; what are the gaps):

(Continued)

continued . . .

DISCUSSION QUESTIONS: EXAMINING OUR LOCAL ASSESSMENT SYSTEM

Tool 28

LAS Indicator 4: Do our assessment processes ensure that assessments and bodies of evidence are of high quality?

Are there common protocols and structures in place for . . .

- clear agreed-upon learning expectations (proficiencies) and performance scales that guide assessment development, evidence-based grading, and interpreting and reporting results?
- establishing validity: content + performance or cognitive rigor alignment (standards, proficiencies)?
- checking reliability: consistency of scoring and interpretations?
- ensuring fairness and engagement: All students are able to access and demonstrate authentic learning?
- combining multiple measures: a process for combining results from different assessments, comparability?
- developing and using common tools: assessment system is articulated by content area and assessment blueprints (alignment), useful in determining proficiency (e.g., standard setting, student work analysis, Body of Evidence), validation protocols (e.g., cognitive labs, performance task review), and classroom observations?
- creating verification methods for evaluating a student's "Body of Assessment Evidence" (Body of Evidence means each student's assessment evidence collected over time, such as in a portfolio)?

Aces (what's useful and relevant right now):

Spaces (where do we need work; what are the gaps):

LAS Indicator 5: Do we have a comprehensive district implementation plan?

Does the district assessment plan . . .
- lay out multiyear implementation for each content area K–12: developing, piloting, refining assessments and curriculum that are proficiency based and responsive to established learning progressions?
- describe and provide for feedback loops and leadership (e.g., to document and support implementation)?
- identify supports to teachers: professional development, curriculum, PLCs, student work analysis?
- systematically collect accreditation evidence?

Aces (what's useful and relevant right now):

Spaces (where do we need work; what are the gaps):

Possible Action Steps			
Steps to be taken	Why is it important to us?	Supports or resources needed	By when?

online resources Available for download at **resources.corwin.com/HessToolkit**

Copyright © 2018 by Corwin. All rights reserved. Reprinted from *A Local Assessment Toolkit to Promote Deeper Learning: Transforming Research into Practice* by Karin Hess. Thousand Oaks, CA: Corwin, www.corwin.com. Reproduction authorized only for the local school site or nonprofit organization that has purchased this book.

BASIC INDIVIDUAL TEST BLUEPRINT ANALYSIS WORKSHEET
One-Way Alignment: Mapping One Assessment Test or Performance Task to Standards and Intended DOK

Use this worksheet to review a single assessment (course exam, common task, project, etc.) being considered for use *in making overall proficiency decisions*.

Assessment Name/Task: _____ Content Area: _____

Course or "Opportunity" of Assessment: _____

List by Item # or Rubric Criterion Assessed	Item Intended DOK	Content Focus *Standards Assessed*	# of Test Points—for Each Item or Part (some items may have multiple points)				Notes Standard Assessed or Emphasis? (F) Fully—(P) Partially?
Totals							

Notes about this test, assessment task, or rubric:

Available for download at **resources.corwin.com/HessToolkit**

Copyright © 2018 by Corwin. All rights reserved. Reprinted from *A Local Assessment Toolkit to Promote Deeper Learning: Transforming Research into Practice* by Karin Hess. Thousand Oaks, CA: Corwin, www.corwin.com. Reproduction authorized only for the local school site or nonprofit organization that has purchased this book.

BASIC INDIVIDUAL TEST BLUEPRINT ANALYSIS WORKSHEET
One-Way Alignment: Mapping One Assessment Test or Performance Task to Standards and Intended DOK (Explained)

Tool 29

Use this worksheet to review an individual assessment (course exam, common task, project, etc.) being considered for use *in making overall proficiency decisions*.

Assessment Name/Task: _____ Content Area: _____

Course or "Opportunity" of Assessment: _____

List by Item # or Rubric Criterion Assessed	Item Intended DOK	Content Focus *Standards Assessed*	# of Test Points—for Each Item or Part (some items may have multiple points)				Notes Standard Assessed or Emphasis? (F) Fully—(P) Partially?
			Skills GUM	Concepts Organization	Reasoning Ideas, Logic	Use of Evidence	
			1 pt	2 pts	3 pts	2 pts	
#1, #4, #5, #8	2						
#2, #3, #6, #7, #10, #11	1	L-1, 2, 3	5 pts				Editing for GUM
#12 Performance task	3	W-1, L-1, 2	1 pt	2 pts	3 pts	2 pts	Develop text-based argument; edit GUM
Totals							

Callouts:
- You may want to determine general categories assessed. Does scoring give more weight to some items (e.g., reasoning vs. GUM)?
- It's important to know whether all (F) or only part (P) of a standard is being assessed. Multiple items *together* might assess all parts.
- If multiple items assess the same standards and the same DOK level, it's easier to see emphasis if you list them together.
- Do totals reflect an appropriate "balance" or emphasis of score points for a high-priority assessment?

Notes about this test, assessment task, or rubric:

Available for download at **resources.corwin.com/HessToolkit**

Copyright © 2018 by Corwin. All rights reserved. Reprinted from *A Local Assessment Toolkit to Promote Deeper Learning: Transforming Research into Practice* by Karin Hess. Thousand Oaks, CA: Corwin, www.corwin.com. Reproduction authorized only for the local school site or nonprofit organization that has purchased this book.

BASIC INDIVIDUAL TEST BLUEPRINT ANALYSIS WORKSHEET
One-Way Alignment: Mapping One Assessment Test or Performance Task to Standards and Intended DOK (Example)

Tool 29

EXAMPLE: *Math Assessment Alignment*

Assessment Task: <u>Intersecting Polygons (see description below)</u> Content Area: <u>Mathematics</u>

Course or "Opportunity" of Assessment: <u>All 9th-grade students</u>

A partial EXAMPLE: This is an on-demand (50-minute) assessment, scored with a rubric. (See notes below.)

List by Item # or Rubric Criterion Assessed	Item DOK	Content Focus *Standards Assessed*	# of Test Points—for Each Item or Part				Notes Standard Assessed or Emphasis? (F) Fully—(P) Partially?
			Concepts Procedure Precision	Problem Solving	Abstract Reasoning, Argue	Modeling	
(1a) F&A 10-3 M&G 10-8	1. 2	Solve & graph	1			1	(F&A 10-3) Solve linear equation—P
(1b) F&A 10-3 M&G 10-8	1, 2	Solve & graph	1			1	(M&G 10-8) Use coordinate system to graph equations—P
(1c) F&A 10-3 M&G 10-8	1, 2	Solve & graph	1			1	
(1d) F&A 10-3 M&G 10-8	1, 2	Solve & graph	1			1	
(2a)	1	Describe					
(2b)	1	Identify Intersection					
(2c)	2/3	Verify			2		
(3a) M&G 10-2	2/3	Recall char of polygon	1				(M&G 10-2) properties of polygon—P
(3b)			1				
(3c) M&G 10-2	2/3		1	1	1		(M&G 10-2) use properties to justify solution—P
TOTALS			7	1	1	4	

Notes about this test, assessment task, or rubric:
Rubric only gives full credit if solved and graphed correctly (1a–1d).

1. Graph these four (linear) equations (1a–d) on the same coordinate plane, labeling axes and including all calculations.
2. Describe how each line relates to the others. (2b) For all lines that intersect, identify points of intersection. (2c) Using algebra, verify points of intersection.
3. (3a) How many polygons are created by the intersecting lines? (3b) Describe in as many ways as possible the characteristics and relationships of the polygons. (3c) Justify each characteristic and relationship mathematically. Be very specific with your descriptions. Write an explanation that includes all mathematical evidence of your findings.

Available for download at **resources.corwin.com/HessToolkit**

Copyright © 2018 by Corwin. All rights reserved. Reprinted from *A Local Assessment Toolkit to Promote Deeper Learning: Transforming Research into Practice* by Karin Hess. Thousand Oaks, CA: Corwin, www.corwin.com. Reproduction authorized only for the local school site or nonprofit organization that has purchased this book.

ASSESSMENT SYSTEM BLUEPRINT—MAPPING CONTENT STANDARDS OR PROFICIENCIES TO ASSESSMENTS

Tool 30

MAPPING ALL HIGH-PRIORITY ASSESSMENTS, TESTS, AND PERFORMANCE TASKS TO ALL STANDARDS AND INTENDED DOK LEVELS

Two-Way Alignment: Alignment Categorical Concurrence, Range of Knowledge, and Balance of Representation

List *all of the major assessment opportunities* that count toward the determination of proficiency in _____. First complete one table for each grade level (common across all classrooms); then combine them across grades for a schoolwide blueprint. For each assessment listed, indicate where or when students have the opportunity to take the assessment, the content focus of this assessment in the system, and generally determine the DOK level assessed with the assessment (1, 2, 3, or 4). The total or approximate number of assessments that will be administered can be analyzed for categorical concurrence (clusters/strands assessed), range of content (depth and breadth—all or only some standards), and balance of representation (emphasis).

Assessment Name or Task	Opportunity: Grade Level or Time of Year	Assessment Type: Common Performance Task (PT), Project, Portfolio, Unit Test (UT), etc.	Content Focus: Most score points are for	Major Clusters (Categories) of Standards or Proficiencies Assessed and Overall DOK or Cognitive Demand for (content area):	Intended DOK (1, 2, 3, or 4)
EMPHASIS					

Available for download at **resources.corwin.com/HessToolkit**

SAMPLE 1 ASSESSMENT SYSTEM BLUEPRINT—MAPPING CONTENT STANDARDS OR PROFICIENCIES TO ASSESSMENTS

ALIGNMENT: CATEGORICAL CONCURRENCE, RANGE OF KNOWLEDGE, AND BALANCE OF REPRESENTATION

List *all of the major assessment opportunities* that count toward the determination of proficiency in Mathematics, Grade K. First complete one table for each grade level (common across all classrooms); then combine them across grades for a schoolwide blueprint. For each assessment listed, indicate where or when students have the opportunity to take the assessment, the content focus of this assessment in the system, and generally determine the DOK level assessed with the assessment (1-2-3-4). The total/approximate number of assessments that will be administered can be analyzed for categorical concurrence (clusters/strands assessed), range of content (depth & breadth—all/only some standards), and balance of representation (emphasis).

Assessment Name or Task	Opportunity Grade Level or Time of Year	Assessment Type Common Performance Task (PT), project Portfolio, Unit Test (UT), etc.	Content Focus Most score points are for	Counting and Cardinality	Operations and Algebraic Thinking	Number and Operations Base Ten	Measurement and Data	Geometry	District Prioritized Standards for K	Intended DOK (1, 2, 3, or 4)	Mathematical Practices 1-PSolve 2-ReasonAb 3-Argu/Crit 4-Models 5-Tools 6-Precision 7-Structure 8-Regularity
Boots and Hats	K–Fall	Interim/benchmark Common PT	Counting and representation strategies	K.CC. 3, 4a, 5	K.OA. 1, 2				K.CC.4a	1, 2, 3	1, 2, 6
Fishbowls—5 objects	K–Fall	Interim/benchmark Common PT	Commutative & associative properties	K.CC. 3, 4a, 5	K.OA. 1, 2, 5				K.CC.4a K.OA.5	1, 2, 3	1, 2, 3, 6
Geometry Task #1	K–Fall	Interim/benchmark Common PT	Identify shapes in environment					KG.1, 2	K.G.2	1	2, 8
Measuring and Comparing	K–Winter	Interim/benchmark Common PT	Attributes, comparing				K.MD. 1, 2		K.MD.1	1, 2	2, 8
Red and Blue Balls—10 objects	K–Winter	Interim/benchmark Common PT	Commutative & associative properties	K.CC. 3, 4a, 5	K.OA. 1, 2, 5				K.CC.4a K.OA.5	1, 2, 3	1, 2, 3, 6
Pigs at the Farm	K–Spring	Interim/benchmark Common PT	Adding and place value	K.CC.3, 5	KOA.1	K.NBT.1			K.NBT.1	1, 2, 3	1, 2, 3, 6
Summative K Place Value and Operations	K–Spring	Summative Common End-of-year	Adding, subtracting, place value	K.CC.3, 5	K.OA.1, 2, 3, 5	K.NBT.1			K.NBT.1 K.OA.5	1, 2, 3	1, 2, 3, 4, 6
Summative K Measurement	K–Spring	Summative Common End-of-year	Attributes, comparing, classifying				K.MD 1, 2, 3		K.MD.1	1, 2, 3	1, 2, 3, 8
Summative K Geometry Task #2	K–Spring	Summative Common PT End-of-year	Analyze, compare, create shapes					K.G.1, 2, 3	K.G.2, 3	1, 2, 3	1, 2, 3, 8
EMPHASIS	—	—	—	K.CC. 3, 4a, 5	K.OA. 1, 2, 5	K.NBT.1	K.MD 1, 2	KG.1, 2	—	1, 2, 3	1-Problem Solve 2-Reason Abstractly 3-Argument/Critique 6-Precision

Available for download at **resources.corwin.com/HessToolkit**

SAMPLE 2 ASSESSMENT SYSTEM BLUEPRINT—MAPPING CONTENT STANDARDS OR PROFICIENCIES TO ASSESSMENTS

Tool 30

ALIGNMENT: CATEGORICAL CONCURRENCE, RANGE OF KNOWLEDGE, AND BALANCE OF REPRESENTATION

List *all of the major assessment opportunities* that count toward the determination of proficiency in ELA, Grade 4. First complete one table for each grade level (common across all classrooms); then combine them across grades for a schoolwide blueprint. For each assessment listed, indicate where/when students have the opportunity to take the assessment, the content focus of this assessment in the system, and generally determine the DOK level assessed with the assessment (1-2-3-4). The total/approximate number of assessments that will be administered can be analyzed for categorical concurrence (clusters/strands assessed), range of content (depth and breadth—all or only some standards), and balance of representation (emphasis).

Assessment Name or Task	Opportunity Grade Level or Time of Year	Assessment Type Common Performance Task (PT), Project, Portfolio, Unit Test (UT), etc.	Weight[1] High-Moderate-Low	Major Clusters (Categories) of Standards or Proficiencies Assessed and Overall DOK or Cognitive Demand for (content area): ELA						Intended DOK (1-2-3-4)	Proficiencies 1-Foundatinal 2-Lit text 3-Infor text 4-Narrative 5-Info writing 6-Opinion 7-S&L 8-Research
				Reading Lit. Text	Reading Info. Text	Language/ Vocab Dev	Narrative Writing	Info. Writing	Opinion Writing	Speaking/ Listening		
District Writing portfolio	4—across school year	4 edited pieces and process	H	X	X		X	X	X		1-2-3-4	4-Narrative 5-Info writing 6-Opinion
Group Oral Presentation	4—Winter or Spring	Optional Social Studies or Science Unit	H		X	X				Formal X	1-2	7-S&L
Literature circles	4—Fall or Winter	Self-select Book or group select	L/M	X		X				Informal X	2-3	2-Lit text 7-S&L
Text based (1 text)	4—Fall and Winter	Common PT	M	FALL X	SPRING X	X	$$$		X		2-3	2-Lit text 3-Infor text 6-Opinion
Text based (2 texts)	4—Winter	Common PT	H	X	X	X		X			2-3-4	2-Lit text 3-Infor text 5-Info writing
Text based (2+ texts)	4—Spring	Common PT	H	X	X	X			X		2-3-4	2-Lit text 3-Infor text 6-Opinion
Local Reading program: Benchmark assessments	4 times/year	Comprehension Fluency and Accuracy	L/M	X	X	X				Informal X	1-2	1-Foundatinal 2-Lit text 3-Infor text 7-S&L
Social Studies Group Research project or paper	4—Winter or Spring	Project: Optional Social Studies Unit	H	X	X	X		X	X	Informal X	1-2-3-4	2-Lit text 3-Infor text 5-Info writing 7-S&L 8-Research
State ELA assessment	4—Spring	State Assmt	M	X	X	X	X	X	X		1-2-3-4	2-Lit text 3-Infor text
EMPHASIS			—	X	X	X		X	X	Informal X	2-3-4	4, 5, or 6 2, 3, 5, 6

[1] Indicate approximate weight or importance of this assessment type (e.g., high, moderate, low). For example, a writing portfolio with several pieces of writing would likely carry more (high) weight or importance in *determining the student's overall proficiency in writing than an on-demand piece of writing*.

Available for download at **resources.corwin.com/HessToolkit**

ADVANCED INDIVIDUAL TEST BLUEPRINT ANALYSIS WORKSHEETS: ONE-WAY ALIGNMENT, WITH ADDITIONAL FACTORS TO CONSIDER

Tool 31

ADVANCED Test Blueprint Sample Coding Form—Reading Assessment		Content: Item or Task Content Standards Alignment		Rigor: Item or Task DOK Alignment				Close reading: Text Evidence directly required in support of analysis			Text Complexity	Item type		SOC?		Alignment Notes—for each item or task (ONLY if item type or text is *not appropriate* to content or depth assessed)
Item/task + Pts if >1	Identify Content assessed	Content Full or Part	Content No above/below	DOK-1	DOK-2	DOK-3	DOK-4	Yes	No	NA	H-M-L	Is type appropriate		If Yes Why?		Describe WHICH part—Partial content standard assessed or WHY No match (above/below grade level)
1 – 3 pts	Topic – Literary text – analyze across 2 texts	P– 5.RL-9					4f - Analyze themes	X			M – 1st poem L – 2nd poem	Long CR		—		5.RL-9 – compare/contrast themes of 2 poems
2	Topic															
3	Topic															

Step 1 Fill in item numbers.

If item or task is worth more than 1 score point, list number of possible points. If 1 score point, do not write anything after item number.

To save time, score point information can be filled in ahead of time by alignment organizers.

Step 2 ID Content
Review each item for broad content or topic assessed. Describe content assessed. This will help you find match with standard(s).

Step 3 Match Content to Standards

Use CCSS for grade level

Review item or task against content or cluster. What standard is assessed?

Is the **Full** standard or only **Part** assessed? (Many items will assess parts.) List code of standard as F or P; if Part—list what part IS assessed in far right column.

If no match with Grade 5, is there a lower or higher grade-level standard match?

List closest lower or higher grade-level standard under "No" with the grade-level standard (e.g., 4.RL-9) and the part assessed in notes to the right.

Step 4 Rigor
Use ELA CRM descriptors—Tools #1 or #3
Match (closest) DOK descriptor(s) to what item is asking the student to do. There may be more than one descriptor. That is OK.

Step 5 Close Reading
Use test item and scoring guide, if appropriate.

Does the answer require locating explicit text details or mostly compiling explicit information (main idea) or making basic inferences? Check "no".

Analyzing the text and making an interpretation or judgment about the content that requires text evidence as proof (e.g., theme), check "yes."

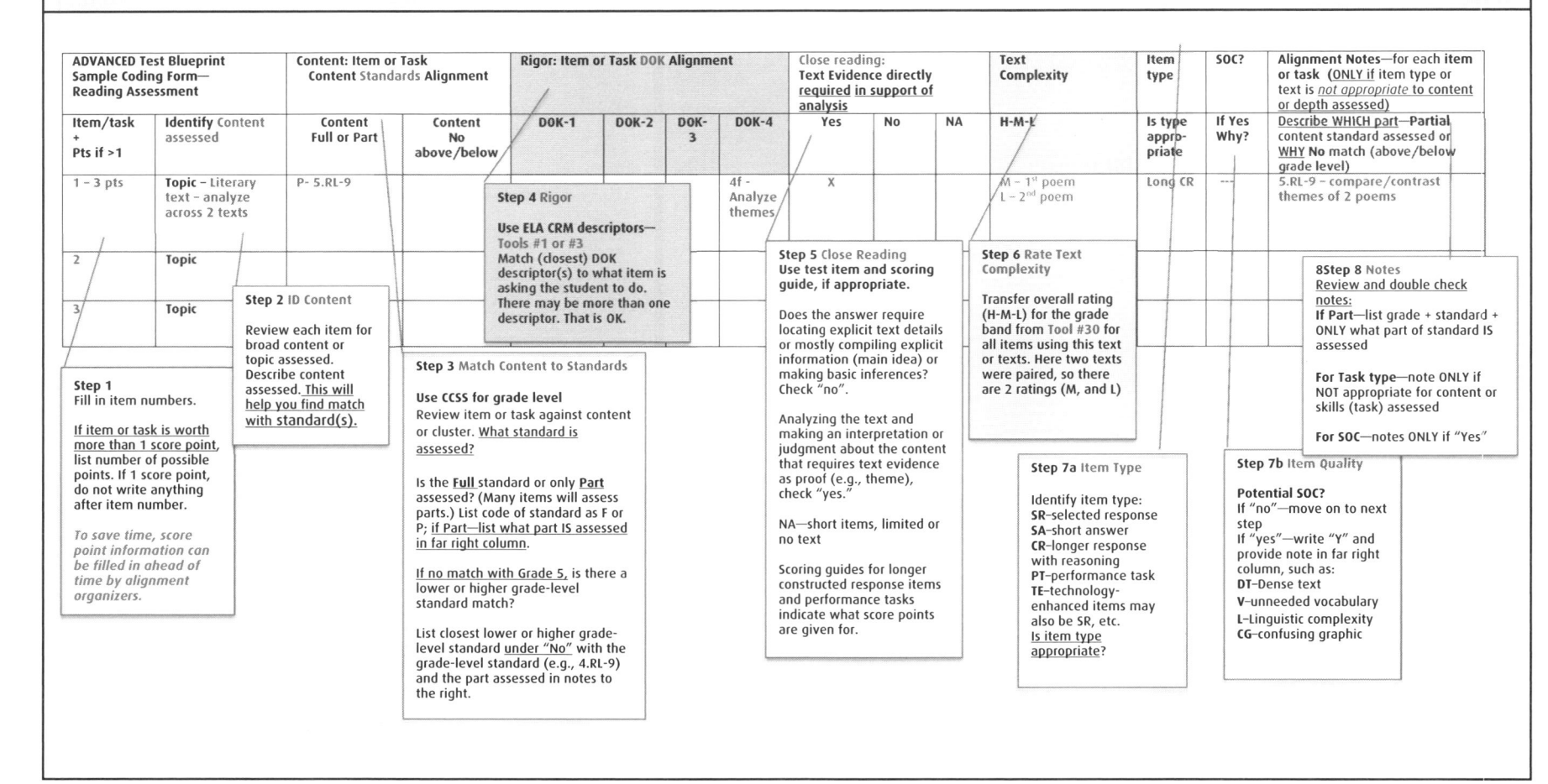

NA—short items, limited or no text

Scoring guides for longer constructed response items and performance tasks indicate what score points are given for.

Step 6 Rate Text Complexity
Transfer overall rating (H-M-L) for the grade band from Tool #30 for all items using this text or texts. Here two texts were paired, so there are 2 ratings (M, and L)

Step 7a Item Type
Identify item type:
SR–selected response
SA–short answer
CR–longer response with reasoning
PT–performance task
TE–technology-enhanced items may also be SR, etc.
Is item type appropriate?

Step 7b Item Quality

Potential SOC?
If "no"—move on to next step
If "yes"—write "Y" and provide note in far right column, such as:
DT–Dense text
V–unneeded vocabulary
L–linguistic complexity
CG–confusing graphic

Step 8 Notes
Review and double check notes:
If Part—list grade + standard + ONLY what part of standard IS assessed

For Task type—note ONLY if NOT appropriate for content or skills (task) assessed

For SOC—notes ONLY if "Yes"

(Continued)

continued...

ADVANCED INDIVIDUAL TEST BLUEPRINT ANALYSIS WORKSHEETS: ONE-WAY ALIGNMENT, WITH ADDITIONAL FACTORS TO CONSIDER

Tool 31

ADVANCED Test Blueprint Sample Coding Form—Math Assessment	Content: Item or Task Content Clusters-Standards Alignment		Rigor Item or Task DOK Alignment				Balance of concepts, procedures, applications)			Connect Practice–Content	Item type	SOC?		Alignment Notes—for each item or task (ONLY if item type or text is *not appropriate* to content/depth assessed)
Item or task + Pts if >1	Match to Topic	Content above/below	DOK-1	DOK-2	DOK-3	DOK-4	Concepts	Procedures	Application	List math practices	Appropriate?	If Yes Why?		Describe WHICH part assessed or WHY **No** match (above/below grade level)
1–2pts	Topic – proportional relationships	P-8.EE.5 F		2e (use tool) 2h (graph data) 2n (interpret)				X routine			Short CR Tech-graphing software			8.EE.5-Graph proportional relationships; connect unit rate
2	Topic													
3	Topic													

Step 1 Fill in item numbers.

If item or task is worth more than 1 score point, list number of possible points. If 1 score point, do not write anything after item number.

To save time, score point information can be filled in ahead of time by

Step 2 ID Content

Review each item for broad content/topic assessed. Describe content assessed. This will help you find match with standard(s).

Step 3 Match Content to Standards

Use CCSS for grade level Review item or task against content or cluster. What standard is assessed?

Review item against content or cluster. What standard is assessed?
Is the **Full** standard or only **Part** assessed? (Many items will assess parts.) List code of standard under F or P AND if Part—list what part IS assessed in far right column.

If no match with Grade 8, is there a lower or higher grade-level standard match?

List closest lower or higher grade-level standard under "No" with the grade-level standard (e.g., 7.EE.1) and part assessed in notes to right.

Step 4 Rigor

Use Math-Science CRM descriptors—Tool #2

Match (closest) DOK descriptor(s) to what item is asking the student to do. There may be more than one descriptor. That is OK.

Step 5 Balance of Emphasis

Use test item and scoring guide, if appropriate. Determine the primary purpose of this item/task—
Conceptual?
Procedural?
Application (routine or non-routine)?

List only one focus for most single items (e.g., multiple choice, short answer).

Longer performance tasks may assess multiple aspects, so check correct answer or solution and what score points are given for.

Step 6 Practices

List math practice(s) assessed with this content.

PS–problem solving
R–reason abstractly
M–modeling
C–critique reasoning
A–math argument
S–use of structure

(Precision is expected for all items.)

Step 7a Item Type

Identify item type:
SR–selected response
SA–short answer
CR–longer response with reasoning
PT–performance task
TE–technology-enhanced items may also be SR, etc.
Is item type appropriate to task?

Step 7b Item Quality

Potential SOC?
If "no"—move on to next step
If "yes"—write "y" and provide note in far right column, such as:
DT–Dense text
V–unneeded vocabulary
L–Linguistic complexity
CG–confusing graphic

Step 8 Notes

Review and double-check notes:
If Part—list grade + standard + ONLY what part of standard IS assessed

For Task type–note ONLY if NOT appropriate for content or skills (task) assessed

For SOC–notes ONLY if "Yes"

Available for download at **resources.corwin.com/HessToolkit**

TEXT COMPLEXITY ANALYSES SUMMARY

Tool 32

Grade Level: _____ Test or Task: _____ Review Date: _____

List texts this test: (R) reading; (W)writing; (R/I) research/inq; (L) Listening	Print or Nonprint	Quant Lexile or text level?[1]	Literary? Published? Text type? Story, novel, play, poem, etc.	Infor text? Published? Text type? Content: L/non SS/H, Sci/Tech	High-Qual and Grade appro? Yes-?-No	Overall Complexity Ratings (see Hess-Hervey text rubric descriptors: Hess Tools #7 informational or #8 literary) 1–4					Paired with other text(s)? Yes–No Comments—use of multi texts	Overall complexity rating 1, 2, 3, or 4 L-M-H for grade band
						Format and Layout	Purpose and meaning	Structure and Discourse	Language features	Background Knowledge		
See example below	P or N[2]	List below										
(R)The People of Mesa Verde	P with Visuals	unknown	—	Web-Published article– SS/H	? – appro complex; not well written	1–2 –sub-headings, photos, inset text	2	2+ chronology, description, comp-contrast	2–3 complex sentences, unfamiliar vocab	2–3	No	2–3 M-Grade 7 H-Grade 6
(R)												
(W)												

(Continued)

continued . . .

Tool 32

TEXT COMPLEXITY ANALYSES SUMMARY

Grade Level: _____ Test or Task: _____ Review Date: _____

List texts this test: (R) reading; (W)writing; (R/I) research/inq; (L) Listening	Print or Nonprint	Quant Lexile or text level?[1]	Literary? Published?	Infor text? Published?	High-Qual and Grade appro?	Overall Complexity Ratings (see Hess-Hervey text rubric descriptors: Hess Tools #7 informational or #8 literary) 1–4	Paired with other text(s)? Yes–No	Overall complexity rating 1, 2, 3, or 4
(R/I)								
(L)								
Summary: Totals and comments for this test form	P = N =	Quant range	%	% L/non % SS/H %Sci/Tech	High-Qual Yes = ? = No =		Standards requiring >1 text assessed?	Qual range H= M= L=

[1] Quantitative text levels are provided by assessment contractor (e.g., Lexile, text-leveling system); Nonprint texts likely will have no Lexiles or levels, so code as "unknown."
[2] Nonprint texts and texts with diverse formats could include Audio (**A**), Visual (**V**), or Graphic (**G**); or Multimedia (**M**); Website (**W**); Presentation, such as a video clip of a play or speech (**Pre**), etc.

Available for download at **resources.corwin.com/HessToolkit**

ITEM OR TASK BANK REVIEW

Tool 33

Individual Teacher Surveys identify items that might potentially be selected for an end-of-year or "grade-level" progress check.

One way teachers and school districts are likely to use an item bank is to select items to create assessments used to gauge whether students are achieving grade-level standards or making progress to achieve them (e.g., a midyear or interim assessment). Grade-level teams complete the survey using available items from the online item bank. Duplicate additional pages as needed. At least fifty items should be evaluated.

Content area: _____
Intended Grade Level _____ (often items in item banks cross grade levels, so consider intended grade levels for this alignment review)
Reviewer ID#(s): _____ (individual or pairs of reviewers—ID#s allow reviews to be anonymous)

Test/Item Bank Reviewed: _____

➤ **Reviewer Question: Which items would you recommend be selected for an assessment to gauge whether students are achieving grade-level standards or making progress at your grade level? Does item align to grade-level standards?** Briefly explain why you would or why you would not select the item (check all comments that apply).

Item #	√ = YES would select item for this grade	Possible Reasons for YES					√ = NO would NOT select item	Possible Reasons for NO			Other Comments?
		Item is like CCSS items	Item is key prerequisite skill	Assesses deeper thinking DOK 3, 4	Goes broader or deeper than CCSS	High-quality item		Already selected enough like this one	Not aligned to CCSS at grade	Poor-quality item	
1											
2											
3											
4											
5											
6											
7											
8											
9											
10											
Totals											

(Continued)

continued...

ITEM OR TASK BANK REVIEW

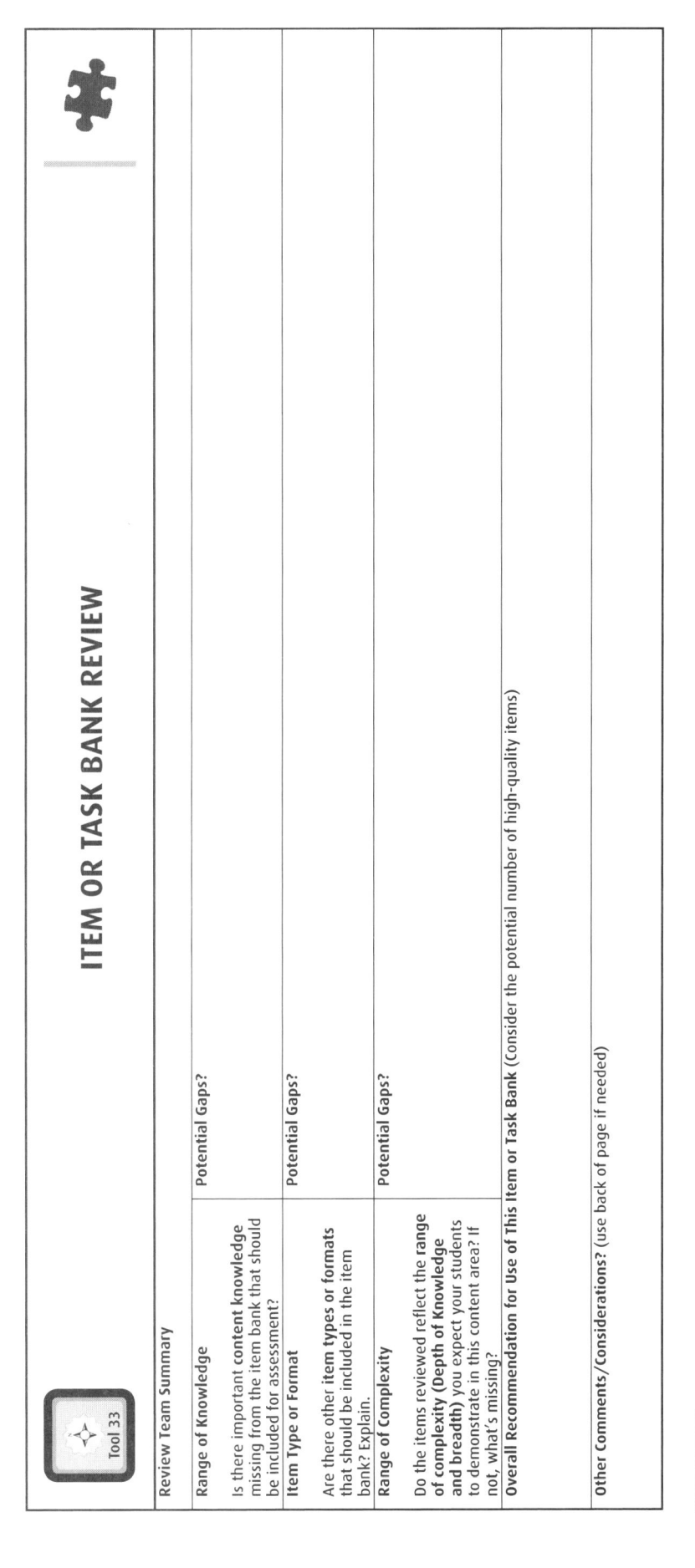

Tool 33

Review Team Summary	
Range of Knowledge Is there important **content knowledge** missing from the item bank that should be included for assessment?	Potential Gaps?
Item Type or Format Are there other **item types or formats** that should be included in the item bank? Explain.	Potential Gaps?
Range of Complexity Do the items reviewed reflect the range of complexity (**Depth of Knowledge and breadth**) you expect your students to demonstrate in this content area? If not, what's missing?	Potential Gaps?
Overall Recommendation for Use of This Item or Task Bank (Consider the potential number of high-quality items)	
Other Comments/Considerations? (use back of page if needed)	

Available for download at **resources.corwin.com/HessToolkit**

Copyright © 2018 by Corwin. All rights reserved. Reprinted from *A Local Assessment Toolkit to Promote Deeper Learning: Transforming Research into Practice* by Karin Hess. Thousand Oaks, CA: Corwin, www.corwin.com. Reproduction authorized only for the local school site or nonprofit organization that has purchased this book.

Appendix A

Summary of Hess Tools to Guide Local Assessment Development, Instructional Planning, and PLC Activities

MODULE	TOOL	TITLE	USE THIS TOOL FOR . . .	PAGE
1: Cognitive Rigor Tools	1	Hess Close Reading CRM	Designing and analyzing **reading and listening** questions, tasks; unit and lesson planning; use with **PLC TOOL #9 or TOOL #10**	53
	2	Hess Math–Science CRM	Designing and analyzing **mathematics and science** questions, tasks; unit and lesson planning; use with **PLC TOOL #9 or TOOL #10**	54
	3	Hess Writing and Speaking CRM	Designing and analyzing **oral and written communication** questions, tasks; unit and lesson planning; use with **PLC TOOL #9 or TOOL #10**	55
	4	Hess Social Studies/Humanities CRM	Designing and analyzing **social studies/humanities** questions, tasks; unit and lesson planning; use with **PLC TOOL #9 or TOOL #10**	56
	5A	Hess Fine Arts CRM	Designing and analyzing **visual arts, music, dance, and theater** questions, tasks; unit and lesson planning; use with **PLC TOOL #9 or TOOL #10**	57
	5B	Hess Health and Physical Education/HPE CRM	Designing and analyzing **health and physical education** questions, tasks; unit and lesson planning; use with **PLC TOOL #9 or TOOL #10**	58
	5C	Hess World Languages CRM	Designing and analyzing **world language** questions, tasks; unit and lesson planning; use with **PLC TOOL #9 or TOOL #10**	59
	5D	Hess Career and Technical Education CRM	Designing and analyzing **CTE** questions, tasks; unit and lesson planning; use with **PLC TOOL #9 or TOOL #10**	60
2: Text Complexity Tools	6	Text Complexity: Analyzing Qualitative Features Worksheet	Making initial notes about qualitative features of texts; lesson and assessment planning	107
	7	Text Complexity: Analytic Rubric for Informational Texts	Conducting a qualitative analysis of complexity in **informational texts**; developing reading and text-based assessments; alignment studies; use with **Alignment TOOL #32**	108
	8	Text Complexity: Analytic Rubric for Literary Texts	Conducting a qualitative analysis of complexity in **literary texts**; developing reading and text-based assessments; alignment studies; use with **Alignment TOOL #32**	109
	9	High-Quality Assessment: Task Quality Validation Protocol	Developing new assessments or analyzing and revising existing assessments; best for summative and performance assessments	189–191

MODULE	TOOL	TITLE	USE THIS TOOL FOR...	PAGE
3: Assessment Development PLC Tools	10	High-Quality Assessment: Strategic Planning Tool: Analyzing Formative Assessments	Analyzing what is being assessed with formative assessments and planning potential next steps for instruction	192
	11	High-Quality Assessment: Rubric Quality Review Worksheet	Providing feedback on seven criteria related to rubric language and format	193
	12	High-Quality Assessment: Student Work Analysis Protocol	Revising assessments and rubrics, planning next steps for instruction, identifying assessment anchors and developing annotations, monitoring progress. FOUR potential performance levels are used to force thinking about what might be close to "got it" and what work might reflect just getting started.	194–195
	13	Calibration Tool: What Is the Evidence?	Making preliminary notes before developing annotations for assessment anchors; locating specific evidence in student work linked to success criteria	196
	14	Calibration Tool: Individual Reviewer Rubric Score Sheet	Preliminary scoring by individuals before compiling consensus scores and developing annotated assessment anchors	197
	15	Calibration Tool: Team Rubric Score Sheet	Compiling team consensus scores into a scoring matrix and developing annotated assessment anchors	198
	16A	Task Validation Summary—Streamlined Version	Summarizing feedback from validation panel to development team; use with PLC TOOL #9. This tool is good for when you are just getting started with validations. It is the "streamlined" version for giving feedback.	199
	16B	Task Validation Summary—In-Depth Version	Summarizing feedback from validation panel to development team; use with PLC TOOL #9. This tool is more detailed for giving validation feedback or unit planning. It can also be used as a conferencing tool during development of performance assessments.	200–202

(Continued)

(Continued)

MODULE	TOOL	TITLE	USE THIS TOOL FOR...	PAGE
	17	Cognitive Labs—Part 2	Thinking aloud with students after they complete the assessment—small group interview template; can also be used as a teacher-student conferencing tool	203
	18	Cognitive Labs—Part 3A	Interpreting student work samples from cognitive lab—some students may have taken different parts of the assessments	204
	19	Cognitive Labs—Part 3B	Collaboratively interpreting evidence in student work—using student work from a cognitive lab to validate evidence elicited by task and to refine rubric language	205
	20	Guide to Performance Task Development	Unpacking the process of developing and designing performance assessments	206–209
	21	Performance Assessment Overview	Providing an overview of when the assessment will be used (unit of study), what it is intended to assess, and how results will be used (e.g., formative, summative)	210–211
4: Learning Progressions Tools	22	Analyzing Learner Characteristics and Student Work Along a Progression	Both examining the characteristics of learners as they move along a learning continuum and documenting the effectiveness of instructional supports at different stages of learning	330–331
	23	Guiding Questions for Developing, Refining, or Validating Learning Progressions	Reviewing or revising draft learning progressions	332–334
	24	Planning Instruction Using a Learning Progressions Mindset	Unpacking a learning progression or analyzing existing units of study along a learning progression	335
	25	Formative-Interim-Summative Assessment Planning Along a Learning Progression	Planning for or analyzing formative and summative assessments within units of study	336–337
	26	Looking for Rigor: Shifting Teacher and Student Roles	Planning a lesson or providing a lesson overview of what a peer or instructional coach will collect data and give feedback on. Use to look for trends, to collect baseline data, or to provide feedback and support to teachers.	338

Module 5: Alignment Tools

TOOL	TITLE	USE THIS TOOL FOR . . .	PAGE
27	Year-at-a-Glance—Mapping Classroom Assessments	Mapping use of existing classroom assessments as the first step to identifying potential assessment overlap and gaps. A completed ELA example is also included.	384–385
28	Discussion Questions: Examining Our Local Assessment System	Using the guiding questions to discuss and examine the current local assessment philosophy and system components and determine next steps for improving the quality and comprehensiveness of the local assessment system.	386–387
29	Basic Individual Test Blueprint Analysis Worksheet: One-Way Alignment	Analyzing current assessments to determine the degree of alignment to intended content and rigor and identify what is being emphasized in the assessment, in terms of the potential number of score points for each item or task. Identifying specific assessment categories using this tool is optional. Use with **PLC TOOL #9.**	388–390
30	Assessment System Blueprint Template: Two-Way Alignment	Analyzing current high-priority assessments to determine the degree of alignment to intended content and rigor, range of knowledge and categories being assessed, and what is being emphasized in each assessment. This is done to build a system overview of assessments in use.	391–393
31	Advanced Individual Test Blueprint Analysis Worksheets: One-Way Alignment, With Additional Factors to Consider	Analyzing current high-priority assessments to determine the degree of alignment to intended content and rigor, range of knowledge and categories being assessed, and determine what is being emphasized in each assessment. Use with **PLC TOOL #9.**	394–395
32	Text Complexity Analyses Summary	Analyzing current high-priority literacy assessments to determine and summarize the complexity of texts used in each assessment. This compiles information from **Text Complexity TOOLS #7 and #8.**	396–397
33	Item/Task Bank Review—Analyzing Online Item Banks	Analyzing item or task banks to determine the degree of alignment with local assessment priorities and developing a rationale for adopting the use of the assessments	398–399

Appendix B

Instructional and Formative Assessment Strategies to Uncover Thinking

STRATEGY	SUGGESTED USES							LOCATION
TEACHER TOOL (T) STUDENT ACTIVITY (S)	SCAFFOLDING	MAKING CONNECTIONS	COLLABORATION	DISCOURSE, ORAL LANGUAGE	QUESTIONING	PEER/SELF-ASSESSMENT	DIFFERENTIATION CHOICE	MODULE
Anatomy of an Opinion/ Argument/ Critique (S)	X	X		X		X		3
Anchor Charts (S) Text Structures	X	X	X	X				2
Anticipation Guides (S)	X	X	X	X	X	X	X	3, 4
Assessment Administration Guides (T)	X				X	X	X	3
Assignment Menus: Quick Tips for Differentiation (S)	X		X			X	X	4
Bookmark (S)	X	X	X	X		X		2
Card Pyramid (S)	X	X	X	X		X	X	2
Carousel/ Progressive Revising (S)	X	X	X	X	X			1
Case Studies (S)	X	X	X	X	X	X	X	3
Character Emojis (S)	X	X	X	X				1
Chocolate Chip Cookie Taste Test (T)		X	X	X				3
Chunking Text (S)	X	X			X			2
CRM Planning: Questioning/ Lesson (T)	X	X	X	X	X	X	X	1

408

STRATEGY — TEACHER TOOL (T) STUDENT ACTIVITY (S)	SUGGESTED USES						LOCATION
	SCAFFOLDING	MAKING CONNECTIONS	COLLABORATION	DISCOURSE, ORAL LANGUAGE	QUESTIONING	PEER/SELF-ASSESSMENT	DIFFERENTIATION CHOICE	MODULE
CRM Planning: Little Red Example (T)	X				X	X	X	1
CRM Planning: Kid-Friendly Language (T)								1
CRM Planning: Units of Study (T)	X				X	X	X	1
Collaborative Inquiry Plan (S)			X			X		1
EKGs—Characters, Events, Interactions (S)	X	X	X	X				1
Favorite "No" (S)	X	X	X	X	X	X		4
Flipped Classroom (T)	X		X				X	4
GRASPS (T/S)	X	X	X	X	X	X	X	3
Hint Cards (S)	X	X					X	1
Infographics (S)		X	X	X			X	4
Interactive Self-Assessments (S)	X	X	X	X	X	X	X	3
Jigsaws to Develop Schemas (S)	X	X	X	X	X	X	X	1
Multisensory Clustering (S)	X	X		X			X	1

(Continued)

(Continued)

STRATEGY TEACHER TOOL (T) STUDENT ACTIVITY (S)	SUGGESTED USES						LOCATION
	SCAFFOLDING	MAKING CONNECTIONS	COLLABORATION	DISCOURSE, ORAL LANGUAGE	QUESTIONING	PEER/SELF-ASSESSMENT	DIFFERENTIATION CHOICE	MODULE

STRATEGY	SCAFFOLDING	MAKING CONNECTIONS	COLLABORATION	DISCOURSE, ORAL LANGUAGE	QUESTIONING	PEER/SELF-ASSESSMENT	DIFFERENTIATION CHOICE	MODULE
Note Facts (S)	X	X				X		4
One-Pager (S)	X	X		X			X	1
Paraphrase Passport (S)		X		X				1
Partner Collaborations/ Dyads (S)	X							1
Pattern Folders (S)	X	X	X	X			X	2
Photo/Picture Search (S)	X	X		X	X		X	1
Probing Questions (S)	X	X	X	X	X	X	X	3
Quick Guide to Rubric Development (T)		X	X	X		X	X	3
Rubric Models (T, S)	X	X	X	X		X		3
Send a Problem (S)	X	X	X	X	X	X		1
Socratic Questioning (S)		X	X	X	X	X		1
SQS—Students Questioning Students (S)		X		X	X	X		1
Stand and Deliver (S)	X	X	X	X			X	1
SWA—6 Purposes (T)	X		X	X			X	3

STRATEGY TEACHER TOOL (T) STUDENT ACTIVITY (S)	SUGGESTED USES							LOCATION
	SCAFFOLDING	MAKING CONNECTIONS	COLLABORATION	DISCOURSE, ORAL LANGUAGE	QUESTIONING	PEER/SELF-ASSESSMENT	DIFFERENTIATION CHOICE	MODULE
SWA—Student Side-by-Side (S)	X	X	X	X		X		3
Systematic Observation (T)		X		X	X	X		3
Talk Moves (S)	X	X		X				1
Task Shells (T)	X	X			X	X	X	3
TBEAR and Kid TBEAR (S)	X	X	X	X				1
Text Decks (S)	X	X	X	X		X		1
Thesis Throwdown (S)	X		X	X		X		1
TV and DOK (T/S)		X		X				1
Unit Planning Prompts (T)	X	X		X	X		X	3
Value Lines (S)		X	X	X	X			1
What Do I Know About These Words? (S)	X	X	X	X	X	X		2
What I Need to Do Rubric (S)	X		X	X		X		3
Word Splash (S)	X	X	X	X	X	X		2

Appendix C

Troubleshooting Tips When Designing Assessment Items and Tasks

Things to Avoid When Developing Selected Response (SR) and Constructed Response (CR) Items and Task Prompts

ISSUE TO BE ADDRESSED	SAMPLES OF BEFORE/AFTER TEST ITEMS		
1. More than one possible correct response in a multiple-choice item	**Underlying Rationale for Item Revision:** While there is a benefit to providing several "plausible" distractors for selected response (SR) items, as well as including a common misconception, there are times when several distractors could be correct.		
ISSUE	POSSIBLE SOLUTION	BEFORE REVISION	AFTER REVISION
More than one possible correct response in a multiple-choice item	Source: Grade 4 NAEP item in Hess Cognitive Lab training and research study (2008) Revise negative in "B" response; change distractor that was too close to correct response. Simplify stem and change distractors—revise negative distractor (B)	1a. Jason probably would have felt better at the birthday party if A. the box had been put in the backyard- B. he decided not to like dogs. C. the party had lasted longer. **D. he had not hidden in the tall weeds.**	1b. Which action **most likely** upset Jason? A. His parents gave Megan a puppy. B. His father talked to him that night. C. The party was over too soon. **D. He hid in the tall weeds.**
2. Avoid use of negatives in stem and possible responses	**Underlying Rationale for Item Revision:** "Difficulty of text may vary due to "Complex Boolean expressions." Such expressions are challenging because "the respondent needs to keep track of different options and possibilities." In the case of negative expressions, an unnecessarily high cognitive loading may be added to items that employ negatives within items (e.g., "Which of the following is not a reason why the captain wanted to turn the ship around?") (Hess, McDivitt, & Fincher, 2008).		
ISSUE	POSSIBLE SOLUTION	BEFORE REVISION	AFTER REVISION
Avoid use of negatives in stem and possible responses	Source: Grade 4 NAEP item in Hess Cognitive Lab training and research study (2008) Eliminate double negatives; simplify stem and make distractors complete sentences.	2a. Jason would **not** have had a problem in the story if he had A. not gone to Megan's party. B. not let the puppy play by the road. **C. not let his curiosity make him open the box.** D. not wanted a puppy of his own so badly.	2b. What caused Jason's problem in the story? A. He went to Megan's party. B. He let the puppy play by the road. **C. He wanted to know what was in the box.** D. He wanted a puppy of his own.

ISSUE	POSSIBLE SOLUTION	BEFORE REVISION	AFTER REVISION
Avoid use of negatives in stem and possible responses	Source: Grade 4 NAEP item in Hess Cognitive Lab training and research study (2008) Stem and distractors modified—removed negatives in A and D distractors	2c. When Megan spoke to Jason in the tall weeds, she was concerned that A. she wouldn't get enough presents. B. **something was wrong with Jason.** C. the puppy was missing from the box. D. her dad wouldn't get back in time for the party.	2d. When Megan spoke to Jason in the tall weeds, she was worried that A. Jason kept her present. B. **something was wrong with Jason.** C. the puppy was missing from the box. D. her dad would miss the party.
Avoid use of negatives in stem and possible responses	Source: Grade 4 NAEP item in Hess Cognitive Lab training and research study (2008) Simplified and removed negative in stem and some distractors.	2e. Why are wombats not often seen by people? A. Wombats look too much like koalas. B. **Wombats usually are active at night.** C. There are not enough wombat-crossing signs. D. Wombats are difficult to see in trees.	2f. Why is it difficult for people to see wombats? A. Wombats look like koalas. B. **Wombats are active at night.** C. There are very few wombats. D. Tree branches hide the wombats.
3. Potentially excessive reading load	**Underlying Rationale for Item Revision:** "Sentences with 'dense clauses'" are sentences that "pack too many constituents or idea units (i.e., propositions) within a single clause"... and/or with "dense noun phrases" as sentences with "too many adjectives and adverbs modifying the head noun." Items with either one of the above sentence types may be problematic to reading comprehension (RAND, p. 96, cited in Hess, McDivitt, & Fincher, 2008).		

(Continued)

(Continued)

ISSUE	POSSIBLE SOLUTION	BEFORE REVISION	AFTER REVISION
Potentially excessive reading load in CR math item	Make the prompt more concise, eliminating extraneous details. Add white space between question context and question. Be consistent with item presentation formatting.	Kathy's parents are remodeling her bedroom and she can have new wall-to-wall carpeting. The room is 12 feet long and 15 feet wide. How large will the carpet have to be in square feet to fit Kathy's room?	Kathy is getting wall-to-wall carpeting for her bedroom. The room is 12 feet long and 15 feet wide. How many square feet of carpet will they buy?
Potentially excessive reading load	Source: Grade 8 NAEP item in Hess Cognitive Lab training and research study (2008) Shorten the question stem.	The main point the author is making in this passage is about the A. hardships of ocean travel in the nineteenth century. B. struggles of the early immigrants entering America. C. many opportunities to make money in America. D. effect of immigration on European countries.	This passage is **mostly** about A. hardships of ocean travel in the nineteenth century. B. struggles of the early immigrants entering America. C. many opportunities to make money in America. D. effect of immigration on European countries.
Potentially excessive reading load	Source: Grade 8 NAEP item in Hess Cognitive Lab training and research study (2008) Simplify (shorten) stem and distractors.	Reread the lines beginning with "I admired" (line 45) and ending with "aching jaw" (line 64). The speaker **most** admires the fish because she thinks it A. has escaped from being caught by fishermen. B. is strong and intelligent. C. has strange movements. D. has the speckled barnacles.	The speaker **most** admires the fish (in lines 45–64) because of its A. ability to escape. B. human-like intelligence. C. strange movements. D. speckled barnacles.

ISSUE	POSSIBLE SOLUTION	BEFORE REVISION	AFTER REVISION
Potentially excessive reading load	Source: Grade 8 NAEP item in Hess Cognitive Lab training and research study (2008) Simplify Stem and make distractors complete sentences instead of long complex sentences.	The United States eventually reduced the number of immigrants allowed to enter the country because A. the United States already had too many people. B. the immigrants were taking away jobs from American workers. C. the immigrants had too many hardships to face in America. D. the country that the immigrants came from was angry about their leaving. NAEP—dense text in distractors	Why did the United States reduce the number of immigrants? A. The United States already had too many people. B. The immigrants were taking away jobs from American workers. C. Immigrants had too many hardships to face in America. D. The country that the immigrants came from was angry about their leaving.
Potentially excessive reading load	Source: Grade 8 NAEP item in Hess Cognitive Lab training and research study (2008) Clarify stem and make distractors complete sentences.	This article **mostly** describes how A. **the wombat's special body parts help it to grow and live.** B. highway signs help to save the wombat. C. the wombat is like the koala and the North American badger. D. wombats feed and raise their young.	What is the **main** idea of the passage? A. **Wombats are unusual and interesting animals.** B. Koalas and wombats have a lot in common. C. Australian marsupials are a lot alike. D. The writer has adventures in Adelaide, Austria. Revised stem and simplified distractors

(Continued)

(Continued)

ISSUE	POSSIBLE SOLUTION	BEFORE REVISION	AFTER REVISION
4. Potential visual discrimination confusion	**Underlying Rationale for Item Revision:** "Graphic organizers are effective instructional supports used during a lesson to assist students in understanding such things as the text structure (e.g., story map for narrative, timeline for chronology, Venn diagram for compare-contrast) (Schumm, 2006). The layout or format of a table, graph, or graphic organizer visually organizes information for conceptual understanding (Robb, Richek, & Spandel, 2002, cited in Hess, McDivitt, & Fincher, 2008). Use of familiar graphics (also used in instruction, such as a visual of a food web) can help students to see how information should be connected (e.g., cause/effect, compare/contrast). However, item developers need to be sure that visuals used in test items have adequate white space, formatting, and text font and size or do not include extraneous information that can be confusing to students with visual discrimination issues."		

ISSUE	POSSIBLE SOLUTION	BEFORE REVISION	AFTER REVISION
Potential visual discrimination confusion	Source: Draft Grade 3 math local assessment Note that the dots in each configuration are close together with little white space between. It might be less confusing to provide one array of dots with four different number sentences OR ask students to "construct" an array to show $4 \times 7 = 28$.	Which model represents the number sentence $4 \times 7 = 28$? A [array of dots] B [array of dots] C [array of dots]	Which number sentence is shown in this model? [5×4 array of dots] A. $10 \times 2 = 20$ B. $4 \times 7 = 28$ C. $5 \times 4 = 20$

ISSUE	POSSIBLE SOLUTION	BEFORE REVISION	AFTER REVISION
5. Increasing Rigor/ deeper thinking in SR items	**Underlying Rationale for Item Revision:** What increases rigor/deeper thinking generally involves delving into more complex applications (DOK 3—nonroutine tasks/contexts); more abstract content or interpretations (e.g., DOK 3—interpret symbolism); asking for justification of a solution or conclusion (e.g., DOK 3—which data or text evidence supports this conclusion); or drawing upon multiple sources or texts for supporting evidence (DOK 4). Often an unintended consequence of asking for deeper thinking in SR items results in increasing the reading load. Consider whether a constructed response prompt will elicit more meaningful assessment data (deeper understanding) than simply selecting the best option given in the SR item.	D •	

ISSUE	POSSIBLE SOLUTION	BEFORE REVISION	AFTER REVISION
Increasing rigor in SR math items	Source: NAEP, Grade 8 (2009) Adding an open-ended or short answer question after SR item will elicit underlying reasoning and deeper thinking. The revised item demonstrates understanding and comparisons of different units, considerations of precision of measurement, and perhaps some background knowledge and thinking about real-world applications to plant growth. **NOTE:** Making an item "harder" is not the same as making it deeper! Identifying a small number of SR items to add a CR reasoning question can be a strategic means of getting at deeper thinking.	Of the following, which is the best unit to use when measuring the growth of a plant every other day during a 2-week period? A. Centimeter B. Meter C. Kilometer D. Foot E. Yard	(SR—part 1) Of the following, which is the best unit to use when measuring the growth of a plant every other day during a 2-week period? A. Centimeter B. Meter C. Kilometer D. Foot E. Yard (CR—part 2) Explain WHY this unit is a better choice than the others.

(Continued)

(Continued)

ISSUE	POSSIBLE SOLUTION	BEFORE REVISION	AFTER REVISION
Increasing rigor in SR reading items, while reducing reading load	Adding an open-ended or short answer question after SR item will elicit underlying reasoning and deeper thinking. The revised item demonstrates understanding of the need for text evidence to support interpretation of theme or author's purpose (DOK 3). Other revisions to the original item: Eliminate clause at beginning of stem and make distractors complete sentences. **NOTE:** Making an item "harder" is not the same as making it deeper! Identifying a small number of SR items to add a CR reasoning question can be a strategic means of getting at deeper thinking.	In the story, what lesson does Jason's father think Jason had learned? A. how to take care of an animal B. how to think about his sister's needs C. **that running away makes a situation worse** D. that only older children should have pets	(SR—part 1) 7. What lesson does Jason learn? A. People should take care of their animals. B. He should think about his sister's needs. C. **Running away makes a situation worse.** D. Only older children should have pets. (CR—part 2) What evidence from the text supports your response?
Increasing rigor in SR items, while reducing reading load (World languages)	Source: draft high school Spanish local assessment World language teachers often struggle with the idea that students have limited vocabulary and therefore cannot be asked very challenging (deeper thinking) questions. Two possible approaches have been tested by Hess (2013–2014) in MD and NH with good success: 1. Add an open-response question to explain reasoning behind answer selected and respond for that part of the question in English.	Look at this advertisement for a product. What item is being sold? (vocabulary being tested is listed as distractors—generally masculine or feminine pronouns and nouns with adjectives) A. B. C. D.	(part 1) Look at this advertisement for a product. What item is being sold? (vocabulary being tested is listed as distractors—generally nouns with adjectives) A. B. C. D. (Optional part 2) What made you select this response or not choose the others?

420

ISSUE	POSSIBLE SOLUTION	BEFORE REVISION	AFTER REVISION
	2. Interpret the visual (e.g., who is the intended audience) and respond for that part of the question in English or the language		(Optional part 2) Who is the intended audience for this product? Use evidence from the visuals or text in the ad to support your thinking. OR What four ideas presented in the ad tell you that this is intended for teens?
	Source: NAEP, Grade 4 (2009) The revised item asks for the ability to calculate perimeter of squares (DOK 1) as well as a generalized conceptual understanding of perimeter (applied to all polygons; DOK 2). In the revised item, students must first calculate perimeter of the triangle (DOK 1) and use that solution to make a decision about how to determine one side of a square, given the perimeter (DOK 2), and then make the second calculation (DOK 1). **NOTE:** This revision involves several routine operations with decision points. A nonroutine problem context would increase the rigor and deeper thinking even more (DOK 3).	What is the length of a side of the square if the perimeter is 20? (visual shows square with no side measures) A. 4 B. 5 C. 6 D. 7	If both the square and the triangle above have the same perimeter, what is the length of each side of the square? (visual shows triangle with sides of 4, 9, and 7 and square with no side measures) A. 4 B. 5 C. 6 D. 7
6. Fairness—Use of nonessential or unfamiliar contexts	**Underlying Rationale for Item Revision:** Similar to using sentences with "dense clauses" ((too many constituents or idea units, too many adjectives and adverbs modifying the head noun, etc.), sometimes the prompt or stimulus for otherwise rich open-ended questions becomes problematic because of students' lack of prior knowledge. The problem context has the potential to confuse some students rather than help them to see how the skills needed to solve the problem can be transferred to a new situation.		

(Continued)

(Continued)

ISSUE	POSSIBLE SOLUTION	BEFORE REVISION	AFTER REVISION
The context provided for the prompt or stimulus is too unfamiliar for some students to know how to apply.	Most students know what a race is; but do all of them know what hurdles or a commentator is? Prior knowledge will advantage some students. Show a short video clip of a hurdles race before giving students the problem. Let them hear how a commentator describes in detail what's happening all along the race.	This graph describes what happened when three athletes A, B, and C, ran a 400-meter hurdles race. Imagine that you are the race commentator and describe what is happening as carefully as you can. (Middle school, DOK 2—interpret a graph)	This graph describes what happened when three athletes A, B, and C, ran a 400-meter (hurdles) race. Use your interpretation of the graph to describe what each runner is probably doing at 100, 200, 300, and 400 meters.
The context provided for the prompt or stimulus is too unfamiliar for some students to know how to apply.	Source: draft local assessment. Not all students will have prior knowledge that a sketchbook is used for drawing. If students don't know the days of the week, they may not know that Friday is day 5 of the pattern, so they may not be able to find the correct solution due to days of the week and not because of the mathematics. Change "sketchbook" to "tablet," or change prompt to "Every day Anna drew apples." (less reading) Use parallel sentence structure and no pronouns.	Every day Anna drew in her sketchbook. On Monday, she drew one apple, on Tuesday she drew three apples, and on Wednesday she drew five apples. What do you think she'll draw on Friday? Explain your thinking. (Grades 1/2, DOK 2—extend a pattern)	Change names of days of the week to "the first day, the second day, . . . the fifth day" or ". . ." Provide a table showing 5 days with one apple filled in for day 1. Every day Anna drew apples. The table shows that on the first day, she drew one apple. | Day 1 | Day 2 | Day 3 | Day 4 | Day 5 | **Part 1:** Complete the table to show that on the second day Anna drew three apples. On the third day Anna drew five apples. **Part 2:** Use <u>words</u> and <u>numbers</u> to describe the pattern **Part 3:** If this pattern keeps going, how many apples will Anna draw on the fifth day? Explain how you know.

Appendix D

Sample "What I Need to Do" Rubrics—Science, ELA, Mathematics, Blank Template

SCORING CRITERIA	"WHAT I NEED TO DO" RUBRIC—SCIENCE (This area provided for you to indicate that you understand the requirements and success criteria of the assessment task.) Task Title:	EVIDENCE OF WHAT I DID (This is for your FINAL self-assessment. You can color-code or provide a key to show where evidence is found in your assessment write-up.)
Scientific Communication Using Data (DOK 2, 3)	My data is organized in ____ (chart, table, graph, diagram, other?) and labeled (__ title __ axes __ parts). Diagrams have a key (__ scale __ time __ other) My data address my question/hypothesis and are used to support my analysis and conclusions (do data support __/refute __ my hypothesis? Raise a new question __?). ____ has reviewed my explanation and data, understands it, sees no design or procedural flaws and *could* replicate my investigation. (Requires peer to review and sign off—both of you are graded, so read critically!)	Peer who reviewed data representations and use in support of conclusions:
Scientific Concepts and Related Content (DOK 1, 2, 3)	Terms/concepts I'll accurately use/understand (list here and underline in your report): Things I need to be sure to observe or pay attention to: A "Big Idea" that might help me to *connect my learning* to other things I know or want to learn more about: I'll connect ____ procedures ____ observations ____ conclusions to a big idea or ____	
Scientific Tools and Technologies (DOK 1, 2)	Tools I need to safely use to collect data and complete the task/investigation: I'll check for data collection mistakes/errors and precision by:	
Scientific Procedures and Reasoning Strategies (DOK 2, 3)	The investigation question: My hypothesis/prediction ____ is based on my prior observation/understandings: Procedures ensure variable(s) ____ are controlled (fair test). Data to be collected: [____ Trials ____ sample size]	

SCORING CRITERIA	"WHAT I NEED TO DO" RUBRIC—ELA (This area provided for you to indicate that you understand the requirements and success criteria of the assessment task.) Task Title:	EVIDENCE OF WHAT I DID (This is for your FINAL self-assessment. You can **color-code/provide a key** to show where evidence is found in your write-up.)
IDEA DEVELOPMENT, ANALYSIS, and SUPPORTING EVIDENCE (DOK 3 or 4)	My thesis/claim is: My analysis makes connections between WHAT information is presented (e.g., by the media) and HOW it is presented to shape interpretation/assumptions. I explain the significance of each citation or specific example I am analyzing—I underline key sentences in my text where I am explaining why this evidence is important. I checked my sources of evidence for accuracy, credibility, and relevancy by: _____ has reviewed my thesis and agrees that it is clear, and defensible; and that my evidence elaborates upon rather than repeats my points. (Requires peer to review and sign-off—both are graded, so read critically!)	Peer who reviewed thesis clarity with significance of evidence:
ORGANIZATION (DOK 2)	My introduction orients the reader by _____ providing historical context _____ summarizing event _____ explaining issue _____ using data/facts _____ referencing text/media _____ raising question _____ other: _____ Body paragraphs are logically ordered to show this progression of ideas: (1) . . . (2) . . . (3) . . . My essay's transitions are logical and help the reader make connections between key ideas. My conclusion summarizes _____ or expands _____ my analysis _____ reflects upon the thesis.	
GRAMMAR, USAGE, AND CONVENTIONS (DOK 1, 2)	I have few or no errors, and my errors do not interfere with the reader's interpretation of my message. _____ has reviewed my conventions and word choice. My intended audience is: Language use and rhetorical devices show that the style of my writing is: Key terms used: My works cited page includes _____ sources and _____ different formats (journal, film, etc.)	Peer who reviewed GUM:

SCORING CRITERIA	"WHAT I NEED TO DO" RUBRIC—MATHEMATICS (This area provided for you to indicate that you understand the requirements and success criteria of the assessment task.) Task Title:	EVIDENCE OF WHAT I DID (This is for your FINAL self-assessment. You can color-code or provide a key to show where evidence is found in your assessment write-up.)
Problem Solving and Data Representation (DOK 2)	My strategy/approach/plan is appropriate to the situation/problem: My data is organized in _____ (chart, table, graph, diagram, other?) and labeled (__ title __ axes __ parts). Diagrams have a key (__ scale __ time __ other) My data address the question and are appropriate to use in support of my solution. _____ has reviewed my explanation/data, understands it, sees no inaccuracies in how they support my solution. (Requires peer to review and sign off—both of you are graded, so read critically!)	Peer who reviewed data representations and use in support of solution: I adjusted my first strategy/plan because
Communication and Related Content (DOK 1, 2)	Terms/concepts I'll accurately use/understand (list here and underline in your solution): Things I need to be sure to pay attention to: __ patterns __ structures __ real-world conditions/applications __ other __ I'll connect my solution to __ diagram/table __ equations __ a big idea or __	
Calculations, Tools, and Technologies (DOK 1, 2)	Tools used to collect data and complete the task: I checked for accuracy in computations and possible data collection mistakes/errors and precision by: (Requires peer to review and sign off)	Peer who reviewed accuracy and precision:
Reasoning and Proof (DOK 3)	The question I answered: My claim is: My argument/proof is supported by how I explain these math concepts/properties: My argument/proof is also supported by how I explain: __ models __ data __ calculations __ My real-world connections were: A "Big Idea" that helped me to connect my solution to other things I know or want to learn more about:	

SCORING CRITERIA	**"WHAT I NEED TO DO" RUBRIC** (This area provided for you to indicate that you understand the requirements and success criteria of the assessment task.) Task Title:	**EVIDENCE OF WHAT I DID** (This is for your FINAL self-assessment. You can **color-code or provide a key** to show where evidence is found in your assessment write-up.) Peer who reviewed:

APPENDICES

Appendix E

Student Profile: Science Inquiry Learning Progression

Student: _____

DOB: _____

Date of Entry: _____

Reentry: _____

YEAR	GRADE	TEACHER	SUPPORT SERVICE PROVIDER	CASE MANAGER

The Individual Student Profile for Science Inquiry Learning provides a guide for instructional planning, progress monitoring, and documentation of essential learning of science inquiry skills and concepts within and across Grades PreK–5. The science skills and concepts listed were developed using student work samples across multiple classrooms. They have been integrated with consideration of developing literacy and numeracy skills at these grade levels. The intent is that *each student* will have a "profile" (folder/portfolio) with the student's work samples and evidence.

At the end of each school year, samples of student work in science could accompany this record when the Profile is passed on to the next year's teacher. When including a sample of student work, *label the student work* with the inquiry indicator letter (e.g., "C" for Conducting Investigations) and the corresponding skills or concepts number(s) assessed with that assessment. (Note that numbers are for ease of use and relate to a general progression, not a specific intended skill sequence. For example, PreK–K skills generally develop before the Grade 1 skills and concepts, but not always in the numbered order.) Also *list the assessment tool* (by name or description) *under column E* with coding notes (e.g., "Ice Melt Performance Task"—A10, A11, C13, C14, D12, D13). Be sure the student work is dated (e.g., 10/2009); and indicate *which content domain* (Earth & Space, Physical, Life Science, STEM) is being assessed with this assessment.

DIRECTIONS for Documenting Progress

/ in the box indicates the skill or concept has been introduced, but the student has not yet demonstrated conceptual understanding or consistently applied the skill *in the context of an investigation*. It may be necessary to scaffold instruction, reteach the concept using another approach or another context or investigation, or reassess acquisition of skills/concepts at earlier levels if not yet mastered. Administering formative assessments prior to conducting extended investigations is highly recommended to guide instructional planning and appropriate timing of the summative assessments.

X in the box indicates the student has met expectations for this grade level, meaning that there is *sufficient evidence* (assessment data from multiple formats—teacher observations, formative assessments, performance tasks, etc.) to support this conclusion.

SCIENCE INQUIRY	A IS THE STUDENT DEVELOPING AN AWARENESS AND CURIOSITY ABOUT OBJECTS, ORGANISMS, AND EVENTS IN THE ENVIRONMENT?	B IS THE STUDENT DEVELOPING THE ABILITY TO PLAN AND ANALYZE SIMPLE INVESTIGATIONS TO TEST PREDICTIONS/ANSWER QUESTIONS?	C TO WHAT EXTENT IS THE STUDENT DEVELOPING SKILLS OF OBSERVING, MEASURING, RECORDING, ORGANIZING, AND SUMMARIZING DATA?
GRADE LEVELS	FORMULATING QUESTIONS AND HYPOTHESIZING	PLANNING AND CRITIQUING INVESTIGATIONS	CONDUCTING INVESTIGATIONS
Grades PreK–K	1. Sustains curiosity and focus during teacher-guided explorations 2. Sustains curiosity and focus during open-ended and self-guided explorations 3. Answers questions about things observed, manipulated, or predicted 4. Uses picture cues, prior knowledge, and observations to make predictions 5. Formulates questions about things observed or manipulated when cued (e.g., What do you wonder?) or on own	1. Selects materials and objects for open-ended explorations 2. Works with others to generate simple testable questions (Will it sink?) 3. Works with others to plan how to answer simple testable questions: What tools or materials to use How to "collect" data Where and how to record data Safety rules	1. Uses multiple senses to collect data and make observations *with teacher guidance* 2. Uses simple tools (e.g., magnifier, scale) to gather data *with teacher guidance* 3. Uses nonstandard units, numbers, words, drawings to record observations 4. Identifies differences in observable characteristics of materials or events 5. Identifies similarities in observable characteristics of materials or events 6. Drawings show some details (size, color)
Grade 1	6. Asks questions about things that can be observed or manipulated (how far . . .)	4. Works with others to generate simple testable questions	7. Follows steps of a plan *with guidance*

(Continued)

(Continued)

SCIENCE INQUIRY GRADE LEVELS	A IS THE STUDENT DEVELOPING AN AWARENESS AND CURIOSITY ABOUT OBJECTS, ORGANISMS, AND EVENTS IN THE ENVIRONMENT? FORMULATING QUESTIONS AND HYPOTHESIZING	B IS THE STUDENT DEVELOPING THE ABILITY TO PLAN AND ANALYZE SIMPLE INVESTIGATIONS TO TEST PREDICTIONS/ANSWER QUESTIONS? PLANNING AND CRITIQUING INVESTIGATIONS	C TO WHAT EXTENT IS THE STUDENT DEVELOPING SKILLS OF OBSERVING, MEASURING, RECORDING, ORGANIZING, AND SUMMARIZING DATA? CONDUCTING INVESTIGATIONS
	7. Connects prior knowledge and evidence to observations and predictions	5. Identifies potential data to collect and tools and materials needed	8. Uses tools and senses to make observations
	8. Identifies variable to change or test (e.g., what if . . . more or less water?)	6. Works with others to develop major steps to follow to collect and record data	9. Drawings show detail of "target" features (size, color, shape, numbers, proportions)
			10. Records similarities and differences in teacher-provided tables, charts, or templates
Grade 2	9. Poses observational questions (e.g., compare differences in speed)	7. Works with others to write a plan to answer observational questions	11. Follows a plan to conduct investigations with peers
	10. Uses prior knowledge or evidence to explain logical predictions	8. Identifies data to collect and tools and materials needed	12. Uses tools and senses to collect data
	11. Identifies variable to change or test	9. Explains safety rules and (steps) procedure for data collection	13. Drawings show detail and completeness (relative proportions, key features, labels)
	12. Generates new inquiry questions		14. Explains similarities and differences
			15. Organizes, labels, and titles drawings, graphs, and charts

SCIENCE INQUIRY	A IS THE STUDENT DEVELOPING AN AWARENESS AND CURIOSITY ABOUT OBJECTS, ORGANISMS, AND EVENTS IN THE ENVIRONMENT?	B IS THE STUDENT DEVELOPING THE ABILITY TO PLAN AND ANALYZE SIMPLE INVESTIGATIONS TO TEST PREDICTIONS/ANSWER QUESTIONS?	C TO WHAT EXTENT IS THE STUDENT DEVELOPING SKILLS OF OBSERVING, MEASURING, RECORDING, ORGANIZING, AND SUMMARIZING DATA?
GRADE LEVELS	FORMULATING QUESTIONS AND HYPOTHESIZING	PLANNING AND CRITIQUING INVESTIGATIONS	CONDUCTING INVESTIGATIONS
Grade 3	13. Poses cause/effect questions	10. Develops a sequential plan to test a prediction or answer a question	16. Records and labels data (e.g., units of measure, labels, titles, trials, order)
	14. Uses observations and evidence to explain predictions (e.g., data patterns, cause/effect observations)	11. Identifies tools, materials, and equipment needed and data to collect	17. Drawings are detailed, complete, keyed
	15. Describes variables that affect systems using "if-then" statements	12. Explains how to ensure a "fair test" (e.g., variables to control, methods) and identifies potential design flaws	18. Selects appropriate representations to display data graph, table and observations
			19. Follows and explains procedures
			20. Interprets data: describes results, makes connections to prediction
Grades 4–5	16. Connects observations to a question	13. Identifies types of evidence that answer a question or test a prediction	21. Uses tools correctly; collects accurate data; measures precisely
	17. Connects observations to prediction	14. Develops a step-by-step plan to answer a question or test a prediction	22. Records and labels *all* relevant data (e.g., observations, measurement units)

(Continued)

(Continued)

SCIENCE INQUIRY GRADE LEVELS	A IS THE STUDENT DEVELOPING AN AWARENESS AND CURIOSITY ABOUT OBJECTS, ORGANISMS, AND EVENTS IN THE ENVIRONMENT?	B IS THE STUDENT DEVELOPING THE ABILITY TO PLAN AND ANALYZE SIMPLE INVESTIGATIONS TO TEST PREDICTIONS/ANSWER QUESTIONS?	C TO WHAT EXTENT IS THE STUDENT DEVELOPING SKILLS OF OBSERVING, MEASURING, RECORDING, ORGANIZING, AND SUMMARIZING DATA?
	FORMULATING QUESTIONS AND HYPOTHESIZING	PLANNING AND CRITIQUING INVESTIGATIONS	CONDUCTING INVESTIGATIONS
	18. Makes reasonable predictions based on available evidence 19. Supports prediction or question with an explanation or reason 20. Analyzes scientific data about systems to generate questions or predictions (showing cause/effect relationships)	15. Explains why a procedure is or is not a "fair test" (e.g., control of variables, multiple trials, data collection method) 16. Explains appropriateness and safe use of tools, materials, and procedures 17. Determines how to collect and record data (e.g., use of table, drawing) 18. Redesigns investigation based on design flaws or designs new investigation using new evidence	23. Uses appropriate representations and accurately organizes and displays data (scale for graph, labels table) and observations, (e.g., keys, scale, and details in drawings) 24. Follows and can explain procedures (e.g., multiple trials, control variables) 25. Interprets *all* data: summarizes results using big ideas; identifies patterns; connects data to prediction (support/refute); shows relationships between variables

D. IS THE STUDENT ABLE TO USE INFORMATION AND/OR DATA TO COMMUNICATE AND SUPPORT IDEAS AND DRAW CONCLUSIONS?	E. LIST COMMON ASSESSMENTS, SPECIFIC IN-DEPTH LEARNING EXPERIENCES (E.G., PROJECTS), AND/OR INVESTIGATIONS USED TO ASSESS SCIENCE INQUIRY.	EARTH & SPACE SCIENCE CONCEPTS	PHYSICAL SCIENCE CONCEPTS	LIFE SCIENCE CONCEPTS	STEM CONCEPTS
DEVELOPING AND EVALUATING EXPLANATIONS	LIST COMMON ASSESSMENTS AND (CODES FOR) RELATED SKILLS	UNITS OF STUDY (AND ASSESSMENT)	UNITS OF STUDY (AND ASSESSMENT)	UNITS OF STUDY (AND ASSESSMENT)	UNITS OF STUDY (AND ASSESSMENT)
1. Nonverbally conveys ideas investigated (drawing, movement, demonstrate with objects)					
2. Verbally conveys ideas investigated					
3. Uses some letters or words to label drawings					
4. Organizes data (e.g., makes pictograph, colors in bar graph, fills in chart, sorts objects)					
5. Explains observations using props (e.g., table, drawing, graph, objects)					
6. Sorts/classifies objects by observable attribute (e.g., color, size, shape, etc.)					

(Continued)

(Continued)

D. IS THE STUDENT ABLE TO USE INFORMATION AND/OR DATA TO COMMUNICATE AND SUPPORT IDEAS AND DRAW CONCLUSIONS?	E. LIST COMMON ASSESSMENTS, SPECIFIC IN-DEPTH LEARNING EXPERIENCES (E.G., PROJECTS), AND/OR INVESTIGATIONS USED TO ASSESS SCIENCE INQUIRY.	EARTH & SPACE SCIENCE CONCEPTS	PHYSICAL SCIENCE CONCEPTS	LIFE SCIENCE CONCEPTS	STEM CONCEPTS
DEVELOPING AND EVALUATING EXPLANATIONS	LIST COMMON ASSESSMENTS AND (CODES FOR) RELATED SKILLS	UNITS OF STUDY (AND ASSESSMENT)	UNITS OF STUDY (AND ASSESSMENT)	UNITS OF STUDY (AND ASSESSMENT)	UNITS OF STUDY (AND ASSESSMENT)
7. Writes a coherent message (1–2 sentences) to describe observations (I saw . . . ; I found out . . .)					
8. Organizes data (e.g., pictograph, diagram, bar graph, chart)					
9. Sorts or classifies objects and explains groupings					
10. Describes results (in table, diagram, drawing)					
11. Describes or writes about a sequence of observed events using some details or evidence					
12. Organizes data (e.g., pictograph, diagram, bar graph, chart, model) and identifies patterns					
13. Sorts or classifies objects and materials and justifies groupings (e.g., with evidence, definitions)					

D IS THE STUDENT ABLE TO USE INFORMATION AND/OR DATA TO COMMUNICATE AND SUPPORT IDEAS AND DRAW CONCLUSIONS?	E LIST COMMON ASSESSMENTS, SPECIFIC IN-DEPTH LEARNING EXPERIENCES (E.G., PROJECTS), AND/OR INVESTIGATIONS USED TO ASSESS SCIENCE INQUIRY.	EARTH & SPACE SCIENCE CONCEPTS	PHYSICAL SCIENCE CONCEPTS	LIFE SCIENCE CONCEPTS	STEM CONCEPTS
DEVELOPING AND EVALUATING EXPLANATIONS	LIST COMMON ASSESSMENTS AND (CODES FOR) RELATED SKILLS	UNITS OF STUDY (AND ASSESSMENT)	UNITS OF STUDY (AND ASSESSMENT)	UNITS OF STUDY (AND ASSESSMENT)	UNITS OF STUDY (AND ASSESSMENT)
14. Uses main points, details, and evidence to summarize results and conclusions					
15. Uses labeled drawings and data tables to support interpretations (e.g., patterns, trends)					
16. Discusses possible errors in data					
17. Relates data to prediction or question					
18. Proposes new questions based on results					
19. Identifies data relevant to task or question					
20. Classifies data into meaningful categories					

(Continued)

(Continued)

D IS THE STUDENT ABLE TO USE INFORMATION AND/OR DATA TO COMMUNICATE AND SUPPORT IDEAS AND DRAW CONCLUSIONS?	E LIST COMMON ASSESSMENTS, SPECIFIC IN-DEPTH LEARNING EXPERIENCES (E.G., PROJECTS), AND/OR INVESTIGATIONS USED TO ASSESS SCIENCE INQUIRY.	EARTH & SPACE SCIENCE CONCEPTS	PHYSICAL SCIENCE CONCEPTS	LIFE SCIENCE CONCEPTS	STEM CONCEPTS
DEVELOPING AND EVALUATING EXPLANATIONS	LIST COMMON ASSESSMENTS AND (CODES FOR) RELATED SKILLS	UNITS OF STUDY (AND ASSESSMENT)	UNITS OF STUDY (AND ASSESSMENT)	UNITS OF STUDY (AND ASSESSMENT)	UNITS OF STUDY (AND ASSESSMENT)

21. Compares own data to other sources (e.g., scientific data given, science concepts, proposed predictions, seemingly inaccurate results)

22. Interprets or analyzes data: Uses evidence to explain interpretations of data trends, justify conclusions, evaluate significance of data

23. Connects task or model to real-world example

24. Identifies possible experimental error (e.g., data collection method, insufficient or inaccurate data)

25. Proposes new questions, new predictions, or modifies procedures based on results

Appendix F

Student Learning Progression Literacy Profile-Grades 7-8

Student: _____

DOB: _____

Date of Entry: _____   Reentry: _____

YEAR	GRADE	TEACHER	SUPPORT SERVICE PROVIDER	CASE MANAGER

The Student Learning Progression Literacy Profile (LPLP) provides a general guide for instructional planning, progress monitoring, and documentation of essential learning of literacy skills and concepts within and across grades. The skills and concepts listed have been integrated with consideration of a research-based learning progression for literacy and the Common Core State Standards at the designated grade levels. At the end of each school year, samples of student work could accompany this record if the Profile is passed on to the next year's teacher or used for reporting to parents.

- Grade-level literacy teams can begin using the Literacy Profile by examining descriptions of Progress Indicators (e.g., **M.RL.k** identify use of literary techniques. e.g., flashback, foreshadowing) and narrative strategies (e.g., dialogue, sensory details) and explain how they advance the plot or impact meaning with the corresponding grade-level CC standards (e.g., **8.RL-3, 4**) in order to develop appropriate instructional building blocks for each unit of study (selecting texts that increase in complexity, developing lesson sequences that move students along the learning continuum). Units of study typically encompass multiple Progress Indicators from several LPF strands (e.g., ***Making Meaning at the Word Level, Reading Literary Texts, and Writing Literary Texts***).

- Next, develop or identify the major common assessments for each unit of study used during the school year, asking this question: **How can we best collect evidence of learning at different entry points along the learning progression**? These assessments should include summative and performance assessments used across all classrooms at the grade level as a starting point, assessing multiple skills described along the learning progression typically taken by most students.

- Additional evidence of learning, using ongoing assessments (preassessments, formative assessments, teacher observations, etc.), mid-assessments, and classroom-specific unit assessments can be documented in the profile throughout the school year. The depth and breadth of assessments used will vary according to intended purpose.

DIRECTIONS for Documenting Progress Along the Learning Progressions

/ in the box to the left of the Progress Indicator indicates the skill or concept has been introduced, but the student has not yet demonstrated conceptual understanding or consistently applied the skills or concepts *in the context of applying them to various texts and text types*. It may be necessary to scaffold instruction; reteach the concept using another approach or another context or text; or reassess acquisition of skills or concepts at earlier levels if not yet mastered. Administering ongoing formative assessments is highly recommended to guide instructional planning and appropriate timing of the summative or interim assessments.

X in the box to the left of the Progress Indicator indicates the student has met expectations for this grade level, meaning that *there is sufficient assessment evidence* (assessment data from multiple formats—teacher observations, formative assessments, student work from performance tasks, etc.) to support this conclusion.

When collecting samples of student work (e.g., for parent conferences, progress monitoring), *label the student work* with the Literacy Profile indicator strand letters ("HD"—Habits & Dispositions; RL—Reading Literary texts, WI—Writing Informational texts, etc.) and include the Progress Indicator code for corresponding skills or concepts assessed with that assessment task. Also be sure the student work is dated. (Note that coding and ordering of the Progress Indicators (a, b, c, etc.) in the profile are for ease of use with the *Learning Progressions Framework* (LPF) *for ELA & Literacy** and relate to a general progression, NOT a specific intended, lock-step skill sequence. For example, many of the same skills and concepts will generally develop and be practiced again and again with different and increasingly more complex texts across a school year. Beginning with an optimal lesson sequencing planning tool (such as the LPF and Literacy Profile) can provide insights into how to best support students with smaller learning steps in order to attain the end-of-year skills and concepts articulated in the Common Core State Standards.

---

* Hess, Karin. (Ed. & Principle author). (2011). *Learning progressions frameworks designed for use with the common core state standards in English language arts & literacy K–12*. Available at http://www.nciea.org/publications/ELA_LPF_12%20 2011_final.pdf.

LPF LITERACY STRANDS	HD	1-LITERACY HABITS & DISPOSITIONS IS THE STUDENT DEMONSTRATING GREATER INDEPENDENCE AND CONFIDENCE WHEN DEVELOPING AND APPLYING LITERACY SKILLS?	RWL	2-MAKING MEANING AT THE WORD LEVEL DOES THE STUDENT READ FLEXIBLY, USING A VARIETY OF STRATEGIES TO MAKE MEANING—LITERAL AND INTERPRETATIVE—AT THE WORD OR PHRASE LEVEL?	NOTES: LIST SAMPLE TEXTS (TITLES, LEVELS, ETC.) USED BY STUDENTS TO DEMONSTRATE INDEPENDENT SKILL ACQUISITION: "MAKING MEANING AT THE WORD LEVEL"
Describe Evidence of Extending Skills		**M.HD.j** Use reading, writing, or discussion to reflect on or modify how self and others see the world (e.g., multiple perspectives, reasoning, evidence). **7.SL-1d** **8.SL-1d**		**M.RWL.l** Analyze intent or impact of language used (e.g., What impact does this word or phrase have on the reader?). **7.RL-4; 7.RI-4** **8.RL-4; 8.RI-4** **M.RWL.k** Interpret use of words or phrasing (e.g., figurative, symbolic, sensory). **7.L-5a; 7.RL-4; 7.RI-4** **8.L-5a; 8.RL-4; 8.RI-4** **M.RWL.j** Utilize specialized reference materials (print/digital) to verify and expand reading, writing, and speaking vocabulary. **7.L-4c** **8.L-4c** **M.RWL.i** Integrate grade-appropriate academic and domain-specific vocabulary in reading, writing, listening, and speaking. **7.L-6; 7.RI-4** **8.L-6; 8.RI-4**	

Grades 7–8 Learning Progression

(Continued)

(Continued)

LPF LITERACY STRANDS	HD	1-LITERACY HABITS & DISPOSITIONS IS THE STUDENT DEMONSTRATING GREATER INDEPENDENCE AND CONFIDENCE WHEN DEVELOPING AND APPLYING LITERACY SKILLS?	RWL	2-MAKING MEANING AT THE WORD LEVEL DOES THE STUDENT READ FLEXIBLY, USING A VARIETY OF STRATEGIES TO MAKE MEANING—LITERAL AND INTERPRETIVE—AT THE WORD OR PHRASE LEVEL?	NOTES: LIST SAMPLE TEXTS (TITLES, LEVELS, ETC.) USED BY STUDENTS TO DEMONSTRATE INDEPENDENT SKILL ACQUISITION: "MAKING MEANING AT THE WORD LEVEL"
Grades 7–8 Learning Progression		**M.HD.i** Sustain efforts to complete complex reading or writing tasks; seek out assistance, models, sources, or feedback to improve understanding or refine final products. 7.W-5 8.W-5 **M.HD.h** Develop a deepening awareness and raise questions about the accuracy and intent of various media messages and texts (e.g., print/non-print, blogs, political cartoons). 7.SL-2, 3 8.SL-2, 3 **M.HD.g** Expand options for reading for pleasure and for academic learning to include new genres, topics, and sources (e.g., newspapers, online/digital media, magazines, historical, scientific, or technical texts). 8.W-7		**M.RWL.h** Use word derivation to expand vocabulary use to new contexts (e.g., historical, cultural, political, mathematical). 7.L-4c; 7.RL-4 8.L-4c; 8.RL-4 **M.RWL.g** Make conceptual connections between known and unknown words, using word structure, word relationships, or context. 7.L-4a, 4b, 4d, 5b 8.L-4a, 4b, 4d, 5b **M.RWL.f** Use connotations and denotations of words to extend and deepen definitional understanding. 7.L-4a, 5c; 7.RL-4; 7.RI-4 8.L-4a, 5c; 8.RL-4; 8.RI-4	

Units & Assessments Used

Record & Date Fluency Checks

Oral reading (O) or (S) Silent reading

LPF LITERACY STRANDS	3-READING LITERARY TEXTS TO WHAT EXTENT DOES THE STUDENT MAKE MEANING OF AND UNDERSTAND THE UNIQUE GENRE FEATURES, STRUCTURES, AND PURPOSES OF LITERARY TEXTS?	NOTES: LIST SAMPLE TEXTS (TITLES, LEVELS, ETC.) USED BY STUDENTS TO DEMONSTRATE SKILL ACQUISITION: "READING LITERARY TEXTS"	4-READING INFORMATIONAL TEXTS TO WHAT EXTENT DOES THE STUDENT MAKE MEANING OF AND UNDERSTAND THE UNIQUE GENRE FEATURES, STRUCTURES, AND PURPOSES OF INFORMATIONAL TEXTS?	NOTES: LIST SAMPLE TEXTS (TITLES, LEVELS, ETC.) USED BY STUDENTS TO DEMONSTRATE SKILL ACQUISITION: "READING INFORMATIONAL TEXTS"
	RL		RI	
Describe Evidence of Transfer ← Grades 7–8 Learning Progression	**M.RL.m** Use supporting evidence to evaluate and respond to a range of literature using given criteria. 7.RL-6, 7, 9; 7.L-5a 8.RL-6, 7, 9; 8.L-5a **M.RL.l** Use supporting evidence to analyze or compare texts according to text structure, genre features, or author's style or tone. 7.RL-5, 7, 8 8.RL-5, 7, 8 **M.RL.k** Identify use of literary techniques (e.g., flashback, foreshadowing) and narrative strategies (e.g., dialogue, sensory details) and explain how they advance the plot or impact meaning. 7.RL-3, 4 8.RL-3, 4 **M.RL.j** Use supporting evidence to identify and analyze how the use of literary elements and point of view influence development of plot, characters (motivation, interactions) or theme. 7.RL-2, 3 8.RL-2, 3		**M.RI.l** Compare or integrate information from multiple sources to develop deeper understanding of the concept, topic, subject, and resolve conflicting information. 7.RI-7, 9 8.RI-9 **M.RI.k** Use supporting evidence to analyze and explain why and how authors: organize, develop, and present ideas; establish a point of view; or build supporting arguments to affect the text as a whole. 7.RI-2, 5, 6, 8 8.RI-2, 5, 6, 8 **M.RI.j** Use supporting evidence to summarize central ideas, draw inferences, or analyze connections within or across texts (e.g., events, people, ideas). 7.RI-1, 2, 3, 9 8.RI-1, 2, 3, 9	

(Continued)

(Continued)

LPF LITERACY STRANDS	RL	3-READING LITERARY TEXTS TO WHAT EXTENT DOES THE STUDENT MAKE MEANING OF AND UNDERSTAND THE UNIQUE GENRE FEATURES, STRUCTURES, AND PURPOSES OF LITERARY TEXTS?	NOTES: LIST SAMPLE TEXTS (TITLES, LEVELS, ETC.) USED BY STUDENTS TO DEMONSTRATE SKILL ACQUISITION: "READING LITERARY TEXTS"	RI	4-READING INFORMATIONAL TEXTS TO WHAT EXTENT DOES THE STUDENT MAKE MEANING OF AND UNDERSTAND THE UNIQUE GENRE FEATURES, STRUCTURES, AND PURPOSES OF INFORMATIONAL TEXTS?	NOTES: LIST SAMPLE TEXTS (TITLES, LEVELS, ETC.) USED BY STUDENTS TO DEMONSTRATE SKILL ACQUISITION: "READING INFORMATIONAL TEXTS"
← Grades 7–8 Learning Progression		**M.RL.i** Use a range of textual evidence to support summaries and interpretations of text (e.g., purpose, plot/subplot, central idea, theme). 7.RL-1, 2 8.RL-1, 2 **M.RL.h** Flexibly use strategies to derive meaning from a variety of texts and literary mediums. 7.RL-4; 7.L-4, 5a, 5c 8.RL-4; 8.L-4, 5a, 5c			**M.RI.i** Utilize knowledge of text structures and genre features to locate, organize, or analyze important information. 7.RI-5 8.RI-5 **M.RI.h** Flexibly using strategies to derive meaning from a variety of print/non-print informational texts. 7.RI-4; 7.L-4, 5a; 7.SL-2 8.RI-4; 8.L-4, 5a; 8.SL-2	

Units & Assessments Used

LPF LITERACY STRANDS	5-WRITING LITERARY TEXTS CAN THE STUDENT APPLY NARRATIVE STRATEGIES AND TEXT STRUCTURES TO CREATE LITERARY TEXTS FOR VARIED PURPOSES?	6-WRITING INFORMATIONAL TEXTS CAN THE STUDENT APPLY ORGANIZATIONAL STRATEGIES, STRUCTURES, AND USE OF SOURCES TO EXPLAIN OR DESCRIBE TOPICS AND IDEAS?	7-WRITING PERSUASIVELY (ARGUMENTS/CRITIQUES) CAN THE STUDENT APPLY ORGANIZATIONAL STRATEGIES AND USE SOURCES TO ANALYZE TOPICS OR TEXTS IN ORDER TO SUPPORT A CLAIM/ OPINION FOR VARIED AUDIENCES?
	WL	WI	WP
Describe Evidence of Transfer	**M.WL.p** Apply editing and revision strategies to full texts that clarify intent and strengthen intended impact on reader. 7.W-3, 4, 5; 7.L-1, 2, 3, 4c, 5, 6 8.W-3, 4, 5; 8.L-1, 2, 3, 4c, 5, 6 **M.WL.o** Write a conclusion that follows the flow of ideas, reflects back on the theme, and leaves readers with something to think about. 7.W-3e 8.W-3e	**M.WI.o** Apply editing (cohesion of subject-verb, pronoun use, verb tense, and impact of word choice and sentence variety) and revision strategies to full texts that clarify intent and meaning; make judgments about completeness and accuracy of information, visual, and auditory components, validity of sources cited. 7.W-2, 4, 5; 7.SL-4, 5; 7.L-1, 2, 3, 4c, 4d, 6; 7.RI-4 8.W-2, 4, 5; 8.SL-4, 5; 8.L-1, 2, 3, 4c, 4d, 6; 8.RI-4 **M.WI.n** Draw and state conclusions by synthesizing information and summarizing key points that link back to focus or thesis. 7.W-2f; 7.SL-3; 7.RI-2 8.W-2f; 8.SL-3; 8.RI-2	**M.WP.o** Apply editing (cohesion of subject-verb, pronoun use, verb tense, and impact of word choice and sentence variety/ complexity) and revision strategies to full texts that clarify intent and meaning: make judgments about completeness and accuracy of information, visual, and auditory components, validity of sources cited, discourse style, and approach to addressing audience needs (e.g., emotion, interest, moral authority, potential objections). 7.W-1, 4, 5; 7.SL-4, 5; 7.L-1, 2, 3, 4c, 4d, 6; 8.W-1, 4, 5; 8.SL-4, 5; 8.L-1, 2, 3, 4c, 4d, 6 **M.WP.n** Draw and state conclusions by synthesizing information, summarizing key points of reasoning chain that link back to focus or thesis, and reflecting a response to the opposition. 7.W-1e; 7.SL-3 8.W-1e; 8.SL-3

Grades 7–8 Learning Progression

(Continued)

(Continued)

Grades 7-8 Learning Progression

LPF LITERACY STRANDS	WL	5-WRITING LITERARY TEXTS: CAN THE STUDENT APPLY NARRATIVE STRATEGIES AND TEXT STRUCTURES TO CREATE LITERARY TEXTS FOR VARIED PURPOSES?	WI	6-WRITING INFORMATIONAL TEXTS: CAN THE STUDENT APPLY ORGANIZATIONAL STRATEGIES, STRUCTURES, AND USE OF SOURCES TO EXPLAIN OR DESCRIBE TOPICS AND IDEAS?	WP	7-WRITING PERSUASIVELY (ARGUMENTS/CRITIQUES): CAN THE STUDENT APPLY ORGANIZATIONAL STRATEGIES AND USE SOURCES TO ANALYZE TOPICS OR TEXTS IN ORDER TO SUPPORT A CLAIM/OPINION FOR VARIED AUDIENCES?
		M.WL.n Refine overall coherence with literary techniques or realistic accuracy (historical, geographic, technical, etc.). 7.L-3, 5, 6 8.L-3, 5, 6		**M.WI.m** Select relevant facts, details, examples, quotations, or text features to support or clarify the focus/controlling idea. 7.W-2a, 2b, 9; 7.SL-4, 5; 7.RI-1 8.W-2a, 2b, 9; 8.SL-4, 5; 8.RI-1		**M.WP.m** Utilize emotive, precise, or technical language, transitional devices, and rhetorical questions for effect, while maintaining an authoritative stance and consistent discourse style and voice. 7.W-1c, 1d; 7.L-3, 5c 8.W-1c, 1d; 8.L-3, 5c
		M.WL.m Use dialogue to advance the plot or theme. 7.W-3a-3d 8.W-3a-3d		**M.WI.l** Include precise language, specialized domain-specific vocabulary, and maintain a knowledgeable stance and consistent (formal) style and voice. 7.W-2d, 2e; 7.L-3, 5c; 7.RI-4 8.W-2d, 2e; 8.L-3, 5c; 8.RI-4		**M.WP.l** Select and organize relevant facts, text evidence or quotes, data, or examples to support focus (claim/thesis) and a response to opposing claims of the audience. 7.W-1a, 1b 8.W-1a, 1b
		M.WL.l Select details and precise or nuanced language to enhance tone and imagery, elaborate on ideas, or evoke an emotional response. 7.W-3a-3d; 7.L-4c 8.W-3a-3d; 8.L-4c				
		M.WL.k Sustain point of view, style, and text structure(s) appropriate to purpose and genre; use transitional devices to control pacing or add interest (e.g., flashback, foreshadowing). 7.W-3a-3d 8.W-3a-3d		**M.WI.k** Select text structure(s) and transitions appropriate to organizing and develop information to support the focus, controlling idea, or thesis. 7.W-2a, 2c; 7.RI-2, 5 8.W-2a, 2c; 8.RI-2, 5		**M.WP.k** Establish a perspective on a topic or text in order to introduce a focus (claim/thesis) and provide context and possible counter claims, and plan a chain of logic to be presented. 7.W-1a 8.W-1a

Grades 7–8 Learning Progression

LPF LITERACY STRANDS	WL	5-WRITING LITERARY TEXTS	WI	6-WRITING INFORMATIONAL TEXTS	WP	7-WRITING PERSUASIVELY (ARGUMENTS/CRITIQUES)
		CAN THE STUDENT APPLY NARRATIVE STRATEGIES AND TEXT STRUCTURES TO CREATE LITERARY TEXTS FOR VARIED PURPOSES?		**CAN THE STUDENT APPLY ORGANIZATIONAL STRATEGIES, STRUCTURES, AND USE OF SOURCES TO EXPLAIN OR DESCRIBE TOPICS AND IDEAS?**		**CAN THE STUDENT APPLY ORGANIZATIONAL STRATEGIES AND USE SOURCES TO ANALYZE TOPICS OR TEXTS IN ORDER TO SUPPORT A CLAIM/OPINION FOR VARIED AUDIENCES?**
		M.WL.j Set the context and tone (e.g., an opening lead to 'hook' readers) and establish a point of view and discourse style. 7.W-3a 8.W-3a		**M.WI.j** Analyze information in order to establish a focus, or controlling idea about a topic, investigation, problem, or issue. 7.W-2a, 9; 7.RI-9 8.W-2a, 9; 8.RI-9		**M.WP.j** Use varied (credible) sources and locate relevant evidence to analyze factual and contextual information on a topic or text to better understand possible perspectives or POV. 7.W-7, 8, 9; 7.SL-3; 7.RI-7, 8, 9 8.W-7, 8, 9; 8.SL-3; 8.RI-7, 8, 9
		M.WL.i Employ strategies (e.g., writing log, mentor texts, peer conferencing, research) to develop images, characters, plot, central message or theme, or discourse style. 7.W-9; 7.RL-2, 3, 6, 9 8.W-9; 8.RL-2, 3, 6, 9		**M.WI.i** Independently locate information from multiple reference sources (print and nonprint) to obtain information on a topic; validate reliability of references, and list or cite them using an established format. 7.W-7, 8, 9; 7.SL-2; 7.RI-7, 9 8.W-7, 8, 9; 8.SL-2; 8.RI-9		**M.WP.i** Use strategies to better understand genres of persuasive writing and their audiences (e.g., discuss opposing perspectives; analyze mentor texts—political cartoons, literary critiques, speeches, propaganda techniques). 7.W-7, 8, 9; 7.SL-1d, 2, 3, 4; 7.RI-8 8.W-7, 8, 9; 8.SL-1d, 2, 3, 4; 8.RI-8

APPENDIX G

Writing Persuasively Learning Progression (Strand 7, LPF)

STRAND 7: Writing Persuasively/Communicating Opinions, Critiques, and Arguments (WP)—Different genres of persuasive writing (literary critiques, persuasive essays, speeches, editorials, etc.) are appropriate for different purposes and require use of genre-specific features, text structures, and strategic use of logic chains with compelling supporting evidence to produce a coherent unit of thought that persuades the intended audience.

(K–4) ELEMENTARY SCHOOL LEARNING TARGETS	(5–8) MIDDLE SCHOOL LEARNING TARGETS	(9–12) HIGH SCHOOL LEARNING TARGETS
E.WP Apply organizational strategies (e.g., description, definition, compare/contrast, cause/effect, proposition/support) and an understanding of topics or texts to develop and support opinions about them for authentic audiences.	**M.WP** Apply organizational strategies (e.g., cause/effect, problem/solution, proposition/support, critique), and use of multiple sources to analyze topics or texts in order to support a claim or thesis for authentic and varied audiences.	**H.WP** Apply organizational structures (e.g., proposition/support, critique, inductive and deductive reasoning), credible sources, and rhetorical strategies to the analysis and synthesis of complex ideas to present and support reasoned arguments/critiques of texts, issues, or problems for authentic and varied audiences.

GRADES K–2	GRADES 3–4	GRADES 5–6	GRADES 7–8	GRADES 9–12
Use a process approach to develop and communicate support for opinions . . .	Use a process approach to develop and communicate support for opinions . . .	Use a process approach to develop and communicate support for claims or thesis . . .	Use a process approach to develop and communicate support for claims or thesis . . .	Use a process approach to develop and communicate compelling and credible evidence to support reasoned arguments and critiques. . . .
E.WP.a generating ideas about a topic, text, or stimulus shared (event, photo, video, peers, etc.) using a range of responses (e.g., discussion, dictation, drawing, letters/invented spelling, writing)	E.WP.i generating their own ideas for writing, using strategies to understand opinion writing (e.g., discuss possible reasons for/against with peers; analyze mentor texts—ads, book/movie reviews, letters to editor)	M.WP.a using strategies to better understand genres of persuasive writing (e.g., discuss opposing perspectives; analyze mentor texts—ads, essays, book/movie reviews, speeches, propaganda techniques)	M.WP.i using strategies to better understand genres of persuasive writing and their audiences (e.g., discuss opposing perspectives, analyze mentor texts—political cartoons, literary critiques, speeches, propaganda techniques)	H.WP.a using advanced searches and analyses to better understand genres and techniques associated with argument and critique and their intended audiences (e.g., discuss reasoning and rebuttals, analyze mentor texts—political commentaries, literary critiques, media messages, editorials, seminal historical and scientific documents)
K.W-1, 7; K.SL-4, 5; K.L-6	3.W-5; 3.SL-1d, 3; 3.L-3, 6	5.W-8, 9; 5.SL-3, 4; 5.RI-8	7.W-7, 8, 9; 7.SL-1d, 2, 3, 4; 7.RI-8	9-10.W-7, 8, 9; 9-10.RI-6, 7, 8, 9
1.W-7, 8; 1.SL-1b, 2, 4, 5; 1.L-6	4.W-5; 4.SL-1d, 3; 4.L-3, 6	6.W-7, 8, 9; 6.SL-1d, 2, 3, 4; 6.RI-8	8.W-7, 8, 9; 8.SL-1d, 2, 3, 4; 8.RI-8	11-12.W-7, 8, 9; 11-12.RI-6, 7, 8
2.W-8; 2.SL-2, 4; 2.L-6	E.WP.j developing an understanding of a topic or text by locating evidence and using note-taking strategies to record and organize information relating to opposing sides of an issue (e.g., why people think/do not think dogs make good pets)	M.WP.b using varied sources and locating evidence to obtain factual and contextual information on a topic or text to better understand possible perspectives or points of view	M.WP.j using varied (credible) sources and locating relevant evidence to analyze factual and contextual information on a topic or text to better understand possible perspectives or points of view	H.WP.b organizing, analyzing, and selectively integrating varied and complex information (facts, principles, examples, quotations, data), determining their significance to potential lines of reasoning (claims/counterclaims) either to support or refute the focus or thesis
E.WP.b with prompting and support, connecting information or facts with personal opinions about a topic or text (e.g., I think it is an informational text because it has facts) using discussion, drawings with details, written words (labels, nouns) or completing statements (e.g., This is what I like about dogs . . . ; That character was funny because . . .) and "reading back" what they have written				9-10.W-1a, 1b, 1c, 7, 8, 9; 9-10.SL-2, 3
				11-12.W-1a, 1b, 1c, 7, 8, 9; 11-12.SL-2, 3
				H.WP.c establishing a critical stance and developing coherence among claims and evidence using nuanced transitions and varied syntax to link the focus or thesis with the major claims/counter claims as appropriate to intended audience

GRADES K–2	GRADES 3–4	GRADES 5–6	GRADES 7–8	GRADES 9–12
K.W-1; K.SL-4, 5; K.L-1f, 6	3.W-1b, 7, 8; 3.RL-2, 3; 3.RI-2	5.W-7, 8, 9; 5.SL-2, 3	7.W-7, 8, 9; 7.SL-3; 7.RI-7, 8, 9	9-10.W-1a, 1b, 1c; 9-10.SL-4
1.W-1; 1.SL-4, 5, 6; 1.L-1j, 6	4.W-1b, 7, 8, 9; 4.RL-1, 2, 3; 4.RI-1, 2	6.W-7, 8, 9; 6.SL-2, 3	8.W-7, 8, 9; 8.SL-3; 8.RI-7, 8, 9	11-12.W-1a, 1b, 1c; 9-10.SL-4
2.W-1; 2.SL-4, 6; 2.L-1f, 6	E.WP.k writing an introduction (e.g., for a letter about a product; for a book talk) of several sentences that sets the context (e.g., title/author of book) and states a focus (opinion), controlling idea about a topic or text	M.WP.c establishing a perspective on a topic or text in order to introduce a focus (claim/thesis), and provide context (e.g., circumstance of the problem; historical time period), and plan a chain of logic to be presented	M.WP.k establishing a perspective on a topic or text in order to introduce a focus (claim/thesis) and provide context and possible counterclaims, and plan a chain of logic to be presented	H.WP.d utilizing emotive, precise, or technical language, transitional devices, and rhetorical techniques for effect, while maintaining a critical stance and consistent discourse style and voice
E.WP.c reading a variety of texts and distinguishing among text genres and their purposes (e.g., stories that entertain, texts that teach or give information, ads—convince you to buy, personal messages, letters—different purposes, include opinions)				9-10.W-1c, 1d; 9-10.L-3, 5c
1.RL-5	3.W-1a; 3.L-1i; 3.RL-2; 3.RI-2	5.W-1a; 5.SL-4	7.W-1a	11-12.W-1c, 1d; 11-12.L-3, 5c
2.RI-6	4.W-1a; 4.L-1f; 4.RL-2; 4.RI-2	6.W-1a; 6.SL-4	8.W-1a	H.WP.e articulating a conclusion that expresses implications, states the significance of the position or thesis, or presents a compelling call to action, while reflecting sensitivity to audience, leaving readers with a clear understanding and respect for what the writer is arguing for
E.WP.d with support, using simple note-taking strategies to record and distinguish facts/opinions or reasons for/against a real-world topic (e.g., t-chart with reasons why people like/do not pizza)	E.WP.l selecting relevant facts, details, or examples to support the controlling idea or opinion, including use of domain-specific vocabulary	M.WP.d selecting and organizing relevant facts, text evidence or quotes, or examples to support focus (claim/thesis) and possible opposing claims of the potential audience	M.WP.l selecting and organizing relevant facts, text evidence or quotes, data, or examples to support focus (claim/thesis) and a response to opposing claims of the audience	
1.W-8	3.W-1a, 1b, 8; 3.SL-4; 3.L-6; 3.RI-4	5.W-1a, 1b, 7, 8, 9; 5.SL-4	7.W-1a, 1b	9-10.W-1e and 11-12.W-1e
2.W-8	4.W-1a, 1b, 9; 4.SL-4; 4.L-6; 4.RI-4	6.W-1a, 1b, 7, 8, 9	8.W-1a, 1b	H.WP.f editing and revising full texts to clarify intent and meaning: making judgments about completeness, accuracy, and significance claims-counterclaims, validity of evidence, overall cohesion, and impact of style, tone and voice on message
E.WP.e locating facts to support stated opinions about a topic (e.g., survey peers) or text; collaboratively describing reasons for/against through illustrations, captions, and simple sentences that connect reasons with evidence; applying basic capitalization and end punctuation	E.WP.m stating reasons in a logical order, elaborating on each reason with relevant details and examples using several related sentences, and making connections using transitions (because, but, for example, etc.)	M.WP.e developing a chain of reasoning for the thesis using elaboration to explain logical reasons or rationale, meaningful transitions showing progression of ideas, propaganda strategies) which contribute to the impact on readers	M.WP.m utilizing emotive, precise, or technical language, transitional devices, and rhetorical questions for effect, while maintaining an authoritative stance and consistent discourse style and voice	9-10.W-1, 4, 5; 9-10.SL-5; 9-10.L-1, 2, 3, 4c, 6
K.W-1; K.SL-4, 5; K.L-1f, 2, 6				11-12.W-1, 4, 5; 11-12.SL-5; 11-12.L-1, 2, 3, 4c, 6
1.W-1; 1.SL-4, 5, 6; 1.L-1j, 2, 6			7.W-1c, 1d; 7.L-3, 5c	
2.W-1; 2.SL-2, 4, 6; 2.L-1f, 2, 6			8.W-1c, 1d; 8.L-3, 5c	

(Continued)

(Continued)

GRADES K-2	GRADES 3-4	GRADES 5-6	GRADES 7-8	GRADES 9-12
E.WP.f selecting a topic or text of personal interest, finding accurate information about the topic or text, and generating statements (in *somewhat random order*) connecting opinion with reasons and supporting evidence (e.g., I like winter because . . .)	3.W-1b,1c, 4; 3.SL-4; 3.L-1i 4.W-1b,1c, 4; 4.SL-4; 4.L-1f **E.WP.n** writing a conclusion or concluding statement that links back to the focus (opinion) and helps to summarize key reasons	5.W-1a, 1b, 1c, 4, 5; 5.S-L-4; 5.L-3 6.W-1a, 1b, 1c; 6.SL-4 **M.WP.f** incorporating text features (e.g., numbering, bullets, captioned pictures, labeled diagrams, data tables) to enhance and justify support for claims	**M.WP.n** drawing and stating conclusions by synthesizing information, summarizing key points of reasoning chain that link back to focus or thesis, and reflecting a response to the opposition	
K.W-1; K.SL-4, 5; K.L-1f, 2, 6 1.W-1; 1.SL-4, 5, 6; 1.L-1j, 2, 6 2.W-1; 2.SL-2, 4, 6; 2.L-1f, 2, 6	3.W-1d; 4.W-1d	5.W-1b; 5.SL-5 6.W-1b; 6.SL-5	7.W-1e; 7.SL-3 8.W-1e; 8.SL-3	
E.WP.g developing an opinion on a topic or text with statements that connect the stated opinion ("You will think/say this story is funny . . .") in *several related sentences* with reasons and relevant details or supporting evidence for an authentic audience	**E.WP.o** with support, editing for clarity and meaning: grade-appropriate spelling (words that follow patterns/rules), end punctuation and capitalization, variety of sentence types	**M.WP.g** writing a conclusion that links back to the focus (claim/thesis), summarizes logic of reasoning, and provides a sense of closure for conclusions drawn	**M.WP.o** applying editing (cohesion of subject-verb, pronoun use, verb tense, and impact of word choice and sentence variety or complexity) and revision strategies to full texts that clarify intent and meaning: making judgments about completeness and accuracy of information, visual and auditory components, validity of sources cited, discourse style, and approach to addressing audience needs (e.g., emotion, interest, moral authority, potential objections)	
K.W-1; K.SL-4, 5; K.L-1f, 2, 6 1.W-1; 1.SL-4, 5, 6; 1.L-1j, 2, 6 2.W-1; 2.SL-2, 4, 6; 2.L-1f, 2, 6	3.W-5 (edit); 3.L-1, 2 4.W-5 (edit); 4.L-1, 2	5.W-1d; 5.SL-3 6.W-1e		
E.WP.h with support and audience feedback, revising by adding relevant details, descriptions, and concluding statement or closure; editing using grade-appropriate grammar, usage, spelling (high-frequency words), and mechanics	**E.WP.p** revising full texts from the reader's perspective: making judgments about clarity of message, intent of word choice, and overall continuity of text, visual and auditory components, peer or audience feedback	**M.WP.h** applying editing (subject-verb, pronoun use, verb tense, transitions, sentence variety, etc.) and revision strategies to full texts that clarify intent and meaning: making judgments about accuracy and relevance of evidence, cohesion of text, visual and auditory components, and approach to addressing audience needs (e.g., emotion, interest, sense of humor, potential objections)	7.W-1, 4, 5; 7.SL-4, 5; 7.L-1, 2, 3, 4c, 4d, 6 8.W-1, 4, 5; 8.SL-4, 5; 8.L-1, 2, 3, 4c, 4d, 6	
K.W-5 (details); K.SL-4, 5; K.L-2 1.W-2 (closure), 5 (details); 1.SL-5; 1.L-2, and 2.W-2 (closure), 5 (revise/edit); 2.L-1, 2, 3	3.W-1, 4, 5 (revise); 3.L-1i, 3, 4, 5 4.W-1, 4, 5 (revise); 4.SL-5; 4.L-1f, 3, 4, 5	5.W-1, 4, 5; 5.SL-4, 5; 5.L-1, 2, 3, 4c, 6 6.W-1, 4, 5; 6.SL-4, 5; 6.L-1, 2, 3, 4c, 6		

452

Appendix H

LPF STRAND 7 (Grades K-2) Sample Lesson Planning Steps Using Learning Progressions

STRAND 7: Writing Persuasively/Communicating Opinions, Critiques, AND Arguments (WP)—Different genres of persuasive writing (literary critiques, persuasive essays, speeches, editorials, etc.) are appropriate for different purposes and require use of genre-specific features, text structures, and strategic use of logic chains with compelling supporting evidence to produce a coherent unit of thought that persuades the intended audience.

(K–4) Elementary School Learning Targets

E.WP Apply organizational strategies (e.g., description, definition, compare/contrast, cause/effect, proposition/support) and an understanding of topics or texts to develop and support opinions about them for authentic audiences.

GRADES K–2	CCSS FOCUS	POSSIBLE INSTRUCTIONAL BUILDING BLOCKS AND LESSONS
Use a process approach to develop and communicate support for opinions . . . . **E.WP.a** generating ideas about a topic, text, or stimulus shared (event, photo, video, peers, etc.) using a range of responses (e.g., discussion, dictation, drawing, letters/invented spelling, writing) K.W-1, 7; K.SL-4, 5; K.L-6 1.W-7, 8; 1.SL-1b, 2, 4, 5; 1.L-6 and 2.W-8; 2.SL-2, 4; 2.L-6 **E.WP.b** with prompting and support, connecting information or facts with personal opinions about a topic or text (e.g., I think it is an informational text because it has facts) using discussion, drawings with details, written words (labels, nouns) or completing statements (e.g., This is what I like about dogs . . . ; That character was funny because . . .) and "reading back" what they have written K.W-1; K.SL-4, 5; K.L-1f, 6 1.W-1; 1.SL-4, 5, 6; 1.L-1j, 6 and 2.W-1; 2.SL-4, 6; 2.L-1f, 6 **E.WP.c** reading a variety of texts and distinguishing among text genres and their purposes (e.g., stories that entertain, texts that teach or give information, ads—convince you to buy, personal messages or letters—different purposes, include opinions) 1.RL-5 and 2.RI-6 **E.WP.d** with support, using simple note-taking strategies to record and distinguish facts or opinions or reasons for/against a real-world topic (e.g., t-chart with reasons why people like/do not pizza)	Step 1: Highlight or circle key words in each progress indicator of the learning progressions to get a general sense of how learning can develop with targeted instruction. Step 2: Review related standards for each progress indicator—make notes (in the middle column) about what parts of the CC standards your lessons will focus on. Note that you will likely have more than one unit addressing and assessing these standards during the school year.	Step 3: Identify what your instruction will focus on. We call these Instructional Building Blocks (Lesson learning targets) Step 4: Generate ideas for lessons or learning activities for each PI. This is the beginning of your Unit outline. You may decide to begin your unit part way along the progression if students have already demonstrated learning on the earlier skills in other units. Your preassessment will help to determine where to begin instruction.

GRADES K–2	CCSS FOCUS	POSSIBLE INSTRUCTIONAL BUILDING BLOCKS AND LESSONS
1.W-8 and 2.W-8 **E.WP.e** locating facts to support stated opinions about a topic (e.g., survey peers) or text; collaboratively describing reasons for/against through illustrations, captions, and simple sentences that connect reasons with evidence; applying basic capitalization and end punctuation **K.W-1; K.SL-4, 5; K.L-1f, 2, 6** **1.W-1; 1.SL-4, 5, 6; 1.L-1j, 2, 6 and 2.W-1; 2.SL-2, 4, 6; 2.L-1f, 2, 6** **E.WP.f** selecting a topic or text of personal interest, finding accurate information about the topic or text, and generating statements (in *somewhat random order*) connecting opinion with reasons and supporting evidence (e.g., I like winter because . . .) **K.W-1; K.SL-4, 5; K.L-1f, 2, 6** **1.W-1; 1.SL-4, 5, 6; 1.L-1j, 2, 6 and 2.W-1; 2.SL-2, 4, 6; 2.L-1f, 2, 6** **E.WP.g** developing an opinion on a topic or text with statements that connect the stated opinion ("You will think/agree this story is funny . . .") in several related sentences with reasons and relevant details or supporting evidence for an authentic audience **K.W-1; K.SL-4, 5; K.L-1f, 2, 6** **1.W-1; 1.SL-4, 5, 6; 1.L-1j, 2, 6 and 2.W-1; 2.SL-2, 4, 6; 2.L-1f, 2, 6** **E.WP.h** with support and audience feedback, revising by adding relevant details, descriptions, and concluding statement or closure; editing using grade-appropriate grammar, usage, spelling (high-frequency words), and mechanics **K.W-5 (details); K.SL-4, 5; K.L-2** **1.W-2 (closure), 5 (details); 1.SL-5; 1.L-2 and 2.W-2 (closure), 5 (revise/edit); 2.L-1, 2, 3**		

Appendix I
An Expanded Glossary for Understanding and Designing Comprehensive Local Assessment Systems

As schools move from having a "collection of tests" to designing a high-quality, comprehensive assessment system, it is essential to establish a common language and deeper understanding of the various system components and how they interrelate. In this expanded glossary, I have included some of the most common terminology associated with proficiency-based learning and comprehensive local assessment systems. Many of these concepts come from the world of educational measurement and large-scale testing (e.g., state assessment programs); others come from educational research and best practices literature. Even school systems with limited resources can implement many of these ideas to increase the quality of their assessments, the local assessment system, and use of assessment data.

These definitions and descriptions are the way I use them in my work, which may not reflect how each state, each testing organization, each publisher or author, or even each school system uses them. Much has been written about most of these terms—sometimes whole books! In some cases, I have "adopted" definitions provided by experts in the field. Others represent a synthesis of ideas, including my own. Educational leadership teams should explore and establish a working vocabulary that best supports the ongoing design and refinements to their local proficiency-based assessment system.

A

Accommodations: Accommodations are allowable supports that ensure two things: (1) all students will be able to demonstrate what they know and (2) the assessment will maintain validity—even with the allowable accommodations. A *modification* is a change in the assessment item resulting in changes to what is actually being assessed, such as reading a text to a student when the assessment was originally designed to assess decoding skills. An *accommodation* of reading a text aloud would not change an item asking for interpretation of theme or author's point of view. Large-scale assessments frequently include these approved accommodations: scribing a student's exact words for writing or providing reasoning in a math problem-solving task; reading the text aloud of a math problem or science prompt or providing bilingual dictionaries to ELL students so that they fully understand what they are being asked to do in the problem; providing additional time or shorter testing sessions; enlarging font side of print; and allowing students to take the assessment in a location other than the classroom. Reorganizing the same reading test questions by chunking the same text passages or grouping math problems by math domains (all subtraction questions grouped together) are proven (and allowable) accommodations that support students with learning disabilities (Hess, McDivitt, & Fincher, 2008). Accommodations should be "designed into" common assessments, rather than become an afterthought. PLC **TOOLS #9 and #16B** (Module 3) help assessment developers to ensure that the assessment is "fair" for all students.

Accountability: Test-based accountability is a process by which results of testing are used to hold schools, school systems, and/or teachers responsible for student performance or stated outcomes. According to Linn (2011), "the primary goals of test-based educational accountability systems are (1) to increase student achievement and (2) to increase equity in performance among racial-ethnic subpopulations and between students who are poor and their more affluent peers" (p. 1). The *quantitative* approach through test-based accountability is not the only approach to holding schools and teachers accountable. *Qualitative* approaches, such as using data from school visits, classroom observations, and student interviews, have enjoyed wider use in some other countries than they have in the United States. The qualitative and quantitative approaches both have strengths and limitations. A hybrid system that capitalizes on the strengths of each approach is preferable to either of the two approaches alone.

Achievement Level (Performance Level) Descriptors (ALDs/PLDs): Two terms—Achievement Level Descriptor and Performance Level Descriptor—are commonly used to name and describe a range of performance levels on a given assessment or when making overall decisions about whether a learner has demonstrated proficiency, such as for course completion or meeting high school graduation requirements. For large-scale assessments (e.g., licensing tests, college entrance exams, state assessments), defining ALDs for "proficient performance" is a policy decision set by a governing board. Simply put, ALDs describe what test takers must know and be able to do to be classified within a particular performance level. Schools often use a similar approach when describing performance levels on scoring rubrics with terms such as *Emergent*, *Approaching*, *Proficient*, or *Advanced*. In competency-based assessment systems, ALDs can be used to guide judgements about proficiency when examining work samples that constitute each student's "body of evidence."

Alignment: Alignment is generally defined as a measure of the extent to which a state's standards and assessments "agree" and the degree to which they work in conjunction with each other to guide and support student learning. It is not a question that yields a simple yes or no response; rather, alignment is a considered judgment based on a number of complex factors that collectively determine the degree to which the assessment tools used and evidence collected will gauge how well students are demonstrating achievement of the standards. *In other words, how effective is the end-of-year summative assessment—and the assessment system as a whole—in measuring the depth and breadth of knowledge and skills set forth in the content standards in relation to the performance goals and expectations for each grade level?* (Hess, 2013). Module 5 describes why alignment is important and how to design and conduct a local alignment study.

Anchor Charts: Anchor charts are visual displays, co-created with students during instruction, and used later by students to support their learning as they apply things that may be difficult to remember at first. This makes the charts an excellent scaffolding strategy to support executive functioning and language acquisition. An anchor chart has one clear focus—such as a big idea or topic, a concept, a strategy, or a vocabulary term—which is listed at the top as a title. Key related ideas and examples are organized by purposefully using simple tables, arrows, color coding, spacing, bullets, and visuals. Module 2 includes examples of text structure anchor charts.

Assessment Anchors/Anchor Papers/Exemplars: High-quality common assessments in all content areas include annotated assessment anchors. These are composed of student work samples usually collected and analyzed when piloting new assessments. It can take more than one administration of an assessment to identify examples at each performance level, and often some anchor papers are replaced with better models as time goes on and performance (and instruction) improves. During calibration and scoring practice, assessment anchors are used to interpret the rubric criteria and illustrate what student work products at different performance levels are expected to look like. Collaborative student work analysis protocols are used to identify the best set of training examples, which should include (a) unambiguous sample (exemplar) at each performance level, (b) multiple ways to achieve a proficient or advanced level, and (c) a few examples to illustrate guidance for how to score "line" papers—those papers that seem to fall between almost proficient and proficient. Many teachers also use anchor papers to help students understand expectations for performance, by collaboratively analyzing and scoring work samples. I recommend beginning with the extreme examples (lowest vs. highest) when asking students, "What do you see in this example?" or "What can be improved upon?" Module 3 explains how to annotate student work and develop anchor papers using PLC **TOOLS #13, #14, and #15**.

Assessment Item and Task Types: A robust assessment system will include a variety of assessment types for each assessment purpose, rather than rely on one standardized assessment given at the end of the school year. Item and task types should include a combination of short answer, short- and longer-constructed response items, systematic observations and conferencing, end-of-unit assessments, common performance tasks, extended response tasks or projects, and peer and self-assessments. Appendix C provides examples of common issues with item development and how to correct them.

Assessment Purposes and Uses: Formative, interim or benchmark, and summative assessments can be used for a variety of purposes within the assessment system. When designing or adopting assessments used to make high-stakes decisions (e.g., identifying students requiring additional supports or determining achievement of proficiency in a content area), it is critical to identify each assessment's specific purpose(s) and intended uses as you design your system. It is a mistake to assume that one assessment will be able to meet all purposes. Module 3 describes and provides examples of assessment types and uses. Assessment purposes include the following:

- **Screening All Students** generally include standardized assessments with a broad scope of lower-level (DOK 1, 2) skills or tasks; intended to determine if further diagnostic testing or observation may be needed

- **Diagnosing Individual Student Needs**—typically used after a screening tool identifies potential learning needs; generally diagnostic tools have many items with a narrow focus (e.g., identifying letters and sounds); strongest examples include eliciting student explanations that uncover thinking and reasoning related to skills demonstrated (DOK 3), as well as acquisition of basic skills and concepts (DOK 1, 2)

- **Monitoring Progress**—may be used both formatively and summatively; best examples are aligned with ongoing instruction and have a mix of item types, tasks, and range of cognitive demand (DOK 1–4); usually include common interim or benchmark assessments at specified periodic times during the school year (e.g., performance tasks each quarter, monthly running records)

- **Informing Instruction**—most closely aligned with current instruction and used formatively, not for grading; best examples are embedded in ongoing instruction and have a mix of item types, tasks, and range of cognitive demand (DOK 1–4); most useful when student work analysis is used to examine misconceptions, common errors, conceptual reasoning, and transfer of learning to new contexts

- **Communicating Student or Program Outcomes**—disaggregated data from these assessments is generally used summatively; include interpretations of performance from a combination of assessments (DOK 2–4), given over time to develop individual learning profiles, to determine student or group progress (proficiency), and/or to evaluate program effectiveness

Assessment (Test) Blueprint: An assessment blueprint is used to analyze an existing assessment or to design comparable (parallel) assessments, such as when using task models to design performance tasks. Information in the test blueprint identifies the number and types of assessment items (multiple-choice, constructed response, performance task, etc.), the content standards assessed, the overall intended cognitive demand (performance standards), and scoring emphasis. For example, a test blueprint can identify whether there are more score points given to items assessing certain (high-priority) standards or some item types (e.g., problem-solving tasks getting more or fewer score points than items assessing routine mathematics operations). Module 5 describes how to develop and use test blueprints, using Alignment **TOOLS #29 and #31**.

Assessment System Blueprint: An assessment system blueprint compiles information about "high priority" assessments used within and across grade levels to determine student proficiency in each content area. The assessments listed in the system blueprint are chosen because they complement each other, in terms of the assessment information they generate. Module 5 describes why system blueprints are useful and how to develop them using Alignment **TOOL #30**.

Authentic Applied Contexts: An instructional and assessment approach that is considered to be the most engaging and relevant to the learner is one that allows students to explore, discuss, and meaningfully construct concepts and relationships in contexts that involve real-world problems and issues. Project-based learning and performance tasks are typically designed with authentic tasks and audiences in mind. PLC **TOOL #20** and the GRASPS example (Module 3) provide protocols for developing performance assessments using authentic contexts.

Authentic Intellectual Work: Newmann, Bryk, and Nagaoka (2001) argue that any sound student assessment system should be based on a broader vision of what students should learn and be able to do. The "contemporary demands of productive work, responsible citizenship, and successful management of personal affairs extend well beyond giving correct answers and following proper procedures for the work traditionally assigned in school" (p. 9). Three key characteristics of authentic intellectual work are

- Construction of knowledge that involves interpretation, evaluation, analysis, synthesis, and organization of prior knowledge or solving new problems or understandings

- Disciplined inquiry or using prior knowledge to gain in-depth understanding that enables one to communicate what he or she comes to know and understand in multiple ways

- Value beyond school in which knowledge has "utilitarian, aesthetic, or personal value"

B

Benchmark: A standard or established outcome by which something can be measured or judged. Quarterly or midyear common benchmark or interim assessments can be used to monitor progress toward meeting annual learning goals.

Benchmark or Interim Assessment: Benchmark (also called interim) assessments are generally standards-based and designed to align with a pacing calendar and grade-level content standards. They are typically used to measure progress on large units of a districts' curriculum and to determine which students are "on track" to meet specified annual academic goals. Interim assessments are designed to inform decisions at both the classroom level and beyond, such as at the school or grade level or district level. Thus, they may be given at the classroom level to provide information for the teacher; but the results can also be meaningfully aggregated and reported at a broader level. One caution I offer about use of short, economical fixed-form assessments used as interim assessments is that they may only provide useful data on the "average" student. In most cases, they will not always provide much useful information for students performing well below or well above the standards measured.

Characteristics of benchmark or interim assessments include the following:

- They are typically administered several times per year (e.g., fall, winter, spring, quarterly) or regularly within specified grade spans (e.g., at the end of Grade K, 2, 4, etc.).
- The timing of the administration is likely to be controlled by the school or district rather than by the individual teacher.
- Often common assessments are designed using task shells or to create task banks to ensure quality and comparability.
- They may serve a variety of purposes, including predicting a student's ability to succeed on a large-scale summative assessment at the end of the year, evaluating a particular educational program or pedagogy, or diagnosing gaps in student learning for groups or individual students.

Benchmark Texts: Similar to annotated assessment anchors and anchor papers, benchmark texts are annotated to illustrate areas of text complexity. Lists of literary benchmark texts for different grade levels are sometimes available from text publishers. However, all texts—especially informational texts—will never appear on a single list. Collaborative processes can be used by PLC teams to identify benchmark texts at each grade level. These texts can then be used to calibrate future text analyses or compare texts of differing complexity. Often lists of benchmark texts are updated with better models as time goes on. Many teachers also use benchmark texts to help students understand how different texts are constructed. Module 2 includes protocols for how to analyze texts for use as benchmark texts.

Benchmarking: The process of identifying assessment anchors for a given assessment task. Module 3 includes PLC **TOOLS #13, #14, and #15** for developing anchor sets and using assessment anchors.

Big Ideas: The concepts of big ideas and enduring understandings have been best operationalized by McTighe and Wiggins in the Understanding by Design framework (2005). Big ideas are broadly defined as the domain-specific core concepts, principles, theories, and reasoning that *should* serve as the focal point of curriculum and assessment if the learning goal is to have students make broader and deeper connections among specific skills and concepts taught. Big ideas tie the learning from multiple units of study together and are the unifying threads connecting the learning targets in learning progressions. Module 4 describes how big ideas and enduring understandings guide development of learning progressions.

Body of Evidence: High-priority assessments identified in the Assessment System Blueprint are administered over an extended time in order to gather *sufficient* evidence that students are making progress toward achieving proficiency in a given content area. Best practices in developing the interpretations of student learning include use of common assessments, collaborative scoring, juried reviews of student work and portfolio products (e.g., involving experts, peers, community), and student self-assessment and reflection.

Body-of-Evidence Verification: As described by Great Schools Partnership, determining proficiency using a body of evidence requires a review and evaluation of student work and assessment scores. The review and evaluation process may vary in both format and intensity, but verifying proficiency requires that educators use common criteria to evaluate student performance consistently from work sample to work sample or assessment to assessment. For example, teachers working independently may use agreed-upon criteria to evaluate student work, a team of educators may review a student portfolio using a common rubric, or a student may demonstrate proficiency through an exhibition of learning that is evaluated by a review committee using the same consistently applied criteria. I suggest developing and using common rubrics, aligned with agreed-upon Achievement Level Descriptors for different grade levels or grade spans, to facilitate discussions about determining proficiency when examining a student's body of evidence.

C

Close Reading: Close reading is characterized by the use of text evidence to support analysis, conclusions, or interpretations of text. Close reading goes beyond simply locating evidence, summarizing, or recalling explicit information presented in the text. Close reading should be practiced with shorter texts or excerpts of longer texts. Fisher, Frey, and Hattie (2016) describe four key strategies that support close reading: repeated reading to build fluency and deepen understanding, annotating chunks of text to mark thinking, teacher questioning to guide analyses, and discussion that helps to elaborate on analysis and thinking.

Cognitive Demand: Cognitive demand describes the potential range of mental processing required to complete a given task, within a given context or scenario. Determining the intended cognitive demand of a test item or task requires more than simply identifying the "verbs" and the "nouns" describing the learning outcomes. Task developers must consider the reasoning and decision making required to complete a task successfully. *"Tasks that ask students to perform a memorized procedure in a routine manner lead to one type of opportunity for student thinking; tasks that require students to think conceptually and that stimulate students to make connections lead to a different set of opportunities for student thinking"* (Stein & Smith, 1998, p. 269). During instruction, the cognitive demand of highly complex tasks can be lessened using strategic scaffolding strategies without significantly changing the constructs being assessed. This might include strategies such as chunking texts for a reading assessment, group data collection for a science investigation, and facilitated discussions as a prewriting activity. Module 1 provides an in-depth discussion of common misconceptions about rigor, depth-of-knowledge (DOK), and cognitive demand.

Cognitive Labs: Using cognitive labs is the least used of three strategies for determining how well a new or draft assessment will "perform"—meaning how effective is this assessment (test items, reading passages, and tasks) in eliciting the intended evidence of learning? A cognitive lab approach does not require the time and number of students that field testing and task piloting require; therefore, it is a good option for smaller schools with limited resources. To set up cognitive labs, teachers identify a small (less than 20) sample of students at varying ability levels to take a draft assessment. Sometimes, several teachers will each take a few students to work with or different students will do different parts of the assessment. Upon completion of the assessment task, students are interviewed about the task and results are analyzed to determine whether revisions are needed. Cognitive labs can also be used as a formative assessment-conferencing strategy. Module 3 describes this think-aloud process in detail, using PLC **TOOLS #17–#19**.

Cognitive Psychology and **Developmental Psychology:** Cognitive psychology refers to the study of human mental processes and their role in perceiving, thinking, memory, attention, feeling, problem solving, and behaving. Developmental psychology is a scientific approach which aims to explain how children and adults change over time.

Cognitive Rigor: Cognitive rigor encompasses the complexity of the content, the cognitive engagement with that content, and the scope of the planned learning activity (Hess, Carlock, Jones, & Walkup, 2009). Module 1 provides an in-depth discussion of what makes learning and assessment tasks more or less complex.

Cognitive Rigor Matrix (CRM): The Hess Cognitive Rigor Matrices (CRMs) are content-specific tools designed to enhance increasingly rigorous instructional and assessment planning and practices at classroom, district, and state levels. Descriptors in each CRM can guide a teacher's use of questioning during a lesson, shifting student roles to be more student directed. Module 1 includes eight content-specific CRM **TOOLS, #1–#5D**, used for examining cognitive rigor. Hess CRMs are available online at http://www.karin-hess.com/free-resources.

Common Assessment/Common Assignment: Common assessments are designed and used to collect *comparable* evidence of learning within and across grade levels. They can include performance tasks (e.g., common writing prompts, parallel tasks with common scoring rubrics, such as internships or capstone projects), district interim or benchmark assessments (given at particular times during the school year to measure progress), and other district-level and state-level assessments. Administration guidelines must accompany common assessments (and common scoring guides) to ensure fidelity of implementation. If assessments are scored locally, calibration training and scoring practice are also essential. Modules 3 through 5 provide guidance in developing and using common assessments.

Competency: The term *competency* is often used interchangeably with the term *proficiency*. As defined by Achieve, Inc., competencies include explicit, measurable, transferable learning objectives that empower students.

Competency-Based Pathways (CBP): Achieve, Inc. has adapted from iNACOL/CCSSO a working definition of CBP (Domaleski et al., 2015) to include these indicators:

- Students advance upon demonstrated mastery and can demonstrate their learning at their own point of readiness.

- Assessment is meaningful and a positive learning experience for students and requires students to actually *demonstrate* their learning.

- Students receive rapid, differentiated support based on their individual learning needs.

- Learning outcomes emphasize competencies that include the application and creation of knowledge.

- The process of reaching learning outcomes encourages students to develop skills and dispositions important for success in college, careers, and citizenship.

Conjunctive and Compensatory Models (of Accountability Systems): Two methods for combining information from multiple assessments, subjects areas, or grade levels (e.g., test scores, artifacts of learning) include using a conjunctive or a compensatory model, or a combination of both. A conjunctive model requires a minimum level of performance on each of several measures, meaning that poor performance on one measure may result in a failure to meet established targets. In a compensatory model, good performance on one measure may offset poor performance on another (see Brennan, 2006, p. 570 for NCME and ACE information).

Construct-Driven Assessment Design: Assessments that are construct driven require three things to be specified to guide the test and item development process: (a) the knowledge, skills and other attributes to be assessed; (b) the expected performance and procedures that will illuminate the intended knowledge and skills assessed; and (c) descriptions of the tasks or situations that apply the knowledge and performance specified for assessment or task design. This approach is intended to strengthen overall test validity and interpretation of scores. Test blueprints and test specifications typically contain this information with samples of test items to illustrate how tasks integrate content knowledge and performance expectations. Module 5 describes how to develop and use test blueprints to ensure that assessments emphasize what instruction focuses on.

Constructed (Open-Ended) Response Item: A constructed or open-ended test question or task is one that requires the student to generate rather than select an answer from a list of possible responses. These items may include constructing or filling in a table or diagram (DOK 1, 2) or are questions that require some supporting evidence (DOK 3) for the answer given (e.g., text evidence to support interpretation of a theme in reading, data to support conclusions from a science investigation).

Criterion-Referenced Test (CRT): A CRT measures an individual's performance against a well-specified set of standards (distinguished from tests that compare students in relation to the performance of other students, known as norm-referenced tests).

Cut Score: A cut score is a specified point on a score scale, such that scores at or above that point are interpreted or acted on differently from scores below that point. In standards-based assessments, cut scores may typically delineate passing from failing, proficient from basic performance, and so on.

D

Data: Data includes factual information (such as measurements or statistics) used as a basis for reasoning, discussion, calculation, or judgements. Data can be qualitative or quantitative. Actionable data must be current or timely, reliable, and valid.

Demographic Data: Demographic data focus on the gender, socioeconomic background, race, and ethnicity of students in a school or district. Disaggregating assessment data by demographics helps to understand what impact the educational system is having on different groups of students. This analysis is often used to interpret and compare how various subgroups of students are performing in relation to the overall population and delineates the context in which the school operates, which is crucial for understanding all other data and potential underlying issues.

Depth-of-Knowledge (DOK): Norman Webb's Depth-of-Knowledge Levels (Webb, 2002) describe the depth of content understanding and scope of a learning activity, which manifests in the skills required to complete a task from inception to finale (e.g., planning, researching, drawing conclusions). The Hess CRM tools integrate Webb levels with Revised Bloom's Taxonomy. Webb's four DOK levels are

- Level 1:   Recall and reproduction
- Level 2:   Basic skills and concepts
- Level 3:   Strategic thinking and reasoning
- Level 4:   Extended thinking

Depth-of-Knowledge (DOK) "ceilings and targets": An important consideration in the development of test items or performance tasks is to use the highest Depth-of-Knowledge (DOK) demand implicit in an assessment blueprint as the "ceiling" for assessment, not a target. A "DOK target" has a more narrow focus (e.g., only assess at DOK 2), whereas a "DOK ceiling" is the highest potential Depth-of-Knowledge level to be assessed, as well as assessing DOK levels up to the ceiling. The DOK ceiling is determined by the intended cognitive demand of the combination of standards assessed. Why is this distinction important? When only the highest DOK level is assessed as a target and only DOK 3 and 4 are assessed, the assessment as a whole may end up being too difficult for many students. Additionally, important information about learning along the achievement continuum would be lost. Multiple items or performance tasks covering a range of DOK levels will provide the most useful instructional information for teachers. Examples of *possible* assessment "ceilings" in science might be (a) DOK 1 ceiling: perform a simple procedure to gather data (DOK 1—measure temperature); (b) DOK 2 ceiling: organize and represent data collected over a period of time, making comparisons and interpretations (DOK 1—measure temperature + DOK 2—graph and compare data); and (c) DOK 3 ceiling: answer a research question related to the environment using data collected to draw and support conclusions (DOK 1—measure temperature + DOK 2—graph and compare data + DOK 3—conduct an investigation to explain the effect of varying temperatures of the river in different locations) (Hess, 2008a).

Disaggregated Data: Assessment data can be broken down by specific targeted student subgroups (representative of a school or district), using criteria such as current grade or age, race, previous achievements, gender, ethnicity, and socioeconomic status, for example. Typically data are disaggregated to examine and make program decisions about assessment equity and fairness, curricular programs, instruction, and quality of local support and intervention programs.

Disciplined Inquiry: The concept of disciplined inquiry was advanced by Newmann, King, and Carmichael (2007) where they argue that students can learn as adults do in various occupations. "To reach an adequate solution to new problems, the competent adult has to construct knowledge because these problems cannot be solved by routine use of information or skills previously learned" (pp. 3–4). Disciplined inquiry involves developing a knowledge base of relevant vocabulary, facts, concepts, and theories and developing a deeper understanding by proposing and testing ideas.

Dispositions/Habits of Mind: Costa and Kallick (2008) describe 16 attributes—or Habits of Mind—that human beings display when they behave intelligently. They are considered the characteristics of what intelligent people do when they are confronted with problems the resolutions to which are not immediately apparent. Habits of Mind seldom are performed in isolation and are not limited to these 16 behaviors of Costa and Kallick: persisting; managing impulsivity; listening with understanding and empathy; thinking flexibly; thinking about thinking (metacognition); striving for accuracy; questing and posing problems; applying past knowledge to new situations; thinking and communicating with clarity and precision; gathering data though all senses; creating, imagining, innovating; responding with wonderment and awe; taking responsible risks; finding humor; thinking interdependently; and remaining open to continuous learning. States now promoting competency-based learning have included many of these 16 Habits of Mind as constructs to be assessed within the context of projects and performance assessments.

E

Executive Functioning: *Executive Functioning* is a broad term describing the neurologically based skills involving mental control and self-regulation. Executive function is employed when performing activities required by complex performance tasks, such as planning, managing time, organizing materials and information, strategizing, and paying attention to and remembering details. Many strategic scaffolding strategies can be used to support students with poor executive functioning when completing complex tasks (e.g., providing assignment checklists, focusing questions, visual calendars, breaking tasks into manageable parts).

Expeditionary Learning/Learning Expeditions: Learning expeditions are interdisciplinary studies, usually lasting six to twelve weeks. They may include a combination of case studies, in-depth projects, fieldwork, working with experts, service learning, and a culminating event that features high-quality student work. Module 3 includes guidance in using learning expeditions as student-designed performance assessments.

F

Feedback: Grant Wiggins used to say that there is a big difference between giving advice and giving feedback. Most people don't really want advice, but will listen to, reflect on, and ultimately make use of specific feedback to improve their performance. Feedback that describes performance in relation to criteria for success can lead to more effort and deeper learning. Wiliam and Leahy (2015) describe the research underlying two different kinds of feedback (corrective and reinforcing) and stress the importance of using feedback to "move learning forward."

Field Testing: Field testing is one of three common strategies used for determining how well a new or draft assessment will "perform"—meaning how effective is this assessment (test items, reading passages, overall difficulty, and tasks) in eliciting the intended evidence of learning? Field testing requires that a large representative sample of students (across gender, income, ability, race/ethnicity, etc.) take an assessment—such as a state reading or science assessment—before it is administered to all students at that grade level in the following year. Student responses from the field test are disaggregated by subgroup and analyzed to determine which test items and tasks can be used as currently written, which items or tasks need to be revised and field-tested a second time before they can be used, and which ones should not be used at all in the operational test. This strategy is used most often by testing companies, either by embedding new (field test) items into an existing test at that grade level, or administering the test to students at the intended grade level who will not be taking this assessment in the future.

Because this approach is costly and time-consuming, it is not ideal for schools to employ. That said, one way I have seen larger schools or consortia of schools successfully use field testing is with development of performance tasks, such as "testing" new writing prompts. A representative sample of at least 100 students at the intended grade level (across several schools or districts) is given the task to complete. Work samples are collected and collaboratively analyzed by teachers. The goal is NOT to score every paper, but to see if a large enough sample (of student work) exhibits the intended assessment evidence. If you find that after looking at the first 25 papers, for example, the prompt was unclear or students did not provide enough evidence to be scored, then you can probably assume that some revision will be needed before the task can be widely used as a common task. If most student samples are scorable but fall into the lower performance levels, the committee may determine that instruction was not adequate or expectations were unreasonable for this grade level. Either way, this task might not be ready for "prime time." Module 3 contrasts this process with piloting and using cognitive labs as a means for validating new assessments brought into the local assessment system.

Flexible Pathways (to Graduation): In Vermont, the Flexible Pathways Initiative, created by Act 77 of 2013, encourages and supports the creativity of school districts as they develop and expand high-quality educational experiences as an integral part of secondary education in the evolving 21st century classroom. Flexible pathways promote opportunities for students to achieve postsecondary readiness through high-quality educational experiences that acknowledge individual goals, learning styles, and abilities and can increase the rates of secondary school completion and postsecondary training. Evidence of flexible pathways can include dual enrollment and early college programs, internships and work-based learning initiatives, virtual or blended learning opportunities, and use of Personalized Learning Plans (PLPs) to design student-centered learning.

Formative Assessment: Formative assessment is as much a process or instructional strategy as it is a measurement tool. Also known as "short-cycle" assessment, formative assessment practices are embedded in instruction and used frequently during a teaching or learning cycle (e.g., to preassess readiness, to target mastery of specific skills, to check conceptual understanding). The primary purposes of using assessment data formatively are to (a) diagnose where students are in their learning along a learning progression, (b) identify gaps in knowledge and student understanding, (c) determine how to help some or all students move ahead in their learning, and (d) provide opportunities for peer and self-assessment as part of the learning process. Formative assessment tasks may be designed for all students (e.g., unit preassessment, planned probing questions during a lesson) or may vary from one student to another depending on the teacher's judgment about the need for specific information about a student at a given point in time. Assessment information gathered from a variety of activities (observations, quick checks for understanding, small-group problem solving and discussion, conferencing, common performance tasks, exit tickets, etc.) can be used formatively. Formative uses of assessment can uncover a range of understanding (DOK 1–4), including deeper levels of reasoning and thinking that lead to student meta-cognition and taking action about their own learning. Learning—not grading—is the primary focus of formative assessment. Hess's **TOOL #10** was designed to examine formative assessments in use. Module 3 contrasts formative, interim, or summative uses of assessment and describes how to use PLC **TOOL #10** to develop formative assessments and interpret results.

K

Kolb's Experiential Learning Model: David Kolb's research (1984) advanced a model of experiential learning that combined two key dimensions in a four-stage cycle: how we perceive new or reintroduction of information (along a continuum from concrete to abstract) and how we then process that information (along an intersecting continuum from reflection to experimentation). In Kolb's theory, the impetus for the development of learning new concepts is provided by new experiences: Learning involves the acquisition of abstract concepts that can be applied flexibly in a range of situations (McLeod, 2013). Each module includes a suggested cycle of workshop activities based on Kolb's experiential learning model.

L

Learning Outcomes/Objectives/Goals: Several terms are used interchangeably by educators to describe what students will understand and be able to perform with regard to the content and skills being taught. An effective learning goal is composed of a clearly stated progression of *learning targets* that demonstrate eventual attainment of the desired performance or proficiency. Smaller-grained learning targets guide day-to-day instruction and formative uses of assessment as a student makes progress toward the broader learning goal.

Learning Progression (LP): Learning progressions, progress maps, developmental continuums, and learning trajectories are all terms that have been used to generally mean *research-based* descriptions of how students develop and demonstrate deeper, broader, and more sophisticated understanding over time. A learning progression can visually and verbally articulate a hypothesis about how learning will typically move toward increased understanding for most students. Learning progressions are based in empirical research and therefore are not the same as curricular progressions or grade-to-grade standards. This is because LPs also include typical misconceptions along the way to reaching learning goals. When developing LPs, cognitive scientists compare novice performers to expert performers. Novice performers generally have not yet developed schemas that help them to organize and connect information. Novice performers use most of their working memory just trying to figure out what all the parts of the task are, not in engaging with the task or assignment. Module 4 describes how to use learning progressions to develop assessments and student profiles to monitor progress.

Learning Target (LT): As defined by Moss and Brookhart (2012, p. 3), learning targets guide learning and therefore should use wording that students can understand and use for peer and self-assessment. LTs can be thought of as "lesson-sized chunks" of information, skills, and reasoning processes that students will come to know deeply over time. In proficiency-based systems, learning targets can be stated as short descriptive or bulleted phrases that create levels of a performance scale. A series of LTs detail the progression of knowledge and skills students must understand and be able to perform to demonstrate achievement of the broader learning goal or proficiency. Module 4 describes how to use learning progressions to develop daily learning targets and formative assessments aligned with progressions.

- **Foundational LTs:** Foundational learning targets contain essential prerequisites, knowledge, and basic processes which may not explicitly be stated in academic standards but are necessary to build the foundational understandings required to reach the overarching learning goal or proficiency. Unit preassessments often focus on foundational learning targets to determine whether students are ready to move on.

- **LTs of Increasing Cognitive Complexity:** A series of learning targets should form a progression of learning with those at the higher end of a performance scale (i.e., Proficient and Advanced levels) describing increasingly more sophisticated understanding and cognitive complexity that exceed expectations of a single academic standard.

Local Assessment System: A comprehensive local assessment system includes multiple components, identifying high-priority local and state-level assessments used in the educational system. The most important characteristic of an assessment system is that it is designed to provide cohesive and actionable information about student performance, using multiple measures. The various components of the system across the different educational levels provide complementary information so that decisions can be based on making valid inferences. Module 5 provides guidance and tools for designing and refining a local comprehensive assessment system. Four critical components make up high-quality comprehensive local assessment systems:

1. Technically sound assessments of academic achievement and assessments of district-based goals for learning (e.g., community service)
2. A theory of action that illustrates how curricular programs, instruction, assessments, and assessment data interact
3. Adequate protocols, professional development, and leadership supporting implementation of assessment principles and practices
4. Explicit and well-coordinated mechanisms (feedback loops) for managing assessments, assessment results, and addressing student and program needs

M

Metacognition: Metacognitive skills are one of the Habits of Mind or dispositions identified in the research as essential college and career readiness skills (Hess & Gong, 2014). They are evidenced when students are able to reflect on their own learning, frame and monitor their own learning goals, and seek out and use evidence of their own progress from one or more sources to improve their performance. Teachers can design instructional tasks that require students to use metacognitive skills to self-assess and to act on feedback from peers.

Multiple (Assessment) Opportunities: Sufficient opportunities or occasions are provided for each student to meet proficiency or other learning expectations or requirements. This can be accomplished in a variety of ways with different assessments, while still scoring performance on a common scale or rubric.

Multiple-Choice (MC) Items: A multiple-choice item—also called selected response—consists of a problem, known as the stem, and a list of suggested solutions, known as alternatives. Traditional MC items have included one correct or best alternative, which is the answer, and three incorrect or inferior alternatives, known as distractors. Next-generation assessments now often include more than four alternatives with several possible correct answers among them. Appendix C includes strong and weak examples of MC items.

N

Norm-Referenced Test (NRT): A norm-referenced test is used to compare individual student performance with a larger (norming) group, usually based on a national sample representing a diverse cross-section of students. NRT results typically are measured in percentile ranks. Examples of NRTs include Iowa Tests of Basic Skills and the Stanford Achievement Test. (Norm-referenced tests differ from criterion-referenced tests, which measure performance compared with a standard or benchmark.)

P

Performance Indicator: This is a term that seems to have many different uses and interpretations in the literature. For this reason, it might be useful to think of a "performance indicator" the way we do for learning targets. A series of LTs—or performance indicators—detail the progression of knowledge and skills students must understand and be able to perform to demonstrate achievement of the broader learning goal or proficiency. Performance indicators are often used in rubrics to further define criteria for success and thus, represent possible assessment evidence.

Performance Task/Performance Assessment: Performance assessments can be used for a variety of purposes—instructional–formative and evaluative–summative. Performance tasks are generally defined as multistep assignments with clear criteria, expectations, and processes that measure how well a student transfers knowledge and applies complex skills to create or refine an original product (Center for Collaborative Education [CCE], 2012). Often common assessments include a performance component because they are designed to integrate multiple skills and concepts within authentic contexts. Performance tasks produce a variety of real-world products such as essays, demonstrations, presentations, artistic performances, solutions to complex problems, and research or investigation projects. They are assessments that may be completed individually or with others. Module 3 includes a variety of tools and examples to support the design of high-quality performance assessments for formative, interim, and summative use.

Personalization: Personalization is a learning process in which schools help students assess their own talents and aspirations, plan a pathway toward their own purposes, work cooperatively with others on challenging tasks, maintain a record of their explorations, and demonstrate learning against clear standards in a wide variety of media, all with the close support of adult mentors and guides (Clarke, 2003). In some states and school districts, every school student is assigned a responsible adult, in addition to a school counselor, to provide this support.

Piloting: Piloting is one of three common strategies used for determining how well a new or draft assessment will "perform"—meaning how effective is this assessment (test items, reading passages, overall difficulty, and tasks) in eliciting the intended evidence of learning? An assessment piloting process requires fewer students than does field-testing a new assessment and is therefore a time-efficient strategy for "trying out" new assessments. In a locally designed pilot, students from a minimum of two or three representative classrooms (within or across schools) will take an assessment. Then educators collect and collaboratively review the results (student work, scoring rubrics, administration guidelines, etc.) to determine whether or not this assessment elicited the intended evidence and can be reliably scored. Student work analysis is used to refine both task prompts and rubrics. For strong assessments, scoring anchors may also be identified during the piloting phase.

Portfolios and Exhibitions: These performance assessment models typically address a wide range of content-area and cross-curricular standards, including critical thinking and problem solving, reading and writing proficiency, and/or work habits, dispositions, and character traits (e.g., teamwork, preparedness, responsibility, persistence). In course-based portfolio and exhibition assessments, individual teachers use common, agreed-upon criteria to evaluate a body of work that students have completed over the course of an instructional period. For cross-curricular portfolios and exhibitions, groups of content-area teachers or review committees evaluate the work. It should be noted that portfolios do not have to require students to create new work, but may require that students collect and present past work, evidence of growth, self-reflection, and accomplishments over time. Exhibitions can also incorporate examples of past work that has been used as a foundation for new products. Module 3 includes a variety of tools and examples to support the design of high-quality performance assessments, including student-designed assessments.

Prerequisites/Preassessment: Prerequisite (foundational) knowledge and skills encompass the discrete learning upon which more complex tasks are built. I recommend that preassessments begin with assessing the core prerequisite skills needed to build up in order to be successful at completing more complex and cognitively demanding tasks. Module 4 describes how learning progressions can be used to develop preassessments based on prerequisite skills or readiness for learning.

Proficiency: The term *proficiency* is often used interchangeably with the term *competency*. The Rhode Island Department of Education defines proficiency as the measure of a student's knowledge and skill demonstrated in a consistent manner across multiple disciplines in various settings over time. The Vermont Agency of Education elaborates on this definition, stating, "Proficiencies include explicit, measurable, transferable learning objectives that empower students."

Proficiency-Based Learning (PBL): PBL (also called competency-based learning) is described by Sturgis and Patrick (2010) as embodying these four characteristics:

- Learning outcomes emphasize proficiencies that include application and creation of knowledge, along with the development of important skills and dispositions.

- Student progress is measured and supported.

- Assessment is meaningful and a learning experience for students; students receive timely, differentiated support and feedback based on their individual learning needs; and students advance upon mastery, not seat time; learning is the constant and time is the variable.

- Learning occurs with the student at the center; students take ownership of their learning; and learning can happen anywhere and anytime.

Project-Based Learning: Project-based learning is designed to make learning more meaningful and relevant to students. Projects require that students go beyond the textbook to study complex topics based on real-world issues (e.g., examining water quality in their communities or the history of their town). Students often work in groups to gather and analyze information from multiple sources, including interviews with experts and collecting survey data. Project-based classwork is generally more demanding than traditional book-based instruction, where students may just memorize facts presented in a single source. Students are expected to utilize original documents and data, applying principles covered in traditional courses to real-world situations. Projects have multiple components and can last weeks or may cover entire courses. Student work is assessed in stages (e.g., gathering and analyzing information, integrating what was learned, presenting information) and presented to "authentic" audiences beyond the teacher, including parents and community groups.

Q

Qualitative data: Qualitative data are based on information gathered from sources such as one-on-one interviews, focus groups, surveys, or systematic observations done over time.

Quantitative data: Quantitative data are based on "hard numbers" such as enrollment figures, dropout rates, and test scores.

R

Reliability: Test *reliability* is defined as the consistency of test scores over different test administrations, multiple raters, or different test questions. Reliability answers the question "How likely is it that a student would obtain the same score if they took the same test a second time (test–retest reliability) or if someone else scored this student's test (interrater reliability)?" In statistics, interrater reliability or agreement—or concordance—is the degree of agreement or consistency with which two or more judges rate the work or performance of assessment takers. Strong interrater reliability is easiest to achieve with selected response test items (questions having only one right answer). Interrater reliability for scoring more complex assessments (projects, portfolios, observations, or performance tasks) is strengthened by the use of clear scoring guides, annotated student work, and periodic calibration practice. Assessments can be reliable and still not be valid (assessing what is intended to be assessed).

Rubrics/Scoring Guides: Rubrics and scoring guides provide a set of rules or guidelines for assigning scores to test takers. Rubrics are often used to elaborate on how to score longer constructed response items, performance tasks, and extended projects. More simplified scoring guides tend to be used for shorter open-ended test items. Scoring criteria fall into several types: **Form criteria** (e.g., following formatting guidelines for documenting sources, editing grammar use, turning in work on time—DOK 1); **Accuracy of Content criteria** (e.g., calculations, definitions, applying concepts or terms appropriately—DOK 1, DOK 2); **Process criteria** (e.g., gathering and organizing information, identifying trends, graphing data—DOK 2); **Impact criteria** (e.g., effectiveness in solving a problem or convincing an audience—DOK 3 or DOK 4); and **Knowledge Production criteria** (e.g., generating new questions for investigation or new insights, reflections on new learning—DOK 3 or DOK 4). There are also several different types of scoring rubrics, each with unique strengths and weaknesses. Module 3 describes differences among rubric criteria and rubric design. PLC **TOOL #11** guides you through a rubric quality review. Rubric types include the following:

- **Analytic rubrics** apply several different, distinct criteria to evaluate products (e.g., process skills, content accuracy, editing skills). A score is given for each separate criterion, thus providing multiple scores and specific feedback to students on strengths and weaknesses of the performance. Analytic rubrics offer opportunities to yield "weighted scoring" such as giving more scoring weight to reasoning and justification (Knowledge Production) than to steps being followed to solve the problem (Process).

- **Holistic rubrics** combine several criteria to yield one generalized—or holistic—score. While these scores can be used to describe overall performance, they are not as useful in providing specific feedback to students on strengths and weaknesses of the performance. Holistic rubrics are frequently used for scoring performance tasks in large-scale assessments because they may be seen as more efficient (taking less time) and tend to be easier to get scoring agreement across raters (interrater reliability) than do analytic rubrics.

- **Task-specific rubrics** are typically designed to score one specific constructed response item or performance task (e.g., essay, open-ended questions on state assessments) and therefore include examples of specific text evidence from a passage or a particular mathematical representation or method expected in the student response. Task-specific scoring rubrics are most useful when scoring large amounts of student work with very particular success criteria or when defining what partial credit looks like.

- **Generalized rubrics** are typically designed to score multiple, similar (comparable) performance tasks at different times during the learning process (e.g., argumentative essay, scientific investigation). Because these are generalized for use with many tasks, it is highly recommended that annotated student work samples include explanations of specific scoring evidence that help to interpret rubric criteria. Generalized scoring rubrics are especially useful when building student understanding of success criteria and learning goals and are most useful when scoring student work products over time with similar success criteria, such as in a portfolio.

S

Scaffolding Strategically: Scaffolding is the purposeful use of supports to achieve a balance between cognitive complexity and student autonomy, as the overall cognitive demand of the task increases. Strategic scaffolding means the intentional steps designed into the instruction that ensure that all students can eventually complete the same complex task independently. The primary difference between scaffolding and differentiating is that differentiating means different—different assignments, different options, student choice. Differentiation is achieved by changing the content, the process skills, and/or the products of learning. Modules 1 and 2 include a variety of strategic scaffolding strategies to support deeper learning.

Scales—Performance, Proficiency, Scoring, Analytical: Various terms are used to describe a continuum of performance descriptors that articulate distinct levels of demonstrated knowledge and skills relative to a learning outcome or proficiency statement. The term *Proficiency Scales* is defined by the Vermont Agency of Education as a single criterion rubric that is task neutral and includes explicit performance expectations for each possible rating (adapted from Gallaudet University). Moore, Garst, and Marzano (2015) use the term *Performance Scale* to mean a continuum that articulates distinct levels of knowledge and skills relative to a specific standard. Great Schools Partnership calls these scales "scoring scales." [*Personally*, I prefer to use the broader term of *performance scale* so as not to imply this is only for scoring; and I do not recommend developing scales for every standard or even for a set of prioritized standards. This to me would end up being somewhat unmanageable to track single standards and quite limiting in that rich performance tasks and proficiency-based learning requires the integration of multiple standards. Consequently, my use of performance or proficiency scales is a hybrid of other models.]

Schema: "A **schema** is a cognitive framework or concept that helps organize and interpret information. Schemas can be useful because they allow us to take shortcuts in interpreting the vast amount of information that is available in our environment. . . . Schemas can (also) contribute to stereotypes and make it difficult to retain new information that does not conform to our established ideas about the world. . . . In Piaget's theory, a schema is both the category of knowledge as well as the process of acquiring that knowledge. As experiences happen and new information is presented, new schemas are developed and old schemas are changed or modified" (Cherry, 2016).

Standard: A standard represents a long-term learning goal, such as for the end of a year's learning. Standards describe "learning destinations" and differ from empirically based learning progressions that describe typical pathways of learning to arrive at the destination. Module 4 contrasts the differences between learning progressions and standards.

Standardized Assessment: When an assessment is administered using specified conditions, protocols, and procedures (e.g., time allotted, allowable accommodations or use of materials such as calculators), it is called a standardized assessment. Common assessments used locally across classrooms and schools should be accompanied by an administration guide which helps teachers to know under what conditions the assessment should be used. Standardized administration guides may include specific prerequisites (e.g., administer after students have completed the unit on Pythagorean theorem) to ensure that all students have had an adequate opportunity to learn the content prior to being tested. Module 3 includes examples and a planning template for developing administration guides for ensuring that common performance assessments are administered similarly by different educators, making assessment results more reliable.

Stanine: A stanine is based on a standard score of nine units in which 1, 2, or 3 indicate below-average performance; 4, 5, or 6 indicate average performance; and 7, 8, or 9 indicate above-average performance. Stanines are still used in some standardized tests.

Student-Centered Learning (SCL): Student-centered learning involves shifting the traditional role of teacher and student so that students are more engaged and more responsible for their own learning. The Nellie Mae Education Foundation has supported schools and districts in implementing SCL practices. In contrast to more traditional, adult-directed approaches to instruction, SCL adheres to four broad principles (Hess & Gong, 2014):

1. *Learning is personalized*: Each student is well known by adults and peers and benefits from individually paced learning tasks, tailored to his or her needs and interests. Collaboration with others and engaging, authentic, increasingly complex tasks deepen learning.

2. *Learning is competency based*: Students move ahead when they demonstrate competency, and they have multiple means and opportunities to do so. Differentiated supports ensure that all students have what they need to achieve college and career readiness goals.

3. *Learning takes place anytime, anywhere*: Students learn outside the typical school day and year in a variety of settings, taking advantage of learning technologies and community resources, and receiving credit for learning, wherever it happens.

4. *Students exert ownership over learning*: Students understand that they improve by applying effort strategically. They have frequent opportunities to reflect on and understand their strengths and learning challenges. They take increasing responsibility for learning and assessment, and they support and celebrate each other's progress.

Success Criteria: Success criteria are the established learning targets for a given task, performance, or project. Success criteria are stated using "kid-friendly" wording that students can understand and use for peer and self-assessment. Success criteria are incorporated into scoring rubrics using several broad criteria (e.g., use of research skills) with performance indicators that further define expectations specific to the given task (e.g., conduct a key word search, check validity of sources). Module 3 discusses how scoring guides and rubrics incorporate success criteria.

Summative Assessment: A summative assessment is given at the end of a period of learning (e.g., unit of study, end of semester) and generalizes how well a student has performed. Summative assessments are typically used for grading and making high-stakes decisions. Modules 3 and 5 discuss formative, interim, and summative uses of assessment.

Systematic Observation: Systematic observation is a formative assessment strategy used to document knowledge and skills of a group of students over a period of time, rather than assessing all students at the same time (on demand). Generally this approach works well for areas that are difficult to assess with pencil and paper tests or when multiple opportunities are provided for students to demonstrate acquisition of skills and knowledge over time. Systematic observation captures the often "missed opportunities" for collecting assessment data during an instructional activity and can document progress being made over time in meeting broader learning goals for the school year. Module 3 provides a recording template for documenting systematic (over time) observations.

T

Task Shell/Task Model: Task shells (also referred to as task models) provide general guidelines for what a performance task should include if it is to effectively measure the stated learning objective(s). For example, a template for test or task developers for science performance tasks might include the following components: (a) a scenario or data related to a real-world phenomenon; (b) a prompt asking students to state a hypothesis (or testable question) based on the data; (c) a list of steps needed to conduct the investigation; and (d) results of the investigation, stating conclusions based on evidence collected. Test developers use task shells to ensure that (parallel) performance tasks will elicit comparable evidence of learning year to year, and can be reliably scored using the same performance criteria. Module 3 describes how task shells can be used to develop common performance assessments.

Technical Quality of Assessments: High-quality assessments, no matter the form, format, or intended purpose, should be evaluated in terms of several research-based criteria. Hess's **TOOL #9** provides PLC teams with a protocol for evaluating and giving feedback on the quality of assessments included in the local assessment system. Hess's **TOOL #9** incorporates the application of these criteria when developing high-quality assessments. Module 3 describes how to use PLC **TOOLS #9 and #16B** to develop, refine, and "validate" local performance assessments.

- **Clarity**—Clarity of expectations and intended student products is the starting point of all high-quality assessment development.

- **Validity**—Determinations of test validity are based on the degree of alignment to both content standards and intended rigor being assessed. Interpretations of student learning cannot be considered "valid" when assessments (items and tasks) are poorly aligned with intended learning outcomes or proficiencies.

- **Reliability**—Test reliability is the consistency with which two or more judges rate the same work products or performances. Interrater reliability for more robust assessment tasks, such as performance tasks and portfolios, is generally highest when calibration training includes annotated work samples that help to differentiate levels of performance on scoring rubrics.

- **Opportunities for Student Engagement**—While not required in all types of assessments, systems that profess to be student centered should review performance tasks and other student-designed learning opportunities for how well they engage students in making decisions about the approach to and quality of their work.

- **Fairness**—"Fair" assessments clearly address the expectations specified by the performance indicators so that all students are afforded an equitable opportunity to demonstrate corresponding skills and knowledge. Assessments should be prescriptive enough to require the demonstration of the expected skills and knowledge so that student interpretation will not dilute the intended demand of the performance indicator.

Text Complexity: Being able to read increasingly more complex texts has always been a driving goal of reading instruction. According to Hiebert (2012), who has written extensively about text complexity, many qualitative and quantitative dimensions—including topic complexity and author's discourse style—contribute to making a text more or less complex. Hess and Biggam (2004) identify additional qualitative dimensions that affect text complexity to include formatting and layout, genre features, text structure, level of reasoning required, and reader background knowledge. But the variable that consistently predicts reading comprehension is vocabulary. The core vocabulary accounts for at least 90% of the words in most texts. Module 2 provides guidance and Text Complexity **TOOLS #6, #7, and #8** for examining text complexity and planning for instruction or assessment.

Text Features: Text features are used to organize, add, or elaborate on information presented in informational texts, including headings and subheadings, captioned photos, labeled diagrams, graphs and charts, and inset text, for example. Features used in informational texts differ from those used in literary texts, such as including illustrations to emphasize character actions or features, or using white space to indicate time lapses in chronology.

Text Pattern Signals: Words or phrases embedded in texts which help to indicate—or signal—the organizational features of the text and indicate to the reader where the text *may be* "heading." Signals, *in combination with the context of their use* and various semantic cues, determine text structure—not signals alone (Hess, 2008c; Vacca & Vacca, 1989). Module 2 includes sample instructional strategies for using signal words for each text structure.

Text Structures: Test structures are the *internal organizational structures* used within paragraphs or longer texts, appropriate to genre and purpose. This is different from genre characteristics that help students to determine whether a text is a fable, fairy tale, or myth based on how it is structured. Increasingly complex structures tend to follow this general progression: sequence (procedure), chronology (time order), description, definition, compare–contrast, cause–effect, problem–solution, proposition–support, critique, and inductive–deductive (Hess, 2008c). Module 2 includes instructional strategies for teaching about text structures and developing text structure anchor charts.

Transfer: "In cognitive theory, knowing means more than the accumulation of factual information and routine procedures; it means being able to integrate knowledge, skills, and procedures in ways that are useful for interpreting situations and solving problems" (National Research Council, 2001, p. 62). The ability to transfer our knowledge and skill effectively involves the capacity to take what we know and use it creatively, flexibly, fluently, in different settings or problems, and on our own (Wiggins & McTighe, 2005, 2012). When a student is able to understand concepts and apply skills beyond what is considered to be "routine understanding" (DOK 1–2), we call that transfer. Module 1 introduces the concept of transfer in the discussion of the Hess Cognitive Rigor Matrix. The theme of designing instruction and assessment for deeper thinking and transferability of learning is carried though all modules of the *Local Assessment Toolkit*.

Transferrable Skills: Also referred to as dispositions, applied learning, soft skills, or "cross-cutting" skills, transferrable skills are not content-specific skills. They should not be taught in isolation; they are best taught and assessed within the context of each content domain (Hess & Gong, 2014). Many states and school districts have identified specific transferrable skills and work habits as part of their proficiency-based systems. For example, the Vermont Agency of Education includes these as their list of transferrable skills:

- Clear and effective communication
- Creative and practical problem solving
- Informed and integrative thinking
- Responsible and involved citizenship
- Self-direction

U

Universal Design: The idea of universal design in assessment comes from architectural practices. Think about how a person might get from the first floor to the second floor of a building. A ladder would only provide access for some people. A set of stairs would work for more people, but not for those using wheelchairs or crutches. An elevator is the most accessible structure and therefore more "universally designed" for access to all who want to get to the second floor. Thompson, Johnstone, and Thurlow (2002) lay out guidelines to ensure that large-scale tests meet the principles of universal design. Application of those guidelines in the construction of assessments ensures that all students have a fair and equitable opportunity to demonstrate their learning. Hess's **TOOL #9** incorporates the application of these principles when developing high-quality local assessments. Module 3 describes how to use PLC **TOOL #9** to develop and refine local performance assessments for "fairness" and universal access. Universally designed assessments incorporate these seven elements:

1. Inclusive assessment population (Assessments are developed in the context of the entire population.)
2. Precisely defined constructs (measuring exactly what they are intended to measure)
3. Accessible, non-biased items (Items are reviewed for content quality, clarity, and lack of ambiguity, and sometimes for sensitivity to gender or cultural issues.)
4. Amendable to accommodations
5. Simple, clear, and intuitive instructions and procedures
6. Maximum readability and comprehensibility (e.g., use of simple, clear, commonly used words or eliminating any unnecessary words)
7. Maximum legibility (e.g., spacing, formatting of text and visuals)

V

Validity: Validity refers to the degree to which tests measure what they purport to measure. Alignment studies are designed to examine how well an assessment design and test items match the intent (standards to be assessed). For example, does this writing assessment actually assess a student's ability to compose and communicate ideas in writing or simply the student's ability to edit a composition? Assessments can be valid (assessing what is intended to be assessed) and still not be reliable in terms of scoring. Module 3 describes how to create validation teams to develop, validate, and refine local assessments. PLC **TOOLS #9, #16A, and #16B** are used to guide the task validation process.

References

ACT, Inc. (2006). *Reading between the lines: What the ACT reveals about college and career readiness in reading*. Iowa City, IA: Author.

Ainsworth, L. (2014). *Common formative assessment 2.0: How teacher teams intentionally align standards, instruction, and assessment*. Thousand Oaks, CA: Corwin.

Allen, J. (1999). *Words, words, words: Teaching vocabulary in Grades 4–12*. York, ME: Stenhouse.

American Association for the Advancement of Science. (2001). *Atlas of science literacy (Vol. 1)*. Washington, DC: American Association for the Advancement of Science and the National Science Teachers Association.

Anderson, L., Krathwohl, D., Airasian, P., Cruikshank, K., Mayer, R., Pintrich, P., Raths, J., & Wittrock, M. (Eds.). (2001). *A taxonomy for learning, teaching, and assessing: A revision of Bloom's Taxonomy of educational objectives*. New York, NY: Addison Wesley Longman.

Andrade, H. (2016). *Arts assessment for learning: What is formative assessment?* [Video]. New York, NY: NYC Department of Education. Retrieved from http://artsassessmentforlearning.org/about-assessment

Bader, E. J. (2014, July 7). *"Alternative high": Raising the bar on public education*. Retrieved from http://www.truth-out.org/news/item/24793-alternative-high-raising-the-bar-on-public-education

Beck, I., McKeown, M., & Kucan, L. (2002). *Bringing words to life: Robust vocabulary instruction.* New York, NY: Guilford Press.

Beck, I., McKeown, M., & Kucan, L. (2008). *Bringing words to life: Robust vocabulary instruction* (2nd ed.). New York, NY: Guilford Press.

Becker, A. (2013). *Journey*. Somerville, MA: Candlewick Press.

Becker, A. (2014). *Quest*. Somerville, MA: Candlewick Press.

Bjork, R. (2012). *Desirable difficulties: Slowing down learning* [Video]. Retrieved from https://www.youtube.com/watch?v=gtmMMR7SJKw&feature=youtu.be

Black, P., Burkhardt, H., Daro, P., Lappan, G., Pead, D., & Stephens, M. (2011). *High-stakes examinations that support student learning: Recommendations for the design, development and implementation of the PARCC assessments* (ISDDE Working Group on Examinations and Policy). Retrieved from http://www.mathshell.org/papers/pdf/ISDDE_PARCC_Feb11.pdf

Black, P., & Wiliam, D. (1998). Assessment and classroom learning. *Assessment in Education, 5*(1), 7–74.

Bloom, B. S. (1968). Learning for mastery. *Evaluation Comment* (UCLA-CSIEP), *1*(2), 1–12.

Bloom, B. S. (Ed.), Englehardt, M. D., Furst, E. J., Hill, W. H., & Krathwohl, D. R. (1956). *The taxonomy of educational objectives, the classification of educational goals, handbook I: Cognitive domain*. New York, NY: David McKay.

Brennan, R. L. (Ed.). (2006). *Educational measurement* (4th ed.). West Port, CT: American Council on Education and Praeger.

Brookhart, S. (2009, November). The many meanings of "multiple measures." *Educational Leadership, 67*(3), 6–12.

Brown, P., Roediger, H. L., & McDaniel, M. A. (2014). *Make it stick: The science of successful learning*. Cambridge, MA: Belknap Press.

Brulles, D., Brown, K., & Winebrenner, S. (2016). *Differentiated lessons for every learner: Standards-based activities and extensions for middle school*. Waco, TX: Prufrock Press.

Center for Collaborative Education. (2012). *Quality performance assessment: A guide for schools and districts*. Boston, MA: Author.

Cherry, K. (2016, June 22). *What is schema in psychology?* Retrieved from https://www.verywell.com/what-is-a-schema-2795873

Clark, B. (1983). *Growing up gifted* (2nd ed.). Columbus, OH: Charles E. Merrill.

Clark, J. (2003). *Changing systems to personalize learning*. Providence, RI: The Education Alliance at Brown University.

Clements, D. H., & Sarama, J. (2009). Learning trajectories in early mathematics—Sequences of acquisition and teaching. In Canadian Language and Literacy Research Network, *Encyclopedia of Language and Literacy Development* (pp. 1–7). Retrieved from https://www.scribd.com/document/22929814/Trajectorias-Aprendizagem-Clemets-Sarama-2009

Corcoran, T., Mosher, F. A., & Rogat, A. D. (2009). *Learning progressions in science: An evidence-based approach to reform*. Philadelphia, PA: Consortium for Policy Research in Education.

Costa, A., & Kallick, B. (2008). *Learning and leading with habits of mind*. Alexandria, VA: ASCD.

Danielson, C. (2013). *The framework for teaching evaluation instrument*. Princeton, NJ: The Danielson Group.

Darling-Hammond, L. (2010). *Performance counts: Assessment systems that support high-quality learning*. Washington, DC: Council of Chief State School Officers and Stanford, CA: Stanford Center for Opportunity Policy in Education.

Daro, P., Mosher, F. A., & Corcoran, T. (2011). *Learning trajectories in mathematics: A foundation for standards, curriculum, assessment, and instruction*. Consortium for Policy Research in Education. Retrieved from http://www.cpre.org/learning-trajectories-mathematics-foundation-standards-curriculum-assessment-and-instruction

DePascale, C. (2011). *Multiple measures, multiple meanings*. Paper presented at the 2011 Reidy Interactive Lecture Series, Boston, MA.

Dickenson, S. V., Simmons, D. C., & Kame'enui, E. J. (1998). Text organization: Research bases. In D. C. Simmons & E. J. Kame'enui (Eds.), *What reading research tells us about children with diverse learning needs* (pp. 239–278). Mahwah, NJ: Erlbaum.

Domaleski, C., Gong, B., Hess, K., Marion, S., Curl, C., & Peltzman, A. (2015). *Assessment to support competency-based pathways*. Washington, DC: Achieve. Retrieved from http://www.karin-hess.com/free-resources

Driver, R., Squires, A., Rushworth, P., & Wood-Robinson, V. (2002). *Making sense of secondary science: Research into children's ideas*. Abingdon, OX, England: RoutledgeFalmer.

Duschl, R., Schweingruber, H., & Shouse, A. (Eds.), & Board on Science Education, Center for Education, & Division of Behavioral and Social Sciences and Education. (2007). *Taking science to school: Learning and teaching science in Grades K–8*. Washington, DC: The National Academies Press.

Education Department of Western Australia. (1994). *First steps: Oral language developmental continuum*. Melbourne: Longman Australia.

Edutopia. (2008). *How should we measure student learning? 5 keys to comprehensive assessment with Linda Darling Hammond* [Video]. Retrieved from https://www.edutopia.org/comprehensive-assessment-introduction

EL Education. (2012). *Austin's butterfly: Building excellence in student work* [Video]. Retrieved from https://vimeo.com/search?q=Austin%E2%80%99s+Butterfly

EL Education. (2013). *Citing evidence from informational and literary texts* [Video]. Retrieved from https://vimeo.com/54871334

Engle, J. (1988). *Students questioning students: A technique to invite student involvement*. Presentation at the Fifth Annual Forum in Gifted Education, Rutgers University, New Brunswick, NJ.

Fisher, D., Frey, N., & Hattie, J. (2016). *Visible learning for literacy: Implementing the practices that work best to accelerate student learning*. Thousand Oaks, CA: Corwin.

Flowers, C., Browder, D., Wakeman, S., & Karvonen, M. (2007). *Links for academic learning: The conceptual framework*. National Alternate Assessment Center (NAAC) and the University of North Carolina at Charlotte.

Foorman, B. R. (2009). Text difficulty in reading assessment. In E. H. Hiebert (Ed.), *Reading more, reading better* (pp. 231–250). New York, NY: Guilford Press.

Francis, E. (2016). *Now that's a good question!* Alexandria, VA: ASCD.

Frey, N., Fisher, D., & Everlove, S. (2009). *Productive group work: How to engage students, build teamwork, and promote understanding*. Alexandria, VA: ASCD.

Goertz, M. E. (2011). *Multiple measures, multiple uses*. Paper presented at the 2011 Reidy Interactive Lecture Series, Boston, MA.

Great Schools Partnership. (2014) *The glossary of education reform*. Retrieved from http://edglossary.org/proficiency

Gregory, G., & Kaufeldt, M. (2015). *The motivated brain: Improving student attention, engagement, and perseverance*. Alexandria, VA: ASCD.

Hammond, W. D., & Nessel, D. (2011). *The comprehension experience: Engaging readers through effective inquiry and discussion*. Portsmouth, NH: Heinemann.

Hattie, J. (2002, October). *What are the attributes of excellent teachers?* Presentation at the New Zealand Council for Educational Research Annual Conference, University of Auckland.

Hattie, J. (2006, July). *Large-scale assessment of student competencies*. Paper presented as part of the Symposium, Working in Today's World of Testing and Measurement: Required Knowledge and Skills (Joint ITC/CPTA Symposium), 26th International Congress of Applied Psychology, Athens, Greece.

Hattie, J. (2009). *Visible learning. A synthesis of over 800 meta-analyses relating to achievement*. Abingdon, OX, England: Routledge.

Hawai'i Department of Education. (2010). *Learning progressions Hawaii progress maps* [Video] (project described in Hess, 2011b). Tri-State Enhanced Assessment Grant. Minneapolis: University of Minnesota, National Center on Educational Outcomes (NCEO). Retrieved from http://youtu.be/8vltv2PaZVU

Hess, K. (1987). *Enhancing writing through imagery*. Unionville, NY: Royal Fireworks Press.

Hess, K. (2000). *Beginning with the end in mind: A cross-case analysis of two elementary schools' experiences implementing Vermont's framework of standards and learning opportunities* (Unpublished Dissertation). University of Vermont, Burlington.

Hess, K. (2004a). *Applying Webb's depth-of-knowledge levels in reading and writing* (White paper developed for the New England Common Assessment Program [NECAP]). Dover, NH: Center for Assessment.

Hess, K. (2004b). *Applying Webb's depth-of-knowledge levels in mathematics* (White paper developed for the New England Common Assessment Program [NECAP]). Dover, NH: Center for Assessment.

Hess, K. (2008a). *Applying Webb's depth-of-knowledge levels in science* (White paper developed for the New England Common Assessment Program [NECAP]). Dover, NH: Center for Assessment.

Hess, K. (2008b). *Developing and using learning progressions as a schema for measuring progress*. Retrieved from http://www.karin-hess.com/learning-progressions

Hess, K. (2008c). *Teaching and assessing understanding of text structures across the grades: A research synthesis*. Dover, NH: Center for Assessment.

Hess, K. (2009). Student profile: Science inquiry learning Grades preK–5. In K. Hess, *Linking research with practice: A local assessment toolkit.* Underhill, VT: Educational Research in Action.

Hess, K. (2010a). Using learning progressions to monitor progress across grades: A science inquiry learning profile for PreK–4. In *Science & Children*, 47(6), 57–61.

Hess, K. (Ed.). (2010b). *Learning progressions frameworks designed for use with the Common Core State Standards in mathematics K–12.* National Alternate Assessment Center at the University of Kentucky and the National Center for the Improvement of Educational Assessment. Retrieved from http://www.karin-hess.com/learning-progressions

Hess, K. (Ed.). (2011a). *Learning progressions frameworks designed for use with the Common Core State Standards for ELA & literacy, K–12.* National Alternate Assessment Center at the University of Kentucky and the National Center for the Improvement of Educational Assessment. Retrieved from http://www.karin-hess.com/learning-progressions

Hess, K. (2011b). *Learning progressions in K–8 classrooms: How progress maps can influence classroom practice and perceptions and help teachers make more informed instructional decisions in support of struggling learners.* (Synthesis Report 87). Minneapolis: University of Minnesota, National Center on Educational Outcomes. Retrieved from http://www.karin-hess.com/learning-progressions

Hess, K. (2011c). *Text-based assessment targets planning worksheets for Grades 3–12*. Underhill, VT. Retrieved from http://www.karin-hess.com/free-resources

Hess, K. (2012a). *Using a research-based learning progression schema in the design of performance-based assessment tasks and interpretation of student progress.* Invited presentation for Roundtable Discussion on Performance Assessment at the April 2012 AERA Annual Meeting, Vancouver, BC.

Hess, K. (2012b). *What is the role of common assessments in local assessment systems?* (White paper developed for WY school districts). Underhill, VT: Educational Research in Action.

Hess, K. (2013a). *Linking research with practice: A local assessment toolkit to guide school leaders.* Underhill, VT: Educational Research in Action.

Hess, K. (2013b). *Text complexity toolkit: A video workshop with Dr. Karin Hess* [Video]. Underhill, VT: Educational Research in Action. Retrieved from http://www.karin-hess.com/free-resources

Hess, K. (2014). *Unit planning tools using the LPF: Strand 7.* Underhill, VT: Educational Research in Action, LLC.

Hess, K. (2015). *Linking research and rigor: A video workshop with Dr. Karin Hess* [Video]. Underhill, VT: Educational Research in Action. Retrieved from http://www.karin-hess.com/free-resources

Hess, K. (2016). *Student work to DIE for: A video workshop with Dr. Karin Hess* [Video]. Underhill, VT: Educational Research in Action. Retrieved from http://www.karin-hess.com/free-resources

Hess, K. (2017). *Piloting new assessments using a cognitive labs approach: A video workshop with Dr. Karin Hess* [Video]. Underhill, VT: Educational Research in Action. Retrieved from http://www.karin-hess.com/free-resources

Hess, K., & Biggam, S. (2004). *A discussion of "increasing text complexity" Grades K–HS* (White paper published by NH, RI, and VT Departments of Education as part of the New England Common Assessment Program (NECAP) Grade Level Expectations for Reading). Dover, NH: Center for Assessment.

Hess, K., Burdge, M., & Clayton, J. (2011). Challenges to developing alternate assessments. In M. Russell (Ed.), *Assessing students in the margins: Challenges, strategies, and techniques.* Charlotte, NC: Information Age Publishing.

Hess, K., Carlock, D., Jones, B., & Walkup, J. (2009). *What exactly do "fewer, clearer, and higher standards" really look like in the classroom? Using a cognitive rigor matrix to analyze curriculum, plan lessons, and implement assessments.* Retrieved from http://www.karin-hess.com/free-resources

Hess, K., Darling-Hammond, L., Abedi, J., Thurlow, M., Hiebert, E. H., Ducummun, C. E., et al. (2012). *Content specifications for the summative assessment of the Common Core State Standards for English Language Arts and literacy in history/social studies, science, and technical subjects.* Santa Cruz: University of California Santa Cruz Silicon Valley Extension, SMARTER Balanced Assessment Consortium.

Hess, K., & Gong, B. (2014). *Ready for college and career? Achieving the Common Core Standards and beyond through deeper, student-centered learning*. Quincy, MA: Nellie Mae Education Foundation. Retrieved from http://www.karin-hess.com/free-resources

Hess, K., & Gong, B. (2015). *An alignment study methodology for examining the content of high-quality summative assessments of college and career readiness in English language arts/literacy and mathematics* (Unpublished white paper). Dover, NH: Center for Assessment.

Hess, K., & Hervey, S. (2010). *Tools for examining text complexity* (White paper). Dover, NH: Center for Assessment.

Hess, K., Kurizaki, V., & Holt, L. (2009). *Reflections on tools and strategies used in the Hawai'i progress maps project: Lessons learned from learning progressions. Final Report, Tri-State Enhanced Assessment Grant*. Minneapolis: University of Minnesota, National Center on Educational Outcomes (NCEO). Retrieved from https://nceo.umn.edu/docs/tristateag/022_HI%201.pdf

Hess, K., McDivitt, P., & Fincher, M. (2008). *Who are the 2% students and how do we design test items and assessments that provide greater access for them? Results from a pilot study with Georgia students*. Atlanta, GA: Tri-State Enhanced Assessment Grant. Retrieved from http://www.nciea.org/publications/CCSSO_KHPMMF08.pdf

Hiebert, E. H. (2012). *Readability and the Common Core's Staircase of Text Complexity (Text Matters 1.3) and The Text Complexity Multi-Index (Text Matters 1.2)*. Retrieved from http://textproject.org/professional-development/text-matters

Hiebert, E. H. (2013). Supporting students' movement up the staircase of text complexity. *Reading Teacher, 66*(6), 459–467.

Hillocks, G. (2011). *Teaching argument writing Grades 6–12*. Portsmouth, NH: Heinemann.

Howard, G. (1991, November). *Sally Forth* comic strip. Orlando, FL: Reed Brennan Media Associates, King Features Syndicate. Retrieved from https://www.bing.com/images/search?q=sally+forth+comic+greg+howard%2c+november%2c+1991&qpvt=Sally+Forth+comic+Greg+Howard%2c+November%2c+1991&qpvt=Sally+Forth+comic+Greg+Howard%2c+November%2c+1991&qpvt=Sally+Forth+comic+Greg+Howard%2c+November%2c+1991&FORM=IGRE

International Society for the Scholarship of Teaching & Learning/ISSTL. (2013). *Studying and designing for transfer: What is transfer?* [Video]. Retrieved from http://blogs.elon.edu/issotl13/studying-and-designing-for-transfer

Jabot, M., & Hess, K. (2010). *Learning progressions 101* (Modules Addressing Special Education and Teacher Education [MAST]). Greenville, NC: East Carolina University. Retrieved from http://mast.ecu.edu/modules/lp

Kagan, S. (1992). *Cooperative learning*. San Juan Capistrano, CA: Resources for Teachers.

Keely, P. (2008). *Science formative assessment: 75 practical strategies for linking assessment, instruction, and learning*. Thousand Oaks, CA: Corwin.

Keeley, P., Eberle, F., & Farrin, L. (2005). *Uncovering student ideas in science: Vol. 1. 25 formative assessment probes*. Arlington, VA: NSTA Press.

Kolb, D. A. (1984). *Experiential learning: Experience as the source of learning and development* (Vol. 1). Englewood Cliffs, NJ: Prentice-Hall.

Maine Department of Education. (2000). *Measured measures: Technical considerations for developing a local assessment system*. Augusta, ME: Maine Department of Education, Maine Comprehensive Assessment System Technical Advisory Committee.

Maloney, A., & Confrey, J. (2013, January 24–26). *A learning trajectory framework for the mathematics common core: Turnonccmath for interpretation, instructional planning, and collaboration*. Presentation at the 17th Annual Conference of the Association of Mathematics Teacher Educators, in Orlando, FL. Retrieved from https://www.fi.ncsu.edu/wp-content/uploads/2013/05/A-Learning-Trajectory-Framework-presentation.pdf

Maloney, A. P., Confrey, J., & Nguyen, K. H. (Eds.). (2014). *Learning over time: Learning trajectories in mathematics education*. Charlotte, NC: Information Age Publishing.

Marston, E. (2005). The lost people of Mesa Verde (NECAP support materials with permission of *Highlights for Children*). Retrieved from http://www.narragansett.k12.ri.us/Resources/NECAP%20support/gle_support/Reading/end7/the_lost_people.htm

Marzano, R. J. (2012). Teaching argument. *Educational Leadership, 70*, 80–81.

Masters, G., & Forster, M. (1996). *Progress maps* (Part of the *Assessment Resource Kit*, pp. 1–58). Melbourne: The Australian Council for Educational Research.

McCarthy, B. (1987). *The 4MAT System: Teaching to learning styles with right/left mode techniques*. Barrington, IL: Excel.

McKenna, M., & Stahl, S. (2003). *Assessment for reading instruction*. New York, NY: Guilford Press.

McLeod, S. A. (2013). *Kolb—Learning styles*. Retrieved from https://www.simplypsychology.org/learning-kolb.html

McTighe, J., & Wiggins, G. (1999, 2004). *Understanding by design professional development workbook*. Alexandria, VA: ASCD.

Moore, C., Garst, L., & Marzano, R. (2015). *Creating and using learning targets and performance scales: How teachers make better instructional decisions*. West Palm Beach, FL: Learning Sciences International.

Moss, C., & Brookhart, S. (2012). *Learning targets: Helping students aim for understanding in today's lesson*. Alexandria, VA: ASCD.

National Center and State Collaborative. (2013). *Learning progressions frameworks* [Video]. Retrieved from https://www.youtube.com/watch?v=ss8fE1dBkE4&t=24s

National Center and State Collaborative/NCSC. (2015, December). *NCSC's content model for grade-aligned instruction and assessment: "The same curriculum for all students."* Retrieved from http://www.ncscpartners.org/Media/Default/PDFs/Resources/NCSCBrief7.pdf

National Center for Learning Disabilities. (2005). *Executive functioning fact sheet*. Retrieved from www.ldonline.org/article/24880

National Governors Association Center for Best Practices & Council of Chief State School Officers. (2010a). *Common Core State Standards for English language arts & literacy in history/social studies, science, and technical subjects: Appendix A*. Washington, DC: Authors.

National Governors Association Center for Best Practices & Council of Chief State School Officers. (2010b). *Common Core State Standards for English language arts & literacy in history/social studies, science, and technical subjects*. Washington, DC: Authors.

National Governors Association Center for Best Practices & Council of Chief State School Officers. (2010c). *Common Core State Standards for mathematics*. Washington, DC: Authors.

National Research Council. (2012). *Education for life and work: Developing transferable knowledge and skills in the 21st century*. Washington, DC: The National Academies Press.

National Research Council, Pellegrino, J., Chudowsky, N., & Glaser, R. (Eds.). (2001). *Knowing what students know: The science and design of educational assessment*. Washington, DC: National Academy Press.

Newmann, F., King, M., & Carmichael, D. (2007). *Authentic instruction and assessment: Common standards for rigor and relevance in teaching academic subjects*. Des Moines: Iowa Department of Education. Retrieved from https://www.centerforaiw.com/phases-of-aiw

Nottingham, J. A., Nottingham, J., & Renton, M. (2017). *Challenging learning through dialogue: Strategies to engage your students and develop their language of learning*. Thousand Oaks, CA: Corwin.

OGAP. (2008, January 18). The Vermont Mathematics Partnership, U.S. Department of Education (Award Number S366A020002) & National Science Foundation (Award Number EHR-0227057). Retrieved from http://www.ogapmath.com

O'Keefe, P. A. (2014, September 5). Liking work really matters. *NY Times*. Retrieved from https://www.nytimes.com/2014/09/07/opinion/sunday/go-with-the-flow.html?_r=3

Pellegrino, J. W. (2002). Understanding how students learn and inferring what they know: Implications for the design of curriculum, instruction and assessment. In M. J. Smith (Ed.), *NSF K–12 mathematics and science curriculum and implementation centers conference proceedings* (pp. 76–92). Washington, DC: National Science Foundation and American Geological Institute.

Perkins, D., & Salomon, G. (1988, September). Teaching for transfer. *Educational Leadership, 46*(1), 22–32.

Pinnell, G. S., & Fountas, I. (2007). *The continuum of literacy learning Grades K–8: Behaviors and understandings to notice, teach, and support*. Portsmouth, ME: Heinemann.

Porter, A., & Smithson, J. (2001). *Defining, developing, and using curriculum indicators: CPRE Research Report Series RR-048*. Philadelphia: University of Pennsylvania, Consortium for Policy Research in Education.

Roediger, H. L., & Marsh, E. J. (2005, September). The positive and negative consequences of multiple-choice testing. *Journal of Experimental Psychology: Learning, Memory, and Cognition, 31*(5), 1155–1159.

Rose, C., Minton, L., & Arline, C. (2007). *Uncovering student thinking in mathematics: 25 formative assessment probes*. Thousand Oaks, CA: Corwin.

Schmidt, W. H., Wang, H. A., & McKnight, C. C. (2005). Curriculum coherence: An examination of U.S. mathematics and science content standards from an international perspective. *Journal of Curriculum Studies, 37*(5), 525–529.

Shin, N., Stevens, S., Short, H., & Krajcik, J. (2009, June). *Learning progressions to support coherence in instructional material, instruction, and assessment design*. Paper presented at the Learning Progression in Science (LeaPS) Conference, Iowa City, IA.

Shwartz, Y., Weizman, A., Fortus, D., Krajcik, J., & Reiser, B. J. (2008). The IQWST experience: Using coherence as a design principle for a middle school science curriculum. *Elementary School Journal, 109*(2), 199–219.

Slavin, R. (1991). Synthesis of research on cooperative learning. *Educational Leadership, 48*(5), 71–82.

Smarter Balanced Assessment Consortium. (2017). *SBAC Mathematics Task Specifications*. Retrieved from http://www.smarterbalanced.org

Sousa, D. A. (2015). *Brain-friendly assessments: What they are and how to use them*. West Palm Beach, FL: Learning Sciences International.

Stiggins, R. (1997). *Student-involved classroom assessment* (3rd ed.). Upper Saddle River, NJ: Prentice-Hall.

Stiggins, R. (2017). *The perfect assessment system*. Alexandria, VA: ASCD.

Sturgis, C., & Patrick, S. (2010, November). *When success is the only option: Designing competency-based pathways for next generation learning*. Quincy, MA: Nellie Mae Education Foundation.

Teachers College Reading Writing Project. (2013). *Learning progression to support self-assessment and writing about themes in literature: Small group* [Video]. Retrieved from https://www.youtube.com/watch?v=8grZFus5OCo

Thompson, S. J., Johnstone, C. J., & Thurlow, M. L. (2002). *Universal design applied to large scale assessments* (Synthesis Report 44). Minneapolis: University of Minnesota, National Center on Educational Outcomes. Retrieved from http://education.umn.edu/NCEO/OnlinePubs/Synthesis44.html

Tucker, C. (2015, February). *Thesis statement throwdown!* Retrieved from http://catlintucker.com/2015/02/thesis-statement-throwdown

Understanding Language/Stanford Center for Assessment, Learning, & Equity. (2016, June). *Evaluating item quality in large-scale assessments: Phase I report of the study of state assessment systems*. Stanford, CA: Author.

Vacca, R. T., & Vacca, J. A. (1989). *Content area reading* (3rd ed.). New York, NY: HarperCollins.

Vermont Agency of Education. *What is proficiency-based learning?* Retrieved from http://education.vermont.gov/student-learning/proficiency-based-learning

Vygotsky, L. S. (1978). *Mind and society: The development of higher mental processes*. Cambridge, MA: Harvard University Press.

Walsh, J. A., & Sattes, B. D. (2015). *Questioning for classroom discussion*. Alexandria, VA: ASCD.

Walsh, J. A., & Sattes, B. D. (2017). *Quality questioning* (2nd ed.). Thousand Oaks, CA: Corwin.

Webb, N. (1997). *Criteria for alignment of expectations and assessments on mathematics and science education* [Research Monograph Number 6]. Washington, DC: CCSSO.

Webb, N. (2002, March 28). *Depth-of-Knowledge levels for four content areas* (White paper shared via personal email).

Webb, N. (2005). *Web alignment tool (WAT): Training manual*. Madison: University of Wisconsin and Council of Chief State School Officers.

Wiggins, A. (2017). *The best class you never taught: How spider web discussion can turn students into learning leaders*. Alexandria, VA: ASCD.

Wiggins, G. (2006). *Healthier testing made easy: The idea of authentic assessment*. Retrieved from https://www.edutopia.org/authentic-assessment-grant-wiggins

Wiggins, G., & McTighe, J. (1999). *The understanding by design handbook*. Alexandria, VA: ASCD.

Wiggins, G., & McTighe, J. (2005). *Understanding by design* (expanded 2nd ed.). Alexandria, VA: ASCD.

Wiggins, G., & McTighe, J. (2012). *The understanding by design guide to advanced concepts in creating and reviewing units*. Alexandria, VA: ASCD.

Wiliam, D. (2015). Designing great hinge questions. *Educational Leadership, 73*(1), 40–44.

Wiliam, D., & Leahy, S. (2015). *Embedding formative assessment: Practical techniques for K–12 classrooms*. West Palm Beach, FL: Learning Sciences International.

Willingham, D. T. (2009). *Why don't students like school? A cognitive scientist answers questions about how the mind works and what it means for the classroom*. San Francisco, CA: Wiley.

Wilson, M., & Bertenthal, M. (Eds.). (2005). *Systems for state science assessment*. Board on Testing and Assessment, Center for Education, National Research Council of the National Academies. Washington, DC: National Academies Press.

Wisconsin Department of Public Instruction. (2016). *Wisconsin's Strategic Assessment Systems Foundational Charts* (revised). Madison, WI: Author. Retrieved from https://dpi.wi.gov/sites/default/files/imce/strategic-assessment/Strategic_Assessment%20CHARTS.pdf

Index

Figures and tables are indicated by f or t following the page number.

Accountability, 25
Accuracy of content criteria, 139
ACT, 89
Action research, 288–289
Adding on, 27
Advanced Individual Test Blueprint, 375, 376, 382t, 394–395
Alignment, 372–377, 375f
Alignment studies, 373–374
Analytic tools for text complexity, 94–96, 104–105, 108–109
Analytic rubrics, 139, 140–141
Analyzing, unpacking of, 23t
Analyzing Formative Assessments, 187t, 192
Analyzing Learner Characteristics/Student Work Samples Along a Progression, 329t, 330–331
Anatomy of an Opinion/Argument/Critique: Planning Tools, 212, 216–223, 218–219t
Anchor charts, 113–115
Anchor paper development, 158–164, 159–161f
Anchor papers, defined, 158
Anchor sets, 158, 159f
Annotations, 159–161, 160f
Antecedent-consequence (cause-effect) text structure, 111
Anticipation guides, 236, 247, 282–283, 339–340
Artifact analysis task shell, 260
Artists. *See* Group roles
Art of questioning, 33
Assessment
  design, 8, 38–40
  gaps in, 376
  to improve instruction, 301, 370–371
  learning progressions and, 297–298, 297f, 314–315, 316f, 318
  quality and learning, 1–2
  reliability and validity of, 372–373
  sample tasks for pre- and mid-assessments, 341–347
  stages of, 298
  teacher use of, 367–368
  text complexity and, 371
  See also Comprehensive local assessment systems; High-quality assessment; Rubrics for assessment

Assessment System Blueprint, 376, 382t, 391–393
Assessment Triangle, 2, 3f, 236, 236f
Assignment menus, 349–357, 350f
Authenticity, 134
Automaticity, 301

Background knowledge for reading, 101–102
Bader, E. J., 131
Balance of representation, 376–377
Basic (closed) questions, 29–30
Basic Individual Test Blueprint, 375, 382t, 388–390
Beck, I., 101
Beginners versus experts, 298
Benchmarking, 158
Benchmark/interim assessment, 136, 137f
Benchmark texts, 92, 96, 97f
Bertenthal, M., 284
Big Ideas, 289, 290t, 308
Black, Paul, 235, 372
Bloom, B. S., 21
Bloom's Cognitive Process Dimensions, 45
Bloom's Taxonomy, 24t, 36, 45, 46–47. *See also* Cognitive Rigor Matrices (CRMs)
Body of evidence, 136
Bookmark-As-You-Read, 117–118, 128
Boots and Hats task, 151–153, 232–233
Brookhart, S., 157, 281
Brown, P., 18

Calibration sets, 158, 159f
Calibration tool, 162
Card Pyramid, 118–119, 129
Career and Technical Education CRM, 52t, 60
Carousel, 28
Case studies, 252
Categorical concurrence, 376, 377
Cause-effect (antecedent-consequence) text structure, 111
CCR (college and career-ready) standards, 1, 16–17, 373
Change, time needed for, 49
Changing your mind, 27
Character analysis task shells, 263–268
Character emojis, 22
Chunking text, 97–98, 298

Clark, Barbara, 37
Classroom visits, 33. *See also* Teacher evaluation
Closed (basic) questions, 29–30
Close Reading and Listening CRM, 51t, 53
Cognition, in Assessment Triangle, 2, 3f
Cognitive demand, 38. *See also* Cognitive rigor
Cognitive dissonance, 18
Cognitive labs, 166–171
Cognitive Labs Part 2, 188t, 203
Cognitive Labs Part 3A, 188t, 204
Cognitive Labs Part 3B, 188t, 205
Cognitive lab tools, 170–171
Cognitive rigor
    overview, 8
    assessment analysis of, 378
    Collaborative Inquiry Plan, 27
    college- and career-readiness standards and, 16–17
    connections and, 17–19
    defined, 16, 35
    higher order thinking and, 23, 23–24t
    learning progressions and, 320–325, 322–324f
    memorization and, 15–16
    misconceptions about, 35–43, 41t
    one-pagers, 19
    questions and, 29–35, 34f
    reflection, 48
    scaffolding and, 21–22
    transfer of learning and, 19–21
    visible thinking and, 25–29
    Walk-Through Tool for, 321, 322–324f, 324–325, 338
Cognitive Rigor Matrices (CRMs), 43–47, 44t
Cognitive Rigor Matrix Tools
    overview, 51–52t
    Career and Technical Education CRM, 52t, 60
    Close Reading and Listening CRM, 51t, 53
    Fine Arts CRM, 52t, 57
    Health and Physical Education CRM, 52t, 58
    Mathematics and Science CRM, 51t, 54
    Social Studies and Humanities CRM, 52t, 56
    walk-throughs and, 320
    World Languages CRM, 52t, 59
    Writing and Speaking CRM, 51t, 55
Cognitive rigor strategies and tools
    Collaborative Inquiry Plan, 77, 81
    DOK "IQ" Test, 48, 61, 64–70
    Experiential Learning Cycle activities, 50–51
    "I Can Rock the Rigor" Kid Tool, 77
    jigsaw, 79
    Multi-sensory Clustering, 78–79, 87
    One-Pagers, 77, 82
    professional development application for teachers, 48–49
    Question-Planning Worksheets, 49, 71–76
    TBEARs, 77–78, 82–86
    text decks, 79–80
    Turn and Talk Frames, 79, 88
    What's TV got to do with DOK? 48, 61, 63
    See also Cognitive Rigor Matrix Tools

Cognitive science research, 288
Coherence, 285–286
Collaboration, 5, 25–29
Collaborative Inquiry Plan, 27, 77, 81
College- and career-readiness (CCR) standards, 1, 16–17, 373
Common assessments, 368–371
Common Core State Standards, 299, 310
Compare-contrast text structure, 111
Competency-based graduation, 317
Complexity versus difficulty, 47
Comprehensive local assessment systems
    overview, 9
    alignment and, 372–377, 375f
    common assessments in, 368–371
    components of, 1–4
    Experiential Learning Cycle and, 380–381
    guiding questions for, 361
    implementation plan for, 366
    indicators of, 364–366
    interpretation of results from analyses of, 377–379
    multiple measures in, 361, 367, 368t
    reflection, 379
    rethinking about, 360–363, 362–363f
    values incorporated in, 359–360
Comprehensive local assessment systems tools
    overview, 381, 382–383t
    Advanced Individual Test Blueprint, 375, 376, 382t, 394–395
    Assessment System Blueprint, 382t, 391–393
    Basic Individual Test Blueprint, 375, 382t, 388–390
    Discussion Questions: Examining Our Local Assessment System, 363, 363f, 382t, 386–387
    Item or Task Bank Review, 383t, 398–399
    Text Complexity Analyses Summary, 383t, 396–397
    Year-at-a-Glance, 361–362, 362f, 382t, 384–385
Conducting investigations learning targets, 286, 287f
Connection making, 17–19, 43
Consolidation, formative assessment and, 19
Constructed-response questions, 38–40
Content alignment, 374
Content-specific empirical research, 288
Content standards
    assessment aligned with, 373–376, 375f
    learning progressions and, 288, 299–300
    limits of, 1
Context, benefits of, 18
Corcoran, T., 300–301
Course-embedded tasks. *See* Performance assessment
Creating, unpacking of, 24t
Critical friends, 181
Critical thinking, 40
CRMs (Cognitive Rigor Matrices), 43–47, 44t. *See also* Cognitive Rigor Matrix Tools

CSI, 63
Culture of assessment, 360
Curie, Marie, 272
Curricular progressions, 299. *See also* Learning progressions
Curriculum, learning progressions and, 288

Darling-Hammond, L., 359
Daro, P., 372
Deeper learning
　assessment of, 377
　Clint Mathews on, 5
　collaboration and, 26
　defined, 3
　as goal for every student, 2–4, 35, 47
　importance of, 1, 4
　methods to teach, 3–4
　professional development application for teachers, 48–49
Deeper questions, 30–31
Definition text structure, 111
Degrees of alignment, 375f
Density of text, 97–98
Depth-of-Knowledge
　assignment menus and, 349–357, 350f
　consistency in, 376, 377
　key ideas from, 46–47
　misconceptions about, 36–40
　teacher-student roles and, 321
　See also Cognitive Rigor Matrices (CRMs)
Descriptive versus judgmental feedback, 182
Developmental continuums. *See* Learning progressions
Dialogue, 26–29
Dickenson, S. V., 110
Dickey, Marie, 32
D-I-E, 149–150t, 149–151
Differentiation, 348–349, 350f, 352
Difficulty versus complexity, 47
Discourse, rigor and, 26–29
Discourse style, 93, 101
Discussion Questions: Examining Our Local Assessment System, 363, 363f, 382t, 386–387
Doing, assessment of, 157
DOK "IQ" Test, 48, 61, 64–70
DOK Wheel of Misfortune, 37
Duschl, R., 285
Dyads, 22

Education Department of Western Australia, 299
Education for Life and Work (NRC), 2–3
Edutopia, 20
Einstein, Albert, 272
EKGs, 22
Embedding Performance Assessments, 188t, 210–211
Engagement, 25–29, 43
Engle, Judy, 33
Episodic predictions, 99
Evaluating, unpacking of, 24t

Evaluation of teachers, 320, 367
Events-enumeration-description text structure, 111
Excellence versus perfection, 143
Expectations, uniformity in, 369–370
Expeditionary learning, 252
　Type-1 learners, 10
　Type-2 learners, 10
　Type-3 learners, 10
　Type-4 learners, 10
Experiential Learning Cycle
　overview, 9–13, 10f
　comprehensive local assessment systems and, 380–381
　high-quality assessment and, 185–186
　learning progressions and, 327–328
　rigor and, 50–51
　text complexity and, 103–104
Experts versus beginners, 298
Extended performance assessment. *See* Performance assessment

Fact checkers. *See* Group roles
Far transfer, 21
Feedback types, 182
Field testing, 165
Fine Arts CRM, 52t, 57
First Steps, 299
Flipped classrooms, 348
Foorman, B. R., 90
Formative, Interim, and Summative Assessment Planning Along a Learning Progression, 329t, 336–337
Formative assessment
　action research and, 288–289
　anticipation guides, 236, 247
　cognitive labs and, 166–167
　defined, 136
　graphic organizers for, 236, 238–239
　key ideas about, 235–236
　learning progression alignment with, 290–291, 291f
　probing questions for, 243, 243t
　purposes and uses of, 137f
　self- and peer-assessment, 243–246
　strategies for, 236
　systematic observation, 236, 240–242
　types of, 236
Formative assessment, connection making and, 19
Format/layout of text, 98
Form criteria, 138–139
Forster, M., 284
Foundational skills, 301
4MAT® model, 10
Frames, text complexity and, 119, 119–120t

Games versus scrimmage, 20–21
Generalized rubrics, 139
Genre, 98–99
Giants of Science task shell, 145, 272–273
The Giver (Lowry), 90

Goal setting, 7
Goldilocks support, 22
Gong, B., 26, 31
Gradients in Complexity rubrics, 94–96
Graduation based on competency, 317
Grapes of Wrath (Steinbeck), 90
Graphic organizers, 78–79, 113, 236, 238–239
GRASPS model, 254, 256–257
Great American Chocolate Chip Cookie Taste Test, 138, 212–215
Growing Up Gifted (Clark), 37
Growth mindset, 236
Guide to Performance Task Development, 188t, 206–209
Guiding Questions for Developing, Refining, or Validating Learning Progressions, 329t, 332–334

Harackiewicz, Judith, 18
Hattie, John, 22, 143, 370
Health and Physical Education CRM, 52t, 58
Hess, K., 26, 31, 367. *See also* Cognitive Rigor Matrices (CRMs)
Hiebert, E. H., 92
Higher order thinking, 23, 23–24t, 40, 41t. *See also* Deeper learning
High-quality assessment
  overview, 131–135
  anchor point development for, 158–164, 159–161f
  Boots and Hats task, 151–153, 232–233
  characteristics of, 135
  cognitive labs for, 166–171
  Experiential Learning Cycle and, 185–186
  field testing of, 165
  formative assessment strategies, 235–237, 236f
  Great American Chocolate Chip Cookie Taste Test, 138, 212–215
  mathematics, guidelines for, 228–231
  piloting of, 165
  purposes and uses of, 136–137, 137f
  reflection, 184
  research on, 135
  types of, 135–136
  writing, guidelines for, 224–228
  See also Formative assessment; Student work analysis (SWA); Task validation teams
High-quality assessment tools
  overview, 187, 187–188t
  Analyzing Formative Assessments, 187t, 192
  Anatomy of an Opinion/Argument/Critique: Planning Tools, 212, 216–223, 218–219t
  anticipation guides, 236, 247
  Cognitive Labs Part 2, 188t, 203
  Cognitive Labs Part 3A, 188t, 204
  Cognitive Labs Part 3B, 188t, 205
  Embedding Performance Assessments, 188t, 210–211
  graphic organizers, 238–239
  Guide to Performance Task Development, 188t, 206–209
  Individual Reviewer Rubric Score Sheet, 187t, 197
  My Writing Checklist, 244–246
  Performance Assessment Overview: Purpose and Use, 188t, 210–211
  Rubric Quality Review Worksheet, 187t, 193
  Student Work Analysis, 187t, 194–195
  Systematic Observation Template, 241–242
  Task Quality Validation Protocol, 187t, 189–191
  Task Validation Summary, 188t, 199–202
  Team Rubric Score Sheet, 187t, 198
  What is the Evidence? tool, 162, 187t, 196
High-road transfer, 21
Hillocks, G., 217
Hinge questions, 29
Hint cards, 22
Holistic rubrics, 139–140
Horse story example of learning progressions, 284–285
Hospital discharge task shell, 258–259
Hulleman, Chris S., 18
Humanities and Social Studies CRM, 52t, 56
Hypothetical (problem-solution) text structure, 111

IBBs (Instructional Building Blocks), 312
Ibonia, Evelyn, 61
"I Can Rock the Rigor" Kid Tool, 77
Ikuma, Margeaux, 61–62
Impact criteria, 139
Implementation plans, 366
Individual Reviewer Rubric Score Sheet, 163, 187t, 197
Inductive-deductive text structure, 111
Infographics, 348
Informational texts, 92
Informational writing task shell, 261
Instructional Building Blocks (IBBs), 312
Interest, 5, 18
Interim assessment, 136, 137f
Interpretation, in Assessment Triangle, 2, 3f
Investigating Sharks assessment, 344–347
Item or Task Bank Review, 383t, 398–399

Jeopardy, 63
Jigsaw, 79
Jobs in group, 26–27
Judgmental versus descriptive feedback, 182
Judgment-critique text structure, 111
Justifications, 161, 161f

Kagan, Spencer, 25, 27–28, 32
Kame'enui, E. J., 110
Kid TBEAR, 77–78, 86
King, Martin Luther, Jr., 102
Knowing What Students Know (NRC), 236
Knowledge production criteria, 139
Kolb, David, 9–13, 10f
Krajcik, J., 285–286
Kucan, L., 101

Language structure, 101
Lappan, G., 372
Layout/format of text, 98

Leadership density, 6
Learning, assessment and, 2
"Learning for Mastery" (Bloom), 21
Learning goals, defined, 286
Learning progressions
    overview, 8, 281–286
    anticipation guides, 282–283, 339–340
    assessment linked with, 297–298, 297f, 318
    background for, 309–310
    benefits of using, 300–302
    Big Ideas and, 289, 290t, 308
    case studies for, 310–317, 311f, 313f, 316f
    content standards and, 288, 299–300
    curriculum and, 288
    as describing increased understanding, 289
    Experiential Learning Cycle and, 327–328
    filling gaps in learning with, 305–307
    formative assessment alignment and, 290–291, 291f
    grain size and, 286–288, 309
    guiding questions for, 307–308
    horse story example of, 284–285
    Mathematics Learning Progressions Framework example, 291–296
    reflection, 326
    resources and strategies for use with students, 348–351, 350f
    rigor and, 320–324, 322–324f
    using to guide instruction and assessment, 317–320
    as validated by research, 288–289
    visuals to see mastery of, 61–62
    zooming in or out with, 302–306, 303–304f, 306f
    See also Learning progression tools
Learning Progressions Frameworks (LPFs)
    assessment case study and, 314–315, 316f
    competency-based graduation case study and, 317
    ELA example and, 302–304, 303–304f
    history of, 309–310
    lesson planning and content monitoring case study and, 310–312, 311f, 313f
Learning progression tools
    overview, 329, 329t
    Analyzing Learner Characteristics/Student Work Samples Along a Progression, 329t, 330–331
    Formative, Interim, and Summative Assessment Planning Along a Learning Progression, 329t, 336–337
    Guiding Questions for Developing, Refining, or Validating Learning Progressions, 332–334
    Guiding Questions for Developing, Refining, or Validating Learning Progressions, 329t
    Looking for Rigor: Shifting Teacher-Student Roles, 329t, 338
    Planning Instruction Using a Learning Progressions Mindset, 329t, 335
Learning style, McCarthy on, 10
Learning targets, defined, 286
Learning trajectories, 156–157. See also Learning progressions

Length of text, 97–98
"Letter from a Birmingham Jail" (King, Jr.), 102
Lexile measures, 89–90, 101
Literary analysis task shells, 263–268
Literary texts, 92
Local assessment system components, 1–4
Local assessment systems. See Comprehensive local assessment systems
Local bibliography of benchmark texts, 96, 97f
Long-term memory, requirements for, 18
Looking for Rigor: Shifting Teacher-Student Roles, 329t, 338
Lower order thinking, 23, 23–24t
Low-road transfer, 21
Lowry, Lois, 90
LPF. See Learning Progressions Frameworks (LPFs)

Marsh, E. J., 40
Masters, G., 284
Materials managers, 27
Mathematics, assessment guidelines for, 228–231
Mathematics and Science CRM, 51t, 54
Mathematics Learning Progressions Framework/LPF, 291–296
Mathes, Christy, 42–43
Mathews, Clint, 5
McCarthy, Bernice, 9, 10
McDaniel, M. A., 18
McKeown, M., 101
McTighe, Jay, 20, 138
"Meaningless" means, 363
Measurement task shell, 269
Memorization, rigor and, 15–16
Memory, rigor and, 17–18
Metacognition, 3, 31, 249
Meyer, Dan, 251
Mid-assessments, 298
Mosher, F. A., 300–301
Moss, C., 157, 281
Motivation, 4–5
Multiple assessment measures, 361, 367, 368t, 371
Multiple choice questions, 38–40
Multiplication strategies task shell, 271
Multi-sensory Clustering, 78–79, 87
Multistep tasks, 42–43
My Favorite No strategy, 348
My Favorite—or Not So Favorite—Holiday, 342–343
My Writing Checklist, 244–246

National Governors Association, 93
National Research Council (NRC), 2–3, 37, 236, 298
NCIS, 63
Near transfer, 21
New Hampshire Model competencies, 317
New York Performance Standards Consortium, 131–133
Nifty 9, 349
Note facts, 305–307, 351, 358
Nottingham, J., 26
Nottingham, J. A., 26
The Novel task shell, 255, 277–278

Index 487

Observation, in Assessment Triangle, 2, 3f
One-Pagers, 19, 77, 82
One-way alignment, 374–375
Open-ended assessments, 369
Opinion writing task shell, 262

Pacing guides, 300. *See also* Learning progressions
Pairs, 22
Paraphrase passport, 27
Partner collaborations, 22
Passage pickers, 27
Pattern Folders-Emerging Themes, 119
PBA. *See* Performance assessment
Pead, D., 372
Peer-assessment, 155, 236, 243–246
Perception, in Experiential Learning Cycle, 9
Perfection versus excellence, 143
Performance assessment
 overview, 132–134
 case studies, 252
 components of, 249
 design, 248–251, 250t
 expeditionary learning, 252
 learning progressions and, 305–307
 rubric criteria for, 250, 250t
 sources for, 251
 transfer and, 248
 types of, 248
 See also High-quality assessment; Task shells
Performance Assessment Overview: Purpose and Use, 188t, 210–211
Performance Task Administration Guidelines, 234
Performance Task Development, 188t, 206–209
Perkins, D., 21
Photo/picture search, 32–33
Physical Education and Health CRM, 52t, 58
PIGS, 25
Piloting, 151, 165
Place value task shell, 254–255, 270
Planning Instruction Using a Learning Progressions Mindset, 329t, 335
Planning Worksheet, 94, 97, 102
Practice, transfer versus, 19
Practice sets, 158, 159f
Preassessments versus postassessments, 136, 148–149, 153, 298, 314
Preconceptions, 300
Predetermined assessment targets, 120–126, 121t
The Price is Right, 63
Probing questions, 236, 243, 243t
Problem-solution (hypothetical) text structure, 111
Process (sequence) text structure, 111
Process criteria, 139
Processing, in Experiential Learning Cycle, 9
Progress indicators, 298
Progress maps. *See* Learning progressions
Progress visuals, 61–62
Proposition-support text structure, 111

Qualitative Text Analysis Planning Worksheet, 94, 97, 102, 107
Qualitative text dimensions, 93
Quantitative text dimensions, 92–93
Question-Planning Worksheets, 49, 61, 71–76
Questions
 formative assessment and, 236
 rigor and, 29–35, 34f
 second questions, 32
 Socratic Questioning, 33
Quick checks for understanding, 19

Range-of-knowledge correspondence, 376, 377
Readability scores, 89–90, 101
Reading. *See* Text complexity
Reading Between the Lines (ACT), 89
Recall, deeper learning compared, 3
Recorders. *See* Group roles
Reflections
 cognitive rigor, 48
 comprehensive local assessment systems and, 379
 high-quality assessment, 184
 learning progressions and, 326
 performance assessment and, 249
 rigorous questions and, 31
 text complexity, 102
Relevance, memory and, 18
Reliability, 134, 372
Renton, M., 26
Repeating, 27
Repiloting, 378
Research, types of, 288–289
Revised Bloom's Taxonomy, 24t, 36
Rigor. *See* Cognitive rigor
Rigor alignment, 374
Rigorous questions, 30–31
Roediger, H. L., 18, 40
Rogat, A. D., 300–301
Role-playing, 254
Roles in group, 26–27
Roll of Thunder (Taylor), 90
Rubric Quality Review Worksheet, 147, 187t, 193
Rubrics for assessment
 overview, 138–139
 assessment analysis of, 378
 development guide, 146–147
 quality of, 141–145
 Rubric Quality Review Worksheet, 147, 187t, 193
 types of, 139–141
 "What I Need to Do" rubric, 144
 See also Student work analysis (SWA)
Rubrics for text complexity, 94–96, 104–105, 108–109

Sally Forth comic, 15
Salomon, G., 21
SBAC (Smarter Balanced Assessment Consortium), 252, 253f
Scaffolding, 21–22, 35–36, 378

Schemas, 99, 298
Schweingruber, H., 285
Science and Mathematics CRM, 51t, 54
Scientific inquiry task shell, 255, 274–276
Scope and sequences. See Learning progressions
Scoring guides. See Rubrics for assessment
Scribes
   guidelines for, 225–226, 229, 230–231
   student work analysis and, 151
   template for, 227
Scrimmage versus games, 20–21
Second questions, 32
Selected response items, 39–40
Self-assessment
   formative assessment and, 235–236, 243–246
   learning progressions and, 319
   motivation and, 5
   student work analysis and, 155
Self-monitoring checklists, 225, 230
Semantic predictions, 99
Send a question, 32
Sequence (process) text structure, 111
Shin, N., 285–286
Short, H., 285–286
Short-cycle assessment. See Formative assessment
Short-term (working) memory, rigor and, 17–18
Shouse, A., 285
Signal words, 112, 113
Silent signals, 27
Simmons, D. C., 110
Simultaneous engagement, 25
Slavin, Robert, 25
Smarter Balanced Assessment Consortium (SBAC), 252, 253f
SOC (source of challenge), 374, 376, 378
Social Studies and Humanities CRM, 52t, 56
Socratic Questioning, 33
Sorting versus scoring, 153–155
Source of challenge (SOC), 374, 376, 378
Sousa, D. A., 18
Speaking and Writing CRM, 51t, 55
Special education students, as capable of deeper learning, 35
SQS - Students Questioning Students, 33
Stand and deliver, 28–29
Standardized testing, alternatives to, 369
Standards. See Common Core State Standards; Content standards
Standards progressions, 299
Statements of purpose, 364
Steinbeck, John, 90
Stephens, M., 372
Stevens, S., 285–286
Stiggins, Rick, 4, 360
Strategically designed performance tasks, 148–151
Strategic Assessment Systems Foundational Charts, 137, 137f
Strategic scaffolding, 22. See also Scaffolding

Student achievement, 301
Student roles, shifting with teachers, 33, 34–35t
"Student Side-by-Side SWA," 155
Student Work Analysis, 187t, 194–195
Student work analysis (SWA)
   overview, 147–148
   purposes of, 149–150t, 149–157
   strategically designed performance tasks and, 148–151
Student Work Analysis tool, 187t, 194–195
Student work samples, 289, 319
Success criteria, 27
Summative assessment, 36–37, 136, 137f
SWA. See Student work analysis (SWA)
Systematic observation, 236, 240–242
Systematic Observation Template, 241–242

Talk moves, 27
Task managers. See Group roles
Task Quality Validation, 187t, 189–191
Task Quality Validation Protocol, 187t, 189–191
Task shells
   overview, 252–255, 253f
   artifact analysis, 260
   character analysis, 263–268
   Giants of Science, 145, 272–273
   GRASPS model, 254, 256–257
   hospital discharge, 258–259
   informational writing, 261
   literary analysis, 263–268
   measurement, 269
   multiplication strategies, 271
   The Novel, 255, 277–278
   opinion writing, 262
   place value, 254–255, 270
   scientific inquiry, 255, 274–276
   Smarter Balanced Assessment Consortium and, 252, 253f
   teacher approval of, 255, 276
   Turning Points in History, 255, 279–280
Task-specific rubrics, 139
Task Validation Summary, 188t, 199–202
Task validation teams
   overview, 172–173
   conducting, 180–183, 181f
   cover page for, 177–179
   members of, 173–175
   preparation for, 173, 175–176
   quality of assessment and, 172
Taxonomies, 24t, 36–37
Taylor, Mildred D., 90
TBEAR, 77–78, 82–86
Teacher approval of task shells, 255, 276
Teacher evaluation, 320, 367
Teachers, 4, 33, 34–35t
Teaching Argument Writing (Hillocks), 217
Teaching Channel, 27, 28, 33
Team learning, 25
Team Rubric Score Sheet, 163–164, 187t, 198
Text-based opinions, 263–268

Text complexity
  overview, 8
  analysis process learnings, 92
  assessment and, 371, 374, 378–379
  Experiential Learning Cycle and, 103–104
  importance of considering, 89–90
  instructional strategies for text structure, 112–115
  qualitative analysis approach to, 94–96, 97f
  qualitative complexity factors, 97–102
  quantitative versus qualitative measures of, 92–93
  reflection, 102
  text structures and, 100, 110–111
Text Complexity Analyses Summary, 383t, 396–397
Text complexity assessment strategies
  Bookmark-As-You-Read, 117–118, 128
  Card Pyramid, 118–119, 129
  frames, 119, 119–120t
  Pattern Folders-Emerging Themes, 119
  predetermined assessment targets, 120–126, 121t
  reading strategy use, 119, 130
  What Do I Know About These Words? 117
  World Splash, 116, 127
Text complexity tools
  overview, 91, 91t, 104–106
  Analytic Rubric for Informational Texts, 105, 108
  Analytic Rubric for Literary Texts, 105, 109
  Analyzing Qualitative Features Worksheet, 104, 107
  local bibliography of benchmark texts, 96, 97f
  Qualitative Text Analysis Planning Worksheet, 94, 97, 102, 107
  rubrics, 94–96, 104–105, 108–109
  sample frames, 112
  thinking behind, 90–91
Text decks, 79–80
Text signals, 112, 113
Text structures, 100, 110–111. *See also* Text complexity
Thesis throwdown, 28
Thinking, 16, 157
3 Acts format, 251
Tier 1 vocabulary, 101
Tier 2 vocabulary, 101
Tier 3 vocabulary, 101
Time order-chronology text structure, 111
Tools by name
  Advanced Individual Test Blueprint, 375, 376, 382t, 394–395
  Analytic Rubric for Informational Texts, 105, 108
  Analytic Rubric for Literary Texts, 105, 109
  Analyzing Formative Assessments, 187t, 192
  Analyzing Learner Characteristics/Student Work Samples Along a Progression, 329t, 330–331
  Analyzing Qualitative Features Worksheet, 104, 107
  Assessment System Blueprint, 382t, 391–393
  Basic Individual Test Blueprint, 375, 382t, 388–390
  Career and Technical Education CRM, 52t, 60
  Close Reading and Listening CRM, 51t, 53
  Cognitive Labs Part 2, 188t, 203
  Cognitive Labs Part 3A, 188t, 204
  Cognitive Labs Part 3B, 188t, 205
  Discussion Questions: Examining Our Local Assessment System, 363, 363f, 382t, 386–387
  Fine Arts CRM, 52t, 57
  Formative, Interim, and Summative Assessment Planning Along a Learning Progression, 329t, 336–337
  Guide to Performance Task Development, 188t, 206–209
  Guiding Questions for Developing, Refining, or Validating Learning Progressions 329t, 332–334
  Health and Physical Education CRM, 52t, 58
  Individual Reviewer Rubric Score Sheet, 187t, 197
  Item or Task Bank Review, 383t, 398–399
  Looking for Rigor: Shifting Teacher-Student Roles, 329t, 338
  Mathematics and Science CRM, 51t, 54
  Performance Assessment Overview: Purpose and Use, 188t, 210–211
  Planning Instruction Using a Learning Progressions Mindset, 329t, 335
  Rubric Quality Review Worksheet, 187t, 193
  Social Studies and Humanities CRM, 52t, 56
  Student Work Analysis, 187t, 194–195
  Task Quality Validation Protocol, 187t, 189–191
  Task Validation Summary, 188t, 199–202
  Team Rubric Score Sheet, 187t, 198
  Text Complexity Analyses Summary, 383t, 396–397
  walk-throughs and, 320
  What is the Evidence? 162, 187t, 196
  World Languages CRM, 52t, 59
  Writing and Speaking CRM, 51t, 55
  Year-at-a-Glance, 361–362, 362f, 382t, 384–385
Transfer of learning
  defined, 3, 20
  importance of, 1
  near or far, 21
  performance assessment and, 248
  rigor and, 19–21, 371
Tucker, Catlin, 28
Turn and Talk Frames, 79, 88
Turning Points in History task shell, 255, 279–280
Two-way alignment, 375–376

Understanding by design, 138
Unsubstantiated generalizations (UG), 45

Validity, 134, 372–373
Value lines - where do I stand, 27–28
Verbs, 23–24t, 37–38, 41t
Visible thinking, rigor and, 25–29
Vocabulary, 101
Vygotsky, Lev, 36

Walk-Through Tool, 321, 322–324f, 324–325, 338
Webb, N., 376
What Do I Know About These Words? 117
"What I Need to Do" rubric, 144
What is the Evidence? tool, 162, 187t, 196
What's TV got to do with DOK? 48, 61, 63
Wiggins, Grant, 20, 138
Wiliam, Dylan, 29, 235
Willingham, Daniel, 301
Wilson, M., 284
Wisconsin Strategic Assessment Systems Foundational Charts, 137, 137f

Word difficulty, 101
Working (short-term) memory, rigor and, 17–18
Workshop planning frame, stages of, 11–13
World Languages CRM, 52t, 59
World Splash, 116, 127
Writing, assessment guidelines for, 224–228
Writing and Speaking CRM, 51t, 55

Year-at-a-Glance, 361–362, 362f, 382t, 384–385

Zone of proximal development (ZPD), 36, 297–298, 297f

CORWIN
A SAGE Publishing Company

Helping educators make the greatest impact

CORWIN HAS ONE MISSION: to enhance education through intentional professional learning.

We build long-term relationships with our authors, educators, clients, and associations who partner with us to develop and continuously improve the best evidence-based practices that establish and support lifelong learning.

Solutions you want. Experts you trust. Results you need.

AUTHOR CONSULTING

Author Consulting

On-site professional learning with sustainable results! Let us help you design a professional learning plan to meet the unique needs of your school or district.
www.corwin.com/pd

INSTITUTES

Institutes

Corwin Institutes provide collaborative learning experiences that equip your team with tools and action plans ready for immediate implementation.
www.corwin.com/institutes

ECOURSES

eCourses

Practical, flexible online professional learning designed to let you go at your own pace.
www.corwin.com/ecourses

READ2EARN

Read2Earn

Did you know you can earn graduate credit for reading this book? Find out how:
www.corwin.com/read2earn

Contact an account manager at (800) 831-6640 or visit **www.corwin.com** for more information.

CORWIN